Street by Street

EAST SUSSEX

PLUS BURGESS HILL, EAST GRINSTEAD, HAYWARDS HEATH, ROYAL TUNBRIDGE WELLS

Enlarged Areas Brighton, Eastbourne, Hastings, Lewes, Newhaven

Ist edition May 2001

© Automobile Association Developments Limited 2001

This product includes map data licensed from Ordnance Survey® with the permission of the Controller of Her Majesty's Stationery Office. © Crown copyright 2000. All rights reserved. Licence No: 399221.

Published by AA Publishing (a trading name of Automobile Association Developments Limited, whose registered office is Norfolk House, Priestley Road, Basingstoke, Hampshire, RG24 9NY. Registered number 1878835).

Mapping produced by the Cartographic Department of The Automobile Association.

A CIP Catalogue record for this book is available from the British Library.

Printed by G. Canale & C. s.p.a., Torino, Italy

Ref: MX019

Key to map pages	ii-iii
Key to map symbols	iv-1
Enlarged scale pages	2-11
Street by Street	12-209
Index – towns & villages	210
Index – streets	211-227
Index – featured places	228-231

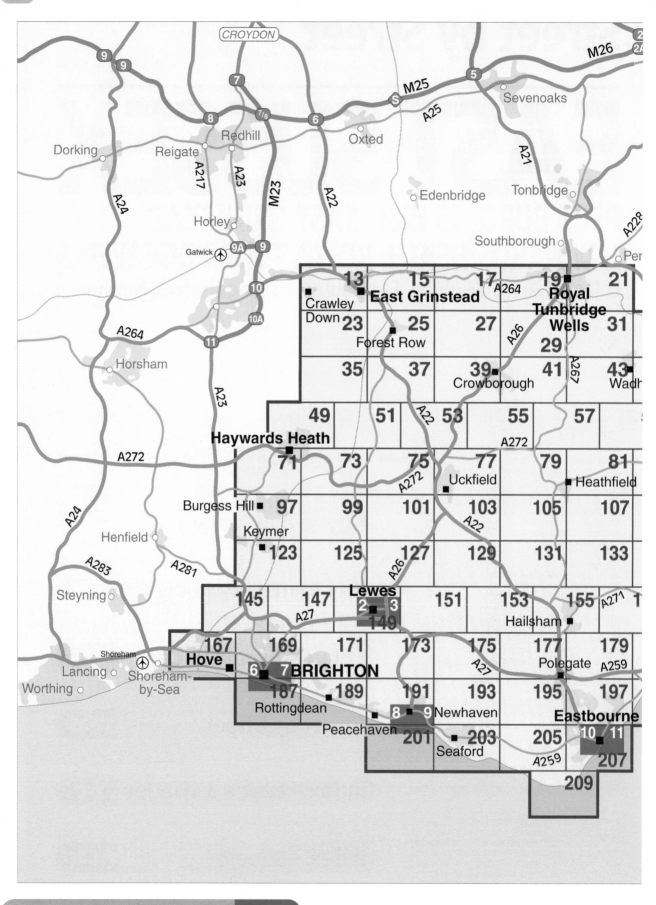

CROYDON

9 9

7

8 7/8 6 M25 5 M26

S A25 Sevenoaks

Dorking Redhill A21 Tonbridge

Reigate A217 A23 M23 A22 Oxted

A24 Edenbridge Southborough A228

Horley A264 Per

Gatwick 9A 9

10

10A

A264 13 15 17 19 21
Crawley East Grinstead A264 Royal
Down 23 25 27 Tunbridge 31
Horsham Forest Row A26 Wells
A23 35 37 39 29 43
Crowborough A267 Wadh

A272 49 51 53 55 57
A22 A272

Haywards Heath 71 73 75 77 79 81
A272 Uckfield Heathfield

Burgess Hill 97 99 101 103 105 107
Keymer A22

Henfield A283 123 125 127 129 131 133
A26

Steyning A281 145 147 Lewes 151 153 155 A271
A27 2 3 Hailsham
149

Shoreham 167 169 171 173 175 177 179
Hove A27 Polegate A259
Lancing 6 7 BRIGHTON
Worthing Shoreham- 187 189 191 193 195 197
by-Sea Rottingdean 8 9 Newhaven Eastbourne
Peacehaven 201 203 205 10 11
Seaford A259 207
209

Enlarged scale pages   1:10,000   6.3 inches to 1 mile

0   1/4   miles   1/2   3/4

0   1/4   1/2   kilometres   3/4   1   1 1/4

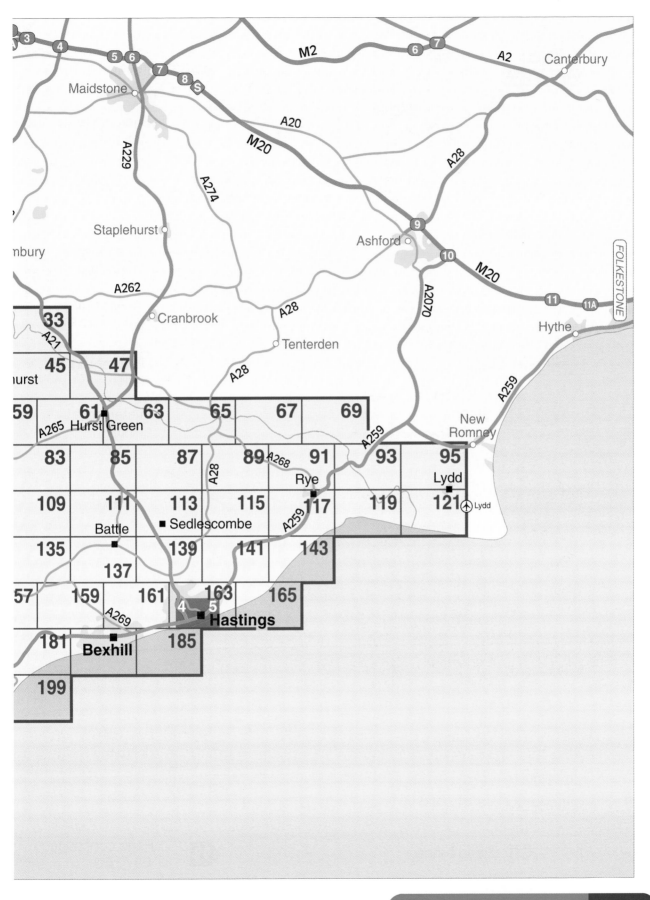

Canterbury

M2

A2

7

6

7

8 S

Maidstone

A20

A229

M20

A274

A28

9

Ashford

10

M20

A2070

11

11A

FOLKESTONE

Staplehurst

A262

Hythe

A259

33

A21

Cranbrook

A28

Tenterden

New
Romney

45

47

nbury

hurst

59

61

63

65

67

69

93

95

A265

Hurst Green

A28

A259

Lydd

83

85

87

89

A268

91

93

Lydd

A28

Rye

109

111

113

115

117

119

121

Lydd

Battle

Sedlescombe

A259

135

139

141

143

137

57

159

161

163

165

A269

4

5

181

Hastings

185

Bexhill

199

Junction 9	Motorway & junction
Services	Motorway service area
	Primary road single/dual carriageway
Services	Primary road service area
	A road single/dual carriageway
	B road single/dual carriageway
	Other road single/dual carriageway
	Restricted road
	Private road
← ←	One way street
	Pedestrian street
	Track/ footpath
	Road under construction
⫶⫶⫶⫶⫶	Road tunnel
P	Parking

P+	Park & Ride
	Bus/coach station
	Railway & main railway station
	Railway & minor railway station
⊖	Underground station
⊖	Light railway & station
+++++++++	Preserved private railway
LC	Level crossing
●—●—●—●	Tramway
- - - - - -	Ferry route
....	Airport runway
- · - · - · -	Boundaries- borough/ district
▼▼▼▼▼▼▼	Mounds
93	Page continuation 1:17,500
7	Page continuation to enlarged scale 1:10,000

	River/canal lake, pier			Toilet with disabled facilities
	Aqueduct lock, weir			Petrol station
465 Winter Hill	Peak (with height in metres)		PH	Public house
	Beach		PO	Post Office
	Coniferous woodland			Public library
	Broadleaved woodland		i	Tourist Information Centre
	Mixed woodland			Castle
	Park			Historic house/ building
	Cemetery		Wakehurst Place NT	National Trust property
	Built-up area		M	Museum/ art gallery
	Featured building		†	Church/chapel
	City wall			Country park
A&E	Accident & Emergency hospital			Theatre/ performing arts
	Toilet			Cinema

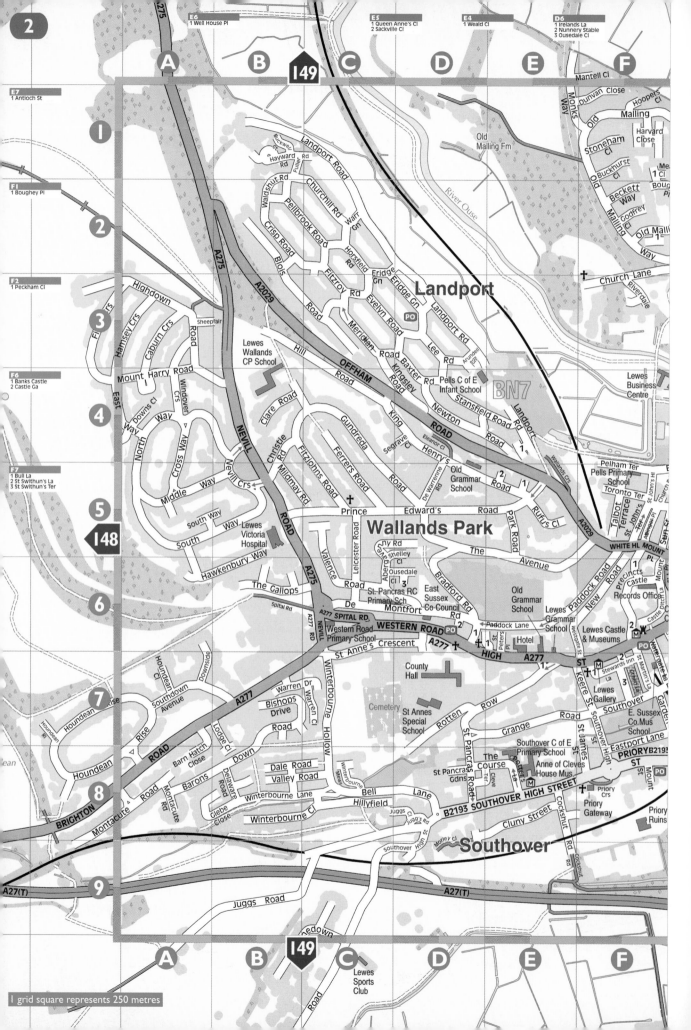

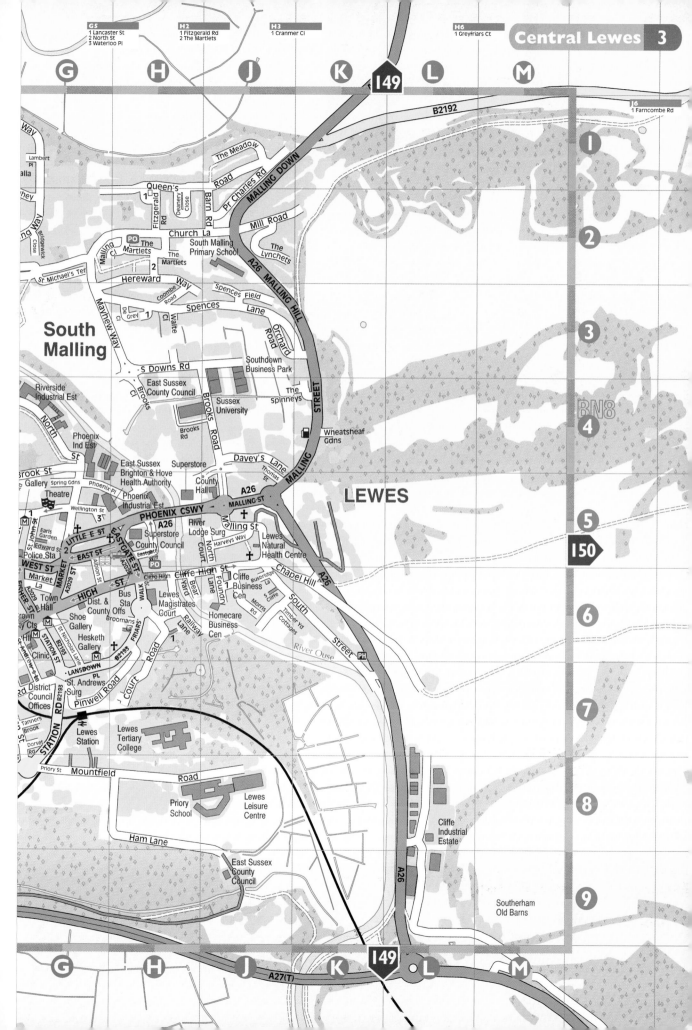

G5
1 Lancaster St
2 North St
3 Waterloo Pl

H2
1 Fitzgerald Rd
2 The Martlets

H3
1 Cranmer Ci

H6
1 Greyfriars Ct

J6
1 Farncombe Rd

G H J K L M

149

B2192

The Meadow Road

Queen's
Fitzgerald Rd
Deanery Close
Barn Rd
Pr Charles Rd
MALLING DOWN

Lambert Pl

Bridgewick Close

Church La
South Malling Primary School
Mill Road
PO The Martlets
The Martlets
2
St Michael's Ter
Malling
The Lynchets
A26 MALLING HILL

Hereward Way
Coombe Road
Spences Field
Mayhew Way
De Grey Cl 1 Waite Cl
Spences Lane
Orchard Road

South Malling

S Downs Rd
Southdown Business Park
Brooks
East Sussex County Council
Sussex University
The Spinneys
STREET

Riverside Industrial Est
North St
Brooks Rd
Brooks Road
MALLING

BN8

Phoenix Ind Est
Superstore
Davey's Lane
Wheatsheaf Gdns
Thomas St

Gallery
Spring Gdns
East Sussex Brighton & Hove Health Authority
Phoenix Pl
County Hall
A26

LEWES

Theatre
Phoenix Industrial Est
MALLING ST

Earls Garden
Wellington St
PHOENIX CSWY
A26
River Lodge Surg
Malling St

M
St John St
Edward St
LITTLE E ST
Superstore
County Council
Lewes Natural Health Centre
150

Police Sta
EAST GATE ST
Eastgate
Harveys Way
149

WEST ST
Market La
HIGH ST
PO
Cliffe High St
Cliffe High
Chapel Hill
A26

Town Hall
Dist. & County Offs
Bus Sta
WALK
Lewes Magistrates Court
Cliffe Business Cen
Bear Yard
Foundry Lane
Morris Rd
S Cliffe
Rusbridge La
South

Shoe Gallery
Broomans
FRIARS
Railway Lane
Homecare Business Cen
Timber Yd Cottages
Street

Clinic
Hesketh Gallery
LANSDOWN PL
1

Crown Cts
STATION ST
B2193
St Nicholas Lane
B2193
Court Road
River Ouse
PH

District Council Offices
St Andrews Surg
Pinwell Road

Tanners Brook
Lewes Station
Lewes Tertiary College

Dorset Rd
STATION RD B2193
Priory St
Mountfield Road

Priory School
Lewes Leisure Centre

Ham Lane

East Sussex County Council
A26
Cliffe Industrial Estate

Southerham Old Barns

G H J K L M
149
A27(T)

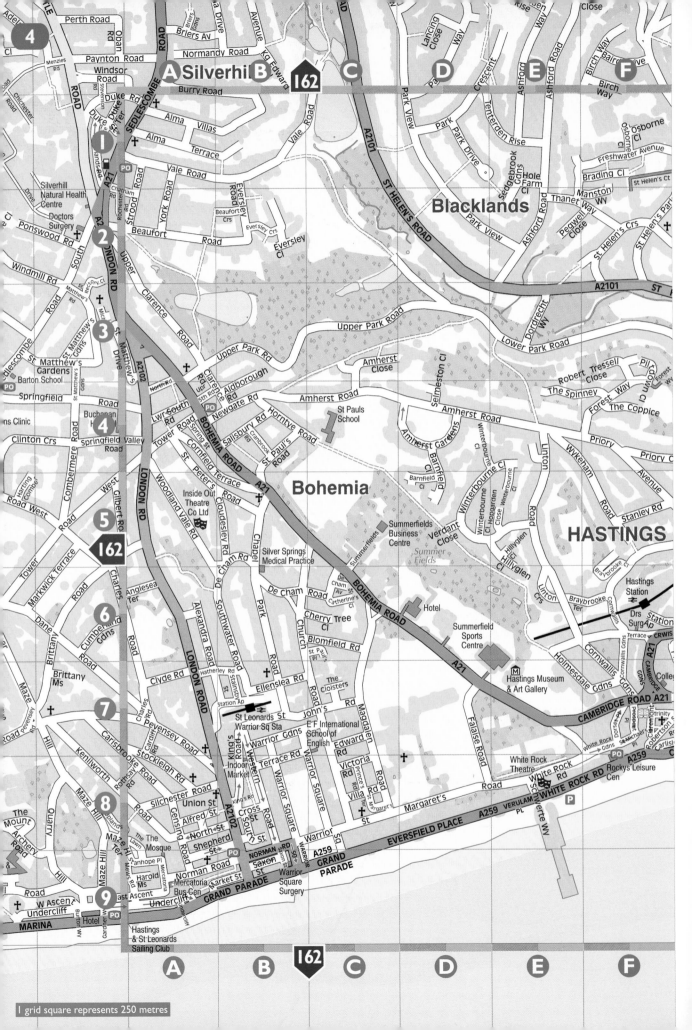

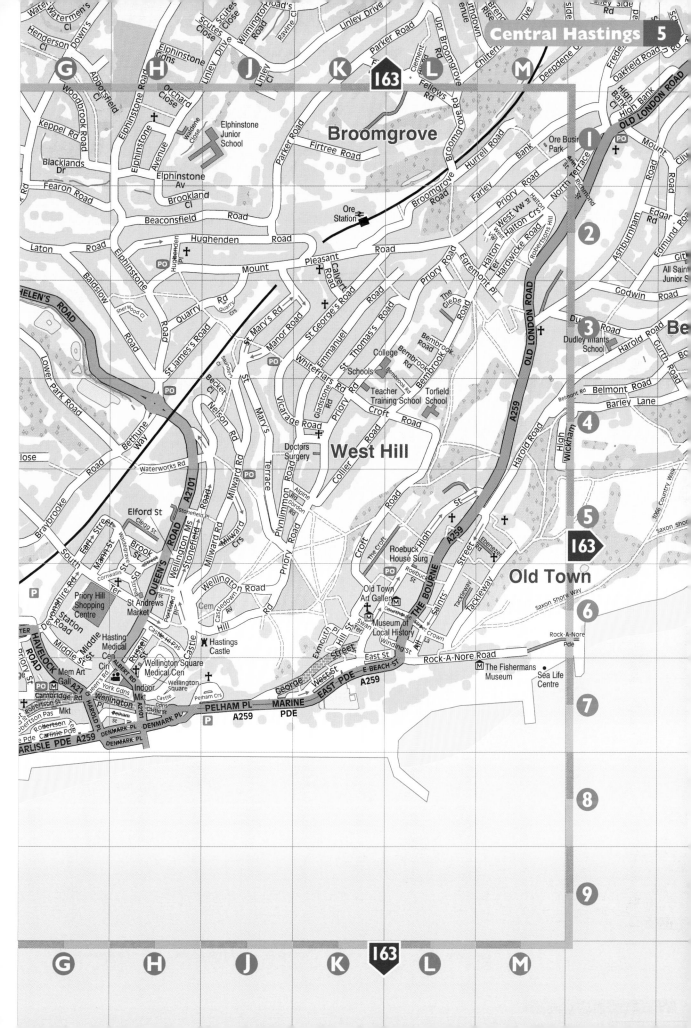

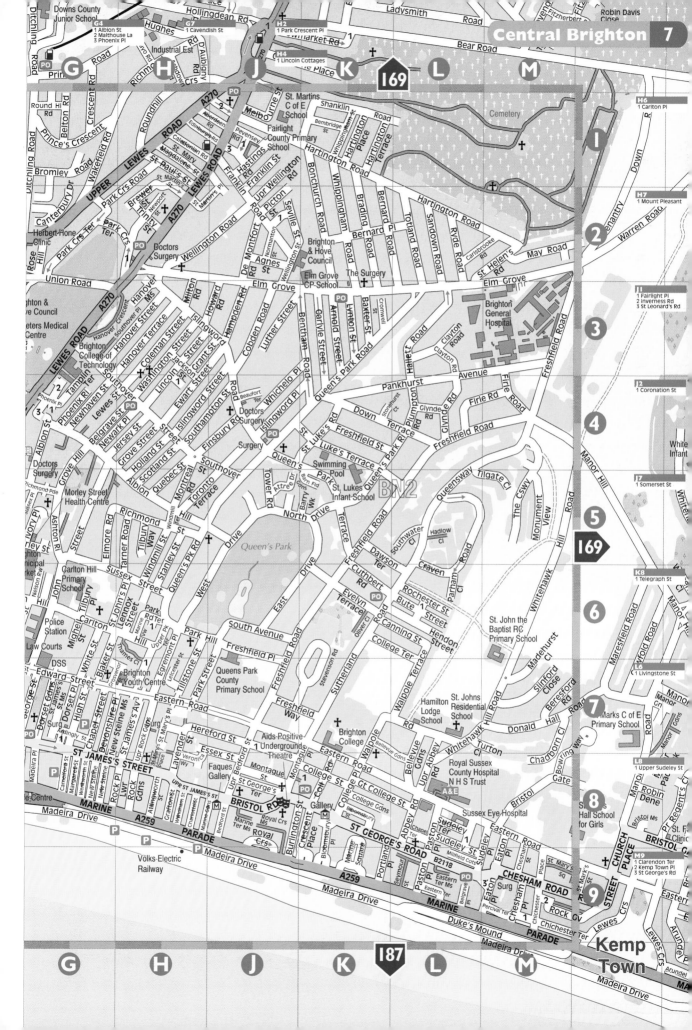

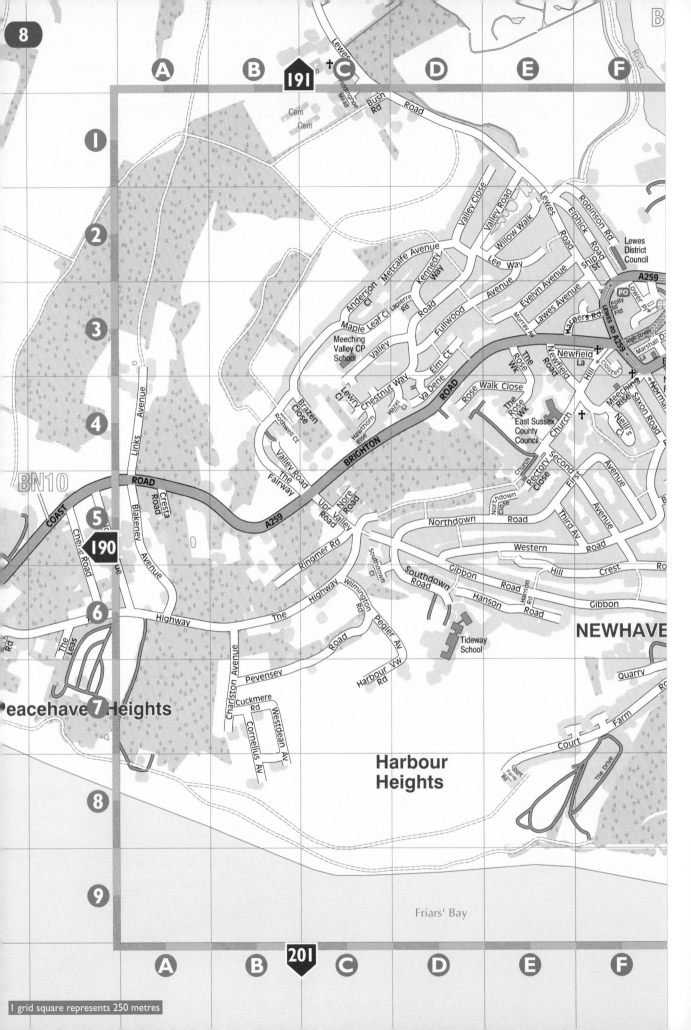

191

201

190

BN10

COAST

Peacehaven Heights

Harbour Heights

NEWHAVEN

Friars' Bay

Lewes District Council

East Sussex County Council

Meeching Valley CP School

Tideway School

A259

PO

Anderson Cl
Metcalfe Avenue
Maple Leaf Cl
Lapierre Rd
Kennedy Road
Valley
Fullwood
Elm Ct
Va Dene
Chestnut Way
Hawthorn
Hazel Cl
Lewry Cl
Brazen Close
Rothwell Ct
Valley Road
The Fairway
ROAD
BRIGHTON
Upr Valley Road
Nore Road
Ringmer Rd
The Highway
Wilmington Rd
Pegler Av
Southdown Cl
Southdown Road
Northdown
Northdown Close
Rectory Close
Church Hill
Second Avenue
First Avenue
Third Av
Western Road
Gibbon Road
Hanson Road
Hanson Rd
Crest Road
Gibbon
Quarry
Court Farm
Court Farm Rd
The drive
Highway
The
Charlston Avenue
Pevensey
Cuckmere Rd
Westdean Av
Cornelius Av
Harbour Vw Rd
The Leas
Rd
Cresta Road
Blakeney Avenue
Links Avenue
Chene Road
Valley Close
Valley Road
Willow Walk
Lee Way
Avenue
Evelyn Avenue
Lewes Avenue
Murray Av
Lewes Road
Elphick Road
Robinson Rd
Snipel St
Harpers Rd
Newfield La
Cloisters
Lewes Rd
Folly Fld
Lower
High Street
Marshall La
Newfield Road
The Rose WK
Rose Walk Close
The Rose WK
Rose Walk
Church
Church Hill
Meeching Rise
Neill's Cl
Saxon Road
Norman Rd
A259
Bush Rd
Bush Road
Piddinghoe Mead
Lewes Rd
Cem
Cem

A   **B**   **C**   **D**   **E**   **F**

B3   1 Kindersley Cl   A6   1 Windsor Pl   A5   1 Warburton Cl   A2   1 Sandhawes Hl

The Approach

Wilderness Rise

Road

1

The Avenue

Wilderwick Road

Wilderwick House

Blockfield Wood

Lower Stonehurst Farm

Lullenden

Shepherdsgrove Lane

Sussex Border Path

Vanguard Way

Gotwick Manor

2

Woodlands Road

Hoskins Rd

Spring

PO

Hollands Way

Jordans Court

Weald

1

Surrey County
West Sussex County

Gotwick Farm

Orchards

Stonequarry

Holtye Av

Quarry Rise

Close Cl

Victoria
I N H S Trust

Blenheim Close

Fulmar

Stirling Way

3

Turner Ct

Merlin Way

Lancaster Drive

Pegasus Drive

7

Holtye Road

Meridian Way

Hilary Close

Linton Park Av

Cleave

East Sussex County
West Sussex County

HOLTYE ROAD
A264

Shovelstrode Manor

Ashplats Wood

Fairlight Farm

Shovelstrode Lane

4

Mindleheim Avenue

East Court

Chestnut

San Feliu

13

Verbania Way

Sussex Border Path

Drive

Maple Drive

Rill Wk

Waterside

Homestall Stud

5

Estcots

Court Crs

Bourg-De-Peage Avenue

Elm Drive

Wagg Close

Lower Dene

7

Sycamore Drive

Sackville School

Freemans Md

The Courtyard

Brook Cl

Potter Wk

Escotts Avenue

The Del

Shovelstrode Farm

Laurel Dene

Old Rd

Escotts County Primary School

Benchfield Close

Farm Cl

The Glades

LEWES RD

Fairfield Road

Richmond

Martyns Place

Tanyard Av

Oak Crs

Barton Crs

York Av

1

The Oaks

Kingdom

LEWES ROAD
A22

Woodbury Close

Worsted Farm

Shovelstrode Farm

6

ow Md

2 Dr

4

3

Glendyne Way

Glendyne Close

Hotel

Worsted Lane

Oakley Close

Stoke Brunswick

Homestall Road

ampton
wy
ay

Buckingham Drive

Brockhurst

Lane

7

Windmill Lane

Westfield

Luxfords La

Sussex Border Path

Box Lane

Dirty Lane

RH19

The Rocks

Ivy Dene La

Beeches Lane

Woods Hill

Maypole Road

Phoenix Lane

School

Allen's

Chapel La

Hammerwood Road

8

PO

Woods Hill Cl

Wr Cl

Ashurst
Wood

A   **B**   **C**   **24**   **D**   **E**   **F**

Brambletye School

Luxfords Lane

Wall

Sussex Border Pth

1 grid square represents 500 metres

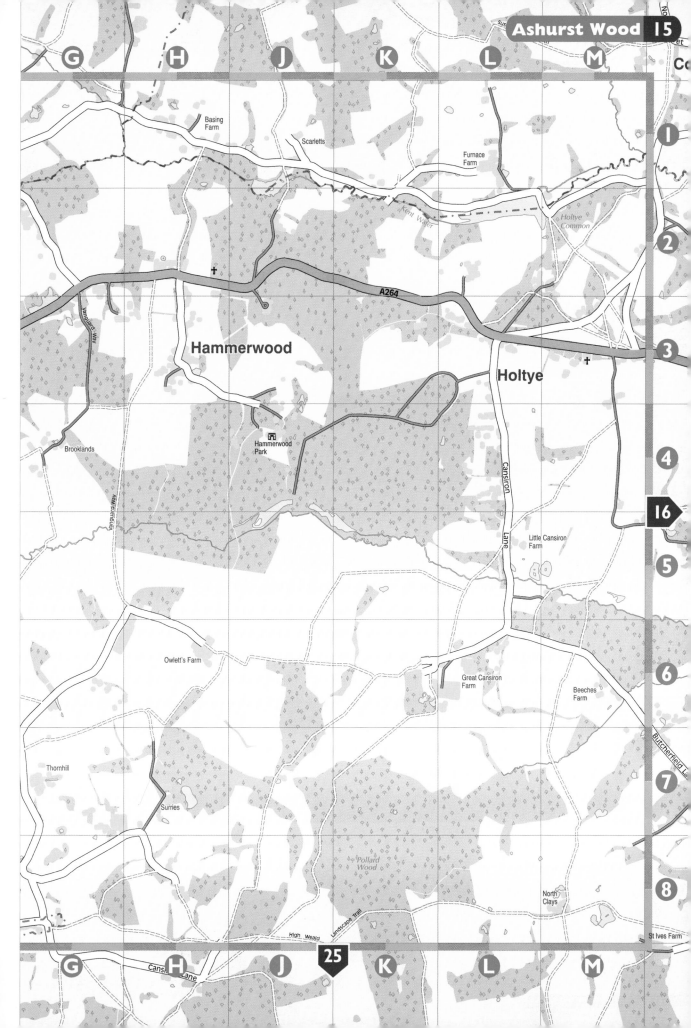

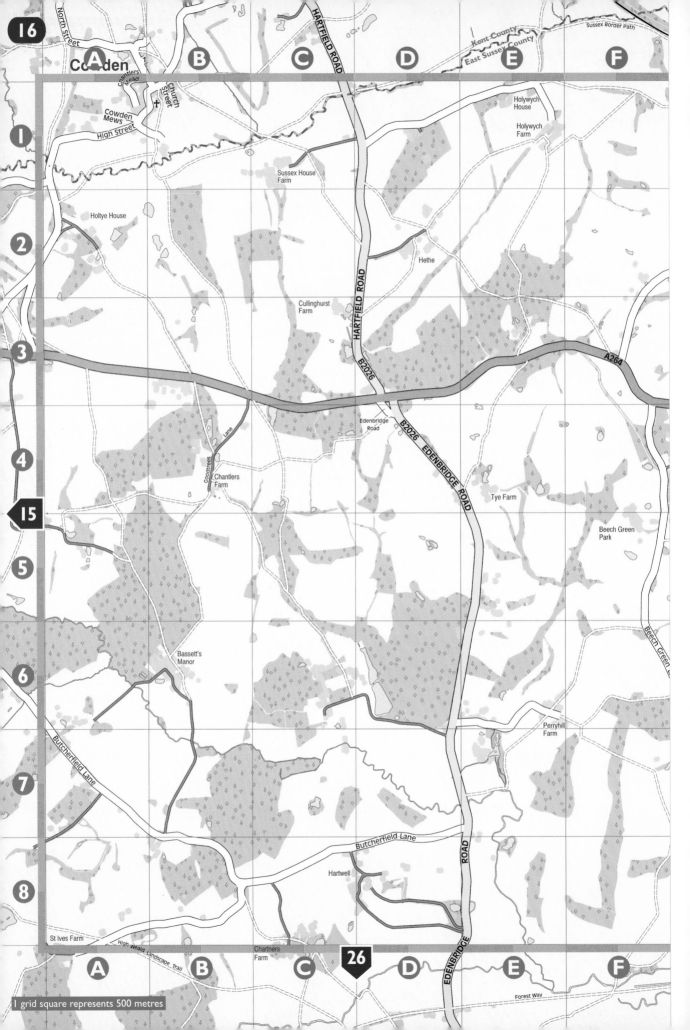

A Cowden B C HARTFIELD ROAD D E F

Chantlers Mead

Church Street

Cowden Mews

High Street

1

North Street

Holtye House

Sussex House Farm

Holywych House

Holywych Farm

2

Hethe

Cullinghurst Farm

HARTFIELD ROAD B2026

3

A264

Edenbridge Road

B2026 EDENBRIDGE ROAD

Goodtrees Lane

Chantlers Farm

Tye Farm

4

15

Beech Green Park

5

Beech Green Lane

Bassett's Manor

6

Perryhill Farm

Butcherfield Lane

7

Butcherfield Lane

8

Hartwell

St Ives Farm

High Weald Landscape Trail

Chartners Farm

EDENBRIDGE ROAD

A B C **26** D E F

Forest Way

Kent County
East Sussex County

Sussex Border Path

1 grid square represents 500 metres

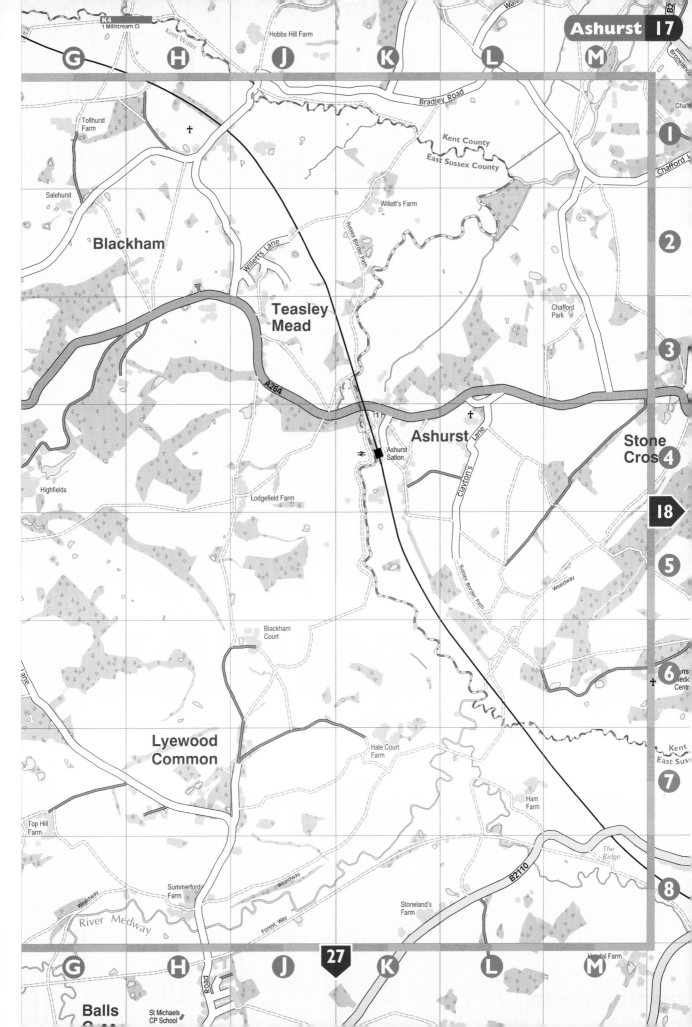

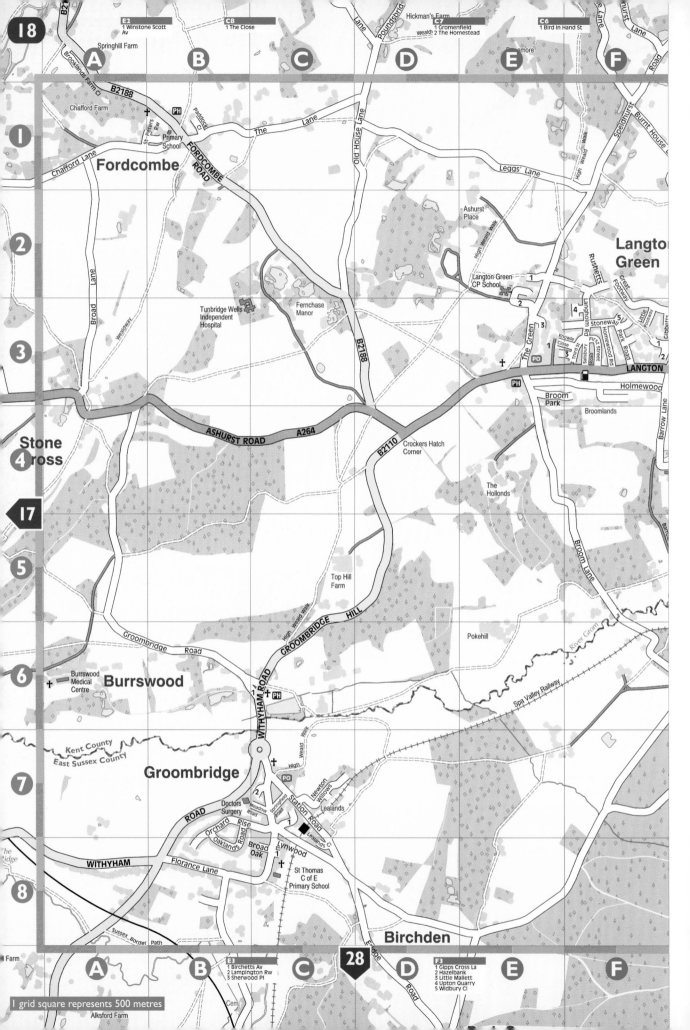

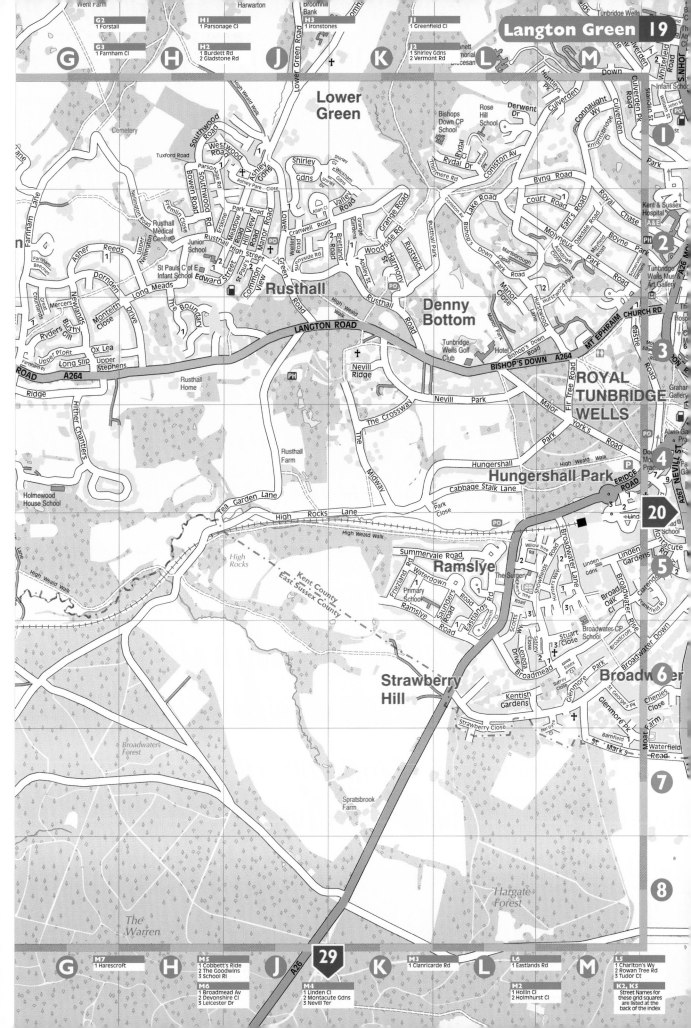

G H J K L M

St Georges School

TN2

PEMBURY

High Street
The Paddock
The Mews
Cornford Pk
Penns Yard
Camden Av
Highfield Close
PO
Henwoods Crescent
Henwoods Mount
Woodside Road
Sandhurst Av

Henwood

PEMBURY RD

Cornford Lane

Chalket Lane

Belfield Rd
Stanam Road

Woodside Close

Kin

A21(T)

HASTINGS ROAD

Pastheap

Elmhu Farm

Larkfield Hall

High Weald Walk

High Weald Walk

Fletchers Farm

Mouseden

Little Bayhall

Chalket Farm

Great Bayhall

High Woods Lane

Dodhurst

River Teise

Dundale Farm

Gr Sa W

Dundale Road

Kent County

East Sussex County

Brown's Wood

Dundale Road

Sunninglye Farm

Furnace Wood

Tollslye

Rushlye Down

Oxpasture Wood

Rushlye Farm

Abbots Down

ews Wood

Bayham Lake

G H J **31** K L M

Middle Road

Bells Yew Green

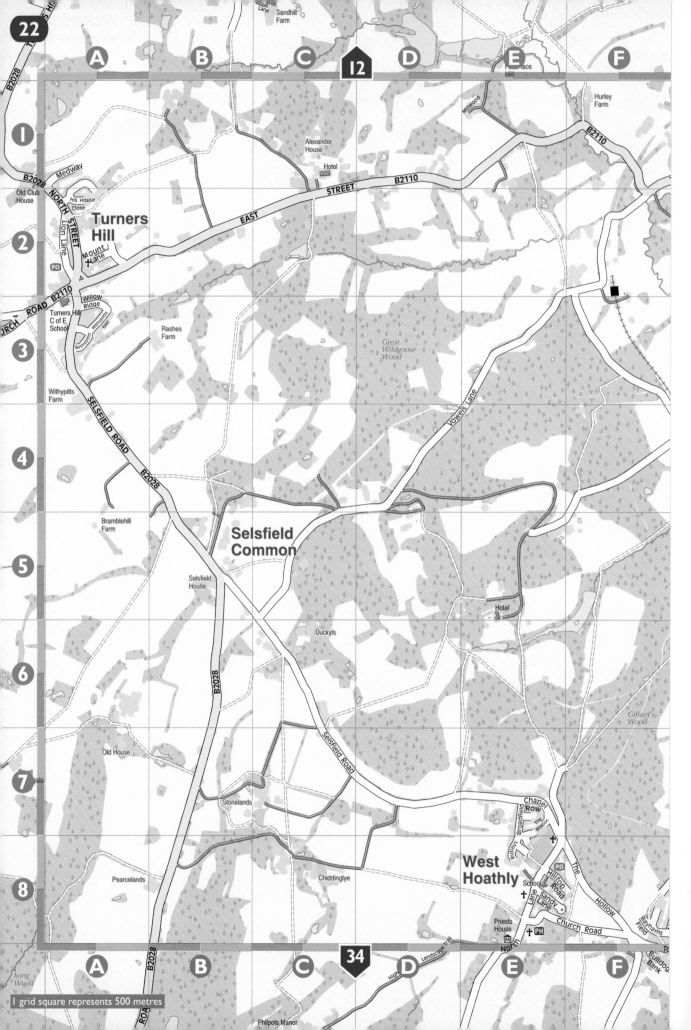

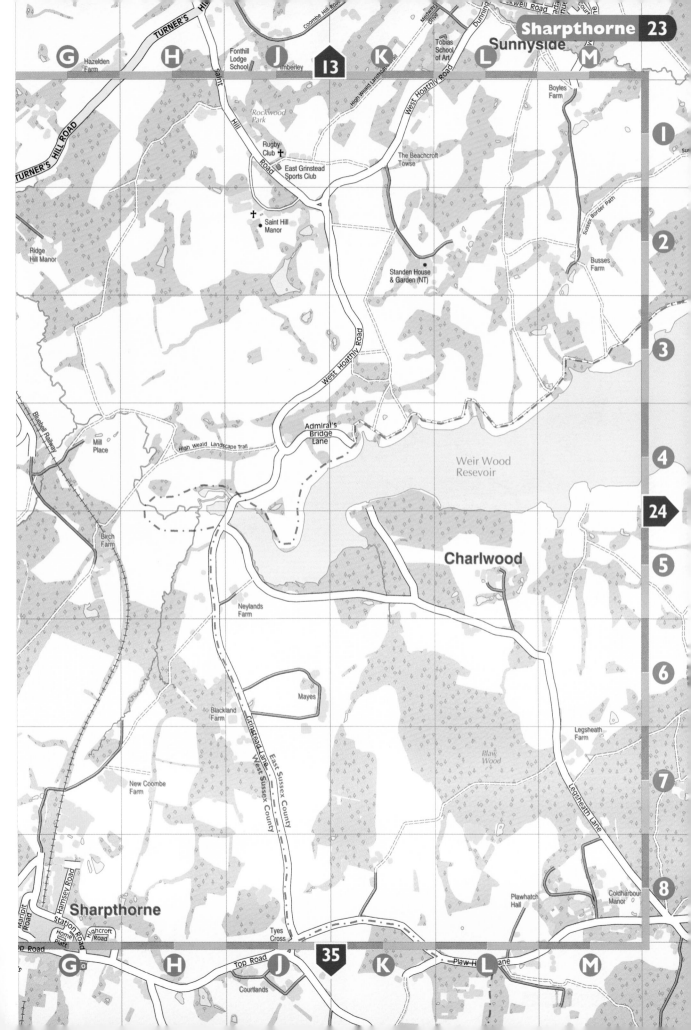

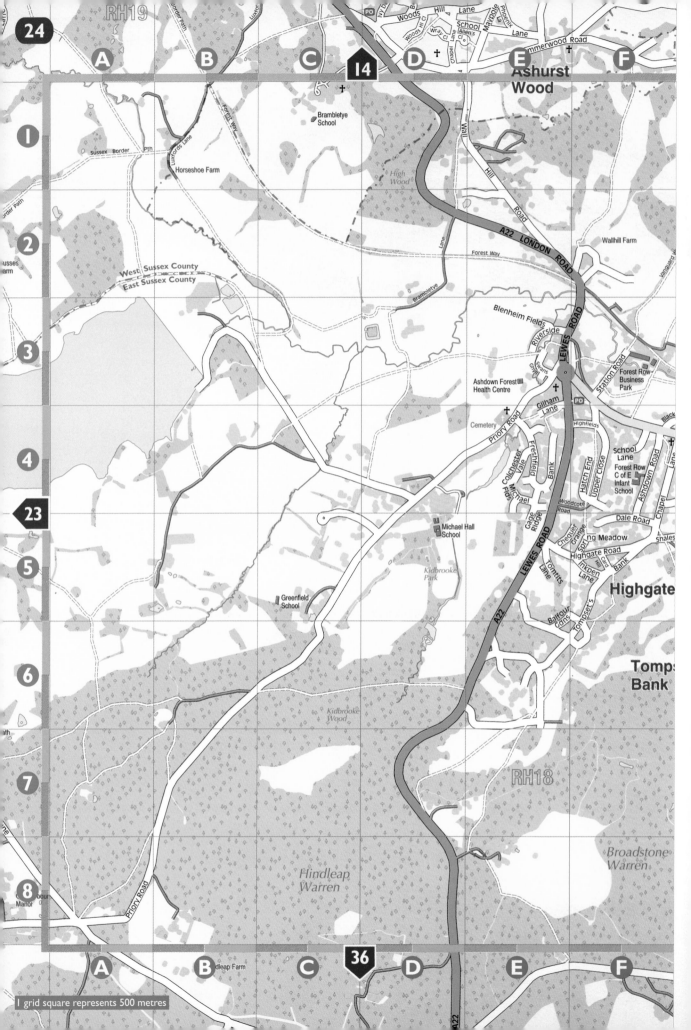

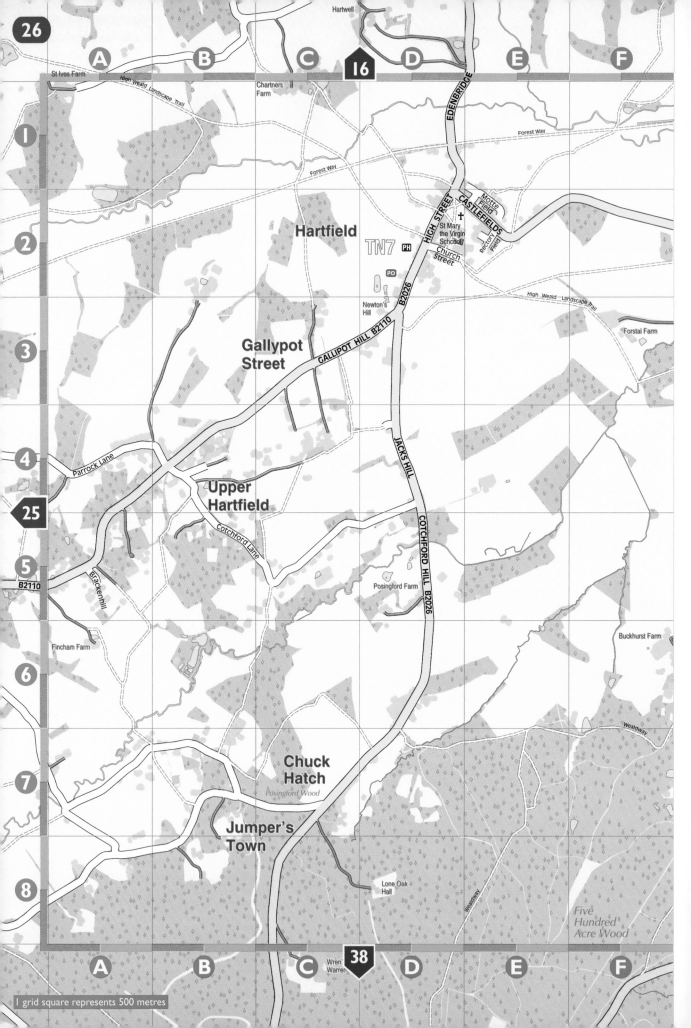

A   B   C   16   D   E   F

I

2

Hartwell

St Ives Farm

High Weald Landscape Trail

Chartners Farm

EDENBRIDGE

Forest Way

Forest Way

Hartfield

Motte Field

CASTLEFIELDS

HIGH STREET

St Mary the Virgin School

Rectory Field

TN7   PH

Church Street

PO

High Weald Landscape Trail

Newton's Hill

Forstal Farm

3   Gallypot Street

GALLIPOT HILL B2110

B2026

4   Parrock Lane

JACKS HILL

25

Cotchford Lane

Upper Hartfield

5   Brackenhill

B2110

Posingford Farm

COTCHFORD HILL B2026

Fincham Farm

Buckhurst Farm

6

Wealdway

7   Chuck Hatch

Posingford Wood

Jumper's Town

Lone Oak Hall

Wealdway

8   Five Hundred Acre Wood

A   B   C   38   D   E   F

Wren' Warren

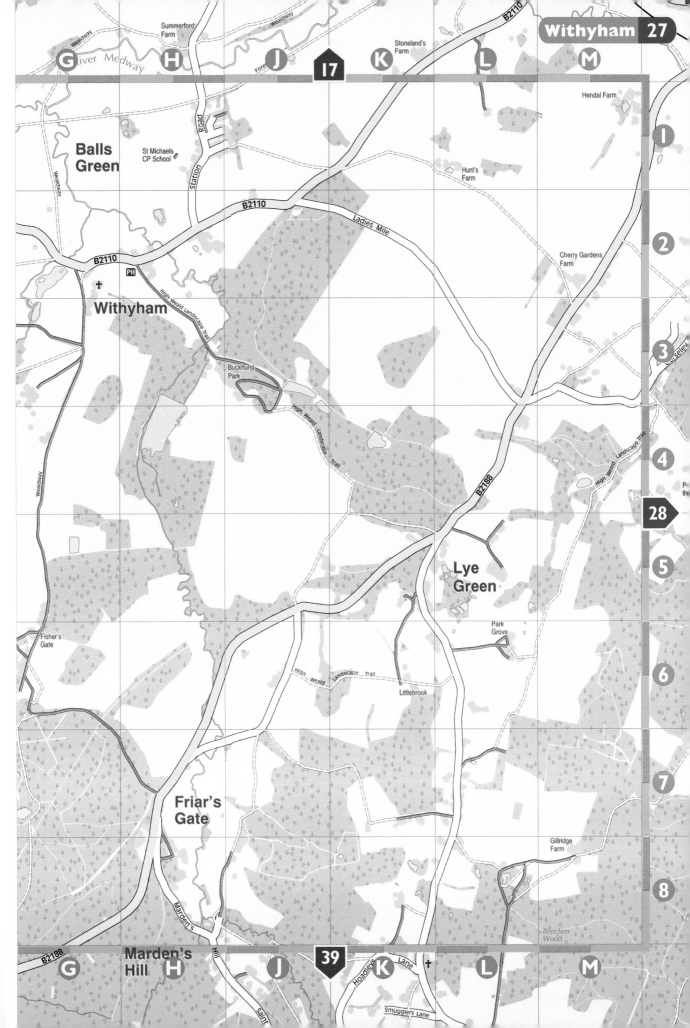

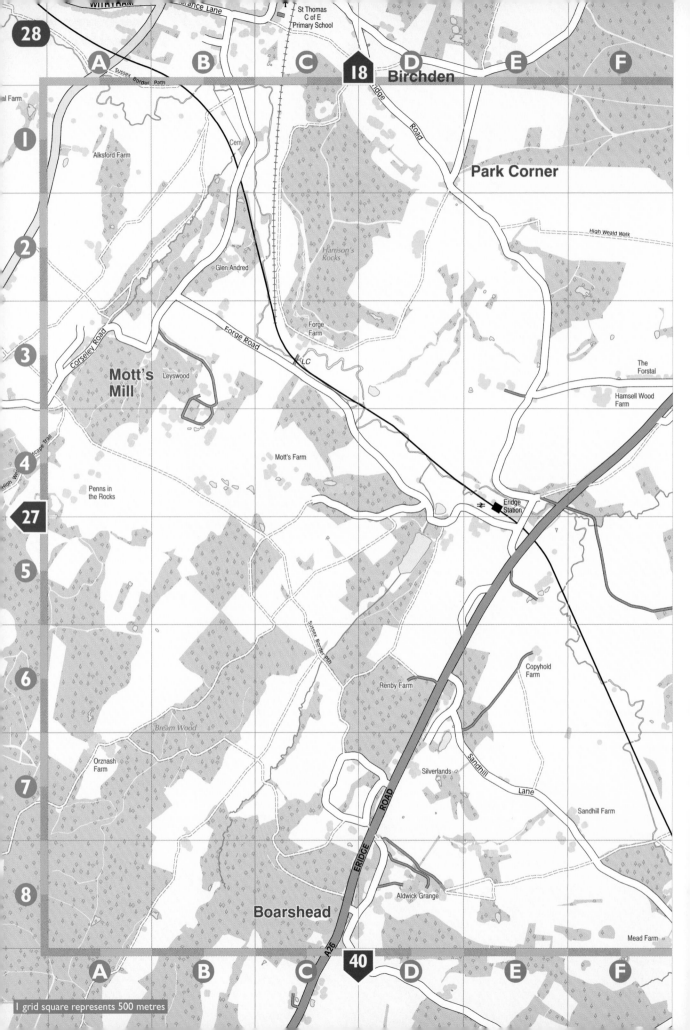

A   B   C   **18** **Birchden**   D   E   F

Park Corner

1

I Farm

Alksford Farm

High Weald Walk

2

Glen Andred

Harrison's
Rocks

3

Corseley Road

**Mott's
Mill**

Leyswood

Forge Road

LC

Forge
Farm

The
Forstal

Hamsell Wood
Farm

High Weald Scarp Trail

4

Mott's Farm

Penns in
the Rocks

Eridge
Station

5

6

Copyhold
Farm

Renby Farm

Bream Wood

7

Orznash
Farm

Silverlands

Sandhill
Lane

Sandhill Farm

8

Eridge Road

Aldwick Grange

Boarshead

Mead Farm

A26

A   B   C   **40** D   E   F

Hargate
Forest

G   H   J   19   K   L   M

The
Warren

I

2

Warren
Farm   Eridge
Park   Whitehill
Wood

3
Warren Farm
Lane   **Eridge Green**

High Weald Walk

4

Forge
Wood

30

5

Hamsell
Manor

6

Danegate   Sussex Border Path

Stonewall

7

Sussex Border Path
Stitches Farm   Great
Danegate   8

Blackdon Hill

Redgate Mill
Farm   Green Hedges
Farm

G   H   J   41   K   L   M

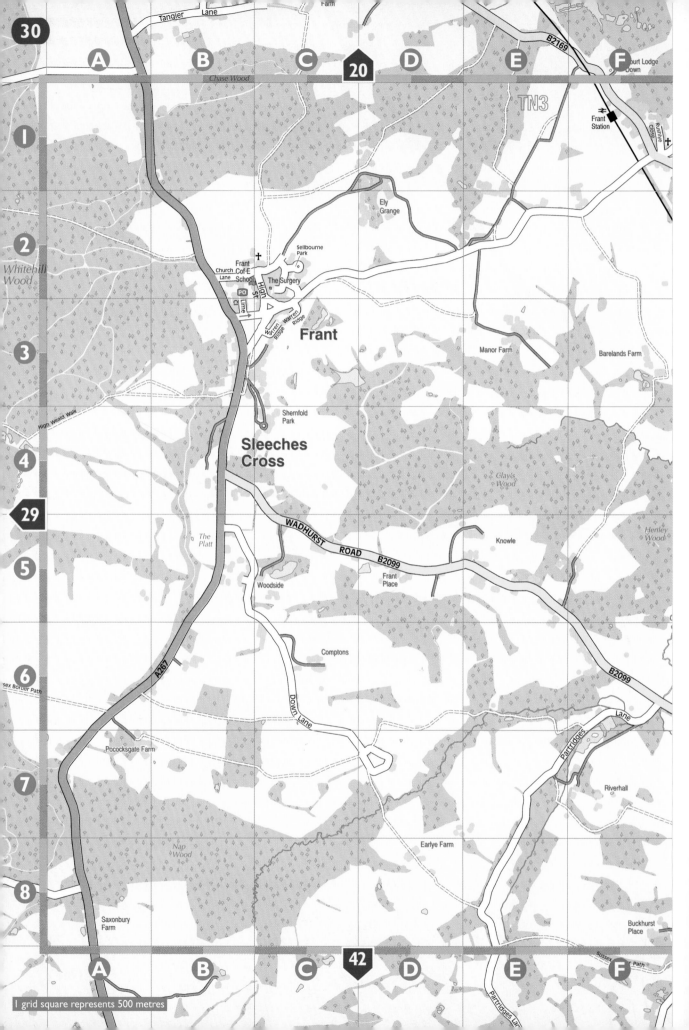

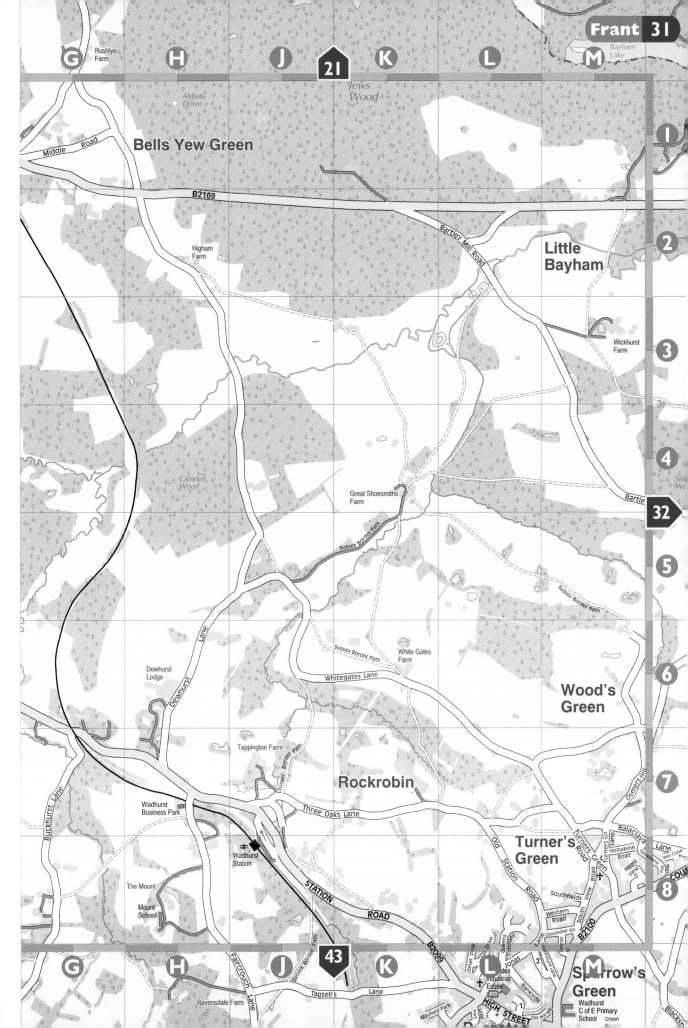

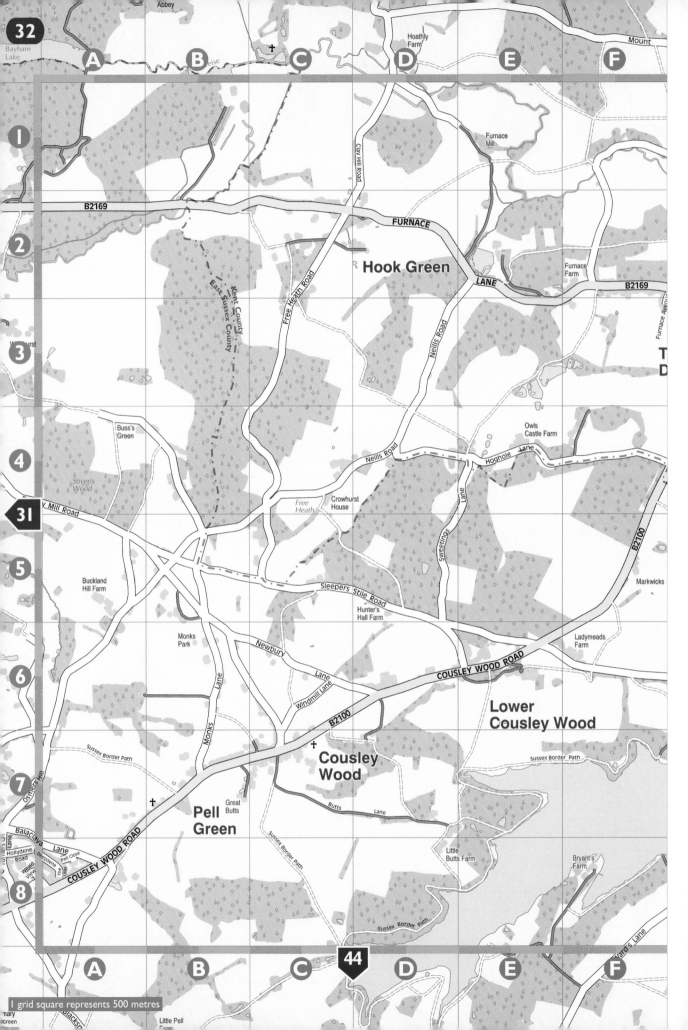

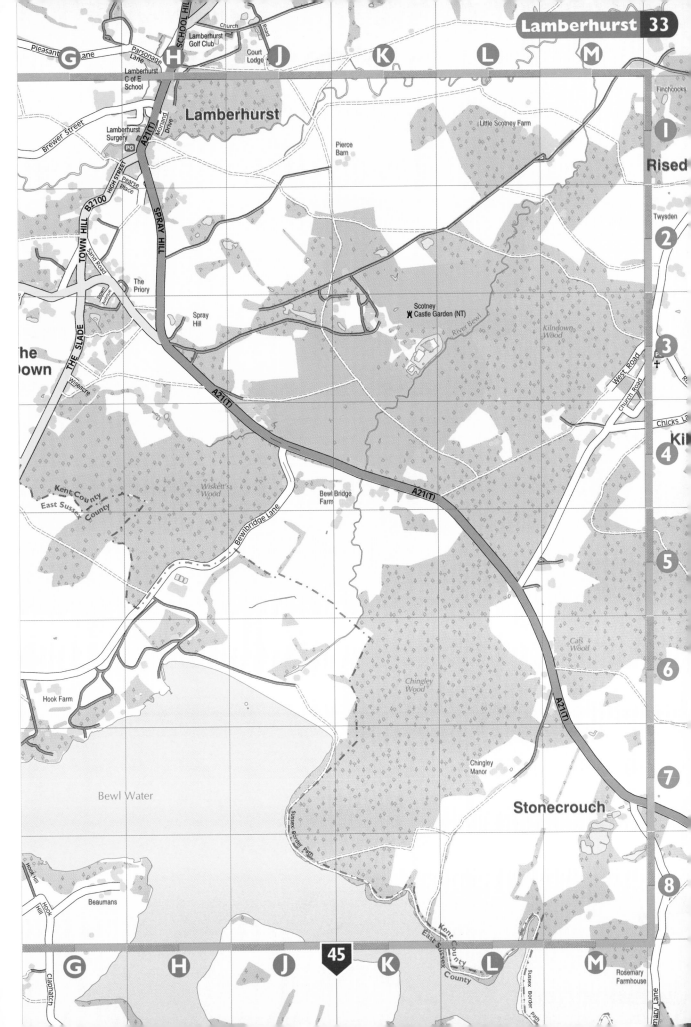

Pleasant Lane
SCHOOL HILL
Church Road
Lamberhurst Golf Club
Court Lodge
G
H
J
K
L
M

Parsonage Lane
Lamberhurst C of E School
Lamberhurst
Finchcocks

Brewer Street
Lamberhurst Surgery
PO
MORLAND DRIVE
Pierce Barn
Little Scotney Farm

I

Rised

Twysden

Pearse Place
SPRAY HILL
HIGH STREET
A21(T)
B2100
TOWN HILL
Sand Road

2

The Priory
Spray Hill

Scotney Castle Garden (NT)
River Bewl
Kilndown Wood

West Road

3

THE SLADE
Down Avenue

Church Road
Chicks Lane

Ki

Wiseacre

A21(T)

4

The
Down

Kent County
East Sussex County

Wiskett's Wood

Bewl Bridge Farm

A21(T)

5

Bewlbridge Lane

6

Hook Farm

Cats Wood

Chingley Wood

A21(T)

Chingley Manor

7

Bewl Water

Sussex Border Path

Stonecrouch

8

Hook Hill
Hook Hill

Beaumans

Kent County
East Sussex County

Sussex Border Path

Rosemary Farmhouse

Clapdatch
Rosemary Lane

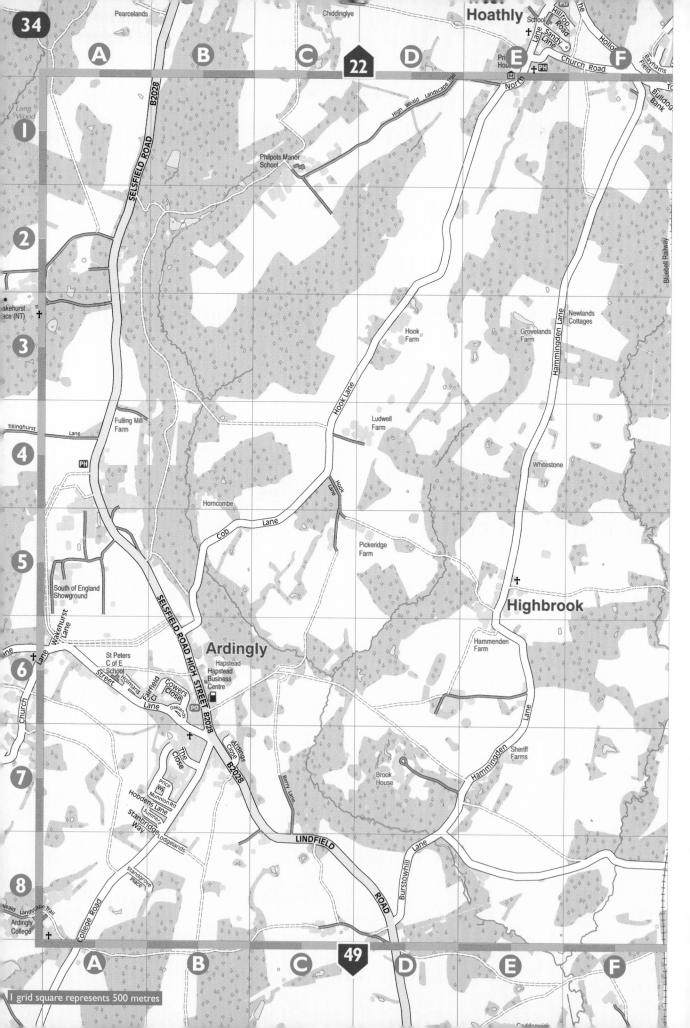

A B C 22 D E F

I

2

3

4

5

6

7

8

A B C 49 D E F

Hoathly

Pearcelands

Chiddinglye

Hilltop Road

School

Sandy Lane

Hollo

Church road

Baynams Field

Bulldog Bank

Long Wood

High Weald Landscape Trail

Philpots Manor School

Pri Hou

North

SELSFIELD ROAD B2028

Hook Farm

Hammingden Lane

Newlands Cottages

Grovelands Farm

akehurst ce (NT)

Tillinghurst

Lane

Fulling Mill Farm

Hook Lane

Ludwell Farm

Whitestone

PH

Horncombe

Cob Lane

Hook Lane

Pickeridge Farm

Highbrook

South of England Showground

Wakehurst Lane

SELSFIELD ROAD HIGH STREET

Ardingly

Hapstead Business Centre

Hammenden Farm

Church

St Peters C of E School

Holmans

Fairfield Lane

Gowers Close

Oaklands

PO

B2028

Hammingden Lane

Sheriff Farms

The Close

Ardings Close B2028

Berry Lane

Brook House

Price Munnion Rd

Hobdens Lane

Summer

Stanbridge Way

Lodgelands

LINDFIELD

Burstowhill Lane

ROAD

Standgrove Place

College Road

Weald Landscape Trail

Ardingly College

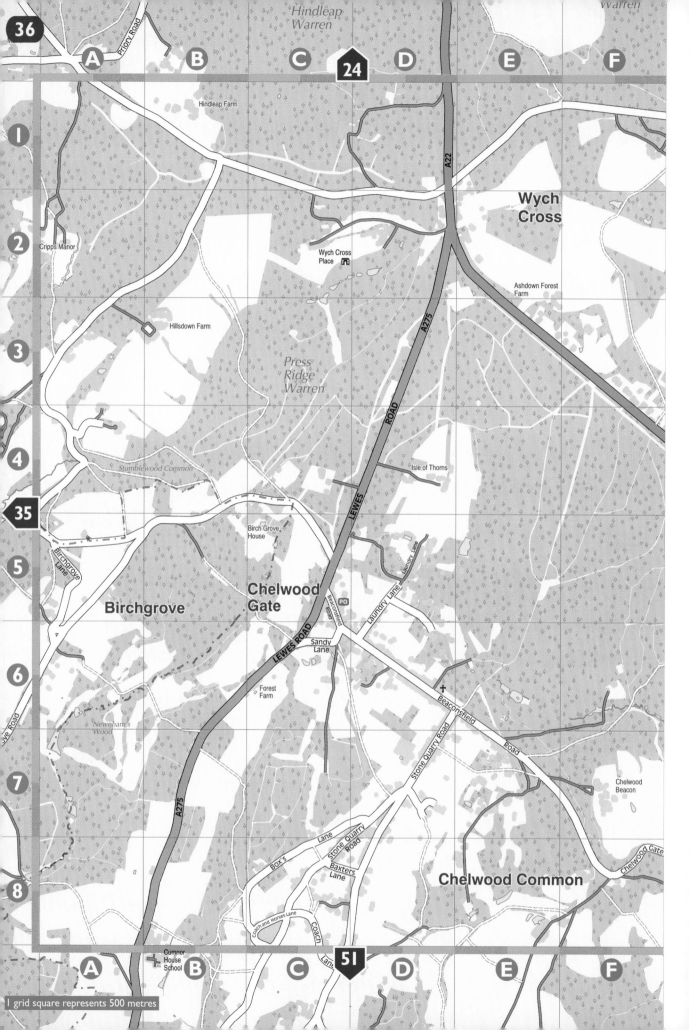

A   B   C   26   D   E   F   Five
                                        Hundred
                                        Acre Wood

Lone Oak
Hall

Wren's
Warren

1

Gills
Lap

Vanguard Way

2

Wood
Eaves

3

Wealdway

B2026

King's
Standing

Greenwood
Gate

4

Vanguard Way

5

Wealdway

B2188

Old Mill
House

6

Wealdway

B2026

Crabtree
Farm

7

Wealdway

Vanguard Way

8

ugh Road

The Doves
Nest

Duddleswell
Manor

Wealdway

A   B   C   53   D   E   F

Vanguard Way

Barnsgate

1 grid square represents 500 metres

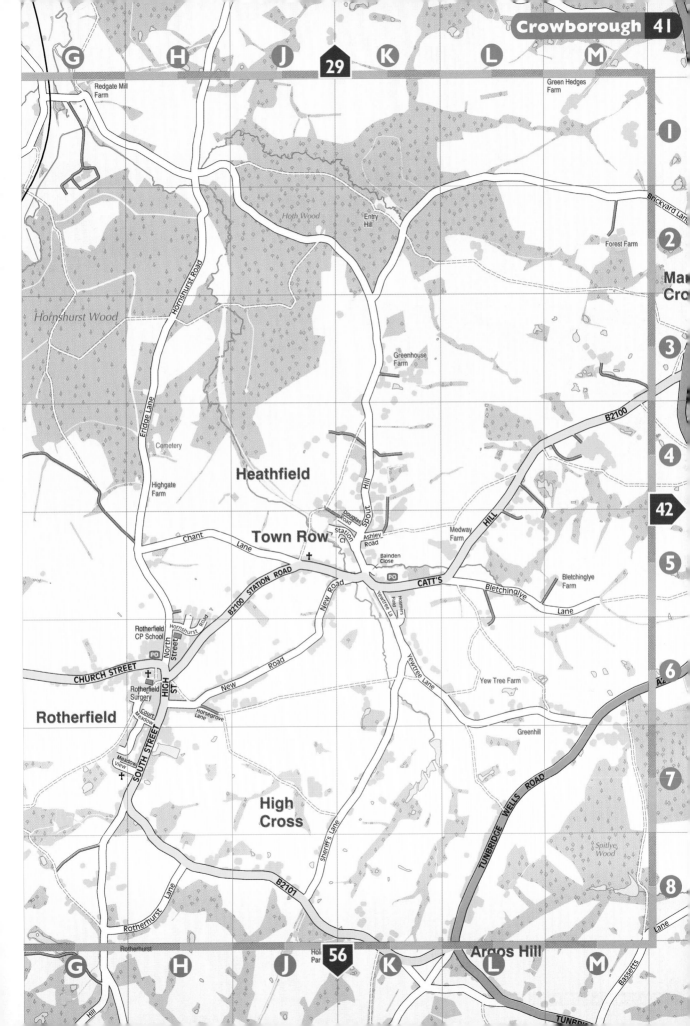

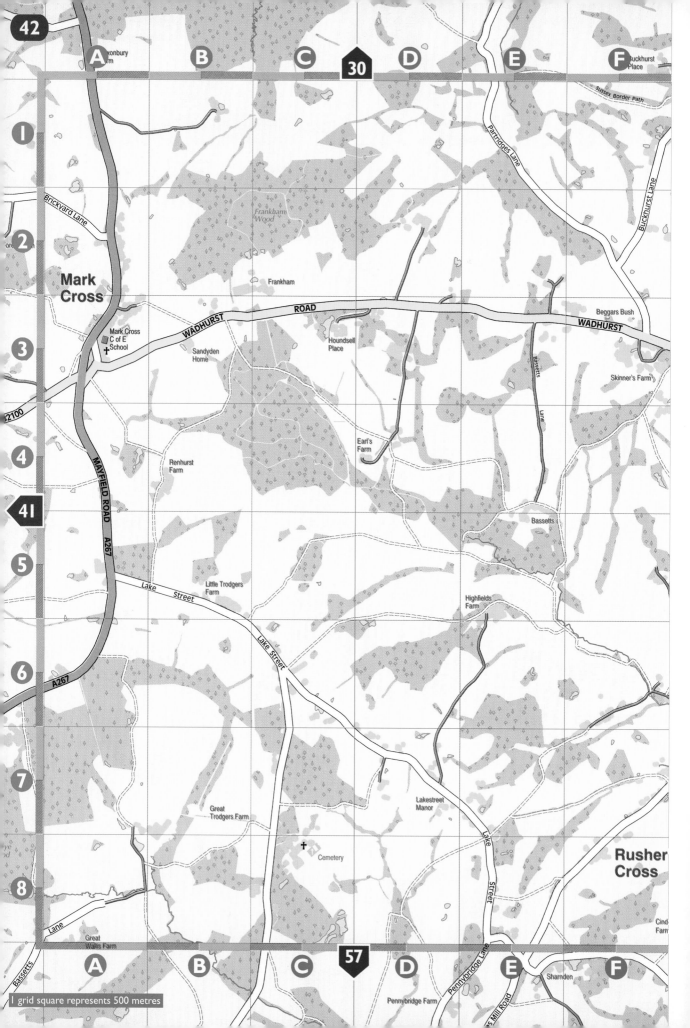

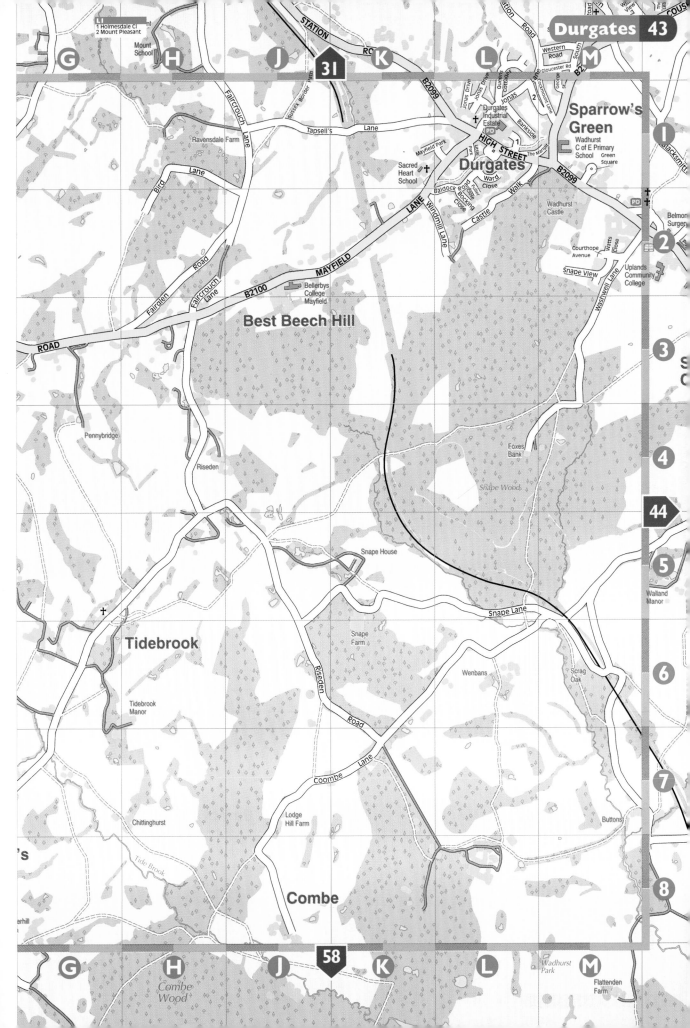

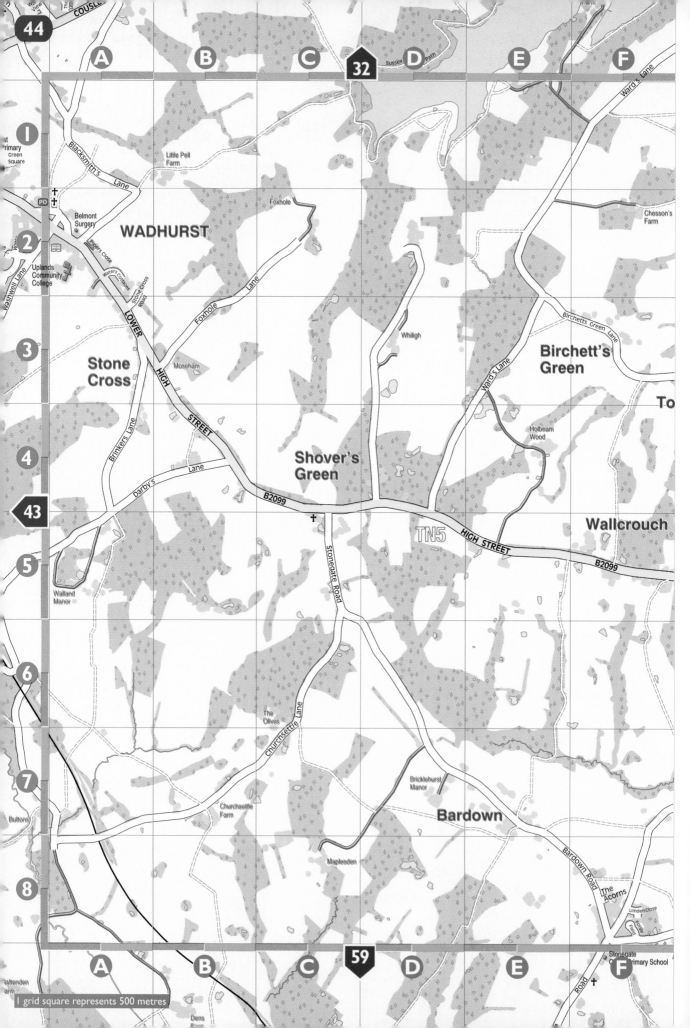

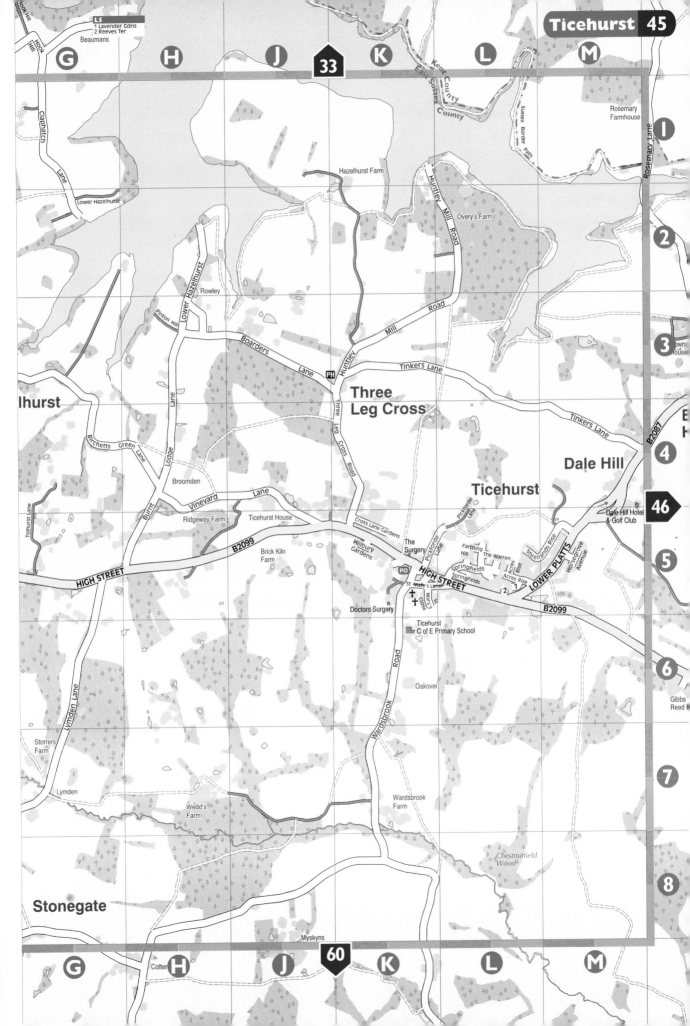

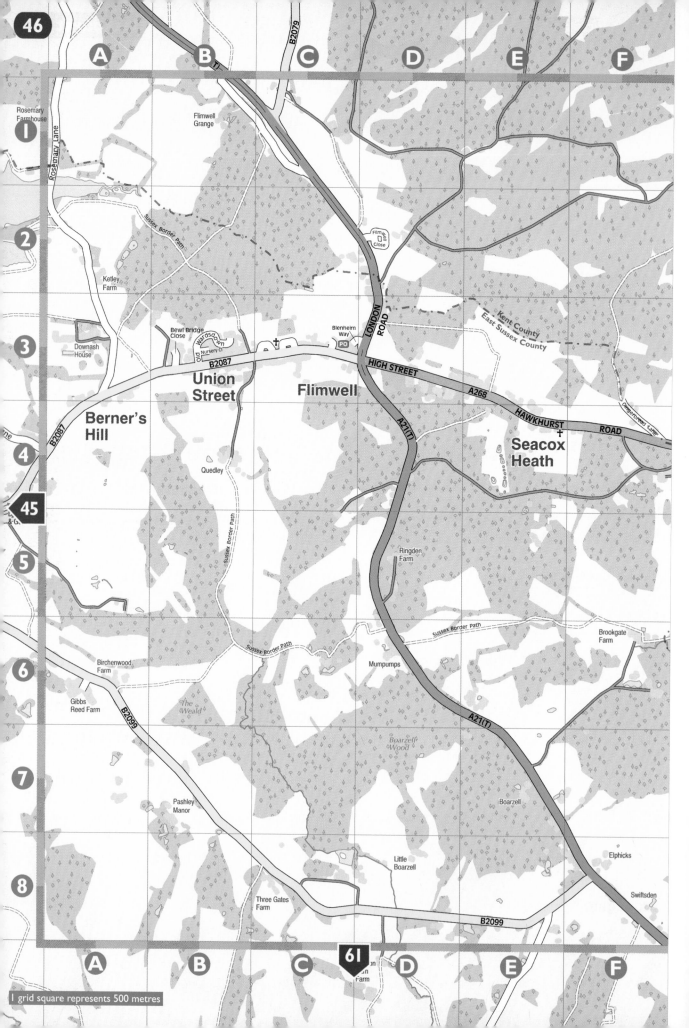

M4
1 Northgrove Rd
2 Post Office Rd

Trenley Farm

Gill's Green

Frith Farm

Tanyard Farm

Limes Grove

Soper's Lane

Siseley Farm

Soper's Lane

Slip Mill Road

Wellington Cottages

Ockley

Ockley Lane

Slip Mill

Cranbrook Road

Springfield Industrial Estate

A229

Little Pix Hall Farm

High Street

Slip Mill Road

Slip Mill Rd

Squash Club

Oakfield

Vale Rd

Woodham Rd

Winchester Rd

Western Road

Terrace

Western Av

Ockley Road

Hospital

A268

HIGH STREET

Slip

Marlborough House School

Hawkhurst

Theobalds

Highgate Hill

Fairview

Doctors Surgery Mercers

Highfield

Elm Hill House

Delmonden Road

North Hill Road

Oaklands Rd

Copt

Delmonden Manor

Sussex Border Path

Sussex Border Path

Hensill House

Wish Valley Surgery

Moor Hill Road

Hall House

Delmonden House

Sussex Border Path

Hawkhurst C of E Primary

Horns Road

Delmonden Road

PO

The Chestnuts

Heansill La

Red Oak

Talbot

The Moor

The Moor

Bokes Farm

A229

HORNS ROAD

Avards Close

Cowden Close

Stream Lane

Horns Corner

Collingwood House

B2244

Cowden Lane

Cowden

Lillesden

HASTINGS ROAD

A229

Kent County

East Sussex County

Cemetery

A21(T)

Coldha

Merriments Lane

Merriments Farm

Stone House

Congh

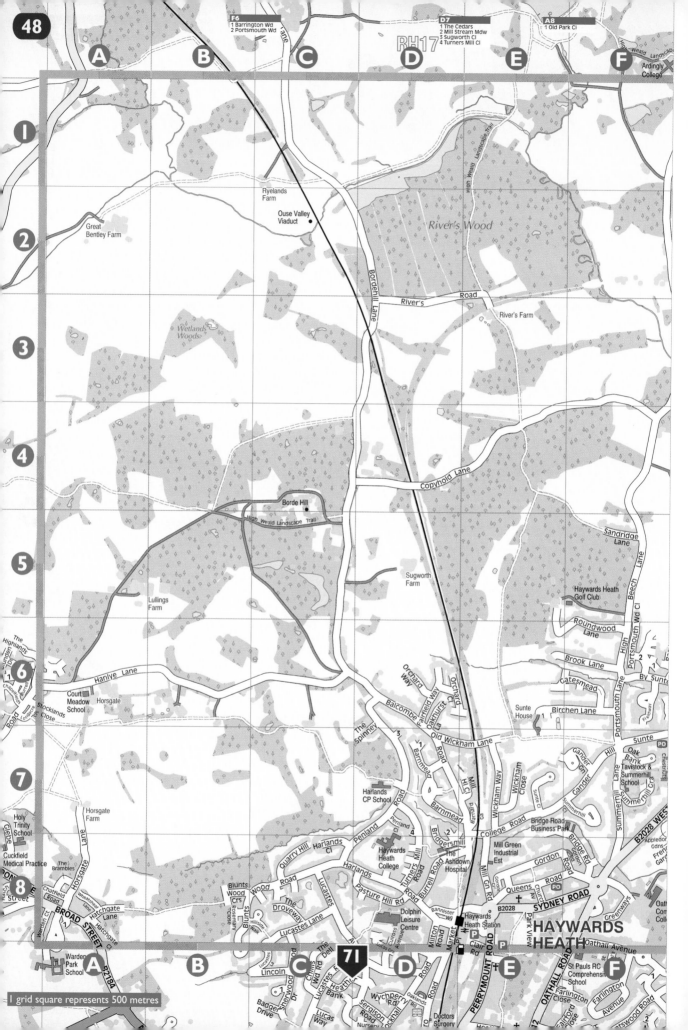

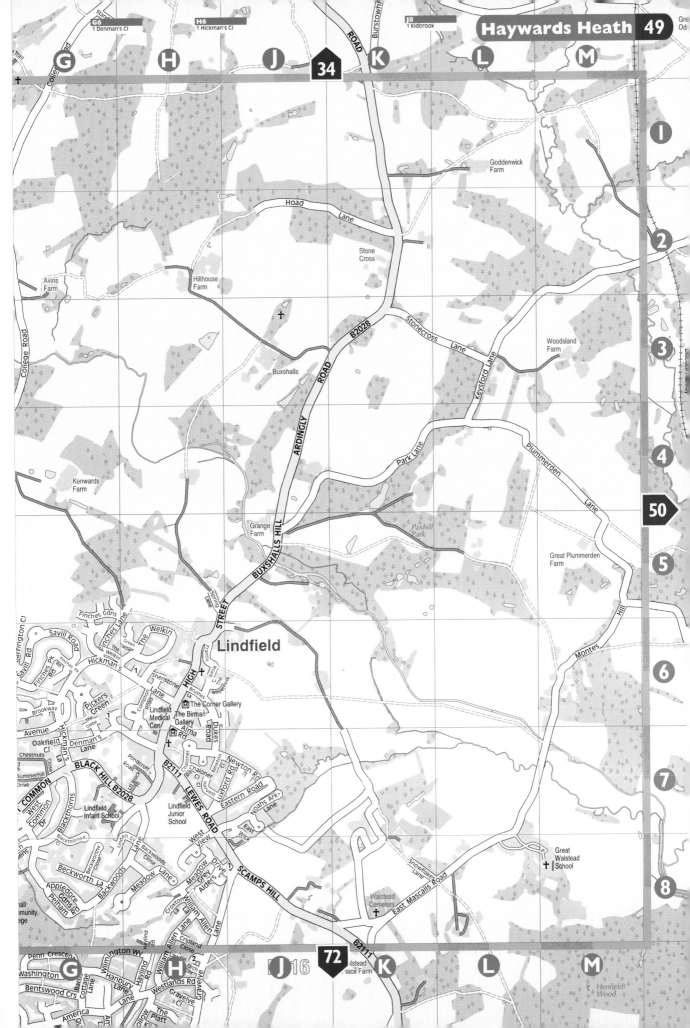

A   B   C   **35**   D   E   F

1
2
49
5
6
7
8

A   B   C   **73**   D   E   F

Great Oddynes

Horsted Keynes
C of E School

**Horsted
Keynes**

Waterbury
Hill

Cheeleys
Leighton Rd
Station Road
Ludwell
Keysford Lane
Sugar Lane
Boxes La
Jefferies
Rixons Cl
Lewes
Church La
Chapel Lane
PO
Bonfire Lane
Challoners
Hamsland
Wyatts Lane
Lucas
Birchgrove Road
Danehill Lane
Horsted

Wyatts

Sussex Border Pth

West Sussex County
East Sussex County

Freshfield Lane

Bluebell Railway

Treemans Road

Latchetts

Stoaches
Farm

Sussex Border Path

Hill

Cockhaise Mill
Farm

Monteswood   Lane

Freshfield
Crossways

Freshfield Lane

Town
Place

Ketche's Lane

Northlands Farm

Sussex Border Path

Slider

Bluebell Railway

enfield

1 grid square represents 500 metres

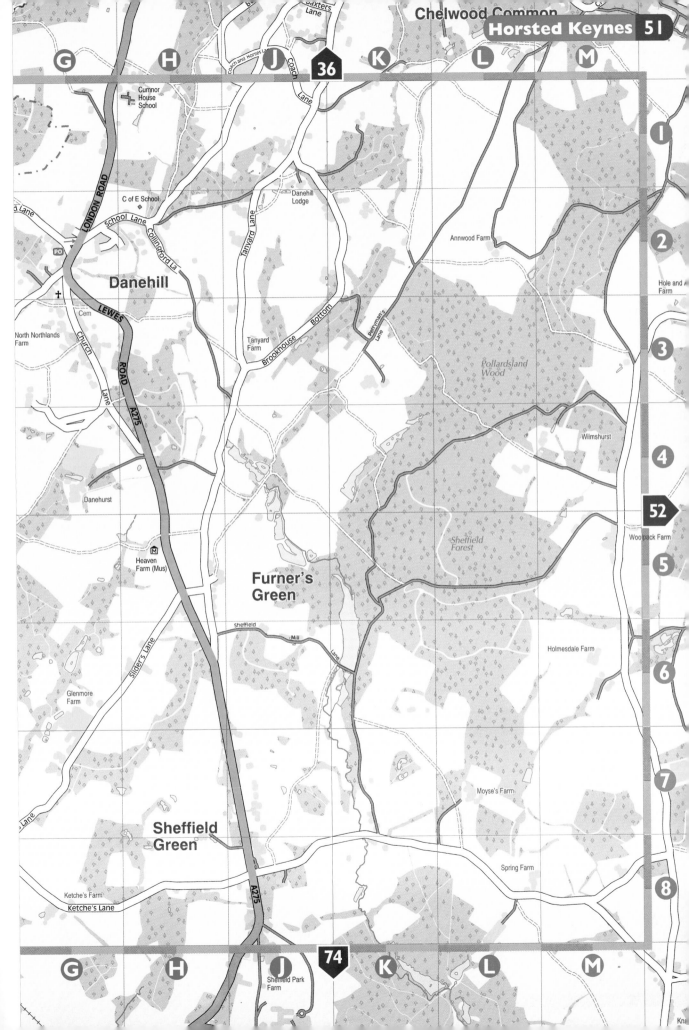

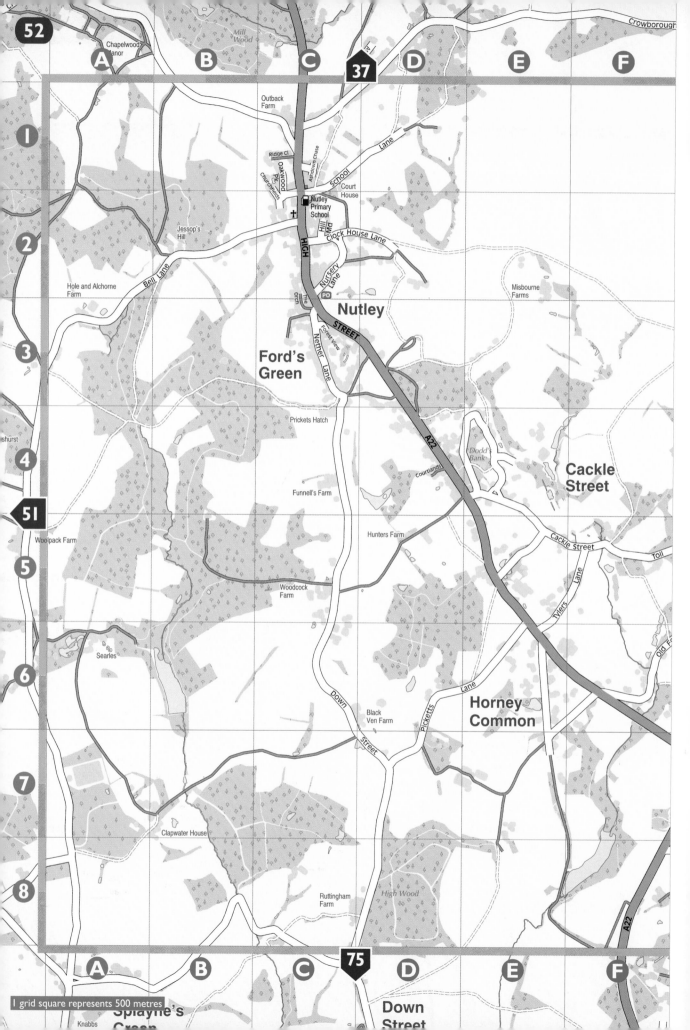

52

37

75

A B C D E F

I
2
3
4
51
5
6
7
8

Chapelwood
Manor

Mill
Wood

Outback
Farm

Ridge Cl

Ashdown Chase

School Lane

Court
House

Oakwood
Pk
Churchfields

Nutley
Primary
School

Jessop's
Hill

Bell Lane

Hole and Alchorne
Farm

HIGH

Mill Hill

Clock House Lane

Nursery Lane

PO

The Torch

STREET

Nutley

Misbourne
Farms

Ford's
Green

Forest View

Nether Lane

Prickets Hatch

Funnell's Farm

Dodd's
Bank

Courtlands

A22

Cackle
Street

Woolpack Farm

Hunters Farm

cackle street

Toll

Tylers Lane

Searles

Woodcock
Farm

Down Street

Black
Ven Farm

Picketts Lane

Horney
Common

Old F

Clapwater House

Ruttingham
Farm

High Wood

A22

A B C D E F

Down
Street

Knabbs

Splayne's
Green

1 grid square represents 500 metres

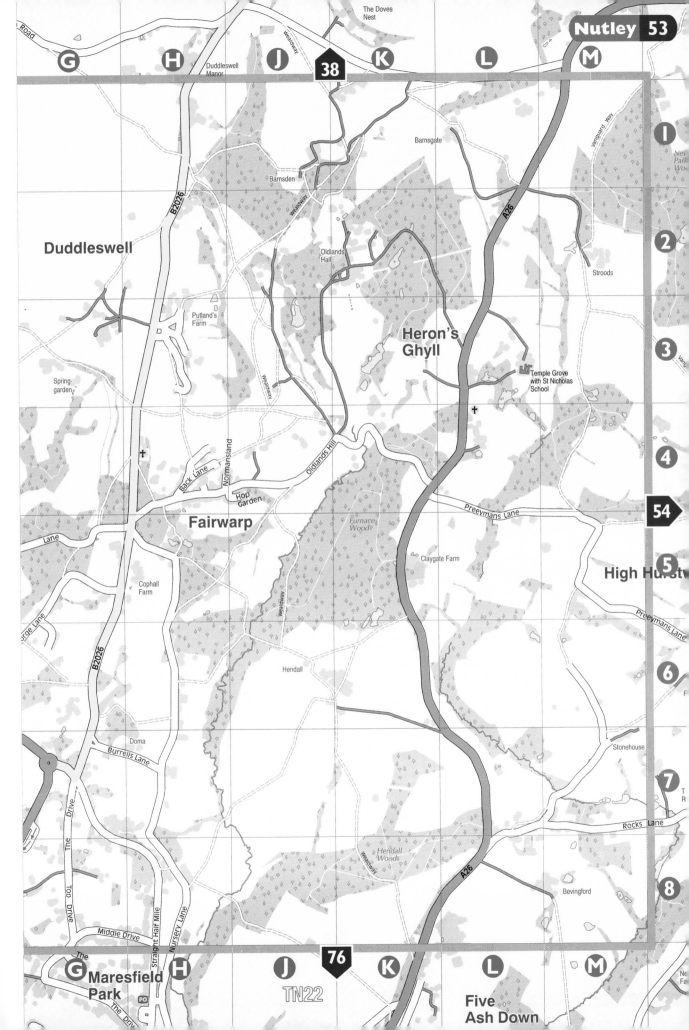

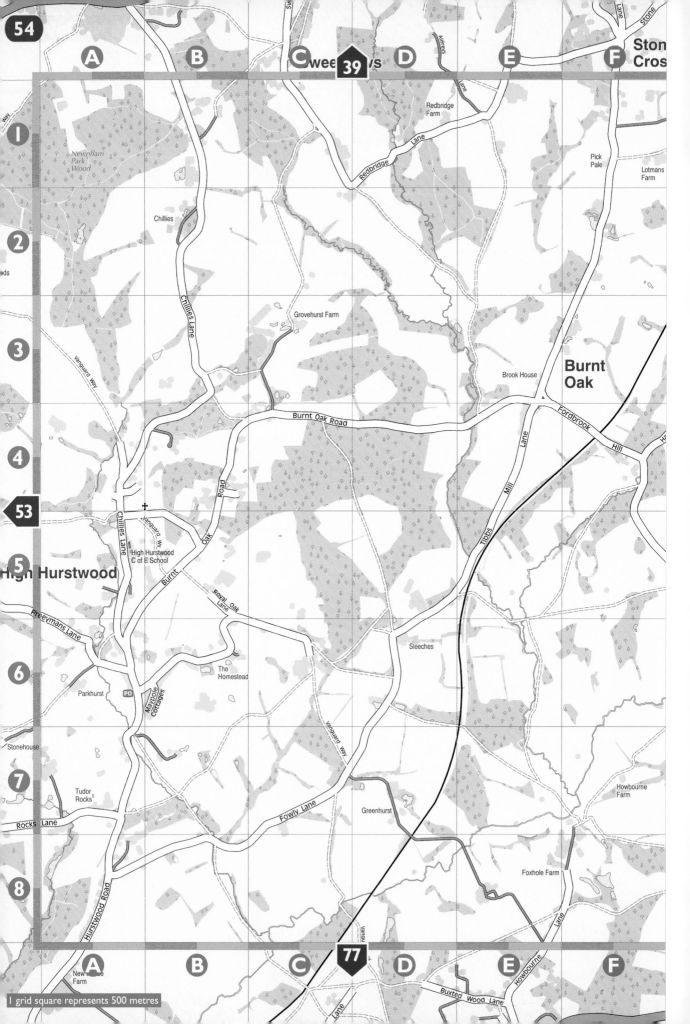

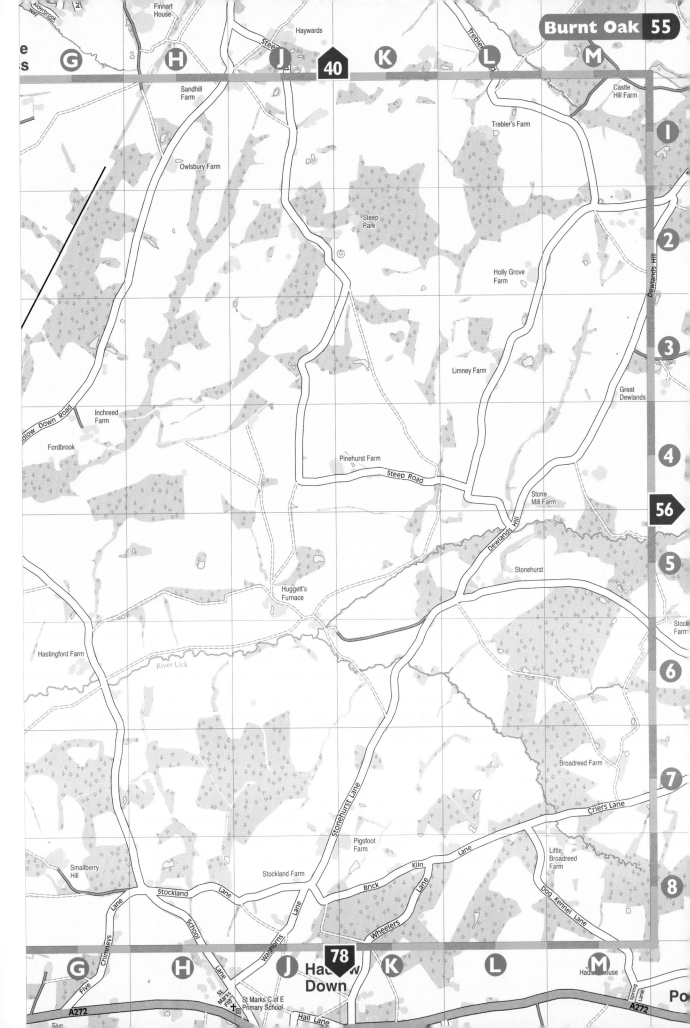

G H J 40 K L M

Finnart House

Haywards

Steep

Sandhill Farm

Owlsbury Farm

Steep Park

Trebler's Farm

Castle Hill Farm

Holly Grove Farm

Treble Lane

Dewlands Hill

1

2

3

Great Dewlands

Limney Farm

Pinehurst Farm

Steep Road

Inchreed Farm

Fordbrook

udlow Down Road

Stone Mill Farm

Dewlands Hill

Stonehurst

56

4

5

Huggett's Furnace

Hastingford Farm

River Uck

Stock Farm

Broadreed Farm

6

7

Criers Lane

Little Broadreed Farm

Stonehurst Lane

Pigsfoot Farm

Smallberry Hill

Stockland Farm

Stockland Lane

School Lane

Waghorns Lane

Brick Lane

Kiln Lane

Lane

Wheelers

Dog Kennel Lane

8

Five Chimneys Lane

G H J 78 K L M

Hadlow Down

St Marks C of E Primary School

Hall Lane

Hadlow House

Spring Lane

Po

A272 A272

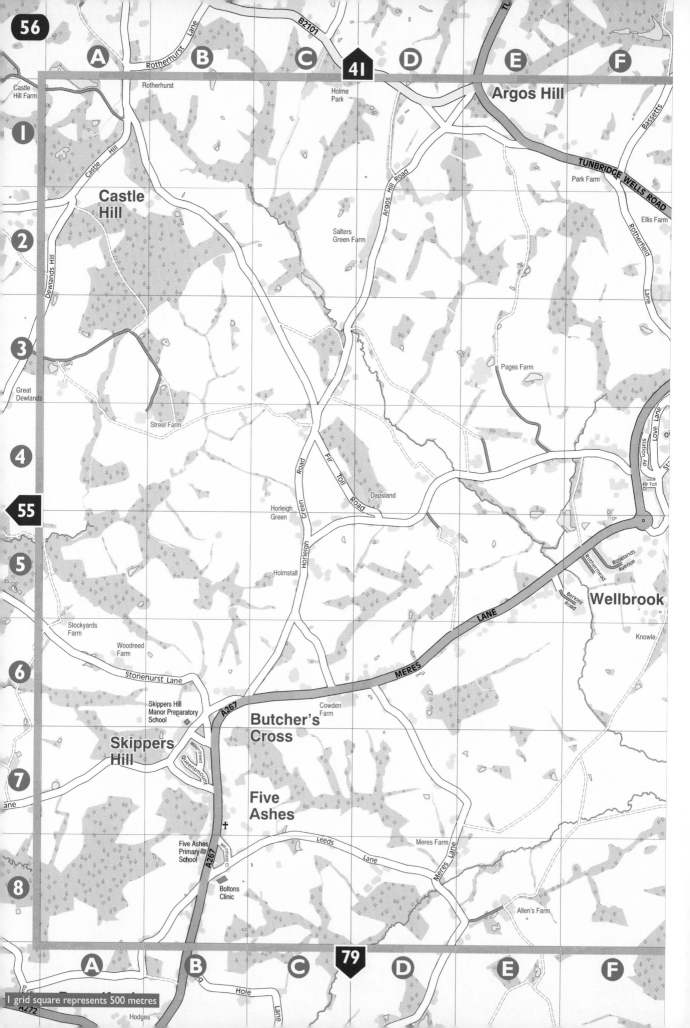

56

A　B　C　**41**　D　E　F

1

Castle Hill Farm

Rotherhurst Lane

Rotherhurst

B2101

Holme Park

Argos Hill

Bassetts

2

Castle Hill

Castle Hill

Dewlands Hill

Salters Green Farm

Argos Hill Road

Park Farm

TUNBRIDGE WELLS ROAD

Ellis Farm

Rotherfield Lane

3

Great Dewlands

Streel Farm

Pages Farm

Love Lane

Station Rd

4

Horleigh Green

Green Road

Fir Toll Road

Dapsland

Fir Toll

55

5

Holmstall

Horleigh

Holmstall

Rothermead

Roselands Avenue

Berkley Road

Wellbrook

Knowle

6

Stockyards Farm

Woodreed Farm

Stonehurst Lane

MERES LANE

7

Skippers Hill Manor Preparatory School

A267

Mountfield

Queensmount

Skippers Hill

Cowden Farm

Butcher's Cross

8

Five Ashes

Five Ashes Primary School

A267

Westfield Cl

Boltons Clinic

Leeds Lane

Meres Farm

Meres Lane

Allen's Farm

A272

Hodges

Hole Lane

A　B　**79**　C　D　E　F

1 grid square represents 500 metres

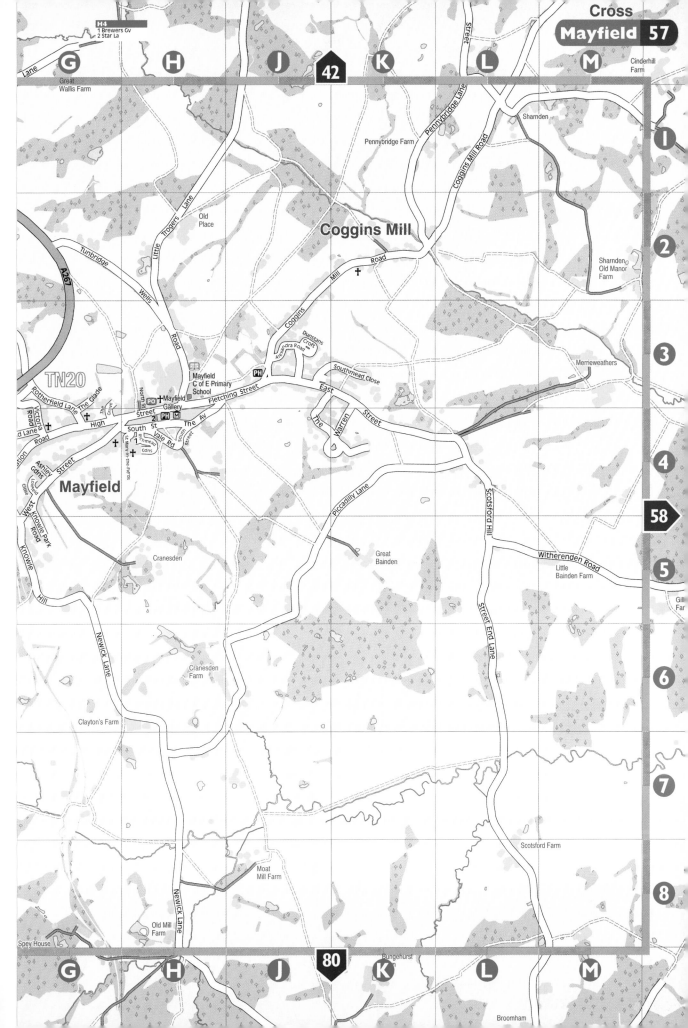

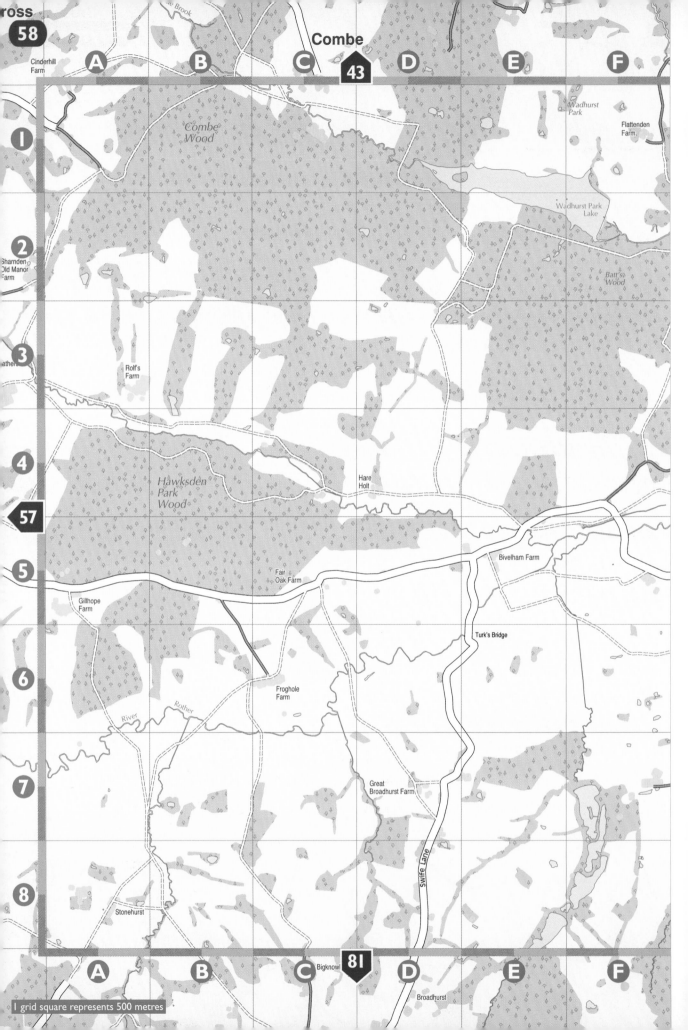

A B C D E F

Cinderhill
Farm

1

Wadhurst
Park

Flattenden
Farm

Combe
Wood

Wadhurst Park
Lake

2

Bharnden
Old Manor
Farm

Batt's
Wood

3

eather

Rolf's
Farm

4

Hawksden
Park
Wood

Hare
Holt

57

Bivelham Farm

5

Fair
Oak Farm

Gillhope
Farm

Turk's Bridge

Brook

6

Froghole
Farm

River Rother

7

Great
Broadhurst Farm

Swife Lane

8

Stonehurst

1 grid square represents 500 metres

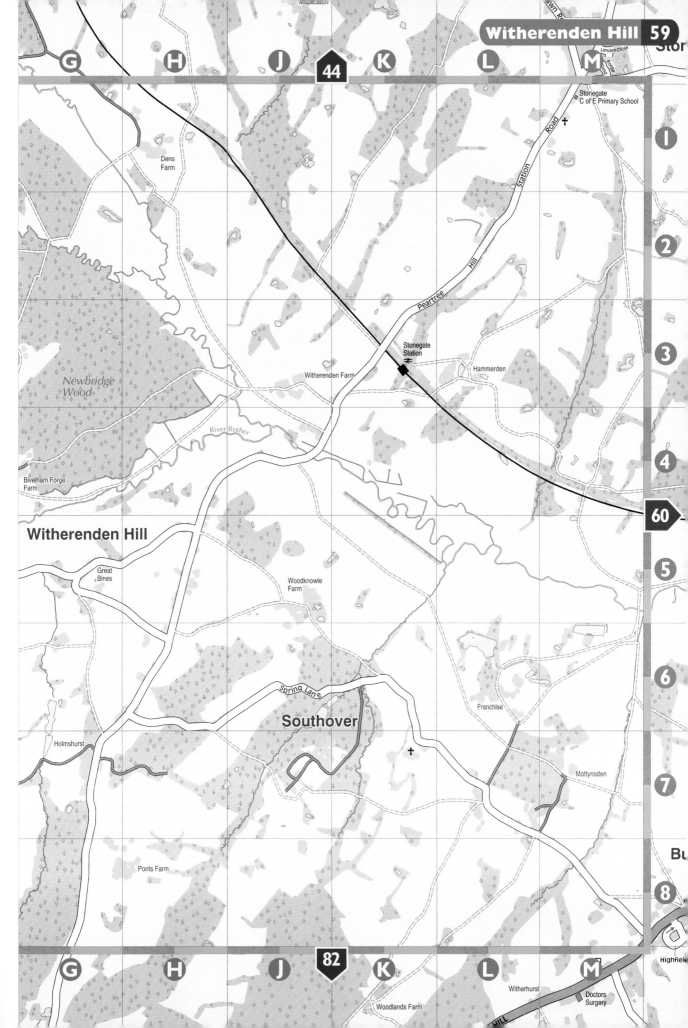

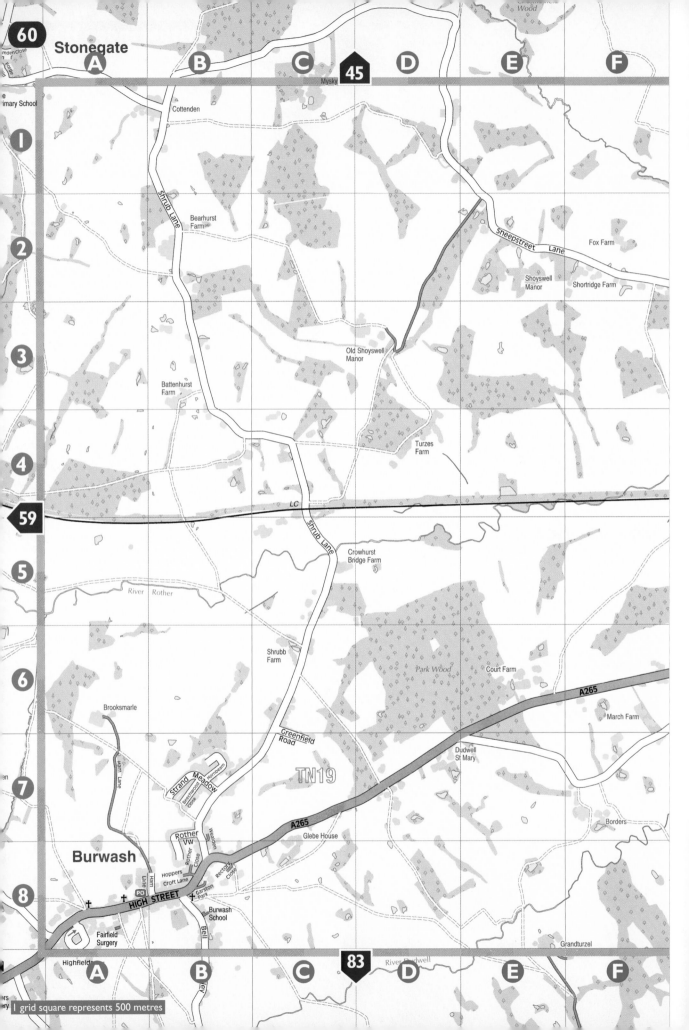

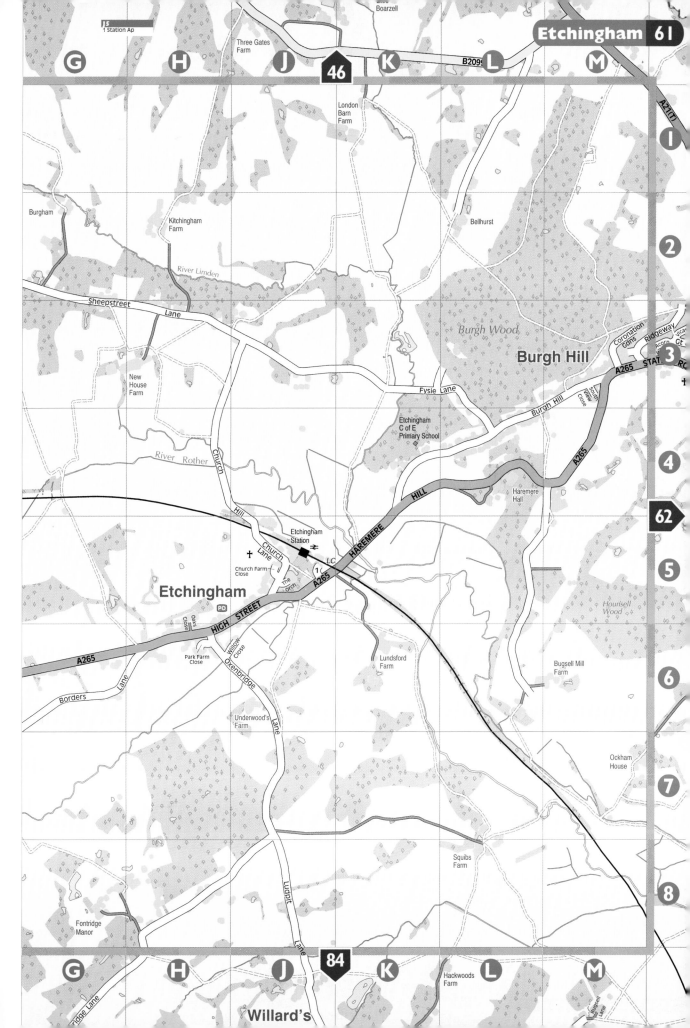

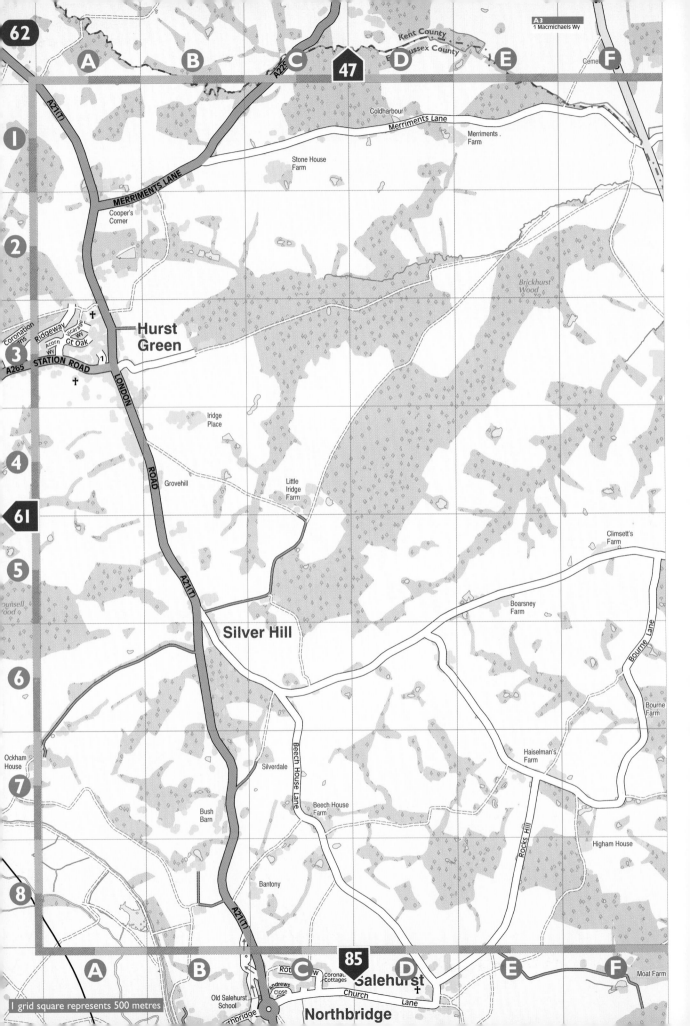

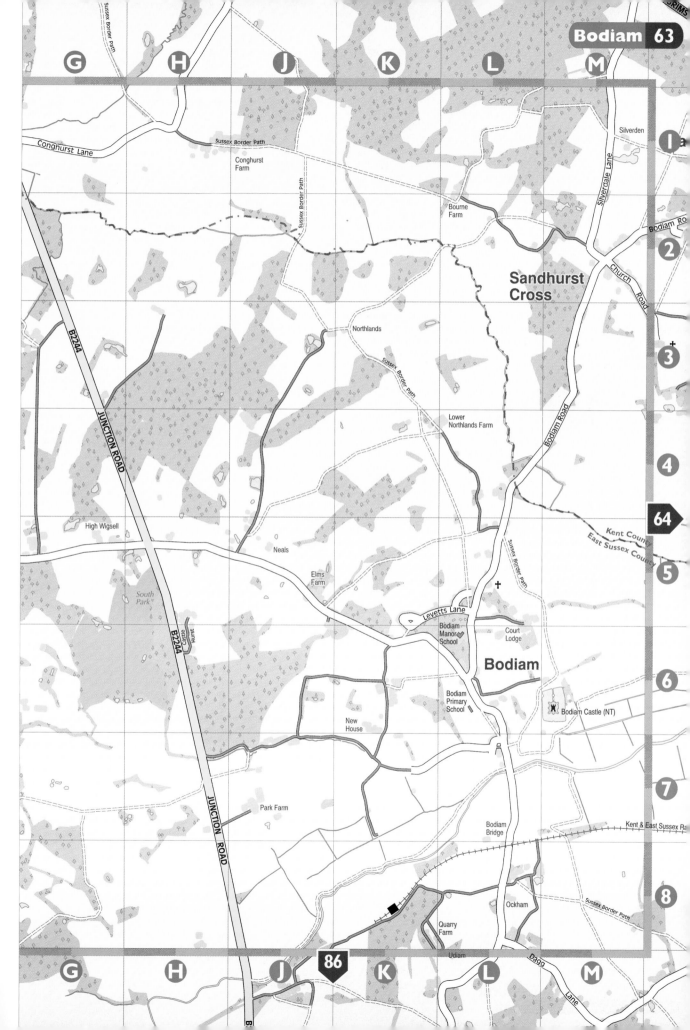

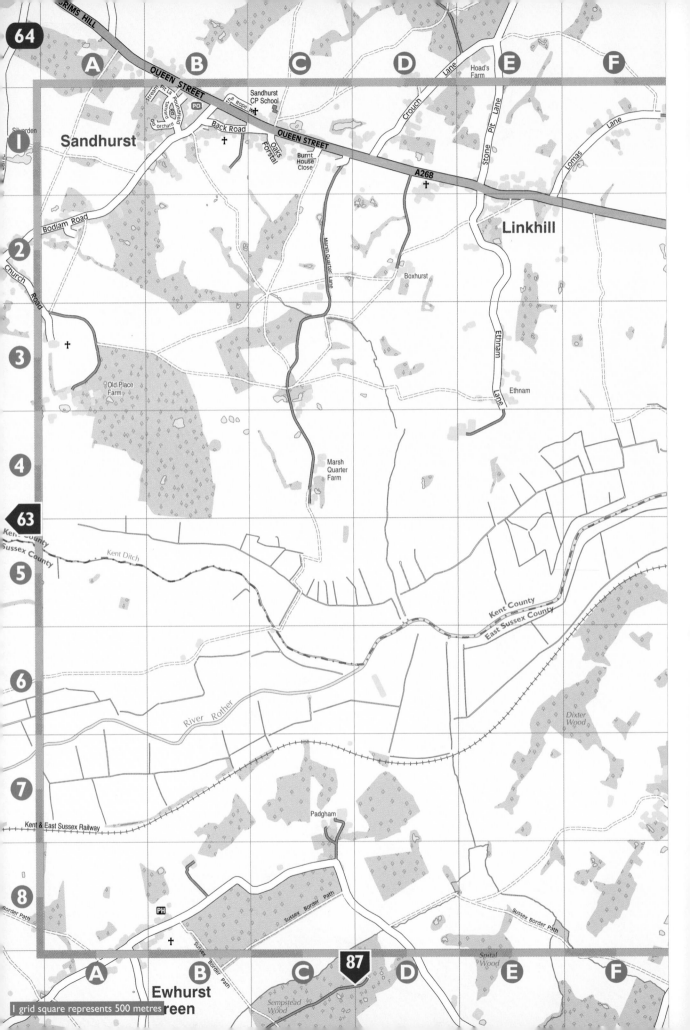

A B C D E F

GRIMS HILL

QUEEN STREET

Sandhurst CP School

Stream Pit La

PO

Tanyard

Old Orchard

Poundfield

The Rope Wk

Back Road

Hoad's Farm

Crouch Lane

Stone Pit Lane

Lomas Lane

Silverden

Sandhurst

QUEEN STREET

Oaks Forstal

Burnt House Close

A268

Linkhill

Bodiam Road

1

Church Road

2

Marsh Quarter Lane

Boxhurst

Ethnam Lane

Ethnam

3

Old Place Farm

Marsh Quarter Farm

4

63

Kent County

Sussex County

Kent Ditch

Kent County

East Sussex County

5

Dixter Wood

6

River Rother

Kent & East Sussex Railway

7

Padgham

PH

Sussex Border Path

Sussex Border Path

Spital Wood

8

Border Path

A B C D E F

87

Ewhurst Green

Sempstead Wood

1 grid square represents 500 metres

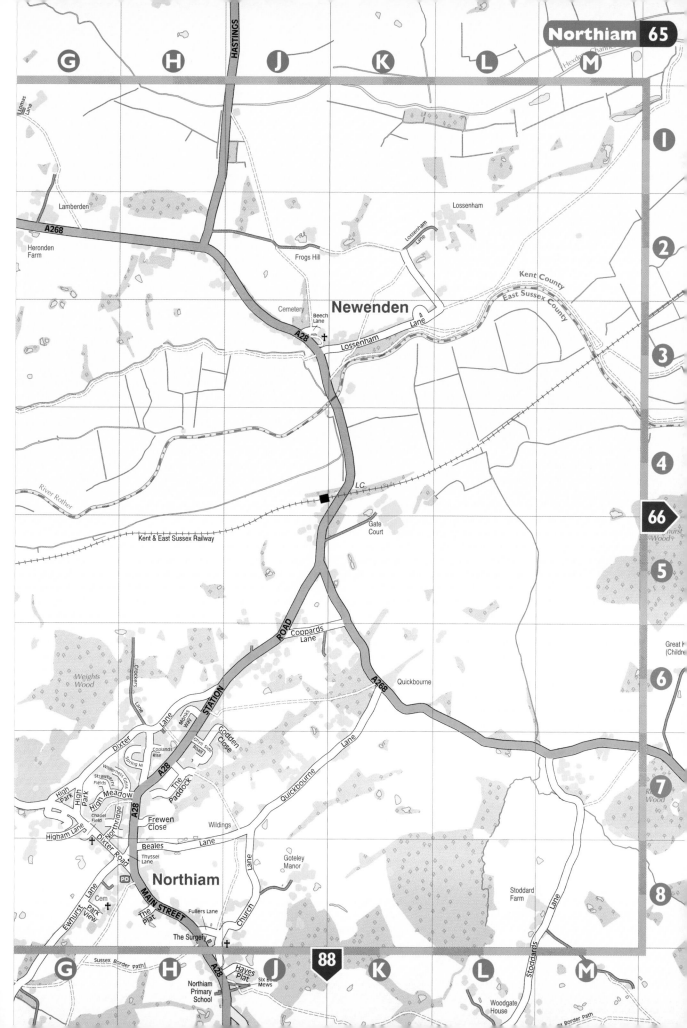

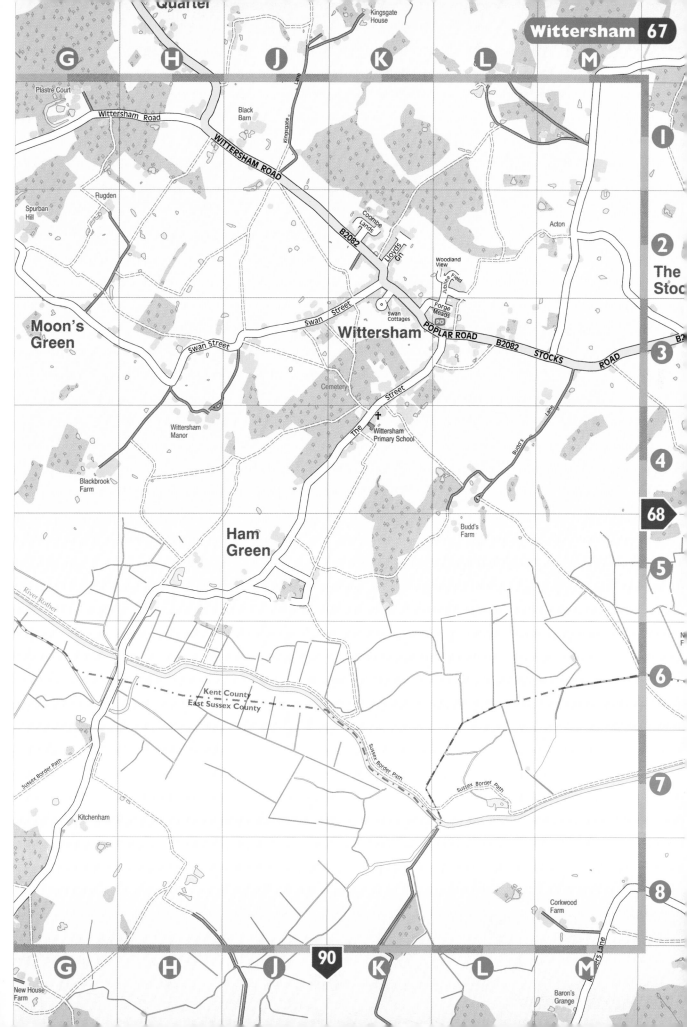

Quarter

Kingsgate
House

G   H   J   K   L   M

1

Plastre Court

Wittersham Road

WITTERSHAM ROAD

Black
Barn

Kingsgate Lane

Acton

2

The
Stoc

Rugden

Spurban
Hill

B2082

Coombe
Lands

Lloyds
Gn

Woodland
View

Jubilee Field

**Moon's
Green**

Swan   Street

Swan Street

Wittersham

Swan
Cottages

Forge
Meads
PO

POPLAR ROAD

B2082   STOCKS   ROAD

B2

3

Cemetery

The   Street

Budd's   Lane

4

Wittersham
Manor

✝
Wittersham
Primary School

68

Blackbrook
Farm

Budd's
Farm

5

**Ham
Green**

River Rother

6

Kent County
East Sussex County

Sussex Border Path

Sussex Border Path

Sussex Border Path

7

Kitchenham

8

Corkwood
Farm

G   H   J   K   L   M

Kingers Lane

New House
Farm

Baron's
Grange

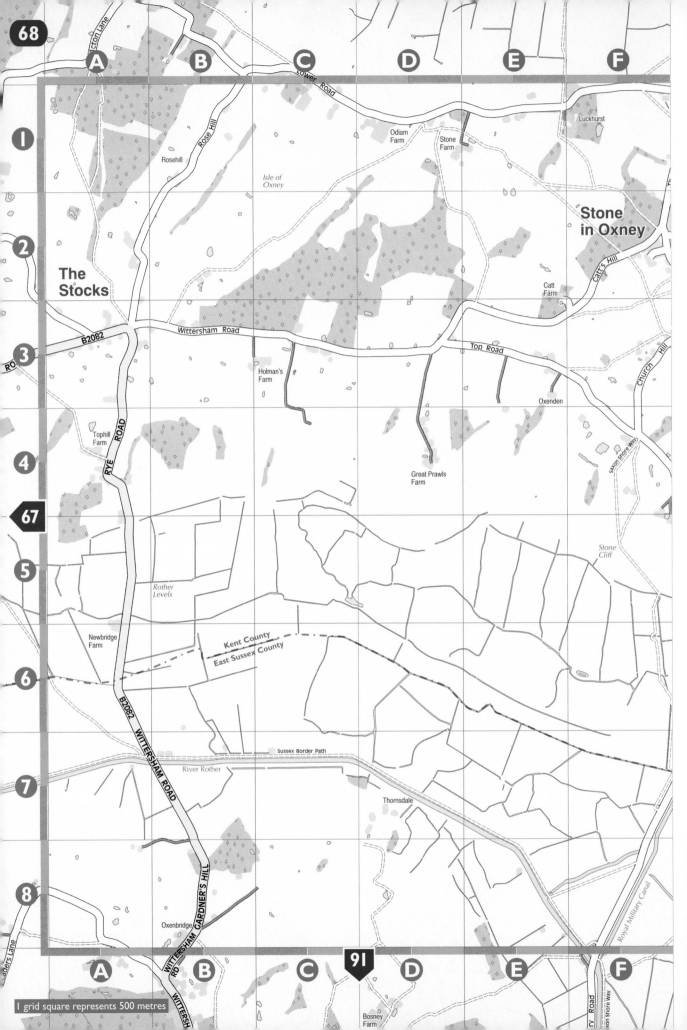

A   B   C   D   E   F

Lower Road

Luckhurst

Rose Hill

Rosehill

Isle of
Oxney

Odiam
Farm

Stone
Farm

Stone
in Oxney

1

2

The
Stocks

Catt's Hill

Catt
Farm

B2082

Wittersham Road

Top Road

3

Holman's
Farm

Oxenden

RO

RYE ROAD

Tophill
Farm

Church Hill

Saxon Shore Way

4

Great Prawls
Farm

67

Stone
Cliff

5

Rother
Levels

Newbridge
Farm

Kent County

East Sussex County

6

B2082

WITTERSHAM ROAD

Sussex Border Path

River Rother

7

Thornsdale

Royal Military Canal

GARDNER'S HILL

8

Oxenbridge

WITTERSHAM RD

Ladders Lane

WITTERSH

A   B   C   D   E   F

91

Bosney
Farm

axon Shore Way

y Road

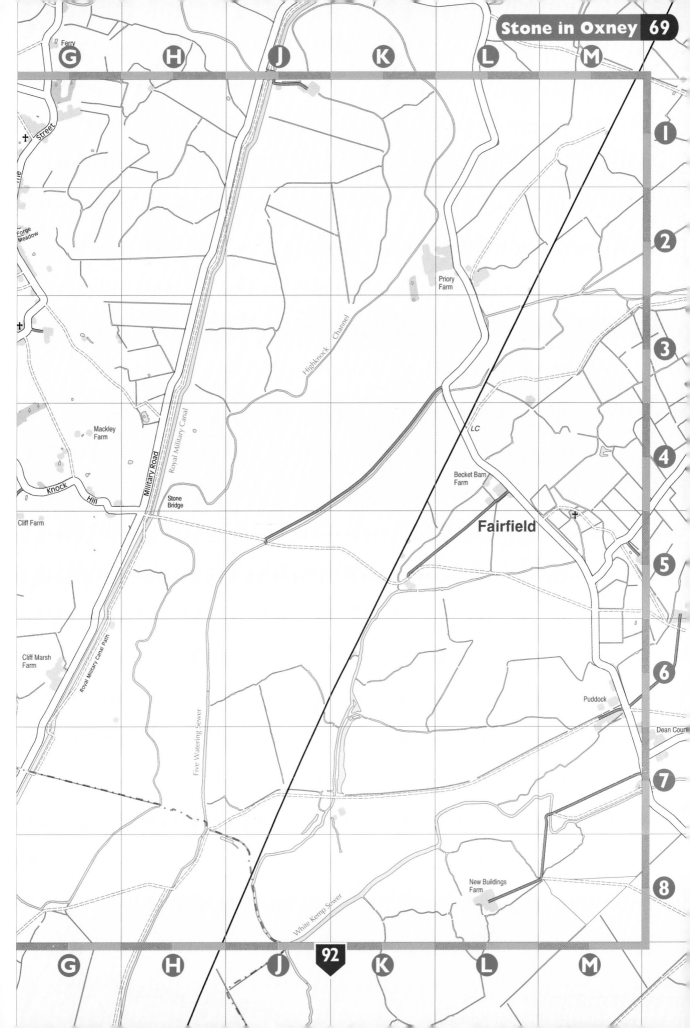

G H J K L M

I
2
3
4
5
6
7
8

Ferry

Street

Forge
Meadow

Priory
Farm

Highknock Channel

Mackley
Farm

Royal Military Canal

Military Road

LC

Becket Barn
Farm

Fairfield

Knock Hill

Stone
Bridge

Cliff Farm

Cliff Marsh
Farm

Royal Military Canal Path

Puddock

Dean Court

Five Watering Sewer

New Buildings
Farm

White Kemp Sewer

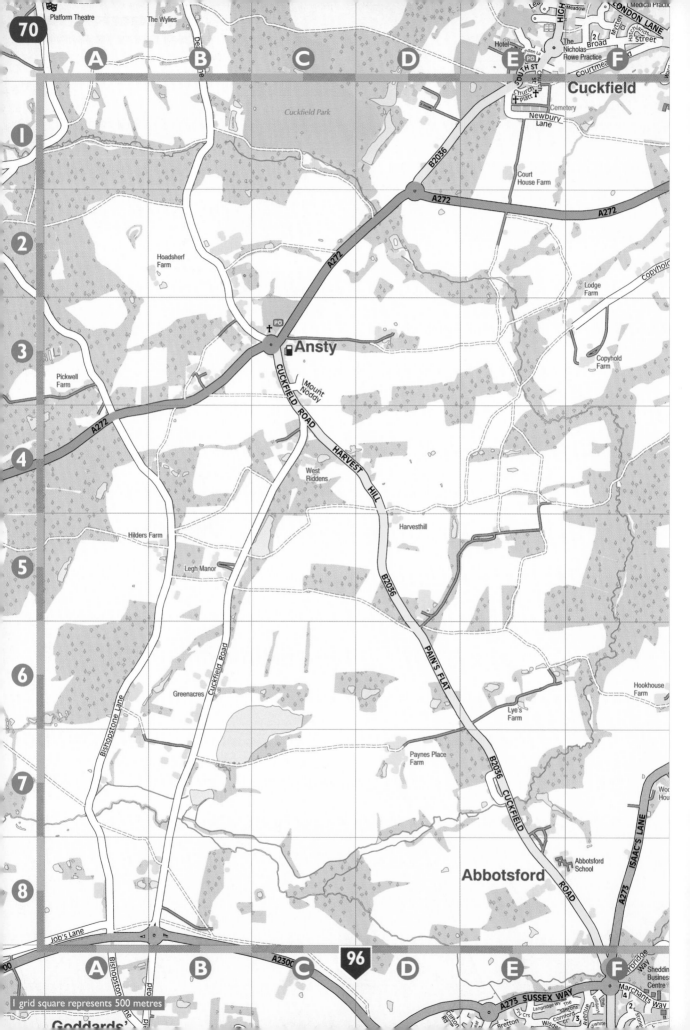

Platform Theatre

The Wylies

Cuckfield Park

Cuckfield

Hotel

The
Nicholas
Rowe Practice

Medical Practice

LONDON LANE

HIGH

Mitten

Broad

Courtmead

Church
Platt

Cemetery

Newbury
Lane

South St
PO

A272

B2036

Court
House Farm

Copyhold

Lodge
Farm

Copyhold
Farm

Hoadsherf
Farm

PO

Ansty

Mount
Noddy

Pickwell
Farm

A272

CUCKFIELD ROAD

HARVEST HILL

West
Riddens

Harvesthill

Hilders Farm

B2036

Legh Manor

Bishopstone Lane

Cuckfield Road

Greenacres

PAIN'S FLAT

Hookhouse
Farm

Lye's
Farm

Paynes Place
Farm

B2036

CUCKFIELD

Abbotsford
School

A273

ISAAC'S LANE

Woo
Hou

Abbotsford

ROAD

Job's Lane

Bishopstone
Road

A2300

Sheddin
Busines
Centre

Marchants Way

A273 SUSSEX WAY

Goddards'

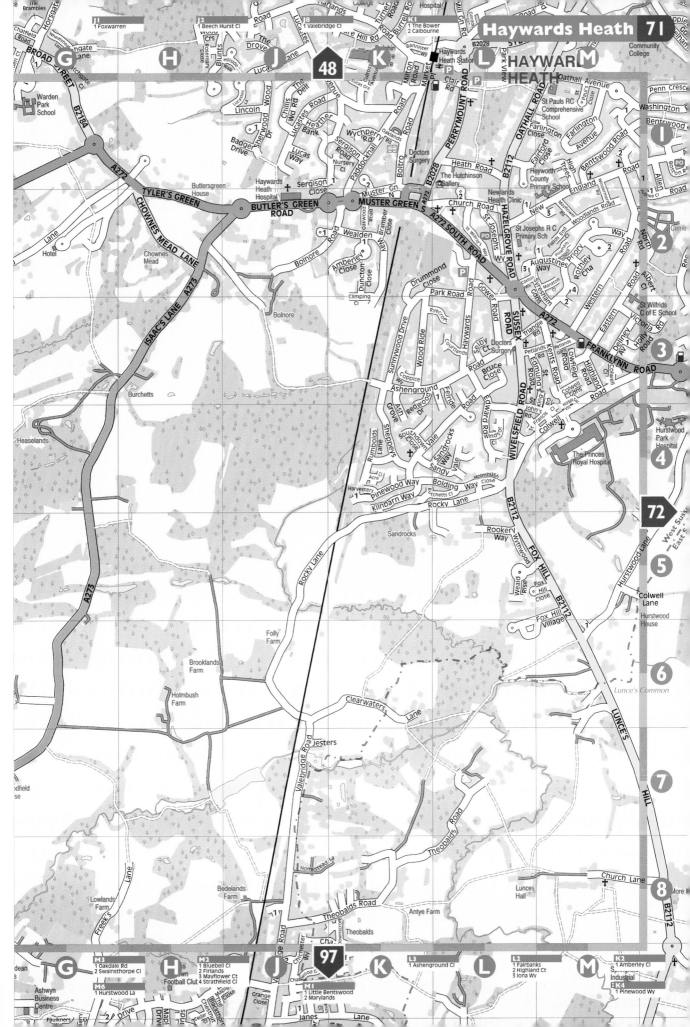

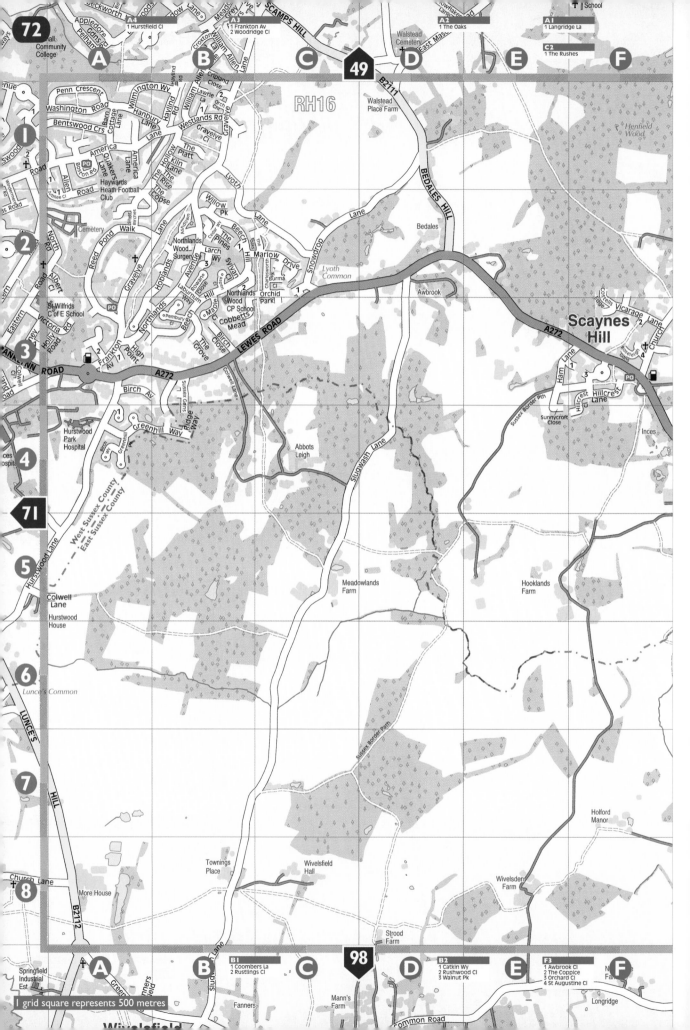

A   B   C   49   D   E   F

1 grid square represents 500 metres

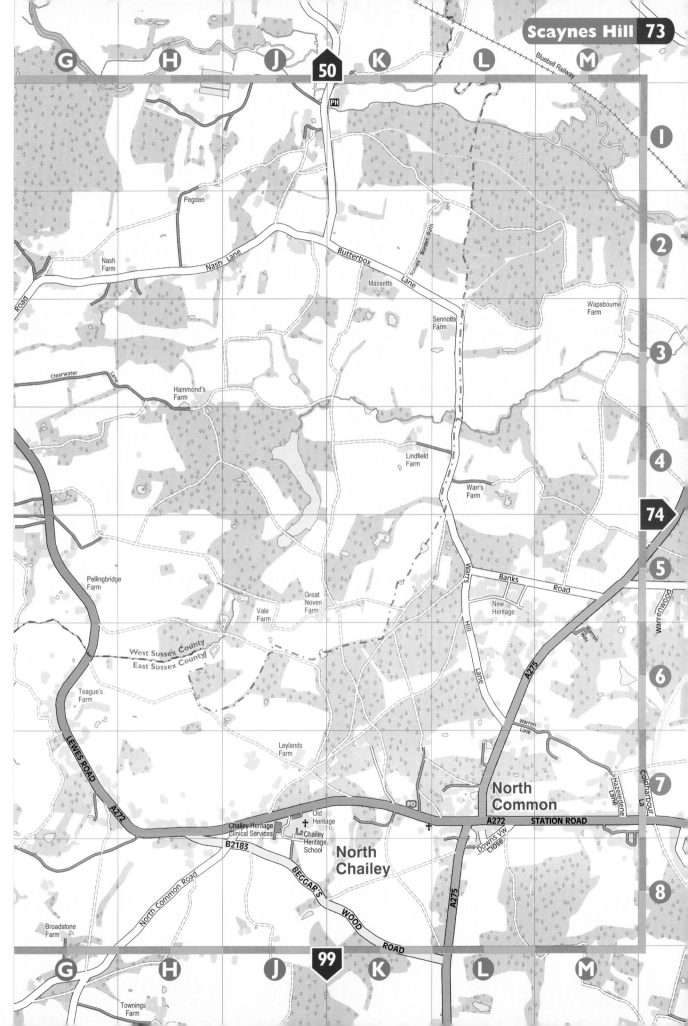

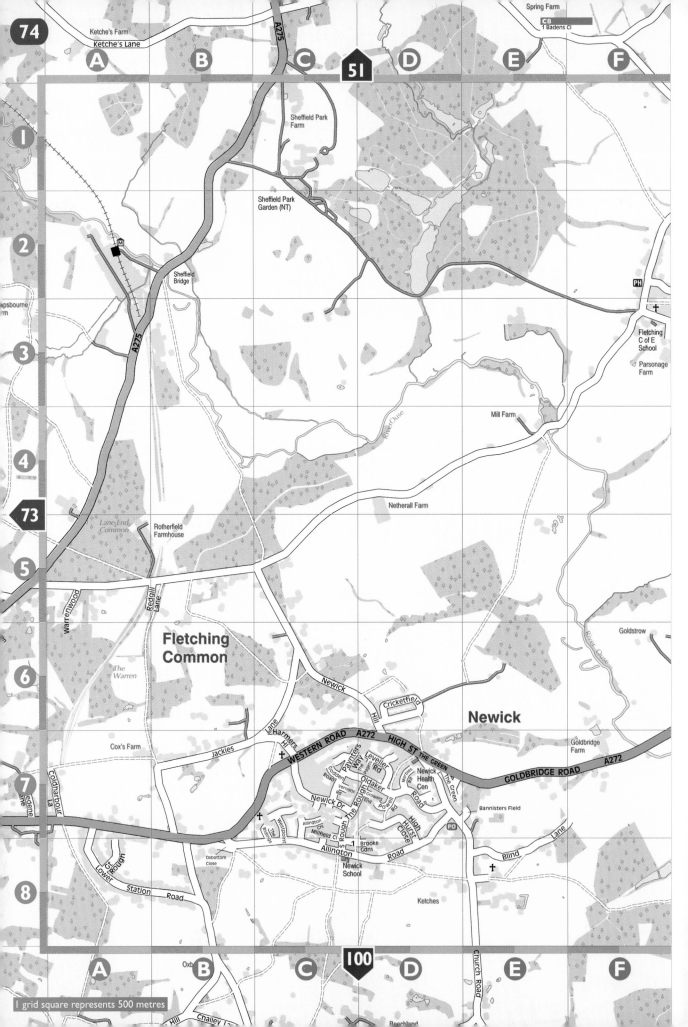

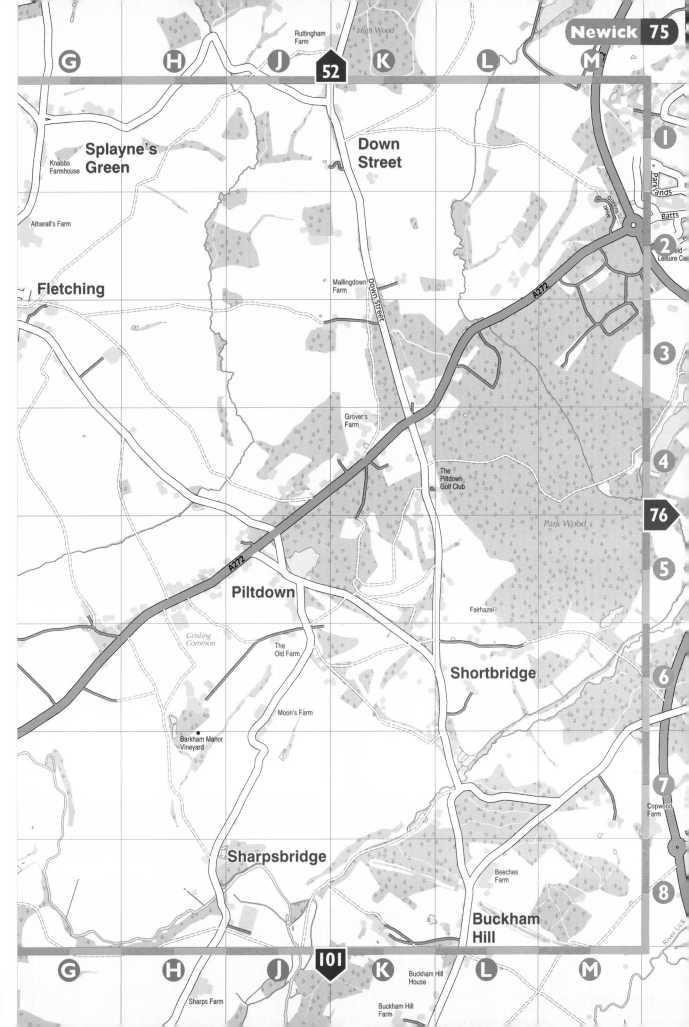

G   H   J   **52**   K   L   M

Ruttingham
Farm

High Wood

**Down
Street**

Parklands

Batts

ield
Leisure Ce

Knabbs
Farmhouse

**Splayne's
Green**

Atherall's Farm

Fletching

Mallingdown
Farm

Down Street

Queens
Drive

A272

Grover's
Farm

The
Piltdown
Golf Club

Park Wood

Piltdown

*Grisling
Common*

The
Old Farm

A272

Fairhazel

Shortbridge

Moon's Farm

Barkham Manor
Vineyard

Sharpsbridge

Beeches
Farm

Copwood
Farm

River Uck

**Buckham
Hill**

G   H   J   **IOI**   K   L   M

Sharps Farm

Buckham Hill
House

Buckham Hill
Farm

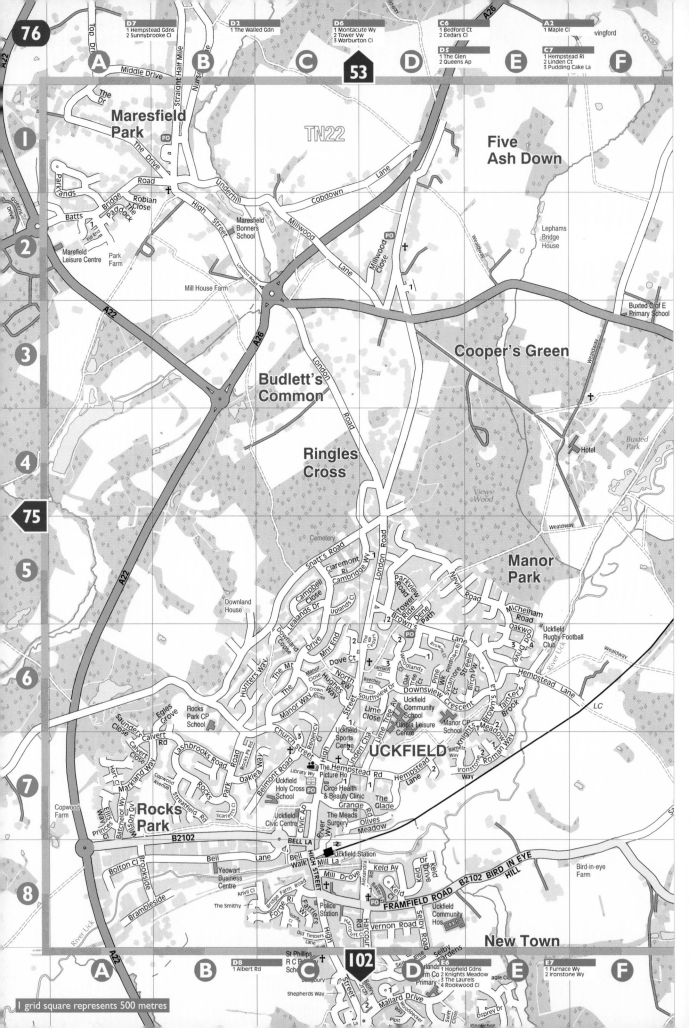

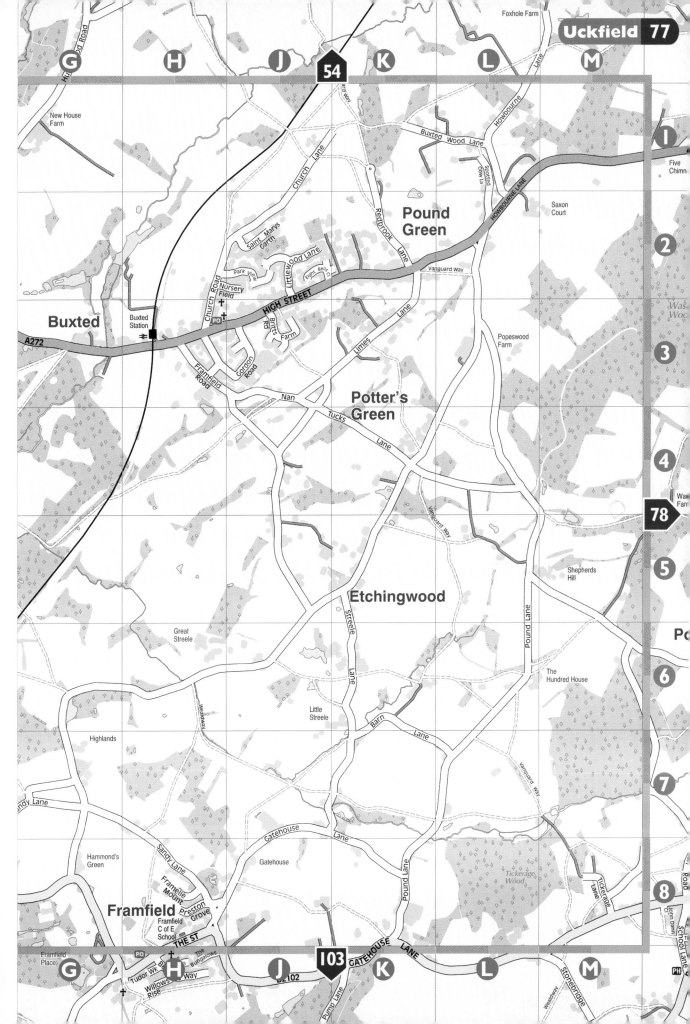

Foxhole Farm

New House Farm

Buxted Wood Lane

Pound Green

Saxon Court

Buxted

Buxted Station

A272

High Street

Saint Marys Garth

Park View

Church Road

Nursery Field

Britts Rd

Britts Farm

Gordon Road

Framfield Road

Nan

Tucks Lane

Potter's Green

Limes Lane

Vanguard Way

Popeswood Farm

Vanguard Way

Shepherds Hill

Etchingwood

Streele Lane

Great Streele

Wealdway

Little Streele

Barn Lane

Pound Lane

The Hundred House

Highlands

Sandy Lane

Hammond's Green

Sandy Lane

Framelle Mount

Preston Grove

Gatehouse Lane

Gatehouse

Pound Lane

Vanguard Way

Tickerage Wood

Tickerage

Framfield

Framfield C of E School

THE ST

Framfield Place

Tudor Wk

Willows Rise

The Bungalows

GATEHOUSE LANE

Pump Lane

Stonebridge

Wealdway

School Lane

Five Chimn

Church Lane

Littlewood Lane

Redbrook Lane

Eight Bells

Howbourne Lane

Spotted Cow La

Howbourne Lane

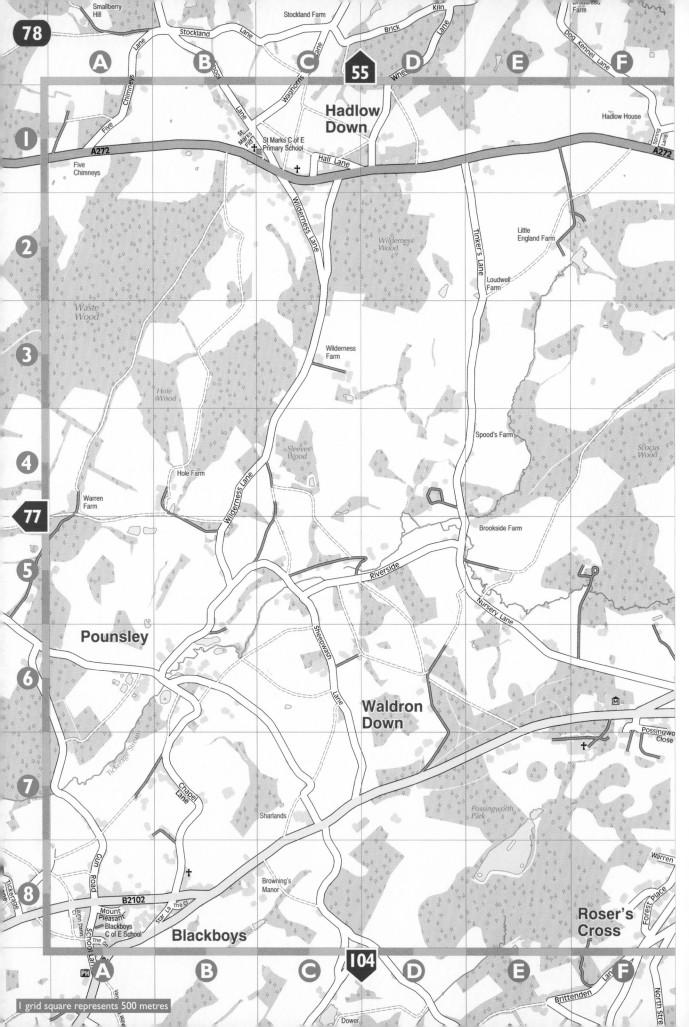

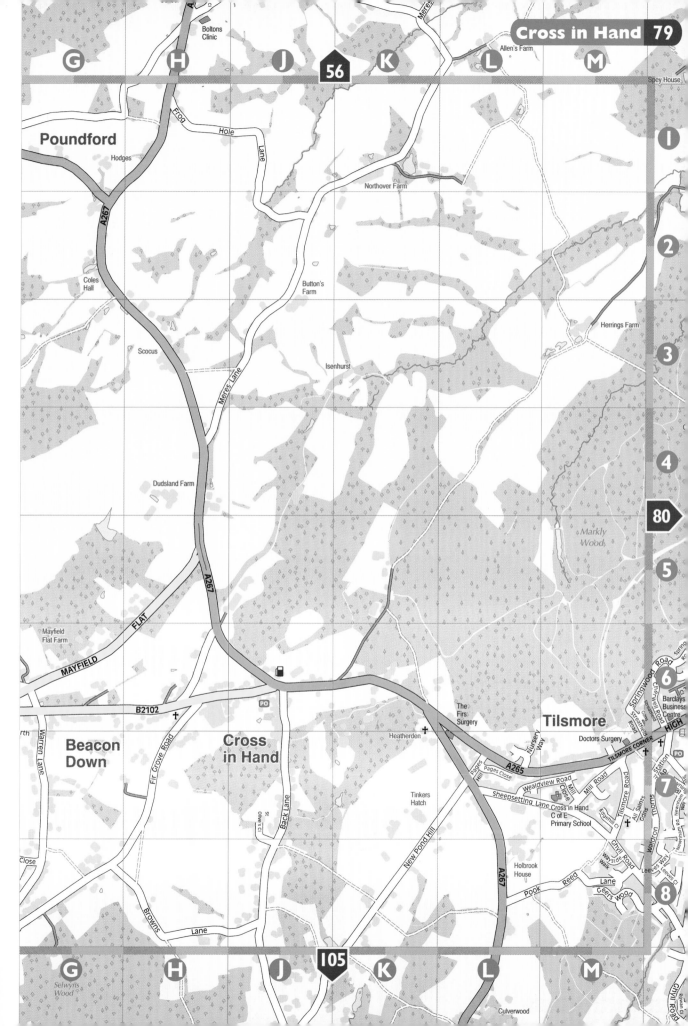

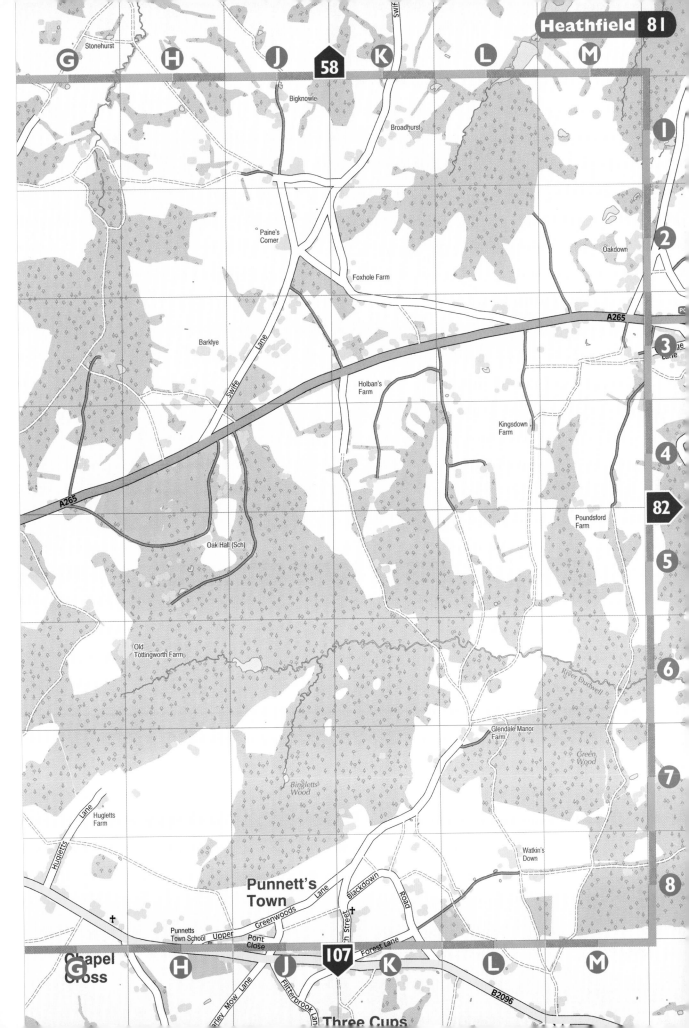

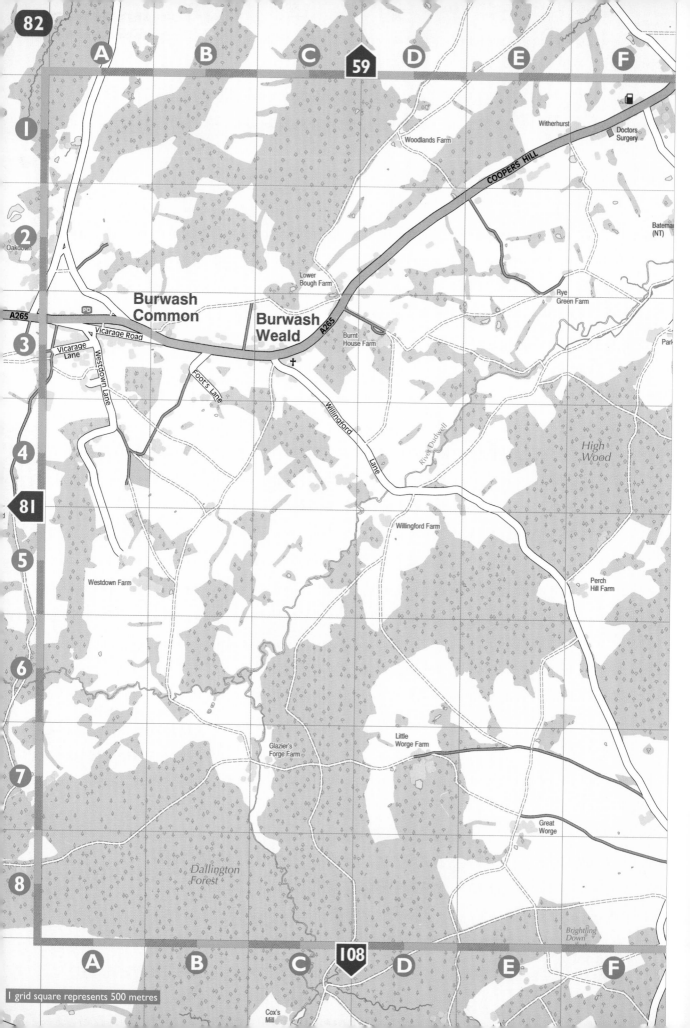

A   B   C   59   D   E   F

I

Witherhurst

Woodlands Farm

COOPERS HILL

Doctors Surgery

Bateman (NT)

2

Oakdown

Lower Bough Farm

Rye Green Farm

A265

Burwash Common

Vicarage Road

Burwash Weald

A265

Park

Burnt House Farm

3

Vicarage Lane

Westdown Lane

Foor's Lane

Willingford Lane

River Dudwell

High Wood

4

81

Willingford Farm

5

Westdown Farm

Perch Hill Farm

6

Glazier's Forge Farm

Little Worge Farm

7

Great Worge

8

Dallington Forest

Brightling Down

A   B   C   108   D   E   F

Cox's Mill

1 grid square represents 500 metres

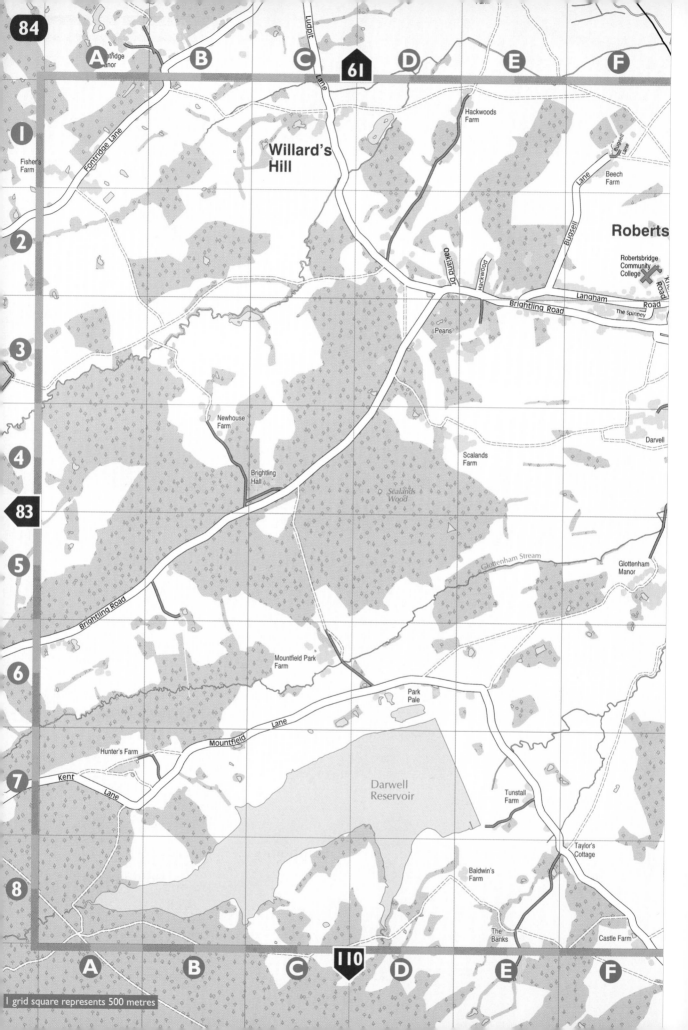

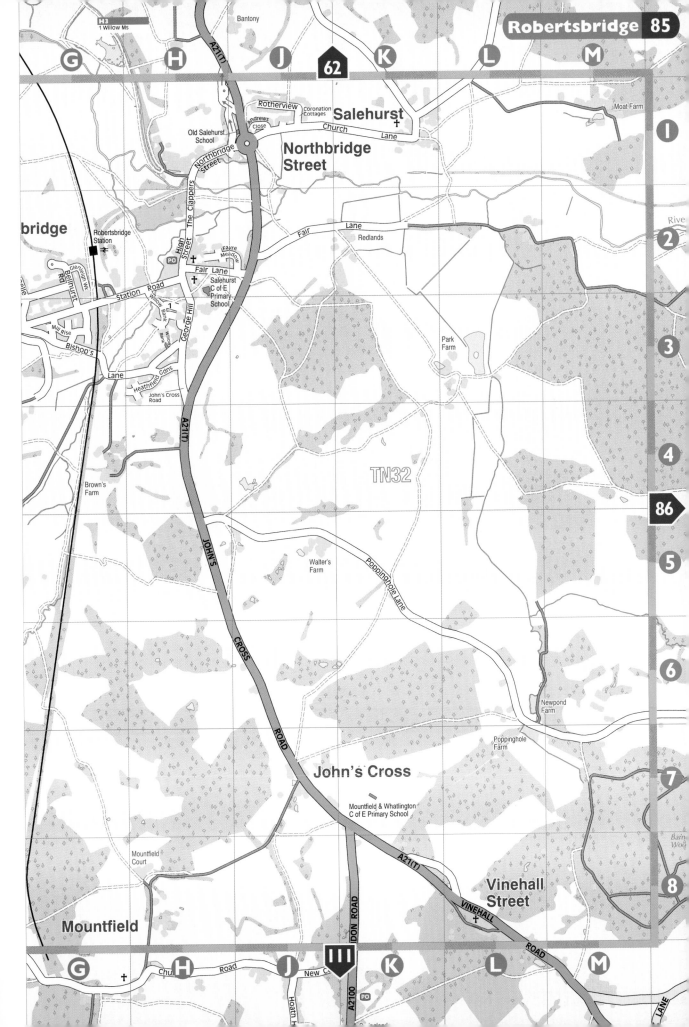

G H J K L M

62

Bantony

1 Willow Ms
H3

Rotherview
Coronation
Cottages
Andrews
Close
Old Salehurst
School

Salehurst

Church Lane

**Northbridge
Street**

Northbridge Street

The Clappers

Robertsbridge
Station

bridge

High Street

PO

Fayre
Meadow

Fair Lane

Redlands

Fair Lane

Glenleigh Wk

Belhurst
Rd

Station Road

Willow Bank

Salehurst
C of E
Primary
School

Mill Rise

Bishop's

George Hill

Heathfield Gdns

Willow Bank

John's Cross
Road

Lane

A21(T)

Park
Farm

TN32

Brown's
Farm

JOHN'S

Walter's
Farm

Poppinghole Lane

CROSS

Newpond
Farm

ROAD

Poppinghole
Farm

John's Cross

Mountfield & Whatlington
C of E Primary School

Mountfield
Court

DON ROAD

A21(T)

**Vinehall
Street**

VINEHALL

Mountfield

G H J K L M

III

Church Road

New C

Hoath

A2100

PO

ROAD

LANE

Moat Farm

Rive

I

2

3

4

86

5

6

7

8

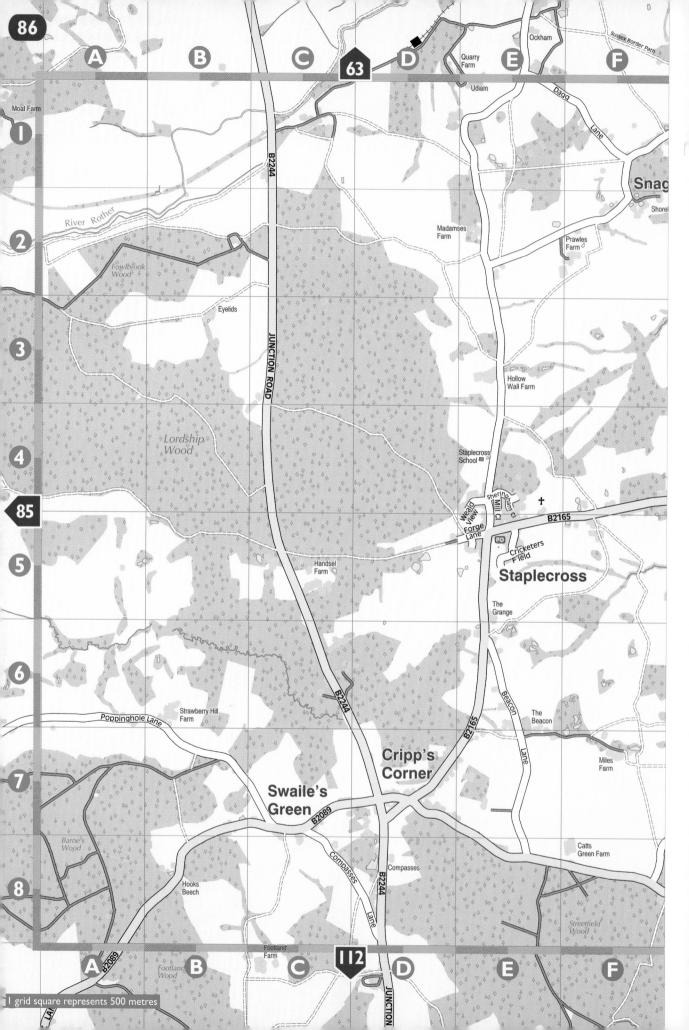

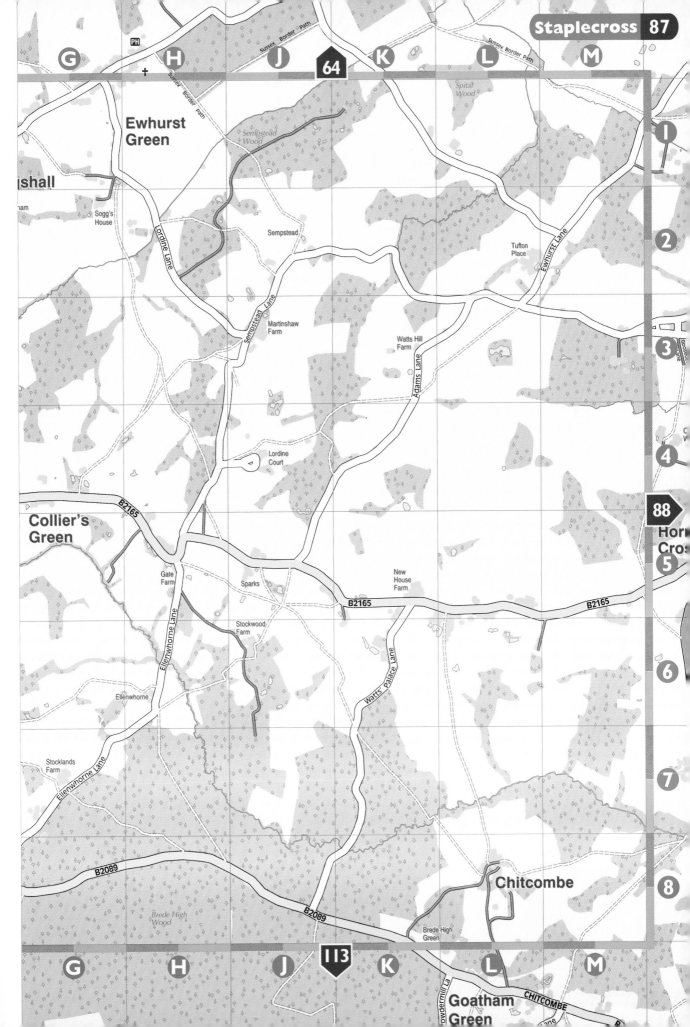

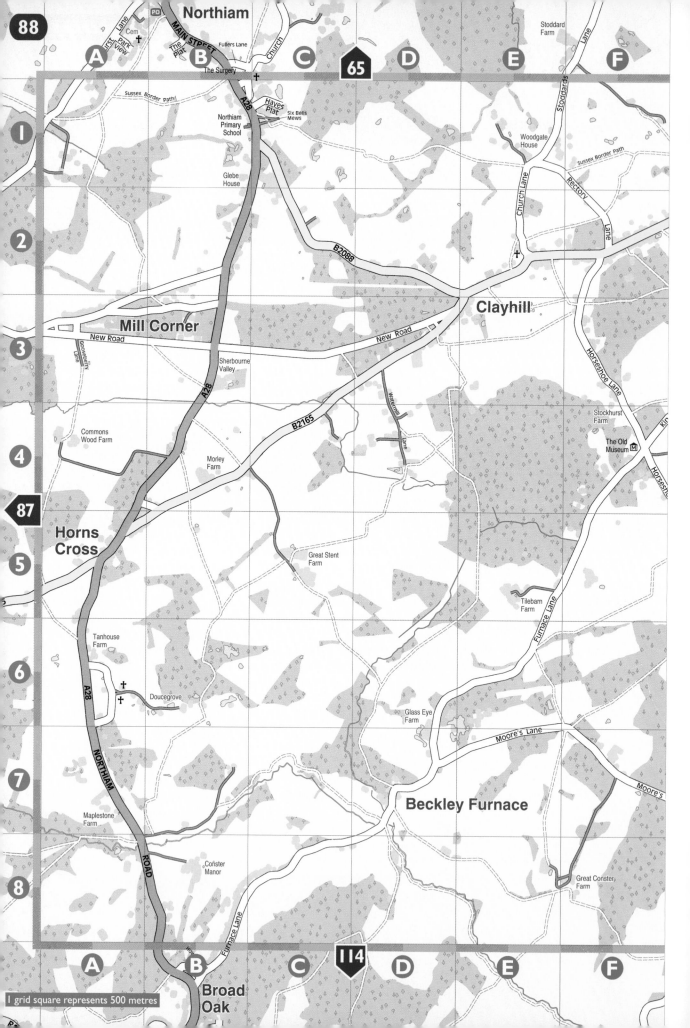

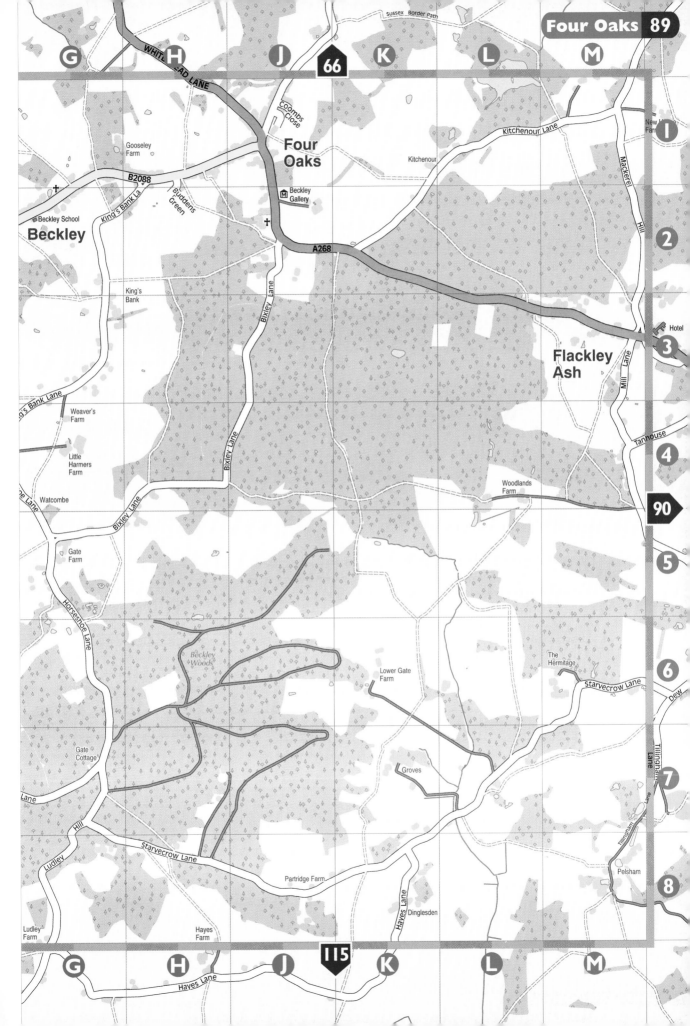

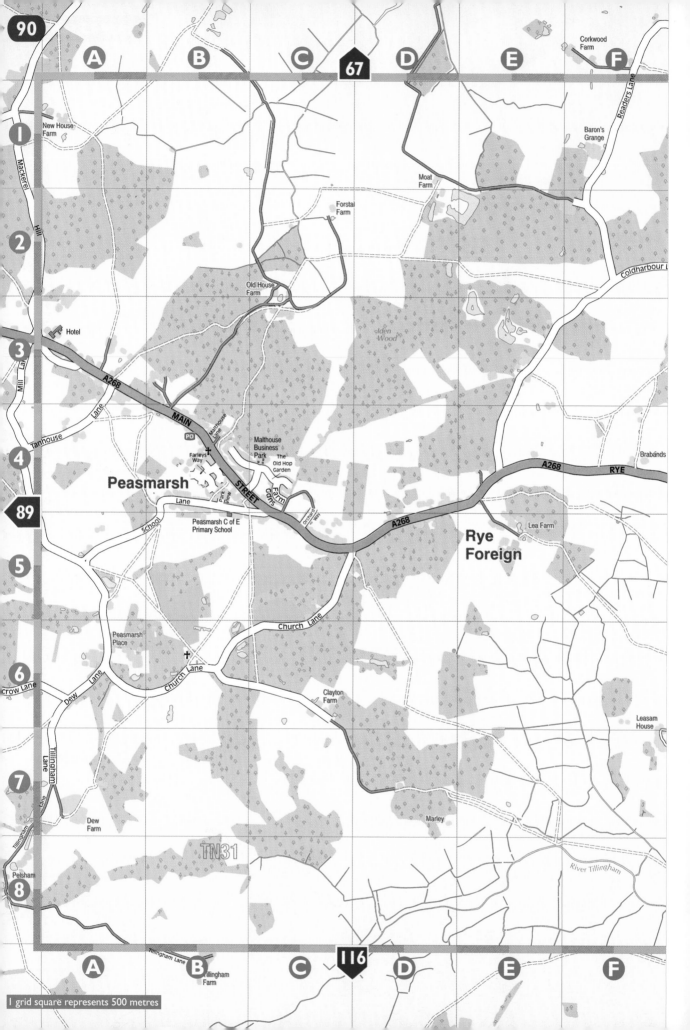

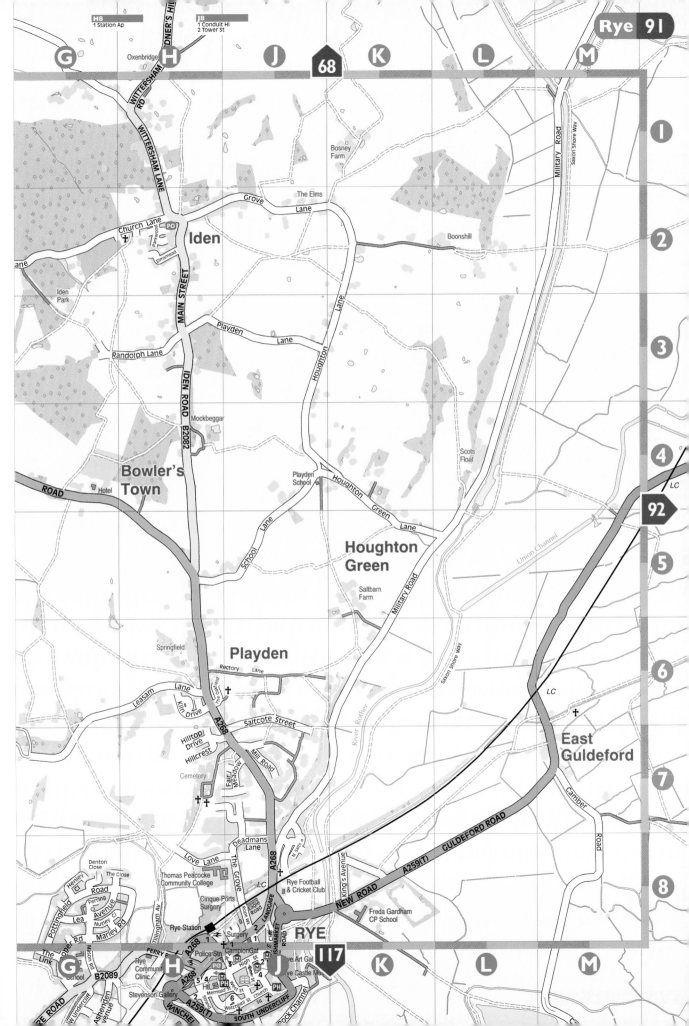

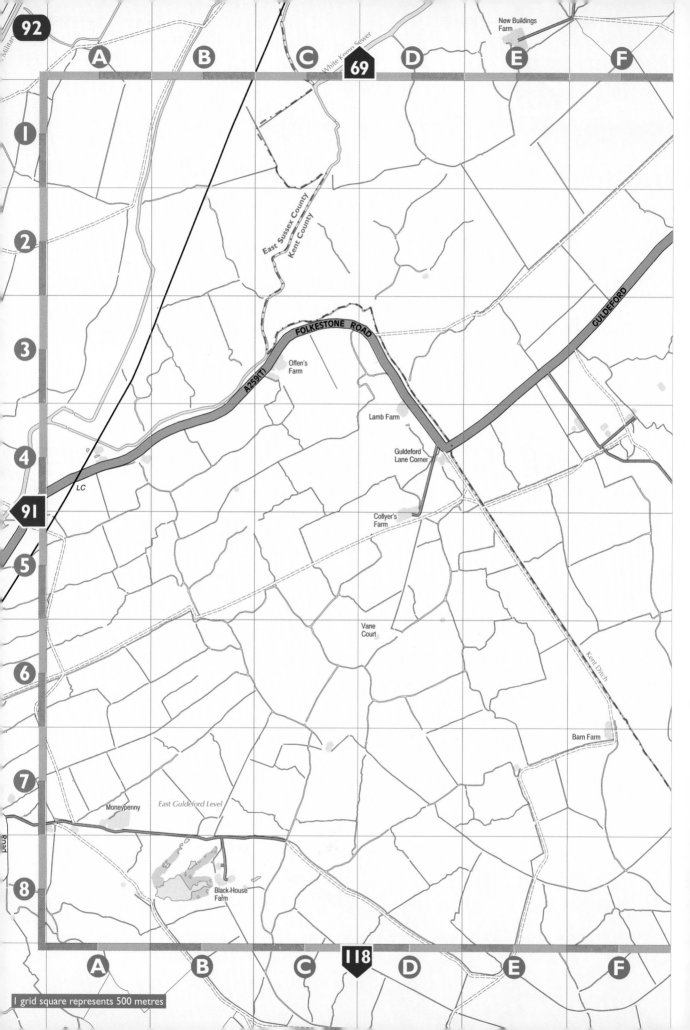

69

New Buildings
Farm

A   B   C   D   E   F

1

2

East Sussex County

Kent County

3

FOLKESTONE ROAD

GULDEFORD

A259(T)

Offen's
Farm

Lamb Farm

Guldeford
Lane Corner

4

LC

91

Collyer's
Farm

5

Kent Ditch

Vane
Court

6

Barn Farm

7

Moneypenny   East Guldeford Level

Military

Road

White Kemp Sewer

8

Black-House
Farm

A   B   C   118   D   E   F

I grid square represents 500 metres

G H J **70** K L M

I

Ashentree

A259(T)

LANE

Whitehouse
Farm

Hook Wall

Walland Marsh

Blue
House
Farm

2

Old Cheyne
Court

3

4

94

5

Little Cheyne
Court

6

Lower
Agney

7

Kent County
East Sussex County

8

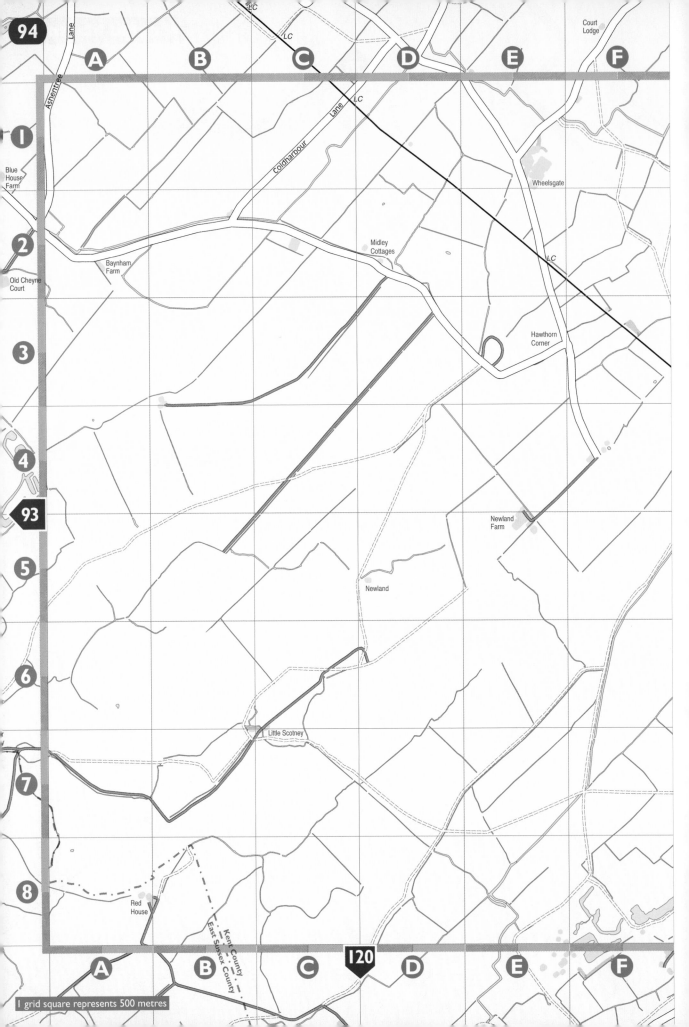

A   B   C   D   E   F

Court
Lodge

Ashentree Lane

Coldharbour Lane

LC

LC

1

Blue
House
Farm

Wheelsgate

2

Baynham
Farm

Midley
Cottages

LC

Old Cheyne
Court

3

Hawthorn
Corner

4

93

Newland
Farm

5

Newland

6

7

Little Scotney

8

Red
House

Kent County
East Sussex County

A   B   C   120   D   E   F

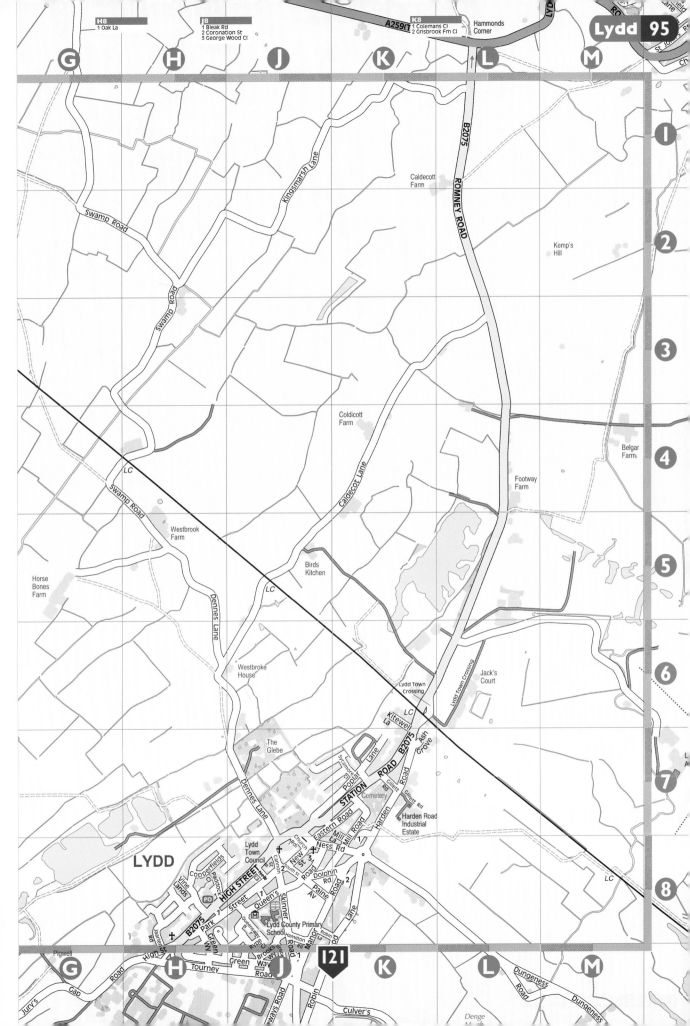

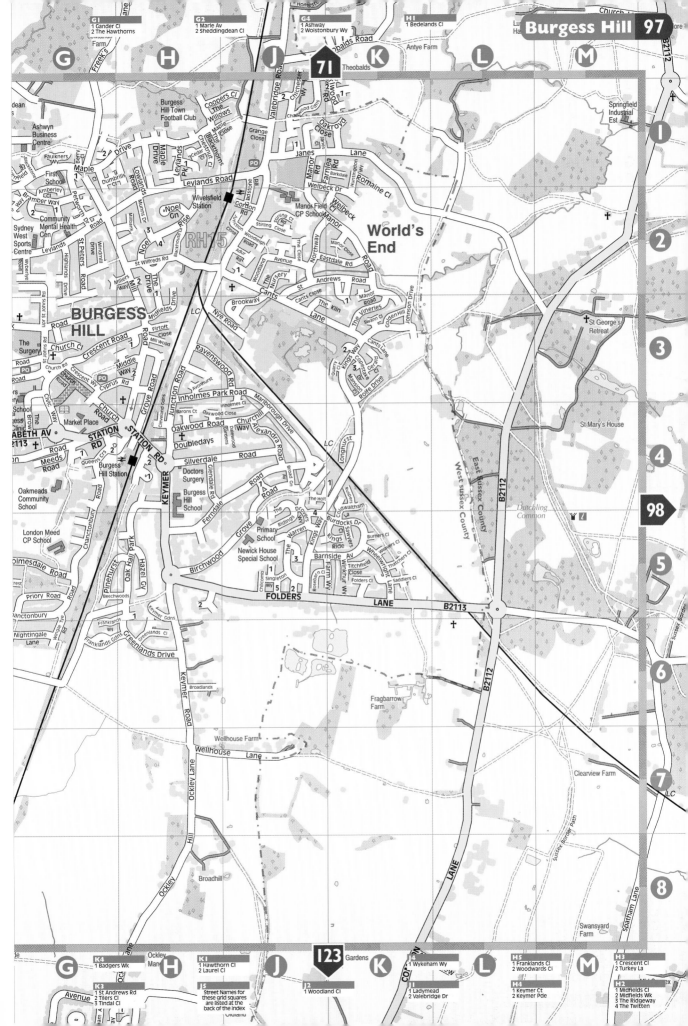

98

B2112

A **B** **C** **72** **D** E8 1 The Paddocks Wivelsden Farm C2 1 Coppards Cl **E** **F**

Church Lane

More House

Place

Hall

Strood
Farm

Newhouse
Farm

Springfield
Industrial
Est

Green Road

Tanners Field

Slugwash Lane

Fanners

Mann's
Farm

North common Road

Longridge

I

Wivelsfield

Green Pk Cl

Street
Gate

Farncombe
Close

PO
CfS
Allwood

Go
Gr

2

St George's
Retreat

Downsview Dr

1

South   Road

Woodlands
Farm

3

West
Wood

Sussex Border Path

ary's House

Heath
Farm

4

Park
Farm

97

Hundred Acre Lane

North America
Farm

St Helena
Farm

Shaw
Park

5

Sussex Border Path

6

Blackbrook
Wood

Gallops

Streat Lane

Captains Farm

Inholms Farm

ew Fa

7

LC

Kent's Lane

Chapel
Rd

Woodgate
Mdw

Wells
Cl

8

Spatham Lane

Station Road

West
Gate

Plumpton Green

Riddens
Lane

Riddens
La

PO
1

A Mid Sussex
Golf Club

B Marchants
Farm

C **124** **D** LC **E**

East Vw
Fields

Barnfield

F Plumpton
Primary
School

Elmgrove

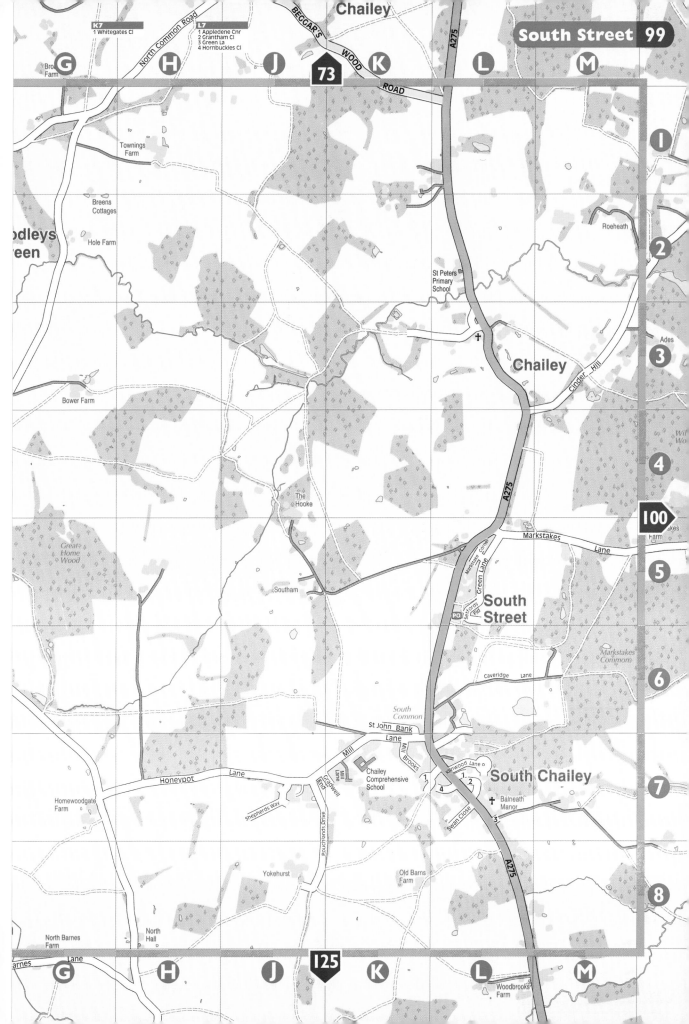

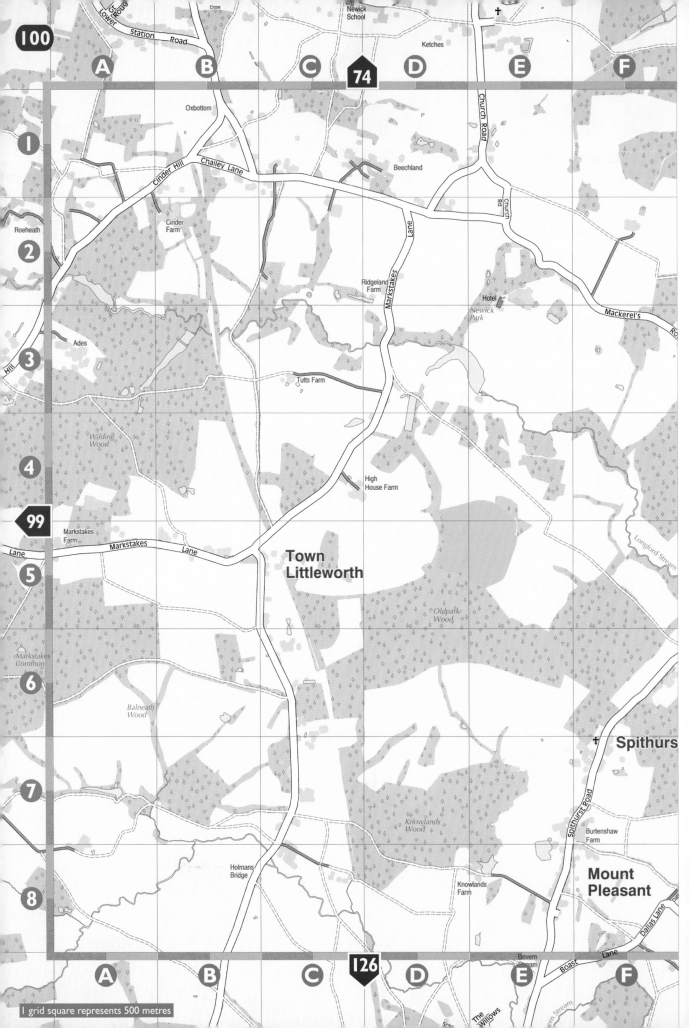

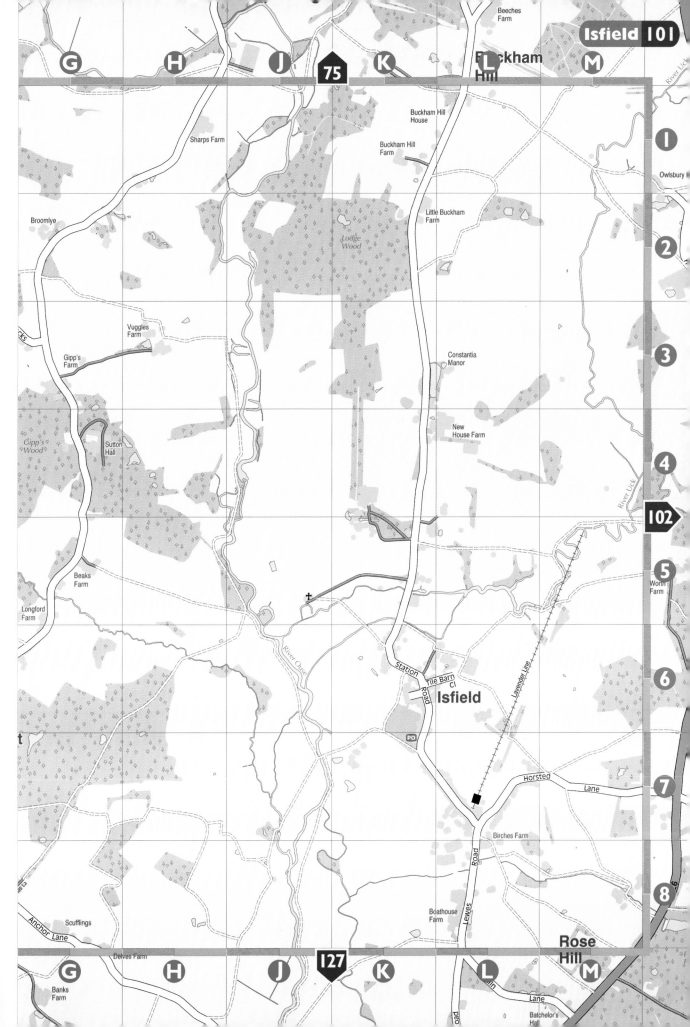

G   H   J   **75**   K   L   M

Beeches
Farm

Buckham
Hill

1

Buckham Hill
House

Owlsbury

Buckham Hill
Farm

Sharps Farm

2

Broomlye

Little Buckham
Farm

River Uck

Lodge
Wood

3

Vuggles
Farm

Gipp's
Farm

Constantia
Manor

4

Gipp's
Wood

Sutton
Hall

New
House Farm

River Uck

102

Beaks
Farm

5

Worth
Farm

Longford
Farm

River Ouse

Station

Tile Barn
Cl

6

Isfield

PO

Lavender Line

Horsted   Lane

7

Birches Farm

Scufflings

Boathouse
Farm

Rose
Hill

8

Anchor Lane

Delves Farm

G   H   J   **127**   K   L   M

Banks
Farm

Batchelor's
Hall

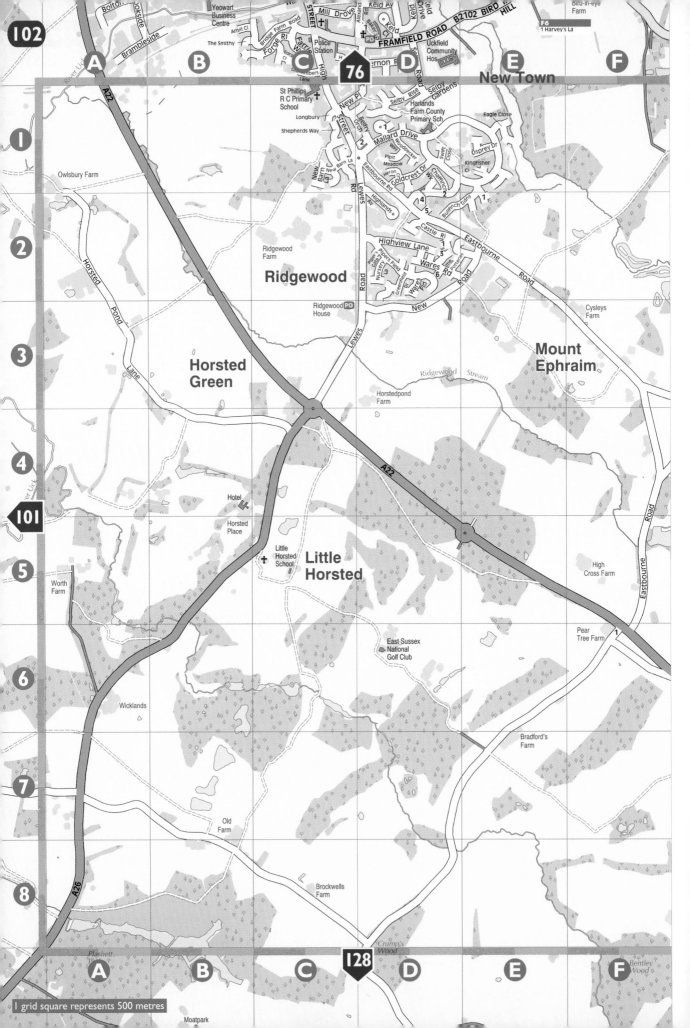

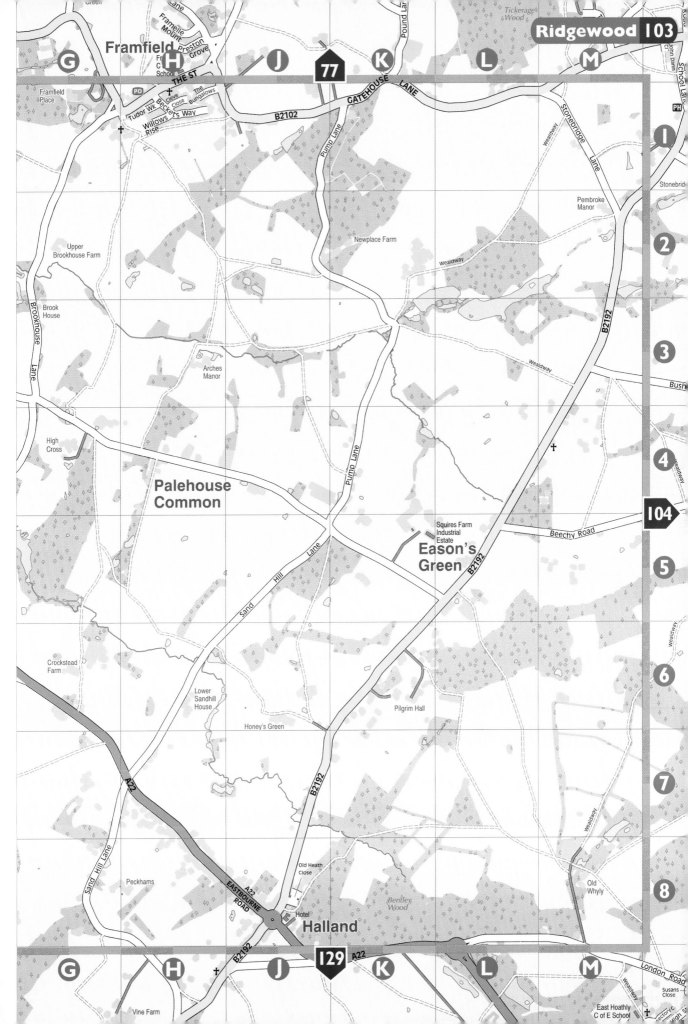

Framfield

G H J **77** K L M

Framelle Mount
Framfield C School
THE ST
PO
Tudor Wk
Cleve Close
The Bungalows
Becket's Way
Willows Rise
Preston Grove
B2102
GATEHOUSE LANE
Pound Lane

Framfield Place

Tickerage Wood

Stonebridge Lane
Wealdway

Pembroke Manor

I

2

Stonebri

Newplace Farm

Wealdway

B2192

Upper Brookhouse Farm

3

Bush

Brook House

Arches Manor

Wealdway

High Cross

4

Pump Lane

104

Palehouse Common

Squires Farm Industrial Estate

Beechy Road

Eason's Green

Sand Lane

B2192

5

Wealdway

Crockstead Farm

6

Lower Sandhill House

Pilgrim Hall

Honey's Green

B2192

7

Sand Hill Lane

A22

Wealdway

Peckhams

Old Whyly

8

Old Heath Close

EASTBOURNE ROAD

A22

Bentley Wood

Hotel

Halland

London Road

G H J **129** A22 K L M

Vine Farm

B2192

Susans Close

East Hoathly C of E School

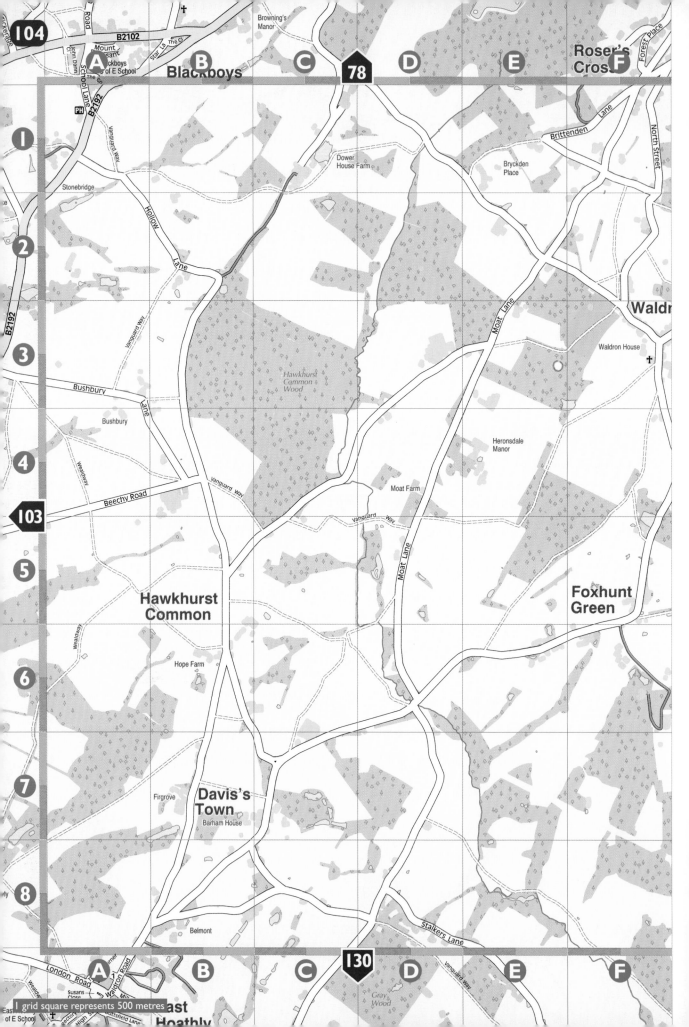

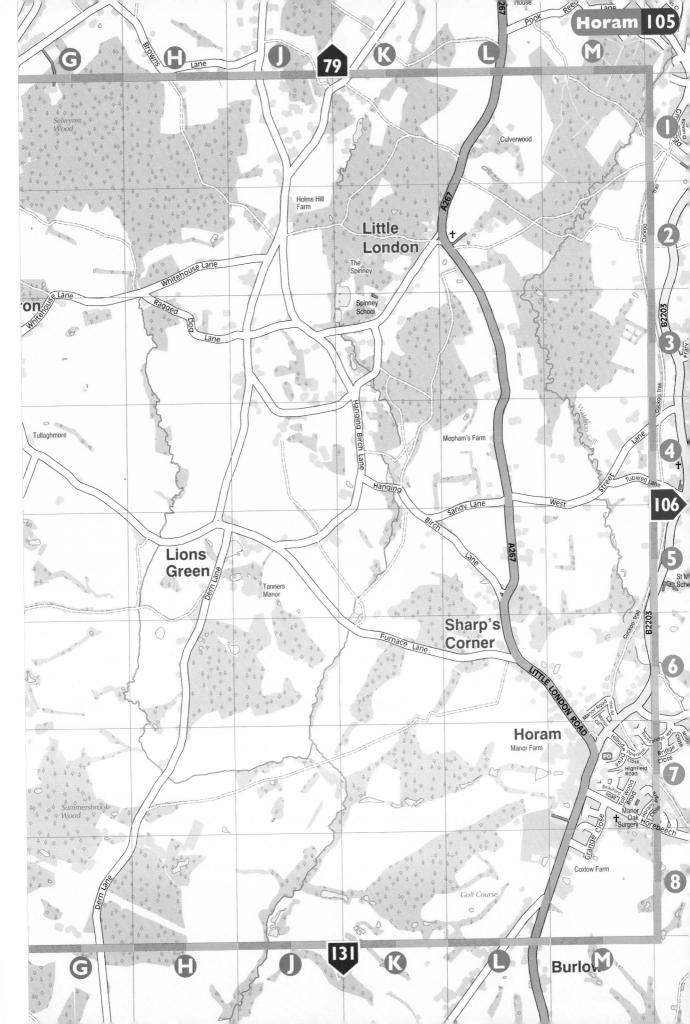

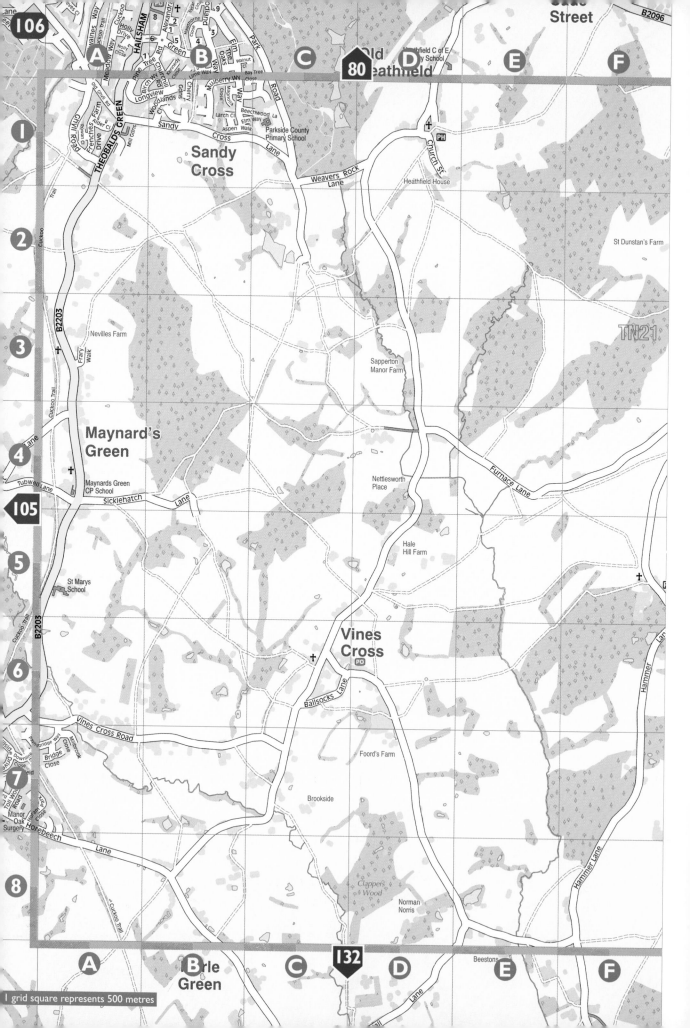

80

Street

B2096

A

B

C

**Old
Heathfield**

D

E

F

Heathfield C of E
Primary School

PH

Church St

Heathfield House

St Dunstan's Farm

I

THEOBALDS GREEN

Frenches Farm

Meadow Way

Old Cuckoo Way

HAILSHAM

Holly Drive

Hollis Close

Pine Tree Wy

Churchill Rd

Kennedy

Longview

Alder Cl

Rowan Cl

Mill Gdns

Woodlands

Longhurst

Alexandra Rd

Green

Cherry Gdns

Magnolia Close

Mulberry Wy

Haseldens

Bay Tree Close

Walnut

Larch Cl

Lime Way

Aspen

Elm Way

Beechwood La

Elm Way Walk

Park Road

Sandy

Cross

Lane

Weavers Rock
Lane

**Sandy
Cross**

Parkside County
Primary School

2

Cuckoo
Trail

B2203

Nevilles Farm

TN21

3

Friary Walk

Cuckoo Trail

Sapperton
Manor Farm

4

Lane

Tubwell Lane

Maynards Green
CP School

**Maynard's
Green**

Sicklehatch

Lane

Nettlesworth
Place

Furnace Lane

105

Hale
Hill Farm

5

St Marys
School

Cuckoo Trail

B2203

6

**Vines
Cross**

PO

Ballsocks Lane

7

Periedge Downlow

Pershridge Way

Millbrook
Close

Bridge
Close

Vines Cross Road

Bridge Drive

Toll Wood
Road

Manor
Oak
Surgery

Horebeech

Lane

Foord's Farm

Brookside

8

Clappers
Wood

Norman
Norris

Hammer Lane

A

**Brle
Green**

132

C

D

Beestons

E

F

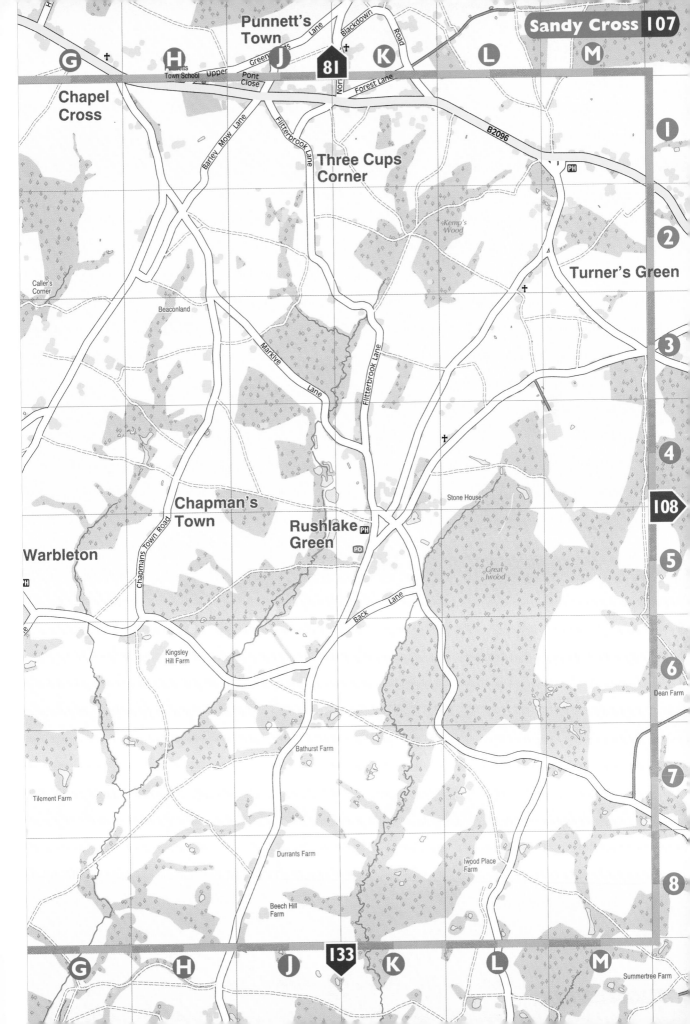

G

**Chapel
Cross**

Caller's
Corner

Beaconland

**Chapman's
Town**

Warbleton

H

**Punnett's
Town**

Punnetts
Town School

Green

Upper

Pont
Close

Barley Mow Lane

Marklye Lane

Chapmans Town Road

Kingsley
Hill Farm

Tilement Farm

J

Blackdown

Fitterbrook Lane

81

**Three Cups
Corner**

Fitterbrook Lane

**Rushlake
Green** PH

PO

Back Lane

Bathurst Farm

Durrants Farm

Beech Hill
Farm

133

K

Road

Nori

Forest Lane

Kemp's
Wood

†

Stone House

†

L

B2096

PH

†

Great
Iwood

Iwood Place
Farm

M

Turner's Green

Dean Farm

Summertree Farm

1

2

3

4

108

5

6

7

8

PH

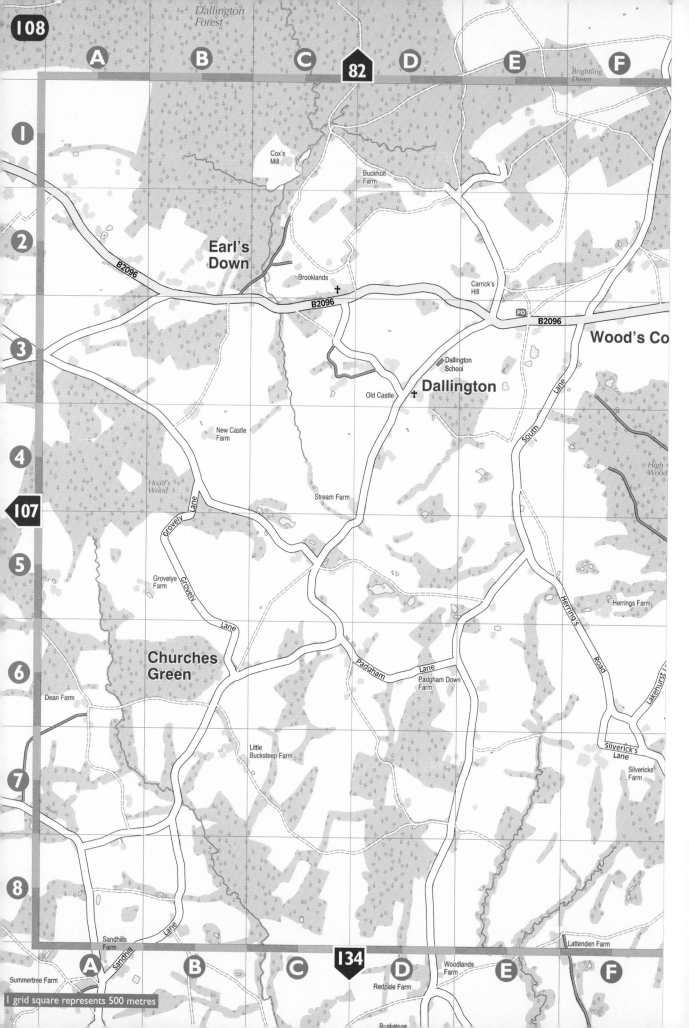

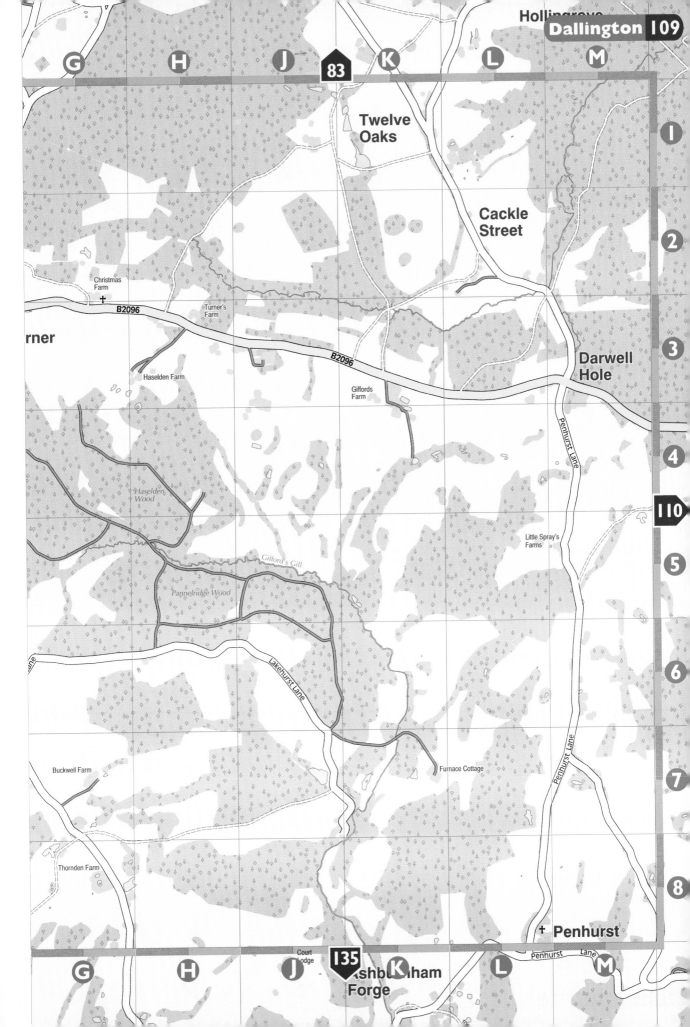

G H J **83** K L M

I

Twelve
Oaks

Cackle
Street

2

Christmas
Farm

rner
† B2096

Turner's
Farm

3

Darwell
Hole

Haselden Farm

B2096

Giffords
Farm

Penhurst Lane

4

Haselden
Wood

110

Little Spray's
Farms

Gifford's Gill

5

Pannelridge Wood

6

Lakehurst Lane

Buckwell Farm

Penhurst Lane

7

Furnace Cottage

Thornden Farm

8

† **Penhurst**

Penhurst Lane

G H J **135** K L M

Court
Lodge

shbu ham
Forge

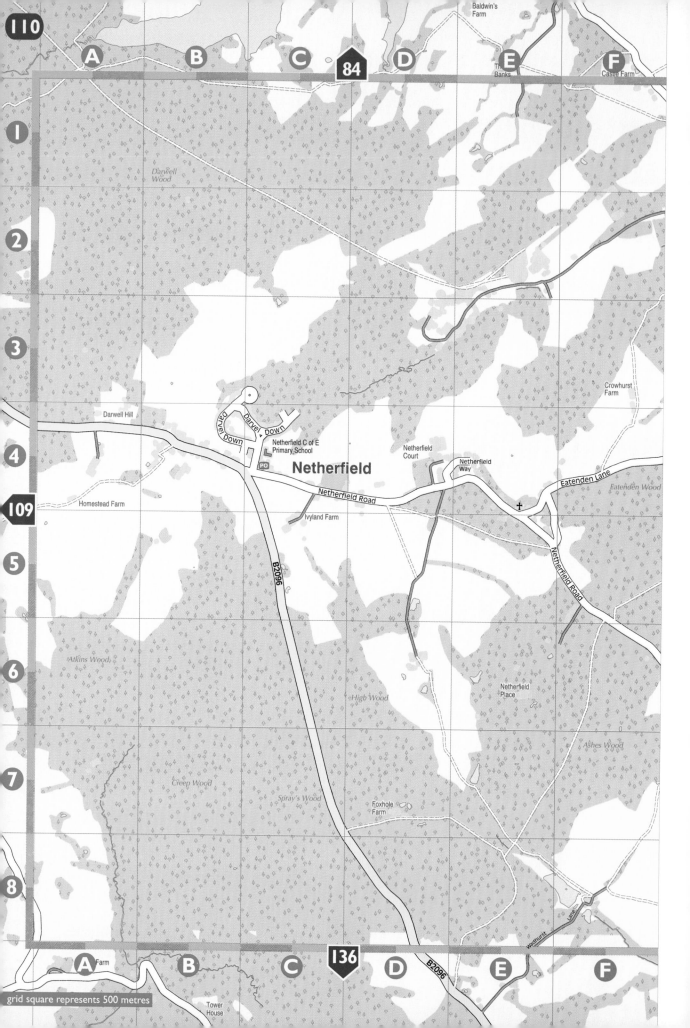

A B C 84 D E F

Baldwin's Farm

The Banks

Castle Farm

1

Darwell Wood

2

3

Crowhurst Farm

Darwell Hill

Darvel Down

Darvel Down

Netherfield C of E Primary School

PO

Netherfield

Netherfield Court

Netherfield Way

Eatenden Lane

Eatenden Wood

4

109

Homestead Farm

Netherfield Road

Ivyland Farm

✝

Netherfield Road

5

B2096

Atkins Wood

6

High Wood

Netherfield Place

Ashes Wood

7

Creep Wood

Spray's Wood

Foxhole Farm

8

A Farm B C 136 D B2096 E F

Wadhurst Lane

Tower House

grid square represents 500 metres

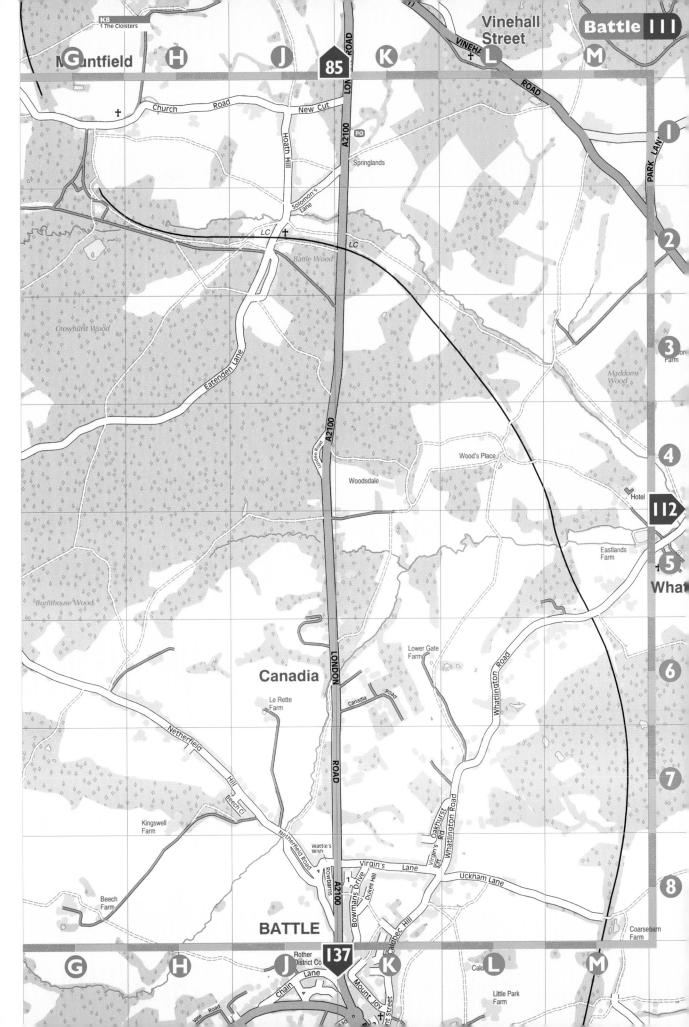

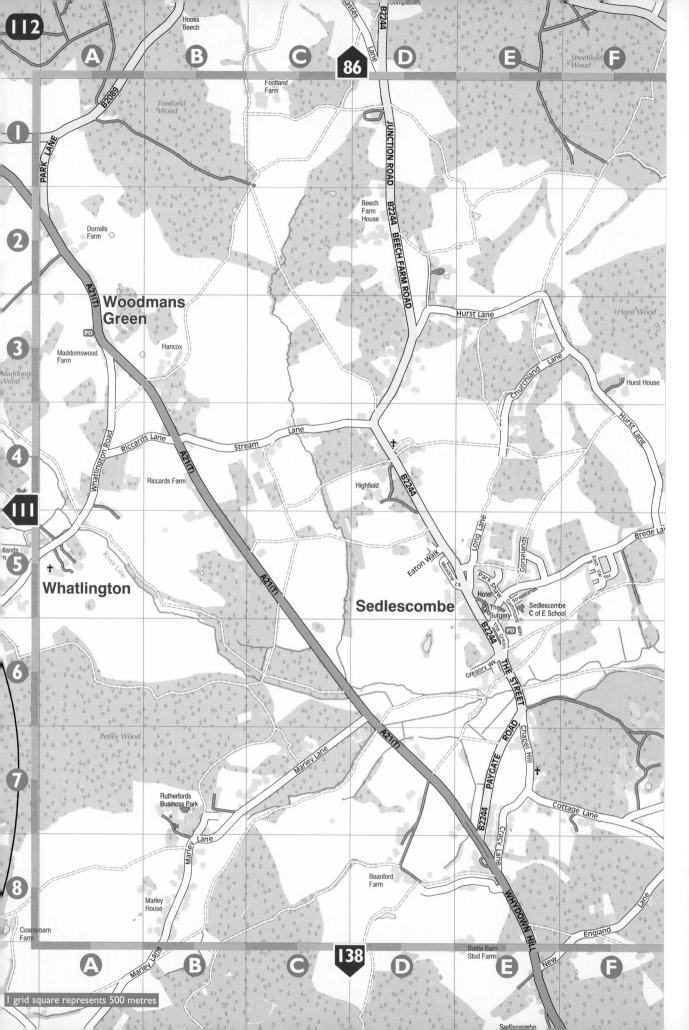

A B C 86 D E F

1

2

3

4

III

5

6

7

8

A B 138 C D E F

Footland Farm

Footland Wood

Hooks Beech

B2089

PARK LANE

B2244

Compasses Lane

JUNCTION ROAD

Dorrells Farm

Woodmans Green

A21(T)

PO

Maddomswood Farm

Hancox

Maddoms Wood

Whatlington Road

Riccards Lane

Riccards Farm

A21(T)

Stream Lane

Highfield

Beech Farm House

B2244

BEECH FARM ROAD

Hurst Lane

Churchland Lane

Hurst Wood

Hurst House

Hurst Lane

+

B2244

tlands m

River Line

Whatlington

+

Eaton Walk

Long Lane

Meadow La

Park Shaw

Hotel

The Surgery

Gregory Wk

B2244

The Green

PO

Gammons Way

Gorselands

Streetlands

Sedlescombe C of E School

East Vw Ter

Brede La

Sedlescombe

Petley Wood

Marley Lane

A21(T)

THE STREET

PAYGATE ROAD

Chapel Hill

+

Cottage Lane

Rutherfords Business Park

Marley Lane

B2244

Cracy Lane

WHYDOWN HILL

New England Lane

Beanford Farm

Marley House

Battle Barn Stud Farm

Coarsebarn Farm

Sedlescombe

Streetfield Wood

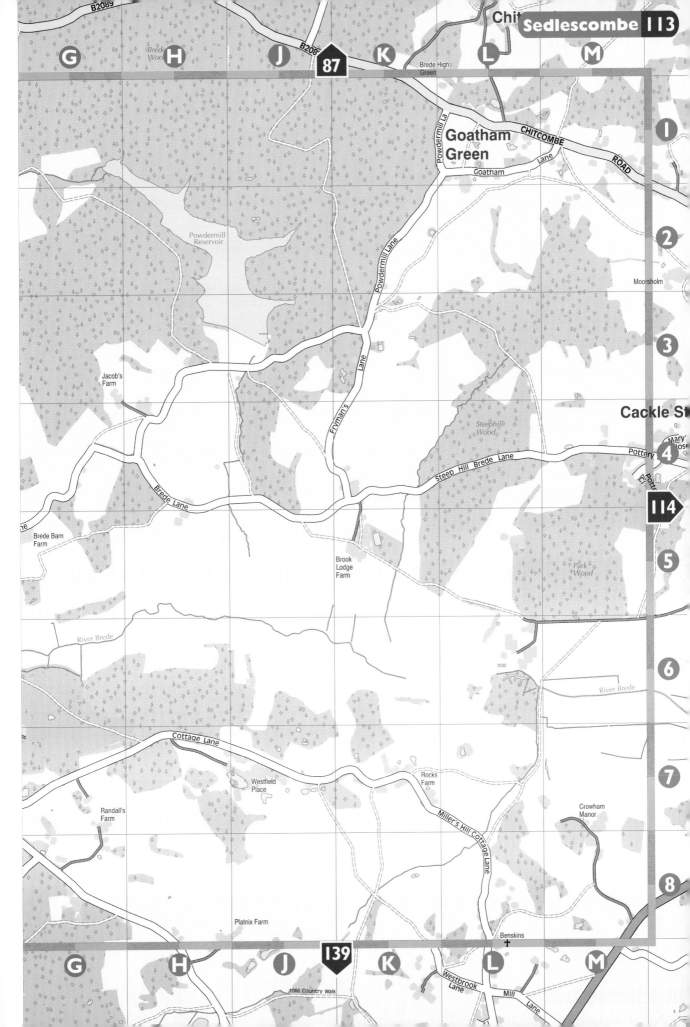

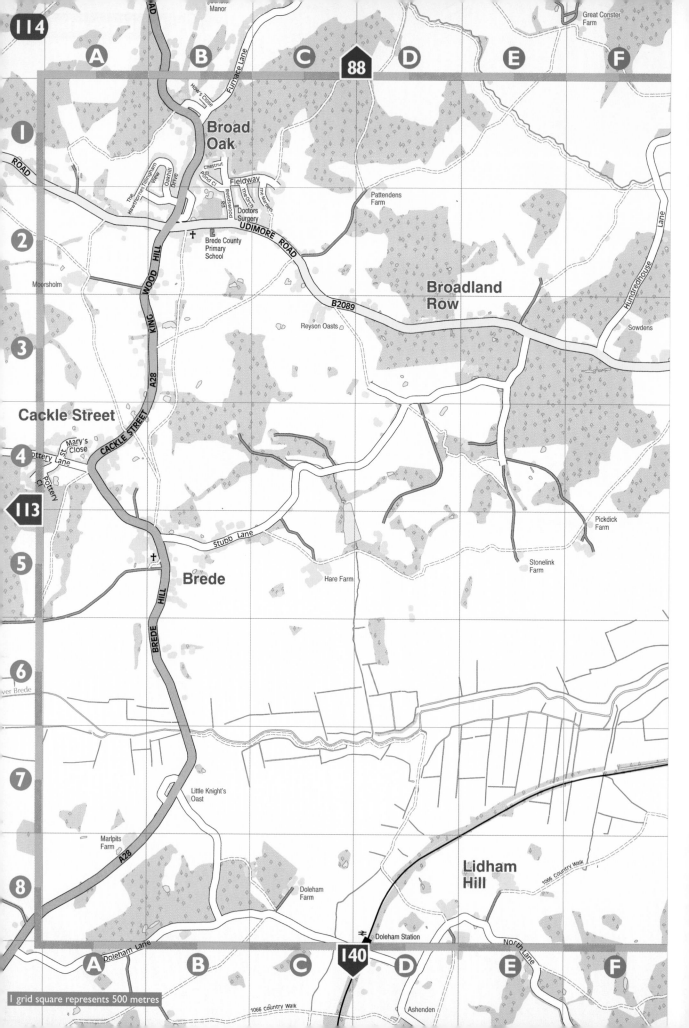

Pelsham

Partridge Farm

L8
1 High Fords Cl

M8
1 Peartree Fld

G Ludley Farm

H Hayes Farm

J

89

K Hayes Lane · Dinglesden

L

M

1

Hayes Lane

River Tillingham

2

Great Sowdens Wood

Billingham Farm

3

Newman's Farm

Billingham Lane

Udimore

4 Knellstone

Little Park Wood

Court Lodge

Cock Marlir

Winchelsea Lane

116

Great Park Wood

5

Fl

River Brede

6

Brede Level

7

Lower Snailham

Brook Farm

8

1066 Country Walk

Broad

Broad Street

Icklesham

Icklesham Primary School

Parsonage Lane

PH

Oast House Fld

G Stocks Farm

H

J

141

K

Toke Farm

High Fords

Brede View

Colourhurst Cn

Manor Cl

L

PO

Workhouse Lane

M

Laurel Lane

4259(T) MAIN ROAD

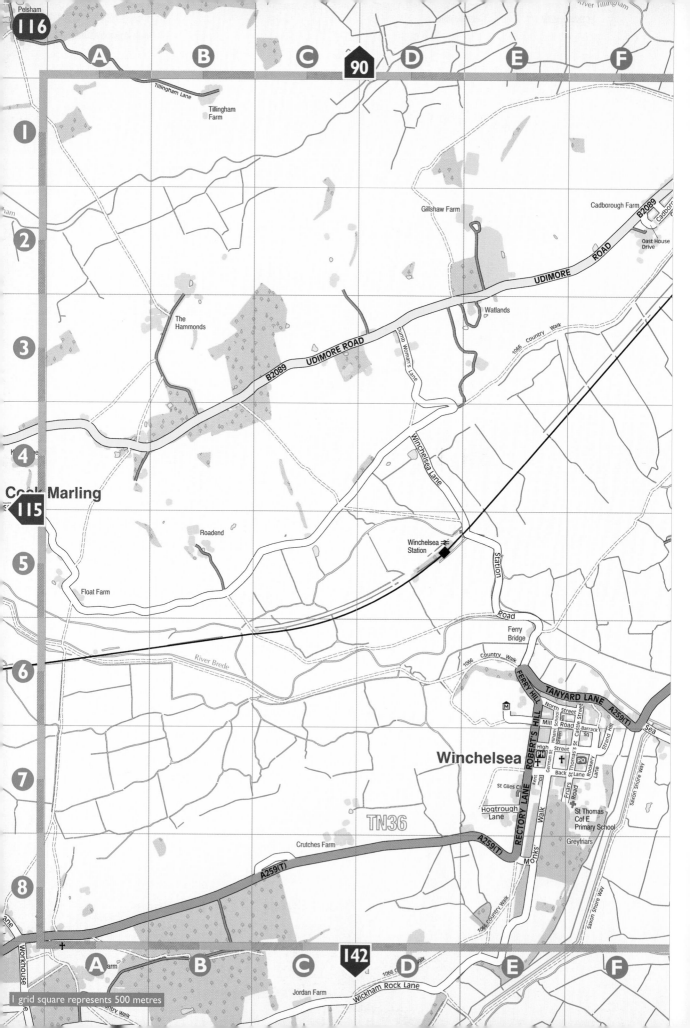

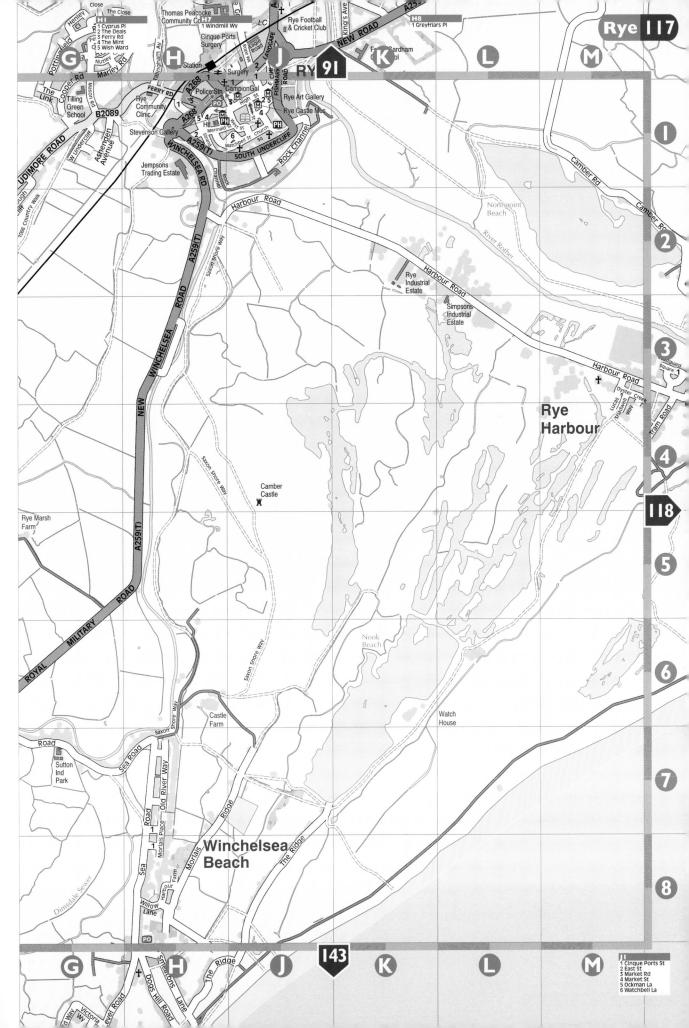

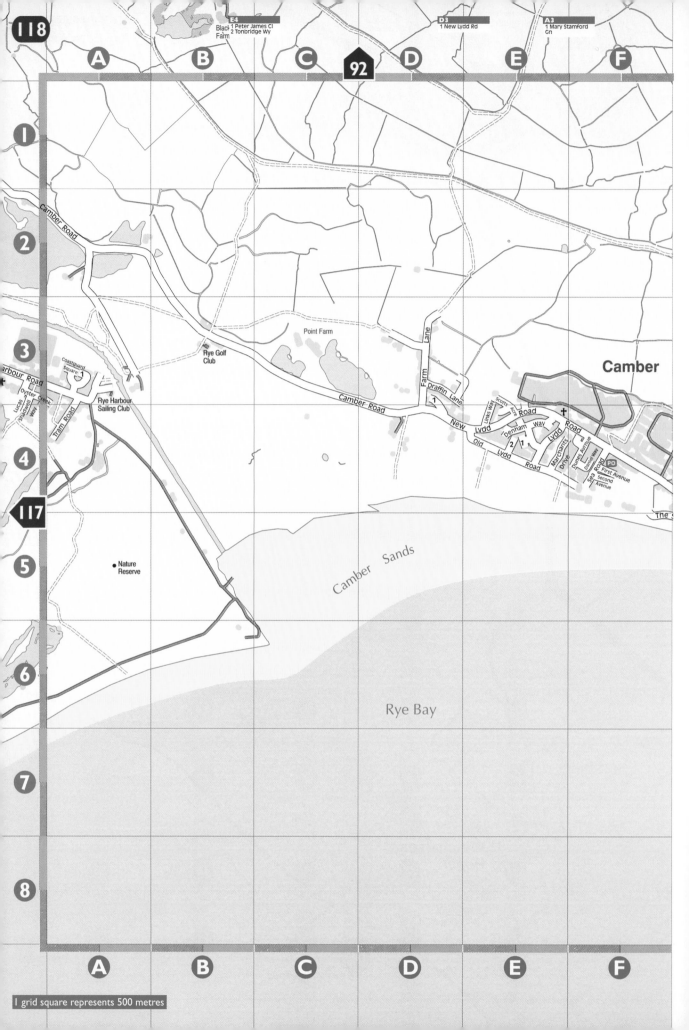

A   B   C   D   E   F

E4
1 Peter James Cl
2 Tonbridge Wy

D3
1 New Lydd Rd

A3
1 Mary Stamford
Gn

1

Camber Road

2

3

Harbour Road

Coastguard
Square

Rye Golf
Club

Point Farm

Lane

Farm

Draffin Lane

Camber

Camber Road

Rye Harbour
Sailing Club

Lucas
Shadwell
Way

Train Road

Oyster Creek

New Lydd

Scotts

Links Way

Acre Road

Dennam Way

Road

Lydd

Marchants
Drive

First Avenue

4

117

Old
Lydd

Road

Dunes Avenue

Daniel Way

Sea Road

second
Avenue

PO

5

Nature
Reserve

Camber   Sands

The

6

Rye Bay

7

8

A   B   C   D   E   F

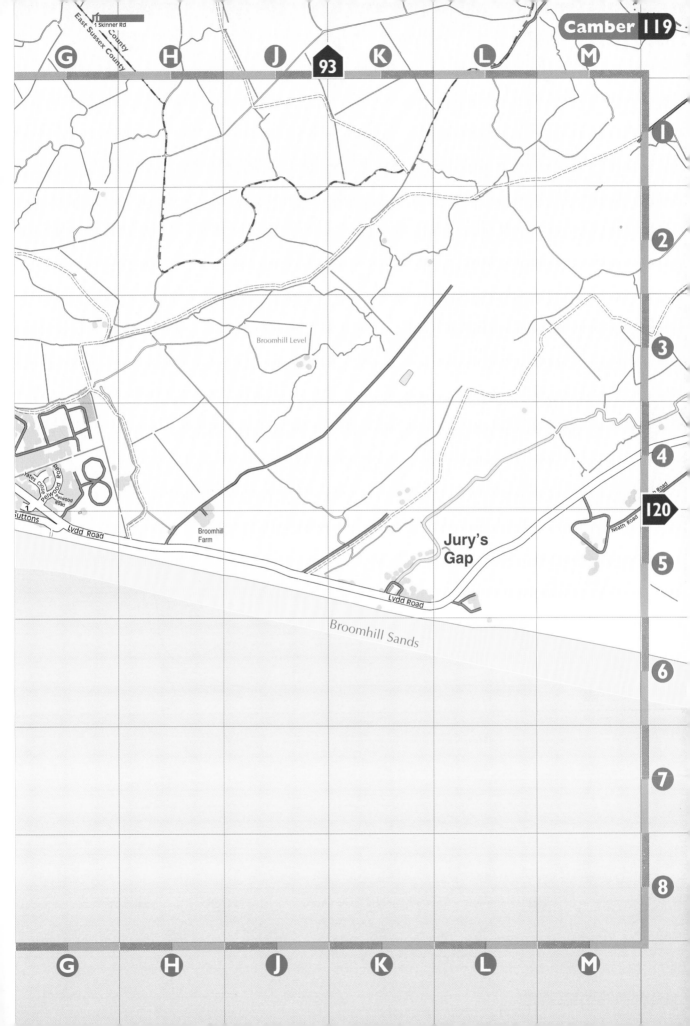

1 Skinner Rd

East Sussex County

93

Broomhill Level

Yates Close

Pelwood Road

Suttons

Lydd Road

Broomhill Farm

Jury's Gap

Neath Road

120

Lydd Road

Broomhill Sands

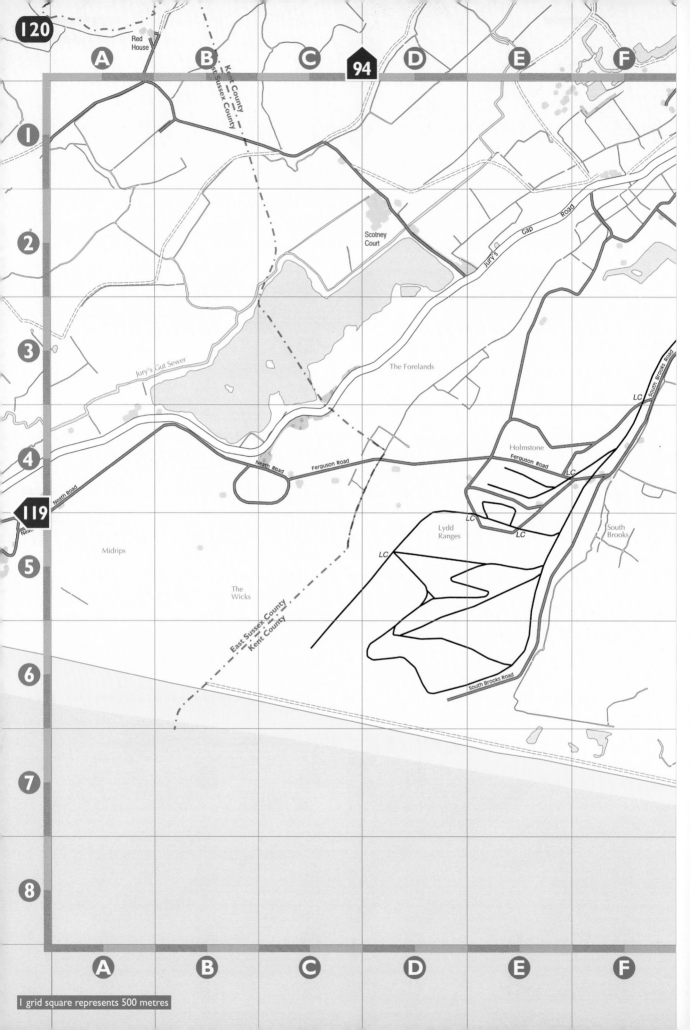

A   B   C   94   D   E   F

I

2

3

4

119

5

6

7

8

A   B   C   D   E   F

Red House

Kent County
East Sussex County

Scotney Court

Jury's Gap Road

Jury's

The Forelands

Jury's Gut Sewer

LC

South Brooks Road

Holmstone

Ferguson Road

LC

Neath Road   Ferguson Road

LC

Neath Road

Midrips

LC

Lydd Ranges

LC

South Brooks

The Wicks

East Sussex County
Kent County

LC

South Brooks Road

1 grid square represents 500 metres

1 Skinner Rd

G H J 95 K L M

I
2
3
4
5
6
7
8

Pigwell

High St

Jury's Gap

West Ripe

LC

LC LC LC

LC

Invicta Road

LC

Galloways Road

Tourney Road

Green Way Road

Green

HIGH STREET

High Street

Queen's

Skinner

B2075

Copper

Park

Vine

Lams

PO

Jaarley Rd

Ryde

Brooks

Paine Av

Dolphin Rd

Rd

Manor Rd

Hamilton Rd

County Primary School

Galloways Road

Robin

Culver's Lane

Dengemarsh Road

Denge Marsh

Dungeness Road

Dungeness Road

Boulderwal Farm

Manor Farm

Brickwall Farm

G2
1 Clerks Acre

G3
1 The Poplars
2 Willowbrook Wy

H1
1 Sweetlands

L3
1 Barnfield Gdns

K3
1 Boddingtons La
2 The Dymock's

97

146

G H J K L M

KEYMER

Avenue
Mackie
Manor Avenue
Ann Cl
Farnham Av
Ockley Way
Bromley Cl
Ockley Way
Avenue
Adastra Avenue
Oakley Lane
Fir Tree Wy
The Quadrant
Parkside
Kymer Gardens
The Minnels
Highlands Cl
Avenue
Windmills County Junior School
Stafford Way
PO
Newlands Close
Damian Way
Mead
Church
The Crescent
Silverdale
Keymer Park
Beacon Hurst

Ockley Lane
Ockley Manor
Oldland

Broadhill

West Sussex County
East Sussex County

Lodge Hill
Lane

Court Gardens Farm

Orchard Lane
North End
B2112

Dumbrells Ct Road

Sussex Border Path

COMMON
South View

Myard Farm
Spatham

Mid Sussex Golf

Stocks Farm

Newtons Farm

Ditchling Museum
Ditchling Gallery
Lodge Hill
Church La
M
WEST ST
HIGH ST
St Dominics Gallery
SOUTH ST

Ditchling
East Gdns
East Mulberry Lane
PO
The Craftsman Gallery
Fieldway
Ditchling Health Centre
Ditchling Primary School

East End Lane
Farm La
Shirleys

Spatham Lane

Park Avenue
Lodge Lane

Clayton Road
B2112

LEWES ROAD
B2116

124

Lodge Farm

Sussex Border Pth
Beacon Road
Nye Lane
The Nye

Park Barn Farm

Nye Lane

Lodge Lane

Whitelands

Burnthouse Bostall

Sussex Border Pth

Underhill Lane
Wick Farm

Westmeston

Nye St

South Downs Way

Ditchling Bostall

248
Ditchling Beacon

Ditchling Road

Heathy Brow

I 1 2 3 4 5 6 7 8

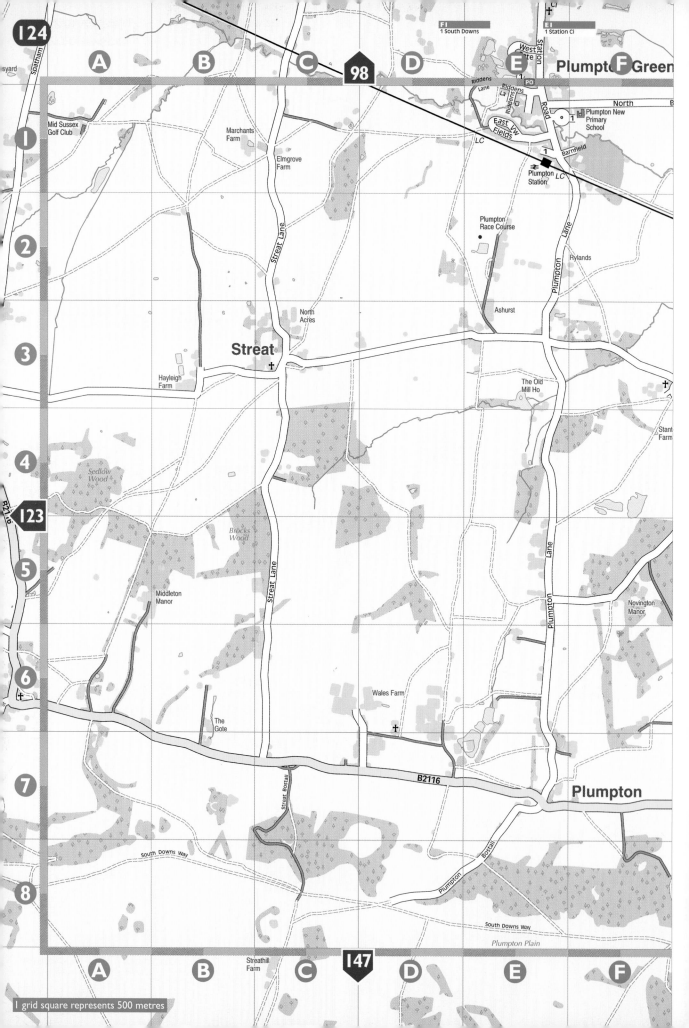

98

123

147

A B C D E F

1 2 3 4 5 6 7 8

B2116

Spatham

Mid Sussex Golf Club

Marchants Farm

Elmgrove Farm

Streat Lane

North Acres

Streat

Hayleigh Farm

Sedlow Wood

Brocks Wood

Middleton Manor

Streat Lane

The Gote

Streat Bostall

South Downs Way

Streathill Farm

Wales Farm

B2116

Plumpton Bostall

South Downs Way

Plumpton Plain

Plumpton

1 South Downs

1 Station Ci

West Gate

Plumpton Green

Riddens Lane

Riddens La

PO

East View Fields

LC

Plumpton Station

LC

North

1

Plumpton New Primary School

Barnfield

Plumpton Race Course

Station Road

Plumpton Lane

Rylands

Ashurst

The Old Mill Ho

Stant Farm

Plumpton Lane

Novington Manor

1 grid square represents 500 metres

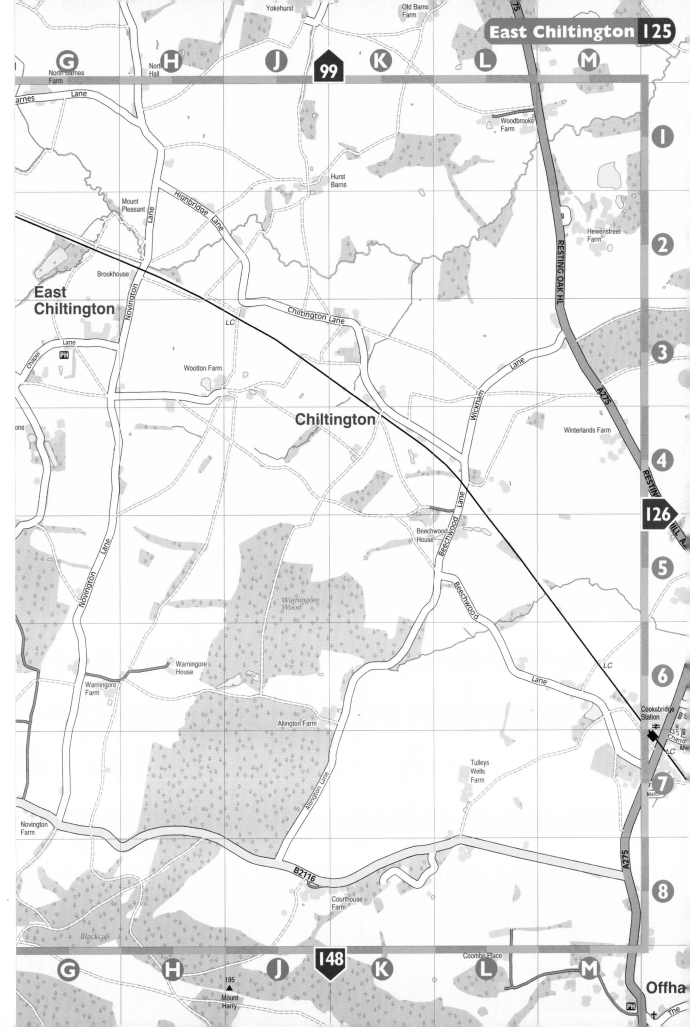

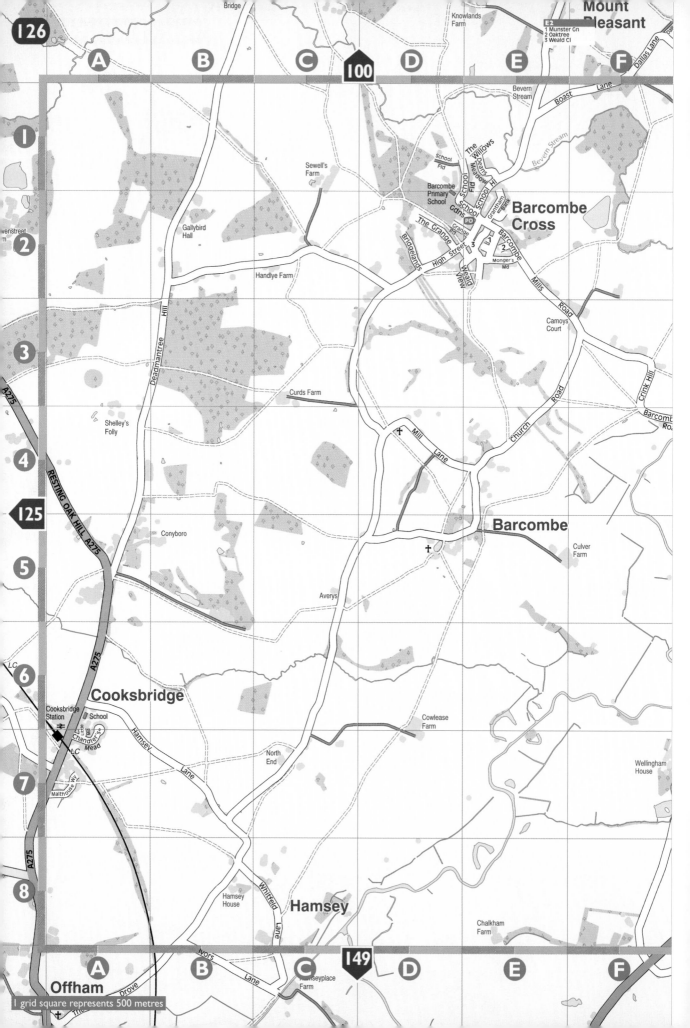

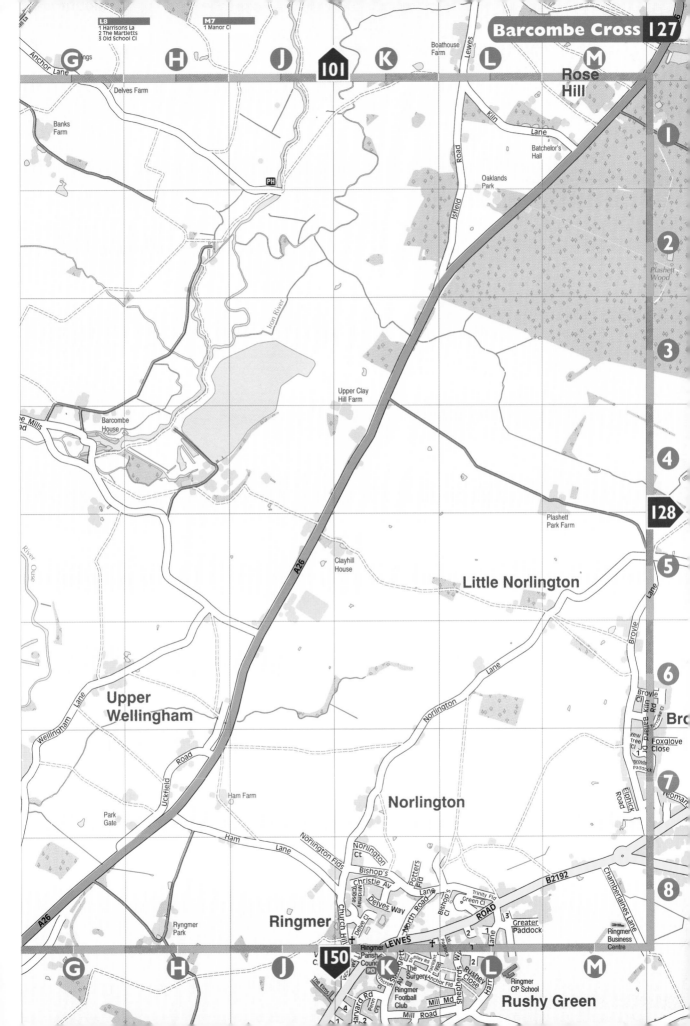

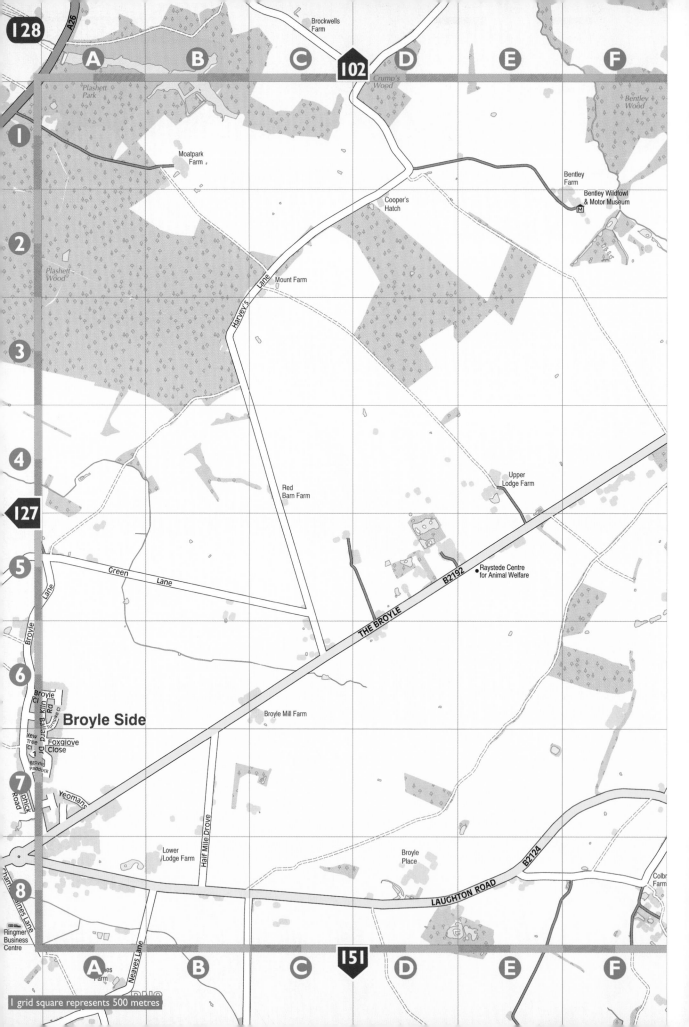

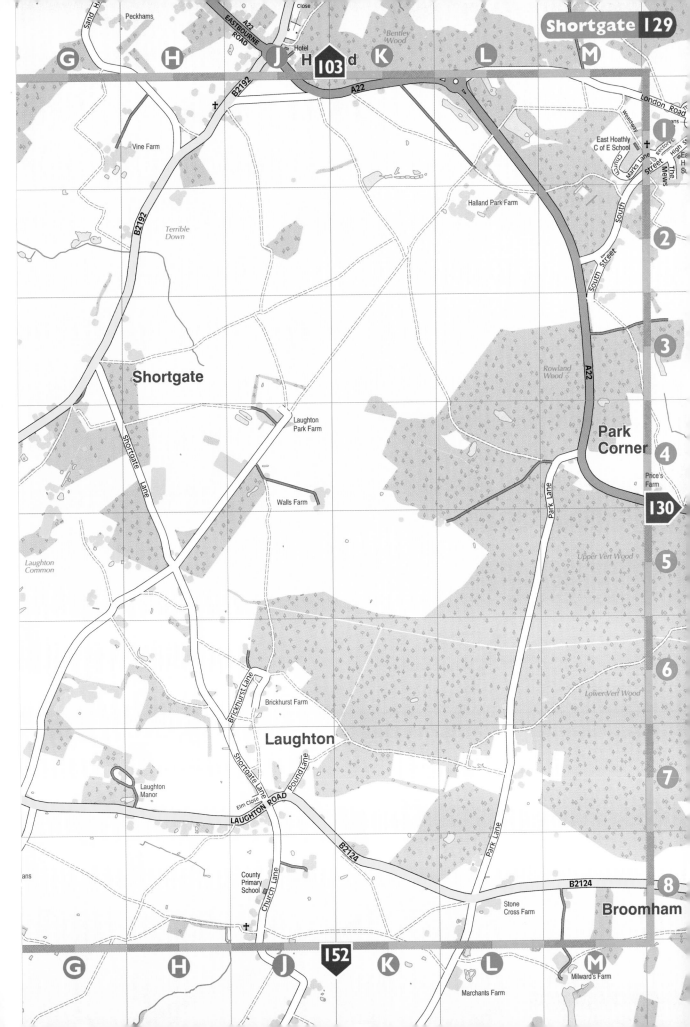

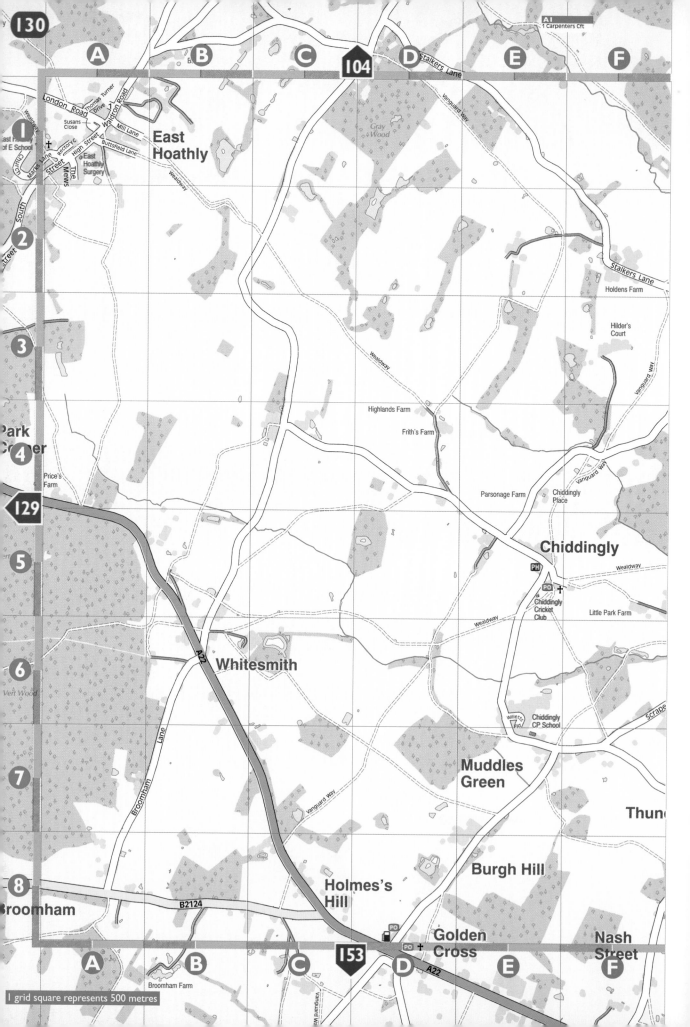

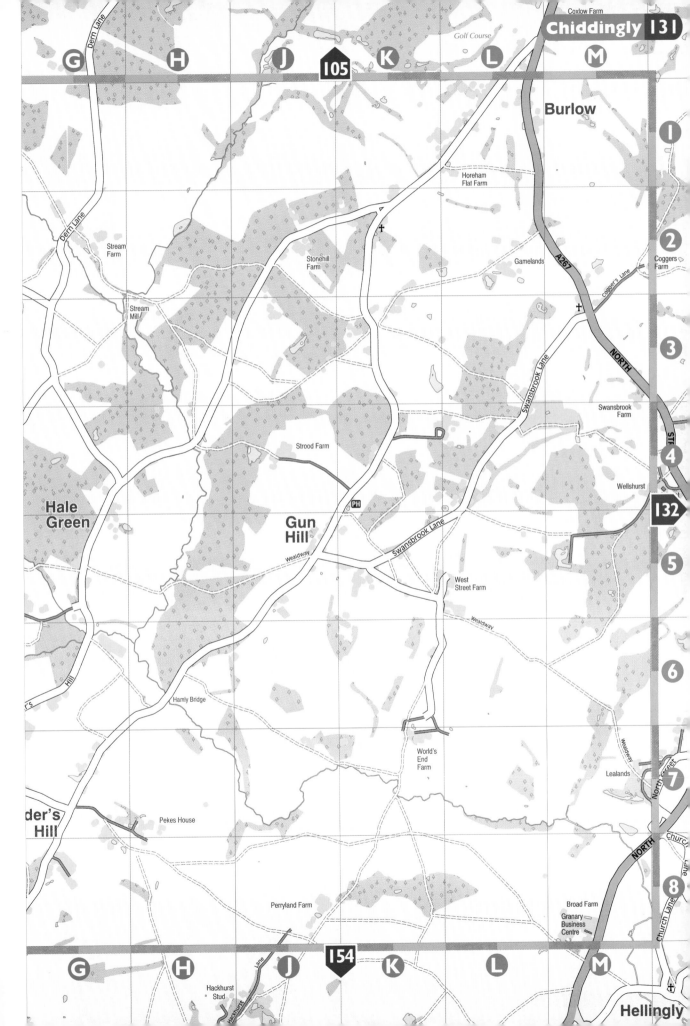

Coxlow Farm

Golf Course

G H J **105** K L M

Burlow

I

Dern Lane

Horeham
Flat Farm

2

Coggers
Farm

Stream
Farm

Stonehill
Farm

Gamelands

A267

Coggers Lane

3

Stream
Mill

NORTH

Swansbrook Lane

Swansbrook
Farm

4

STS

Wellshurst

Hale
Green

Strood Farm

132

PH

5

Gun
Hill

Swansbrook Lane

Wealdway

West
Street Farm

Wealdway

6

Hamly Bridge

World's
End
Farm

North Street

Wealdway

Lealands

7

der's
Hill

Pekes House

NORTH

Church Lane

8

Perryland Farm

Broad Farm

Granary
Business
Centre

Hackhurst
Stud

Hackhurst Lane

Hellingly

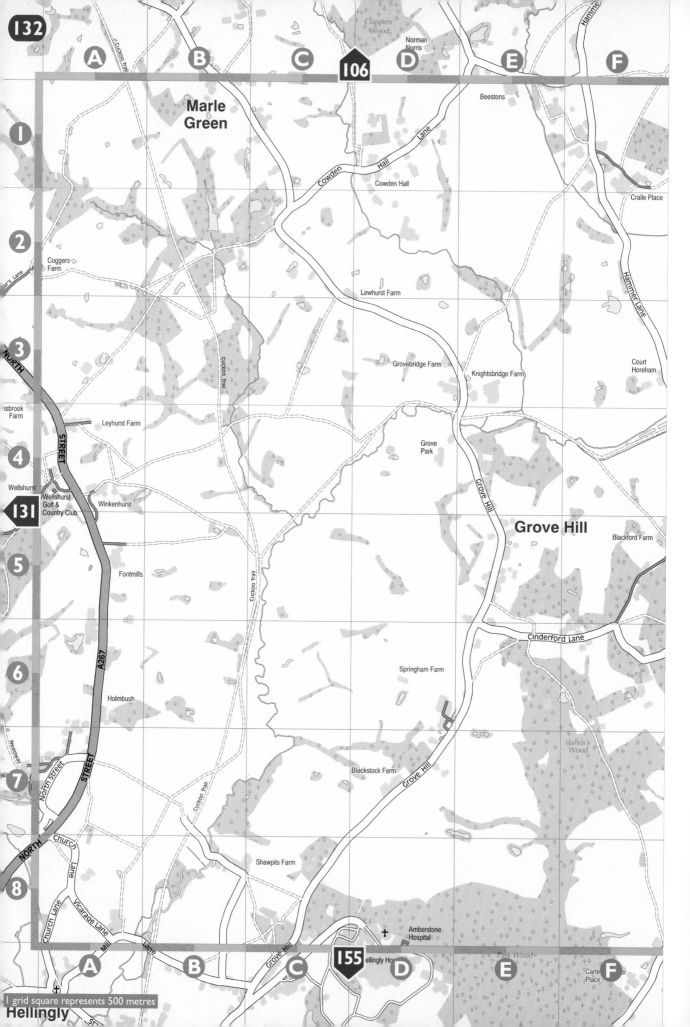

A B C **106** D E F

I

Marle
Green

Beestons

Cralle Place

2

Coggers
Farm

Cowden Hall
Cowden Hall

Lewhurst Farm

NORTH

3

Cuckoo Trail

Grovebridge Farm

Knightsbridge Farm

Court
Horeham

nsbrook
Farm

Leyhurst Farm

STREET

4

Grove
Park

Wellshurst

Wellshurst
Golf &
Country Club

Winkenhurst

131

Grove Hill

Grove Hill

Blackford Farm

5

Fontmills

Cuckoo Trail

A267

6

Holmbush

Springham Farm

Cinderford Lane

Jarvis's
Wood

Weaverway

STREET

7

North Street

Cuckoo Trail

Blackstock Farm

Grove Hill

NORTH

Church Lane

8

Shawpits Farm

Amberstone
Hospital

Park Wood

Church Lane

Vicarage Lane

A B **155** C D E F

Mill Lane

Grove Hill

ellingly Ho

Carter
Place

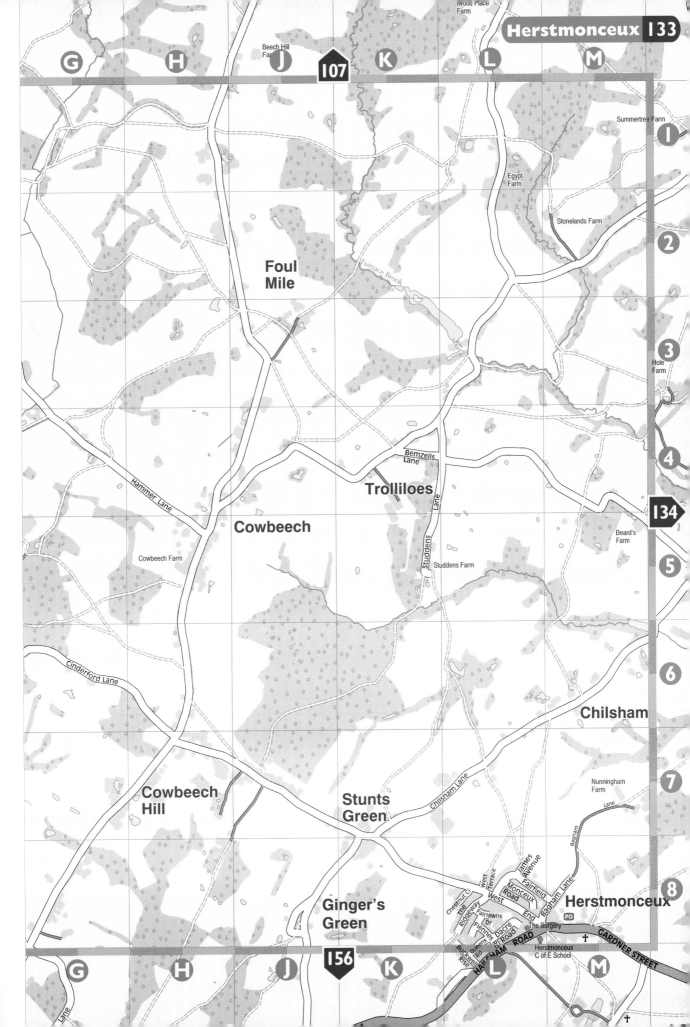

G   H   J   107   K   L   M

Beech Hill Farm

Iwood Place Farm

Summertree Farm

I

Egypt Farm

Stonelands Farm

2

Foul Mile

Furnace Brook

Hole Farm

3

Bemzells Lane

4

Trolliloes

134

Hammer Lane

Cowbeech

Beard's Farm

5

Studdens Lane

Cowbeech Farm

Studdens Farm

Cinderford Lane

6

Chilsham

Cowbeech Hill

Nunningham Farm

7

Stunts Green

Chilsham Lane

Bagham Lane

James Avenue

Fairfield

West Terrace

Monceux Road

8

Ginger's Green

Chestnut Cl

The Ridgeway

Fairlawns Dr

West End

The Surgery

Herstmonceux

PO

Plennes

Dacre Road

Queens Rd

Buckwell Rise

Herstmonceux C of E School

GARDNER STREET

G   H   J   156   K   L   M

HAILSHAM ROAD

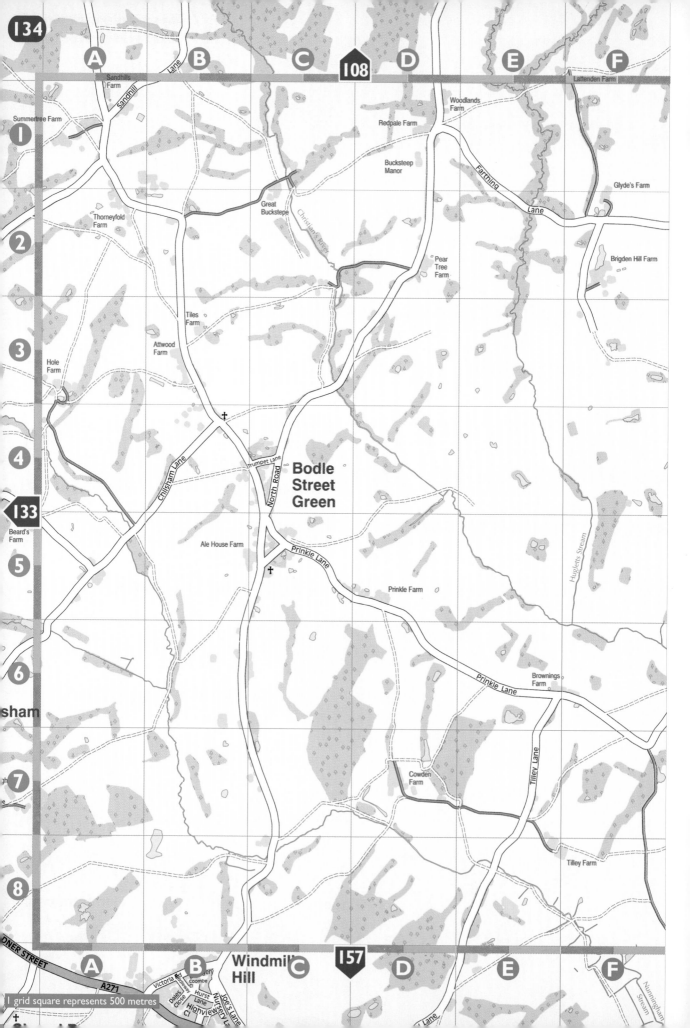

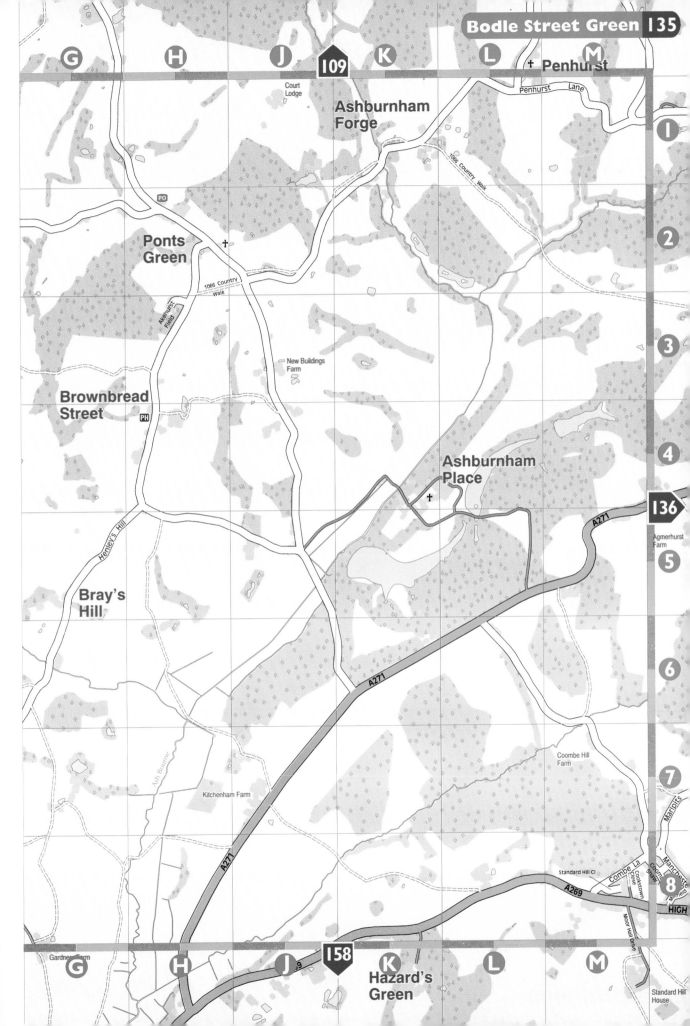

G
H
J
109
K
L
M

† **Penhurst**

Penhurst   Lane

Court
Lodge

**Ashburnham
Forge**

1066 Country Walk

1

PO

2

† **Ponts
Green**

1066 Country
Walk

Akehurst
Field

3

New Buildings
Farm

**Brownbread
Street**

PH

**Ashburnham
Place**

4

†

A271   **136**

Agmerhurst
Farm

5

Henley's Hill

**Bray's
Hill**

A271

6

Ash Bourne

Coombe Hill
Farm

7

Kitchenham Farm

Marlpits

A271

Combe La

Standard Hill Cl

Coom. Shaw

Manchester

Cookstown Close

8

A269

Moor Hall Drive

HIGH

Gardner Farm

G
H
J   9
158
K

**Hazard's
Green**

L
M

Standard Hill
House

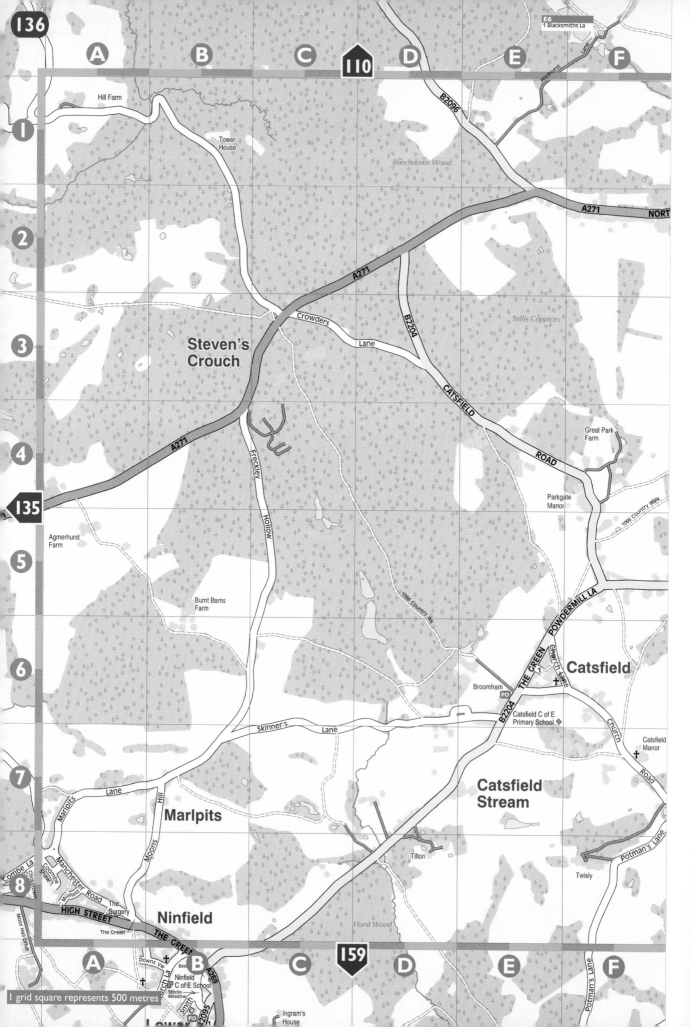

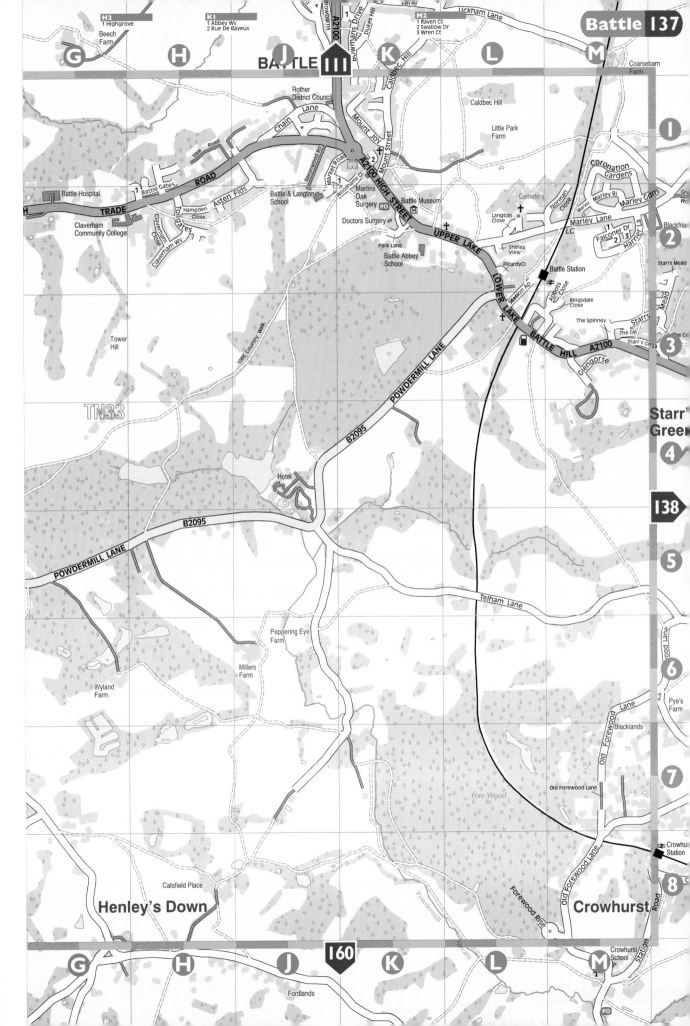

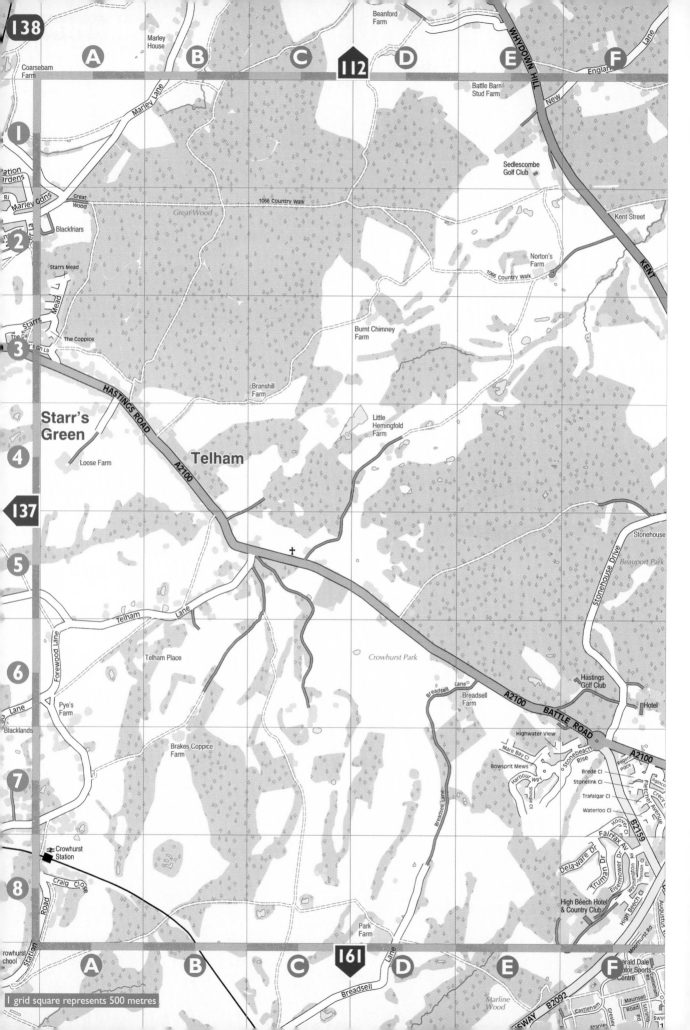

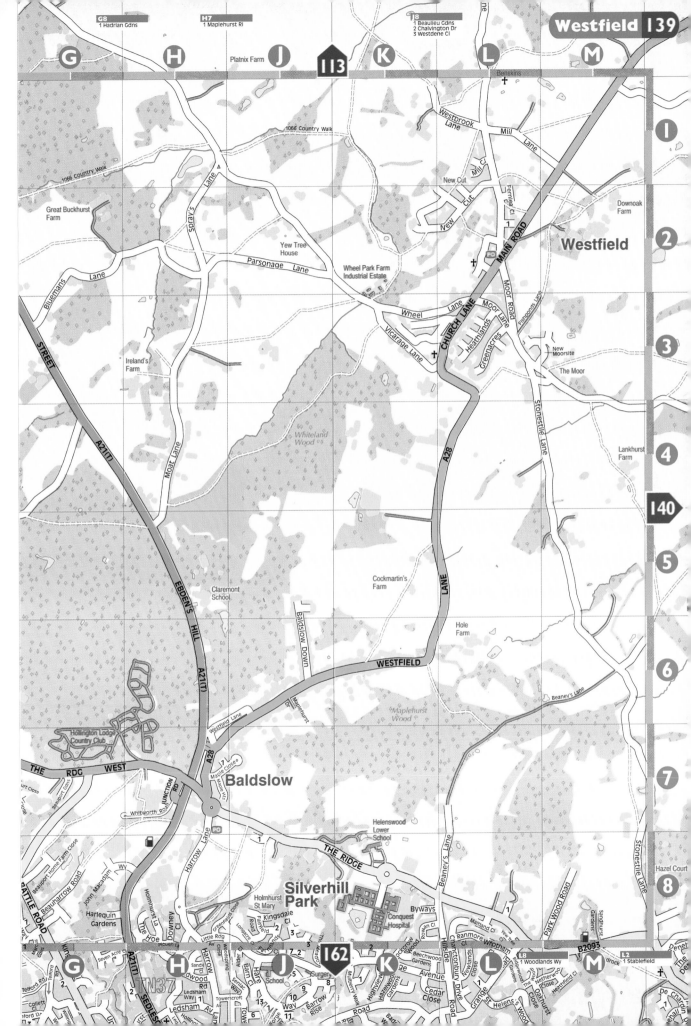

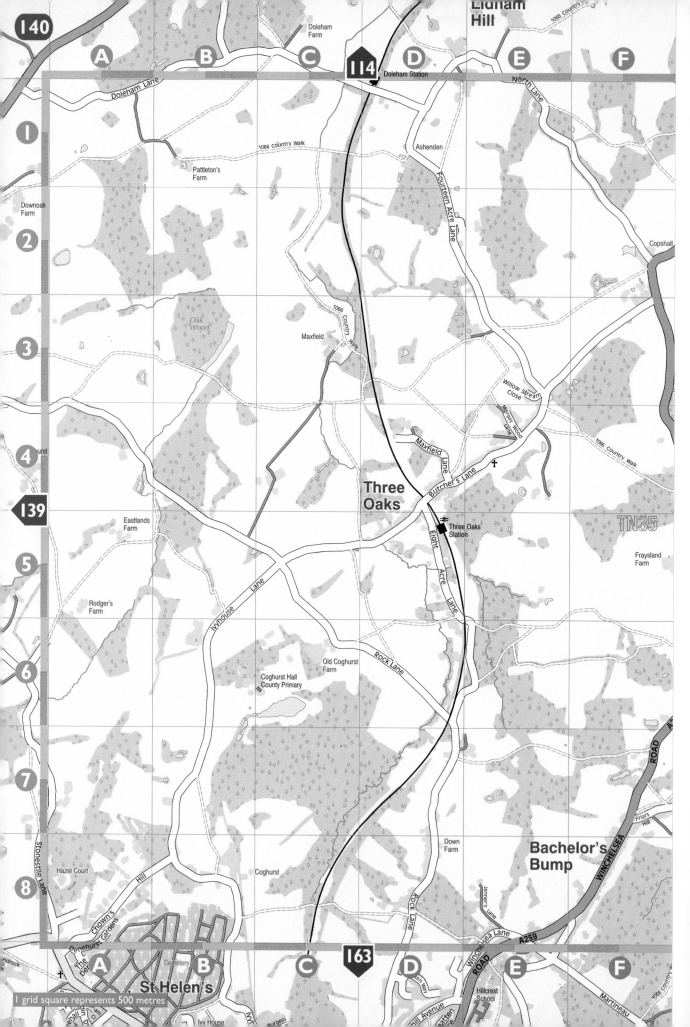

A　B　C　114　D　E　F

Doleham Lane

Doleham Station

Lidham Hill

North Lane

Doleham Farm

1066 Country Walk

Ashenden

Pattleton's Farm

Downoak Farm

Copshall

Fourteen Acre Lane

1066 Country Walk

Oak Wood

Maxfield

Willow Stream Close

1066 Country Walk

Maxfield Lane

Maxfield Lane

Morass Wood Lane

Three Oaks

Butcher's Lane

Eastlands Farm

TN35

Three Oaks Station

Frayland Farm

Eight Acre Lane

Rodger's Farm

Ivyhouse Lane

Old Coghurst Farm

Rock Lane

Coghurst Hall County Primary

Down Farm

Friars Hill

Bachelor's Bump

Stonestile Lane

Hazel Court

Hill

Coghurst

Rock Lane

Jenner's Lane

WINCHELSEA ROAD

Chown's

Denehurst Gardens

The Dell

Cemetery

St Helen's

Winchelsea Lane

A259

ROAD

Hillcrest School

Martineau

A　B　C　163　D　E　F

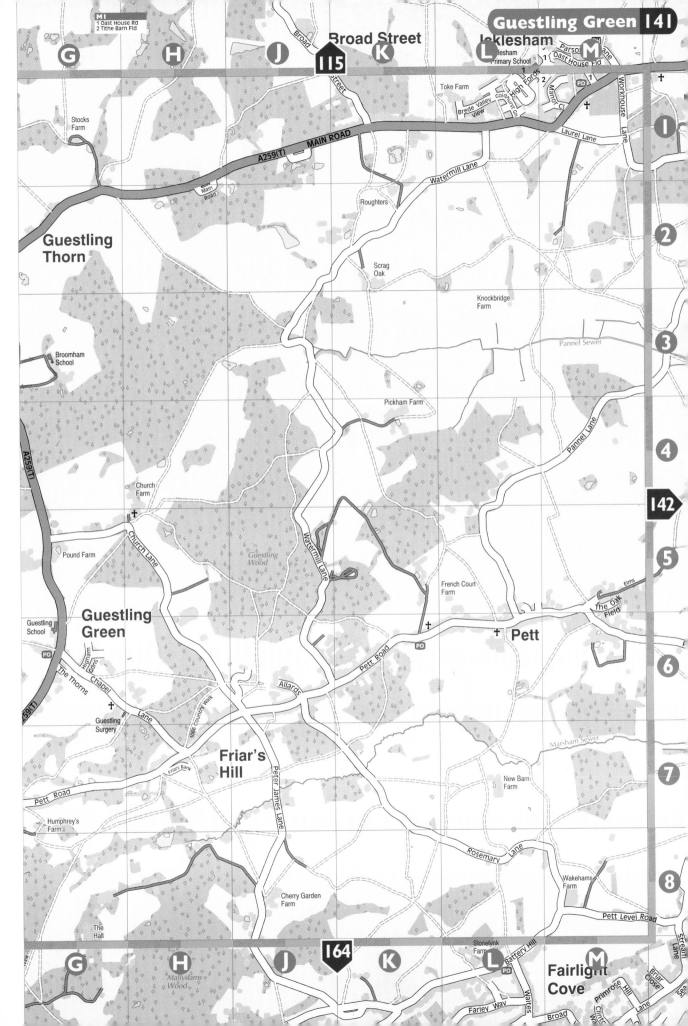

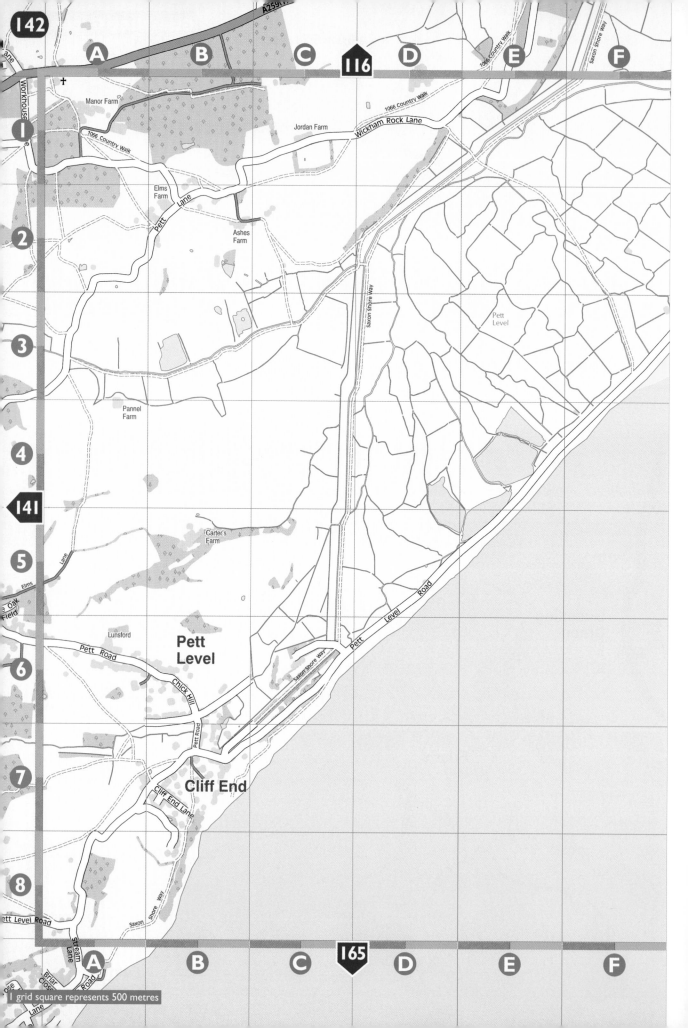

G   H   J   117   K   L   M

Dimsdale Sewer

Willow Lane

Harbour Farm

Smeatons Lane

The Ridge

Dogs Hill Road

Pett Level Road

Donald Way

Victoria Way

Windsor Way

PO

Rye Bay Club House

Pett Level Road

1
2
3
4
5
6
7
8

G   H   J   K   L   M

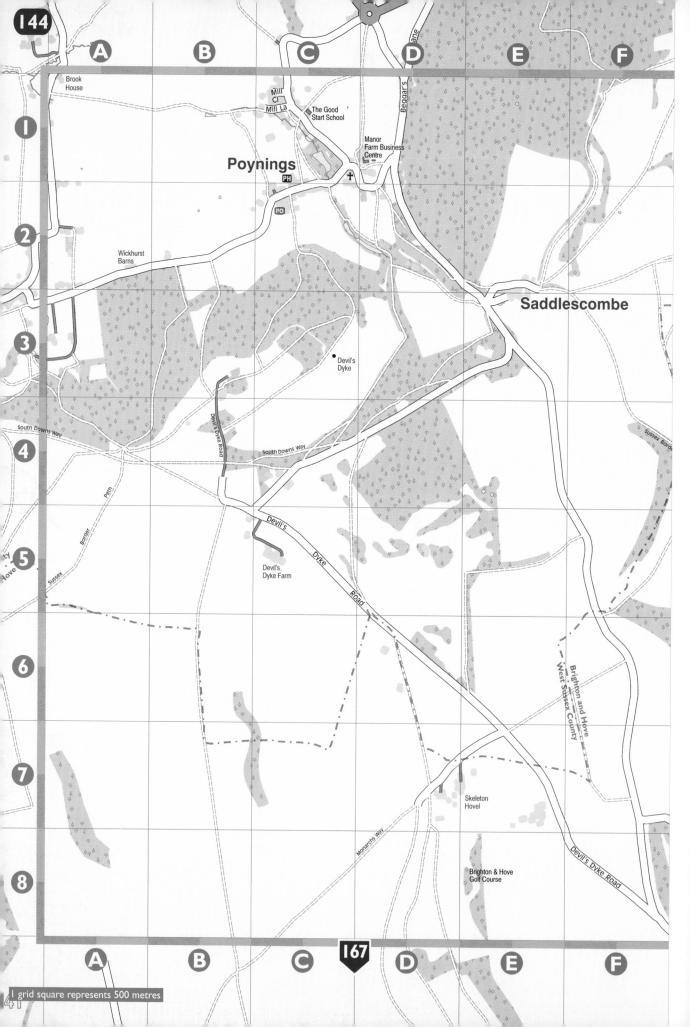

A   B   C   D   E   F

1

Brook
House

Mill
Cl
Mill La

The Good
Start School

Manor
Farm Business
Centre

Poynings

PH

PO

2

Wickhurst
Barns

Saddlescombe

3

Devil's
Dyke

Devil's Dyke Road

South Downs Way

South Downs Way

4

Sussex Border

Path

Border

Sussex

5

Devil's
Dyke Farm

Devil's

Dyke

Road

Brighton and Hove
West Sussex County

6

7

Skeleton
Hovel

Monarchs Way

Devil's Dyke Road

8

Brighton & Hove
Golf Course

A   B   C   D   E   F

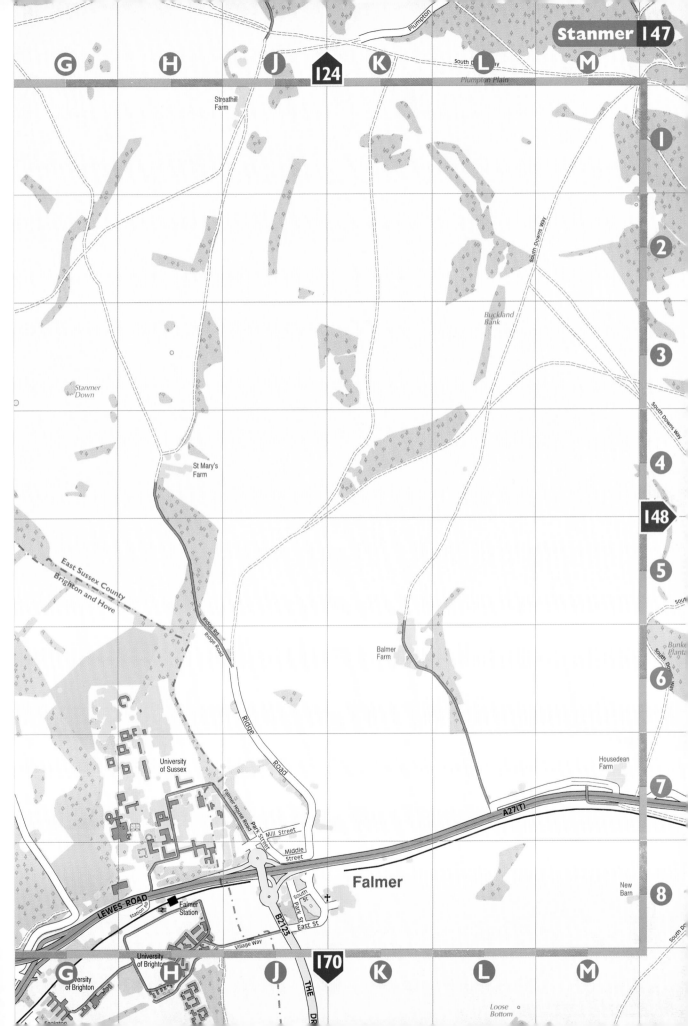

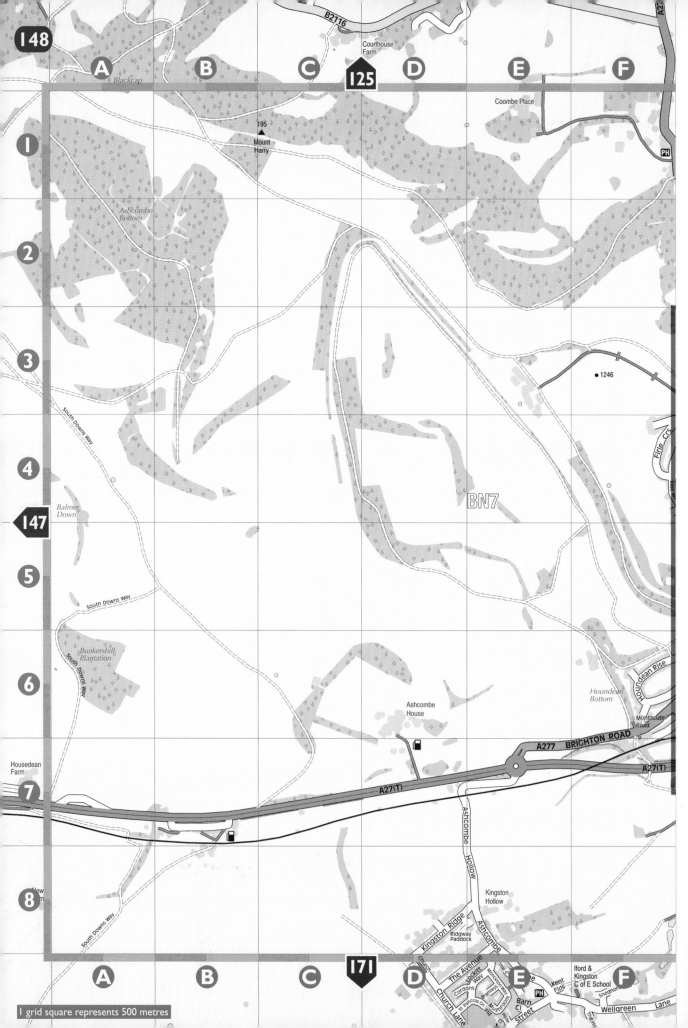

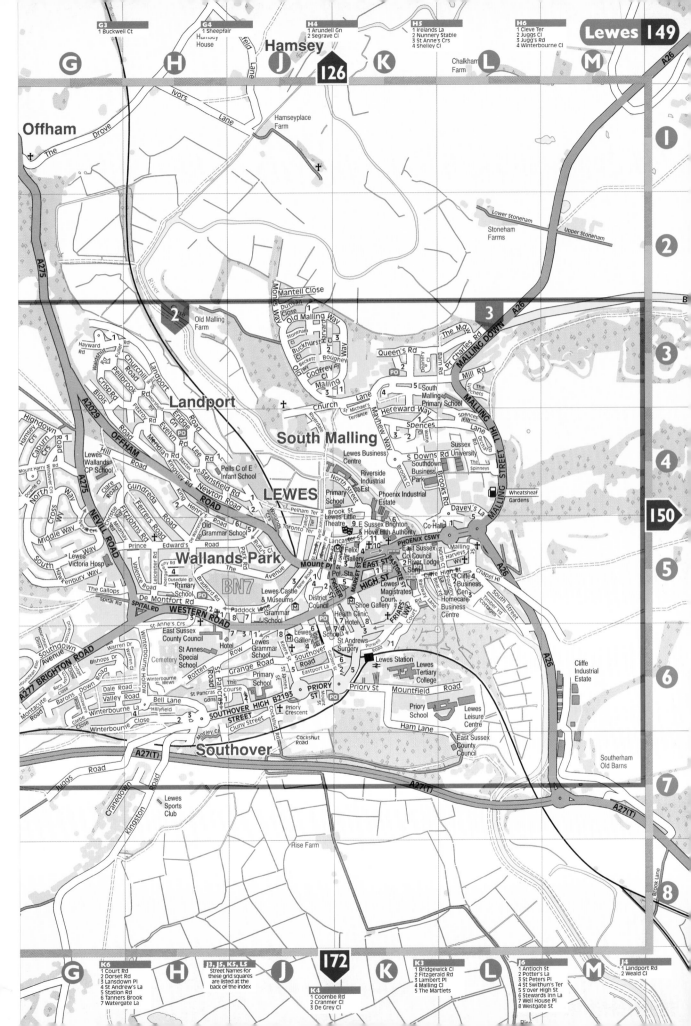

126

Offham

Hamsey

Chalkham
Farm

Ivors
Lane

The
Drove

Hamseyplace
Farm

Lower Stoneham

Stoneham
Farms

Upper Stoneham

River

Mantell Close

Old Malling
Farm

2

Dunyan
Close

Old Malling Way

Stoneham
Cl

Buckhurst

Harvey's
Way

Beckett
Way

Boughey
Pl

Godfrey
Cl

Malling

Church
Lane

Riverdale

Queen's Rd

PO

St Michael's
Terrace

Mayhew Way

South
Malling
Primary School

The Maw

Barn Rd

Pr Charles Rd

MALLING DOWN

Mill Rd

The
Wrchets

MALLING HILL STREET

Hereward Way

Spences

Landport

Hayward
Rd

Waldshut

Fuller
Rd

Churchill
Road

Pelbrook

Elrig Rd

Crisp Rd

Biols

Landport
Road

Fitzroy Rd

Chesterfield

Eridge
Gn

Evelyn
Rd

Lee
Rd

Meridian Rd

Baxter

King
Henry's

Kingsley Rd

Newton Road

Stansfield Rd

Pells C of E
Infant School

South Malling

Spences
Water

Spences
Field

Sussex

S Downs Rd

Sussex
University

Orchard

Lane

The
Spinneys

Highdown
Road

Hamsey Crs

Caburn
Crs

Mount Harry

North
Cross Wy

Middle Way

South
Way

Kenbury Way

A275

A2029

NEVILL ROAD

Clare
Road

Gundreda
Road

Ferrers Road

Fitzjohn's Rd

Mayhew

Prince
Edward's
Road

Valence
Road

Leicester Rd

Lewes
Wallands
CP School

Hill

OFFHAM Road

ROAD

Wallands

Toronto Ter

Pelham Ter

LEWES

Old
Grammar School

Lewes Business
Centre

Southdown
Business Park

Lewes
Victoria Hosp

The Gallops

Spital Rd

De Montfort Rd

WESTERN ROAD

SPITAL RD

Ousedale Cl

Bradford Rd

Primary
School

PO

The
Avenue

BN7

Wallands Park

Mount Pl

Lewes Castle
& Museums

District
Council

Grammar
School

Paddock Lane

Riverside
Industrial
Est

Primary
School

North Street

Brook St

Lewes Little
Theatre

Felix
Gallery

Lancaster St

MARKET ST

EAST ST

HIGH ST

Pol. Sta.

Phoenix Industrial
Estate

E Sussex Brighton
& Hove Hlth Authority

East Sussex
Co Council

River Lodge

Friars Wlk

Court Rd

Cliffe
High St

Chapel Hl

Phoenix
Business
Cen

Homecare
Business Centre

Harvey's

Malling

Brooks Rd

Davey's La

Wheatsheaf
Gardens

150

Co-Hall

Phoenix Cswy

Lewes
Magistrates
Court

Shoe Gallery

Health Clinic

Hotel

Timber Yd
Cottages

South Street

Cliffe
Industrial
Estate

A26

Southdown
Avenue

BRIGHTON ROAD

A277

Montacute
Road

Warren Dr

Warren Cl

Bishops Dr

Cemetery

St Annes
Special
School

Hotel

East Sussex
County Council

Lewes
Grammar
School

ROW

St Anne's Crs

Felix
Gallery

Keere St

St Andrews
Surgery

School

Southover
Road

St Andrew's
Primary
School

PINwell

Eastport La

Barons Down

Dale Road

Valley Road

Bell Lane

Winterbourne

Glebe

Hillyfield

Winterbourne Close

Down

Rotten Row

The
Course

St Pancras Gdns

SOUTHOVER HIGH STREET

St James
St

Cluny Street

Grange Road

Priory
Crescent

PRIORY ST

Mount
St

B2193

PO

Cockshut Rd

Motley Cl

Cockshut
Road

Priory St

Mountfield

Lewes Station

St James

Southover

Lewes
Tertiary
College

Priory
School

Ham Lane

Lewes
Leisure
Centre

East Sussex
County Council

Southerham
Old Barns

A27(T)

Southover

Juggs
Road

Cranedown
Lane

Kingston

Lewes
Sports
Club

Rise Farm

Brook Lane

A27(T)

G H J K L M

A26

A

B

Bishop's
Christie Av
Millway
Close
Delves Way
Ashtonville Cl
2 Shepherds Cl
Trinity Fld
Green Cl
ROAD
B2192
Chamberlaines Lane
D1
1 Butlers Wy
2 Hayes Cl
3 Langham Cl
4 Stephens Cl

C

cgm

127

D

North Road

Bish

E

Greater
Paddock

F

Ringmer
Business
Centre

LEWES

Vicarage
Close

Ringmer
Parish
Council
PO

Springett Av

The
Surgery
Anchor Fld

Mill Md

Rushey
Close

Harrisons

Ringmer
CP School

Rushy Green

1

The Elms

Middleham

Harvard Rd

Penn Cres

Ringmer
Football
Club

Mill
Gdns

Mill Road

Cote Lane

Potato Lane

Oakmead
Wy

Greenacres
Dr

Sadlers

Way

Gote
Farm

2

B2192

Middleham Cl

Mill
Wy

3

Little
Heaven

New
Road

Oldhouse
Farm

A
G

Glyndebourne

4

Week
Lane

149

Saxon
Down

Glyndebourne
Farm

5

6

Lacys

Lacys

Southerham
Old Barns

Glynde
Palace

7

A27(T)

Glynde

Brook Lane

RANSCOMBE
HILL

Mount
Caburn

PO

8

Ranscombe Farm

Glynde Station

Ranscombe
Lane

Glynde Reach

A

B

C

173

D

E

F

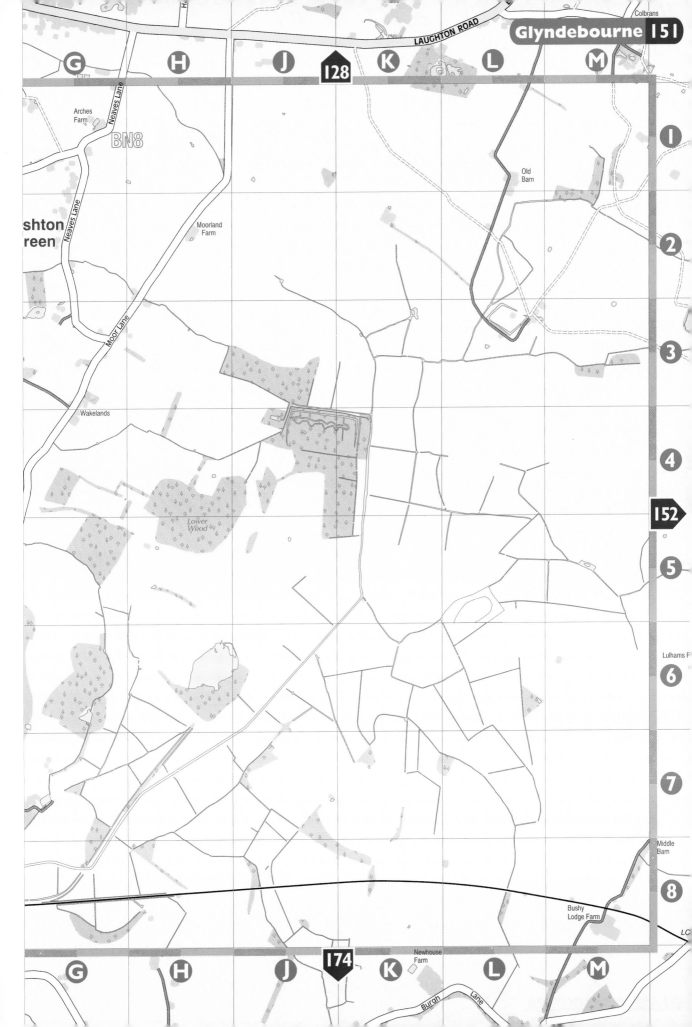

LAUGHTON ROAD

Colbrans

G H J **128** K L M

BN8

Arches Farm

Neaves Lane

I

Old Barn

shton reen

Neaves Lane

Moorland Farm

2

Moor Lane

3

Wakelands

4

152

Lower Wood

5

Lulhams F

6

7

Middle Barn

8

Bushy Lodge Farm

LO

G H J **174** K L M

Newhouse Farm

Burgh Lane

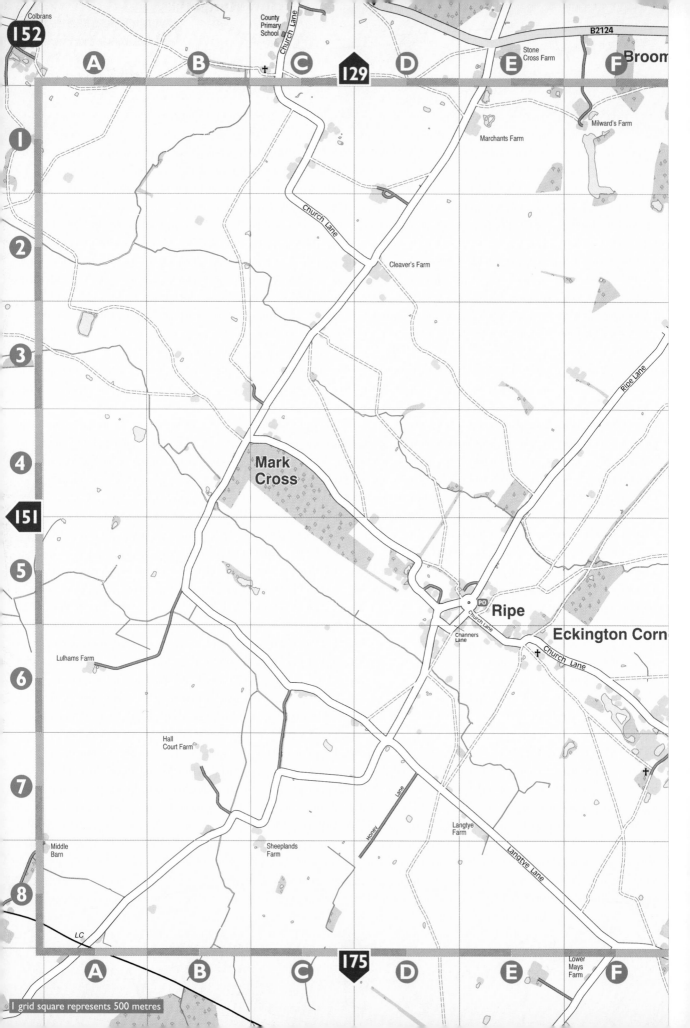

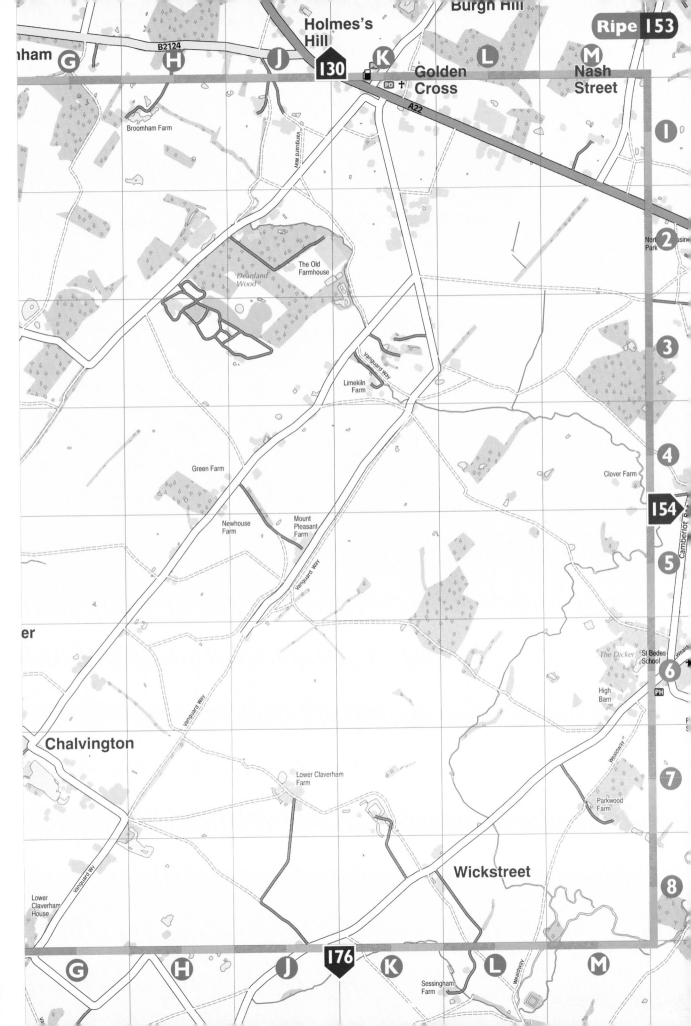

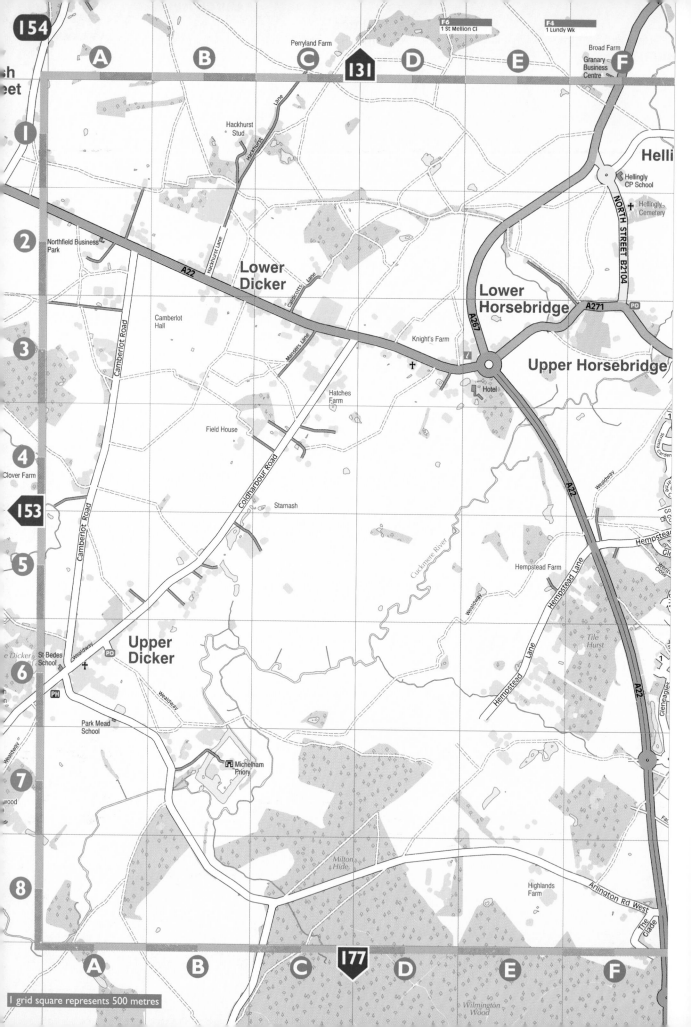

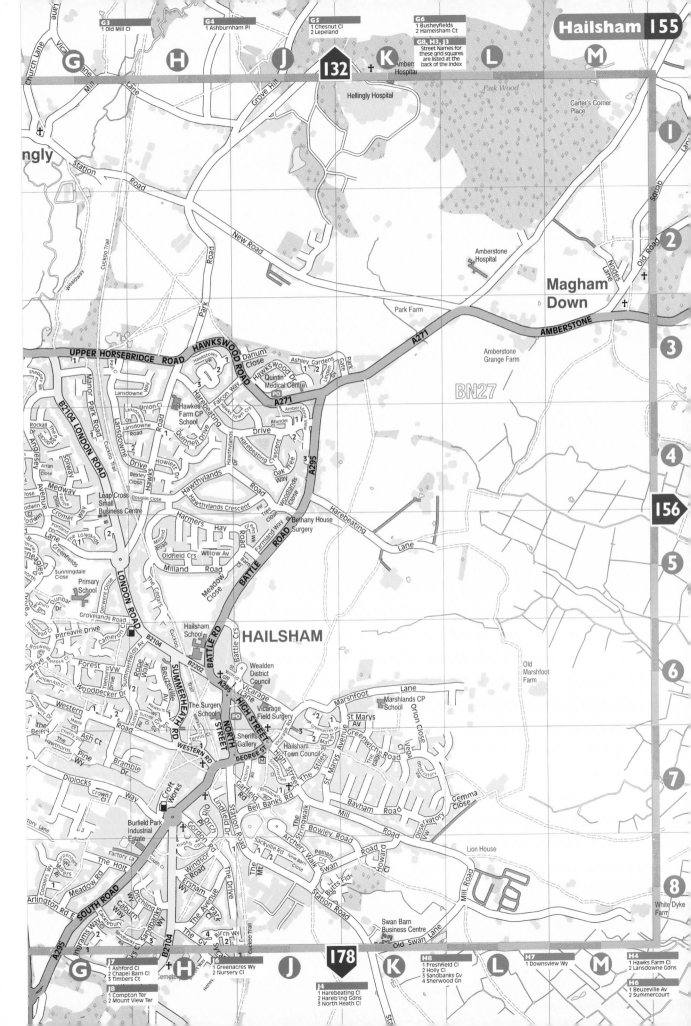

G3
1 Old Mill Cl

G4
1 Ashburnham Pl

G5
1 Chesnut Cl
2 Lepeland

G6
1 Busheyfields
2 Hamelsham Ct

G8, H3, I3
Street Names for
these grid squares
are listed at the
back of the index

G · H · J · 132 · K · L · M

I · 2 · 3 · 4 · 156 · 5 · 6 · 7 · 8

Park Wood

Carter's Corner Place

Hellingly Hospital

Amberstone Hospital

AMBERSTONE

Magham Down

Park Farm

Amberstone Grange Farm

BN27

ngly

Station Road

New Road

Grove Hill

Park Road

UPPER HORSEBRIDGE ROAD

HAWKSWOOD ROAD

Danum Close

Hawkstown Dr

Quintin Medical Centre

A271

Hawkes Farm CP School

Harebeating Drive

Harebeating Crescent

Oak Tree Way

A295

Hawthylands Road

Hawthylands Crescent

Fir Tree Close

Bethany House Surgery

Harebeating Lane

Harmers

Hay

Oldfield Crs

Willow Av

Milland Road

Meadow Close

BATTLE ROAD

Old Marshfoot Farm

B2104 LONDON ROAD

Leap Cross Small Business Centre

LONDON ROAD

Primary School

Grovelands Road

Pitreavie Drive

Cameron Cl

Hailsham School

BATTLE RD

B2104

B2202

HAILSHAM

Wealden District Council

Vicarage Lane

VICARAGE

The Surgery School

HIGH STREET

PO

Vicarage Field Surgery

Marshfoot Lane

Marshlands CP School

Orion Close

SUMMERHEATH RD

Belzeville Av

NORTH STREET

GEORGE ST

Sheriffs Gallery

Hailsham Town Council

St Marys Av

Greenwich Road

St Marys Avenue

The Stiles

Vegal Crescent

observatory

WESTERN RD

Ash Ct

Pine Wy

Bramble Dr

Croft Works

Lindfield Dr

Station Road

Bell Banks Rd

Bayham Road

Gemma Close

Diplocks

Burfield Park Industrial Estate

Windsor Road

Ersham Wy

The Drive

The Avenue

Archery Walk

Bowley Road

Swan

Howard Road

Lion House

SOUTH ROAD

Meadow Rd

A295

B2104

Station Road

Swan Barn Business Centre

Old Swan Lane

Mill Road

White Dyke Farm

G · H · J · 178 · K · L · M

H8
1 Freshfield Cl
2 Holly Cl
3 Sandbanks Gv
4 Sherwood Gn

H7
1 Downsview Wy

H4
1 Hawks Farm Cl
2 Lansdowne Gdns

H6
1 Beuzeville Av
2 Summercourt

J7
1 Ashford Cl
2 Chapel Barn Cl
3 Timbers Ct

J8
1 Compton Ter
2 Mount View Ter

J4
1 Harebeating Cl
2 Hareb'ing Gdns
3 North Heath Cl

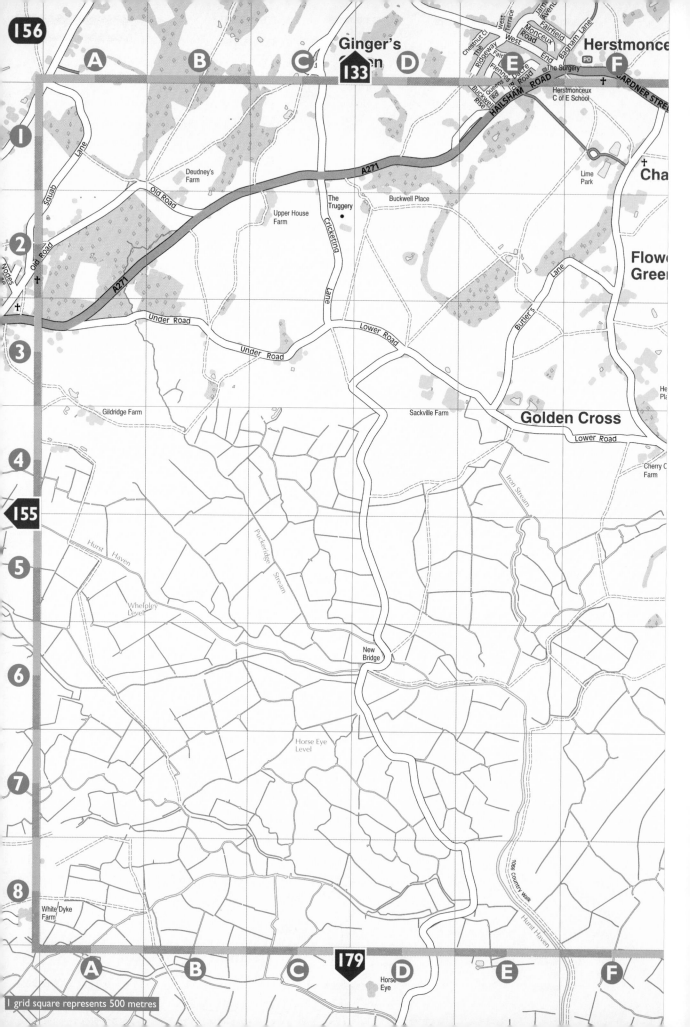

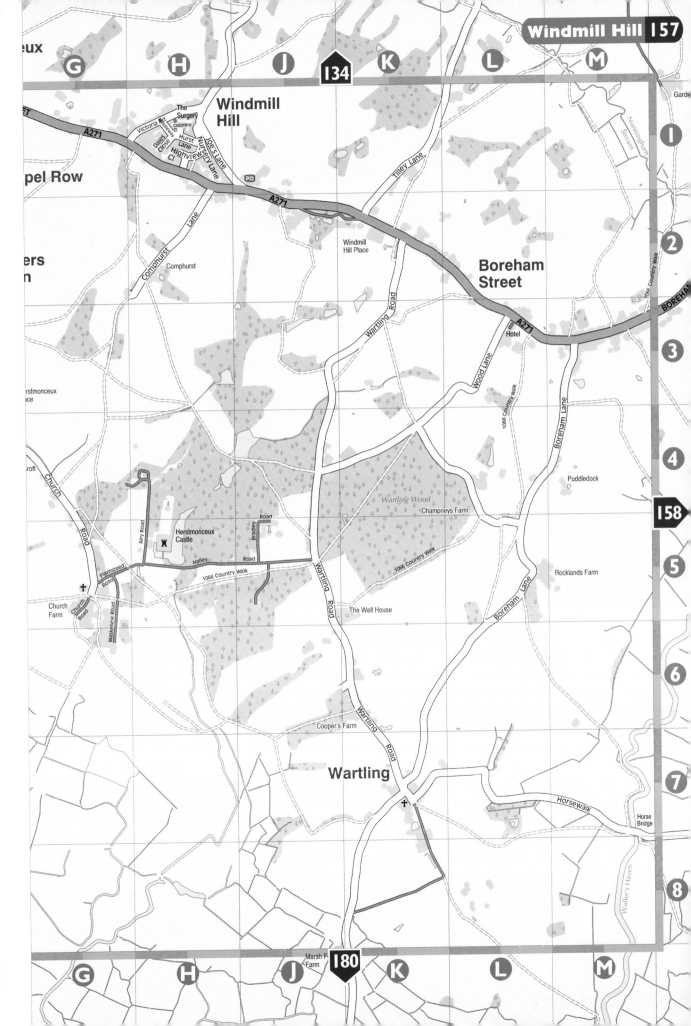

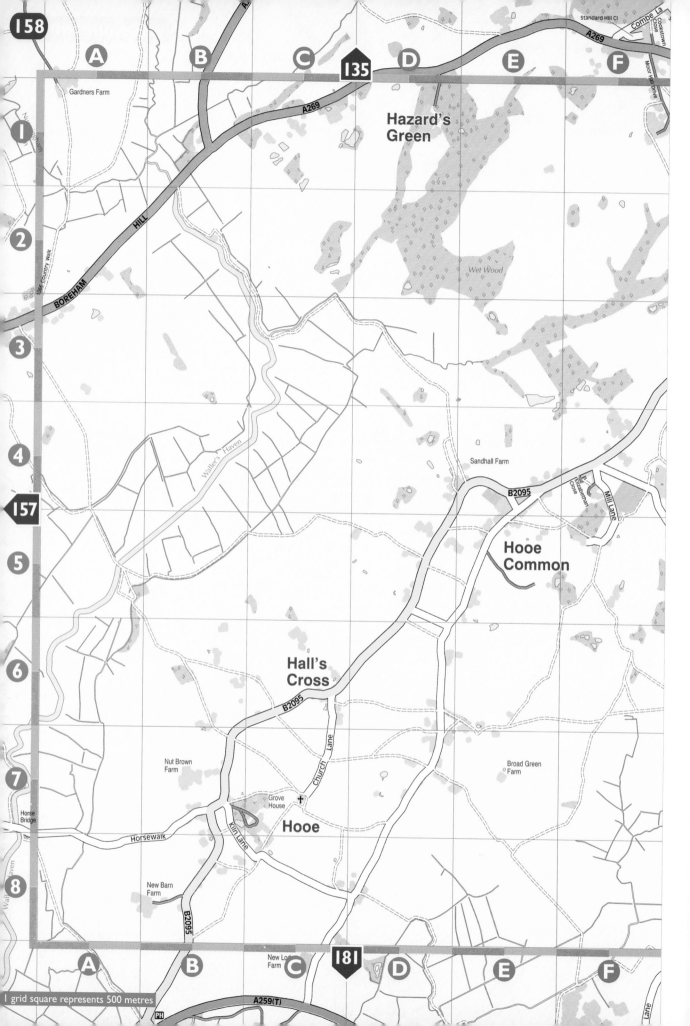

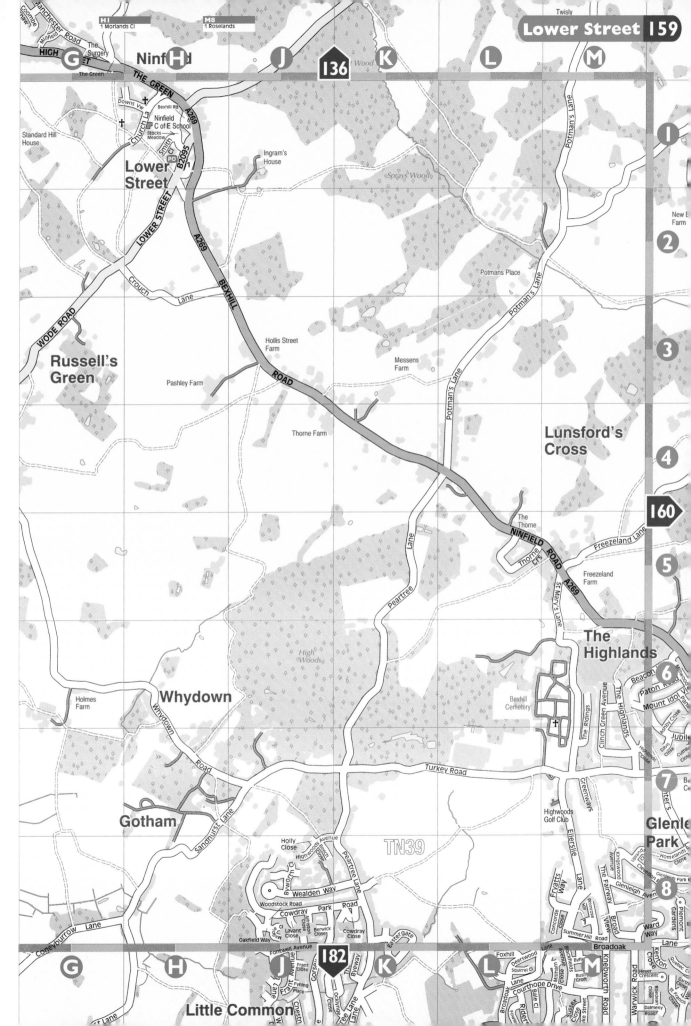

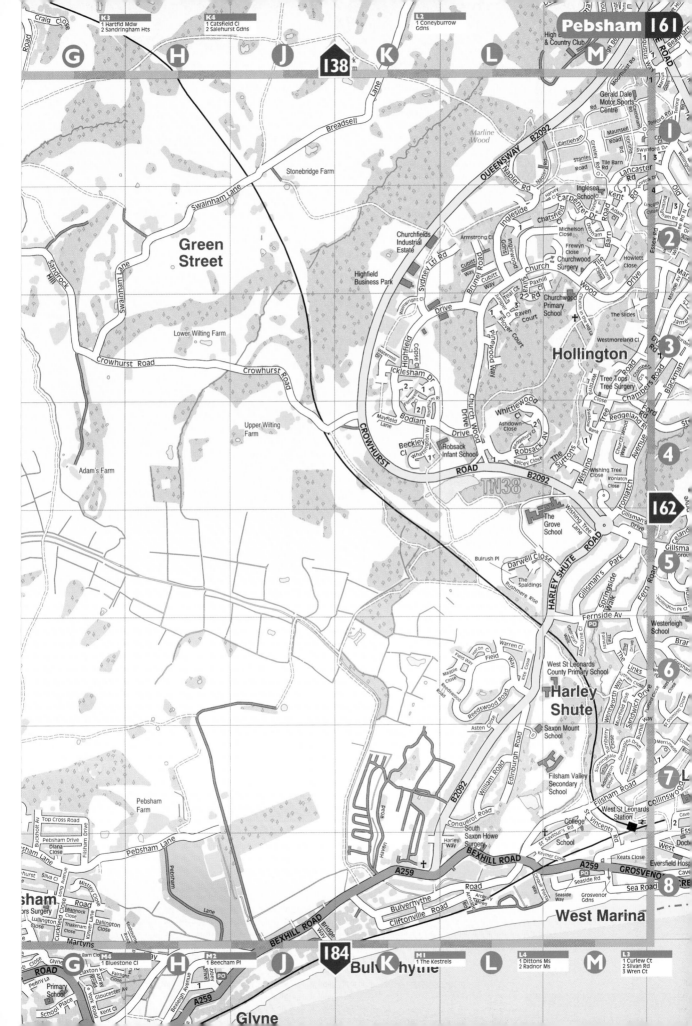

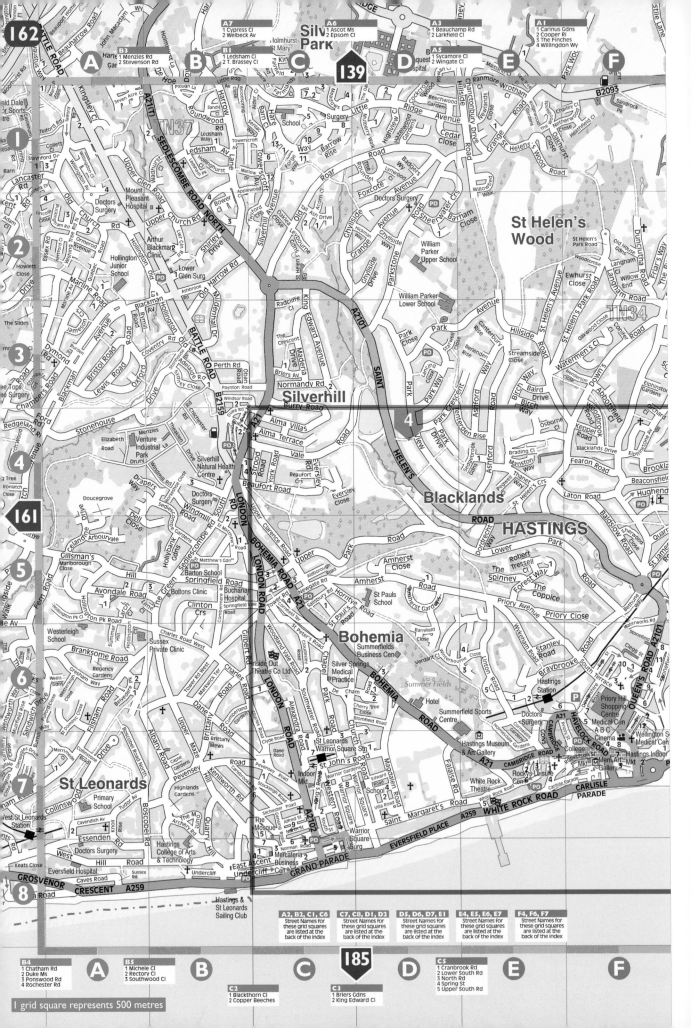

164

A B C **141** D E F

The Hall

Cherry Garden Farm

F2 1 Fairlight Gdns   E1 1 Knowle Av   akehams Farm

ett Level Ro

I

Mallydams Wood

Stonelynk Farm

PO

Battery Hill

Waites

Fairlight Cove

Farley Way

Primrose Hill

Hill

Road

Knowle Road

Broad Way

Clinton

Cliff Way

Woodland Way

Lane

Way

2

Fairlight Road

Battery Hill

Coastguard

The Close

Warren

Fairlight

Road

New Road

Meadow Way

Lower Waites

Rockmead Road

Lane

Commanders Walk

The Avenue

Smugglers Way

Stock

Dale

Blackthorn Way

Bramble Wy

Corsethorn Way

Shepherds Way

Heather Way

Way

3

Lane

Hastings County Park

Fyrsway

Channel

Fire Hills

Saxon Shore Way

4

Fairlight Glen

Covehurst Bay

163

5

6

7

8

A B C D E F

1 grid square represents 500 metres

A   B   C   D   E   F

1

2   BN43

3

4

5

6

7

8

A   B   C   D   E   F

1 grid square represents 500 metres

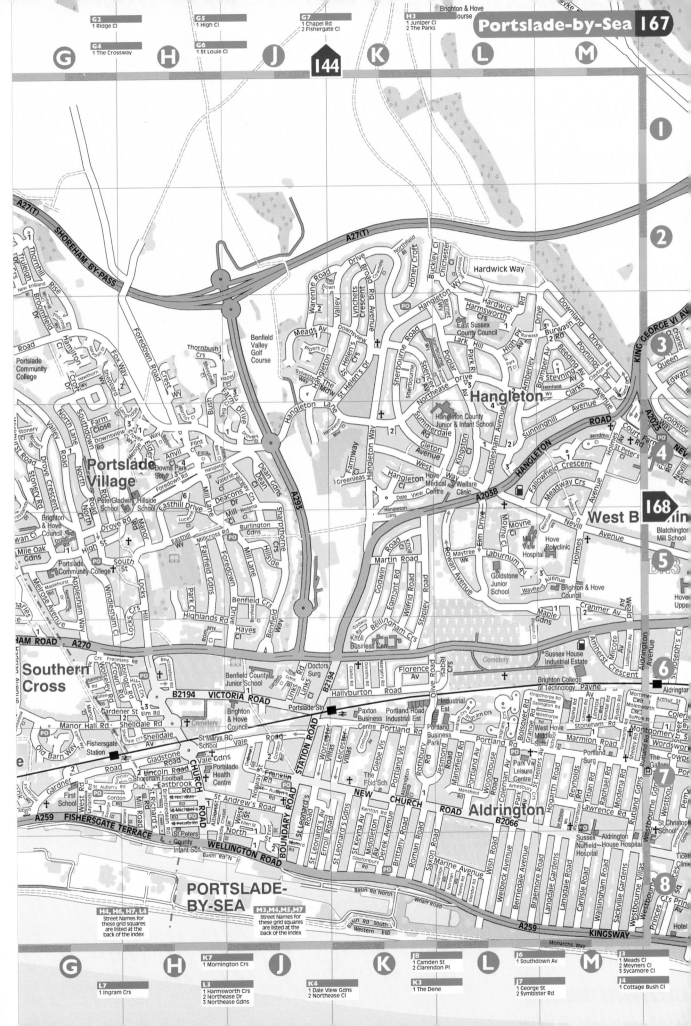

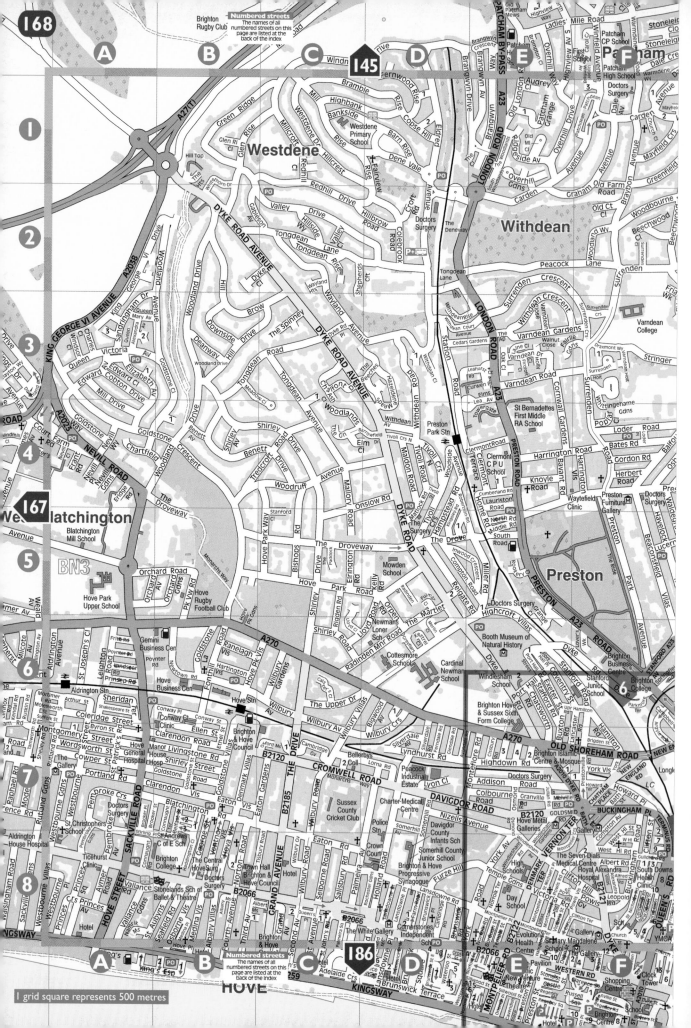

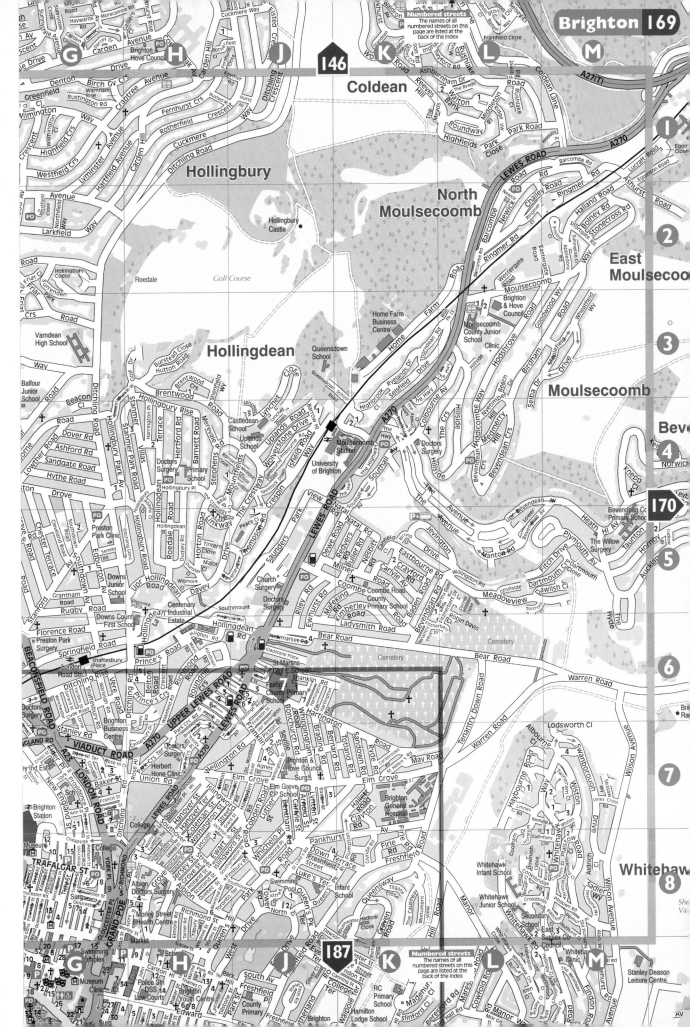

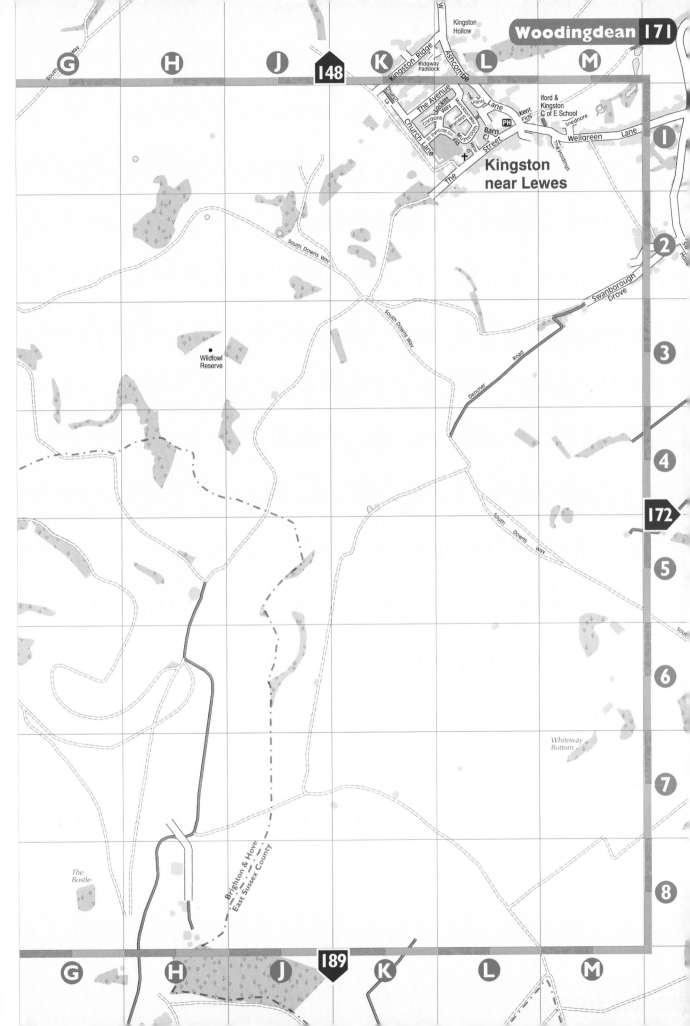

G H J **148** K Kingston Ridge Ashcombe L M I

W
Kingston
Hollow

Kingston Ridge
Ridgway
Paddock

Church
La

The Avenue
Lockitt Way
Cordons
St Pancras Cn Rd
Monkton Way
Hyde
Bramble Way
M/shroom
The Flints
Kent Flds

PH

Iford &
Kingston
C of E School

Sneanore

Wellgreen Lane

Sw Ho

Barn
Cl
Street

Church Lane

The

**Kingston
near Lewes**

The Holdings

2

Swanborough Drove

South Downs Way

3

Dencher Road

South Downs Way

Wildfowl
Reserve

4

172

South Downs Way

5

6

Whiteway
Bottom

7

The
Bostle

Brighton & Hove
East Sussex County

8

G H J **189** K L M

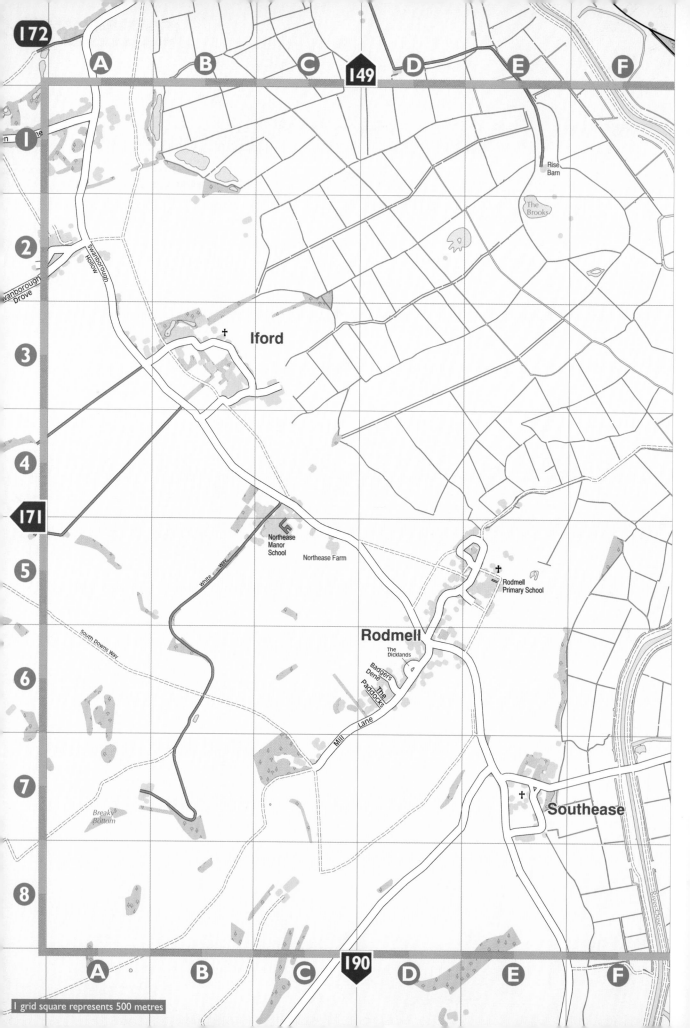

172

A   B   C   149   D   E   F

1

Rise
Barn

The
Brooks

2

Swanborough
Hollow

Swanborough
Drove

3   † Iford

4

171

White Way

Northease
Manor
School

Northease Farm

5   † Rodmell
Primary School

South Downs Way

Rodmell

The Dicklands

Badgers
Dene

The Paddocks

6

Mill Lane

7   Breaky
Bottom   † Southease

River Ouse

8

A   B   C   190   D   E   F

I grid square represents 500 metres

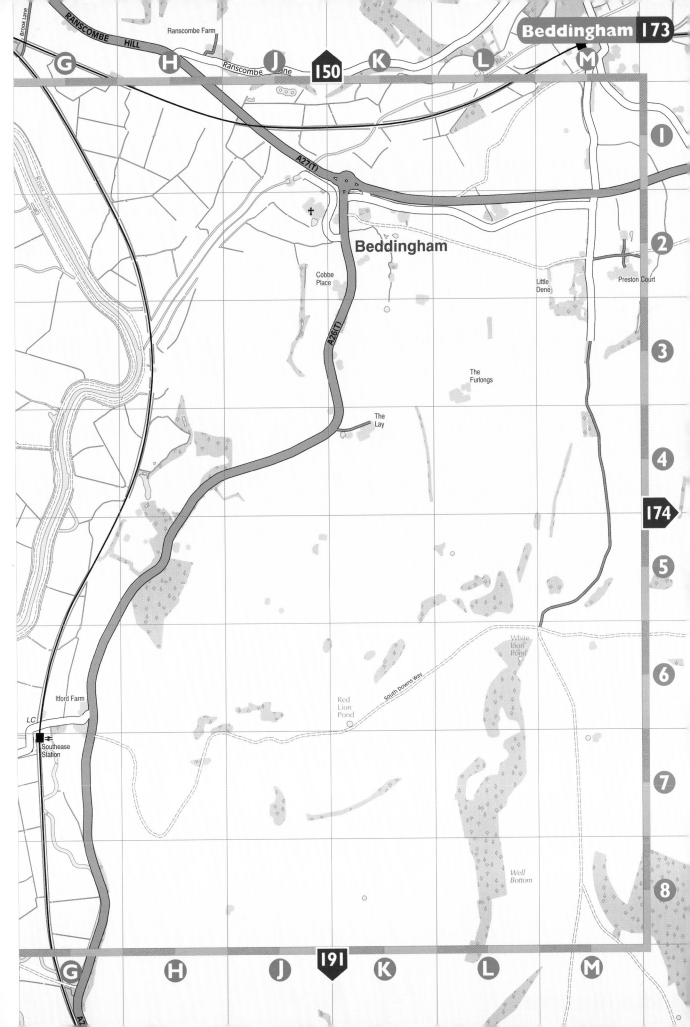

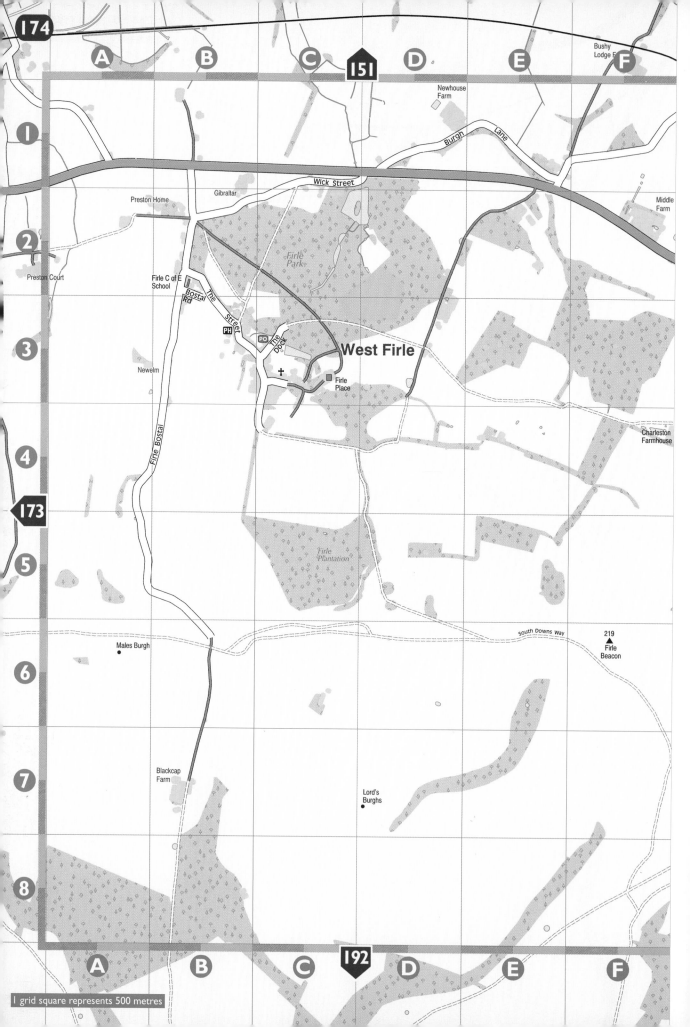

A   B   C   151   D   E   Bushy Lodge F   F

Newhouse Farm

Burgh Lane

1

Wick Street

Middle Farm

Preston Home

Gibraltar

Firle Park

Firle C of E School

Preston Court

2

Bostal Rd

The Street

PH

PO

The Dock

West Firle

3

Newelm

✝

Firle Place

Firle Bostal

Charleston Farmhouse

4

5

Firle Plantation

South Downs Way

219
▲ Firle Beacon

Males Burgh

6

Blackcap Farm

7

Lord's Burghs

8

A   B   C   192   D   E   F

I grid square represents 500 metres

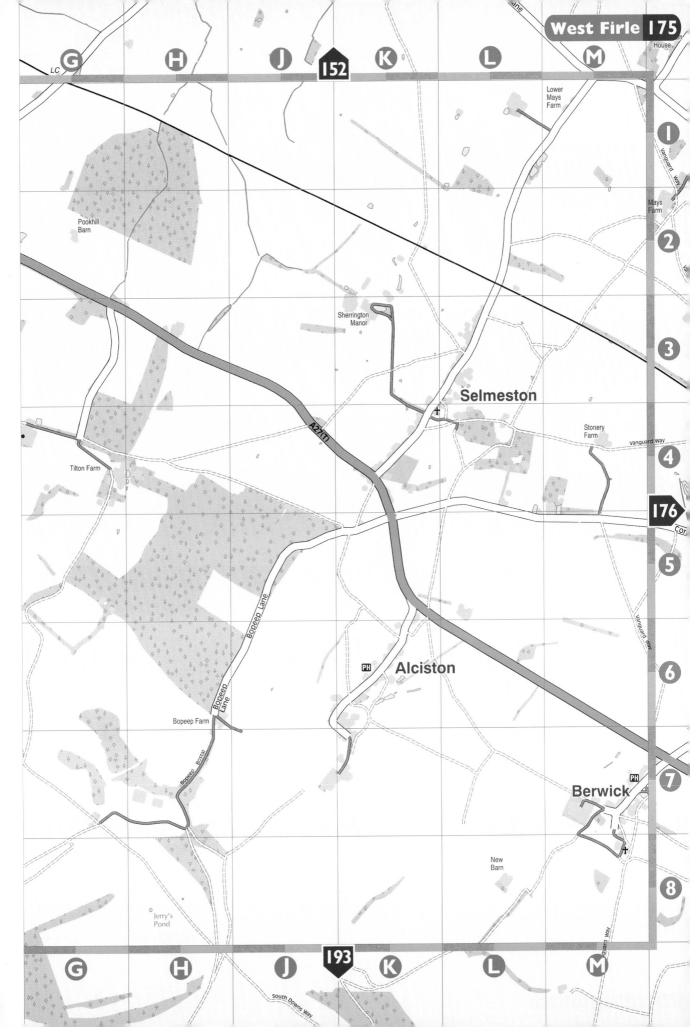

G   H   J   **152**   K   L   M

I

2

3

Pookhill
Barn

LC

Sherrington
Manor

Selmeston

†

A27(T)

Tilton Farm

Stonery
Farm

Vanguard Way

4

176

Cor.

5

Bopeep Lane

PH   **Alciston**

6

Bopeep Lane

Bopeep Farm

Bopeep Bostall

Vanguard Way

PH

7

Berwick

†

New
Barn

8

Jerry's
Pond

Lower
Mays
Farm

Mays
Farm

Vanguard Way

House

G   H   J   **193**   K   L   M

south downs way

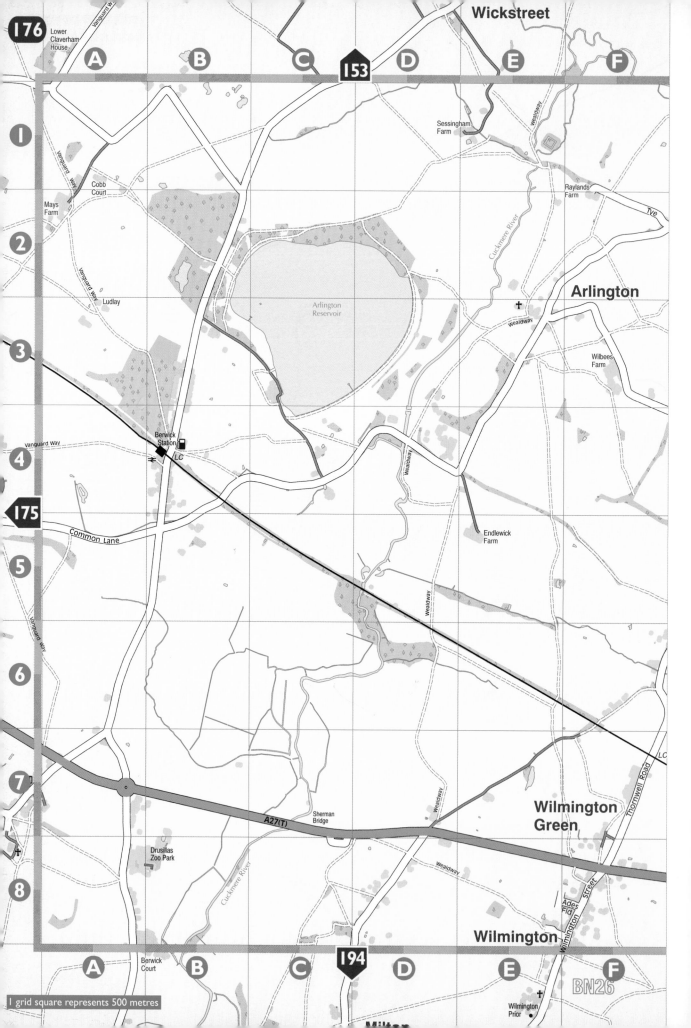

M8
1 Brown Jack Av
2 Diplock Cl
3 Grand Pde
4 Reynoldstown La

G   H   J   **154**   K   L   M   I

Highlands
Farm

The Glade

A205

2

Woodside
Hall

Wilmington
Wood

3

A22

PH

Hill
Road

Abbot's
Wood

● Nature Reserve

Caneheath

4

178

Bayley's
Lane

Nate
Wood

5

Post   Lane

Hayreed

Robin   Lane

Bay Tree Lane

Thornwell Road

6

Monkyn
Pyn

A22

Saverland Road

Polegate By-pass

A271(T)

HAILSHAM ROAD

7

Wootton
Manor

St Leona

Victoria Road

Brook Street

Cosford Wy

Cosford Wy

8

A27(T)   LEWES ROAD

Hyperion Avenue

Sunstar Lane

Bahram Rd

Golden Miller
Lane

Manor Park
Medical Centre

A22

Polegate Town
Council Office

G   H   J   **195**   K   L   M

Southfield

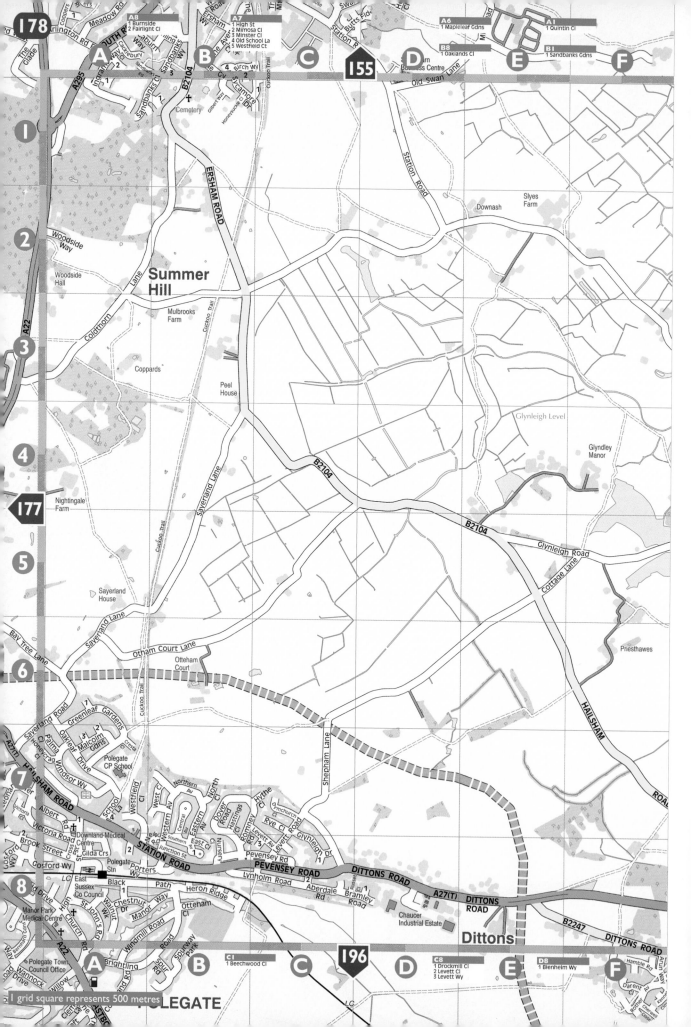

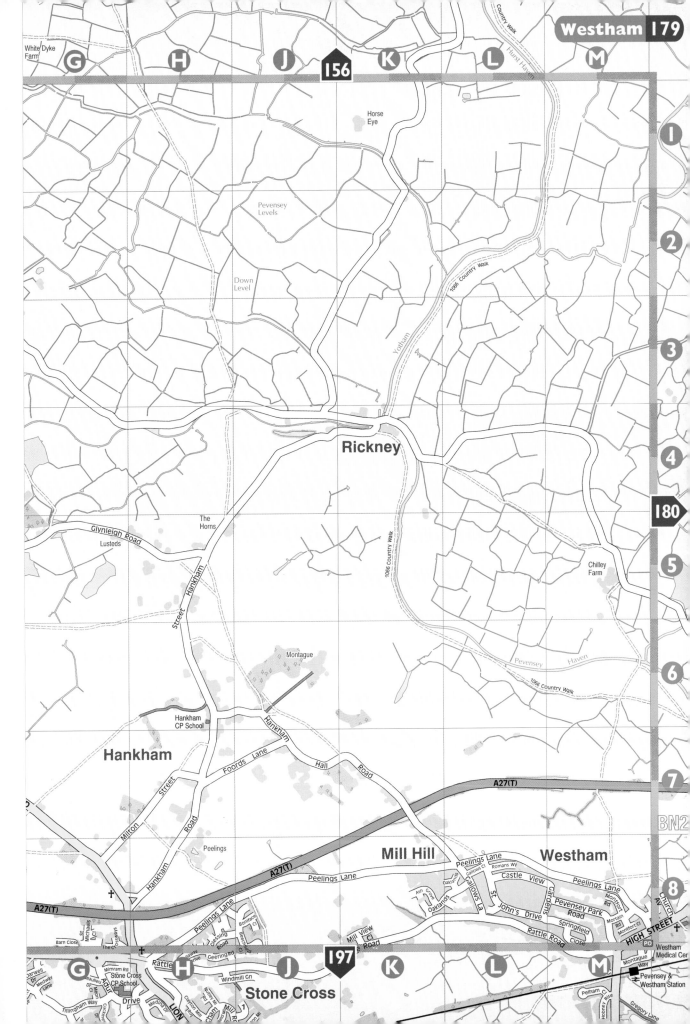

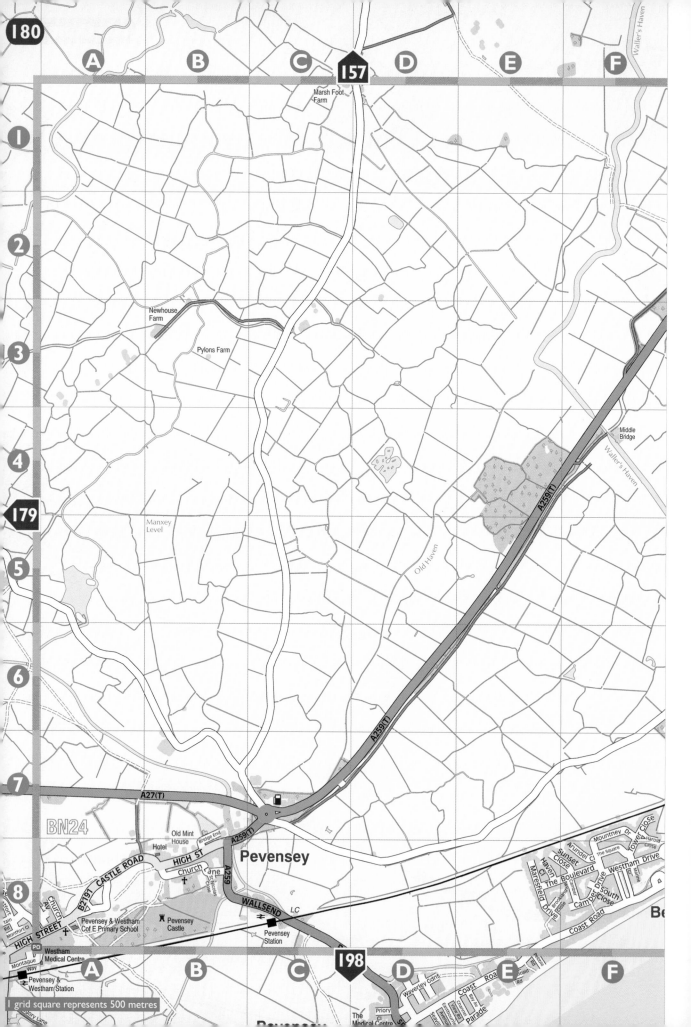

G H J 158 K L M

I

New Barn
Farm

New Lodge
Farm

PH

A259(T)

Coney

Wartling Drive

Coneyburrow Lane

Ticehurst
Avenue

Pleyden Rise

A259(T)

A259(T)

2

BARNHORN   ROAD

Hill Farm

Barnhorn
Manor

A259(T)

Old Road
Farm

3

Hooe
Level

4

182

5

LC

Herbrand Walk

6

Rockhouse
Bank

Norman's Bay
Station

Coast   Road

Norman's
Bay

7

Westham
Dr

Coast Road

8

eachlands

G H J 199 K L M

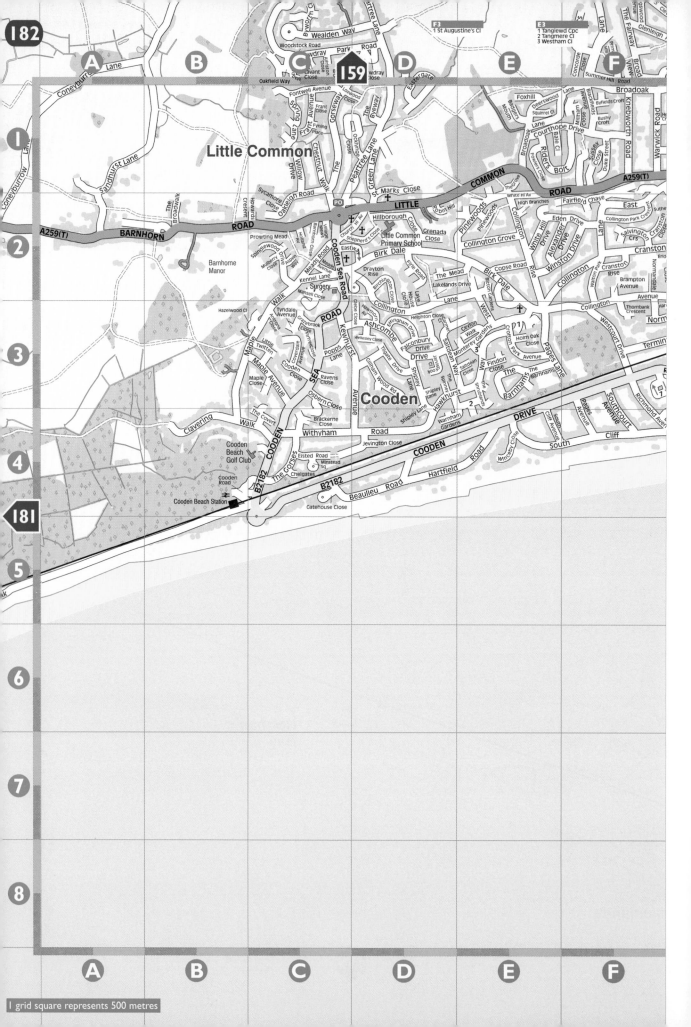

Bexsham

Doctors Surgery

Grand Avenue

Second Avenue

First Avenue

HASTINGS

ROAD

Primary School

School Place

Kent Cl

Martyns

Way

Gloucester Av

York Road

A259

A259(T)

Brett Drive

Megabowl

Boxgrove Close

Cuckfield Close

Long Lane

Silva Ci

Mister Close

Dallington Close

Glyne Barn Close

Claxton Road

Fairlight Close

Abbey Drive

PO

Petsham

Lane

BEXHILL ROAD

Bulverhythe

Glyne Gap

Bexhill Road

A259

Bulverhythe

Road

Ashburnham

Road

Grosvenor Gdns

Seaside Rd

Sea Ro

A259

GROSV

A259

PO

Seaside Way

West **F**larina

A

B

C

D

E

F

1

2

3

4

5

6

7

8

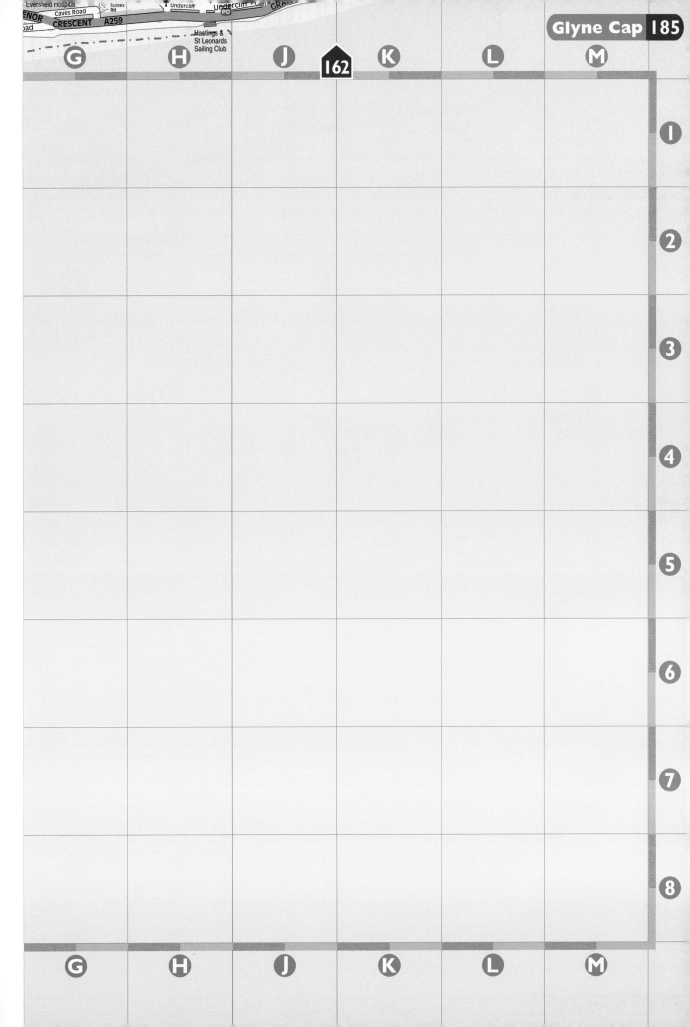

G H J 162 K L M

1
2
3
4
5
6
7
8

Eversfield Hospital
Caves Road
CRESCENT A259
Uncliff
Undercliff
PO
Hastings &
St Leonards
Sailing Club

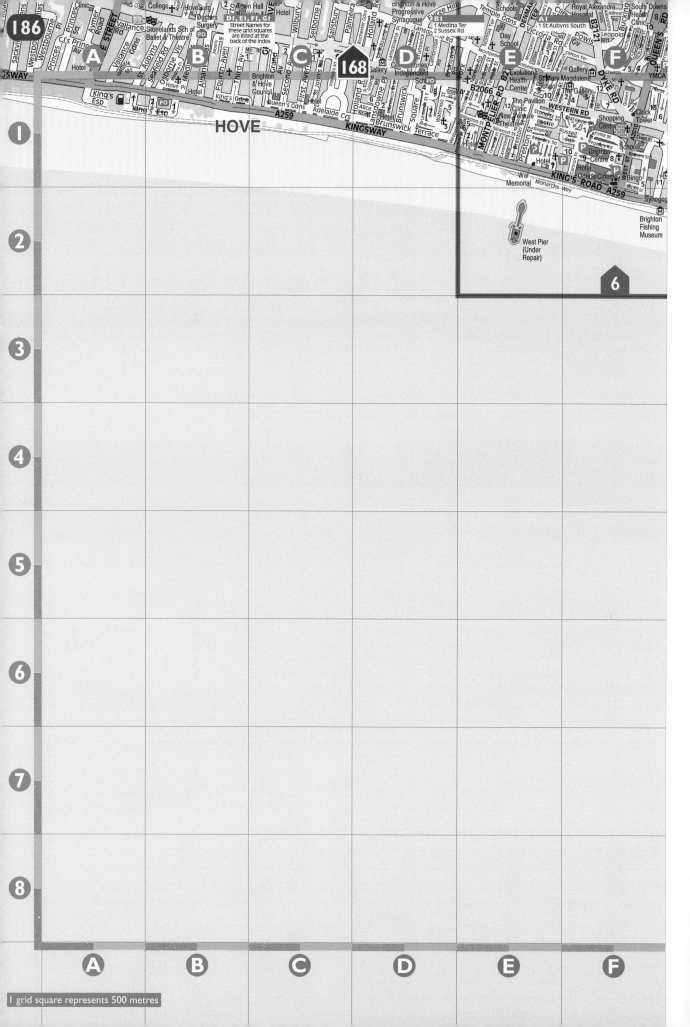

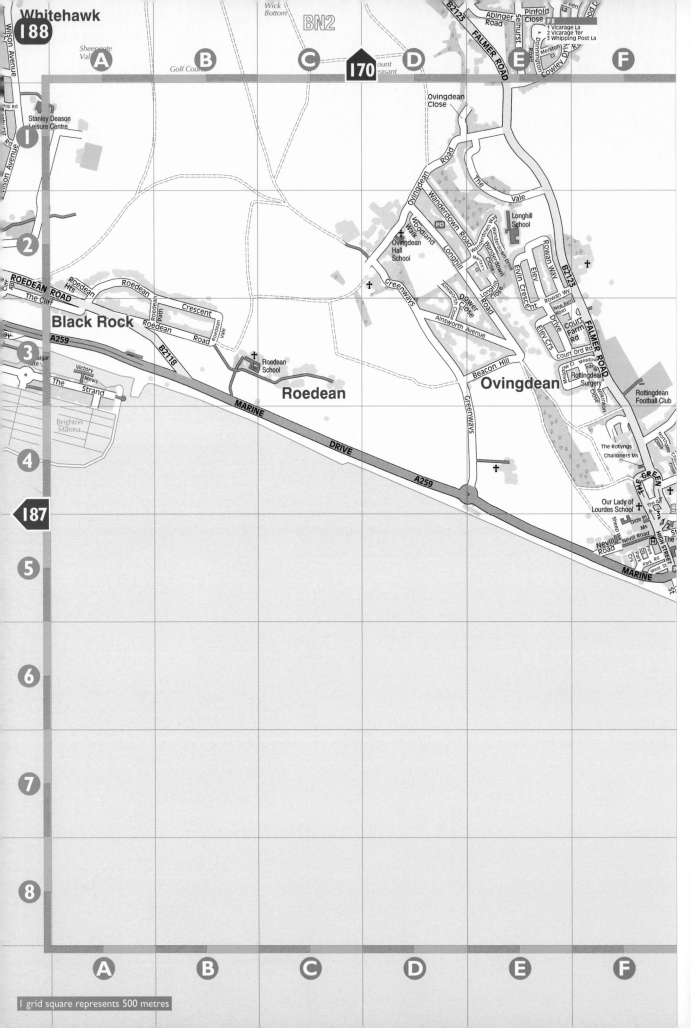

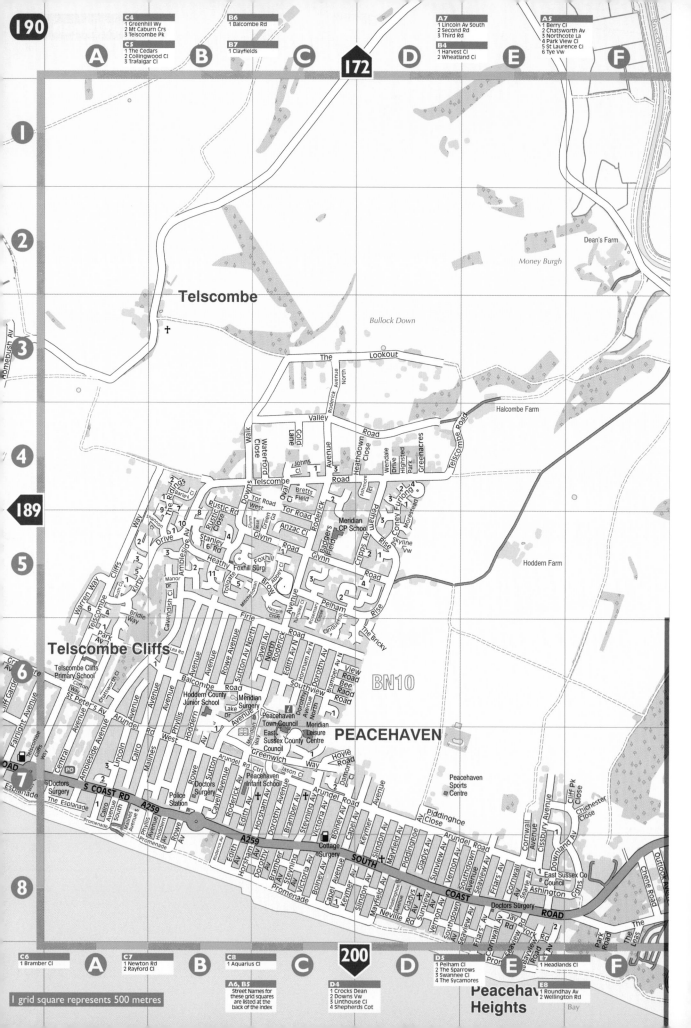

190

172

189

200

C6
1 Bramber Cl

C7
1 Newton Rd
2 Rayford Cl

C8
1 Aquarius Cl

1 grid square represents 500 metres

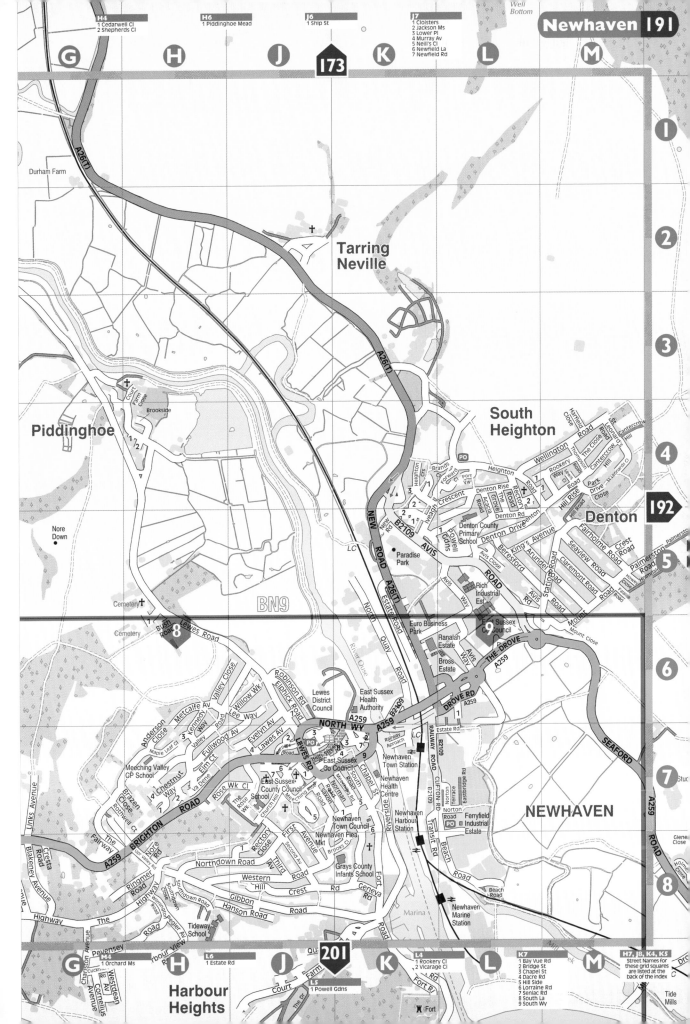

Well Bottom

G **H** **J** 173 **K** **L** **M**

H4
1 Cedarwell Cl
2 Shepherds Cl

H6
1 Piddinghoe Mead

J6
1 Ship St

J7
1 Cloisters
2 Jackson Ms
3 Lower Pl
4 Murray Av
5 Neill's Cl
6 Newfield La
7 Newfield Rd

I

2

Durham Farm

3

Tarring Neville

South Heighton

Piddinghoe

4

Brookside

192

Denton

Nore Down

Paradise Park

5

Cemetery

BN9

6

8 Lewes Road

9

Euro Business Park

Ranalah Estate

Bross Estate

THE DROVE
A259

Lewes District Council

East Sussex Health Authority

SEAFORD ROAD A259

7

Meeching Valley CP School

NORTH WY

East Sussex Go Council

Newhaven Town Station

Newhaven Health Centre

NEWHAVEN

East Sussex County Council

Newhaven Harbour Station

Ferryfield Industrial Estate

8

Meeching Valley School

Newhaven Town Council

Newhaven Flea Mkt

Grays County Infants School

BRIGHTON ROAD A259

Northdown Road

Tideway School

Newhaven Marine Station

Marina

Newhaven Marine Station

M4
1 Orchard Ms

L5
1 Powell Gdns

L6
1 Estate Rd

L4
1 Rookery Cl
2 Vicarage Cl

K7
1 Bay Vue Rd
2 Bridge St
3 Chapel St
4 Dacre Rd
5 Hill Side
6 Lorraine Rd
7 Senlac Rd
8 South La
9 South Wy

H7, J8, K4, K5
Street Names for these grid squares are listed at the back of the index

Harbour Heights

Tide Mills

A B C **176** D E F

Wilmington

I

BN26

Berwick
Court

Wilmington
Prior

Milton
Street

Winton

Hunter's
Burgh

2

Winton Street

Milton
Court Farm

West

Wearaway

Hotel

Primary
School

Sloe Lane

North St

South Downs Way

•The Long Man
of Wilmington

3

Waterloo
Square

River Lane

The Alfriston Gallery

PH

South Downs Way

South Downs Way

Tenantry
Ground

Road

Star
La

Alfriston Clergy
House (NT)

High St

Hotel

Vanguard Way

4

Lullington
Court

193

5

Church Farm

Winchester's
Pond

South Downs Way

Cow Lane

Vanguard Way

Litlington

Lullington Heath
Nature Reserve

6

PH

Fore
Down

Clapham
Lane

Clapham
House

7

8

Vanguard Way

A B C **204** D E F

I grid square represents 500 metres

Charlston
Bottom

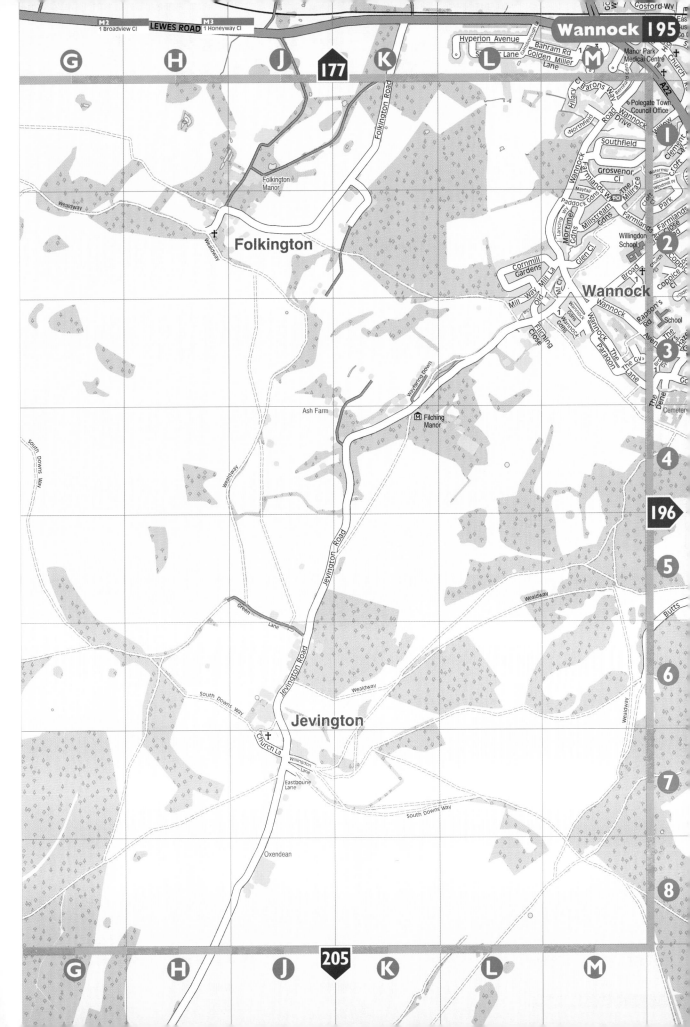

G H J 177 K L M I

M2
1 Broadview Cl
LEWES ROAD
M3
1 Honeyway Cl

Cosford Wy

Hyperion Avenue
Silver Lane
Bahram Rd
Golden Miller Lane

Manor Park
Medical Centre

Hilary Cl
Barons Way
Northfield Rd

Polegate Town
Council Office

Wannock
Road
Southfield

Willow

Clement Cort

Watermill Rd
Windmill Pl

Wealdway

Folkington
Manor

Folkington

Grosvenor
Cl
Mayfair
Mortimer Gdns
Paddock Gdns
Lancing Way
Glen Cl
Farmlands Way
Millstream Gdns
The Millrace
Farmlands Av
Farmlands Close

Willingdon
School

Cornmill
Gardens

Mill Way
Old Mill Way
Mill La
Mill Cl
1 Wannock Gdns
Wannock Gdns

Broad St

Wannock

Folkington Road

Filching
Close

Rapson's Rd
School

Wayfaring Down

Ash Farm

Filching
Manor

Wannock
The Paragon

The Lane
The GV
GC

The Dene
Cemetery

Wealdway

Wealdway

South Downs Way

196

Jevington Road

Green
Lane

Wealdway

Butts

Wealdway

South Downs Way

Jevington

Church La

Willingdon Lane

Eastbourne
Lane

South Downs Way

Oxendean

G H J 205 K L M

Wealdway

I 1 2 3 4 5 6 7 8

A22
East...
Church

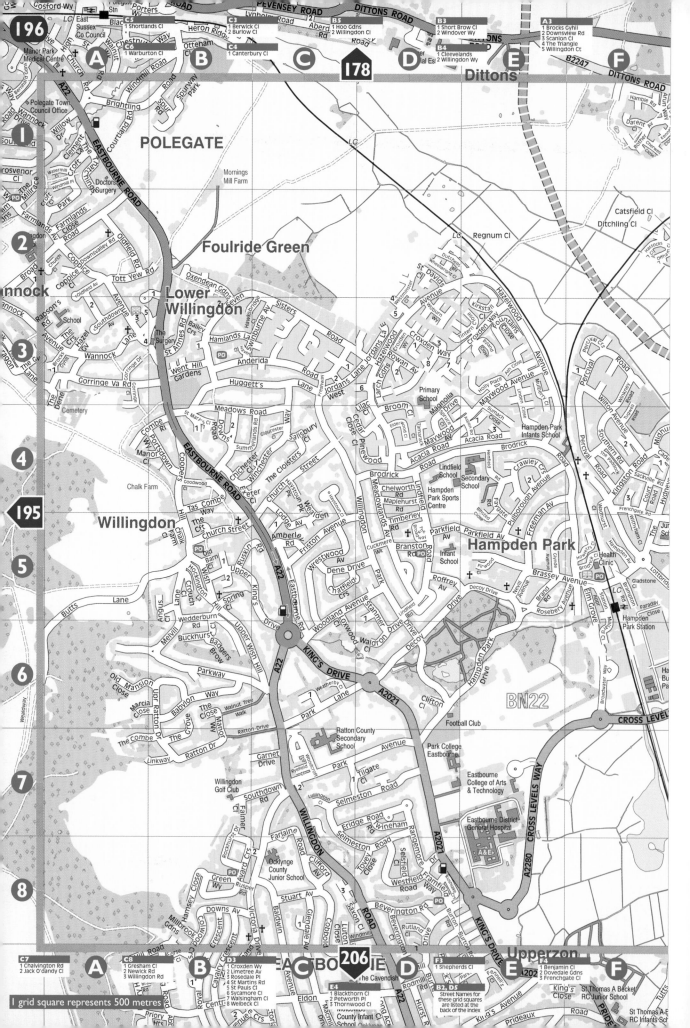

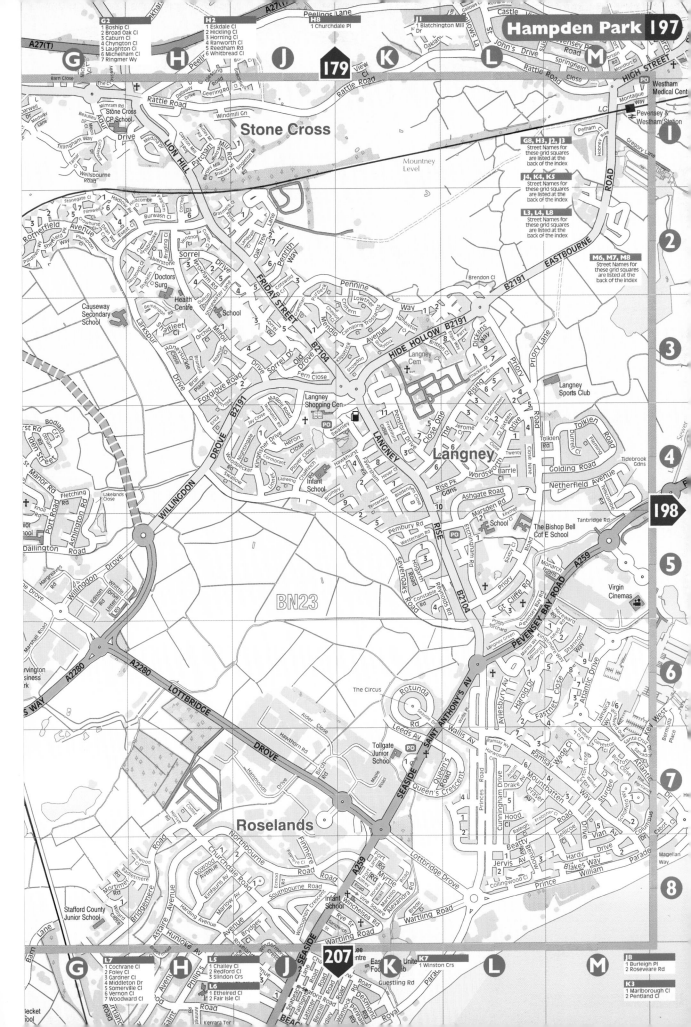

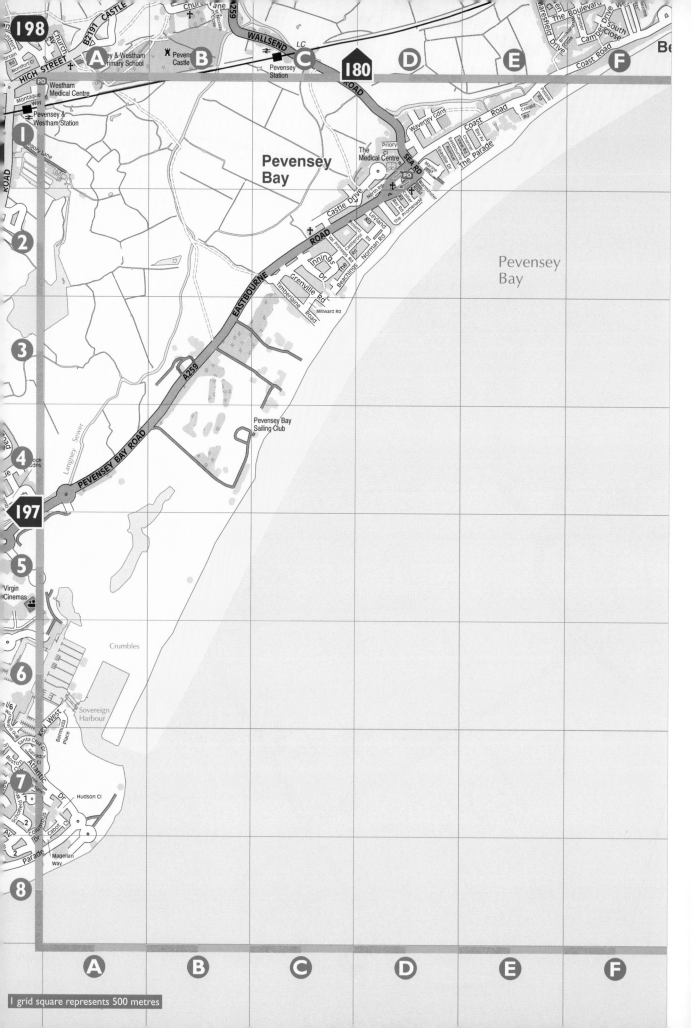

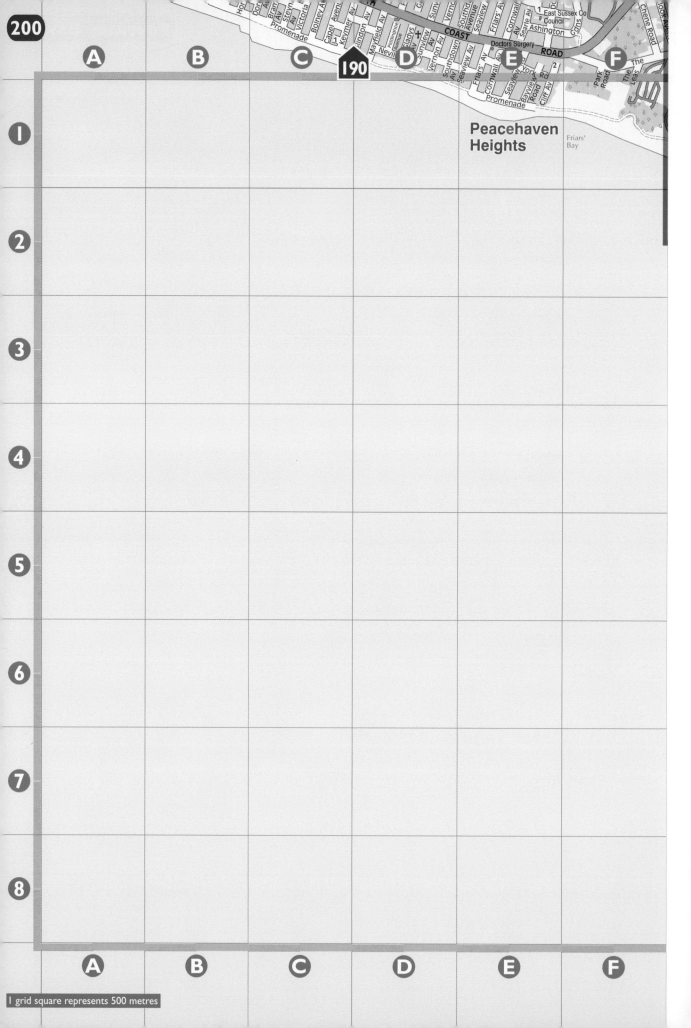

Peacehaven
Heights

Friars'
Bay

I grid square represents 500 metres

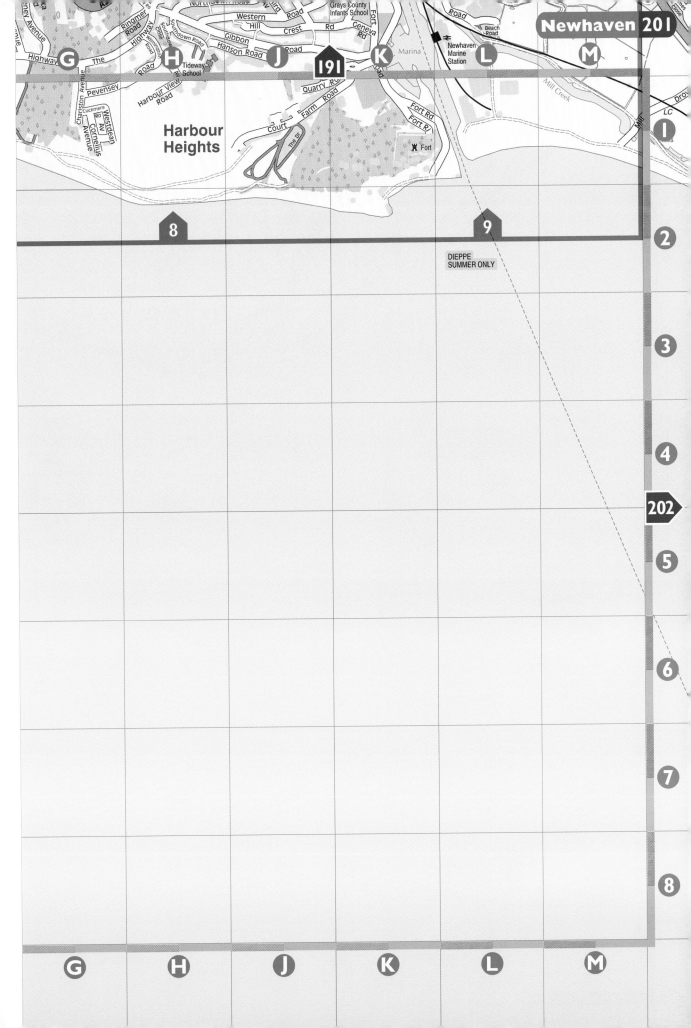

Harbour
Heights

DIEPPE
SUMMER ONLY

193

I

2

Exceat

BN25

Dymock Farm

EASTBOURNE ROAD

A259

Exceat Bridge

PH

3

Cuckmere River

4

204

Foxhole

South

5

6

Cliff End

Cuckmere Haven

Nature Reserve

Cuckmere Haven

South Hill

7

8

Seaford Head

Vanguard Way

Vanguard Way

Hill Fort

Golf Course

Lullington Cl

South-Way

Chyngton Way

PO

Chyngton Farm

Chyngton Lane

Fairways Road

Chyngton Pl

Cuckmere Road

Rother Road

Bracken Road

Chyngton Road

Headland Avenue

Downsview Road

Hartfield Road

Downs Leisure Centre

A259

Sutton

Cradle Hill School

Quarry Valley Lane

Vale Road

Alfriston Road

Kammond Avenue

Cemetery

Hill Road

Chyngton Gardens

Walmer Road

Hythe Crs

Battle Rd

Deal Av

Hastings Aven

Landsdown Rd

Alinston Pk

Hythe Cl

Dymock Farm

Elgin Gardens

Perth Close

Chesterton Drive

Kingston

May Av

Steyning Road

Lindfield Avenue

Hamsey Lane

Vanguard Way

G   H   J   K   L   M

204

A   B   C   194   D   E   F

I

Charlston
Bottom

2

Westdean

Exceat

Vanguard Way

Friston
Forest

A259

3

South Downs Way

The Living World

River

4

South Downs Way

Seven
Sisters
Country Park

Exceat
New Barn

203

Foxhole

5

South Downs Way

Gayles

6

Cliff
End

Crowlink

7

South Downs Way

Seven
Sisters

south Downs Way

8

A   B   C   D   E   F

Fris

I grid square represents 500 metres

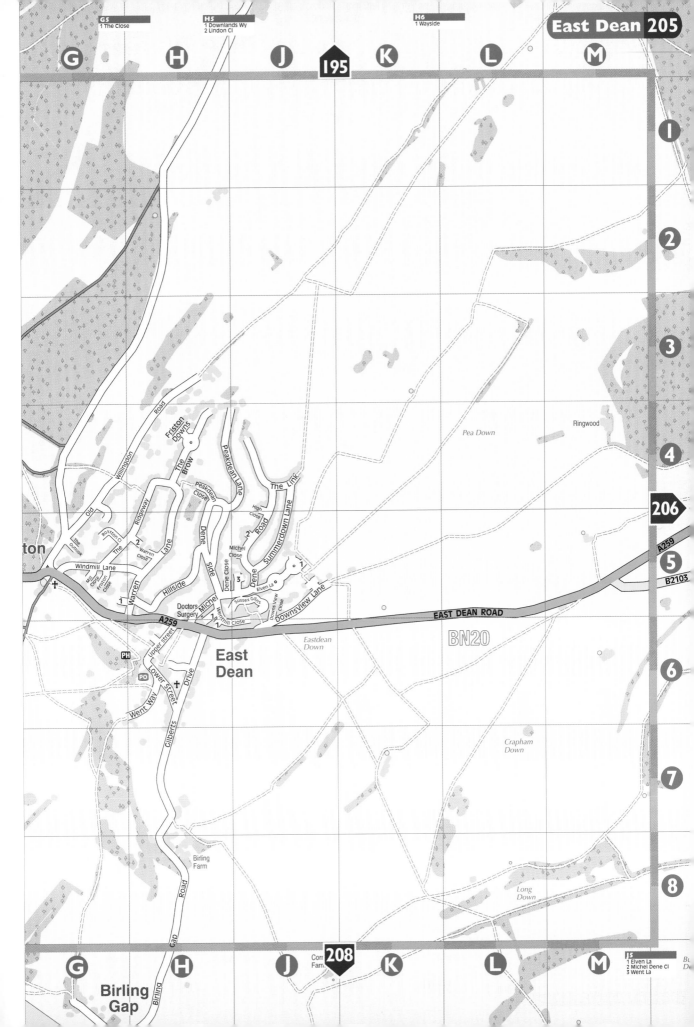

G5
1 The Close

H5
1 Downlands Wy
2 Lindon Cl

H6
1 Wayside

G H J 195 K L M

I

2

3

Friston Downs

4

Pea Down   Ringwood

The Brow

Peakdean Lane

The Link

206

High Close

A259

5

B2103

Willingdon Road

Old

Royston Cl

The Outlook

Ridgeway

Warren Close

Dene

Peakdean Close

2

Summerdown Lane

Dene Road

3

Michel Close

Elven La

ton

†

Mill Close Friston Close

Windmill Lane

Warren

Hillside

Side

Michel

Dene Close

Sussex Gdns

Downs View Close

Downsview Lane

EAST DEAN ROAD

A259

Doctors Surgery

Wenhill Close

1

Eastdean Down

BN20

6

East Dean

PH

PO

Upper Street

Lower Way

Went Way

Lower Street

Drive

†

Gilberts Road

Crapham Down

7

Birling Farm

Long Down

8

G H J 208 K L M

Birling Gap

Birling Gap Road

Corner Farm

J5
1 Elven La
2 Michel Dene Cl
3 Went La

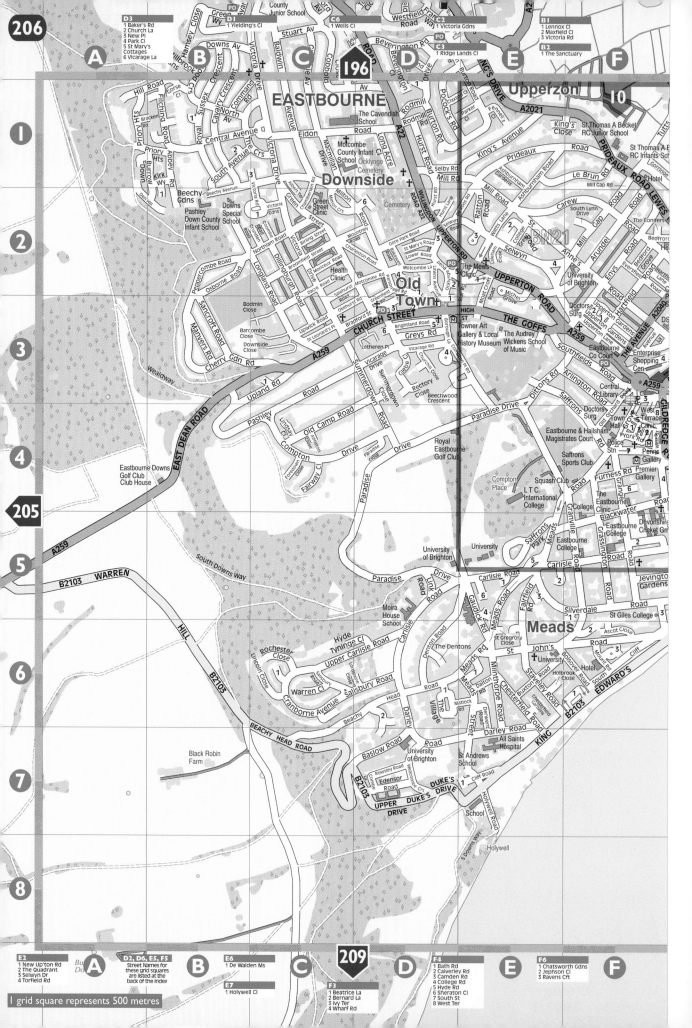

G
H
J
197
K
L
M

I

2

3

4

5

6

7

8

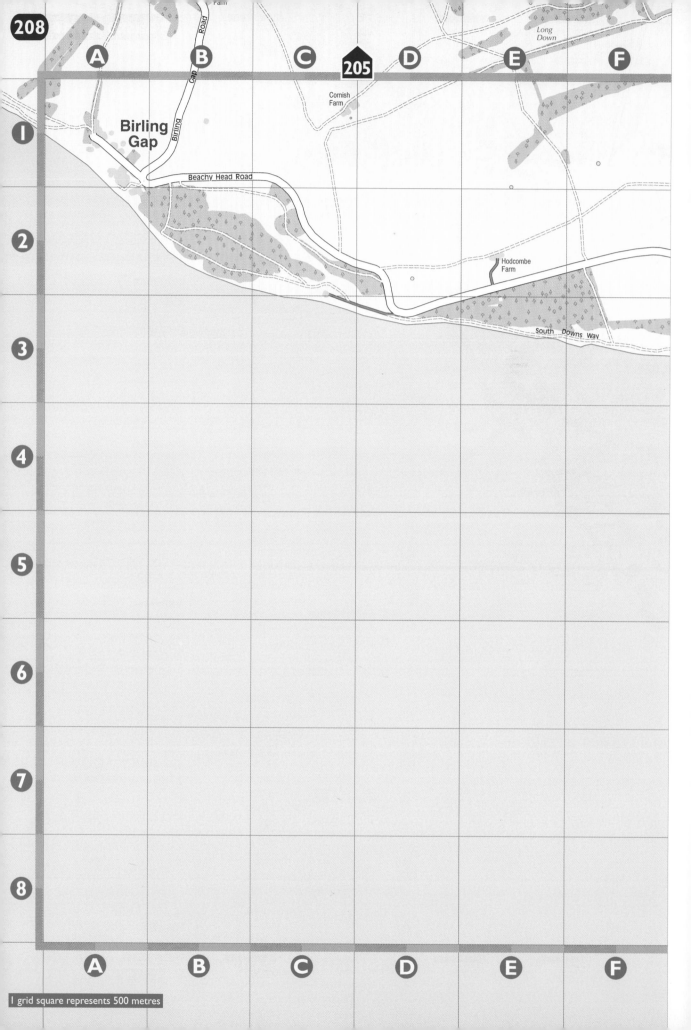

205

A   B   C   D   E   F

Long
Down

Cornish
Farm

**Birling
Gap**

Birling Gap Road

Beachy Head Road

Hodcombe
Farm

South   Downs   Way

1
2
3
4
5
6
7
8

A   B   C   D   E   F

1 grid square represents 500 metres

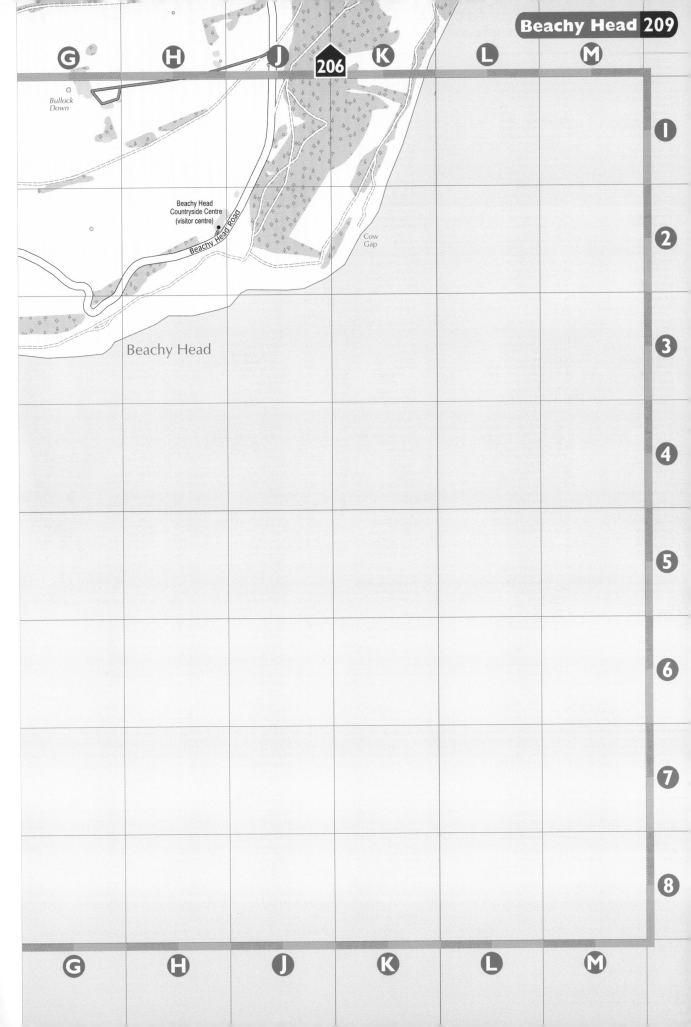

G H J 206 K L M

Bullock Down

Beachy Head
Countryside Centre
(visitor centre)

Beachy Head Road

Cow
Gap

Beachy Head

1
2
3
4
5
6
7
8

G H J K L M

Abbotsford	70 E8	Collier's Green	87 G5
Alciston	175 K6	Combe	43 J8
Alderbrook	39 M7	Cooden	182 D3
Aldrington	167 L7	Cooksbridge	126 A6
Alfriston	193 M4	Cooper's Green	76 D3
Ansty	70 C3	Cousley Wood	32 C7
Ardingly	34 B6	Cowbeech	133 J5
Argos Hill	56 E1	Cowbeech Hill	133 H7
Arlington	176 F2	Crawley Down	12 A7
Ashburnham Forge	135 K1	Cripp's Corner	86 D7
Ashburnham Place	135 L4	Cross in Hand	79 H7
Ashton Green	150 F2	Crowborough	39 M5
Ashurst	17 K4	Crowborough Warren	39 J4
Ashurst Wood	14 E8	Crowhurst	137 M8
Bachelor's Bump	140 E8	Cuckfield	70 F1
Baldslow	139 H7	Dale Hill	45 M4
Baldwins Hill	13 J5	Dallington	108 D3
Balls Green	27 G1	Danegate	29 J6
Barcombe	126 E5	Danehill	51 G2
Barcombe Cross	126 E2	Darwell Hole	109 M3
Bardown	44 D7	Davis's Town	104 B7
Battle	111 J8	Denny Bottom	19 K3
Beachlands	180 F8	Denton	191 M5
Beacon Down	79 C7	Ditchling	123 K3
Beckley	89 G2	Dittons	178 E8
Beckley Furnace	88 D7	Domewood	12 B1
Beddingham	173 K2	Down Park	12 A5
Bells Yew Green	31 H1	Downside	206 C1
Belmont	163 J5	Down Street	75 K1
Berner's Hill	46 A4	The Down	32 F3
Berwick	175 M7	Duddleswell	53 G2
Best Beech Hill	43 J3	Durgates	43 L1
Bevendean	170 A4	Earl's Down	108 B2
Bexhill	183 G2	Eason's Green	103 K5
Birchden	18 D8	East Blatchington	202 E2
Birchett's Green	44 E3	Eastbourne	10 C4
Birchgrove	36 A5	Eastbourne	206 C1
Birling Gap	208 A1	East Chiltington	125 G2
Bishopstone	192 C7	East Dean	205 H6
Blackboys	78 B8	East Grinstead	13 L5
Blackham	17 G2	East Guldeford	91 M7
Blacklands	4 D2	East Hoathly	130 B1
Blackness	40 A5	East Moulsecoomb	169 M2
Black Rock	188 A3	Eckington Corner	152 E6
Blackwell	13 L4	Eridge Green	29 J2
Boarshead	28 B8	Etchingham	61 H5
Bodiam	63 L6	Etchingwood	77 K5
Bodle Street Green	134 C4	Ewhurst Green	87 H1
Bohemia	4 B5	Exceat	203 M2
Boreham Street	157 L2	Fairfield	69 L5
Bowler's Town	91 H4	Fairlight	164 C2
Bray's Hill	135 G5	Fairlight Cove	164 F1
Brede	114 B5	Fairwarp	53 H5
Brightling	83 K8	Falmer	147 K8
Brighton	6 E8	Felbridge	12 F2
Broadland Row	114 D2	Ferndale	20 C1
Broad Oak	80 F5	Fishersgate	166 F7
Broad Oak	114 B1	Five Ash Down	76 E1
Broad Street	115 J8	Five Ashes	56 C7
Broadwater Down	19 M6	Flackley Ash	89 M3
Broomham	129 M8	Fletching	75 G2
Broomsgrove	5 K1	Fletching Common	74 B6
Brownbread Street	135 G3	Flimwell	46 C3
Broyle Side	128 A6	Flowers Green	156 F2
Buckham Hill	75 L8	Folkington	195 J2
Budlett's Common	76 C3	Fordcombe	18 A1
Bulverhythe	184 D1	Ford's Green	52 C3
Burgess Hill	97 G3	Forest Row	24 F5
Burgh Hill	61 L3	Foul Mile	133 J2
Burgh Hill	130 E8	Foulride Green	196 B2
Burlow	131 M1	Four Oaks	89 J1
Burnt Oak	54 F3	Foxhunt Green	104 F5
Burrswood	18 A6	Framfield	77 G8
Burwash	60 A8	Frant	30 C3
Burwash Common	82 A3	Friar's Gate	27 H7
Burwash Weald	82 C3	Friar's Hill	141 H7
Butcher's Cross	56 C6	Friston	204 F5
Buxted	77 G3	Furnace Wood	12 C3
Cackle Street	52 E4	Furner's Green	51 J5
Cackle Street	109 L2	Gallypot Street	26 B3
Cackle Street	113 M4	Gill's Green	47 M1
Cade Street	80 E8	Ginger's Green	133 J8
Camber	118 F3	Glenleigh Park	160 A7
Camden Park	20 C4	Glynde	150 E7
Canadia	111 J6	Glyndebourne	150 E4
Castle Hill	56 A2	Glyne Gap	184 C1
Catsfield	136 F6	Goatham Green	113 L1
Catsfield Stream	136 E7	Goddards' Green	96 A1
Chailey	99 L3	Godleys Green	98 F2
Chalvington	153 G7	Golden Cross	130 D8
Chapel Cross	107 G1	Golden Cross	156 E4
Chapel Row	156 F1	Gotham	159 G7
Chapman's Town	107 H4	Green Street	161 H2
Charlwood	23 L5	Groombridge	18 A7
Chelwood Common	36 D8	Grove Hill	132 E5
Chelwood Gate	36 C5	Guestling Green	141 G6
Chiddingly	130 E5	Guestling Thorn	141 G2
Chilsham	133 M6	Gun Hill	131 J5
Chiltington	125 C4	Hadlow Down	78 C1
Chitcombe	87 L8	Hailsham	155 J6
Chuck Hatch	26 C7	Hale Green	131 G5
Churches Green	108 B6	Halland	103 J8
Cinder Hill	35 G6	Hall's Close	158 C6
Clayhill	88 E3	Ham Green	67 J5
Clayton	122 E6	Hammerwood	15 H3
Cliff End	142 B7	Hampden Park	196 E5
Clive Vale	163 K4	Hamsey	126 C3
Cock Marling	115 M4	Hangleton	167 L4
Coggins Mill	57 J2	Hankham	179 G7
Coldean	169 K1	Harbour Heights	8 C8
Coleman's Hatch	25 L5	Harley Shute	161 M6
Hartfield	26 C2	Ninfield	136 B8
Hassocks	122 E2	Norlington	127 K7
Hastings	4 E5	Norman's Bay	181 K6
Hawkenbury	20 D4	Northbridge Street	85 J1
Hawkhurst	47 L5	North Chailey	73 K8
Hawkhurst Common	104 A5	North Common	73 L7
Haywards Heath	48 B8	North End	13 H2
Hazard's Green	158 D1	Northiam	65 H8
Heathfield	41 A4	North Moulsecoomb	169 K2
Heathfield	80 B7	Norton	192 C6
Hellingly	154 F1	Nutley	52 C3
Henley's Down	137 G8	Offham	149 G1
Heron's Ghyll	53 K3	Old Heathfield	80 D8
Herstmonceaux	133 M8	Old Town	5 M6
Highbrook	34 E5	Old Town	160 C8
High Cross	41 J7	Old Town	206 D2
Highgate	24 F5	Ore	163 J5
High Hurstwood	53 M5	Ovingdean	188 E3
The Highlands	159 M6	Oxley's Green	83 L6
High Street	47 K4	Palehouse Common	103 H4
Hollingbury	169 H1	Park Corner	28 E1
Hollingdean	169 H3	Park Corner	129 M4
Hollingrove	83 L8	Patcham	145 M8
Hollington	161 M3	Peacehaven	190 C7
Holmes's Hill	130 C8	Peacehaven Heights	200 E1
Holtye	15 L3	Peasmarsh	90 A4
Hooe	158 C7	Pebsham	160 F8
Hooe Common	158 E5	Pell Green	32 B7
Hook Green	32 D2	Penhurst	109 M8
Horam	105 L7	Pett	141 L6
Horney Common	52 E6	Pett Green	77 K3
Horns Cross	88 A5	Pett Level	142 B6
Horsted Green	102 B3	Pevensey	180 B8
Horsted Keynes	50 C1	Pevensey Bay	198 C1
Houghton Green	91 K5	Piddinghoe	191 G4
Hove	186 B1	Piltdown	75 J5
Hungershall Park	19 L4	Playden	91 J6
Hurst Green	62 A3	Plumpton	124 F7
Hurst Wickham	96 C3	Plumpton Green	98 E8
Icklesham	115 L8	Polegate	196 A1
Iden	91 H2	Ponts Green	135 H2
Iford	172 B3	Portslade-by-Sea	167 H8
Isfield	101 L6	Portslade Village	167 G4
Jarvis Brook	40 D6	Potman's Heath	66 E1
Jevington	195 J6	Potter's Green	77 K3
John's Cross	85 J7	Poundfield	40 B4
Jumper's Town	26 B7	Poundford	79 G1
Jury's Gap	119 L5	Poundgate	39 G7
Kemp Town	187 K3	Pound Green	77 K2
Keymer	123 H2	Pounsley	78 A6
Kingston by Sea	166 B7	Poynings	144 B1
Kingston near Lewes	171 L1	Preston	168 E5
Lamberhurst	33 H1	Punnett's Town	81 J8
Landport	2 D3	Pyecombe	122 B8
Langney	197 K4	Quabrook	25 J5
Langton Green	18 F2	Ramslye	19 K5
Laughton	129 J7	Rickney	179 K4
Lewes	3 K5	Ridgewood	102 C2
Lidham Hill	114 E8	Ringles Cross	76 C4
Lindfield	49 H6	Ringmer	127 J8
Linkhill	64 E2	Ripe	152 E5
Lions Green	105 H5	Robertsbridge	84 F2
Litlington	194 A6	Rockrobin	31 K7
Little Bayham	31 M2	Rocks Park	76 A7
Little Common	182 B1	Rodmell	172 D6
Little Horsted	102 C5	Roedean	188 C3
Little London	105 K2	Rose Hill	101 M8
Little Norlington	127 L5	Roselands	197 J7
Lower Cousley Wood	32 E6	Roser's Cross	78 F8
Lower Dicker	154 B2	Rotherfield	41 G6
Lower Green	19 J1	Rottingdean	189 G4
Lower Horsebridge	154 E2	Royal Tunbridge Wells	19 M3
Lower Street	159 H1	Rusher's Cross	42 F8
Lower Willingdon	196 B3	Rushlake Green	107 J5
Lunsford's Cross	159 M4	Rushy Green	150 E1
Lydd	95 H8	Russell's Green	159 G3
Lye Green	27 L5	Rusthall	19 J2
Lyewood Common	17 H7	Rye	91 J8
Magham Down	155 M2	Rye Foreign	90 E5
Manor Park	76 E5	Rye Harbour	117 M4
Marden's Hill	39 H1	Saddlescombe	144 E3
Maresfield Park	76 A1	St Helen's	163 G1
Mark Cross	42 A2	St Helen's Wood	162 E2
Mark Cross	152 C4	St John's	39 J2
Marle Green	132 B1	St Leonards	162 A7
Marlpits	37 K8	Salehurst	85 J1
Marlpits	136 B7	Saltdean	189 K4
Mayfield	57 G4	Sandhurst	64 A1
Maynard's Green	106 A4	Sandhurst Cross	63 L2
Meads	206 E6	Sandy Cross	106 B1
Mile Oak	166 F3	Scayne's Hill	72 E3
Mill Corner	88 A3	Seacox Heath	46 E4
Mill Hill	179 K8	Seaford	202 D4
Milton Street	194 D1	Sedlescombe	112 D5
Moon's Green	67 G3	Selmeston	175 L3
The Moor	47 M6	Selsfield Common	22 B5
Mott's Mill	28 A3	Sharpsbridge	75 J2
Moulsecoomb	169 M3	Sharp's Corner	105 L6
Mount Ephraim	102 E3	Sharpthorne	23 G8
Mountfield	85 G8	Sheffield Green	51 H7
Mount Pleasant	100 F8	Shortbridge	75 L6
Mount Pleasant	192 A5	Shortgate	129 H3
Muddles Green	130 E7	Shover's Green	44 C4
Mutton Hall	80 B5	Sidley	160 B8
Nash Street	130 F8	Silver Hill	62 B6
Netherfield	110 C4	Silverhill	162 C3
Newbridge	25 L8	Silverhill Park	139 J8
Newenden	65 K3	Skippers Hill	56 A7
Newhaven	8 F6	Sleeches Cross	30 B4
Newick	74 E6	Snagshall	86 F1
New Town	76 E8	South Chailey	99 L7
		Southease	172 E7
Southern Cross	167 G6		
South Heighton	191 L4		
South Malling	3 G3		
Southover	2 D9		
Southover	59 J6		
South Street	99 L5		
Southwick	166 E6		
Sparrow's Green	43 M1		
Spithurst	100 F7		
Splayne's Green	75 G1		
Stanmer	146 E6		
Staplecross	86 E5		
Starr's Green	138 A4		
Steel Cross	40 B3		
Steven's Crouch	136 B3		
The Stocks	68 A2		
Stone Cross	17 M4		
Stone Cross	39 M8		
Stone Cross	44 A3		
Stone Cross	197 J1		
Stonecrouch	33 L7		
Stonegate	45 G8		
Stone in Oxney	68 F2		
Stonequarry	14 A3		
Strawberry Hill	19 K6		
Streat	124 B3		
Stunts Green	133 K7		
Summer Hill	178 A2		
Sunnyside	13 L8		
Sutton	203 C2		
Swaile's Green	86 C7		
Sweethaws	39 J8		
Tarring Neville	191 K2		
Teasley Mead	17 J3		
Telham	138 B4		
Telscombe	190 B3		
Telscombe Cliffs	190 A6		
Three Cups Corner	107 J1		
Three Leg Cross	45 K3		
Three Oaks	140 D4		
Thunder's Hill	130 F7		
Ticehurst	45 L4		
Tidebrook	43 H6		
Tilsmore	79 M6		
Tolhurst	44 F4		
Tompset's Bank	24 F6		
Town Littleworth	100 C5		
Town Row	41 J5		
Trollilces	133 K4		
Turner's Green	31 L8		
Turner's Green	107 M2		
Turners Hill	22 A2		
Twelve Oaks	109 K1		
Uckfield	76 D7		
Udimore	115 K4		
Union Street	46 B3		
Upper Dicker	154 A6		
Upper Hartfield	26 B4		
Upper Horsebridge	154 E3		
Upperton	10 B3		
Upper Wellingham	127 G6		
Vinehall Street	85 L8		
Vines Cross	106 C6		
Wadhurst	44 A2		
Waldron	104 F3		
Waldron Down	78 D6		
Wallands Park	2 C5		
Wallcrouch	44 F5		
Wannock	195 M2		
Warbleton	107 C5		
Wartling	157 J7		
Watermill	160 B2		
Wellbrook	56 F5		
West Blatchington	167 M5		
Westdean	204 B2		
Westdene	168 B1		
Westfield	139 M2		
West Firle	174 C3		
Westham	179 L8		
West Hill	5 K4		
West Hoathly	22 B8		
West Marina	161 M8		
Westmeston	123 L6		
Whatlington	112 A5		
Whitehawk	169 M8		
Whitehill	39 L6		
Whitesmith	130 B6		
Whydown	159 H6		
Wickstreet	153 L8		
Willard's Hill	84 C1		
Willingdon	196 A5		
Wilmington	176 E8		
Wilmington Green	176 E7		
Winchelsea	116 D7		
Winchelsea Beach	117 H8		
Windmill Hill	157 H1		
Winton	194 A2		
Withdean	168 E2		
Witherenden Hill	59 G5		
Withyham	27 G3		
Wittersham	67 K3		
Wivelsfield	98 A1		
Woodingdean	170 C2		
Woodmans Green	112 A3		
Wood's Corner	108 F3		
Wood's Green	31 M6		
World's End	97 K2		
Wych Cross	36 E2		

USING THE STREET INDEX

Street names are listed alphabetically. Each street name is followed by its postal town or area locality, the Postcode District, the page number, and the reference to the square in which the name is found.

Abbey Wy *BAT* TN33 .... 137 K1 🔟

Some entries are followed by a number in a blue box. This number indicates the location of the street within the referenced grid square. The full street name is listed at the side of the map page.

211

GENERAL ABBREVIATIONS

ACC	ACCESS
ALY	ALLEY
AP	APPROACH
AR	ARCADE
ASS	ASSOCIATION
AV	AVENUE
BCH	BEACH
BLDS	BUILDINGS
BND	BEND
BNK	BANK
BR	BRIDGE
BRK	BROOK
BTM	BOTTOM
BUS	BUSINESS
BVD	BOULEVARD
BY	BYPASS
CATH	CATHEDRAL
CEM	CEMETERY
CEN	CENTRE
CFT	CROFT
CH	CHURCH
CHA	CHASE
CHYD	CHURCHYARD
CIR	CIRCLE
CIRC	CIRCUS
CL	CLOSE
CLFS	CLIFFS
CMP	CAMP
CNR	CORNER
CO	COUNTY
COLL	COLLEGE
COM	COMMON
COMM	COMMISSION
CON	CONVENT
COT	COTTAGE
COTS	COTTAGES
CP	CAPE
CPS	COPSE
CR	CREEK
CREM	CREMATORIUM
CRS	CRESCENT
CSWY	CAUSEWAY
CT	COURT
CTRL	CENTRAL
CTS	COURTS
CTYD	COURTYARD
CUTT	CUTTINGS
CV	COVE
CYN	CANYON
DEPT	DEPARTMENT
DL	DALE
DM	DAM
DR	DRIVE
DRO	DROVE
DRY	DRIVEWAY
DWGS	DWELLINGS
E	EAST
EMB	EMBANKMENT
EMBY	EMBASSY
ESP	ESPLANADE
EST	ESTATE
EX	EXCHANGE
EXPY	EXPRESSWAY
EXT	EXTENSION
F/O	FLYOVER
FC	FOOTBALL CLUB
FK	FORK
FLD	FIELD
FLDS	FIELDS
FLS	FALLS
FLS	FLATS
FM	FARM
FT	FORT
FWY	FREEWAY
FY	FERRY
GA	GATE
GAL	GALLERY
GDN	GARDEN
GDNS	GARDENS
GLD	GLADE
GLN	GLEN
GN	GREEN
GND	GROUND
GRA	GRANGE
GRG	GARAGE
GT	GREAT
GTWY	GATEWAY
GV	GROVE
HGR	HIGHER
HL	HILL
HLS	HILLS
HO	HOUSE
HOL	HOLLOW
HOSP	HOSPITAL
HRB	HARBOUR
HTH	HEATH
HTS	HEIGHTS
HVN	HAVEN
HWY	HIGHWAY
IMP	IMPERIAL
IN	INLET
IND EST	INDUSTRIAL ESTATE
INF	INFIRMARY
INFO	INFORMATION
INT	INTERCHANGE
IS	ISLAND
JCT	JUNCTION
JTY	JETTY
KG	KING
KNL	KNOLL
L	LAKE
LA	LANE
LDG	LODGE
LGT	LIGHT
LK	LOCK
LKS	LAKES
LNDG	LANDING
LTL	LITTLE
LWR	LOWER
MAG	MAGISTRATE
MAN	MANSIONS
MD	MEAD
MDW	MEADOWS
MEM	MEMORIAL
MKT	MARKET
MKTS	MARKETS
ML	MALL
ML	MILL
MNR	MANOR
MS	MEWS
MSN	MISSION
MT	MOUNT
MTN	MOUNTAIN
MTS	MOUNTAINS
MUS	MUSEUM
MWY	MOTORWAY
N	NORTH
NE	NORTH EAST
NW	NORTH WEST
O/P	OVERPASS
OFF	OFFICE
ORCH	ORCHARD
OV	OVAL
PAL	PALACE
PAS	PASSAGE
PAV	PAVILION
PDE	PARADE
PH	PUBLIC HOUSE
PK	PARK
PKWY	PARKWAY
PL	PLACE
PLN	PLAIN
PLNS	PLAINS
PLZ	PLAZA
POL	POLICE STATION
PR	PRINCE
PREC	PRECINCT
PREP	PREPARATORY
PRIM	PRIMARY
PROM	PROMENADE
PRS	PRINCESS
PRT	PORT
PT	POINT
PTH	PATH
PZ	PIAZZA
QD	QUADRANT
QU	QUEEN
QY	QUAY
R	RIVER
RBT	ROUNDABOUT
RD	ROAD
RDG	RIDGE
REP	REPUBLIC
RES	RESERVOIR
RFC	RUGBY FOOTBALL CLUB
RI	RISE
RP	RAMP
RW	ROW
S	SOUTH
SCH	SCHOOL
SE	SOUTH EAST
SER	SERVICE AREA
SH	SHORE
SHOP	SHOPPING
SKWY	SKYWAY
SMT	SUMMIT
SOC	SOCIETY
SP	SPUR
SPR	SPRING
SQ	SQUARE
ST	STREET
STN	STATION
STR	STREAM
STRD	STRAND
SW	SOUTH WEST
TDG	TRADING
TER	TERRACE
THWY	THROUGHWAY
TNL	TUNNEL
TOLL	TOLLWAY
TPK	TURNPIKE
TR	TRACK
TRL	TRAIL
TWR	TOWER
U/P	UNDERPASS
UNI	UNIVERSITY
UPR	UPPER
V	VALE
VA	VALLEY
VIAD	VIADUCT
VIL	VILLA
VIS	VISTA
VLG	VILLAGE
VLS	VILLAS
VW	VIEW
W	WEST
WD	WOOD
WHF	WHARF
WK	WALK
WKS	WALKS
WLS	WELLS
WY	WAY
YD	YARD
YHA	YOUTH HOSTEL

POSTCODE TOWNS AND AREA ABBREVIATIONS

BAT	Battle
BEX	Bexhill
BEXW	Bexhill west
BRI	Brighton
BUR/ETCH	Burwash/Etchingham
BURH	Burgess Hill
CRAWE	Crawley east
CRBK	Cranbrook
CROW	Crowborough
EAST	Eastbourne
EDEN	Edenbridge
EDN/EASTW	East Dean/Eastbourne west
EGRIN	East Grinstead
FROW	Forest Row
HAIL	Hailsham
HAS	Hastings
HAWK	Hawkhurst
HFD	Henfield
HOVE	Hove
HPPT/KEY	Hurstpierpoint/Keymer
HRTF	Hartfield
HTHF	Heathfield
HWH	Haywards Heath
LEW	Lewes
LGNY	Langney
LW/ROSE	Lower Willingdon/Roselands
LYDD	Lydd
MAYF	Mayfield
NEWHV	Newhaven
NROM	New Romney
PEAHV	Peacehaven
PEV	Pevensey
POLE	Polegate
POY/PYE	Poynings/Pyecombe
PTSD	Portslade
RBTBR	Robertsbridge
RHAS	Rural Hastings
RHWH	Rural Haywards Heath
RING/NEW	Ringmer/Newick
ROTT	Rottingdean
RRTW	Rural Royal Tunbridge Wells
RTW	Royal Tunbridge Wells

Index - streets

106 - Ast

1066 Country Wk *BAT* TN33 **138** C2
HAIL BN27 **156** E8
RHAS TN350 **140** C3
RHAS TN35 **163** J6
WSEA TN36 **115** K8

A

Abberton Fld *HPPT/KEY* BN6 **122** B1
Abbey Cl *PEAHV* BN10 **190** C5
Abbey Dr *STLEO* TN38 **184** B1
Abbey Rd *EDN/EASTW* BN20 **206** B1
ROTT BN2 **7** L8
Abbey Vw *BEX* TN40 **160** D8
Abbey Wy *BAT* TN33 **137** K1 [1]
Abbotsbury Cl *ROTT* BN2 **189** H5 [1]
Abbots Cl *BAT* TN33 **137** M3
HPPT/KEY BN6 **122** E2
Abbotsfield Cl *HAS* TN34 **162** F3
Aberdale Rd *POLE* BN26 **178** C8
Aberdeen Rd *ROTT* BN2 **7** H1
Abergavenny Rd *LEW* BN7 **2** C6
Abinger Pl *LEW* BN7 **2** F5
Abinger Rd *PTSD* BN41 **167** H6
ROTT BN2 **170** E8
Acacia Av *HOVE* BN3 **167** M5 [1]
Acacia Rd *LW/ROSE* BN22 **196** D4
NEWHV BN9 **191** L4
Acer Av *RTWE/PEM* TN2 **20** C6
Acorn Cl *EGRIN* RH19 **13** L6
SLVH TN37 **162** C2
The Acorns *HPPT/KEY* BN6 **96** D2
WADH TN5 **44** F8
Acorn Wy *BUR/ETCH* TN19 **62** A3
Acre Cl *HWH* RH16 **71** K4
Acres Ri *WADH* TN5 **45** L5
Adam Cl *CROW* TN6 **40** A8
STLEO TN38 **161** M2
Adams Cl *BRI* BN1 **169** H4
Adams La *RYE* TN31 **87** K3
Adastra Av *HPPT/KEY* BN6 **123** G2
Addingham Rd *LW/ROSE* BN22 **11** J3
Addington Cl *STLEO* TN38 **161** M7
Addison Rd *HOVE* BN3 **6** A3
Adelaide Cl *SEAF* BN25 **202** E1 [1]
Adelaide Crs *HOVE* BN3 **186** C1
Adelaide Rd *STLEO* TN38 **162** B3
Adelaide Sq *SHOR* BN43 **166** B7
Ades Fld *POLE* BN26 **176** F8
Admiral's Bridge La
EGRIN RH19 **23** J4
Adur Dr *PEV* BN24 **197** G1
SHOR BN43 **166** A7
Adur Rd *BURH* RH15 **97** J2
Agincourt Cl *STLEO* TN38 **138** F7
Agnes St *ROTT* BN2 **7** J2
Ainsworth Av *ROTT* BN2 **188** D3
Ainsworth Cl *ROTT* BN2 **188** D2
Airy Rd *HAIL* BN27 **157** H5
Akehurst Fld *BAT* TN33 **135** H3
Alan Wy *ROTT* BN2 **169** M8
Albany Hl *RTWE/PEM* TN2 **20** C1
Albany Ms *HOVE* BN3 **168** B8
Albany Rd *BEX* TN40 **183** J3
SEAF BN25 **202** C3
STLEO TN38 **162** B6
Albany Vls *HOVE* BN3 **186** B1
Albert Cl *HWH* RH16 **72** A2
Albert Dr *BURH* RH15 **96** E4
Albert Ms *HOVE* BN3 **168** B8
Albert Rd *BEX* TN40 **183** J3
BRI BN1 **6** C4
HAS TN34 **5** H7
POLE BN26 **177** M7
STHW BN42 **166** D7
UCK TN22 **76** D8 [1]
Albert Ter *EAST* BN21 **206** C1
Albion Ct *BURH* RH15 **96** F4 [1]
Albion Hl *ROTT* BN2 **7** H5
Albion Rd *LW/ROSE* BN22 **11** G3
RTW TN1 **20** B1
Albion St *LEW* BN7 **3** G5
PTSD BN41 **166** D8
PTSD BN41 **167** H7
ROTT BN2 **7** G4 [1]
STHW BN42 **167** G7
Albourne Cl *ROTT* BN2 **169** L7
STLEO TN38 **161** M6
Aldborough Rd *SLVH* TN37 **4** B4
Alderbrook Cl *CROW* TN6 **40** A8
Alderbrook Wy *CROW* TN6 **40** A8
Alder Cl *CRAWE* RH10 **12** B6
HTHF TN21 **106** A1
SLVH TN37 **162** C1
Alders Av *EGRIN* RH19 **13** K3
Alders View Dr *EGRIN* RH19 **13** L2 [1]
Aldervale Cottages *CROW* TN6 **40** A7
Aldrich Cl *ROTT* BN2 **169** M8
Aldrington Av *HOVE* BN3 **168** A6
Aldrington Cl *HOVE* BN3 **167** K7
Alexander Dr *BEXW* TN39 **182** E2
Alexandra Cl *SEAF* BN25 **202** E1 [2]
Alexandra Rd *BURH* RH15 **97** J4
HTHF TN21 **80** B8
LW/ROSE BN22 **197** K8
MAYF TN20 **57** J3
SLVH TN37 **4** A6
UCK TN22 **76** D8
Alexandra Vls *BRI* BN1 **6** C4
Alford Wy *BEX* TN40 **160** E8
Alfray Rd *BEX* TN40 **184** A1
Alfred Rd *BRI* BN1 **6** C4
LGNY BN23 **197** M6
RHAS TN35 **163** J3
Alfred St *STLEO* TN38 **4** A8
Alfriston Cl *BEXW* TN39 **159** J8
EDN/EASTW BN20 **206** C4
ROTT BN2 **169** M8
Alfriston Pk *SEAF* BN25 **203** J1
Alfriston Rd *SEAF* BN25 **203** H1
Alice Bright La *CROW* TN6 **39** M7
Alice St *HOVE* BN3 **186** D1
Allan Cl *SBGH/RUST* TN4 **19** J2
Allards *RHAS* TN35 **141** J6
Allen Rd *HWH* RH16 **72** A1
Allen's Cl *EGRIN* RH19 **14** D8
Allen Wy *BEX* TN40 **160** F8
Allfrey Rd *LW/ROSE* BN22 **197** K8
Allfreys La *CROW* TN6 **39** K8
Allington Crs *RING/NEW* BN8 **74** C7
Allington La *LEW* BN7 **125** J7
Allington Rd *RING/NEW* BN8 **74** C8
All Saints Gdns *HTHF* TN21 **79** M7
All Saints La *BEXW* TN39 **160** B7
All Saints' St *HAS* TN34 **5** L6
Allwood Crs *RHWH* RH17 **98** C2
Alma Rd *HWH* RH16 **49** H6
Alma Ter *SLVH* TN37 **4** A1
Alma Vls *SLVH* TN37 **4** A1
Alpine Rd *HAS* TN34 **5** K5
HOVE BN3 **167** M6
Alverstone Cl *LGNY* BN23 **197** H2
Amanda Cl *BEX* TN40 **160** F7
Amberley Cl *BURH* RH15 **97** G2
HWH RH16 **71** K2 [1]
Amberley Dr *HOVE* BN3 **167** L3
Amberley Rd *LW/ROSE* BN22 **196** C5
Amberstone *HAIL* BN27 **155** L3
Amberstone Cl *HAS* TN34 **163** G2 [1]
Amberstone Vw *HAIL* BN27 **155** J4
Ambleside Av *PEAHV* BN10 **190** A7
America La *HWH* RH16 **72** A1
Amesbury Crs *HOVE* BN3 **167** L7
Amherst Cl *SLVH* TN37 **4** C3
Amherst Crs *HOVE* BN3 **167** M6
Amherst Gdns *HAS* TN34 **4** D4
Amherst Rd *BEX* TN40 **183** J2
SBGH/RUST TN4 **20** A1
SLVH TN37 **4** B4
Amhurst Rd *PEAHV* BN10 **189** M7
Anchor Cl *SHOR* BN43 **166** A8
Anchor Fld *RING/NEW* BN8 **150** D1
Anchor La *RING/NEW* BN8 **101** G8
Anderida Rd *LW/ROSE* BN22 **196** B3
Anderson Cl *NEWHV* BN9 **8** C3
Andrews Cl *RBTBR* TN32 **85** J1
RTWE/PEM TN2 **20** D1 [1]
Angela Cl *BEX* TN40 **160** F7 [1]
Anglesey Av *HAIL* BN27 **155** G4
Angus Cl *EDN/EASTW* BN20 **196** B6
Ann Cl *HPPT/KEY* BN6 **123** G1
Annington Rd *LW/ROSE* BN22 **11** H2
Ann St *BRI* BN1 **6** E3
HAS TN34 **5** M1
Anson Cl *LGNY* BN23 **197** L7
Ansty Cl *ROTT* BN2 **187** L1
Antioch St *LEW* BN7 **2** E7 [1]
Antony Cl *SEAF* BN25 **192** B8
Antrona Cl *BEXW* TN39 **182** C3
Anvil Cl *PTSD* BN41 **167** H4
UCK TN22 **76** B8
Anvil Ct *SLVH* TN37 **162** C1 [1]
Anzac Cl *PEAHV* BN10 **190** C5
Appledene Cnr
RING/NEW BN8 **99** L7 [1]
Appledore Cl *LGNY* BN23 **197** K4 [1]
Appledore Gdns *HWH* RH16 **48** F8
Appledore Rd *ROTT* BN2 **169** M2
Applesham Av *HOVE* BN3 **167** L4
Applesham Wy *PTSD* BN41 **167** G5
Applewood Cl *SLVH* TN37 **162** B2
The Approach *BRI* BN1 **168** E3
Apsley St *SBGH/RUST* TN4 **19** K2
Aquarius Cl *PEAHV* BN10 **190** C8 [1]
Aquila Pk *SEAF* BN25 **203** G3 [1]
Arbourvale *STLEO* TN38 **162** A5
Archery Rd *STLEO* TN38 **162** B7
Archery Wk *HAIL* BN27 **155** J8
Ardingly Rd *HWH* RH16 **49** J4
ROTT BN2 **189** K6
Ardingly St *ROTT* BN2 **7** G7
Ardings Cl *RHWH* RH17 **34** B7
Argent Cl *SEAF* BN25 **203** G1
Argos Hill Rd *MAYF* TN20 **56** D2
Argyle Rd *BRI* BN1 **6** D2
Arlington Crs *BRI* BN1 **169** L1 [1]
Arlington Gdns *ROTT* BN2 **189** K4
Arlington Rd *EAST* BN21 **10** C6
Arlington Rd East *HAIL* BN27 **154** F8
Arlington Rd West *HAIL* BN27 **154** F8
Armstrong Cl *STLEO* TN38 **161** L2
Arnbury Ms *STLEO* TN38 **161** L8
Arnold St *ROTT* BN2 **7** K3
Arnside Rd *STLEO* TN38 **161** L8
Arran Cl *HAIL* BN27 **155** G4
Arthur Rd *BEXW* TN39 **183** H2
Arthur St *HOVE* BN3 **168** A6
Arundel Cl *HAIL* BN27 **155** J4
PEV BN24 **180** F8
SHOR BN43 **166** C6
Arundel Dr East *ROTT* BN2 **189** J5
Arundel Dr West *ROTT* BN2 **189** H5
Arundell Gn *LEW* BN7 **2** D3
Arundel Pl *ROTT* BN2 **187** L2
Arundel Rd *EAST* BN21 **10** B4
NEWHV BN9 **191** L5
PEAHV BN10 **190** C7
ROTT BN2 **187** L3
RTW TN1 **20** B4
SEAF BN25 **203** G3
Arundel Road Central
PEAHV BN10 **190** B7
Arundel Rd West *PEAHV* BN10 **190** A6
Arundel St *ROTT* BN2 **187** L3
Arundel Ter *ROTT* BN2 **187** L3
Arun Wy *PEV* BN24 **196** F1
Ascham Pl *EDN/EASTW* BN20 **206** E5 [1]
Ascot Cl *EDN/EASTW* BN20 **206** F6
Ascot Ms *STLEO* TN38 **162** A6 [1]
Ashbrook Rd *SLVH* TN37 **162** B2
Ashburnham Cl *BRI* BN1 **169** L1 [2]
Ashburnham Dr *BRI* BN1 **146** D8
Ashburnham Gdns *EAST* BN21 **10** A2
Ashburnham Pl *HAIL* BN27 **155** G4 [1]
Ashburnham Rd *EAST* BN21 **10** B3
RHAS TN35 **163** J5
Ashby Cl *BEXW* TN39 **160** A7
Ash Cl *CRAWE* RH10 **12** C5
HOVE BN3 **168** C3
LW/ROSE BN22 **196** E3
RTWE/PEM TN2 **20** D6
Ashcombe Dr *BEXW* TN39 **182** D3
Ashcombe Hollow *LEW* BN7 **148** D7
Ashcombe La *LEW* BN7 **148** E8
Ash Ct *HAIL* BN27 **155** G7
Ashcroft Cl *RING/NEW* BN8 **150** D1
SHOR BN43 **166** D7
Ashdown Av *ROTT* BN2 **189** H5
Ashdown Cha *UCK* TN22 **52** C1
Ashdown Cl *FROW* RH18 **25** G4
HWH RH16 **72** B2
SBGH/RUST TN4 **19** M2
STLEO TN38 **161** L4
Ashdown Pl *HTHF* TN21 **80** B8 [1]
Ashdown Rd *BEX* TN40 **183** L2
FROW RH18 **24** F4
ROTT BN2 **169** H6
Ashdown Vw *EGRIN* RH19 **13** L7
UCK TN22 **37** K8
Ash Dr *SEAF* BN25 **203** J3
Ashenden Av *RYE* TN31 **117** G1
Ashenground Cl *HWH* RH16 **71** L3 [1]
Ashenground Rd *HWH* RH16 **71** K3
Ashentree La *LYDD* TN29 **94** A1
Asher Reeds *RRTW* TN3 **19** G2
Ashford Cl *HAIL* BN27 **155** J7 [1]
Ashford Rd *BRI* BN1 **169** G4
EAST BN21 **10** F5
HAS TN34 **4** E2
Ashford Sq *EAST* BN21 **10** F5
Ashford Wy *HAS* TN34 **4** E1
Ashgate Rd *LGNY* BN23 **197** L4
Ash Gv *HWH* RH16 **71** K4
LYDD TN29 **95** K7
PEV BN24 **179** K8
Ashington Gdns *PEAHV* BN10 **190** E8
Ashington Rd *LW/ROSE* BN22 **197** G5
Ashleigh Gdns *CROW* TN6 **39** L2
Ashley Cl *BRI* BN1 **145** L7
Ashley Gdns *HAIL* BN27 **155** J3
MAYF TN20 **57** G4
SBGH/RUST TN4 **19** J1
Ashley Park Cl *SBGH/RUST* TN4 **19** J1
Ashley Rd *CROW* TN6 **41** K5
Ashlings Wy *HOVE* BN3 **167** L4 [1]
SHOR BN43 **166** B5
Ashmore Cl *PEAHV* BN10 **190** D4
Ashton Ri *ROTT* BN2 **7** G5
Ashtonville Cl
RING/NEW BN8 **150** E1 [1]
Ash Tree Cl *HTHF* TN21 **80** A7
Ashurst Av *ROTT* BN2 **189** L6
Ashurst Rd *ROTT* BN2 **169** M1
RRTW TN3 **18** B4
SEAF BN25 **202** F4
Ashway *BURH* RH15 **97** G4 [1]
Aspen Cl *HWH* RH16 **72** B2
Aspen Rd *LW/ROSE* BN22 **196** E4
Aspen Wk *HTHF* TN21 **106** B1
Aspen Wy *BEXW* TN39 **182** C2
Astaire Av *LW/ROSE* BN22 **11** G1
Asten Cl *STLEO* TN38 **161** L7
Asten Flds *BAT* TN33 **137** H2

Athelstan Cl *LGNY* BN23 ...... 197 M6
Athelstan Rd *RHAS* TN35 ...... 163 K4
Atlantic Dr *LGNY* BN23 ...... 197 M7
Atlingworth St *ROTT* BN2 ...... 7 H8
Attree Dr *ROTT* BN2 ...... 169 M5
Auckland Dr *ROTT* BN2 ...... 169 M5
Audrey Cl *BRI* BN1 ...... 168 E1
  SEAF BN25 ...... 202 D1
Augustines Wy *HWH* RH16 ...... 71 L2
Augustus Wy *STLEO* TN38 ...... 138 F8
Austen Cl *EGRIN* RH19 ...... 13 H5
Austen Wy *RHAS* TN35 ...... 163 K4
Avard Crs *EDN/EASTW* BN20 ...... 196 B8
Aviary La *LEW* BN7 ...... L6
Avenue La 10 D5
The Avenue *EAST* BN21 ...... 10 D5
  HAIL BN27 ...... 155 H8
  HTHF TN21 ...... 80 E3
  HTHF TN21 ...... 105 M6
  LEW BN7 ...... 2 D5
  LEW BN7 ...... 171 L1
  MAYF TN20 ...... 57 H4
  RHAS TN35 ...... 164 F2
  ROTT BN2 ...... 169 K4
Avery Cl *PTSD* BN41 ...... 166 F2
Aviary Wy *CRAWE* RH10 ...... 12 C5
Aviemore Rd *CROW* TN6 ...... 39 K4
Avis Cl *NEWHV* BN9 ...... 191 L5
Avis Rd *NEWHV* BN9 ...... 191 L5
Avis Wy *NEWHV* BN9 ...... 9 J1
Avondale Rd *HOVE* BN3 ...... 168 D7
  LW/ROSE BN22 ...... 11 H3
  SEAF BN25 ...... 202 F3
  STLEO TN38 ...... 162 A5
Avonhurst *BURH* BN15 ...... 97 H3
Avon St *RTW* TN1 ...... 20 C1
Awbrook Cl *RHWH* RH17 ...... 72 F3
Aylesbury Av *LGNY* BN23 ...... 197 L6
Aymer Rd *HOVE* BN3 ...... 168 A8
Ayscue Cl *LGNY* BN23 ...... 197 M7

B

Babylon Wy *EDN/EASTW* BN20.. 196 B6
Back La *HTHF* TN21 ...... 79 J7
  HTHF TN21 ...... 107 K6
  UCK TN22 ...... 53 H4
  WSEA TN36 ...... 116 E7
Back Rd *HAWK* TN18 ...... 64 B1
Backwoods Cl *HWH* RH16 ...... 49 H8
Backwoods La *HWH* RH16 ...... 49 G8
Baden Rd *ROTT* BN2 ...... 7 L8
Badens Cl *RING/NEW* BN8 ...... 74 C8
Badger Cl *PTSD* BN41 ...... 167 H4
Badger Dr *RHWH* RH17 ...... 71 J1
Badgers Brow
  EDN/EASTW BN20 ...... 196 B6
Badgers Cl *CROW* TN6 ...... 39 L3
Badgers Copse *SEAF* BN25 ...... 203 J3
Badgers Dene *LEW* BN7 ...... 172 D6
Badgers Fld *PEAHV* BN10 ...... 190 C5
Badgers Holt *RTWE/PEM* TN2 ...... 20 E1
Badgers Mt *BEXW* TN39 ...... 182 E1
Badgers Wk *BURH* RH15 ...... 97 K4
  HAS TN34 ...... 162 D1
Badger Wy *BRI* BN1 ...... 146 B8
Badlesmere Rd
  LW/ROSE BN22 ...... 197 G8
Bagham La *HAIL* BN27 ...... 133 M8
Bahram Rd *POLE* BN26 ...... 177 L8
Bailey Crs *LW/ROSE* BN22 ...... 196 B3
Baillie Av *LW/ROSE* BN22 ...... 11 L1
Bainbridge Cl *SEAF* BN25 ...... 202 F4
Bainden Cl *CROW* TN6 ...... 41 K5
Baird Dr *HAS* TN34 ...... 162 E3
Baker's Rd *EAST* BN21 ...... 206 D3
Baker St *BRI* BN1 ...... 6 F3
  NEWHV BN9 ...... 9 J4
  UCK TN22 ...... 76 D8
Bakewell Rd *EAST* BN21 ...... 206 D4
Balaclava La *WADH* TN5 ...... 31 M7
Balcombe Rd *RHWH* RH17 ...... 35 L4
Balcombe Rd *HWH* RH16 ...... 48 D6
  PEAHV BN10 ...... 190 B6
Baldock Rd *EAST* BN21 ...... 43 K2
Baldslow Down *SLVH* TN37 ...... 139 J3
Baldslow Rd *HAS* TN34 ...... 5 C2
Baldwin Av *EAST* BN21 ...... 196 C8
Bale Cl *BEXW* TN39 ...... 182 E1
Balfour Gdns *FROW* RH18 ...... 24 E6
Balfour Rd *BRI* BN1 ...... 168 F4
Ballard Dr *RING/NEW* BN8 ...... 127 M6
Ballards Hl *BAT* TN33 ...... 160 F2
Ballsocks La *HTHF* TN21 ...... 106 C6
Balmoral Cl *SEAF* BN25 ...... 193 G8
Balsdean Rd *ROTT* BN2 ...... 170 A4
Bamford Cl *ROTT* BN2 ...... 170 A4
Bampfield St *PTSD* BN41 ...... 167 H6
Bancroft Rd *BEXW* TN39 ...... 183 H1
Bank Rd *BEXW* TN39 ...... 160 C7
Banks Castle *LEW* BN7 ...... 2 F6
Bankside *BRI* BN1 ...... 168 A4
  HPPT/KEY BN6 ...... 122 F1
  WADH TN5 ...... 43 L1
Banks Rd *RING/NEW* BN8 ...... 73 G3
Banner Farm Rd
  RTWE/PEM TN2 ...... 20 B4
Bannings V *ROTT* BN2 ...... 189 K6
Bannisters Fld *RING/NEW* BN8 ...... 74 E7
Bannister Wy *HWH* RH16 ...... 48 D8
Baranscraig Av *BRI* BN1 ...... 146 A7
Barcombe Av *SEAF* BN25 ...... 203 J3
Barcombe Cl *SEAF* BN25 ...... 203 J3
Barcombe Mills Rd
  RING/NEW BN8 ...... 126 F4
Barcombe Rd *BRI* BN1 ...... 169 L2
Barcombe Rd *LW/ROSE* BN22 ...... 11 J3
Bardown Rd *WADH* TN5 ...... 44 E8
Bargate Cl *ROTT* BN2 ...... 160 C7
Barham Cl *HAS* TN34 ...... 162 D1
Barkdale *BURH* RH15 ...... 97 H5
Barley Cl *PEAHV* BN10 ...... 190 B4
Barley Dr *BURH* RH15 ...... 96 C2
Barley La *RHAS* TN35 ...... 163 J5
Barley Mow La *HTHF* TN21 ...... 107 H1

Barming Cl *LGNY* BN23 ...... 197 K4
Barnard Ga *HWH* RH16 ...... 48 E7
Barn Cl *HAIL* BN27 ...... 155 L5
  LEW BN7 ...... 171 L1
  PEV BN24 ...... 179 G8
  SEAF BN25 ...... 193 G8
Barn Cottage La *HWH* RH16 ...... 72 A1
Barnes Rd *PTSD* BN41 ...... 167 H6
Barnett Rd *BRI* BN1 ...... 169 H4
Barnett Rd *UCK* TN22 ...... 76 D7
Barnet Wy *HOVE* BN3 ...... 167 L3
Barnfield *CROW* TN6 ...... 40 A4
  LEW BN7 ...... 124 E1
  RTWE/PEM TN2 ...... 19 M7
Barnfield Cl *HAS* TN34 ...... 4 C3
Barnfield Gdns
  HPPT/KEY BN6 ...... 123 L3
The Barnhams *BEXW* TN39 ...... 182 E3
Barn Hatch Cl *LEW* BN7 ...... 2 A8
Barnhorn Cl *BEXW* TN39 ...... 182 C2
Barnhorn Rd *BAT* TN33 ...... 181 K2
  BEXW TN39 ...... 182 A2
Barn La *UCK* TN22 ...... 77 K6
Barnmead *HWH* RH16 ...... 48 D7
Barn Ri *BRI* BN1 ...... 168 D1
  SEAF BN25 ...... 203 G1
Barn Rd *LEW* BN7 ...... 3 J2
Barnside Av *BURH* BN15 ...... 97 J5
Barons Cl *SEAF* BN25 ...... 202 C1
Barons Ct *BURH* RH15 ...... 97 H4
Barons Down Rd *LEW* BN7 ...... 2 A8
Barons Wy *POLE* BN26 ...... 195 M1
Barrack Rd *BEX* TN40 ...... 183 J1
Barrack Sq *WSEA* TN36 ...... 116 F7
Barrhill Av *BRI* BN1 ...... 145 M7
Barrie Cl *LGNY* BN23 ...... 197 L4
Barrington Cl *HWH* RH16 ...... 49 G6
Barrington Wd *HWH* RH16 ...... 48 F6
Barrow Cl *BRI* BN1 ...... 169 J4
Barrowfield Cl *HOVE* BN3 ...... 168 C3
Barrowfield Dr *HOVE* BN3 ...... 168 C4
Barrow Hl *BRI* BN1 ...... 169 J4
Barrow La *RRTW* TN3 ...... 18 F5
Barrow Ri *SLVH* TN37 ...... 162 C1
Barry Wk *ROTT* BN2 ...... 7 K5
Bartholomews *BRI* BN1 ...... 6 E7
Bartley Mill La *PEV* BN24 ...... 197 H1
Bartley Mill Rd *RRTW* TN3 ...... 31 L2
Barton Crs *EGRIN* RH19 ...... 14 A6
Basin Rd South *PTSD* BN41 ...... 166 F8
Baslow Rd *EDN/EASTW* BN20 ...... 206 D7
Bassetts La *CROW* TN6 ...... 42 E3
Batchelor Wy *UCK* TN22 ...... 76 A7
Bateman's La *BUR/ETCH* TN19 ...... 83 G2
Batemans Rd *ROTT* BN2 ...... 170 E7
Bates Rd *BRI* BN1 ...... 168 F4
Bathford Cl *LGNY* BN23 ...... 197 K4
Bath Rd *EAST* BN21 ...... 10 D7
Bath St *BRI* BN1 ...... 6 C3
Battery Hl *RHAS* TN35 ...... 164 B3
Battle Cl *SEAF* BN25 ...... 203 J1
Battle Crs *HAIL* BN27 ...... 155 J6
  SLVH TN37 ...... 162 B2
Battle Gates *BAT* TN33 ...... 137 H2
Battle Hl *BAT* TN33 ...... 137 L3
Battle Rd *BAT* TN33 ...... 138 E6
  HAIL BN27 ...... 155 H6
  SLVH TN37 ...... 138 F8
Batts Bridge Rd *UCK* TN22 ...... 76 A2
Bavant Rd *BRI* BN1 ...... 168 E4
Baxter Rd *LEW* BN7 ...... 2 D3
Baxters La *RHWH* RH17 ...... 36 C8
Baxter St *ROTT* BN2 ...... 7 K3
Bay Av *PEV* BN24 ...... 198 E1
Bayencourt North *BEXW* TN39 ...... 183 H1
Bayhall Rd *RTWE/PEM* TN2 ...... 20 D3
Bayham Rd *HAIL* BN27 ...... 155 K7
  LW/ROSE BN22 ...... 11 J4
  RTWE/PEM TN2 ...... 20 A6
Bayhams Fld *EGRIN* RH19 ...... 22 F8
Bayley's La *POLE* BN26 ...... 177 G3
Baylis Crs *BURH* RH15 ...... 96 E2
Bay Pond Rd *EAST* BN21 ...... 206 D2
Bay Rd *PEV* BN24 ...... 198 D2
Bay Tree Cl *HTHF* TN21 ...... 80 B8
  SHOR BN43 ...... 166 C5
Bay Tree La *POLE* BN26 ...... 177 M6
Baywood Gdns *ROTT* BN2 ...... 170 C5
Bazehill Rd *ROTT* BN2 ...... 189 G3
Beach Cl *SEAF* BN25 ...... 202 D3
The Beachings *PEV* BN24 ...... 198 C2
Beach Rd *LW/ROSE* BN22 ...... 11 K2
  NEWHV BN9 ...... 9 J5
Beachy Head Rd
  EDN/EASTW BN20 ...... 206 B6
  EDN/EASTW BN20 ...... 208 B1
Beacon Cl *BRI* BN1 ...... 169 G4
  CROW TN6 ...... 39 L4
  SEAF BN25 ...... 202 D1
Beacon Dr *SEAF* BN25 ...... 202 D1
Beacon Gdns *CROW* TN6 ...... 39 L3
Beacon Hl *BEXW* TN39 ...... 159 M6
  ROTT BN2 ...... 188 E3
Beacon Hurst *HPPT/KEY* BN6 ...... 123 H3
Beacon La *RBTBR* TN32 ...... 86 E6
  CROW TN6 ...... 39 J6
  HPPT/KEY BN6 ...... 123 K5
  RHAS TN35 ...... 163 L2
  SEAF BN25 ...... 202 D2
Beacon Rd West *CROW* TN6 ...... 39 K4
Beaconsfield Rd *BEX* TN40 ...... 160 C8
  BRI BN1 ...... 6 E2
  BRI BN1 ...... 169 G6
  HAS TN34 ...... 5 H1
  PTSD BN41 ...... 167 H6
  RHWH RH17 ...... 36 C1
Beaconsfield Vls *BRI* BN1 ...... 168 F5
The Beacon *EGRIN* RH19 ...... 22 E7
Beal Cts *BRI* BN1 ...... 169 H4
Beales La *RYE* TN31 ...... 65 H8
Beale St *BURH* RH15 ...... 96 E5
Beamsley Rd *LW/ROSE* BN22 ...... 11 J3
Beaney's La *HAS* TN34 ...... 139 L8

  RHAS TN35 ...... 139 M6
Bear Rd *ROTT* BN2 ...... 169 J6
Bear Yd *LEW* BN7 ...... 3 H6
Beatrice La *EAST* BN21 ...... 10 C5
Beatrice Wk *BEXW* TN39 ...... 160 A8
Beatty Av *BRI* BN1 ...... 146 D7
Beatty Rd *LGNY* BN23 ...... 197 L8
Beauchamp Rd *STLEO* TN38 ...... 162 A5
  STLEO 162 A2
Beauford Rd *HTHF* TN21 ...... 105 M7
Beaufort Crs *SLVH* TN37 ...... 4 A2
Beaufort Rd *SLVH* TN37 ...... 4 A2
Beaufort Ter *ROTT* BN2 ...... 7 J4
Beauharrow Rd *SLVH* TN37 ...... 139 G8
Beaulieu Dr *PEV* BN24 ...... 197 G1
Beaulieu Gdns *SLVH* TN37 ...... 139 J8
Beauport Home Farm Cl
  SLVH TN37 ...... 139 G8
  SLVH TN37 ...... 182 C4
Beau Nash Wy
  RTWE/PEM TN2 ...... 20 B5
Beaver Cl *CROW* TN6 ...... 40 A5
Beckenham Cl *HAIL* BN27 ...... 155 H3
Becket Cl *HAS* TN34 ...... 5 J4
Beckets Wy *UCK* TN22 ...... 103 H1
Beckett Wy *EGRIN* RH19 ...... 13 M6
Beckley Cl *ROTT* BN2 ...... 187 L1
  STLEO TN38 ...... 161 K4
Beckworth Cl *HWH* RH16 ...... 49 C8
Beckworth Cl *HWH* RH16 ...... 49 C8
Bedales Hl *HWH* RH16 ...... 72 D1
Bedelands Cl *BURH* RH15 ...... 97 H1
Bedford Av *BEX* TN40 ...... 183 K2
Bedford Ct *UCK* TN22 ...... 76 C6
Bedford Gv *EAST* BN21 ...... 10 C4
Bedford Pl *BRI* BN1 ...... 6 A4
Bedford Rd *RHAS* TN35 ...... 163 J4
Bedford Sq *BRI* BN1 ...... 6 A7
Bedford St *ROTT* BN2 ...... 7 J8
Bedfordwell Rd *EAST* BN21 ...... 10 D3
  LW/ROSE BN22 ...... 10 D3
Bedgebury Cl *STLEO* TN38 ...... 161 L4
Beecham Pl *STLEO* TN38 ...... 161 M2
Beech Cl *BAT* TN33 ...... 111 H7
  BEXW TN39 ...... 159 J8
  PTSD BN41 ...... 166 F3
  UCK TN22 ...... 76 D6
Beechers Rd *PTSD* BN41 ...... 166 F3
Beeches Cl *HTHF* TN21 ...... 80 B6
Beeches Farm Rd *CROW* TN6 ...... 40 A5
Beeches La *EGRIN* RH19 ...... 14 D8
The Beeches *BRI* BN1 ...... 168 D3
Beech Farm Rd *BAT* TN33 ...... 112 D2
Beechfield Cl *PEV* BN24 ...... 179 J8
Beech Flds *LGNY* BN23 ...... 197 K4
Beech Gdns *CRAWE* RH10 ...... 12 A7
Beech Green La *HRTF* TN7 ...... 16 F6
Beech Gv *ROTT* BN2 ...... 169 L3
Beech Hl *HWH* RH16 ...... 72 B3
Beech Holme *CRAWE* RH10 ...... 12 A6
Beech House La *RBTBR* TN32 ...... 62 C7
Beech Hurst Cl *HWH* RH16 ...... 71 J2
Beeching Cl *BEXW* TN39 ...... 183 H2
Beeching Rd *BEXW* TN39 ...... 183 H2
Beeching Wy *EGRIN* RH19 ...... 13 L5
Beech La *HAWK* TN18 ...... 65 J3
Beech St *RTW* TN1 ...... 20 B1
Beechwood Av *BRI* BN1 ...... 168 F2
Beechwood Cl *BRI* BN1 ...... 168 F2
  BUR/ETCH TN19 ...... 60 B8
  HAIL BN27 ...... 178 C1
Beechwood Crs
  EDN/EASTW BN20 ...... 206 B2
Beechwood Gdns *HAS* TN34 ...... 162 D1
Beechwood La *HTHF* TN21 ...... 106 D1
  LEW BN7 ...... 125 L5
Beechwood Ms *RTWE/PEM* TN2.. 20 C2
Beechwoods *BURH* RH15 ...... 97 C5
Beechy Av *EDN/EASTW* BN20 ...... 206 B2
Beechy Gdns
  EDN/EASTW BN20 ...... 206 B2
Beechy Rd *UCK* TN22 ...... 103 M5
Beeding Av *HOVE* BN3 ...... 167 M3
Bee Rd *PEAHV* BN10 ...... 190 C6
Beggar's La *POY/PYE* BN45 ...... 144 D1
Beggar's Wood Rd
  RING/NEW BN8 ...... 73 J8
Belfast St *HOVE* BN3 ...... 168 B8
Belfry Orch *UCK* TN22 ...... 102 D1
The Belfry *HAIL* BN27 ...... 155 G6
Belgrave Crs *SEAF* BN25 ...... 202 F1
Belgrave Pl *ROTT* BN2 ...... 7 L9
Belgrave Rd *RTW* TN1 ...... 20 A2
  SEAF BN25 ...... 202 D2
Bell Alley Rd *BUR/ETCH* TN19 ...... 60 B8
Bell Banks Rd *HAIL* BN27 ...... 155 J7
Belle Hl *BEX* TN40 ...... 183 J1
Bellevue Gdns *ROTT* BN2 ...... 7 K7
Belle Vue Rd *LW/ROSE* BN22 ...... 11 J1
Bell Hammer *EGRIN* RH19 ...... 13 L6
Bellhurst Rd *RBTBR* TN32 ...... 85 G8
Bellingham Cl *SLVH* TN37 ...... 162 B2
Bellingham Crs *HOVE* BN3 ...... 167 K6
Bell La *LEW* BN7 ...... 2 D1
  UCK TN22 ...... 52 A2
  UCK TN22 ...... 76 C8
Bell Wk *UCK* TN22 ...... 76 B8
Belmont *BRI* BN1 ...... 6 B2
Belmont Cl *HPPT/KEY* BN6 ...... 122 C1
Belmont La *HPPT/KEY* BN6 ...... 122 C2
Belmont Rd *RHAS* TN35 ...... 5 M4
  UCK TN22 ...... 76 C7
Belmont St *BRI* BN1 ...... 6 F3
Belmore Rd *LW/ROSE* BN22 ...... 11 G4
Belton Rd *ROTT* BN2 ...... 7 L1
Beltring Rd *LW/ROSE* BN22 ...... 11 H4
Beltring Ter *LW/ROSE* BN22 ...... 11 H3
Belvedere Gdns *CROW* TN6 ...... 40 A5
  SEAF BN25 ...... 203 G1
Belvedere Pk *STLEO* TN38 ...... 162 A6
Bembridge Rd *LGNY* BN23 ...... 197 H3
Bembridge St *ROTT* BN2 ...... 7 L1
Bembrook Rd *HAS* TN34 ...... 5 L4
Bemzells La *HAIL* BN27 ...... 133 K4

  WADH TN5 ...... 44 A1
Blackstone Wy *BURH* RH15 ...... 97 G1
Blackthorn Cl *BRI* BN1 ...... 168 D3
  LW/ROSE BN22 ...... 196 E4
  PTSD BN41 ...... 167 H4
  SLVH TN37 ...... 162 C2
Blackthorns *HWH* RH16 ...... 49 G7
Blackthorns Cl *HWH* RH16 ...... 49 G7
The Blackthorns *BURH* RH15 ...... 97 H1
Blackthorn Wy *RHAS* TN35 ...... 164 F2
Blackwater Rd
  EDN/EASTW BN20 ...... 10 C9
Blackwell Farm Rd *EGRIN* RH19.. 13 M3
Blackwell Hollow *EGRIN* RH19 ...... 13 M4
Blackwell Rd *EGRIN* RH19 ...... 13 M4
Blakeney Av *PEAHV* BN10 ...... 8 A5
Blaker St *ROTT* BN2 ...... 7 G7
Blakes Wy *LGNY* BN23 ...... 197 M8
Blatchington Cl *SEAF* BN25 ...... 202 F2
Blatchington Hl *SEAF* BN25 ...... 202 E2
Blatchington Mill Dr
  PEV BN24 ...... 197 J1
Blatchington Rd *HOVE* BN3 ...... 168 B7
  RTW TN1 ...... 20 A5
  SEAF BN25 ...... 202 E3
Bleak Rd *LYDD* TN29 ...... 95 J8
Blenheim Cl *EGRIN* RH19 ...... 14 A3
Blenheim Flds *FROW* RH18 ...... 24 E3
Blenheim Pl *BRI* BN1 ...... 6 F5
Blenheim Wy *POLE* BN26 ...... 178 D8
  WADH TN5 ...... 46 C3
Bletchinglye La *CROW* TN6 ...... 41 L5
Blind La *RING/NEW* BN8 ...... 74 E8
Blois Rd *LEW* BN7 ...... 2 B2
Blomfield Rd *SLVH* TN37 ...... 4 B6
Bloomsbury Pl *ROTT* BN2 ...... 7 K9
Bloomsbury St *ROTT* BN2 ...... 7 K8
Blount Av *EGRIN* RH19 ...... 13 J5
Bluebell Cl *EGRIN* RH19 ...... 13 H5
  HWH RH16 ...... 71 M2
Blue Haze Av *SEAF* BN25 ...... 203 H2
Bluemans La *BAT* TN33 ...... 139 G3
Bluestone Cl *STLEO* TN38 ...... 161 M4
Blunts Wood Crs *RHWH* RH17 ...... 48 B8
Blunts Wood Rd *RHWH* RH17 ...... 48 B8
The Blytons *EGRIN* RH19 ...... 13 H5
Boarders La *WADH* TN5 ...... 45 J3
Boast La *RING/NEW* BN8 ...... 126 E1
Bocking La *WADH* TN5 ...... 43 L2
Boddingtons La
  HPPT/KEY BN6 ...... 123 K3
Bodiam Av *BEX* TN40 ...... 160 D8
Bodiam Cl *ROTT* BN2 ...... 170 D5
  SEAF BN25 ...... 203 J2
Bodiam Crs *LW/ROSE* BN22 ...... 197 G4
Bodiam Dr *STLEO* TN38 ...... 161 K4
Bodiam Rd *HAWK* TN18 ...... 63 M4
Bodle Crs *BEXW* TN39 ...... 160 B7
Bohemia Rd *SLVH* TN37 ...... 4 A4
  STLEO TN38 ...... 162 B5
Bolding Wy *HWH* RH16 ...... 71 K4
Bolebrooke Rd *BEX* TN40 ...... 183 K3
Bolney Av *PEAHV* BN10 ...... 190 C8
Bolney Rd *ROTT* BN2 ...... 169 M2
Bolnore Rd *HWH* RH16 ...... 71 J2
  HOVE BN3 ...... 167 L7
Bolton Cl *UCK* TN22 ...... 76 A8
Bolton Rd *EAST* BN21 ...... 10 F7
Boltro Rd *RHWH* RH16 ...... 71 K1
Bonchurch Rd *ROTT* BN2 ...... 7 L1
Bond St *BRI* BN1 ...... 6 E6
Bonfire La *RHWH* RH17 ...... 50 C2
Boniface Cl *PEV* BN24 ...... 179 J8
Bonny Wood Rd
  HPPT/KEY BN6 ...... 122 E3
Booker Cl *CROW* TN6 ...... 40 A5
Bopeep Bostal *POLE* BN26 ...... 175 H7
Bopeep La *POLE* BN26 ...... 175 H6
Bordehill La *HWH* RH16 ...... 48 D2
Border Ct *EGRIN* RH19 ...... 13 M2
Borders La *BUR/ETCH* TN19 ...... 61 G3
Boreham Hl *HAIL* BN27 ...... 158 A3
Boreham La *HAIL* BN27 ...... 157 L5
Borough La *EDN/EASTW* BN20 ...... 206 D3
Borough St *BRI* BN1 ...... 6 A6
Borrowdale Cl *LGNY* BN23 ...... 197 G2
Borrow King Cl *ROTT* BN2 ...... 169 K5
Boscawen Cl *LGNY* BN23 ...... 197 M7
Boscobel Rd *STLEO* TN38 ...... 162 A7
Boscobel Rd North
  STLEO TN38 ...... 162 A6
Boship Cl *LGNY* BN23 ...... 197 G2
Bostal Rd *RING/NEW* BN8 ...... 174 B2
Boston La *LGNY* BN23 ...... 197 M7
Boston Rd *HWH* RH16 ...... 72 A1
Boston St *BRI* BN1 ...... 6 E4
Bough Beeches *BURH* RH15 ...... 97 J5
Boughey Pl *LEW* BN7 ...... 2 F1
The Boulevard *PEV* BN24 ...... 180 E8
Boundary & Station Roads
  PTSD BN41 ...... 187 J8
Boundary Rd *ROTT* BN2 ...... 187 L3
  RTWE/PEM TN2 ...... 20 D5
The Boundary *RRTW* TN3 ...... 19 H3
  SEAF BN25 ...... 202 E4
Bourg-de-peage Av
  EGRIN RH19 ...... 14 A5
Bourne La *RBTBR* TN32 ...... 62 F6
Bourne St *LW/ROSE* BN22 ...... 11 G5
The Bourne *HAS* TN34 ...... 5 L5
  HPPT/KEY BN6 ...... 96 B3
Bowden Ri *SBGH/RUST* BN4 ...... 192 E8
Bowen Rd *SBGH/RUST* TN4 ...... 19 H1
Bower Cl *SLVH* TN37 ...... 162 B2
The Bower *RHWH* RH17 ...... 71 K1
Bowers Pl *CRAWE* RH10 ...... 12 B6
Bowley Rd *HAIL* BN27 ...... 155 J7
Bowmans Dr *BAT* TN33 ...... 111 K8
Bowood Av *LW/ROSE* BN22 ...... 197 H6
Bowring Wy *ROTT* BN2 ...... 7 M8
Bowsprit Ms *STLEO* TN38 ...... 138 E7
Boxes La *RHWH* RH17 ...... 50 C2
Boxgrove Cl *BEX* TN40 ...... 183 M2
Box La *EGRIN* RH19 ...... 14 E8
Box's La *RHWH* RH17 ...... 36 C8

Boyce's St *BRI* BN1 .... 6 D7
Boyne Pk *SBGH/RUST* TN4 .... 19 M2
Boyne Rd *RHAS* TN35 .... 163 J5
Brackenbury Cl *PTSD* BN41 .. 167 H4 ▣
Bracken Cl *CROW* TN6 .... 40 C5 ▣
RTWE/PEM TN2 .... 20 E1 ▣
Brackendale *RHAS* TN35 .... 163 K4
Brackenhill *HRTF* TN7 .... 26 A5
Bracken Rd *EDN/EASTW* BN20 .. 206 A4 ▣
RTWE/PEM TN2 .... 20 E1
SEAF BN25 .... 203 G4
Bracken Wy *HTHF* TN21 .... 80 E5
Brackerne Cl *BEXW* TN39 .... 182 C4
Bradford Rd *LEW* BN7 .... 2 D6
Bradford St *EAST* BN21 ...... 206 C4
Brading Cl *HAS* TN34 .... 4 F1
LGNY BN23 .... 197 H2
Brading Rd *ROTT* BN2 .... 7 K2
Bradley Rd *HAIL* BN27 .... 157 J5
RRTW TN3 .... 17 K1
Braemore Rd *HOVE* BN3 .... 167 L8
Braeside Av *BRI* BN1 .... 145 K7
Brailsford Rd *HOVE* BN3 ..... 167 M3
PEAHV BN10 .... 190 C7
Bramber Av North
PEAHV BN10 .... 190 C6
Bramber Cl *HWH* RH16 .... 71 K2
PEAHV BN10 .... 190 C6 ▣
SEAF BN25 .... 202 F4 ▣
Bramber La *SEAF* BN25 .... 202 F4
Bramber Rd *SEAF* BN25 .... 202 F4
Bramber Wy *BURH* RH15 .... 97 G2
Bramble Cl *LGNY* BN23 .... 197 H3
Bramble Cft *CROW* TN6 .... 40 D5
Brambledean Rd *PTSD* BN41 .. 167 H7
Bramble Dr *HAIL* BN27 .... 155 G8
Bramble Gdns *BURH* RH15 .... 96 D2
Bramble Ri *BRI* BN1 .... 168 C1
Brambles *HPPT/KEY* BN6 ...... 122 F1 ▣
Brambleside *UCK* TN22 .... 76 A8
The Brambles *RHWH* RH17 ..... 48 A8
Brambletye La *FROW* RH18 .... 24 D3
Brambletye La *ROTT* BN2 ..... 189 K5
Bramble Wy *RHAS* TN35 .... 164 F2
Bramley Rd *POLE* BN26 .... 178 C8
Bramleys *LEW* BN7 .... 171 L1
Brampton Av *BEXW* TN39 ...... 182 F2
Brampton Rd *LW/ROSE* BN22 .. 196 F5
Brand Rd *LW/ROSE* BN22 ...... 196 E5
Brands Cl *NEWHV* BN9 .... 191 K4
Brangwyn Av *BRI* BN1 .... 145 L8
Brangwyn Crs *BRI* BN1 .... 145 L8
Brangwyn Dr *BRI* BN1 .... 145 K8
Brangwyn Wy *BRI* BN1 .... 168 E1
Branksome Rd *STLEO* TN38 .... 162 A6
Branston Rd *LW/ROSE* BN22 .. 196 D5
Brassey Av *LW/ROSE* BN22 .... 196 D5
Brassey Rd *BEX* TN40 .... 183 K3
Brasslands Dr *PTSD* BN41 .... 166 F5
Braybon Av *BRI* BN1 .... 168 F2
Braybrooke Cl *HAS* TN34 ..... 4 F5
Braybrooke Rd *HAS* TN34 ..... 5 C5
Braybrooke Ter *HAS* TN34 .... 4 F5
Braypool La *BRI* BN1 .... 145 K6
Brazen Cl *NEWHV* BN9 .... 191 J5
Breadsell La *BAT* TN33 ...... 138 D7
BAT TN33 .... 161 J1
Bread St *BRI* BN1 .... 6 E6
Brede Cl *LW/ROSE* BN22 ...... 197 K8
ROTT BN2 .... 187 L1
STLEO TN38 .... 138 F7
Brede HI *RYE* TN31 .... 114 A4
Brede La *BAT* TN33 .... 112 F5
Brede Valley Vw *WSEA* TN36 .. 141 L1
Brendon Cl *LGNY* BN23 .... 197 L2
RTWE/PEM TN2 .... 20 D1 ▣
Brendon Ri *HAS* TN34 .... 163 H5
Brentwood Cl *BRI* BN1 .... 169 H3 ▣
Brentwood Crs *BRI* BN1 ...... 169 H3
Brentwood Rd *BRI* BN1 .... 169 H3
Bretland Rd *SBGH/RUST* TN4 .. 19 K2
Brett Dr *BEX* TN40 .... 183 M1
Bretton *BURH* RH15 .... 96 E1
Bretts Fld *PEAHV* BN10 ...... 190 C4
Brewers Gv *MAYF* TN20 .... 57 H4 ▣
Brewer St *ROTT* BN2 .... 7 H2
RRTW TN3 .... 33 J1
Briar Cl *RHAS* TN35 .... 165 G1
ROTT BN2 .... 170 D7
Briarcroft Rd *ROTT* BN2 ..... 170 D7
Briar Pl *LGNY* BN23 .... 197 H3
Brickhurst La *RING/NEW* BN8 .. 129 J6
Brick Kiln La *UCK* TN22 ..... 55 K8
Bricklands *CRAWE* RH10 ...... 12 B7
Brickyard La *CRAWE* RH10 .... 12 B6
CROW TN6 .... 41 M2
The Bricky *PEAHV* BN10 ...... 190 D6
Bridge Cl *BURH* RH15 .... 96 F2
HTHF TN21 .... 106 A7
Bridge End *PEV* BN24 .... 180 B8
Bridge Farm Rd *UCK* TN22 .... 76 C8
Bridgelands *RING/NEW* BN8 .. 126 D2
Bridgemere Rd
LW/ROSE BN22 .... 197 H8
Bridge Rd *HWH* RH16 .... 48 F7
Bridgersmill *HWH* RH16 ...... 48 D7
Bridger Wy *CROW* TN6 .... 39 M5
Bridge St *NEWHV* BN9 .... 9 G3
Bridge Wy *STLEO* TN38 .... 161 J8
Bridgewick Cl *LEW* BN7 ...... 3 G2
Bridle Wy *PEAHV* BN10 .... 190 A7
Briers Av *SLVH* TN37 .... 162 C3
Briers Gdns *SLVH* TN37 ...... 162 C3 ▣
Brigden St *BRI* BN1 .... 6 C2
Brightland Rd
EDN/EASTW BN20 .... 206 D3
Brightling Av *RHAS* TN35 .... 163 K2
Brightling Rd *POLE* BN26 .... 196 A1
RBTBR TN32 .... 84 A6
Brighton Pl *BRI* BN1 .... 6 E7 ▣
Brighton Rd *HPPT/KEY* BN6 .. 122 D4
LEW BN7 .... 148 E2
NEWHV BN9 .... 8 C4
Brills La *BRI* BN1 .... 6 E8 ▣
Brincliffe *CROW* TN6 .... 39 L3
Brinkers La *WADH* TN5 .... 44 A4
Bristol Gdns *ROTT* BN2 ...... 187 L2 ▣
Bristol Ga *ROTT* BN2 .... 7 M8

Bristol Ms *ROTT* BN2 .... 187 L2
Bristol Pl *ROTT* BN2 .... 187 L2
Bristol Rd *ROTT* BN2 .... 7 J8
STLEO TN38 .... 162 A3
Bristol St *ROTT* BN2 .... 187 L2
Brittany Ms *STLEO* TN38 ..... 162 B7
Brittany Rd *HOVE* BN3 .... 167 K8
STLEO TN38 .... 162 B7
Britten Cl *LGNY* BN23 .... 197 K3
Brittenden La *HTHF* TN21 .... 104 F3
Britts Farm Rd *UCK* TN22 .... 77 J3
Broadcroft *RTWE/PEM* TN2 .. 19 M6
Broadfield *EGRIN* RH19 ...... 24 E2
Broadfields *ROTT* BN2 .... 169 L3 ▣
Broadfields Rd *ROTT* BN2 .... 169 L3 ▣
Broad Gn *ROTT* BN2 .... 170 E8
Broad Green Av *BURH* RH15 .. 97 J4
Broad Gv *FROW* RH18 .... 20 A5 ▣
Broadhill Cl *HTHF* TN21 ..... 80 E5
Broadlands *BURH* RH15 .... 97 H6
RHAS TN35 .... 163 K2
Broad La *RRTW* TN3 .... 18 A3
Broadmead
RTWE/PEM TN2 .... 19 L6
Broadmead Av
RTWE/PEM TN2 .... 19 M6 ▣
Broad Oak *BRI* BN1 .... 18 B8
Broad Oak Cl *LW/ROSE* BN22 .. 197 G2 ▣
RTWE/PEM TN2 .... 19 M5
Broadoak La *BEXW* TN39 ...... 182 C4
Broad Rig Av *RHAS* TN35 ..... 167 K2
Broad Rd *EDN/EASTW* BN20 .. 195 M3
Broadstone Cl *FROW* RH18 .... 25 G4
Broad St *RHWH* RH17 .... 48 A8
ROTT BN2 .... 6 F8
SEAF BN25 .... 202 E3
WSEA TN36 .... 115 J3
Broad Vw *BEXW* TN39 .... 159 M8
HTHF TN3 .... 80 E5
Broadview Cl
EDN/EASTW BN20 .... 195 M2 ▣
The Broadwalk *BEXW* TN39 .. 182 B2
Broadwater Down
RTWE/PEM TN2 .... 19 M6
Broadwater La *RTWE/PEM* TN2 .. 19 M5
Broadwater Ri *RTWE/PEM* TN2 .. 19 M5
Broadwater Wy
LW/ROSE BN22 .... 196 F6
Broad Wy *RHAS* TN35 .... 164 F1
The Broadway *CROW* TN6 .... 39 M4
HWH RH16 .... 71 K1
LW/ROSE BN22 .... 196 D5
POLE BN26 .... 193 M3
RHAS TN35 .... 163 K2 ▣
RRTW TN3 .... 33 H1
Brockley Rd *BEXW* TN39 ...... 183 G3
Brocks Gyhll
EDN/EASTW BN20 .... 196 A3 ▣
Brodie Pl *EAST* BN21 .... 206 D2 ▣
Brodrick Cl *LW/ROSE* BN22 .. 196 F5
Brodrick Rd *LW/ROSE* BN22 .. 196 D4
Bromley Cl *HPPT/KEY* BN6 .. 123 G2
LGNY BN23 .... 197 J4
Bromley Rd *ROTT* BN2 .... 7 G1
SEAF BN25 .... 203 H2
Brompton Cl *BRI* BN1 .... 145 L8
The Brontes *EGRIN* RH19 .... 13 K5 ▣
Brook Av *HPPT/KEY* BN6 ...... 122 F3
Brook Cl *CROW* TN6 .... 40 D5
EGRIN RH19 .... 14 B5
Brooke Gdns *RING/NEW* BN8 .. 74 D8
Brooker Pl *HOVE* BN3 .... 168 A7
Brooker St *HOVE* BN3 .... 168 A7
Brookfield Rd *BEX* TN40 ..... 183 L2 ▣
Brookhouse Bottom
RHWH RH17 .... 51 J3
Brookhouse La *UCK* TN22 .... 103 G3
Brookland Cl *HAS* TN34 ...... 5 H2
PEV BN24 .... 180 E2
Brooklands Av *CROW* TN6 .. 39 M7
Brooklands Wy *EGRIN* RH19 .. 13 K6
Brook La *HWH* RH16 .... 48 F7
RING/NEW BN8 .... 150 A8
Brooklyn Rd *SEAF* BN25 ...... 202 E3
Brookmead Cl *LW/ROSE* BN22 .. 11 G1
Brooks Cl *LEW* BN7 .... 3 H4
NEWHV BN9 .... 8 F5
Brookside *NEWHV* BN9 .... 191 H4
UCK TN22 .... 76 A8
Brookside Av *POLE* BN26 .... 177 M7
Brooks Rd *LEW* BN7 .... 3 H4
The Brooks *BURH* RH15 .... 96 E1
Brook St *HAS* TN34 .... 5 H5
LEW BN7 .... 2 F5
POLE BN26 .... 177 M8
Brooks Wy *LYDD* TN29 .... 121 J1
Brookway *BURH* RH15 .... 97 J3
HWH RH16 .... 49 G6
Broomans La *LEW* BN7 .... 3 G5
Broom Cl *LW/ROSE* BN22 ...... 196 D4
Broomfield Av *PEAHV* BN10 .. 189 M7
Broomfield Dr *PTSD* BN41 .... 167 H7
Broomfield St
EDN/EASTW BN20 .... 206 C2
Broomgrove Rd *HAS* TN34 .... 5 L2
Broomham La *RING/NEW* BN8 .. 130 A7
Broom La *RRTW* TN3 .... 18 F5
Broom Pk *RRTW* TN3 .... 18 E3
Browning Rd *HTHF* TN21 ...... 80 A7
The Brownings *EGRIN* RH19 .. 13 J5 ▣
Brown Jack Av *POLE* BN26 .. 177 M4 ▣
Brownleaf Rd *ROTT* BN2 ...... 170 D8
Browns Cl *UCK* TN22 .... 76 D6
Browns La *HTHF* TN21 .... 79 H8
UCK TN22 .... 76 D5
Browns Wd *EGRIN* RH19 .... 13 L2
The Brow *BURH* RH15 .... 97 G4
EDN/EASTW BN20 .... 205 H4
ROTT BN2 .... 170 D6
Broyle Cl *RING/NEW* BN8 .... 127 M6
Broyle La *RING/NEW* BN8 .... 127 M5
Broyle Paddock
RING/NEW BN8 .... 127 M7
The Broyle *RING/NEW* BN8 .. 128 D6
Bruce Cl *HWH* RH16 .... 71 L3
Brunel Rd *STLEO* TN38 .... 161 L3
Brunswick Ms *HOVE* BN3 ...... 186 D1 ▣
Brunswick Pl *HOVE* BN3 ...... 168 D8
Brunswick Rd *HOVE* BN3 ...... 168 D8

Brunswick Sq *HOVE* BN3 .. 186 D1
Brunswick St East *HOVE* BN3 .. 186 D1
Brunswick St West
HOVE BN3 .... 186 D1 ▣
Brunswick Ter *HOVE* BN3 .. 186 D1
Brushes La *HWH* RH16 .... 49 H6
Bryants Fld *CROW* TN6 .... 39 J3
Brydges Cl *LW/ROSE* BN22 .. 197 J8
Buci Crs *SHOR* BN43 .... 166 C6
Buckholt Av *BEX* TN40 .... 161 C8
Buckhurst Cl
EDN/EASTW BN20 .... 196 B6
EGRIN RH19 .... 13 J3
LEW BN7 .... 2 F1
Buckhurst La *CROW* TN6 ...... 42 F2
Buckhurst Rd *BEX* TN40 ...... 183 J2
PEAHV BN10 .... 189 M7
Buckhurst Wy *EGRIN* RH19 .. 13 J3
Buckingham Cl *SEAF* BN25 .. 202 E2 ▣
SHOR BN43 .... 166 A6 ▣
Buckingham Dr *EGRIN* RH19 .. 14 A7
Buckingham Pl *BRI* BN1 ...... 6 C3
Buckingham Rd *BRI* BN1 ...... 6 C4
RTW TN1 .... 20 B4
STLEO TN38 .... 162 A2
Buckingham St *BRI* BN1 ...... 6 D4 ▣
Buckland Rd *SEAF* BN25 ...... 202 F1
Buckle By-pass *SEAF* BN25 .. 202 C2
Buckle Cl *SEAF* BN25 .... 202 C2
Buckle Dr *SEAF* BN25 .... 202 C2
Buckle Ri *SEAF* BN25 .... 202 C2
Bucklers Cl *RTWE/PEM* TN2 .. 20 C3 ▣
Buckler St *PTSD* BN41 .... 167 H6 ▣
Buckley Cl *HOVE* BN3 .... 167 L2 ▣
Buckley Pl *CRAWE* RH10 .... 12 A6
Buckthorn Cl *SEAF* BN25 .... 203 J3 ▣
Buckwell Ct *LEW* BN7 .... 2 B1
Buckwell Ri *HAIL* BN27 ...... 156 E1
Buddens Gn *RYE* TN31 .... 89 H2
Budd's La *LEW* BN7 .... 67 L4
Bugsell La *RBTBR* TN32 ...... 84 F1
Bulbeck Cl *BURH* RH15 .... 96 E5
Bulldogs Bank *EGRIN* RH19 .. 34 F1
Buller Cl *CROW* TN6 .... 40 A5
Buller Rd *ROTT* BN2 .... 169 K5
Bullfinch Gdns *UCK* TN22 .. 102 D2
Bull La *LEW* BN7 .... 2 F7 ▣
Bulrush Pl *STLEO* TN38 ...... 161 L5
Bulverhythe Rd *STLEO* TN38 .. 161 K8
Bungalows *UCK* TN22 .... 103 H1
The Bungalows *UCK* TN22 .. 103 H1
Burchetts Cl *HWH* RH16 ...... 71 K4
Burden Pl *STLEO* TN38 .... 162 A3
Burdett Rd *CROW* TN6 .... 40 C5
SBGH/RUST TN4 .... 19 H2 ▣
Burdocks Dr *BURH* RH15 ...... 97 J5
Burfield Cl *LW/ROSE* BN22 .. 11 H5
Burgh Hl *BUR/ETCH* TN19 .. 61 L4
Burgh La *RING/NEW* BN8 .... 174 D1
Burhill Wy *STLEO* TN38 ...... 161 M7
Burleigh Cl *CRAWE* RH10 .. 12 B6
Burleigh Cl *CRAWE* RH10 .. 12 C7
Burleigh Pl *LW/ROSE* BN22 .. 197 J8 ▣
Burleigh Wy *CRAWE* RH10 .. 12 B6
Burlington Gdns *PTSD* BN41 .. 167 J5
Burlington Pl *EAST* BN21 .... 10 F8
Burlington Rd *EAST* BN21 .. 11 G7
Burlington St *ROTT* BN2 ..... 7 J9
Burlow Cl *LW/ROSE* BN22 .. 196 C3 ▣
ROTT BN2 .... 187 L1
Burma Cl *HWH* RH16 .... 72 C2
Burners Cl *BURH* RH15 .... 97 K5
Burnham Cl *ROTT* BN2 .... 170 F7
Burnside *POLE* BN26 .... 178 A8 ▣
Burns Wy *EGRIN* RH19 .... 13 J5
Burnthouse Bostall
HPPT/KEY BN6 .... 123 J7
Burnt House Cl *HAWK* TN18 .. 64 C1
Burnt House La *RRTW* TN3 .... 18 F1
Burnt Lodge La *WADH* TN5 .... 45 H5
Burnt Oak Rd *UCK* TN22 ...... 54 B5
Burrell Rd *HWH* RH16 .... 48 D8
Burrells La *UCK* TN22 .... 53 G7
The Burrells *SHOR* BN43 .... 166 B8
Burrow Down
EDN/EASTW BN20 .... 206 A1
Burry Rd *SLVH* TN37 .... 162 C1
Burstead Cl *BRI* BN1 .... 169 H3
Burston Gdns *EGRIN* RH19 .. 13 K2
Burstowhill La *RHWH* RH17 .. 34 D8
Burton Rd *EAST* BN21 .... 10 A1
Burton Vls *HOVE* BN3 .... 168 D6 ▣
Burwash Cl *HAS* TN34 .... 163 G1 ▣
LGNY BN23 .... 197 H2
Burwash Rd *HOVE* BN3 .... 167 L3
HTHF TN21 .... 80 C6
Bushbury La *UCK* TN22 .... 104 A3
Bush Cl *PEAHV* BN10 .... 190 A5
ROTT BN2 .... 170 D5
Busheyfields *HAIL* BN27 .... 155 G6 ▣
Bush Farm Dr *PTSD* BN41 .... 167 H4
Bush Rd *NEWHV* BN9 .... 8 C1
Bushy Cft *ROTT* BN2 .... 182 F1
Bushy Gill *RRTW* TN3 .... 19 G3
Butcherfield La *HRTF* TN7 .... 16 A7
Butcher's La *RHAS* TN35 .... 140 D4
Bute St *ROTT* BN2 .... 7 L6
Butler's Green Rd *HWH* RH16 .. 71 J2
Butler's La *HWH* RH16 .... 71 J1
Butlers Wy *RING/NEW* BN8 .. 150 D1 ▣
Butterbox La *RHWH* RH17 .... 73 K2
Buttercup Wk *BRI* BN1 .... 146 B8
Butterfield *EGRIN* RH19 .. 13 H5
Buttermere Wy *LGNY* BN23 .. 197 J2 ▣
Butts Fld *HAIL* BN27 .... 155 J8
Buttsfield La *RING/NEW* BN8 .. 147 J4
Butts La *EDN/EASTW* BN20 .. 196 A5
WADH TN5 .... 43 L4
Butts Rd *STHW* BN42 .... 166 E7
Buxshalls HI *HWH* RH16 ...... 49 J5
Buxted Cl *BRI* BN1 .... 169 H1
Buxted Wood La *UCK* TN22 .. 77 K1
Buxton Dr *BEXW* TN39 .... 160 B8
Buxton Rd *BRI* BN1 .... 6 B2
EDN/EASTW BN20 .... 206 E6
Bydown *SEAF* BN25 .... 203 G2
The Byeways *SEAF* BN25 ...... 202 F2
The Byeway *BEXW* TN39 .... 182 D1

HAS TN34 .... 162 F2
Byfields Cft *BEXW* TN39 .... 182 F1
Byland Cl *LW/ROSE* BN22 .... 196 E3
Byng Rd *SBGH/RUST* TN4 ...... 19 L1
Byron Gv *EGRIN* RH19 .... 13 J6
Byron St *HOVE* BN3 .... 168 A7
By Sunte *HWH* RH16 .... 48 F6
Byways *HAS* TN34 .... 139 K8
The Byway *HAS* TN34 .... 139 K8
The Byway *BRI* BN1 .... 169 L1
Byworth Cl *BEXW* TN39 .... 159 J8
ROTT BN2 .... 169 M8

C

Cabbage Stalk La
SBGH/RUST TN4 .... 19 L4
Cabot Cl *LGNY* BN23 .... 198 A3
Caburn Cl *LW/ROSE* BN22 .... 197 G2 ▣
Caburn Crs *LEW* BN7 .... 2 A3
Caburn Rd *HOVE* BN3 .... 6 B2
Caburn Wy *HAIL* BN27 .... 155 G8
Cackleberry La *HAIL* BN27 .. 155 G8
Cackle St *RYE* TN31 .... 114 A4
UCK TN22 .... 52 E5
Cadborough Cliff *RYE* TN31 .. 116 F2
Cade St *HTHF* TN21 .... 81 M2
Cairngorm Cl *LGNY* BN23 .... 197 K3
Cairo Av *PEAHV* BN10 .... 190 A7
Cairo Av South *PEAHV* BN10 .. 190 A7
Caister's Cl *HOVE* BN3 ...... 168 C6
Calbourne *HWH* RH16 .... 71 K1 ▣
Caldbec HI *BAT* TN33 .... 137 K1
Caldecot La *LYDD* TN29 ...... 95 K4
Caldicotts La *HAIL* BN27 .. 154 C3
Caledonian Rd *ROTT* BN2 ..... 7 H1
Calgary Rd *BEXW* TN39 .... 160 B7
Callums Wk *BEX* TN40 .... 183 L1
Calverley Ct *RTWE/PEM* TN2 .. 20 C3 ▣
Calverley Pk *RTWE/PEM* TN2 .. 20 B3
Calverley Park Crs
RTWE/PEM TN2 .... 20 B3
Calverley Park Gdns *RTW* TN1 .. 20 B3
RTW TN1 .... 20 B2
RTWE/PEM TN2 .... 20 B3
Calverley St *RTW* TN1 .... 20 B2
Calvert Cl *UCK* TN22 .... 76 A7
Calvert Rd *HAS* TN34 .... 5 K2
UCK TN22 .... 76 A7
Camber Cl *BEX* TN40 .... 160 E8
Camber Dr *PEV* BN24 .... 180 F8
Camberlot Rd *HAIL* BN27 .. 154 A5
Camber Rd *RYE* TN31 .... 117 M2
Camber Wy *PEV* BN24 .... 180 F8
Cambridge Gdns *HAS* TN34 .... 4 F7
RTWE/PEM TN2 .... 20 B4 ▣
Cambridge Gv *HOVE* BN3 ...... 168 C7
Cambridge Rd *BEXW* TN39 .... 160 C8
HAS TN34 .... 4 E7
HOVE BN3 .... 168 C7
LW/ROSE BN22 .... 11 H4
Cambridge St
RTWE/PEM TN2 .... 20 C3 ▣
Cambridge Wy *UCK* TN22 .. 76 C5
Camden HI *RTWE/PEM* TN2 .. 20 B3 ▣
RTWE/PEM TN2 .... 20 B3 ▣
Camden Pk *RTWE/PEM* TN2 .. 20 B3 ▣
RTWE/PEM TN2 .... 20 B3 ▣
Camden Rd *EAST* BN21 .... 10 D7
RTW TN1 .... 20 B3
Camden St *PTSD* BN41 .... 167 J8 ▣
Camelford St *ROTT* BN2 ..... 7 G8
Cameron Cl *HAIL* BN27 .... 155 G6
Campbell Cl *UCK* TN22 .... 76 C5
Campbell Crs *EGRIN* RH19 .. 13 H5
Campbell Rd *BRI* BN1 .... 6 D1
Camperdown St *BEXW* TN39 .. 160 A7
Canada Cl *PEAHV* BN10 .... 190 B5 ▣
Canada Wy *BEXW* TN39 .... 160 B7
Canadia Rd *BAT* TN33 .... 111 K6
Canfield Cl *ROTT* BN2 .... 169 K5
Canfield Rd *ROTT* BN2 .... 169 K5 ▣
Canning St *ROTT* BN2 .... 7 K6
Cannon Pl *BRI* BN1 .... 6 C6
Cannon St *LYDD* TN29 .... 95 J8
Cansiron La *EDEN* TN8 .... 15 L4
FROW RH18 .... 25 L1
Cantelupe Rd *BEX* TN40 ...... 183 K3
EGRIN RH19 .... 13 M5
Canterbury Cl
LW/ROSE BN22 .... 196 C4 ▣
Canterbury Ri *HAS* TN34 .... 162 E3
Canterbury Ri *HAS* TN34 .... 162 E3
Cantercrow HI *NEWHV* BN9 .. 191 M4
Cants Cl *BURH* RH15 .... 97 J2
Cants La *BURH* RH15 .... 97 J2
Canute Cl *LGNY* BN23 .... 197 M6 ▣
Canute Rd *RHAS* TN35 .... 163 G3
Capel Av *PEAHV* BN10 .... 190 B5
Capenors *BURH* RH15 .... 96 F5
Caple Gdns *STLEO* TN38 ...... 162 B3
Carden Av *BRI* BN1 .... 168 F1
Carden Cl *BRI* BN1 .... 146 A8
Carden Crs *BRI* BN1 .... 146 A8
Carden HI *BRI* BN1 .... 169 H1
Card HI *FROW* RH18 .... 24 F5
Cardiff St *STLEO* TN38 ...... 4 A7
Cardinals Cl *BEX* TN40 ...... 160 F8
Carew Rd *EAST* BN21 .... 206 C2
Carey Down *PEAHV* BN10 ...... 190 B5 ▣
Carfax Cl *BEXW* TN39 .... 160 B6
Carinus Gdns *STLEO* TN38 .. 162 A1 ▣
Carisbrooke Cl *LGNY* BN23 .. 197 H2
Carisbrooke Rd *ROTT* BN2 ... 7 L2
STLEO TN38 .... 162 B7
Carlisle Pde *HAS* TN34 ...... 4 E6
Carlisle Rd *EAST* BN21 ...... 10 E9
EDN/EASTW BN20 .... 206 C4 ▣
HOVE BN3 .... 167 M8
Carlton Cl *SEAF* BN25 .... 202 D2
Carlton Crs *RTWE/PEM* TN2 .. 20 C2 ▣
Carlton HI *ROTT* BN2 .... 7 H5 ▣
Carlton Pl *ROTT* BN2 .... 7 H6 ▣
Carlton Rd *LW/ROSE* BN22 .. 11 J2
RTWE/PEM TN2 .... 20 C2
SEAF BN25 .... 202 D1

Carlton Ter *HOVE* BN3 .... 167 J6
Carlyle Av *BRI* BN1 .... 169 K5
Carlyle St *ROTT* BN2 .... 7 K3
Carmel Cl *BEXW* TN39 .... 182 D3
Carol Cl *BRI* BN1 .... 145 K2
Caroline Cl *SEAF* BN25 ...... 202 D1 ▣
Carpenter Dr *STLEO* TN38 .. 161 K2
Carpenters Cft
RING/NEW BN8 .... 130 A1 ▣
Carpenters Wy *HAIL* BN27 .. 155 G8
Castle Ditch La *LEW* BN7 .... 2 F6
Castledown Av *HAS* TN34 .... 5 H7
Castle Dr *PEV* BN24 .... 198 C2
Castlefields *HRTF* TN7 ...... 26 D2
Castle Gdns *HAS* TN34 .... 5 H7
Castle Ga *LEW* BN7 .... 2 F6 ▣
Castle HI *MAYF* TN20 .... 56 A1
Castle Hill Pas *HAS* TN34 .. 5 H7
Castle Hill Rd *HAS* TN34 .. 5 H8
Castle Hurst *RBTBR* TN52 .. 63 H6
Castle Ri *UCK* TN22 .... 102 D2
Castle Rd *PEV* BN24 .... 180 A8
SBGH/RUST TN4 .... 19 M3
Castleross Rd *PEV* BN24 ..... 198 C2
Castle Sq *BRI* BN1 .... 6 E7
Castle St *BRI* BN1 .... 192 E6
HAS TN34 .... 5 H7
RTW TN1 .... 20 A4 ▣
WSEA TN36 .... 116 F7
Castle View Gdns *PEV* BN24 .. 179 L8
Castle Wk *WADH* TN5 .... 43 L2
Castle Wy *UCK* TN22 .... 102 D2 ▣
Catherine Pl *RTW* TN1 .... 20 B3 ▣
Catherine V *ROTT* BN2 .... 170 E6
Catkin Wy *HWH* RH16 .... 72 B2
Catsfield Cl *POLE* BN26 ..... 161 K4 ▣
STLEO TN38 .... 161 K4 ▣
Catsfield Rd *BAT* TN33 ...... 136 D3
Cat St *HRTF* TN7 .... 25 M5
Catt's HI *CROW* TN6 .... 41 K5
TENT TN30 .... 68 F2
The Causeway *ROTT* BN2 ...... 7 M5
SEAF BN25 .... 202 E4
Cavalier Wy *EGRIN* RH19 .. 13 M7
Cavalry Crs *EDN/EASTW* BN20 .. 206 B1
Cavell Av *PEAHV* BN10 .... 190 B7
Cavell Av North *PEAHV* BN10 .. 190 C6
Cavendish Av *LW/ROSE* BN22 .. 11 G4
STLEO TN38 .... 162 A7
Cavendish Cl *PEAHV* BN10 .. 190 B6
Cavendish Dr *RTWE/PEM* TN2 .. 20 B4
Cavendish Pl *BRI* BN1 .... 6 A7
EAST BN21 .... 10 F5
Cavendish St *ROTT* BN2 ...... 7 G7 ▣
Caveridge La *RING/NEW* BN8 .. 99 L6
Caves Rd *STLEO* TN38 .... 162 A8
Caxton Wy *HWH* RH16 .... 71 L2
Cedar Cl *BURH* RH15 .... 97 H1
HAS TN34 .... 162 D1
LW/ROSE BN22 .... 196 C4
Cedars Cl *UCK* TN22 .... 76 C6 ▣
Cedars Gdns *BRI* BN1 .... 168 D3
The Cedars *HAIL* BN27 .... 155 H5
HWH RH16 .... 48 D7 ▣
PEAHV BN10 .... 190 C5
UCK TN22 .... 76 D6
Cedar Wy *HWH* RH16 .... 72 B2
Cedarwell Cl *NEWHV* BN9 .. 191 H4 ▣
Celandine Dr *STLEO* TN38 .. 162 A5
Central Av *EDN/EASTW* BN20 .. 206 A1
PEAHV BN10 .... 190 A7
POLE BN26 .... 178 B7
Centurion Ri *HAS* TN34 ...... 162 E1
Centurion Rd *BRI* BN1 .... 6 D5 ▣
Ceylon Pl *LW/ROSE* BN22 .. 11 G6
Ceylon Wk *BEXW* TN39 .... 182 C5
Chadborn Cl *ROTT* BN2 .... 7 M8
Chaffinch Cl *BURH* RH15 .. 96 D2 ▣
Chaffinch Rd *LGNY* BN23 .... 197 J4
Chaffinch Wk *UCK* TN22 .. 102 C3
Chafford La *RRTW* TN3 .... 18 A1
Chailey Av *ROTT* BN2 .... 189 G5
Chailey Cl *HAS* TN34 .... 162 E1
LGNY BN23 .... 197 L5 ▣
Chailey Crs *ROTT* BN2 .... 189 G5
Chailey La *RING/NEW* BN8 .. 100 B1
Chailey Rd *BRI* BN1 .... 169 L2
Chain La *BAT* TN33 .... 137 J1
Chalfont Dr *HOVE* BN3 .... 168 C3
Chalkers La *HPPT/KEY* BN6 .. 96 B3
Chalket La *RTWE/PEM* TN2 .. 21 J1
Chalk Farm Cl
EDN/EASTW BN20 .... 196 B5
Chalkland Ri *ROTT* BN2 ...... 170 A6
Chalky Rd *PTSD* BN41 .... 166 F3
Challoners *RHWH* RH17 .... 50 C2
Challoners Cl *ROTT* BN2 .... 188 F4
Challoners Ms *ROTT* BN2 .... 188 F4
Challow Cl *HPPT/KEY* BN6 .. 122 E2 ▣
Chaloner Cl *HWH* RH16 .... 49 H7
Chaloner Rd *HWH* RH16 .... 49 H7
Chalvington Cl *BRI* BN1 ..... 146 E8
SEAF BN25 .... 192 F8
Chalvington Dr *SLVH* TN37 .. 139 J8
Chalvington Rd *EAST* BN21 .. 196 C7 ▣
Chamberlaines La
RING/NEW BN8 .... 127 M8
Chamberlain Rd *EAST* BN21 .. 206 C2
Chambers Crs *STLEO* TN38 .. 161 M3
Chambers Rd *STLEO* TN38 .. 161 M3
Chancellors Pk *HPPT/KEY* BN6 .. 122 F2
Chanctonbury Dr *HAS* TN34 .. 139 L8
Chanctonbury Rd *BURH* RH15 .. 96 F5
HOVE BN3 .... 6 A2
Chandler Rd *BEXW* TN39 ...... 183 G1
Chandler's Md *RING/NEW* BN8 .. 152 D5
Chandos Rd *RTW* TN1 .... 20 C1 ▣
Channel Vw East *BEX* TN40 .. 183 L3
Channel View Rd
LW/ROSE BN22 .... 11 K1
PEV BN24 .... 198 C2
ROTT BN2 .... 170 B6
Channel Vw West *BEX* TN40 .. 183 L3
Channel Wy *RHAS* TN35 .... 164 E3
Channers La *RING/NEW* BN8 .. 152 D6
Chant La *CROW* TN6 .... 41 H5
Chantiers Cl *EGRIN* RH19 .. 13 J4
Chantlers Md *EDEN* TN8 ...... 16 A1

Chantry Av BEX TN40 160 C8
Chantry La BEX TN40 183 J1
Chapel Barn Cl HAIL BN27 155 J7 2
Chapel Cl BURH RH15 96 F1
SEAF BN25 202 E2
Chapel Fld RYE TN31 65 G7
Chapel Gn CROW TN6 39 M4 1
Chapel Hl BAT TN33 112 E6
BAT TN33 160 F2
LEW BN7 3 J6
Chapel La EGRIN RH19 14 D8
FROW RH18 24 F5
LEW BN7 125 G3
RHAS TN35 141 G6
RHWH RH17 50 C1
UCK TN22 78 B7
Chapel Ms HOVE BN3 186 D1 3
Chapel Park Rd SLVH TN37 4 B5
Chapel Pl PTSD BN41 167 H7
Chapel Rd LEW BN7 98 E7
PTSD BN41 167 G7 1
Chapel Rw EGRIN RH19 22 E7
Chapel St NEWHV BN9 9 G3
ROTT BN2 7 G7
Chapel Ter ROTT BN2 7 L8
Chapman's La EGRIN RH19 13 K5 2
Chapmans Town Rd
HTHF TN21 107 H5
Charity Farm Wy CROW TN6 40 A3
Charles Av BURH RH15 96 E4
Charles Cl HOVE BN3 168 A3
SEAF BN25 202 D1 2
Charles Rd STLEO TN38 4 A7
Charles Rd West STLEO TN38 162 B6
Charles St ROTT BN2 6 F8
Charleston Rd EAST BN21 206 C2
Charlesworth Pk HWH RH16 72 C2
Charlotte St ROTT BN2 7 H8
Charlston Av NEWHV BN9 8 B7
The Charltons BRI BN1 146 D8 1
Charlton's Wy
SBGH/RUST TN4 19 L5 1
Charlwood Gdns BURH RH15 97 J1
Charlwood Rd BURH RH15 97 J1
Charlwoods Business Centre
EGRIN RH19 13 K4 1
Charlwoods Pl EGRIN RH19 13 L3 2
Charlwoods Rd EGRIN RH19 13 K4
Chartfield HOVE BN3 168 A4
Chartres BEX TN40 160 D8
Chartres Cl BEX TN40 160 D8
Chartwell Cl SEAF BN25 192 E8 1
Chatfield Crs LW/ROSE BN22 196 C5
Chatfield Rd RHWH RH17 48 A8
Chatham Pl BRI BN1 6 C3
SEAF BN25 202 E4 1
Chatham Rd SLVH TN37 162 B4 1
Chatsfield Cl STLEO TN38 161 L2
Chatsworth Av PEAHV BN10 190 A5 2
Chatsworth Cl PEAHV BN10 190 A6
Chatsworth Gdns
EDN/EASTW BN20 206 F6 1
Chatsworth Pk PEAHV BN10 190 B5 1
Chatsworth Rd BRI BN1 6 B1
Chaucer Av EGRIN RH19 13 J6
Chawbrook Rd LW/ROSE BN22 11 G3
Cheal Cl SHOR BN43 166 A8
Cheapside BRI BN1 6 E4
Cheeleys RHWH RH17 50 C1
Chelgates BEXW TN39 182 C4
Chelsea Cl BEX TN40 183 K2
Chelston Av HOVE BN3 167 K7
Cheltenham Pl BRI BN1 6 F5
Chelwood Cl BRI BN1 146 C8
Chelwood Gate Rd UCK TN22 36 F8
Chelworth Rd LW/ROSE BN22 196 D4
Chene Rd PEAHV BN10 190 F8
Chenies Cl RTWE/PEM TN2 20 A6
Chepbourne Rd BEX TN40 183 H2
Chequer Gra FROW RH18 24 E5
Chequer Rd EGRIN RH19 13 M5 1
Chequers Cl CROW TN6 40 A4 1
Chequers Wy CROW TN6 40 A4
Cherington Cl
HPPT/KEY BN6 122 B1 1
Cherry Cl BURH RH15 96 E3
Cherry Garden Rd
EDN/EASTW BN20 206 B3
Cherry Gdns HTHF TN21 106 B1
Cherry Side HAIL BN27 155 G7
Cherry Tree Cl SLVH TN37 4 B6
Cherry Tree Gdns BEX TN40 160 F8
Cherry Tree Rd RTWE/PEM TN2 19 L5
Cherwell Cl POLE BN26 196 F1
Cherwell Rd HTHF TN21 80 A6
Chesham Pl ROTT BN2 7 M9
Chesham Rd ROTT BN2 7 M9
Chesham St ROTT BN2 7 M9
Chesnut Cl HAIL BN27 155 G5 1
Chester Av RTWE/PEM TN2 20 D4
Chesterfield Cl CRAWE RH10 12 C2
Chesterfield Gdns
EDN/EASTW BN20 206 E6
Chesterfield Rd
EDN/EASTW BN20 206 E6
Chester Ter BRI BN1 169 G5
Chesterton Av SEAF BN25 203 H3
Chesterton Cl EGRIN RH19 13 M7
Chesterton Dr SEAF BN25 203 H3
Chestnut Cl BURH RH15 97 H1
EGRIN RH19 14 A5
HAIL BN27 133 L8
RYE TN31 114 B1
Chestnut Dr POLE BN26 178 A8
Chestnuts Cl HWH RH16 49 G7
The Chestnuts HAWK TN18 47 L6
HWH RH16 48 F7
Chestnut Wk BEXW TN39 182 C1
Chestnut Wy NEWHV BN9 8 C4
Cheviot Cl LGNY BN23 197 J3
The Cheviots HAS TN34 163 H2
Chichester Cl BEXW TN39 160 B8
HOVE BN3 167 L2
LW/ROSE BN22 196 B4
PEAHV BN10 190 F7
Chichester Dr East ROTT BN2 189 J6
Chichester Dr West ROTT BN2 189 H5
Chichester Pl ROTT BN2 7 M9
Chichester Rd SEAF BN25 202 E3
Chichester Ter ROTT BN2 7 M9
Chichester Wy BURH RH15 97 J1
Chick Hl RHAS TN35 142 B6
Chiddingley Cl ROTT BN2 187 M1
Chieveley Dr RTWE/PEM TN2 20 C5
Chilcomb BURH RH15 97 J5
Chilham Cl LGNY BN23 197 K4 4
Chillies La UCK TN22 54 A5
Chilling St EGRIN RH19 35 H6
Chillis Wood Rd HWH RH16 71 J1
Chilsham La HAIL BN27 133 K7
Chilston Cl SBGH/RUST TN4 20 A1
Chilston Rd SBGH/RUST TN4 20 A1
Chiltern Cl LGNY BN23 197 K3
SHOR BN43 166 C6
Chiltern Dr HAS TN34 163 H3
Chiltington Cl BURH RH15 96 F1 1
ROTT BN2 189 J4
Chiltington La LEW BN7 125 J3
Chiltington Wy ROTT BN2 189 J4
Chiswick Pl EAST BN21 10 F8
Chitcombe Rd RYE TN31 113 L1
Chorley Av ROTT BN2 189 H4
Chownes Mead La RHWH RH17 71 H2
Chown's Hl HAS TN34 140 A8
Chrisdory Rd PTSD BN41 166 E3
Christie Av RING/NEW BN8 127 K8
Christie Rd LEW BN7 2 B5
Christies EGRIN RH19 13 K6 1
Christopher Rd EGRIN RH19 13 L5
Church Av HWH RH16 48 E8
PEV BN24 180 A8
Church Cl BRI BN1 168 F1
BURH RH15 97 G3
EDN/EASTW BN20 196 A2
Churchdale Pl
LW/ROSE BN22 197 H8 1
Churchdale Rd LW/ROSE BN22 197 H8
Church Farm Cl
BUR/ETCH TN19 61 J5
Churchfields UCK TN22 52 C1
Church Gn SHOR BN43 166 C7
Church Hl BRI BN1 145 L8
BUR/ETCH TN19 61 H4
NEWHV BN9 8 E5
POY/PYE BN45 122 C8
RING/NEW BN8 127 K8
TENT TN30 68 F3
Church Hill Av BEXW TN39 182 C2
Church House Cl STHW BN42 166 E5
Churchill Av RHAS TN35 163 K1
Churchill Cl EDN/EASTW BN20 206 D3
Churchill Rd HTHF TN21 80 B8
LEW BN7 2 C2
SEAF BN25 202 D1
SHOR BN43 166 C6
Churchill Wy BURH RH15 97 J4
Church in the Wood La
STLEO TN38 161 M3
Churchland La BAT TN33 112 E3
Church La BAT TN33 136 E6
BAT TN33 158 C7
BAT TN33 159 H1
BUR/ETCH TN19 61 J5
EAST BN21 206 D3 2
EGRIN RH19 13 M5
HAIL BN27 132 A8
HAIL BN27 155 G1
HPPT/KEY BN6 123 J3
HWH RH16 71 M8
LEW BN7 2 F3
LEW BN7 171 K1
PEV BN24 180 B8
POLE BN26 195 J7
POY/PYE BN45 122 C8
RBTBR TN32 85 J1
RHAS TN35 139 L3
RHAS TN35 141 H5
RHWH RH17 35 J8
RHWH RH17 51 G3
RING/NEW BN8 129 J8
RING/NEW BN8 152 E6
RRTW TN3 30 B2
RYE TN31 65 J8
RYE TN31 88 E2
RYE TN31 90 B6
RYE TN31 91 H2
SEAF BN25 202 E4 2
STHW BN42 166 D7
UCK TN22 77 J1
Church Marks La
RING/NEW BN8 129 M1
Church Md HPPT/KEY BN6 123 G3
Church Pl ROTT BN2 187 L2
Church Platt RHWH RH17 70 E1
Church Rd BAT TN33 136 F6
BURH RH15 97 G4
CRBK TN17 33 M4
CROW TN6 39 L4
EGRIN RH19 22 E8
HAIL BN27 157 G5
HAWK TN18 63 M2
HOVE BN3 168 B8
HWH RH16 71 L2
LEW BN7 2 F5
LYDD TN29 95 J7
POLE BN26 178 A8
PTSD BN41 167 H7
RBTBR TN32 111 H1
RHWH RH17 72 F3
RING/NEW BN8 100 E2
RING/NEW BN8 126 E4
SBGH/RUST TN4 19 M3
SLVH TN37 4 B6
UCK TN22 77 H3
Churchsettle La WADH TN5 44 C7
Church Sq RYE TN31 117 J1
Church St BEX TN40 183 K1
BRI BN1 6 C5
CROW TN6 41 G6
EDEN TN8 16 B1
EDN/EASTW BN20 196 B5
EDN/EASTW BN20 206 D3
HRTF TN7 26 D2
HTHF TN21 106 D1
LW/ROSE BN22 196 C4
PTSD BN41 167 H7 1
RHAS TN35 163 J3
SEAF BN25 202 E3
UCK TN22 76 C6
Church Vale Rd BEX TN40 183 J1
Church Wood Dr STLEO TN38 161 L2
Church Wood Wy STLEO TN38 161 M4
Chyngton Av SEAF BN25 203 H2
Chyngton Cl LGNY BN23 197 G2 4
Chyngton Gdns SEAF BN25 203 H2
Chyngton La SEAF BN25 203 J3
Chyngton La North SEAF BN25 203 J3
Chyngton Pl SEAF BN25 203 H4
Chyngton Rd SEAF BN25 203 G4
Chyngton Wy SEAF BN25 203 J4
Cinderford La HAIL BN27 132 E6
Cinder Hl EGRIN RH19 35 H5
RING/NEW BN8 99 M3
RING/NEW BN8 100 B1
Cinquefoil PEAHV BN10 190 C6
Cinque Ports St RYE TN31 117 J1 1
Cinque Ports Wy SEAF BN25 203 J2
STLEO TN38 161 L8
Circus St ROTT BN2 6 F6
The Circus LGNY BN23 197 K6
Cissbury Av PEAHV BN10 190 E8
Cissbury Crs ROTT BN2 189 L5
Cissbury Rd BURH RH15 96 E2
HOVE BN3 6 A2
Civic Ap UCK TN22 76 C7
Civic Wy BURH RH15 97 G3
Clackhams La CROW TN6 40 D7
Clair Rd HWH RH16 71 L1
Clanricarde Gdns RTW TN1 20 A3 1
Clanricarde Rd
SBGH/RUST TN4 19 M3 1
Clapham La POLE BN26 194 A6
Claphatch La WADH TN5 45 G1
The Clappers RBTBR TN32 85 H2
Claremont HAS TN34 4 F7
Claremont Gdns RTW TN1 20 B4
Claremont Ri UCK TN22 76 C5
Claremont Rd BEXW TN39 160 B7
NEWHV BN9 191 M5
RTW TN1 20 B4
SEAF BN25 202 D3
Clarence Dr EGRIN RH19 13 M7
Clarence Rd LW/ROSE BN22 11 G3
RTW TN1 20 A3 2
SLVH TN37 4 A3
Clarence Rw RTW TN1 20 A2 2
Clarence Sq BRI BN1 6 C6
Clarendon Cl SLVH TN37 162 B2 2
Clarendon Gdns
RTWE/PEM TN2 20 A5 2
Clarendon Pl PTSD BN41 167 J8 2
Clarendon Rd HOVE BN3 168 B7
SHOR BN43 166 C6
Clarendon Ter ROTT BN2 7 M9 1
Clarendon Vls HOVE BN3 168 A7
Clarendon Wy RTWE/PEM TN2 19 M5
Clare Rd LEW BN7 2 B4
Clarke Av HOVE BN3 167 M3
Claverham Cl BAT TN33 137 H2
Claverham Wy BAT TN33 137 H2
Clavering Wk BEXW TN39 182 B4
Claxton Cl EAST BN21 206 D1
Claxton Rd BEX TN40 184 A1
Clayfields PEAHV BN10 190 B7 1
Clay Hill Rd RRTW TN3 32 D1
Clays Cl EGRIN RH19 13 L6 1
Clayton Av HPPT/KEY BN6 122 E3
Clayton Dr BURH RH15 96 F5
Clayton Hl POY/PYE BN45 122 D7
Clayton Mill Rd PEV BN24 197 H1
Clayton Rd HPPT/KEY BN6 123 J4
ROTT BN2 7 L3
Clayton's La RRTW TN3 17 L4
Clayton Wy HOVE BN3 167 M3
Clearwater La RHWH RH17 73 G3
Clearwaters La BURH RH15 71 K6
Cleeve Av RTWE/PEM TN2 20 D4
Cleevelands LW/ROSE BN22 196 B4 1
Clegg St HAS TN34 5 H5
Clement Hill Rd HAS TN34 163 H3 1
Clementine Av SEAF BN25 202 D1
Clement La POLE BN26 196 A1
Clerks Acre HPPT/KEY BN6 123 G2 1
Clermont Rd BRI BN1 168 D4
Clermont Ter BRI BN1 168 E4
Cleve Cl UCK TN22 103 H1
Clevedon Rd BEXW TN39 159 M8
Cleveland RTWE/PEM TN2 20 D1
Cleveland Cl LGNY BN23 197 J3 1
Cleveland Gdns BURH RH15 97 H4
Cleveland Rd BRI BN1 169 G5
Cleve Ter LEW BN7 2 E8
Cliff Ap ROTT BN2 187 M2
Cliff Av PEAHV BN10 200 E1
Cliff Cl SEAF BN25 202 F5
Cliffe High St LEW BN7 3 H6
Cliff End La RHAS TN35 142 B7
Cliff Gdns PEAHV BN10 189 M6
SEAF BN25 202 F5
Clifford Av EAST BN21 196 C8
Clifford Rd BEX TN40 183 J2
Cliff Park Cl PEAHV BN10 190 F7
Cliff Rd EDN/EASTW BN20 206 E7
ROTT BN2 187 M3
SEAF BN25 202 F5
The Cliff ROTT BN2 187 M2
Cliff Wy RHAS TN35 164 F1
Clifton Cl LW/ROSE BN22 196 D6
Clifton Hl BRI BN1 6 B4
Clifton Pl BRI BN1 6 B5
RTW TN1 20 B4 2
Clifton Ri BEX TN40 183 M1
Clifton Rd BRI BN1 6 C4
BURH RH15 96 D1
NEWHV BN9 9 H4
RHAS TN35 163 J3
Clifton St BRI BN1 6 D4
Clifton Ter BRI BN1 6 C5
Cliftonville Rd STLEO TN38 161 K8
Clifton Wy PEAHV BN10 190 A6
Climping Cl HWH RH16 71 K3
Clinch Green Av BEXW TN39 159 M7
Clinton Crs STLEO TN38 162 B5
Clinton La SEAF BN25 202 E3
Clinton Pl SEAF BN25 202 E3
Clinton Wy RHAS TN35 164 F1
Clive Av RHAS TN35 163 J4
Clock House La UCK TN22 52 C2
Cloisters NEWHV BN9 8 F3
The Cloisters BAT TN33 111 K8 1
LW/ROSE BN22 196 C4
SLVH TN37 4 C7
Close Eight LGNY BN23 197 L3 1
Close Eighteen LGNY BN23 197 L4 1
Close Eleven LGNY BN23 197 L3 2
Close Fifteen LGNY BN23 197 L4 2
Close Five LGNY BN23 197 L3 3
Close Four LGNY BN23 197 L4 3
Close Fourteen LGNY BN23 197 L3 3
Close Nine LGNY BN23 197 L4
Close One LGNY BN23 197 K4
Close Seven LGNY BN23 197 L3 5
Close Seventeen LGNY BN23 197 L4
Close Six LGNY BN23 197 L3 6
Close Sixteen LGNY BN23 197 L4
Close Ten LGNY BN23 197 L4 4
The Close BRI BN1 168 D1
BURH RH15 97 J2
CROW TN6 39 L3
EDN/EASTW BN20 196 B6
EDN/EASTW BN20 205 G5 1
EGRIN RH19 13 K6
HPPT/KEY BN6 122 F2
NEWHV BN9 191 M4
RHAS TN35 164 C2
RHWH RH17 34 B7
RRTW TN3 18 C8 1
RYE TN31 91 G8
SEAF BN25 202 F4
UCK TN22 78 B8
Close Three LGNY BN23 197 K4 5
Close Twelve LGNY BN23 197 L4 5
Close Twenty LGNY BN23 197 L4
Close Twentyfive
LGNY BN23 197 K4 6
Close Twentyfour
LGNY BN23 197 L4 6
Close Two LGNY BN23 197 K4 7
Cloudesley Rd SLVH TN37 4 A5
Cloverlea HAS TN34 162 E1 1
Clovers End BRI BN1 146 B7
Clover Wy PTSD BN41 167 H4
Cluny St LEW BN7 2 E8
Clyde Rd BRI BN1 6 E1
STLEO TN38 4 A7
Coach & Horses La RHWH RH17 36 C8
Coach La RHWH RH17 36 C8
Coastguard La RHAS TN35 164 B2
Coastguard Sq RYE TN31 118 A3
Coast Rd PEV BN24 198 E1
Cobald Rd PEV BN24 198 E1
Cobbetts Md HWH RH16 72 B3
Cobbett's Ride
RTWE/PEM TN2 19 M5 1
Cobbold Av EAST BN21 196 C8
Cob Cl CRAWE RH10 12 C6
Cobden Rd ROTT BN2 7 J3
Cobdown La UCK TN22 76 C2
Cob La RHWH RH17 34 B5
Cobton Dr HOVE BN3 168 A3
Cochrane Cl LGNY BN23 197 L7 1
Cockcrow Wd HAS TN34 162 D1
Cockmount La WADH TN5 31 L8
Cockshut Rd LEW BN7 2 E9
Cogger's La HTHF TN21 131 M3
Coggins Mill Rd MAYF TN20 57 J3
Coghurst Rd RHAS TN35 163 J2
Colbourne Av ROTT BN2 169 K4
Colbourne Rd HOVE BN3 6 A3
Colchester V FROW RH18 24 E4
Colchins BURH RH15 96 F5 1
Coldean La BRI BN1 146 C6
Coldharbour Cl CROW TN6 40 A5 1
Coldharbour La LYDD TN29 94 C1
RING/NEW BN8 74 A7
RYE TN31 90 F2
Coldharbour Rd HAIL BN27 154 B4
Coldthorn La HAIL BN27 178 A3
Coldwaltham La BURH RH15 97 K5
Colebrooke Rd BEXW TN39 183 G3
Colebrook Rd BRI BN1 168 D2
STHW BN42 166 F7
Coleman Av HOVE BN3 167 L7
Colemans Cl LYDD TN29 95 K8 1
Colemans Hatch Rd
FROW RH18 37 H1
Coleman St ROTT BN2 7 H3
Coleridge St HOVE BN3 168 A6
Colgate Cl ROTT BN2 169 M8
College Cl EGRIN RH19 13 M5 2
PTSD BN41 166 F3
College Dr RTWE/PEM TN2 20 D2
College Gdns ROTT BN2 7 K8
College Gn EAST BN21 10 B3
College La EGRIN RH19 13 M5
HPPT/KEY BN6 122 C1
College Pl HPPT/KEY BN6 96 C8
ROTT BN2 7 K8
College Rd BEX TN40 183 L2
EAST BN21 10 D8
HWH RH16 48 E8
ROTT BN2 7 K8
SEAF BN25 202 E4
College St ROTT BN2 7 K8
College Ter ROTT BN2 7 K6
Collier Cl LW/ROSE BN22 197 H7
Collier Rd HAS TN34 5 K5
PEV BN24 198 D2
Collingford La RHWH RH17 51 H2
Collington Av BEXW TN39 182 F3
Collington Cl
EDN/EASTW BN20 206 E5 3
Collington Gv BEXW TN39 182 E2
Collington La East BEXW TN39 182 E2
Collington La West
BEXW TN39 182 D3
Collington Park Crs
BEXW TN39 182 F2
Collington Ri BEXW TN39 182 E2
Collingwood Av HTHF TN21 80 A7
Collingwood Cl EGRIN RH19 13 M7 3
LGNY BN23 197 L8
PEAHV BN10 190 C5 2
Collingwood Ri HTHF TN21 80 A7
Collinstone Rd STLEO TN38 162 A7
Collinswood Dr STLEO TN38 162 A7
Colmer Ct BURH RH15 96 E3
Colmer Pl BURH RH15 96 E3 1
Colonnade Rd LW/ROSE BN22 11 H6
Coltstocks Rd
EDN/EASTW BN20 206 D6 1
Columbus Dr LGNY BN23 197 M8
Colwell Cl HWH RH16 71 M3
Colwell Gdns HWH RH16 71 M3
Colwell La HWH RH16 72 B3
RHWH RH17 71 M5
Colwell Rd HWH RH16 71 M4
Colwood Crs
EDN/EASTW BN20 196 B8
Combe End CROW TN6 39 M6
Combe La BAT TN33 135 M8
EDN/EASTW BN20 206 D7
Combe Ri EDN/EASTW BN20 196 A4
Combermere Rd STLEO TN38 162 B5
The Combe EDN/EASTW BN20 196 A7
Commanders Wk RHAS TN35 164 E2
Command Rd
EDN/EASTW BN20 206 B1
Commercial Rd BURH RH15 96 F3 1
EAST BN21 10 E5
RTW TN1 20 B1
Common La HPPT/KEY BN6 123 K1
POLE BN26 176 A5
Common Vw SBGH/RUST TN4 19 J3
Common Wood Ri CROW TN6 39 M2
Compasses La RBTBR TN32 86 C8
Comphurst La HAIL BN27 157 H2
Compton Av BRI BN1 6 C4
Compton Cl BEX TN40 183 L1 1
Compton Dr EDN/EASTW BN20 206 C4
Compton Place Rd
EDN/EASTW BN20 206 D3
Compton Rd BRI BN1 168 D5
HWH RH16 49 H6
Compton St EAST BN21 10 F9
EDN/EASTW BN20 207 G5
Compton Ter HAIL BN27 155 J8 1
The Compts PEAHV BN10 190 B5 1
Concord Cl RTWE/PEM TN2 20 C2 2
Concorde Cl BEXW TN39 159 M8
Condor Wy BURH RH15 96 E3
Conduit Hl RYE TN31 91 J8 1
Coneyburrow Gdns
STLEO TN38 161 L2 1
Coneyburrow La BEXW TN39 181 M2
Coneyburrow Rd
RTWE/PEM TN2 20 E1
Coney Furlong PEAHV BN10 190 D5
Conghurst La HAWK TN18 63 G1
Conifer Cl HAS TN34 162 F3
The Conifers EAST BN21 10 D3
Coniston Av SBGH/RUST TN4 19 L2
Coniston Rd LGNY BN23 197 J2 3
Connaught Rd EAST BN21 10 E7
HOVE BN3 168 A8
SEAF BN25 202 C3
Connaught Ter HOVE BN3 168 B7
Connaught Wy SBGH/RUST TN4 19 M1
Connell Dr ROTT BN2 170 E7
Conqueror Rd STLEO TN38 161 M7
Consort Wy BURH RH15 96 E4
Constable Rd LGNY BN23 197 K5
Constable Wy BEX TN40 160 D8
Conway Pl HOVE BN3 168 B6
Conway St HOVE BN3 168 B6
Cooden Cl BEXW TN39 182 C3
Cooden Dr BEXW TN39 182 D4
Cooden Sea Rd BEXW TN39 182 B4
Cook Av LGNY BN23 197 L8 1
Cookham Dene BEX TN40 183 J2 1
Cooksbridge Rd ROTT BN2 169 L8
Cookstown Cl BAT TN33 135 M8
Coolham Dr ROTT BN2 169 L8
Coombe Cl HAIL BN27 157 H1
Coombe Hill Rd EGRIN RH19 13 J8
Coombe Lands TENT TN30 67 K2
Coombe La WADH TN5 43 J7
Coombe Ri ROTT BN2 189 K3
Coombe Rd EDN/EASTW BN20 206 C2
LEW BN7 3 H3
ROTT BN2 169 K5
Coombers La HWH RH16 72 B1 1
Coombe Shaw BAT TN33 136 A8
Coombe V ROTT BN2 189 K3
Coombs Cl RYE TN31 89 J1
Cooper Dr BEXW TN39 160 A6
Cooper Ri STLEO TN38 162 A1 2
Cooper Rd RYE TN31 117 G1
Coopers Cl BURH RH15 97 H1
Coopers Hl EDN/EASTW BN20 196 B4
Coopers La CROW TN6 39 K2
Coopers Wy HAIL BN27 155 G8
Coopers Wd CROW TN6 39 K2
Copestake Dr BURH RH15 97 K3
Coplands Ri RYE TN31 65 H7
Coppards Cl RHWH RH17 98 C2 1
Coppards La RYE TN31 65 J6
Copper Beeches SLVH TN37 162 C2 1
Copperfields LYDD TN29 95 H8
Coppice Av EDN/EASTW BN20 196 A2
Coppice Cl EDN/EASTW BN20 196 A2
The Coppice BAT TN33 138 A3
CRAWE RH10 12 B6
HAS TN34 4 F4
RHWH RH17 72 F3 2
Coppice Vw HTHF TN21 80 B8 3
Coppice Wy HWH RH16 71 K3
Copse Cl CRAWE RH10 12 B6 1
EGRIN RH19 13 M3
STLEO TN38 161 K3
Copse Hl BRI BN1 168 D1
Copse Rd BEXW TN39 182 E2
The Copse HWH RH16 72 B1
Copthall Av HAWK TN18 47 M5
Copthorne Rd CRAWE RH10 12 B2
EGRIN RH19 12 E2
Copwood Av UCK TN22 76 B7
Copyhold La HWH RH16 48 D4
RHWH RH17 70 F2
Copyhold Rd EGRIN RH19 13 K6
Corbyn Crs SHOR BN43 166 A7

Cordons *LEW* BN7 .... 171 K1
Cormorant Cl *LGNY* BN23.... 197 J4
Cornelius Av *NEWHV* BN9 ...... 8 B7
Cornfield Cl *SEAF* BN25 ... 202 F3 ▣
Cornfield La *EAST* BN21 .... 10 E8
Cornfield Rd *EAST* BN21 .... 10 E7
   SEAF BN25 .... 202 F3
Cornfield Ter *EAST* BN21 ...... 10 E8
   SLVH TN37 .... 4 A4
Cornford Cl *BURH* RH15 ...... 96 E1
   CROW TN6 .... 40 A5
   PTSD BN41 .... 167 H4 ▣
Cornford La *RTWE/PEM* TN2 ... 20 E2
Cornish Cl *LGNY* BN23......... 197 H2
Cornmill Gdns *POLE* BN26 .. 195 L2
Cornwall Av *PEAHV* BN10.... 190 E8
   PEAHV BN10 .... 200 E1
Cornwall Gdns *BRI* BN1 ...... 168 E3
   EGRIN RH19 .... 13 M6 ▣
Cornwallis Cl *LGNY* BN23 ... 197 M7 ▣
Cornwallis Gdns *HAS* TN34 ..... 4 F7
Cornwallis St *HAS* TN34 .... 5 C6
Cornwallis Ter *HAS* TN34 ...... 4 F6
Cornwall Rd *NEWHV* BN9 ... 183 H3
Coronation Cottages
   RBTBR TN32 .... 85 J1
Coronation Gdns *BAT* TN33 .. 137 M1
   BUR/ETCH TN19 .... 61 M3
Coronation Rd *EGRIN* RH19 ... 13 L7
Coronation St *LYDD* TN29 ... 95 J8 ▣
   ROTT BN2 .... 7 J2 ▣
Corseley Rd *RRTW* TN3 .... 28 A3
Corsica Cl *SEAF* BN25 .... 202 F5
Corsica Rd *SEAF* BN25 .... 202 F5
Costells Edge *RHWH* RH17 ... 72 F2
Cotchford Hl *HRTF* TN7 .... 26 D5
Cotchford La *HRTF* TN7 .... 26 B5
Cotswold Cl *HAS* TN34 .... 163 H2
   LGNY BN23 .... 197 J2
The Cotswolds *STHW* BN42 .. 166 E7 ▣
Cottage Bush Cl *PTSD* BN41 .. 167 J4 ▣
Cottage Cl *NEWHV* BN9 ..... 191 K5 ▣
Cottage La *BAT* TN33 .... 112 E7
   PEV BN24.................. 178 E5
Coulstock Rd *HPPT/KEY* BN6 .. 96 C2
County Oak Av *BRI* BN1 ...... 146 B8
The Course *LEW* BN7 .... 2 D8
Court Cl *BRI* BN1 .... 145 L1
   EGRIN RH19................ 13 M5
Court Crs *EGRIN* RH19......... 14 A5
Court Farm Cl *NEWHV* BN9 .. 191 H3
Court Farm Rd *HOVE* BN3 ... 167 M4
   NEWHV BN9 .... 8 E7
   ROTT BN2 .... 188 E3
Courthope Av *WADH* TN5...... 43 M2
Courthope Dr *BEXW* TN39 ... 182 E1
Courthouse St *HAS* TN34 .... 5 K6
Courtland Rd *POLE* BN26 .... 196 A1
   UCK TN22 .... 52 D4
Courtlands Pl *CROW* TN6 ...... 39 L5
Courtlands Rd *LW/ROSE* BN22 .. 10 F1
Court Meadow *CROW* TN6 ...... 41 H6
Court Ord Rd *ROTT* BN2 ...... 188 E3
Court Rd *LEW* BN7 .... 3 H7
   LW/ROSE BN22 .... 196 F4
   SBGH/RUST TN4 .... 19 L2
The Courtyard *EGRIN* RH19 ... 14 B5
Cousley Wood Rd *WADH* TN5 .. 32 A8
Coventry St *STLEO* TN38 .... 162 A3
Coventry St *BRI* BN1 .... 168 E6
Coverdale Av *BEXW* TN39 ... 182 C3
The Covers *SEAF* BN25 .... 202 F4
The Covert *BEXW* TN39 ...... 182 C4
Cowden Cl *HAWK* TN18......... 47 L6
Cowden Hall La *HTHF* TN21 ... 132 A7
Cowden La *HAWK* TN18 .... 47 L7
Cowden Ms *EDEN* TN8 .... 16 A1
Cowden Rd *ROTT* BN2 .... 189 K6
Cowdens Cl *HOVE* BN3 .... 167 K2
Cowdray Cl *BEXW* TN39 ...... 159 K8
Cowdray Park Rd *BEXW* TN39 .. 159 J8
Cowfold Rd *ROTT* BN2 .... 187 L1
Cowhurst La *BEXW* TN39 ..... 160 C7
Cow La *POLE* BN26 .... 193 M6
Cowley Dr *ROTT* BN2 .... 170 E8
Cowper St *HOVE* BN3 .... 168 A7
Cox Gv *BURH* RH15 .... 96 E1
Crabtree Av *BRI* BN1 .... 169 C1
Cradle Hill Rd *SEAF* BN25 ... 193 G8
Craig Cl *BAT* TN33 .... 138 A8
Craignair Av *BRI* BN1 .... 145 M7
Cranborne Av
   EDN/EASTW BN20 ...... 206 C6
Cranbrook Rd *HAWK* TN18 ...... 47 M2
   SLVH TN37 .... 4 B4
Cranedown *LEW* BN7 .... 149 C7
Cranfield Rd *BEX* TN40 .... 183 J2
Cranleigh Av *ROTT* BN2 ...... 189 H5
Cranleigh Cl *BEXW* TN39 .... 183 G2
Cranmer Av *HOVE* BN3 .... 167 M5
Cranmer Cl *LEW* BN7 .... 3 H3 ▣
Cranston Av *BEXW* TN39 .... 182 F3
Cranston Cl *BEXW* TN39 ..... 182 F2
Cranston Ri *BEXW* TN39 ..... 182 F2
Cranston Rd *EGRIN* RH19 ..... 13 M4
Cranwell Rd *SBGH/RUST* TN4 .. 19 J2
Craven Rd *ROTT* BN2 .... 7 L6
Crawfurd Wy *EGRIN* RH19 ... 13 M3 ▣
Crawley Crs *LW/ROSE* BN22 .. 196 E4
Crawley Down Rd *EGRIN* RH19.. 12 E3
Crawley Rd *BRI* BN1 .... 146 D8
Crayford Rd *ROTT* BN2 .... 169 K5
Crazy La *BAT* TN33............ 112 E7
Crecy Cl *SLVH* TN37 .... 138 F7
Crescent Rd *BURH* RH15 ...... 97 H3 ▣
   ROTT BN2 .... 170 E6
Crescent Dr North *ROTT* BN2 .. 170 E6
Crescent Dr South *ROTT* BN2 .. 170 E8
Crescent Pl *ROTT* BN2 .... 7 K9
Crescent Rd *BURH* RH15 .... 97 H3
   EGRIN RH19 .... 13 K5
   ROTT BN2 .... 7 G1
The Crescent
   DN/EASTW BN20 .... 196 A3
   EDN/EASTW BN20 .... 206 A1
   HPPT/KEY BN6 .... 123 H3
   ROTT BN2 .... 169 L4

SLVH TN37 column

SLVH TN37 .... 162 C3
   STHW BN42 .... 166 F6
Crescent Wy *BURH* RH15...... 97 G3
Crespin Wy *BRI* BN1 .... 169 J5
Cresta Cl *POLE* BN26 .... 178 C8
Cresta Rd *NEWHV* BN9 .... 8 A5
Crest Rd *NEWHV* BN9 .... 8 A5
Crest Wy *PTSD* BN41 .... 167 H3
The Crestway *BRI* BN1 .... 169 J5
Cricket Ct *EGRIN* RH19 .... 13 L3
Cricketers Fld *RBTBR* TN32 .... 86 E5
Cricketfield La *HAIL* BN27 ... 156 C2
Cricketfield Rd *SEAF* BN25 .. 202 F4
Cricketing La *HAIL* BN27 ..... 156 C2
Criers La *MAYF* TN20 .... 55 M7
Crink Hl *RING/NEW* BN8 ..... 126 F3
Cripland Cl *HWH* RH16 .... 48 H8
Cripps Av *PEAHV* BN10 .... 190 D5
Crisp Rd *LEW* BN7 .... 2 B2
Crockers La *RYE* TN31 .... 65 H6
Crocks Dean *PEAHV* BN10 ... 190 D4 ▣
Croft Av *STHW* BN42 .... 166 E7
Croft Cl *POLE* BN26 .... 195 M2
Croft Ct *SEAF* BN25 .... 202 E3 ▣
Croft Dr *PTSD* BN41 .... 167 G3
Croft La *SEAF* BN25 .... 202 E3
Crofton Park Av *BEXW* TN39 .. 182 E5
Croft Rd *BRI* BN1 .... 168 D2
   CROW TN6 .... 39 M5
   HAS TN34 .... 5 K5
The Croft *EDN/EASTW* BN20 .. 196 B5
   HAS TN34 .... 5 K5
   HPPT/KEY BN6 .... 122 F1
Croft Works *HAIL* BN27 ...... 155 H7
Croham Rd *CROW* TN6 .... 39 M3
Cromer Wy *HAIL* BN27 .... 155 G4
Cromleigh Wy *STHW* BN42 .... 166 B5
Cromwell Pl *EGRIN* RH19 ..... 13 M7 ▣
Cromwell Rd *BURH* RH15 ...... 96 F3
   HOVE BN3 .... 168 C4
   RTWE/PEM TN2 .... 20 C3
Cromwell St *ROTT* BN2 .... 7 K3
Crooked La *SEAF* BN25 .... 202 F4
Crossbush Rd *ROTT* BN2 ...... 169 L8
Cross Lane Gdns *WADH* TN5 ... 45 K5
Cross Levels Wy *EAST* BN21 .. 196 E6
Cross Rd *STHW* BN42 .... 166 D6
Crossroad St *STHW* BN42 .... 166 D6 ▣
Cross St *BRI* BN1 .... 6 E2 ▣
   HOVE BN3 .... 186 D1
   POLE BN26 .... 178 A8
   SLVH TN37 .... 4 B8
Cross Wy *LEW* BN7 .... 2 A5
Crossways Av *EGRIN* RH19 .... 13 J5
The Crossways *PEV* BN24 .... 197 G1
The Crossway *BRI* BN1 .... 169 G1
   PTSD BN41 .... 167 G4 ▣
   SBGH/RUST TN4 .... 19 K4
Crouch Cl *EDN/EASTW* BN20 .. 196 B5
Crouch La *BAT* TN33 .... 159 H2
   HAWK TN18 .... 64 D1
   SEAF BN25 .... 202 E4
Crowborough Hl *CROW* TN6 .... 40 A3
Crowborough Rd *RHAS* TN35 .. 163 K2
   ROTT BN2 .... 189 G6
   UCK TN22 .... 37 M8
Crowders La *BAT* TN33 .... 136 C3
Crowhurst Cl *LGNY* BN23 .... 197 G2
Crowhurst Rd *BAT* TN33 ...... 161 G3
   STLEO TN38 .... 161 K4
Crowmere Av *BEX* TN40 ...... 183 J1
Crowmere Ter *BEX* TN40 ..... 183 J1
Crown Cl *HAIL* BN27 .... 155 G7
   UCK TN22 .... 76 C6
Crown Hl *SEAF* BN25 .... 192 E8
Crown La *HAS* TN34 .... 5 L6
Crown Rd *PTSD* BN41 .... 167 G6
   SHOR BN43 .... 166 B6
Crown St *BRI* BN1 .... 6 B6
Croxden Wy *LW/ROSE* BN22 .. 196 D3 ▣
Croxton La *HWH* RH16 .... 49 H8
Crunden Rd *EDN/EASTW* BN20 .. 206 B2
Cubitt Wy *STLEO* TN38 .... 161 L2
Cuckfield Cl *BEX* TN40 .... 161 G8
Cuckfield Rd *BURH* RH15 ...... 70 F3
   HPPT/KEY BN6 .... 96 A8
   RHWH RH17 .... 70 E3
Cuckmere Dr *PEV* BN24 ...... 197 G1
Cuckmere Ri *HTHF* TN21 ...... 80 B7
Cuckmere Rd *NEWHV* BN9 ..... 8 B7
   SEAF BN25 .... 203 H6
Cuckmere Wk *LW/ROSE* BN22 .. 196 D5
Cuckmere Wy *BRI* BN1 .... 146 B8
   BRI BN1 .... 169 H1
Cuckoo Dr *HTHF* TN21 .... 80 A8
Cuckoo Trail *HAIL* BN27 ..... 155 H6
   HTHF TN21 .... 80 A8
   HTHF TN21 .... 105 M2
   POLE BN26 .... 178 A6
Culpepper *BURH* RH15 .... 96 E1
Culpepper Cl *ROTT* BN2 ...... 169 K4 ▣
Culross Av *HWH* RH16 .... 71 K1
Culver Cl *LGNY* BN23 .... 197 H2
Culverden Down
   SBGH/RUST TN4 .... 19 M1
Culverden Pk *SBGH/RUST* TN4 .. 19 M1
Culverden Sq *SBGH/RUST* TN4 .. 20 A1
Culverden St *RTW* TN1 .... 20 A2 ▣
Culver's La *LYDD* TN29 .... 121 K1
Cumberland Dr *BRI* BN1 ...... 168 E4 ▣
Cumberland Gdns *STLEO* TN38 .. 162 B6
Cumberland Rd *BEXW* TN39 .. 160 B7
   BRI BN1 .... 168 E4
Cumberland Yd *RTW* TN1 ..... 20 A4 ▣
Cunningham Dr *LGNY* BN23 .. 197 L7
Curlew Ct *STLEO* TN38 .... 161 L3 ▣
The Curlews *SHOR* BN43 ...... 166 A6
Curwen Pl *BRI* BN1 .... 168 E3
Cuthbert Cl *BEXW* TN39 ...... 160 A7
Cuthbert Rd *ROTT* BN2 .... 7 K6
Cuttinglye La *CRAWE* RH10 ... 12 A5
Cuttinglye Rd *CRAWE* RH10 .. 12 A4
Cypress Cl *STLEO* TN38 ...... 162 A7 ▣
Cypress Gv *RTWE/PEM* TN2 .... 20 B3
Cyprus Pl *RYE* TN31 .... 117 H1 ▣
Cyprus Rd *BURH* RH15 .... 97 G3

D column

D

Dacre Rd *EDN/EASTW* BN20 .. 206 C2
   HAIL BN27 .... 133 L8
The Dakins *EGRIN* RH19 ...... 13 L6 ▣
Dale Av *BRI* BN1 .... 168 F1
   HPPT/KEY BN6 .... 122 F3
Dale Crs *BRI* BN1 .... 145 M8
Dale Dr *BRI* BN1 .... 145 M8
Dale Hl *POY/PYE* BN45 .... 122 A8
Dale Rd *FROW* RH18 .... 24 C7
   LEW BN7 .... 2 B8
Dales Cl *HAIL* BN27 .... 157 H1
Dale Vw *HOVE* BN3 .... 167 K4
Dale View Gdns *HOVE* BN3 .. 167 K4 ▣
Dalewood Gdns *BURH* RH15 ... 97 J4
Dallas La *RING/NEW* BN8 ..... 100 F3
Dallaway Dr *PEV* BN24 .... 197 H1
Dallaway Gdns *EGRIN* RH19 ... 13 L5
Dallington Cl *BEX* TN40 ...... 161 G8
Dallington Rd *HOVE* BN3 ..... 167 L6
   LW/ROSE BN22 .... 196 F5
Dalmeny Rd *BEXW* TN39 ..... 183 G1
Dalton Rd *EDN/EASTW* BN20 .. 206 E6
Damian Wy *RYE* TN31 .... 118 F4
Danum Cl *HAIL* BN27 .... 155 J3
Danworth La *HPPT/KEY* BN6 .. 96 B3
Darby's La *WADH* TN5 .... 44 A4
Darcey Dr *BRI* BN1 .... 146 A8
Darent Cl *POLE* BN26 .... 196 F1
Daresbury Cl *BEXW* TN39 .... 160 A8
Darley Rd *EDN/EASTW* BN20 .. 206 D6
Dartmouth Cl *ROTT* BN2 ...... 169 M5
Dartmouth Crs *ROTT* BN2 .... 169 L5
Darwell Down *BAT* TN33 ..... 110 B4
Darwell Dr *SEAF* BN25 .... 203 G3
Darwell Cl *STLEO* TN38 ...... 161 L5
   POLE BN26 .... 196 F1
Davey Dr *BRI* BN1 .... 169 H5
Davey's La *LEW* BN7 .... 3 J4
Davidgor Rd *HOVE* BN3 ...... 168 D7
Davis Cl *BEXW* TN39 .... 160 A7
Dawlish Cl *ROTT* BN2 .... 169 L5
Dawson Ter *ROTT* BN2 .... 7 K5
Daynes Wy *BURH* RH15 .... 96 E5
Deacons Dr *PTSD* BN41 ...... 167 H4
Deadmans La *RYE* TN31 ...... 91 J8
Deadmantree Hl
   RING/NEW BN8 .... 126 B3
Deal Av *SEAF* BN25 .... 203 J1
The Deals *RYE* TN31 .... 117 H1 ▣
Dean Cl *PTSD* BN41 .... 167 J4
Dean Court Rd *ROTT* BN2 .... 189 G4
Deanery Cl *LEW* BN7 .... 3 H2
Dean Gdns *PTSD* BN41 .... 167 J4
Dean Rd *SEAF* BN25 .... 202 F4
Deans Cl *BEXW* TN39 .... 160 B7
   ROTT BN2 .... 170 E6
Dean Dr *BEXW* TN39 .... 160 A8
Deans Meadow
   RING/NEW BN8 .... 126 C1
Deans Rd *POLE* BN26 .... 193 M3
Dean St *BRI* BN1 .... 6 B6
Deanway *HOVE* BN3 .... 168 B3
Dean Wood Cl *LGNY* BN23 ... 197 G2
De Cham Av *SLVH* TN37 .... 4 C6
De Cham Rd *SLVH* TN37 .... 4 B6
De Chardin Dr *HAS* TN34 .... 163 H1
De Courcel Rd *ROTT* BN2 .... 187 L3 ▣
Decoy Dr *LW/ROSE* BN22 .... 196 D6
Deepdene *WADH* TN5 .... 31 M8
Deepdene Gdns *HAS* TN34 ... 163 H3
Deerswood La *BEXW* TN39 ... 182 E1
The Deeside *BRI* BN1 .... 146 A7
De Grey Cl *LEW* BN7 .... 3 H3
Delaware Dr *STLEO* TN38 .... 138 F8
Delaware Rd *LEW* BN7 .... 2 B8
De La Warr Pde *BEX* TN40 ... 183 K3
De La Warr Rd *BEX* TN40 .... 183 K1
Dell Cl *STLEO* TN38 .... 162 A4
Dell Dr *RTWE/PEM* TN2 .... 20 D2
Dellney Av *HWH* RH16 .... 71 M3
The Dell *EGRIN* RH19 .... 14 B5
   HWH RH16 .... 71 J1
Delmonden Rd *HAWK* TN18 ... 47 J6
Delves Av *RTWE/PEM* TN2 .... 20 C5
Delves Cl *RING/NEW* BN8 .... 127 K8
Delves Wy *RING/NEW* BN8 ... 127 K8
De Moleyns Cl *BEX* TN40 .... 183 K2 ▣
De Montfort Rd *LEW* BN7 ...... 2 C6
   ROTT BN2 .... 7 J2
Dencher Rd *LEW* BN7 .... 171 L3
Dene Cl *EDN/EASTW* BN20 ... 205 H5
Dene Dr *LW/ROSE* BN22 ..... 196 C5
Denehurst Gdns *HAS* TN34 .. 163 G1
Dene Pth *UCK* TN22 .... 76 D5
Deneside *BRI* BN1 .... 168 D1 ▣
The Dene *EDN/EASTW* BN20 .. 196 A4
   HAS TN34 .... 163 G1
   HOVE BN3 .... 167 K3
Dene V *BRI* BN1 .... 168 D1
The Deneway *BRI* BN1 .... 168 D2
Dengemarsh Rd *LYDD* TN29 .. 121 J3
Denham Cl *STLEO* TN38 ...... 161 M2
Denham Rd *BURH* RH15 ...... 96 D2
Denham Wy *RYE* TN31 .... 118 E4
Den Hl *EDN/EASTW* BN20 .... 206 A2
Denman's La *HWH* RH16 ...... 49 G7
Denmark Ms *BRI* BN1 .... 6 B4
Denmark Pl *HAS* TN34 .... 5 G4
Denmark Rd *PTSD* BN41 ...... 167 J7
Denmark Ter *BRI* BN1 .... 6 B4

Denmark Vls column

Denmark Vls *HOVE* BN3 ...... 168 B7
Dennes La *LYDD* TN29 .... 95 H5
Dennis Hobden Cl *ROTT* BN2 .. 169 L5
Denton Cl *RYE* TN31 .... 91 G8
Denton Dr *BRI* BN1 .... 169 G1
   NEWHV BN9 .... 191 L5
Denton Ri *NEWHV* BN9 .... 191 L4
Denton Rd *EDN/EASTW* BN20 .. 206 D6
   NEWHV BN9 .... 191 L5
The Dentons
   EDN/EASTW BN20 .... 206 D6
Derek Av *HOVE* BN3 .... 167 K8
De Roos Rd *EAST* BN21 ...... 206 D2
Derwent Cl *HAIL* BN27 .... 155 G5
Derwent Dr *SBGH/RUST* TN4 ... 19 L1
Derwent Rd *LW/ROSE* BN22 .. 206 E6
Desmond Rd *LW/ROSE* BN22 .. 11 G2
Desmond Wy *ROTT* BN2 ...... 169 M8
Devil's Dyke Rd *HOVE* BN3 .. 144 F8
   POY/PYE BN45 .... 144 B4
   PTSD BN41 .... 144 C5
Devonshire Cl
   RTWE/PEM TN2 .... 19 M6 ▣
Devonshire Pl *EAST* BN21 .... 10 F7
   ROTT BN2 .... 7 G8
Devonshire Rd *BEX* TN40 .... 183 J3
   HAS TN34 .... 5 C6
De Walden Ms
   EDN/EASTW BN20 .... 206 E6 ▣
De Warrenne Rd *LEW* BN7 ..... 2 D5
Dewe Rd *ROTT* BN2 .... 169 J5
Dewhurst La *WADH* TN5 .... 31 H6
Dewlands Hl *MAYF* TN20 ...... 55 L5
Dew La *RYE* TN31 .... 90 A6
The Dewpond *PEAHV* BN10 .. 190 D5 ▣
Dexter Dr *EGRIN* RH19 .... 13 L6
Diana Cl *BEX* TN40 .... 161 G8
Dickens Cl *EGRIN* RH19 ...... 13 J5
Dickens Wy *LGNY* BN23 ...... 197 J5
Dillingburgh Rd
   EDN/EASTW BN20 .... 206 C2
Diplock Cl *POLE* BN26 .... 177 M8 ▣
Diplocks Wy *HAIL* BN27 ...... 155 G7
Dirty La *EGRIN* RH19 .... 14 E8
Ditchling Bostall
   HPPT/KEY BN6 .... 123 K7
Ditchling Cl *POLE* BN26 ..... 196 F1
Ditchling Dr *HAS* TN34 ...... 163 J1
Ditchling Gdns *BRI* BN1 ..... 169 G5
Ditchling Ri *BRI* BN1 .... 6 E1
Ditchling Rd *BRI* BN1 .... 146 C6
   ROTT BN2 .... 6 F3
Ditchling Wy *HAIL* BN27 ..... 155 H8
Dittons Ms *STLEO* TN38 ...... 161 L4 ▣
Dittons Rd *EAST* BN21 .... 10 B6
   POLE BN26 .... 178 C8
Dixter La *RYE* TN31 .... 65 G7
Dixter Rd *RYE* TN31 .... 65 G7
The Dock *RING/NEW* BN8 .... 174 C3
Dodshill *CROW* TN6 .... 40 A5
Dog Kennel La *UCK* TN22 ..... 55 L8
Dogs Hill Rd *WSEA* TN36 .... 143 H1
Doleham La *RHAS* TN35 ...... 140 A1
Dolphin Rd *LYDD* TN29 .... 95 J8
   SHOR BN43 .... 166 B7
Dolphin Wy *SHOR* BN43 ...... 166 B7
Donald Hall Rd *ROTT* BN2 ..... 7 M7
Donald Wy *WSEA* TN36 ...... 143 G1
Donkey Ms *HOVE* BN3 .... 186 D1 ▣
Donnington Rd *ROTT* BN2 .... 170 E8
Dordrecht Wy *HAS* TN34 .... 4 E3
Dormans Park Rd *EGRIN* RH19 .. 13 K3
Dornden Dr *RRTW* TN3 .... 19 G2
Dorothy Av *PEAHV* BN10 .... 190 C6
Dorothy Av North
   PEAHV BN10 .... 190 C6
Dorothy Rd *HOVE* BN3 .... 167 K6
Dorset Av *EGRIN* RH19 .... 13 J3
Dorset Gdns *EGRIN* RH19 ..... 13 J3
   ROTT BN2 .... 7 G7
Dorset Pl *HAS* TN34 .... 4 F7
Dorset Rd *BEX* TN40 .... 183 K2
   LEW BN7 .... 3 G7
   RTWE/PEM TN2 .... 20 D4
Dorset Rd South *BEX* TN40 .. 183 K2
Dorset St *ROTT* BN2 .... 7 G7
Doubledays *BURH* RH15 ...... 97 H5
Doucegrove *STLEO* TN38 ..... 162 A4
Douglas Cl *HAIL* BN27 .... 155 H4
Douglas Rd *CROW* TN6 .... 41 K5
Dove Ct *UCK* TN22 .... 76 C6
Dovedale Gdns
   LW/ROSE BN22 .... 196 F4 ▣
Dover Cl *SEAF* BN25 .... 203 J1
Dover Rd *BRI* BN1 .... 169 C4
   POLE BN26 .... 178 B7
Dower Cl *ROTT* BN2 .... 188 D3
Downash Cl *ROTT* BN2 .... 169 L8
Down Av *RRTW* TN3 .... 33 G3
Downey Cl *SLVH* TN37 .... 139 H8
Downland Av *PEAHV* BN10 ... 190 E8
   STHW BN42 .... 166 D5
Downland Cl *ROTT* BN2 ...... 170 B6 ▣
   STHW BN42 .... 166 D5
Downland Copse *UCK* TN22 .. 76 D5
Downland Crs *HOVE* BN3 ..... 167 M3
Downland Dr *HOVE* BN3 ...... 167 M3
Downland Rd *ROTT* BN2 ...... 170 B6
Downlands Av *BEXW* TN39 .. 183 H2
Downlands Cl *BEXW* TN39 .. 183 G2 ▣
Downlands Wy
   EDN/EASTW BN20 .... 205 H5 ▣
Down La *RRTW* TN3 .... 30 C6
Downline Cl *HTHF* TN21 ..... 105 M7
Down Rd *ROTT* BN2 .... 170 D4
Downs Av *EDN/EASTW* BN20 .. 196 B8
Downs Cl *LEW* BN7 .... 2 B7
Downscroft *BURH* RH15 ...... 97 K1
Downside *BRI* BN1 .... 168 D1 ▣
   HOVE BN3 .... 168 B3
   LEW BN7 .... 3 G3
   SHOR BN43 .... 166 A5
Downs Rd *BURH* RH15 .... 96 F3
   HAS TN34 .... 162 F3
   LW/ROSE BN22 .... 196 B4

SEAF column (rightmost)

SEAF BN25 .... 203 G3
Down St *UCK* TN22 .... 52 C6
Downsvalley Rd
   EDN/EASTW BN20 .... 196 A2
Downs Valley Rd *ROTT* BN2 .. 170 E6
Downs Vw *HAS* TN33 .... 159 G1
Downsview *HOVE* BN3 .... 167 K3
   HTHF TN21 .... 80 B6
Downs Vw *PEAHV* BN10 ..... 190 D4 ▣
Downsview Av *ROTT* BN2 .... 170 C5
Downs View Cl
   EDN/EASTW BN20 .... 205 J6
   RING/NEW BN8 .... 73 L8
Downsview Crs *UCK* TN22 .... 76 D6
Downsview Dr *RHWH* RH17 ... 98 C2
Downs View La
   EDN/EASTW BN20 .... 205 J6
Downsview Rd
   EDN/EASTW BN20 .... 196 A3 ▣
   HPPT/KEY BN6 .... 122 F3
Downsview Rd *PTSD* BN41 ... 167 G4
   SEAF BN25 .... 203 C3
Downsview Wy *HAIL* BN27 ... 155 H7 ▣
Downs Wk *PEAHV* BN10 ..... 190 E6
Downsway *ROTT* BN2 .... 170 D6
   STHW BN42 .... 166 F4
Down Ter *ROTT* BN2 .... 7 K4
The Down *HOVE* BN3 .... 167 J2
Draffin La *RYE* TN31 .... 118 D3
Drake Av *LGNY* BN23 .... 197 L7
Drapers Wy *STLEO* TN38 ..... 162 A4
Draxmont Wy *BRI* BN1 .... 168 F3
Drayton Ri *BEXW* TN39 ...... 182 D2
The Drive *BURH* RH15 .... 97 J2
   CROW TN6 .... 39 K4 ▣
   HAIL BN27 .... 155 H8
   HOVE BN3 .... 168 C7
   NEWHV BN9 .... 8 F8
   RTWE/PEM TN2 .... 20 A5
   STHW BN42 .... 166 F3
   STLEO TN38 .... 161 M6
   UCK TN22 .... 53 G8
   UCK TN22 .... 76 A1
   UCK TN22 .... 76 C6
Drockmill Cl *POLE* BN26 .... 178 C8 ▣
Drove Av *ROTT* BN2 .... 170 D4
Drove Crs *PTSD* BN41 .... 167 G4
Drove Rd *NEWHV* BN9 .... 9 J2
   PTSD BN41 .... 167 G5
   ROTT BN2 .... 170 C5
Drovers Cl *PTSD* BN41 ...... 167 J4
Drovers Wy *BURH* RH15 ...... 97 H5
The Drove *BRI* BN1 .... 168 D5
   BRI BN1 .... 170 C1
   NEWHV BN9 .... 9 K1
   RING/NEW BN8 .... 149 C1
The Droveway *HOVE* BN3 .... 168 C5
   RHWH RH17 .... 48 D3
Drummond Cl *HWH* RH16 ..... 71 K2
Duchess Dr *SEAF* BN25 ...... 192 E8
Dudley Rd *BRI* BN1 .... 169 H5
   LW/ROSE BN22 .... 11 G3
   RTW TN1 .... 20 A2 ▣
Dudwell Rd *ROTT* BN2 .... 170 D4
Duke Ms *SLVH* TN37 .... 162 B6 ▣
Duke Rd *SLVH* TN37 .... 162 B4
Dukes Cl *SEAF* BN25 .... 202 D1
Duke's Dr *EDN/EASTW* BN20 .. 206 D7
Dukes Hl *BAT* TN33 .... 111 K8
Duke's Mound *ROTT* BN2 ...... 7 L9
Dukes Rd *HWH* RH16 .... 49 H6
   RTW TN1 .... 20 C1
Duke St *BEXW* TN39 .... 182 F1
   BRI BN1 .... 6 D7
   SLVH TN37 .... 162 B4
Duke Ter *SLVH* TN37 .... 162 B4
Dulwich Cl *SEAF* BN25 ...... 203 H2 ▣
Dumbrells Court Rd
   HPPT/KEY BN6 .... 123 K2
Dumbrills Cl *BURH* RH15 ..... 97 C1
Dumb Woman's La *RYE* TN31 .. 116 D3
Dunbar Dr *HAIL* BN27 .... 155 G5
Dunclutha Rd *HAS* TN34 .... 162 F2
Duncton Cl *HWH* RH16 .... 71 K2
Dundale Rd *RRTW* TN3 .... 21 L5
Dunes Av *RYE* TN31 .... 118 F4
Dungeness Rd *LYDD* TN29 ... 121 M1
Dunning's Rd *EGRIN* RH19 ... 13 L7
   EGRIN RH19 .... 13 L8
Dunstall Av *BURH* RH15 ...... 96 F1
Dunstall Farm Rd *BURH* RH15 .. 96 F2
Dunstan Gv *SBGH/RUST* TN4 .. 20 B1
Dunstans Cft *MAYF* TN20 ..... 57 J3
Dunster Cl *BRI* BN1 .... 169 J4
Dunvan Cl *LEW* BN7 .... 2 F1
Durham Cl *ROTT* BN2 .... 170 A5
Durkins Rd *EGRIN* RH19 ..... 13 K3
Durrell Cl *LGNY* BN23 .... 197 H3
Dursley Rd *LW/ROSE* BN22 .. 10 F4
Dutchells Wy *LW/ROSE* BN22 .. 196 D2
Dyall Cl *BURH* RH15 .... 96 E2
Dyke Cl *HOVE* BN3 .... 168 B2
Dyke Rd *BRI* BN1 .... 6 D6 ▣
   HOVE BN3 .... 6 B2
   HOVE BN3 .... 168 C4
Dyke Road Av *HOVE* BN3 .... 168 B2
Dyke Road Dr *BRI* BN1 ...... 168 E4
Dyke Road Pl *HOVE* BN3 .... 168 C3
Dymchurch Cl *POLE* BN26 ... 178 C7
   SEAF BN25 .... 203 H1
Dymock Cl *SEAF* BN25 ...... 203 J2 ▣
The Dymock's
   HPPT/KEY BN6 .... 123 K3 ▣
Dymond Rd *STLEO* TN38 ..... 162 A3

E

Eagle Cl *UCK* TN22 .... 102 E1
Eagle Rd *RYE* TN31 .... 91 J8
Earls Cl *SEAF* BN25 .... 202 C1 ▣
Earls Gdn *LEW* BN7 .... 3 G5
Earl's Rd *SBGH/RUST* TN4 ... 19 M2
Earl St *HAS* TN34 .... 5 C5
East Albany Rd *SEAF* BN25 .. 202 F2
East Ascent *STLEO* TN38 .... 162 B8

Eastbank *STHW* BN42 .... 166 F5
East Beach St *HAS* TN34 .... 5 K7
East Beeches Rd *CROW* TN6 .... 40 C4
Eastbourne La *POLE* BN26 .... 195 J7
Eastbourne Rd
  EDN/EASTW BN20 .... 196 B4
  LGNY BN23 .... 197 M2
  LW/ROSE BN22 .... 196 C5
  PEV BN24 .... 198 D3
  POLE BN26 .... 196 A1
  RING/NEW BN8 .... 103 J3
  ROTT BN2 .... 169 K5
  SEAF BN25 .... 203 J3
  UCK TN22 .... 102 F5
Eastbridge Rd *NEWHV* BN9 .... 9 J4
Eastbrook Rd *PTSD* BN41 .... 167 H7
Eastbrook Wy *STHW* BN42 .... 167 G2
East Cliff *RYE* TN31 .... 117 J1
Eastdale Rd *BURH* RH15 .... 97 J2
East Dean Ri *SEAF* BN25 .... 203 G1
East Dean Rd
  EDN/EASTW BN20 .... 205 K6
East Dr *ROTT* BN2 .... 7 L9
East End La *HPPT/KEY* BN6 .... 123 K3
Eastergate *BEXW* BN39 .... 182 D1
Eastergate Rd *ROTT* BN2 .... 169 L2
Eastern Av *POLE* BN26 .... 178 B8
  SHOR BN43 .... 166 A4
Eastern Cl *SHOR* BN43 .... 166 A4
Eastern Pl *ROTT* BN2 .... 187 L2
Eastern Rd *HWH* RH16 .... 49 H7
  HWH RH16 .... 71 M3
  LYDD TN29 .... 95 J8
  ROTT BN2 .... 7 K7
  ROTT BN2 .... 187 L2
Eastern Ter *ROTT* BN2 .... 7 L9
Eastern Terrace Ms *ROTT* BN2 .... 7 L9
East Gdns *HPPT/KEY* BN6 .... 123 K3
Eastgate St *BRI* BN1 .... 3 C5
Eastgate Whf *LEW* BN7 .... 3 F5
Easthill Dr *PTSD* BN41 .... 167 H5
Easthill Wy *PTSD* BN41 .... 167 H5
Eastlands Cl *SBGH/RUST* TN4 .... 19 L6
Eastlands Rd *SBGH/RUST* TN4 .... 19 L6
East Mascalls Rd *HWH* RH16 .... 49 K8
East Meadway *SHOR* BN43 .... 166 A8
East Pde *HAS* TN34 .... 5 K7
Eastport La *LEW* BN7 .... 2 F8
East St *BRI* BN1 .... 6 E7
  CRAWE RH10 .... 22 B2
  HAS TN34 .... 5 K7
  LEW BN7 .... 3 G5
  MAYF TN20 .... 57 J3
  PTSD BN41 .... 167 J8
  RYE TN31 .... 117 J1
  SEAF BN25 .... 202 E3
East View Flds *LEW* BN7 .... 124 E1
East View Ter *BAT* TN33 .... 112 F5
Eastway *BEXW* BN39 .... 182 C2
East Wy *LEW* BN7 .... 148 F4
East Wick *HWH* RH16 .... 49 J7
Eastwick Cl *BRI* BN1 .... 146 E7
Eastwood Rd *BEXW* BN39 .... 183 C2
Eatenden La *BAT* TN33 .... 110 F4
Eaton Gdns *HOVE* BN3 .... 168 C7
Eaton Gv *HOVE* BN3 .... 168 C7
Eaton Pl *ROTT* BN2 .... 7 M9
Eaton Rd *HOVE* BN3 .... 168 C8
Eaton Vls *HOVE* BN3 .... 168 C8
Eaton Wk *BAT* TN33 .... 112 D5
Ebden's Hl *BAT* TN33 .... 139 H5
Ebenezer Rd *HAS* TN34 .... 5 M5
Ecmod Rd *LW/ROSE* BN22 .... 197 J3
Edburton Av *BRI* BN1 .... 169 C5
Edenbridge Rd *EDEN* TN8 .... 16 D4
  HRTF TN7 .... 16 D4
Eden Dr *BEXW* BN39 .... 182 E2
Eden Rd *RTW* TN1 .... 20 A4
Edensor Rd *EDN/EASTW* BN20 .... 206 D7
Eden V *EGRIN* RH19 .... 13 L2
Edgar Rd *RHAS* TN35 .... 163 J4
Edgehill Cl *HTHF* TN21 .... 79 M7
Edgehill Wy *PTSD* BN41 .... 166 F4
Edinburgh Rd *BEX* TN40 .... 183 J1
  ROTT BN2 .... 7 H1
  SEAF BN25 .... 202 D3
  STLEO TN38 .... 161 L7
Edinburgh Wy *EGRIN* RH19 .... 13 M7
Edith Av *PEAHV* BN10 .... 190 D7
Edith Av North *PEAHV* BN10 .... 190 C6
Edith Rd *RHAS* TN35 .... 163 K3
Edmond Cl *LGNY* BN23 .... 197 H4
Edmonton Rd *BEXW* BN39 .... 160 B7
Edmund Rd *RHAS* TN35 .... 163 J4
Edward Av *HOVE* BN3 .... 168 A3
  ROTT BN2 .... 189 K3
Edward Cl *HOVE* BN3 .... 168 A3
  SEAF BN25 .... 192 A8
Edward Rd *HWH* RH16 .... 71 L3
  SLVH TN37 .... 4 C7
Edward St *LEW* BN7 .... 3 G5
  ROTT BN2 .... 7 C7
  SBGH/RUST TN4 .... 19 H2
Edward Ter *STLEO* TN38 .... 162 A2
Edwin Rd *RHAS* TN35 .... 163 J4
Effingham Cl *ROTT* BN2 .... 189 J4
Effingham Dr *BEXW* BN39 .... 182 D3
Egerton Rd *BEXW* BN39 .... 183 H5
Egginton Cl *BRI* BN1 .... 170 A1
Egginton Rd *ROTT* BN2 .... 169 M2
Egles Gv *UCK* TN22 .... 77 J2
Egmont Rd *HOVE* BN3 .... 167 K5
Egremont Pl *HAS* TN34 .... 5 L2
  ROTT BN2 .... 7 G7
Eight Acre La *RHAS* TN35 .... 140 D5
Eight Bells Cl *UCK* TN22 .... 77 J2
Eileen Av *ROTT* BN2 .... 189 H5
Eisenhower Dr *STLEO* TN38 .... 138 F8
Elder Cl *PTSD* BN41 .... 167 K2
Elder Pl *BRI* BN1 .... 6 E2
Elderwood Cl *BEXW* BN39 .... 160 C2
  LW/ROSE BN22 .... 197 J3
Eldon Rd *EAST* BN21 .... 206 C1
Eldred Av *BRI* BN1 .... 168 D1
Eleanor Cl *LEW* BN7 .... 2 F6
  SEAF BN25 .... 202 D1

Eley Crs *ROTT* BN2 .... 188 E3
Eley Dr *ROTT* BN2 .... 188 E2
Elford St *HAS* TN34 .... 5 H5
Elgar Wy *LGNY* BN23 .... 197 L3
Elim Court Gdns *CROW* TN6 .... 39 L2
Elizabethan Ct *BAT* TN33 .... 158 F4
Elizabeth Av *HOVE* BN3 .... 168 A3
Elizabeth Cl *HOVE* BN3 .... 168 A3
  SEAF BN25 .... 192 A8
Elizabeth Crs *EGRIN* RH19 .... 13 M3
Elizabeth Rd *SHOR* BN43 .... 166 C6
Ellenslea Rd *SLVH* TN37 .... 4 B7
Ellen St *HOVE* BN3 .... 168 B7
  ROTT BN2 .... 167 J7
Ellenwhorne La *RBTBR* TN32 .... 87 L3
Ellerslie La *BEXW* BN39 .... 159 M7
Elliots Wy *HTHF* TN21 .... 80 A6
Ellison Cl *CROW* TN6 .... 39 L2
Ellis Wy *UCK* TN22 .... 76 A7
Elm Cl *HOVE* BN3 .... 168 C4
  RING/NEW BN8 .... 129 J7
  SEAF BN25 .... 203 J3
Elm Ct *NEWHV* BN9 .... 8 D3
Elm Dr *EGRIN* RH19 .... 14 A5
  HOVE BN3 .... 167 L5
Elm Gv *LW/ROSE* BN22 .... 196 F5
  ROTT BN2 .... 7 J3
Elmore Rd *ROTT* BN2 .... 7 G5
Elm Rd *PTSD* BN41 .... 167 H6
Elms Av *EAST* BN21 .... 11 G7
Elmsdown Pl *HAIL* BN27 .... 155 J7
Elms La *RHAS* TN35 .... 141 M5
Elms Lea Av *BRI* BN1 .... 168 E3
Elmsmead *RYE* TN31 .... 91 H2
Elmstead Rd *BEX* TN40 .... 11 G7
Elmstead Rd *BEX* TN40 .... 183 L1
The Elms *RING/NEW* BN8 .... 150 C1
Elm Wy *HTHF* TN21 .... 80 B8
  HTHF TN21 .... 106 B1
Elmwood Cl *LGNY* BN23 .... 197 J2
Elmwood Gdns *LGNY* BN23 .... 197 J2
Elphick Pl *CROW* TN6 .... 39 M3
Elphick Rd *NEWHV* BN9 .... 8 E2
  RING/NEW BN8 .... 127 M7
Elphick's Pl *RTWE/PEM* TN2 .... 20 B6
Elphinstone Av *HAS* TN34 .... 5 H1
Elphinstone Rd *HAS* TN34 .... 162 F3
Elphinstone Rd *HAS* TN34 .... 5 H2
Elrington Rd *HOVE* BN3 .... 168 C5
Elsted Crs *BRI* BN1 .... 146 C8
Elsted Rd *BEXW* BN39 .... 182 C4
Elven La *EDN/EASTW* BN20 .... 205 J5
Elvin Crs *ROTT* BN2 .... 188 C2
Elwood Cl *BURH* RH15 .... 96 F5
Emerald Quay *SHOR* BN43 .... 166 A8
Emmanuel Rd *BEX* TN40 .... 183 J3
Endwell Rd *BEX* TN40 .... 183 L3
Engalee *EGRIN* RH19 .... 13 J4
English Cl *HOVE* BN3 .... 167 L6
Enys Rd *EAST* BN21 .... 10 C5
Epsom Cl *STLEO* TN38 .... 162 A6
Erica Cl *LGNY* BN23 .... 197 H4
Eridge Cl *BURH* RH15 .... 182 F2
Eridge Dr *CROW* TN6 .... 39 M3
Eridge Gdns *CROW* TN6 .... 40 A3
Eridge Gn *LEW* BN7 .... 2 C5
Eridge La *CROW* TN6 .... 41 H4
Eridge Rd *CROW* TN6 .... 28 D8
  CROW TN6 .... 40 C2
  EAST BN21 .... 196 C7
  HOVE BN3 .... 168 A4
  RRTW TN3 .... 18 D8
  SBGH/RUST TN4 .... 19 M4
Erin Wy *BURH* RH15 .... 96 E3
Erroll Rd *HOVE* BN3 .... 167 J8
Ersham Rd *HAIL* BN27 .... 178 B1
Ersham Wy *HAIL* BN27 .... 155 H8
Erskine Park Rd
  SBGH/RUST TN4 .... 19 J2
Esher Cl *SEAF* BN25 .... 202 F2
Eshton Rd *LW/ROSE* BN22 .... 11 J2
Eskbank Av *BRI* BN1 .... 146 A7
Eskdale Cl *LGNY* BN23 .... 197 H2
Esplanade *SEAF* BN25 .... 202 F5
Esplanade Ms *SEAF* BN25 .... 202 E4
The Esplanade *PEAHV* BN10 .... 189 M7
Essenden Rd *STLEO* TN38 .... 162 A8
Essex Cl *RTWE/PEM* TN2 .... 19 M6
Essex Rd *STLEO* TN38 .... 162 A2
Essex St *ROTT* BN2 .... 7 H7
Estate Rd *NEWHV* BN9 .... 9 H3
Estcots Dr *EGRIN* RH19 .... 14 B5
Etchingham Rd *LGNY* BN23 .... 197 L5
Ethelred Cl *LGNY* BN23 .... 197 L6
Ethel St *HOVE* BN3 .... 168 B7
Etherton Wy *SEAF* BN25 .... 203 G2
Ethnam La *HAWK* TN18 .... 64 E3
Eton Cl *SEAF* BN25 .... 203 G2
Evelyn Av *NEWHV* BN9 .... 8 E3
Evelyn Rd *LEW* BN7 .... 2 C5
Evelyn Ter *ROTT* BN2 .... 7 K6
Eversfield Pl *SLVH* TN37 .... 4 D8
Eversfield Rd *EAST* BN21 .... 10 D4
Eversley Cl *SLVH* TN37 .... 4 B2
Eversley Crs *SLVH* TN37 .... 4 B2
Eversley Rd *BEX* TN40 .... 183 J3
  SLVH TN37 .... 4 B1
Ewart St *ROTT* BN2 .... 7 H4
Ewhurst Cl *HAS* TN34 .... 162 F2
Ewhurst La *RYE* TN31 .... 87 M2
Ewhurst Rd *ROTT* BN2 .... 169 H6
Exceat Cl *ROTT* BN2 .... 169 L8
Exeat Cl *LGNY* BN23 .... 197 G6
Exeter Cl *LW/ROSE* BN22 .... 196 B4
Exeter St *BRI* BN1 .... 6 B1
Exmouth Pl *HAS* TN34 .... 5 K7

F

Factory La *HAIL* BN27 .... 155 G8
Fairbanks *HWH* RH16 .... 71 L2
Fairbridge Wy *BURH* RH15 .... 96 F1
Faircrouch La *WADH* TN5 .... 43 H1
Fairdene *STHW* BN42 .... 166 F5
Fairfax Av *STLEO* TN38 .... 138 F7

Fairfield *HAIL* BN27 .... 133 L8
Fairfield Av *RTWE/PEM* TN2 .... 20 C1
Fairfield Cha *BEXW* BN39 .... 182 F2
Fairfield Cl *BURH* RH15 .... 96 F2
  RHWH RH17 .... 34 A6
  SHOR BN43 .... 166 B5
Fairfield Crs *HPPT/KEY* BN6 .... 96 A8
Fairfield Gdns *PTSD* BN41 .... 167 H5
Fairfield Rd *BURH* RH15 .... 96 F3
  EDN/EASTW BN20 .... 206 E5
  EGRIN RH19 .... 13 M6
  SLVH TN37 .... 139 J8
Fairfield Wy *HWH* RH16 .... 48 D6
Fairford Cl *HWH* RH16 .... 71 L1
Fairglen Rd *WADH* TN5 .... 43 H3
Fairholme Rd *NEWHV* BN9 .... 191 M5
Fairisle Cl *LGNY* BN23 .... 197 L6
Fairlawn Crs *EGRIN* RH19 .... 13 H4
Fairlawn Dr *EGRIN* RH19 .... 13 H4
Fairlawns *SHOR* BN43 .... 166 A6
Fairlawns Dr *HAIL* BN27 .... 133 L8
Fairlea Cl *BURH* RH15 .... 96 F2
Fairlea Cl *BURH* RH15 .... 96 F2
Fairlie Gdns *BRI* BN1 .... 168 E3
Fairlight Av *PEAHV* BN10 .... 189 M7
  RHAS TN35 .... 163 K3
  POLE BN26 .... 178 A8
Fairlight Cl *BEX* TN40 .... 184 A1
Fairlight Fld *RING/NEW* BN8 .... 150 D1
Fairlight Gdns *RHAS* TN35 .... 164 F2
Fairlight Pl *ROTT* BN2 .... 7 J1
Fairlight Rd *LW/ROSE* BN22 .... 11 K2
  RHAS TN35 .... 163 K3
Fair Meadow *RYE* TN31 .... 91 J7
Fairmile Rd *RTWE/PEM* TN2 .... 20 E1
Fairmount Rd *BEX* TN40 .... 183 K1
Fair Oak Cl *HTHF* TN21 .... 80 A7
Fairstone Cl *RHAS* TN35 .... 163 L2
Fairview *HAWK* TN18 .... 47 M4
Fairview La *CROW* TN6 .... 39 L2
Fairview Ri *BRI* BN1 .... 168 D1
Fairway Cl *EDN/EASTW* BN20 .... 206 C4
Fairway Crs *PTSD* BN41 .... 167 J4
Fairways Cl *SEAF* BN25 .... 203 J4
Fairways Rd *SEAF* BN25 .... 203 H4
The Fairway *BEXW* BN39 .... 159 M8
  NEWHV BN9 .... 8 B5
  STLEO TN38 .... 161 M6
Falaise Rd *HAS* TN34 .... 4 D7
  NEWHV BN9 .... 191 M5
Falconbury Dr *BEXW* BN39 .... 182 D3
Falcon Cl *SHOR* BN43 .... 166 C8
Falconer Dr *BAT* TN33 .... 137 M2
Falcon Wy *HAIL* BN27 .... 155 H4
Fallowfield Cl *HOVE* BN3 .... 167 M4
Fallowfield Crs *HOVE* BN3 .... 167 L4
Falmer Av *ROTT* BN2 .... 189 H4
Falmer Cl *EDN/EASTW* BN20 .... 196 B7
Falmer Gdns *ROTT* BN2 .... 170 D6
Falmer House Rd *BRI* BN1 .... 147 J7
Falmer Rd *ROTT* BN2 .... 170 D6
Falmouth Cl *LGNY* BN23 .... 197 M6
Faraday Av *EGRIN* RH19 .... 13 M8
Farlaine Rd *EAST* BN21 .... 196 C8
Farley Bank *HAS* TN34 .... 5 L2
Farleys Wy *RHAS* TN35 .... 164 E1
Farley Wy *RHAS* TN35 .... 164 E1
Farlington Av *HWH* RH16 .... 71 M1
Farlington Rd *HWH* RH16 .... 71 L1
Farlin Rd *EGRIN* RH19 .... 14 B6
Farm Cl *HWH* RH16 .... 122 E2
  PTSD BN41 .... 167 G4
  SEAF BN25 .... 203 G2
Farmcombe Cl *RTW* TN1 .... 20 B4
Farmcombe La *RTW* TN1 .... 20 B4
Farmcombe Rd *RTW* TN1 .... 20 B4
Farm Gdns *RYE* TN31 .... 90 C4
Farm Hl *ROTT* BN2 .... 170 C6
Farmlands Av *POLE* BN26 .... 195 M2
Farmlands Cl *POLE* BN26 .... 196 A2
  SLVH TN37 .... 162 C1
Farmlands Wy *POLE* BN26 .... 195 M1
Farmland Wy *HAIL* BN27 .... 155 J5
Farm La *HPPT/KEY* BN6 .... 123 L3
Farm Ms *HOVE* BN3 .... 168 D8
Farm Rd *HOVE* BN3 .... 168 D8
Farm Wy *BURH* RH15 .... 97 J5
  STHW BN42 .... 167 G2
Farmway Cl *HOVE* BN3 .... 167 K4
Farncombe Cl *RHWH* RH17 .... 98 D1
Farncombe Rd *LEW* BN7 .... 3 J6
Farne Cl *HAIL* BN27 .... 155 G4
Farnham Av *HPPT/KEY* BN6 .... 123 G1
Farnham Beeches *RRTW* TN3 .... 19 G2
Farnham La *RRTW* TN3 .... 19 G2
Farnham Rd *RRTW* TN3 .... 19 G3
Farningham Rd *CROW* TN6 .... 40 C7
Farnina Rd *BURH* RH15 .... 97 K1
Farriers Wy *UCK* TN22 .... 76 C2
Farrington Hl *WADH* TN5 .... 45 L5
Farthing La *HAIL* BN27 .... 134 E1
The Farthings *CROW* TN6 .... 40 A3
Fastnet Cl *LGNY* BN23 .... 197 L6
Faulkners Wy *BURH* RH15 .... 97 G1
Faversham Rd *LGNY* BN23 .... 197 K4
Faygate Cl *BEXW* BN39 .... 160 B6
Faygate Rd *LW/ROSE* BN22 .... 196 E4
Fayre Meadow *RBTBR* TN32 .... 85 H2
Fearon Rd *HAS* TN34 .... 5 G2
Felbridge Cl *EGRIN* RH19 .... 13 J3
Felbridge Ct *EGRIN* RH19 .... 13 G3
Felbridge Rd *EGRIN* RH19 .... 12 D3
Felcot Rd *CRAWE* RH10 .... 12 C3
Fellows Rd *HAS* TN34 .... 163 G3
Felride *HWH* RH16 .... 71 L3
Fennell's Cl *EAST* BN21 .... 10 A1
Ferguson Rd *LYDD* TN29 .... 120 C4
Fermandy La *CRAWE* RH10 .... 12 A5
Fermor Rd *CROW* TN6 .... 39 M7
Fermor Wy *CROW* TN6 .... 39 M6
Fern Cl *LGNY* BN23 .... 197 J3
Ferndale *RTWE/PEM* TN2 .... 20 D1
Ferndale Rd *RTWE/PEM* TN2 .... 20 C2
  RTWE/PEM TN2 .... 20 C2
Ferndale Rd *BURH* RH15 .... 97 H5

Fernhill *HAIL* BN27 .... 133 L8
Fernhurst Cl *BRI* BN1 .... 146 C8
Fernhurst Crs *BRI* BN1 .... 169 H1
Fernlea Cl *RHAS* TN35 .... 139 L2
Fern Rd *STLEO* TN38 .... 161 M5
Fernside Av *STLEO* TN38 .... 161 M6
The Ferns *RTW* TN1 .... 20 B2
Fernwood Ri *BRI* BN1 .... 168 D1
Ferrers Rd *LEW* BN7 .... 2 C4
Ferry Rd *RYE* TN31 .... 91 G8
Ferry Hl *WSEA* TN36 .... 116 E6
Ferry Rd *RYE* TN31 .... 117 H3
Festival Gdns *BEXW* BN39 .... 160 C7
Feversham Cl *SHOR* BN43 .... 166 B8
Field Cl *BURH* RH15 .... 96 E2
  SEAF BN25 .... 203 H4
Field End *UCK* TN22 .... 76 A2
Fielden La *CROW* TN6 .... 39 K5
Fielden Rd *CROW* TN6 .... 39 J6
Fields End *HWH* RH16 .... 71 M2
Fieldway *HPPT/KEY* BN6 .... 123 K3
  HWH RH16 .... 48 F6
  HAS TN34 .... 4 F4
Field Wy *STLEO* TN38 .... 161 L6
Fiennes Rd *HAIL* BN27 .... 133 L8
Figg La *CROW* TN6 .... 39 M6
Filching Cl *CROW* TN6 .... 195 L3
Filching Rd *EDN/EASTW* BN20 .... 206 B1
Filder Cl *LW/ROSE* BN22 .... 197 G8
Filsham Dr *BEX* TN40 .... 161 G8
Filsham Rd *STLEO* TN38 .... 161 M7
Filsham Va *STLEO* TN38 .... 161 M7
Finches Gdns *HWH* RH16 .... 49 G5
Finches La *HWH* RH16 .... 49 G6
Finches Park Rd *HWH* RH16 .... 49 G6
The Finches *BEX* TN40 .... 183 M2
  SHOR BN43 .... 166 A7
  STLEO TN38 .... 162 A1
Findon Av *ROTT* BN2 .... 189 L5
Findon Cl *BEXW* BN39 .... 182 E3
  HOVE BN3 .... 167 M3
  SEAF BN25 .... 203 J3
Findon Rd *ROTT* BN2 .... 187 M1
Finistere Av *LGNY* BN23 .... 197 M6
Finmere Cl *LW/ROSE* BN22 .... 197 J8
Finmere Rd *LW/ROSE* BN22 .... 197 J8
Finsbury Rd *ROTT* BN2 .... 7 H4
Fir Cl *ROTT* BN2 .... 170 F7
Fircroft Cl *BRI* BN1 .... 168 E3
Fir Grove Rd *HTHF* TN21 .... 79 H7
Firlands *HWH* RH16 .... 71 M2
Firle Bostal *RING/NEW* BN8 .... 174 B4
Firle Cl *RHAS* TN35 .... 163 L2
  SEAF BN25 .... 202 E1
Firle Crs *LEW* BN7 .... 148 F4
Firle Dr *SEAF* BN25 .... 202 E1
Firle Gra *SEAF* BN25 .... 202 E1
Firle Rd *BEXW* BN39 .... 182 D2
  LW/ROSE BN22 .... 11 G3
  PEAHV BN10 .... 190 B5
  ROTT BN2 .... 7 M3
  SEAF BN25 .... 202 E1
First Av *BEX* TN40 .... 183 M1
  HOVE BN3 .... 186 C1
  NEWHV BN9 .... 8 E5
  RYE TN31 .... 118 F4
First St *RRTW* TN3 .... 18 F3
Firtoft Cl *BURH* RH15 .... 97 H3
Fir Toll Cl *MAYF* TN20 .... 56 F4
Fir Toll Rd *MAYF* TN20 .... 56 F4
Fir Tree Cl *BEXW* BN39 .... 182 C3
  HAIL BN27 .... 155 J4
Firtree Rd *HAS* TN34 .... 5 K1
Fir Tree Rd *SBGH/RUST* TN4 .... 19 H4
Fir Tree Wy *HPPT/KEY* BN6 .... 123 G2
Firwood Cl *HTHF* TN21 .... 80 A6
  LW/ROSE BN22 .... 196 E5
Firwood Ri *HTHF* TN21 .... 80 A6
Fisher Cl *LGNY* BN23 .... 197 M7
Fishergate Cl *PTSD* BN41 .... 167 G7
Fishersgate Ter *PTSD* BN41 .... 167 G7
Fisher St *LEW* BN7 .... 2 F6
Fishmarket Rd *RYE* TN31 .... 117 J1
Fishponds La *RHAS* TN35 .... 139 L3
Fitch Dr *ROTT* BN2 .... 169 L5
Fitzgerald Av *SEAF* BN25 .... 202 F4
Fitzgerald Cl
  EDN/EASTW BN20 .... 206 F5
Fitzgerald Pk *SEAF* BN25 .... 202 F4
Fitzgerald Rd *LEW* BN7 .... 3 H2
Fitzherbert Dr *ROTT* BN2 .... 169 K6
Fitzjohns Rd *LEW* BN7 .... 2 C2
Fitzmaurice Av *LW/ROSE* BN22 .... 11 H1
Fitzroy Rd *LEW* BN7 .... 2 C2
Five Chimneys La *UCK* TN22 .... 78 A1
Flamsteed Rd *HAIL* BN27 .... 157 G5
Fleming Cl *LGNY* BN23 .... 197 M4
Fletcher Av *STLEO* TN38 .... 138 F7
Fletching Cl *ROTT* BN2 .... 169 M8
Fletching Rd *LW/ROSE* BN22 .... 197 J1
Fletching St *MAYF* TN20 .... 57 H3
Flimwell Cl *LGNY* BN23 .... 197 G2
  ROTT BN2 .... 187 L1
  STLEO TN38 .... 161 K4
  WADH TN5 .... 46 D2
Flint Cl *PTSD* BN41 .... 167 H4
  SEAF BN25 .... 192 E8
The Flints *ROTT* BN2 .... 171 L1
Flitterbrook La *HTHF* TN21 .... 107 K4
Florance La *RRTW* TN3 .... 18 B8
Florence Av *HOVE* BN3 .... 167 K6
Florence La *HOVE* BN3 .... 167 K6
Florence Pl *BRI* BN1 .... 169 K6
Florence Rd *BRI* BN1 .... 169 G6
Folders Cl *BURH* RH15 .... 97 K5
Folders La *BURH* RH15 .... 97 J5
Foley Cl *LGNY* BN23 .... 197 L7
Folkestone Cl *SEAF* BN25 .... 203 J1
Folkestone Rd *RYE* TN31 .... 92 C3
Folkington Gdns *SLVH* TN37 .... 162 C1
Folkington Rd *POLE* BN26 .... 195 K1
Folly Fld *NEWHV* BN9 .... 8 F3
Fonthill Rd *HOVE* BN3 .... 168 B6
Fontridge La *BUR/ETCH* TN19 .... 83 K3
Fontwell Av *BEXW* BN39 .... 182 C1
Foords La *PEV* BN24 .... 179 H7
Foot's La *BUR/ETCH* TN19 .... 82 B3
Fordbrook Hl *CROW* TN6 .... 54 E4

Fordcombe Rd *RRTW* TN3 .... 18 D3
Ford Rd *STLEO* TN38 .... 161 M4
Foredown Cl
  EDN/EASTW BN20 .... 206 C4
  PTSD BN41 .... 167 H4
Foredown Dr *PTSD* BN41 .... 167 H5
Foredown Rd *PTSD* BN41 .... 167 H3
The Ferns *RTW* TN1 .... 20 B2
Forest Dene *CROW* TN6 .... 40 D5
Forest La *HTHF* TN21 .... 107 K1
Forest Pk *CROW* TN6 .... 39 K4
Forest Pl *HTHF* TN21 .... 78 F8
Forest Ri *CROW* TN6 .... 40 D5
Forest Rd *BRI* BN1 .... 169 L1
  FROW RH18 .... 25 H5
  RTWE/PEM TN2 .... 20 C5
Forest Vw *HAIL* BN27 .... 155 G6
  UCK TN22 .... 52 C3
Forest View Rd *EGRIN* RH19 .... 13 L8
Forest Wy *EGRIN* RH19 .... 24 B1
  HAS TN34 .... 4 F4
  HRTF TN7 .... 17 J8
  RTWE/PEM TN2 .... 20 C5
Forewood La *BAT* TN33 .... 138 A6
Forewood Ri *BAT* TN33 .... 137 L8
Forge Cl *PTSD* BN41 .... 167 H4
  UCK TN22 .... 76 C8
Forge Fld *WADH* TN5 .... 44 F8
Forge La *RBTBR* TN32 .... 86 E5
Forge Meadow *TENT* TN30 .... 69 G2
Forge Meads *TENT* TN30 .... 67 L3
Forge Ri *UCK* TN22 .... 76 C8
Forge Rd *RRTW* TN3 .... 28 B3
Forge Wy *BURH* RH15 .... 96 F2
  SLVH TN37 .... 162 C1
Forstall *RRTW* TN3 .... 19 G2
Fort Hvn *SHOR* BN43 .... 166 C8
Fort La *LW/ROSE* BN22 .... 197 K8
Fort Ri *NEWHV* BN9 .... 9 H7
Fort Rd *LW/ROSE* BN22 .... 197 K8
  NEWHV BN9 .... 9 G5
Forward Cl *NEWHV* BN9 .... 191 L4
Foster Cl *SEAF* BN25 .... 202 E2
Foundry La *LEW* BN7 .... 3 J6
Foundry St *BRI* BN1 .... 6 E5
Fountains Cl *BRI* BN1 .... 169 H4
  LW/ROSE BN22 .... 196 E3
Founthill Av *ROTT* BN2 .... 189 H5
Founthill Rd *ROTT* BN2 .... 189 H5
Fourteen Acre La *RHAS* TN35 .... 140 D3
Fourth Av *HOVE* BN3 .... 186 B1
Fowey Cl *SHOR* BN43 .... 166 B8
Fowlers Cl *BEXW* BN39 .... 182 E1
Fowly La *UCK* TN22 .... 54 C7
Fox Cl *BURH* RH15 .... 96 F3
Foxcote *SLVH* TN37 .... 162 D2
Foxdown Rd *ROTT* BN2 .... 170 F7
Foxglove Cl *BURH* RH15 .... 96 D2
  RING/NEW BN8 .... 128 A7
Foxglove Rd *LGNY* BN23 .... 197 H3
Foxhill *BEXW* BN39 .... 182 E1
Fox Hl *HWH* RH16 .... 71 L5
Foxhill *PEAHV* BN10 .... 190 C5
Fox Hill Cl *HWH* RH16 .... 71 L5
Fox Hill Village *HWH* RH16 .... 71 M6
Foxhole La *WADH* TN5 .... 44 B3
Foxhunters Rd *PTSD* BN41 .... 166 F5
Foxwarren *HWH* RH16 .... 71 J1
Fox Wy *PTSD* BN41 .... 167 G3
Framelle Mt *UCK* TN22 .... 77 H8
Framfield Cl *BRI* BN1 .... 146 E8
Framfield Rd *UCK* TN22 .... 76 D8
  UCK TN22 .... 77 H3
Framfield Wy *EAST* BN21 .... 196 D8
Francis Rd *HWH* RH16 .... 49 H6
Francis St *BRI* BN1 .... 6 F3
Frankfield Ri *RTWE/PEM* TN2 .... 19 M5
Franklands Cl *BURH* RH15 .... 97 H5
Franklands Gdns *BURH* RH15 .... 97 G6
Franklands Wy *BURH* RH15 .... 97 G6
Franklin Rd *PTSD* BN41 .... 167 H5
  ROTT BN2 .... 7 H1
  SHOR BN43 .... 166 C6
Franklin St *ROTT* BN2 .... 7 J2
Franklynn Rd *HWH* RH16 .... 71 M3
Frankton Av *HWH* RH16 .... 72 A3
Frant Av *BEXW* BN39 .... 182 C1
Frant Cl *BEXW* BN39 .... 182 C1
Frant Rd *HOVE* BN3 .... 168 A4
  RTWE/PEM TN2 .... 20 A7
Frary Wk *HTHF* TN21 .... 106 A3
Fraser Av *LGNY* BN23 .... 197 L7
Freckley Hollow *BAT* TN33 .... 136 B4
Frederick Pl *BRI* BN1 .... 6 E4
Frederick Rd *RHAS* TN35 .... 163 J3
Frederick St *BRI* BN1 .... 6 D5
Free Heath Rd *RRTW* TN3 .... 32 C3
Freehold Ter *ROTT* BN2 .... 169 H6
Freek's La *BURH* RH15 .... 71 G8
Freeland Cl *SEAF* BN25 .... 192 D8
Freeman Av *LW/ROSE* BN22 .... 196 E5
Freemans Rd *PTSD* BN41 .... 167 G6
Freezeland La *BEXW* BN39 .... 159 M5
Fremlin Cl *SBGH/RUST* TN4 .... 19 H2
Frenches Farm Dr *HTHF* TN21 .... 106 A1
French Gdns *HWH* RH16 .... 48 F3
Frenchgate Cl
  LW/ROSE BN22 .... 196 F4
Frenchgate Rd
  LW/ROSE BN22 .... 196 F4
Freshfield Bank *FROW* RH18 .... 24 E4
Freshfield Cl *HAIL* BN27 .... 155 H8
Freshfield La *RHWH* RH17 .... 50 C6
Freshfield Pl *ROTT* BN2 .... 7 J6
Freshfield Rd *ROTT* BN2 .... 7 J7
Freshfield St *ROTT* BN2 .... 7 K4
Freshfield Wy *ROTT* BN2 .... 7 J7
Freshford Cl *LGNY* BN23 .... 197 K4
Freshwater Av *HAS* TN34 .... 4 F1
Freshway *LW/ROSE* BN22 .... 196 C3
Frewen Cl *RYE* TN31 .... 65 H7
Frewyn Cl *STLEO* TN38 .... 161 M2
Friar Cl *BRI* BN1 .... 169 G2
Friar Crs *BRI* BN1 .... 168 F3
Friar Rd *BRI* BN1 .... 169 G2
Friars' Av *PEAHV* BN10 .... 190 E8
  PEAHV BN10 .... 200 C1
Friars Bank *RHAS* TN35 .... 141 H7

Friars Cl *HPPT/KEY* BN6 .... 122 E3
Friars Hl *RHAS* TN35 .... 140 F7
Friars Oak Rd *HPPT/KEY* BN6 .... 122 E1
Friars Rd *WSEA* TN36 .... 116 F7
Friars' Wk *LEW* BN7 .... 3 H6
Friday St *LGNY* BN23 .... 197 J2
Friezland Rd *SBGH/RUST* TN4 ... 19 K5
Frimley Cl *ROTT* BN2 .... 170 E7
Friston Av *LW/ROSE* BN22 ...... 196 C5
Friston Cl *EDN/EASTW* BN20 .... 205 C5
ROTT BN2 .... 169 M2
SEAF BN25 .... 202 C2
Friston Downs
EDN/EASTW BN20 .... 205 H4
Frith Pk *EGRIN* RH19 .... 13 L3
Frith Rd *HOVE* BN3 .... 168 A6
Frobisher Cl *LGNY* BN23 .... 197 L7
Frog Hole La *MAYF* TN20 .... 79 H1
Frog La *RTW* TN1 .... 20 A4
Fryatts Wy *BEXW* TN39 .... 159 M8
Fry Crs *BURH* RH15 .... 96 E1
Fryman's La *RYE* TN31 .... 113 K4
Fulford Cl *STLEO* TN38 .... 162 A6
Fuller Cl *WADH* TN5 .... 43 L1
Fuller Rd *LEW* BN7 .... 2 B1
Fullers La *RYE* TN31 .... 65 H8
Fullwood Av *NEWHV* BN9 .... 8 D3
Fulmar Cl *HOVE* BN3 .... 168 D5
Fulmar Dr *EGRIN* RH19 .... 14 A3
The Furlongs *POLE* BN26 .... 193 M3
Furnace Av *RRTW* TN3 .... 32 F3
Furnace La *HTHF* TN21 .... 105 K6
HTHF TN21 .... 106 E4
RRTW TN3 .... 32 D2
RYE TN31 .... 114 B1
Furnace Rd *CRAWE* RH10 .... 12 C3
Furnace Wy *UCK* TN22 .... 76 E7
Furness Rd *EDN/EASTW* BN20 ... 12 A6
Furzefield Rd *EGRIN* RH19 ..... 13 K2
Furze Hl *HOVE* BN3 .... 168 D8
Furze La *EGRIN* RH19 .... 13 H3
Fyning Pl *BEXW* TN39 .... 182 C1
Fyrsway *RHAS* TN35 .... 164 C3
Fysie La *BUR/ETCH* TN19 .... 61 K3

G

Gableson Av *BRI* BN1 .... 168 B2
Gage Cl *CRAWE* RH10 .... 12 C5
Gage Rdg *FROW* RH18 .... 24 E5
The Gages *HAIL* BN27 .... 155 K7
Gainsborough Crs
LGNY BN23 .... 197 K5
Gainsborough La *POLE* BN26 .... 177 L8
Gainsborough Rd *BEX* TN40 ..... 160 E8
Galley Hill Vw *BEX* TN40 ...... 183 L2
Galliers Cl *BRI* BN1 .... 146 B8
Gallipot Hl *HRTF* TN7 .... 26 C3
The Gallops *LEW* BN7 .... 2 F7
Galloways Rd *LYDD* TN29 .... 121 J5
Gallows Cl *PEV* BN24 .... 179 L8
Gallows La *PEV* BN24 .... 179 L8
Galveston Cl *LGNY* BN23 .... 197 M7
Gammons Wy *BAT* TN33 .... 112 E5
Gander Cl *BURH* RH15 .... 97 G1
Gander Gn *HWH* RH16 .... 48 F7
Gander Hl *HWH* RH16 .... 48 F7
Garden Cl *BEX* TN40 .... 183 K2
EGRIN RH19 .... 13 M7
PTSD BN41 .... 167 J6
SHOR BN43 .... 166 B5
Gardener St *PTSD* BN41 .... 167 G6
Garden House La *EGRIN* RH19 .. 13 L7
Garden Rd *RTW* TN1 .... 20 B3
The Gardens *PTSD* BN41 .... 167 J6
STHW BN42 .... 166 F7
Garden St *LEW* BN7 .... 2 F7
RTW TN1 .... 20 B2
Garden Wood Rd *EGRIN* RH19 ... 13 J5
Gardner Cl *LGNY* BN23 .... 197 L7
Gardner La *CRAWE* RH10 .... 12 C4
Gardner Rd *PTSD* BN41 .... 167 G7
Gardner's Hl *RYE* TN31 .... 68 B8
Gardner St *BRI* BN1 .... 6 E6
HAIL BN27 .... 133 M8
Garfield Rd *HAIL* BN27 .... 155 H7
Garland Rd *EGRIN* RH19 .... 13 K5
Garnet Dr *EDN/EASTW* BN20 .... 196 C4
Garston Pk *BUR/ETCH* TN19 .... 60 B8
Garth Cl *BEXW* TN39 .... 183 G1
Gatehouse Cl *BEXW* TN39 ...... 182 C4
Gatehouse La *BURH* RH15 ...... 96 E1
HPPT/KEY BN6 .... 96 B1
UCK TN22 .... 77 J8
UCK TN22 .... 103 K1
Gatelands Dr *BEXW* TN39 ...... 160 A8
Gatesmead *HWH* RH16 .... 48 E6
The Gattons *BURH* RH15 .... 96 E3
Gaudick Cl *EDN/EASTW* BN20 ... 206 E5
Gaudick Rd *EDN/EASTW* BN20 ... 206 E5
Geering Rd *PEV* BN24 .... 197 H1
Geers Wd *HTHF* TN21 .... 79 M8
Gemma Cl *HAIL* BN27 .... 155 L7
Geneva Rd *NEWHV* BN9 .... 9 G6
Gensing Rd *STLEO* TN38 .... 4 A8
George Hl *RBTBR* TN32 .... 85 H3
George St *HAIL* BN27 .... 155 J7
HAS TN34 .... 5 J7
HOVE BN3 .... 168 B8
PTSD BN41 .... 167 J7
PTSD BN41 .... 167 J6
ROTT BN2 .... 7 G7
WADH TN5 .... 43 M1
George Wood Cl *LYDD* TN29 .... 95 J8
Georgian Cl *BEX* TN40 ...... 160 E8
BEX TN40 .... 183 L1
Georgian Wk *STLEO* TN38 ...... 161 M6
Gerald Cl *BURH* RH15 .... 97 K3
Gerald Rd *SEAF* BN25 .... 202 F5
Gerard St *BRI* BN1 .... 6 E1
German St *WSEA* TN36 .... 116 E7
Ghyll Rd *CROW* TN6 .... 39 K2
HTHF TN21 .... 79 M8
Ghyllside *ROTT* BN2 .... 169 L5

Ghyllside Av *SLVH* TN37 .... 162 C2
Ghyllside Dr *HAS* TN34 .... 162 D2
Ghyll Side Rd *RYE* TN31 .... 65 H7
Ghyllside Wy *HAS* TN34 .... 162 D2
Gibb St *BEX* TN40 .... 183 M1
Gibbetts *RRTW* TN3 .... 18 F3
Gibbon Rd *NEWHV* BN9 .... 8 D6
Gibraltar Ri *HTHF* TN21 .... 80 A7
Giffards Cl *EGRIN* RH19 .... 13 M5
STLEO TN38 .... 162 B6
Gilberts Dr *EDN/EASTW* BN20 .. 205 H7
Gilbert Rd *LW/ROSE* BN22 ..... 11 H3
Gilbert Wy *HAIL* BN27 .... 178 B1
Gilda Crs *POLE* BN26 .... 178 A8
Gildredge Rd *EAST* BN21 ...... 10 D7
SEAF BN25 .... 202 F3
Gilham La *FROW* RH18 .... 24 E4
Gillett Rd *LYDD* TN29 .... 95 K7
Gillham Wood Rd *BEXW* TN39 ... 182 D3
The Gilligans *BURH* RH15 ..... 96 F1
Gillridge Gn *CROW* TN6 .... 39 M2
Gillsmans Dr *STLEO* TN38 ..... 161 M8
Gillsmans Hl *STLEO* TN38 ..... 162 A5
Gillsman's Pk *STLEO* TN38 .... 161 M5
Gingerbread La *HAWK* TN18 .... 46 F3
Gipps Cross La *RRTW* TN3 ..... 18 F3
Githa Rd *RHAS* TN35 .... 163 J4
The Glades *BEX* TN40 .... 160 E8
EGRIN RH19 .... 14 B5
The Glade *HAIL* BN27 .... 154 F8
MAYF TN20 .... 57 G4
UCK TN22 .... 76 D7
Gladstone Cl *LW/ROSE* BN22 ... 196 F5
Gladstone Pl *ROTT* BN2 .... 169 J6
Gladstone Rd *BURH* RH15 ...... 97 J1
CROW TN6 .... 39 M6
HAS TN34 .... 5 K4
PTSD BN41 .... 167 H7
SBGH/RUST TN4 .... 19 H2
Gladys Av *PEAHV* BN10 .... 190 D8
Gladys Rd *HOVE* BN3 .... 167 K6
Glassenbury Dr *BEX* TN40 ..... 183 M4
Glastonbury Rd *HOVE* BN3 ..... 167 K8
Gleave Cl *EGRIN* RH19 .... 14 A4
Glebe Cl *BEXW* TN39 .... 182 D2
EDN/EASTW BN20 .... 206 D3
LEW BN7 2
STHW BN42 .... 166 F7
Glebe Dr *SEAF* BN25 .... 202 E3
Glebelands *CRAWE* RH10 .... 12 A6
Glebelands *SHOR* BN43 .... 166 B6
The Glebelands *CROW* TN6 ..... 39 M4
The Glebe *EGRIN* RH19 .... 13 G2
HAS TN34 .... 5 L3
HWH RH16 .... 49 G6
Glebe Vls *HOVE* BN3 .... 167 K7
Glen Cl *POLE* BN26 .... 195 M2
Glendale Av *EAST* BN21 .... 196 C8
Glendale Rd *BURH* RH15 .... 97 H4
HOVE BN3 .... 168 D7
Glendor Rd *HOVE* BN3 .... 167 L8
Glendyne Cl *EGRIN* RH19 ...... 14 A6
Glendyne Wy *EGRIN* RH19 ...... 14 A6
Gleneagles Cl *BEX* TN40 ...... 183 L1
SEAF BN25 .... 192 A8
Gleneagles Dr *HAIL* BN27 ..... 154 F6
STLEO TN38 .... 161 M7
Glenfalls Av *BRI* BN1 .... 146 A7
Glengorse *BAT* TN33 .... 137 M3
Glenleigh Av *BEXW* TN39 ...... 159 M8
Glenleigh Park Rd *BEXW* TN39 . 160 A8
Glenleigh Wk *RBTBR* TN32 ..... 85 G2
Glenmore Pk *RTWE/PEM* TN2 .... 19 M6
Glenmore Rd *CROW* TN6 .... 39 J3
Glenmore Rd East *CROW* TN6 ... 39 K3
Glen Ri *BRI* BN1 .... 168 B1
Glen Rise Cl *BRI* BN1 .... 168 B1
The Glen *UCK* TN22 .... 76 D5
Glenthorn Rd *BEXW* TN39 ...... 183 G2
Glenview Cl *RHAS* TN35 .... 163 K5
Glen Vue *EGRIN* RH19 .... 13 L5
Glessing Rd *PEV* BN24 .... 197 H1
Gleton Av *HOVE* BN3 .... 167 K4
Gloucester Dr *BEX* TN40 ...... 184 A1
Gloucester Cl *LW/ROSE* BN22 .. 196 C4
Gloucester Pas *BRI* BN1 ...... 6 F5
Gloucester Pl *BRI* BN1 .... 6 F5
Gloucester Rd *BRI* BN1 .... 6 E5
BURH RH15 .... 96 F3
WADH TN5 .... 31 M8
Gloucester St *BRI* BN1 .... 6 F5
Glovers La *BEX* TN40 .... 160 D7
BEXW TN39 .... 160 C7
ROTT BN2 .... 189 J4
Glynde Av *LW/ROSE* BN22 ...... 196 E5
ROTT BN2 .... 189 J5
Glyndebourne Gdns
SLVH TN37 .... 162 C1
Glynde Cl *NEWHV* BN9 .... 191 K4
Glynde Rd *ROTT* BN2 .... 7 L4
Glyne Ascent *BEX* TN40 .... 183 M1
Glyne Barn Cl *BEX* TN40 ...... 184 A1
Glyne Dr *BEX* TN40 .... 184 A1
Glynleigh Dr *POLE* BN26 ...... 178 C8
Glynleigh Rd *PEV* BN24 .... 178 E5
Glynn Ri *PEAHV* BN10 .... 190 B5
Glynn Rd *PEAHV* BN10 .... 190 B5
Goatham La *RYE* TN31 .... 113 L1
Godden Cl *RYE* TN31 .... 65 H6
Godden Rd *RING/NEW* BN8 ..... 74 C7
Godfrey Cl *LEW* BN7 .... 2 F1
Godwin Rd *HOVE* BN3 .... 167 K6
RHAS TN35 .... 163 J5
The Goffs *EAST* BN21 .... 10 A5
Goldbridge Rd *RING/NEW* BN8 .. 74 E7
Goldcrest Dr *UCK* TN22 .... 102 D1
Golden Hl *BURH* RH15 .... 97 K3
Golden Miller La *POLE* BN26 .. 177 L8
Goldhurst Gn *WSEA* TN36 ...... 141 L1
Golding Rd *LGNY* BN23 .... 197 M4
Gold La *PEAHV* BN10 .... 190 C4
Goldsmid Rd *HOVE* BN3 .... 6 B3
Goldsmith Cl *LGNY* BN23 ...... 197 L3
Goldsmiths Av *CROW* TN6 ...... 39 K3
Goldstone Cl *HOVE* BN3 .... 168 B3
Goldstone Crs *HOVE* BN3 ...... 168 A3
Goldstone La *HOVE* BN3 .... 168 B6
Goldstone Rd *HOVE* BN3 .... 168 A7

Goldstone St *HOVE* BN3 .... 168 B7
Goldstone Vls *HOVE* BN3 ...... 168 B5
Goldstone Wy *HOVE* BN3 .... 168 A4
Golf Dr *BRI* BN1 .... 169 H3
Goods Station Rd *RTW* TN1 .... 20 B2
Goodtrees La *EDEN* TN8 .... 16 B2
Goodwin Cl *HAIL* BN27 .... 154 F4
Goodwins Cl *EGRIN* RH19 ...... 13 K3
The Goodwins
RTWE/PEM TN2 .... 19 M5
Goodwood Cl
EDN/EASTW BN20 .... 196 B4
Goodwood Wy *ROTT* BN2 .... 169 L3
Gooseberry La *RYE* TN31 ...... 88 A3
Gordon Av *SHOR* BN43 .... 166 A7
Gordon Cl *HWH* RH16 .... 48 E8
Gordon Rd *BRI* BN1 .... 168 F4
BURH RH15 .... 97 J2
CROW TN6 .... 39 M4
HAIL BN27 .... 155 H7
HAS TN34 .... 5 J5
HWH RH16 .... 48 E8
PTSD BN41 .... 167 G7
SEAF BN25 .... 202 E4
Gore Park Av *EAST* BN21 ...... 206 D3
Gore Park Rd *EAST* BN21 ...... 206 D2
Gorham Av *ROTT* BN2 .... 189 G4
Gorham Cl *ROTT* BN2 .... 189 G4
Gorham Wy *PEAHV* BN10 .... 189 L6
Gorringe Cl *EDN/EASTW* BN20 .. 196 A3
SHOR BN43 .... 166 D7
Gorringe Dr *EDN/EASTW* BN20 .. 196 A3
Gorringe Rd *EAST* BN21 .... 10 D7
Gorringe Valley Rd
EDN/EASTW BN20 .... 196 A3
Gorse Cl *EDN/EASTW* BN20 ..... 206 B1
Gorse Dr *SEAF* BN25 .... 192 F8
Gorse Rd *RTWE/PEM* TN2 ...... 20 E1
Gorse Wd *HTHF* TN21 .... 80 E4
Gorselands *BAT* TN33 .... 112 E5
Gorse Rd *RTWE/PEM* TN2 ...... 20 E1
The Gorses *BEXW* TN39 .... 182 C4
Gorsethorn Wy *RHAS* TN35 ..... 164 C2
The Gorseway *BEXW* TN39 ...... 182 C1
Gosford Wy *POLE* BN26 .... 177 M8
Gote La *RING/NEW* BN8 .... 72 B3
Goudhurst Cl *LGNY* BN23 ...... 197 K5
Gower Rd *HWH* RH16 .... 71 L2
Gowers Cl *RHWH* RH17 .... 34 B6
Gradwell End *RING/NEW* BN8 ... 99 J7
Graffham Cl *ROTT* BN2 .... 169 L3
Grafton St *ROTT* BN2 .... 7 H8
Graham Av *BRI* BN1 .... 168 C2
PTSD BN41 .... 166 F2
Graham Crs *PTSD* BN41 .... 166 F2
Grampian Cl *LGNY* BN23 .... 197 J3
Grand Av *BEX* TN40 .... 160 F8
HOVE BN3 .... 168 C8
HPPT/KEY BN6 .... 122 F2
SEAF BN25 .... 202 C1
Grand Crs *ROTT* BN2 .... 189 G5
Grand Junction Rd *BRI* BN1 ... 6 F7
Grand Pde *EAST* BN21 .... 10 F8
POLE BN26 .... 177 M8
ROTT BN2 .... 6 F5
STLEO TN38 .... 4 A9
Grand Parade Ms *ROTT* BN2 .... 6 F6
Grange Av *SLVH* TN37 .... 162 C2
Grange Cl *BRI* BN1 .... 168 E5
BURH RH15 .... 97 J1
CROW TN6 .... 39 L6
HTHF TN21 .... 105 M8
Grange Court Dr *BEXW* TN39 ... 160 B8
Grange Crs *CRAWE* RH10 .... 12 B7
Grange Gdns *SBGH/RUST* TN4 ... 19 K2
Grange Rd *CRAWE* RH10 .... 12 A7
EAST BN21 .... 10 D8
HAS TN34 .... 162 D1
HOVE BN3 .... 167 L7
LEW BN7 2
RING/NEW BN8 .... 126 D2
SBGH/RUST TN4 .... 19 K2
UCK TN22 .... 76 C7
The Grange *RING/NEW* BN8 ..... 126 D2
Grangeways *BRI* BN1 .... 168 E1
Grantham Bank
RING/NEW BN8 .... 126 E2
Grantham Cl *RING/NEW* BN8 .... 99 L7
Grantham Rd *BRI* BN1 .... 169 G5
Grant St *ROTT* BN2 .... 7 H3
Granville Rd *EDN/EASTW* BN20 . 10 C9
HOVE BN3 .... 6 A3
RTW TN1 .... 20 B1
Grasmere Cl *LGNY* BN23 ...... 197 H2
Grassington Rd
EDN/EASTW BN20 .... 10 C9
Grassmere Av *PEAHV* BN10 .... 189 M6
Gravelye Cl *HWH* RH16 .... 72 B1
Gravelye La *HWH* RH16 .... 72 B1
Gravett Ct *BURH* RH15 .... 96 F4
Graycoats Dr *CROW* TN6 ...... 39 M4
Graystone La *RHAS* TN35 ..... 163 J3
Grazebrook Cl *BEXW* TN39 .... 182 C3
Great Cliffe Rd *LGNY* BN23 .. 197 L5
Great College St *ROTT* BN2 .. 7 K8
Great Courtlands *RRTW* TN3 .. 19 C3
Greater Paddock
RING/NEW BN8 .... 127 L8
Great Footway *RRTW* TN3 ..... 18 F2
Great Oak *BUR/ETCH* TN19 .... 62 A3
Great Rough *RING/NEW* BN8 ... 74 A8
Great Wd *BAT* TN33 .... 138 A2
Grecian Rd *RTW* TN1 .... 20 B4
Greenacres *PEAHV* BN10 ...... 190 D4
RHAS TN35 .... 139 L1
Greenacres Dr *HAIL* BN27 .... 155 J6
Greenbank Av *ROTT* BN2 ...... 189 J5
Green Bank *RING/NEW* BN8 .... 127 L8
STHW BN42 .... 166 E7
Greenfield Cl *BRI* BN1 ...... 169 G1
SBGH/RUST TN4 .... 19 J1
Green Field *STHW* BN42 ...... 166 E6
Greenfield Crs *BRI* BN1 ..... 168 F1

Greenfield Dr *UCK* TN22 ...... 102 D2
Greenfield Rd *BUR/ETCH* TN19 . 60 C7
EAST BN21 .... 206 D3
Greenfields *HAIL* BN27 ...... 155 G5
Greenfields Cl *SLVH* TN37 ... 139 H8
Green Ga *PEAHV* BN10 .... 190 C5
Green Gv *HAIL* BN27 .... 155 J6
Green Hedges Av *EGRIN* RH19 . 13 K4
Green Hedges Cl *EGRIN* RH19 . 13 K4
Greenhill Pk *HWH* RH16 ...... 72 A4
Greenhill Wy *HWH* RH16 ...... 72 A4
Greenlands Cl *BURH* RH15 .. 97 H6
Greenlands Dr *BURH* RH15 .... 97 H6
Green La *BEXW* TN39 .... 182 D1
CROW TN6 .... 40 B3
HTHF TN21 .... 80 B8
LEW BN7 .... 2 F7
POLE BN26 .... 195 J5
RING/NEW BN8 .... 99 L7
RING/NEW BN8 .... 99 L5
RING/NEW BN8 .... 128 A5
ROTT BN2 .... 170 E8
SEAF BN25 .... 202 E4
Greenleaf Gdns *POLE* BN26 ... 178 A7
Greenleas *HOVE* BN3 .... 167 K6
Green Mdw *HWH* RH16 .... 49 H6
Green Park Cnr *RHWH* RH17 ... 98 A2
Green Rdg *BRI* BN1 .... 168 B1
Green Rd *RHWH* RH17 .... 98 A1
Green Sq *HAIL* BN27 .... 155 M1
Greenstede Av *EGRIN* RH19 ... 13 M3
Green St *EDN/EASTW* BN20 .... 206 C2
The Green *BAT* TN33 .... 112 E6
HOVE BN3 .... 168 C4
RING/NEW BN8 .... 74 D7
ROTT BN2 .... 188 F4
RRTW TN3 .... 18 E3
STLEO TN38 .... 162 B5
UCK TN22 .... 78 A8
Green Wk *HAIL* BN27 .... 155 J5
SEAF BN25 .... 203 H4
Green Wy *EDN/EASTW* BN20 .... 195 K8
LYDD TN29 .... 95 H8
LYDD TN29 .... 121 J1
Greenways *BEXW* TN39 .... 159 M7
HWH RH16 .... 48 F6
ROTT BN2 .... 188 D2
STHW BN42 .... 166 F7
Greenways Crs *SHOR* BN43 .... 166 A5
Greenwell Cl *SEAF* BN25 ..... 203 H2
Greenwich Rd *HAIL* BN27 ..... 155 K7
Greenwich Wy *PEAHV* BN10 .... 190 B7
Gregory La *PEV* BN24 .... 197 M1
Gregory Wk *BAT* TN33 .... 112 E6
Grenada Cl *BEXW* TN39 .... 182 D2
Grenville Rd *PEV* BN24 ...... 198 C2
Grenville St *BRI* BN1 .... 6 C6
Gresham Cl *EAST* BN21 .... 196 C8
Gresham Wy *STLEO* TN38 ...... 162 A6
Greville Rd *RHAS* TN35 ...... 163 J3
Grey Alders *HWH* RH16 .... 49 H8
Greyfriars *HOVE* BN3 .... 168 D6
Greyfriars Pl *WSEA* TN36 .... 117 H8
Greys Rd *EDN/EASTW* BN20 .... 206 D3
Grinstead La *EGRIN* RH19 .... 23 J6
Grisbrook Farm Cl *LYDD* TN29 . 95 K8
Gromenfield *RRTW* TN3 .... 18 C7
Groombridge Hl *RRTW* TN3 .... 18 A6
Groombridge Rd *RRTW* TN3 .... 18 A6
Grosvenor Br *SBGH/RUST* TN4 . 20 B1
Grosvenor Cl *POLE* BN26 ..... 195 M1
Grosvenor Crs *STLEO* TN38 ... 161 M8
Grosvenor Gdns *STLEO* TN38 .. 161 M8
Grosvenor Pk *RTW* TN1 .... 20 A1
Grosvenor Rd *EGRIN* RH19 .... 13 K5
SEAF BN25 .... 202 E4
Grosvenor St *ROTT* BN2 ...... 7 C7
Grove Av *RTW* TN1 .... 20 A4
Grove Hl *HAIL* BN27 .... 132 E4
HAIL BN27 .... 155 J1
ROTT BN2 .... 7 C5
Grove Hill Gdns *RTW* TN1 .... 20 A4
Grove Hill Rd *RTW* TN1 ...... 20 A3
Grovelands Cl *BURH* RH15 .... 96 F5
Grovelands Rd *HAIL* BN27 .... 155 G5
Grove La *RYE* TN31 .... 91 J2
Grovely La *HTHF* TN21 .... 108 B5
Grove Rd *BURH* RH15 .... 97 H4
EAST BN21 .... 10 D7
RHAS TN35 .... 163 K2
SEAF BN25 .... 202 F3
Grove St *ROTT* BN2 .... 7 H4
The Grove *BAT* TN33 .... 137 M3
BEXW TN39 .... 182 E1
CROW TN6 .... 39 L5
EDN/EASTW BN20 .... 195 M3
EDN/EASTW BN20 .... 196 B7
HAIL BN27 .... 155 M3
HWH RH16 .... 72 B3
MAYF TN20 .... 57 H4
NEWHV BN9 .... 191 L4
RYE TN31 .... 91 J3
Growers End *RING/NEW* BN8 ... 74 D7
Guardswell Pl *SEAF* BN25 .... 202 E3
Guestling Rd *LW/ROSE* BN22 .. 11 L2
Guildford Rd *BRI* BN1 .... 6 D4
RTW TN1 .... 20 B3
Guildford St *BRI* BN1 .... 6 D4
Guldeford La *RYE* TN31 ...... 92 F1
Guldeford Rd *RYE* TN31 ...... 91 L8
Gundreda Rd *LEW* BN7 .... 2 C4
Gun Rd *UCK* TN22 .... 78 A8
Gunter's La *BEXW* TN39 ...... 160 A7
Gurth Rd *RHAS* TN35 .... 163 J5
Gwyneth Gv *BEX* TN40 .... 160 F7
Gwynne Gdns *EGRIN* RH19 ..... 13 J4

H

Hackenden Cl *EGRIN* RH19 .... 13 L3
Hackenden La *EGRIN* RH19 .... 13 L3
Hackhurst La *HAIL* BN27 ..... 154 B1

Hackwood *RBTBR* TN32 .... 84 E2
Haddington Cl *HOVE* BN3 ..... 168 B8
Haddington St *HOVE* BN3 ..... 168 B7
Hadlow Av *LGNY* BN23 .... 197 G3
Hadlow Cl *ROTT* BN2 .... 7 L5
Hadlow Down Rd *CROW* TN6 .... 54 F4
Hadrian Av *STHW* BN42 .... 166 F6
Hadrian Gdns *STLEO* TN38 .... 139 C8
Haig Av *BRI* BN1 .... 146 D8
Hailsham Av *ROTT* BN2 .... 189 K3
Hailsham Rd *HAIL* BN27 ...... 156 E1
HTHF TN21 .... 80 A8
POLE BN26 .... 177 M7
POLE BN26 .... 178 F6
Hairpin Cft *PEAHV* BN10 ..... 190 C5
Half Mile Dro *RING/NEW* BN8 . 128 B8
Halland Cl *LW/ROSE* BN22 .... 196 D5
Halland Rd *ROTT* BN2 .... 169 M2
Hallett Rd *ROTT* BN2 .... 7 L3
Halley Rd *HAIL* BN27 .... 157 H5
HTHF TN21 .... 80 E6
Hall La *UCK* TN22 .... 78 C1
Hall's Hole Rd *RTWE/PEM* TN2 . 20 E1
Hallsland *CRAWE* RH10 .... 12 C6
Hallyburton Rd *HOVE* BN3 .... 167 K6
Halsford La *EGRIN* RH19 ..... 13 H4
Halsford Park Rd *EGRIN* RH19 . 13 J4
Halton Crs *HAS* TN34 .... 5 M2
Halton Pl *HAS* TN34 .... 5 M2
Halton Rd *LW/ROSE* BN22 ..... 11 J4
Halton Ter *HAS* TN34 .... 5 M2
Hamble Rd *POLE* BN26 .... 196 F1
Hambleton Cl *LGNY* BN23 ..... 197 J3
Hambrook *BURH* RH15 .... 97 J5
Hamelsham Ct *HAIL* BN27 ..... 155 G6
Hamilton Cl *PTSD* BN41 ...... 167 G3
Hamilton Gdns *RHAS* TN35 .... 163 K3
Hamilton Rd *BRI* BN1 .... 6 C1
LYDD TN29 .... 95 J8
Hamilton Ter *BEXW* TN39 ..... 183 G2
Hamlands La *LW/ROSE* BN22 ... 196 B3
Ham La *BUR/ETCH* TN19 .... 60 A7
LEW BN7 .... 3 H8
RHWH RH17 .... 72 E3
RING/NEW BN8 .... 127 H8
Hammer La *HTHF* TN21 .... 106 F6
Hammerwood Rd *EGRIN* RH19 ... 14 E7
Hammingden La *EGRIN* RH19 ... 34 E3
RHWH RH17 .... 34 E7
Hammonds Gdns *BURH* RH15 .... 96 F5
Hammonds Rdg *BURH* RH15 ..... 96 E5
Hammy Cl *ROTT* BN2 .... 166 B6
Hammy La *SHOR* BN43 .... 166 B6
Hammy Wy *SHOR* BN43 .... 166 B6
Hampden Av *LW/ROSE* BN22 .... 196 F5
Hampden Cl *BAT* TN33 .... 137 H2
Hampden Park Dr
LW/ROSE BN22 .... 196 E6
Hampden Rd *ROTT* BN2 .... 7 J3
Hampstead Rd *BRI* BN1 .... 168 D5
Hampton Pl *BRI* BN1 .... 6 B6
Hampton St *BRI* BN1 .... 6 B6
Hampton Wy *EGRIN* RH19 ...... 13 M7
Hamsey Cl *EDN/EASTW* BN20 ... 196 B8
ROTT BN2 .... 187 M1
Hamsey La *RING/NEW* BN8 ..... 126 A7
SEAF BN25 .... 203 J4
Hamsey Rd *EGRIN* RH19 .... 23 G3
ROTT BN2 .... 189 K6
Hamsland *RHWH* RH17 .... 50 C2
Hanbury La *RHWH* RH17 .... 72 A1
Hanging Birch La *HTHF* TN21 . 105 K3
Hangleton Cl *HOVE* BN3 ...... 167 K4
Hangleton Gdns *HOVE* BN3 .... 167 K5
Hangleton La *HOVE* BN3 ...... 167 J4
PTSD BN41 .... 167 H4
Hangleton Manor Cl
HOVE BN3 .... 167 J4
Hangleton Rd *HOVE* BN3 ...... 167 L4
Hangleton Valley Dr
HOVE BN3 .... 167 J3
Hangleton Wy *HOVE* BN3 ...... 167 K4
Hankham Hall Rd *PEV* BN24 ... 179 H5
Hankham Rd *PEV* BN24 .... 179 H8
Hankham St *PEV* BN24 .... 179 H5
Hanlye La *RHWH* RH17 .... 48 A6
Hannington Pl *HPPT/KEY* BN6 . 96 A1
Hanover Cl *BEX* TN40 .... 183 J1
SEAF BN25 .... 192 B8
Hanover Crs *ROTT* BN2 .... 7 G3
Hanover Ms *ROTT* BN2 .... 7 H3
Hanover Rd *LW/ROSE* BN22 .... 11 J4
RTW TN1 .... 20 A2
Hanover St *ROTT* BN2 .... 7 H3
Hanover Ter *ROTT* BN2 ...... 7 H3
Hanson Rd *NEWHV* BN9 .... 8 D4
Harbour Farm *WSEA* TN36 .... 117 H8
Harbour Rd *RYE* TN31 .... 117 J2
Harbour View Cl *SEAF* BN25 . 192 B8
Harbour View Rd *NEWHV* BN9 .. 8 C7
Harbour Wy *SHOR* BN43 ...... 166 C8
STLEO TN38 .... 138 E7
Harcourt Cl *UCK* TN22 ...... 76 C8
Harcourt Rd *UCK* TN22 ...... 76 D8
Harden Rd *LYDD* TN29 .... 95 K7
Harding Av *LW/ROSE* BN22 ... 197 H8
Hardwicke Rd *HAS* TN34 ..... 5 M2
Hardwick Rd *EAST* BN21 ..... 10 E8
HOVE BN3 .... 167 L3
Hardwick Wy *HOVE* BN3 ...... 167 L3
Hardy Dr *LGNY* BN23 .... 197 M8
Harebeating Cl *HAIL* BN27 .. 155 J4
Harebeating Crs *HAIL* BN27 . 155 J4
Harebeating Dr *HAIL* BN27 .. 155 J4
Harebeating Gdns *HAIL* BN27 . 155 J4
Harebeating La *HAIL* BN27 .. 155 J4
Harebell Cl *LGNY* BN23 ..... 197 J3
Harebell Dr *PTSD* BN41 ..... 167 G3
Harecombe Rd *CROW* TN6 ..... 39 L6
Harecombe Ri *CROW* TN6 ..... 39 L6
Haremere Hl *BUR/ETCH* TN19 . 61 K5
Harescroft *RTWE/PEM* TN2 ... 19 M7
Hare Wy *SLVH* TN37 .... 162 C1
Harewood Cl *BEXW* TN39 ..... 182 F3
Harfield Cl *NEWHV* BN9 ..... 191 M4
Hargate Cl *RTWE/PEM* TN2 ... 19 M7
Harison Rd *SEAF* BN25 ...... 203 G2
Harkness Dr *HAS* TN34 ...... 163 H1

Harlands Cl RHWH RH17....48 C8
Harlands Rd HWH RH16....48 C8
Harlequin Gdns SLVH TN37 ....139 C8
Harlequin Pl CROW TN6....39 L6
Harlequin La CROW TN6....39 L6
Harley La HTHF TN21....80 A8
Harley Shute Rd STLEO TN38 ..161 L7
Harley Wy STLEO TN38....161 L8
Harmans Md EGRIN RH19....14 A5
Harmers Hay Rd HAIL BN27....155 H5
Harmers Hl RING/NEW BN8 ....74 C7
Harmony St SBGH/RUST TN4 ....19 K2
Harmsworth Crs HOVE BN3 ..167 L3 🔲
Harold Cl PEV BN24....180 F7
Harold Dr LGNY BN23....197 L6
Harold Ms STLEO TN38....5 G7
Harold Pl HAS TN34....5 C7
Harold Rd HAS TN34....5 K4
  RHAS TN35....163 K4
Harpers Rd NEWHV BN9....8 E3
Harrier La BAT TN33....137 M2
Harrington Pl BRI BN1....169 H4
Harrington Rd BRI BN1....168 E4
Harrington Vls BRI BN1....168 E4
Harris Ct EAST BN21....10 F6
Harrisons La RING/NEW BN8 ..127 L8 🔲
  RING/NEW BN8....150 E1
Harrow Cl SEAF BN25....203 C2
Harrow La SLVH TN37....139 H8
  SLVH TN37....162 B1
Hart Cl UCK TN22....76 A7
Hartfield Av BRI BN1....169 G2
Hartfield La EAST BN21....10 D4 🔲
Hartfield Meadow
  STLEO TN38....161 K3 🔲
Hartfield Rd BEXW TN39....182 D4
  EAST BN21....10 D4
  EDEN TN8....16 D3
  FROW RH18....25 G4
  ROTT BN2....189 K4
  SEAF BN25....203 C2
Hartington Pl EAST BN21....10 F7
  ROTT BN2....7 K1
Hartington Rd ROTT BN2....7 K1
Hartington Ter ROTT BN2....7 K1
Hartington Vls HOVE BN3....168 B6
Harvard Cl LEW BN7....2 F1
Harvard Rd RING/NEW BN8....150 D7
Harvest Cl HWH RH16....49 H7
  PEAHV BN10....190 B4 🔲
Harvesters HWH RH16....71 K4
Harvest Hl EGRIN RH19....13 L6
  RHWH RH17....70 C5
Harvest Wy SLVH TN37....162 C1 🔲
Harvey Cl RING/NEW BN8....128 B3
  UCK TN22....102 F6 🔲
Harveys Wy LEW BN7....3 J5
Harwarden Cl CRAWE RH10....12 C6
Harwood Cl LGNY BN23....197 L2
Harwoods Cl EGRIN RH19....13 M7 🔲
  EGRIN RH19....13 M8
Haslam Crs BEX TN40....160 F8
Hassocks Av SEAF BN25....196 F2
Hassocks Rd HPPT/KEY BN6....122 B1
Hastings Av SEAF BN25....203 J1
Hastings La POLE BN26....178 E7
Hastings Rd BAT TN33....138 A3
  BEX TN40....183 K1
  HAWK TN18....47 M7
  ROTT BN2....7 J1
  STPH/PW TN12....21 M1
Hatch End FROW RH18....24 F4
Hatchgate Cl RHWH RH17....48 A8
Hatchgate La RHWH RH17....48 A8
Hatherley Rd SLVH TN37....4 A7
Havelock Rd BEXW TN39....160 C8
  BRI BN1....168 F5
  HAS TN34....5 G6
  LW/ROSE BN22....11 G3
Haven Brow SEAF BN25....203 C2
Haven Cl LW/ROSE BN22....196 B3
  PEV BN24....180 E8
Haven Gdns CRAWE RH10....12 A5
Haven Rd STLEO TN38....161 K8
Hawkenbury Cl
  RTWE/PEM TN2....20 D4 🔲
Hawkenbury Md
  RTWE/PEM TN2....20 D5 🔲
Hawkenbury Rd
  RTWE/PEM TN2....20 E5
Hawkenbury Wy LEW BN7....2 J6
Hawkhurst La LGNY BN23....197 J4
Hawkhurst Rd BRI BN1....146 D8
  BUR/ETCH TN19....46 F4
Hawkhurst Wy BEXW TN39....182 D4
Hawkins Cl SHOR BN43....166 D5
Hawkins Crs SHOR BN43....166 D5
Hawkins Rd SHOR BN43....166 D5
Hawkins Wy HAIL BN27....155 H6
Hawksbridge Cl
  LW/ROSE BN22....196 B3
Hawks Farm Cl HAIL BN27 ..155 H4 🔲
Hawks Rd HAIL BN27....155 H3
Hawkstown Cl HAIL BN27 ....155 H3 🔲
Hawks Town Crs HAIL BN27....155 H3
Hawkstown Gdns HAIL BN27 ..155 H3 🔲
Hawkstown Vw HAIL BN27 ....155 H3 🔲
Hawkswood Dr HAIL BN27....155 J3
Hawkswood Rd HAIL BN27....155 H3
Hawmead CRAWE RH10....12 C6
Hawth Cl SEAF BN25....202 C2
Hawth Crs SEAF BN25....202 C2
Hawth Gv SEAF BN25....202 C1 🔲
Hawth Hl SEAF BN25....202 B1
Hawthorn Av BEXW TN39....182 B3
Hawthorn Cl BURH RH15....97 K1 🔲
  ROTT BN2....189 J4
Hawthorne Cl HTHF TN21....80 B8 🔲
The Hawthornes RYE TN31....114 A2
Hawthorn Ri NEWHV BN9....8 C4
Hawthorn Rd RHAS TN35....163 K4 🔲
The Hawthorns BURH RH15 ..97 G1 🔲
  HAIL BN27....155 J7
Hawthorn Wy PTSD BN41....167 G3
Hawth Park Rd SEAF BN25 ..202 C1 🔲
Hawth Ri SEAF BN25....202 C1 🔲

Hawth Wy SEAF BN25....202 D2
Hawthylands Crs HAIL BN27 ..155 H4
Hawthylands Dr HAIL BN27 ..155 H4
Hawthylands Rd HAIL BN27 ..155 H4
Haybourne Cl ROTT BN2....169 L7 🔲
Haybourne Rd ROTT BN2....169 L7
Hayes Cl PTSD BN41....167 J4
  RING/NEW BN8....150 D1 🔲
Hayes La RYE TN31....115 H1
Hayes Plat RYE TN31....88 C1
Haylind Rd HAS TN34....72 B1
Haystoun Cl LW/ROSE BN22 ..196 C4
Haystoun Pk LW/ROSE BN22 ..196 C4
Hayward Rd LEW BN7....2 B1
Haywards BRI BN1....146 A8
  HWH RH16....71 L3
Hazelbank RRTW TN3....18 F3 🔲
Hazel Cl CRAWE RH10....12 C6
  NEWHV BN9....8 C4
  PTSD BN41....167 H3
Hazeldene SEAF BN25....203 F3
Hazeldene Meads BRI BN1....168 D4
Hazeldene La RING/NEW BN8 ..73 M7
Hazel Gv BURH RH15....97 H5
  EDN/EASTW BN20....196 A3
Hazelgrove Rd HWH RH16....71 L2
Hazelwood Av LW/ROSE BN22 ..196 D3
Hazelwood Cl BEXW TN39....182 B3
Hazelwood Gdns HAS TN34....162 D1
Hazelwood Rd SEAF BN25 ....203 G3
Headland Cl PEAHV BN10 ....190 E7 🔲
Heansill La WADH TN18....47 L6
Heathcote Dr EGRIN RH19....13 H4
Heathdown Cl PEAHV BN10 ..190 D4
Heather Bank HWH RH16....71 J1
Heather Cl LGNY BN23....197 H3
Heatherdune Rd BEXW TN39 ..183 C1
Heather Wy RHAS TN35....164 F2
Heathfield Av ROTT BN2....189 K4
Heathfield Cl HAS TN34....162 F1
Heathfield Crs PTSD BN41....166 F2
Heathfield Dr PTSD BN41....166 F3
Heathfield Gdns RBTBR TN32 ..85 H3
Heathfield Rd SEAF BN25....202 F3
Heath Hill Av ROTT BN2....169 M5
Heathlands RHAS TN35....139 L3
Heath Rd HWH RH16....71 L1
Heathy Brow PEAHV BN10....190 B5
Heavegate Rd CROW TN6....39 J6
Heighton Cl BEXW TN39....182 D3
Heighton Crs NEWHV BN9....191 K4
Heighton Rd NEWHV BN9....191 L4
The Heights BRI BN1....168 B1
  RHAS TN35....163 L2
Helena Cl PTSD BN41....187 L1
Helena Rd ROTT BN2....170 D5 🔲
Hellingly Cl ROTT BN2....187 L1
Hempstead Gdns UCK TN22 ..76 D7 🔲
Hempstead La HAIL BN27....154 E6
  UCK TN22....76 E6
Hempstead Ri UCK TN22....76 C7 🔲
Hempstead Rd UCK TN22....189 K4
  UCK TN22....76 C7
Henderson Cl HAS TN34....162 F3
Hendon St ROTT BN2....7 L6
Henfield Cl ROTT BN2....187 M2
Henfield Rd LW/ROSE BN22 ..196 E4
Henfield Wy HOVE BN3....167 M3
Henge Wy PTSD BN41....167 H4
Hengist Cl LGNY BN23....197 M6 🔲
Henley Cl RTWE/PEM TN2....20 C2
  RYE TN31....91 G8
Henley Rd ROTT BN2....187 M2
Henley's Hl BAT TN33....135 G5
Henry Burt Wy BURH RH15....96 E5
Herbert Rd BRI BN1....168 F4
Herbrand Wk ROTT BN2....181 M5
Hereford Rd ROTT BN2....7 H7
Hereward Rd LGNY BN23....197 M5
Hereward Wy LEW BN7....3 J7
Hermitage La EGRIN RH19....13 M6
Hermitage Rd EGRIN RH19....13 K3
Herne Down CROW TN6....39 M7
Herne Rd CROW TN6....39 M6
Heron Cl LGNY BN23....197 J4
  STLEO TN38....161 L6
  UCK TN22....102 D1
Heron Pl EGRIN RH19....13 M6
Heron Rdg POLE BN26....178 B8
Herons Cl CRAWE RH10....12 A1
Heronsdale Rd ROTT BN2....170 F6
Herons Lea CRAWE RH10....12 A1
Herontye Dr EGRIN RH19....13 M6
Herring's Rd HTHF TN21....108 E5
Hertford Cl STLEO TN38....162 A2
Hertford Rd BRI BN1....169 H4
Heston Av BRI BN1....145 M7
Hever Cl CRAWE RH10....197 K4
Hever Crs BEXW TN39....182 F1
Heyworth Cl ROTT BN2....197 M2
Hickling Cl LGNY BN23....197 H2 🔲
Hickman's Cl HWH RH16....49 H6 🔲
Hickman's La HWH RH16....49 G6
Hickman Wy SLVH TN37....162 D2
Hide Hollow LGNY BN23....197 K3
High Wickham RHAS TN35....5 M4
Higham Gdns RHAS TN35....141 G6
Higham La RYE TN31....65 G8
Highbank BRI BN1....168 B1
High Bank RHAS TN35....163 J4 🔲
High Bank Cl RHAS TN35 ....163 J4 🔲
High Beech Cl STLEO TN38 ..138 F8
High Beech La HWH RH16....48 F6
High Branches BEXW TN39 ..182 E2
Highbridge La LEW BN7....125 H2
Highbrook Cl ROTT BN2....169 K4
High Broom La CROW TN6....39 L7
High Broom Rd CROW TN6....39 L7
High Cl EDN/EASTW BN20....205 J4
  PTSD BN41....167 G5 🔲
Highcroft Crs HTHF TN21....80 A7
Highcroft Rd EGRIN RH19....23 G8
Highcroft Vls BRI BN1....168 E5
High Cross Flds CROW TN6....39 M3
Highdown STHW BN42....166 F5
Highdown Cl STHW BN42....166 F5
Highdown Rd HOVE BN3....6 A2
  LEW BN7....2 A3

Highfield Crs BRI BN1....169 G1
Highfield Dr HPPT/KEY BN6 ..122 B1
  STLEO TN38....161 K3
Highfield Rd EGRIN RH19....13 K3
  HTHF TN21....80 E5
  HTHF TN21....105 M7
Highfields BRI BN1....169 L1
  BUR/ETCH TN19....83 G1
  FROW RH18....24 F4
High Fords Cl WSEA TN36....141 L1
High Fords Cl WSEA TN36 ..115 L8 🔲
Highgate Hl HAWK TN18....47 M5
Highgate Rd FROW RH18....24 F5
Highgrove BAT TN33....137 H2 🔲
  RTWE/PEM TN2....20 A6
High Hurst Cl RING/NEW BN8 ..74 D7
Highland Ct HWH RH16....71 L2 🔲
Highland Rd HWH RH16....71 M3
Highlands Av UCK TN22....102 D2
Highlands Cl BEXW TN39....159 M7
  CROW TN6....39 L3
  HPPT/KEY BN6....123 G3
Highlands Dr BURH RH15....97 G2
Highlands Gdns HAS TN34....162 B7
Highlands Rd PTSD BN41....167 H5
  SEAF BN25....202 F3
The Highlands BEXW TN39....159 M6
Highlea Cl SLVH TN37....162 C1 🔲
High Meadow RYE TN31....65 G7
High Pk RYE TN31....65 G7
High Park Av HOVE BN3....167 L3
High Point HWH RH16....72 A3
High Rocks La RRTW TN3....19 J5
High St LEW BN7....3 C6
  LEW BN7....190 D4
  RING/NEW BN8....130 A1
High St BAT TN33....136 A8
  BAT TN33....137 K1
  BUR/ETCH TN19....60 A8
  BUR/ETCH TN19....61 H6
  CROW TN6....39 M3
  CROW TN6....41 H6
  EAST BN21....10 A5
  EDEN TN8....16 A1
  EGRIN RH19....13 M6
  HAIL BN27....155 J7
  HAS TN34....5 L5
  HPPT/KEY BN6....122 A1
  HPPT/KEY BN6....123 K3
  HRTF TN7....26 D2
  HTHF TN21....80 A7
  HTHF TN21....105 M7
  LEW BN7....2 C7
  LYDD TN29....95 H8
  LYDD TN29....121 H1
  MAYF TN20....57 G4
  NEWHV BN9....8 F3
  PEV BN24....180 E8
  POLE BN26....178 A7 🔲
  POLE BN26....193 M4
  PTSD BN41....167 G5
  RBTBR TN32....85 H2
  RHWH RH17....34 B6
  RING/NEW BN8....74 D7
  RING/NEW BN8....126 D2
  RING/NEW BN8....130 A1
  ROTT BN2....7 G7
  ROTT BN2....188 F5
  RRTW TN3....30 C2
  RRTW TN3....33 G2
  RTW TN1....20 A4
  RYE TN31....117 J1
  SEAF BN25....202 F4
  UCK TN22....52 C2
  UCK TN22....76 B2
  UCK TN22....77 J3
  WADH TN5....43 L1
  WADH TN5....44 D5
  WADH TN5....46 D3
  WSEA TN36....116 E7
High Trees BRI BN1....71 M1
Highview Av North BRI BN1 ..145 L8
Highview Av South BRI BN1 ..168 L1
Highview Cl HAIL BN27....157 H1
  HAS TN34....162 D1
Highview La UCK TN22....102 D2
Highview Rd BRI BN1....145 L8 🔲
  PEAHV BN10....189 L7
Highwater Vw BAT TN33....138 E7
Highway Cl ROTT BN2....169 K4
Highways PTSD BN41....167 H4 🔲
  ROTT BN2....169 K3
High Weald Landscape Trail
  CROW TN6....27 J6
  EGRIN RH19....13 K7
  EGRIN RH19....15 J8
  EGRIN RH19....34 D1
  HRTF TN7....27 J4
  RHWH RH17....48 B5
High Weald Wk RRTW TN3....18 C7
  RTWE/PEM TN2....20 E6
  SBGH/RUST TN4....19 M4
High Wickham RHAS TN35 ....5 M4
Highwoods Av BEXW TN39 ..159 J8
High Woods La RTWE/PEM TN2 ..20 F4
Hiham Gn WSEA TN36....116 E7
Hilary Cl POLE BN26....195 M1
Hilbert Cl RTW TN1....20 C1
Hilders Farm Cl CROW TN6....40 B5
Hilgrove Rd ROTT BN2....189 K3
Hillary Cl EGRIN RH19....14 A4
Hillbank Cl PTSD BN41....166 F3
Hillborough Cl BEXW TN39 ..182 D2
Hill Brow HOVE BN3....168 B2
Hillbrow Rd BRI BN1....168 C2
Hillbury Gdns WADH TN5....45 L5
Hill Cl CROW TN6....39 L5
Hillcrest BRI BN1....168 C1
  RYE TN31....91 H7
Hillcrest Av BEXW TN39....160 A8
Hillcrest Cl RHWH RH17....72 F4
Hillcrest La RHWH RH17....72 E4
Hill Crest Rd NEWHV BN9....8 E6
Hillcroft PTSD BN41....166 F4
Hill Dr HOVE BN3....168 B3

Hill Farm Wy STHW BN42....166 D4
Hill House Cl CRAWE RH10....22 A2
Hill Md UCK TN22....52 C2
Hillrise CROW TN6....40 B4
Hill Ri NEWHV BN9....191 M5
  SEAF BN25....202 C1
Hill Rd EDN/EASTW BN20....206 A1
  LEW BN7....2 B3
  NEWHV BN9....191 M5
  RHAS TN35....164 C3
  ROTT BN2....189 H5
Hill Side NEWHV BN9....9 G4
Hillside CRAWE RH10....12 B6
  EDN/EASTW BN20....205 H5
  PTSD BN41....167 J5
  ROTT BN2....169 K4
  STHW BN42....166 F5
Hillside Av SEAF BN25....203 H1 🔲
Hillside Cl EGRIN RH19....13 L3
Hillside Dr HTHF TN21....105 M7
Hillside Rd BEX TN40....183 H1
  HAS TN34....139 L8
  HAS TN34....162 E3
Hillside Wk RHWH RH17....48 C8
Hillside Wy BRI BN1....168 C2
Hill St LEW BN7....2 C8
  HAS TN34....5 K6
  RTW TN1....20 B1 🔲
Hill Top BRI BN1....168 B1
Hill Top Cl PTSD BN41....166 F4
Hilltop Dr RYE TN31....91 H7
Hilltop Rd EGRIN RH19....22 E8
Hillview Rd SBGH/RUST TN4 ..19 J2
Hill View Rd BRI BN1....168 B1
Hillydale LEW BN7....2 J8
Hillyglen Cl HAS TN34....4 E5
Hindover Crs SEAF BN25....203 G3 🔲
Hindover Rd SEAF BN25....203 G2
Hinton Cl BRI BN1....169 J4
Hither Chantlers RRTW TN3 ..19 G3
Hoad La HWH RH16....49 J2
Hoadleys La CROW TN6....39 K1
Hoad Rd LW/ROSE BN22....11 H4
Hoad's Wood Rd HAS TN34 ..162 F3
Hoath Hl RBTBR TN32....111 J1
Hobbs La RYE TN31....66 D8
Hobdens La RHWH RH17....34 A7
Hoblands HWH RH16....72 B2
Hobney Ri PEV BN24....197 M1
Hockington La
  EDN/EASTW BN20....196 B5
Hodcombe Cl LGNY BN23....197 H2
Hoddern Av PEAHV BN10....190 B7
Hodshrove Rd ROTT BN2....169 L3
The Hoe SLVH TN37....139 H8
Hogarth Rd HOVE BN3....167 M7
Hoggarth St ROTT BN2....197 K5
Hoghole La RRTW TN3....32 E4
Hogtrough La WSEA TN36....116 E7
Holbrook Cl EDN/EASTW BN20 ..206 E6
The Holdings LEW BN7....171 M1
Hole Farm Cl HAS TN34....4 E1
Holland Av BEXW TN39....182 C2
Holland Ms HOVE BN3....186 D1
Holland Rd HOVE BN3....168 D8
Hollands Wy EGRIN RH19....14 A5
Hollier's Hl BEX TN40....183 J1
Hollin Cl SBGH/RUST TN4 ....19 M2 🔲
Hollingbury Copse BRI BN1 ..169 H5
Hollingbury Crs BRI BN1....169 H5
Hollingbury Park Av BRI BN1 ..169 H5
Hollingbury Pl BRI BN1....169 H4
Hollingbury Ri BRI BN1....169 H3
Hollingbury Ri West BRI BN1 ..169 H3
Hollingbury Rd BRI BN1....169 H5
Hollingbury Ter BRI BN1....169 G4 🔲
Hollingdean La BRI BN1....169 G5
Hollingdean Rd ROTT BN2....169 H5
Hollingdean St BRI BN1....169 H5
Hollingdean Ter BRI BN1....169 G5
Hollington Cl SLVH TN37....162 B2 🔲
Hollington Old La SLVH TN37 ..162 A4
Hollington Park Cl STLEO TN38 ..162 A5
Hollington Park Rd
  STLEO TN38....162 A5
Hollow La UCK TN22....104 A2
The Hollow EGRIN RH19....22 F8
  HWH RH16....72 B1
Hollybank Gdns STLEO TN38 ..162 B5
Holly Cl BEXW TN39....159 J8
  BRI BN1....168 E3
  HAIL BN27....155 H8 🔲
  HTHF TN21....80 A8
Holly Ct CROW TN6....39 L4 🔲
Hollydene Rd WADH TN5....31 M8
Holly Pl LW/ROSE BN22....196 E3
Holly Rd HWH RH16....71 M3
Hollyshaw Cl RTWE/PEM TN2 ..20 C4 🔲
Holmans RHWH RH17....34 A6
Holmbush Cl HWH RH16....71 L4
  SHOR BN43....166 D4
Holmbush Wy STHW BN42....166 D5
Holmdale Rd NEWHV BN9....191 M5
Holmes Av HOVE BN3....167 M4
Holmes Cl SEAF BN25....192 A8
Holmesdale Cl WADH TN5....43 L1 🔲
Holmesdale Gdns HAS TN34 ....4 E6
Holmesdale Rd BEXW TN39 ..183 G2
  BURH RH15....96 F5
Holmewood Rdg RRTW TN3....18 F3
Holmhurst Cl
  SBGH/RUST TN4....19 M2 🔲
Holmhurst La SLVH TN37....139 H8
Holm Oak Cl BEXW TN39....182 E3
Holters Wy SEAF BN25....202 F1
Holton Hl ROTT BN2....170 E7
The Holt BURH RH15....97 J4
  HAIL BN27....155 G8
  SEAF BN25....202 F1
Holtye Av BEXW TN39....160 A8
Holtye Rd EGRIN RH19....13 M6
  EGRIN RH19....14 E3
Holyhead Cl HAIL BN27....155 G5

Holywell Cl
  EDN/EASTW BN20....206 E7 🔲
Holywell Rd EDN/EASTW BN20 ..206 E7 🔲
Homebush Av ROTT BN2....189 M3
  ROTT BN2....189 K5
Home Farm Rd BRI BN1....169 K3
Homefield Cl SEAF BN25....202 F2 🔲
Homefield Rd SEAF BN25....202 F1
Homelands Cl BEXW TN39....160 A8
Home Platt EGRIN RH19....23 G8
Home Rd BRI BN1....168 E4
Homestall Rd EGRIN RH19....14 E6
Homestead La BURH RH15....71 J8
The Homestead RRTW TN3....18 C7 🔲
Homewood Cl LW/ROSE BN22 ..197 H8
Homewood Rd RRTW TN3....18 F3
Honeycrag Cl POLE BN26....177 M7
Honey Cft HOVE BN3....167 K2
Honey La RING/NEW BN8....152 D7
Honeypot La RING/NEW BN8 ....99 H7
Honeysuckle Cl HAIL BN27....178 B1
  LGNY BN23....197 H3
  SLVH TN37....162 D1 🔲
Honeyway Cl POLE BN26....195 M3 🔲
Hood Cl LGNY BN23....197 L7
Hoo Gdns EDN/EASTW BN20 ..196 B5 🔲
Hook Hl WADH TN5....33 G8
Hook La EGRIN RH19....34 C4
  RHWH RH17....34 C4
Hookswood Cl CROW TN6....40 A3
Hook Wall LYDD TN29....93 K1
Hoopers Cl LEW BN7....2 B1
Hoover Cl STLEO TN38....138 F7
Hopfield Gdns UCK TN22....76 E6 🔲
Hop Gdn UCK TN22....53 J4
Hopgarden Rd HAS TN34....4 E5
Hophurst Cl CRAWE RH10....12 B6 🔲
Hophurst Dr CRAWE RH10....12 B6
Hophurst Hl CRAWE RH10....12 B6
Hophurst La CRAWE RH10....12 B5
Hoppers Croft La
  BUR/ETCH TN19....60 B8
Horam Park Cl HTHF TN21....105 M7
Horebeech La HTHF TN21....105 M7
Horleigh Green Rd MAYF TN20 ..56 C5
Horley Pl ROTT BN2....169 L8
Hornbeam BUR/ETCH TN19....60 B7
Hornbuckles Cl
  RING/NEW BN8....99 L7 🔲
Hornby Rd ROTT BN2....189 M5
Horning Cl LGNY BN23....197 H2 🔲
Hornshurst Rd CROW TN6....41 H6
Horns Rd HAWK TN18....47 K6
Horntye Rd SLVH TN37....4 B4
Horse Br BAT TN33....157 M7
Horsegrove Av WADH TN5....45 M5
Horsegrove La CROW TN6....41 H6
Horseshoe Cl STLEO TN38....162 B4
Horseshoe La RYE TN31....88 F3
Horsewalk HAIL BN27....157 M7
Horsfield Rd LEW BN7....2 C2
Horsgate La RHWH RH17....48 A8
Horsham Av North BRI BN10 ..190 B8
Horsham Av North
  PEAHV BN10....190 C6
Horsham Cl ROTT BN2....169 M8 🔲
Horsted La EGRIN RH19....35 H2
  RHWH RH17....50 F3
  UCK TN22....101 L7
Horsted Pond La UCK TN22 ....102 A2
Horsye Rd LW/ROSE BN22....197 H1
Horton Rd BRI BN1....169 H5
Hoskins Pl EGRIN RH19....13 M2
Hosmers Fld CROW TN6....41 K5
Hospital Vls HWH RH16....71 M4
Houghton Green La RYE TN31 ..91 K4
Houghton La RYE TN31....91 J3
Houndean Cl LEW BN7....2 A7
Houndean Ri LEW BN7....148 F6
Hova Vls HOVE BN3....168 B8
Hove Park Gdns HOVE BN3....168 C5
Hove Park Rd HOVE BN3....168 C5
Hove Park Vls HOVE BN3....168 C5
Hove Park Wy HOVE BN3....168 C5
Hove Pl HOVE BN3....186 B1
Hove St HOVE BN3....168 A8
Howard Av BURH RH15....96 E2
Howard Cl HAIL BN27....155 K8
Howard Pl BRI BN1....6 C3
Howard Rd ROTT BN2....7 J3
Howards Crs BEXW TN39....182 C2
Howard Sq EAST BN21....10 F8
Howard Ter BRI BN1....6 C3
Howbourne La UCK TN22....77 L1
Howey Cl NEWHV BN9....8 A8
Howlett Cl STLEO TN38....161 M2
Howlett Dr HAIL BN27....155 H4
Howletts Cl LW/ROSE BN22....196 F5
How's Cl RYE TN31....114 B1
Hoyle Rd PEAHV BN10....190 C7
Hudson Cl LGNY BN23....198 A1
Huggett's La LW/ROSE BN22 ..196 B3
Hughenden Pl HAS TN34....5 J2
Hughenden Rd HAS TN34....169 H6
Hughes Rd ROTT BN2....169 H6
Hughes Wy UCK TN22....76 C6
Hugletts La HTHF TN21....81 G8
Humboldt Ct RTWE/PEM TN2 ..20 D1
Humphrey's Gap SHOR BN43 ..166 A8
Hundred Acre La
  HPPT/KEY BN6....98 B5
Hundredhouse La RYE TN31 ..114 F3
Hungershall Pk
  SBGH/RUST TN4....19 L4
Hunloke Av LW/ROSE BN22 ..197 H8
Hunston Cl ROTT BN2....170 F7
Hunters Wy RTWE/PEM TN2 ..19 M5
  UCK TN22....76 B6
Hunting Cl BEX TN40....183 J1
Huntingdon Wy BURH RH15 ..97 K1
Huntley Mill Rd WADH TN5....45 K3
Hurdis Rd SEAF BN25....192 A4
Hurrell Rd HAS TN34....5 L1
Hurst Crs PTSD BN41....167 G3
Hurst Farm Rd EGRIN RH19 ..13 K6
Hurstfield Cl HWH RH16....72 A4 🔲
Hurst Hl BRI BN1....169 J1
Hurst La BAT TN33....112 E3

EAST BN21 206 D2
HAIL BN27 157 H1
Hurst Rd EAST BN21 206 D1
HPPT/KEY BN6 122 D2
Hurstwood Cl BEX TN40 184 B1
Hurstwood La HWH RH16 71 M6 1
RHWH RH17 35 K5
SBGH/RUST TN4 19 L3
Hurstwood Pk SBGH/RUST TN4 19 M3
Hurstwood Rd UCK TN22 54 A8
Hurtis Hl CROW TN6 39 L7
Hutton Rd BRI BN1 169 H3
Hyde Cl LEW BN7 171 L1
Hyde Gdns EAST BN21 10 E7
Hydehurst Cl CROW TN6 39 M5
Hyde Rd EAST BN21 10 D7
The Hyde ROTT BN2 169 M5
Hyde Tynings Cl
EDN/EASTW BN20 206 C6
The Hydneye LW/ROSE BN22 196 F5
Hydney St LW/ROSE BN22 11 J2
Hylden Cl ROTT BN2 170 B6 2
Hyperion Av POLE BN26 177 L8
Hythe Av STLEO TN38 184 B1 1
Hythe Cl POLE BN26 178 C7
SEAF BN25 203 J1
Hythe Crs SEAF BN25 203 J2 3
Hythe Rd BRI BN1 169 G4
Hythe Vw SEAF BN25 203 J2 4

I

Ian Cl BEX TN40 160 F7
Icklesham Dr STLEO TN38 161 K3
Iden Cl ROTT BN2 187 L1
Iden Hurst HPPT/KEY BN6 96 A7
Iden Rd RYE TN31 91 H3
Iden's La HTHF TN21 80 D6
Iden St LW/ROSE BN22 197 G4
Ifield Cl ROTT BN2 189 L4
Ifield Mill Cl PEV BN24 197 H1
Iford Cl NEWHV BN9 191 K4 2
Imberhorne Wy EGRIN RH19 13 H3
Ingham Dr BRI BN1 146 D8
Ingleside STLEO TN38 161 L2
Ingleside Dr CROW TN6 39 L4
Inglewood Gdns STLEO TN38 161 L2
Ingram Crs HOVE BN3 167 L7 1
Ingram Crs East HOVE BN3 167 L7
Ingram Crs West HOVE BN3 167 L7
Ingrams Av BEXW TN39 160 C7
Ingrams Wy HAIL BN27 178 A1
Inholmes Cl BURH RH15 97 H4
Inholmes Park Rd BURH RH15 97 H3
Inkpen La FROW RH18 24 F5
Innham's Wd CROW TN6 39 K2
Innings Dr PEV BN24 198 C2
Innovation Dr HPPT/KEY BN6 96 D4
Inverness Rd ROTT BN2 7 J1 2
Invicta Rd LYDD TN29 121 G4
Inwood Crs BRI BN1 168 D5
Iona Wy HWH RH16 71 L2 3
Irelands La LEW BN7 2 D6 1
Ironlatch Av STLEO TN38 161 M5
Ironlatch Cl STLEO TN38 161 M4
Ironstones RRTW TN3 19 H3 1
Ironstone Wy UCK TN22 76 E7 2
Isaac's La BURH RH15 70 F8
Isabel Cl SEAF BN25 202 E1
Isabel Crs HOVE BN3 167 L6
Isfield Rd BRI BN1 169 J4
UCK TN22 127 L1
Islingword Pl ROTT BN2 7 J4
Islingword Rd ROTT BN2 7 H3
Islingword St ROTT BN2 7 H4
Iveagh Crs NEWHV BN9 191 K5
Ivor Rd ROTT BN2 170 C5
Ivors La RING/NEW BN8 149 H1
Ivory Pl ROTT BN2 7 G5
Ivy Dene La EGRIN RH19 14 D8
Ivyhouse La HAS TN34 163 H1
RHAS TN35 140 B6
Ivy Pl HOVE BN3 186 D1 3
Ivy Ter EAST BN21 10 D6

J

Jaarlen Rd LYDD TN29 95 H8
The Jackdaws UCK TN22 102 E2 1
Jackies La RING/NEW BN8 74 B7
Jack O'dandy Cl EAST BN21 196 C7 2
Jacks Hl HRTF TN7 26 D4
Jackson St ROTT BN2 7 H3
Jacobs Acre BEX TN40 183 J1 3
Jamaica Wy LGNY BN23 197 M6
James Av HAIL BN27 133 L8
Jameson Crs STLEO TN38 162 A3
Jameson Rd BEX TN40 183 K3
Jane Murray Wy BURH RH15 96 E5
HPPT/KEY BN6 96 C4
Janes Cl BURH RH15 97 J1
Janes La BURH RH15 97 J1
Japonica Cl SHOR BN43 166 B5
Jardine Ct CROW TN6 39 M4
Jarvisbrook Cl BEXW TN39 159 M8
BEXW TN39 182 D3
Jason Cl PEAHV BN10 190 C7
Jay Cl LGNY BN23 197 J4
Jay Rd PEAHV BN10 190 E8
The Jays BURH RH15 96 E2
UCK TN22 102 D2 2
Jefferies RHWH RH17 50 C2
Jefferies Wy CROW TN6 39 M2
Jellicoe Cl LGNY BN23 197 M8
Jenner's La RHAS TN35 140 E8
Jephson Cl
EDN/EASTW BN20 206 F6 2
Jerome Cl LGNY BN23 197 L4
Jersey St ROTT BN2 7 G4
Jervis Av LGNY BN23 197 L8
Jesmond Rd HOVE BN3 167 L7
Jesters BURH RH15 71 J7
Jevington Cl BEXW TN39 182 D4
Jevington Dr ROTT BN2 169 K5
SEAF BN25 202 C2
Jevington Gdns
EDN/EASTW BN20 206 F5
Jevington Rd POLE BN26 195 J6
Jew St BRI BN1 6 E6
Job's La HPPT/KEY BN6 70 A8
Joe's La HAIL BN27 157 H1
John Dann Cl UCK TN22 78 A8
John Macadam Wy SLVH TN37 139 G8
Johns Cl PEAHV BN10 190 C4
John's Cross Rd RBTBR TN32 85 H3
Johnson Cl STLEO TN38 138 F8
Johnson Dr BURH RH15 97 K3
John St ROTT BN2 7 G6
SBGH/RUST TN4 20 A1
Jonas Dr WADH TN5 43 L1
Jonas La WADH TN5 43 L1
Jordans La East
LW/ROSE BN22 196 D3
Jordans La West
LW/ROSE BN22 196 C3
The Jordans EGRIN RH19 13 L6
Jubilee Cl HWH RH16 72 A2
Jubilee Fld TENT TN30 67 L2
Jubilee Gdns SEAF BN25 203 G1 1
Jubilee Rd BEXW TN39 160 A7
BURH RH15 96 E4
PTSD BN41 167 G6
Jubilee St BRI BN1 6 E6
Judge's Ter EGRIN RH19 13 L6 3
Juggs Cl LEW BN7 2 C8
Juggs Rd LEW BN7 2 B9
LEW BN7 2 D8
LEW BN7 149 G7
Julian Rd HOVE BN3 6 B3
Junction Cl BURH RH15 97 J2
Junction Rd BRI BN1 6 D4 2
BURH RH15 97 H4
EAST BN21 10 E6
RBTBR TN32 63 G4
RBTBR TN32 112 D1
SLVH TN37 139 H7
Junction St POLE BN26 178 B8
Juniper Cl PTSD BN41 167 H3 1
SEAF BN25 203 J3
STLEO TN38 161 L3
Jury's Gap Rd LYDD TN29 120 E2
LYDD TN29 121 G1

K

Kammond Av SEAF BN25 203 H1
Katherine Wy SEAF BN25 202 D1
Keats Cl STLEO TN38 161 M8
Keats Pl EGRIN RH19 13 K5 3
Kedale Rd SEAF BN25 202 E2
Keere St LEW BN7 2 E7
Keld Av UCK TN22 76 D8
Keld Cl UCK TN22 76 D8
Keld Dr UCK TN22 76 D8
Kelly Rd HOVE BN3 168 D5
Kemps Farm Rd CROW TN6 40 B5 1
Kemp St BRI BN1 6 E5
Kemp Town Pl ROTT BN2 7 M9 2
Kendal Pk SBGH/RUST TN4 19 L1
Kendal Rd HOVE BN3 167 M6
Kenilworth Cl ROTT BN2 170 A4
Kenilworth Rd STLEO TN38 162 B7
Kenmure Av BRI BN1 146 A7
Kennedy Av EGRIN RH19 13 K3
Kennedy Cl HTHF TN21 80 B8
Kennedy Rd BEX TN40 183 L2
Kennedy Wy NEWHV BN9 8 D3
Kennel La BEXW TN39 182 C2
Kennett Cl POLE BN26 196 F1
Kensington Gdns BRI BN1 6 E5
Kensington Pl BRI BN1 6 E5
Kensington St BRI BN1 6 E5
Kent Cl BEX TN40 184 A1
SHOR BN43 166 C7
WSEA TN36 116 E7
Kent Flds LEW BN7 171 L1
Kentish Gdns RTWE/PEM TN2 19 L6
Kent La RBTBR TN32 84 A7
Kenton Cl BEXW TN39 183 G1
Kenton Rd HOVE BN3 167 K7
Kent Rd STLEO TN38 161 M2
Kent's La HPPT/KEY BN6 98 C7
Kents Rd HWH RH16 71 M3
Kent St BAT TN33 138 F2
Kenwards BRI BN1 146 D7
Kenwood Cl HAS TN34 163 H2 1
Keppel Rd HAS TN34 5 G1
Kerrara Ter LW/ROSE BN22 11 H2
Kestrel Cl BEX TN40 183 L2
HOVE BN3 168 D6
The Kestrels STLEO TN38 161 M1 1
Ketche's La RHWH RH17 50 E7
UCK TN22 51 G8
Kevin Gdns ROTT BN2 170 E6
Kewhurst Av BEXW TN39 182 C3
Kew St BRI BN1 6 D5
Keymer Av PEAHV BN10 190 D8
Keymer Cl LGNY BN23 197 L5
STLEO TN38 161 L8
Keymer Ct BURH RH15 97 H4 1
Keymer Gdns BURH RH15 97 H5
Keymer Pde BURH RH15 97 H4 2
Keymer Pk HPPT/KEY BN6 123 H3
Keymer Rd BRI BN1 146 B8
BURH RH15 97 H6
HPPT/KEY BN6 122 F3 1
Keysford La HWH RH16 49 L3
Key West LGNY BN23 197 M7
Kidbrook HWH RH16 49 J8 1
Kidd's Hl HRTF TN7 37 M1
Kildare Cl HAS TN34 163 H2
Kilda St LW/ROSE BN22 11 H3
Kilnbarn Wy HWH RH16 71 K4
Kiln Cl UCK TN22 102 D2 3
Kiln Dr RYE TN31 91 H6
Kiln La BAT TN33 158 B7
HWH RH16 72 B1
UCK TN22 127 L1
Kiln Rd CRAWE RH10 12 B7
RING/NEW BN8 128 A6
The Kiln BURH RH15 97 J3
Kilnwood La RING/NEW BN8 99 L7
Kilpatrick Cl LGNY BN23 197 K3
Kimberley Rd ROTT BN2 169 K6
SEAF BN25 202 C2
Kindersley Cl EGRIN RH19 14 B3 1
Kinfauns Av LW/ROSE BN22 197 H8
King Edward Av SLVH TN37 162 C2
King Edward Cl SLVH TN37 162 C3 2
King Edward's Pde
EDN/EASTW BN20 206 E7
Kingfisher Cl UCK TN22 102 E1
Kingfisher Dr LGNY BN23 197 J4
Kingfisher Ri EGRIN RH19 13 M6
King George Av EGRIN RH19 13 J3
King George Rd SHOR BN43 166 C6
King George V Hl RTW TN1 20 C1
King George Vi Av HOVE BN3 167 M3
King George Vi Dr HOVE BN3 168 A3
King Henry's Rd LEW BN7 2 C4
King Offa Wy BEX TN40 183 J1
King Pl BRI BN1 6 D6
King's Av EAST BN21 10 A2
NEWHV BN9 191 L5
RYE TN31 91 K8
King's Bank La RYE TN31 88 F4
Kingsbury Rd BRI BN1 6 F2
Kings Cha CROW TN6 39 K3
Kings Cl BEX TN40 183 J2
EAST BN21 10 C1
PEAHV BN10 190 B5 3
Kings Copse EGRIN RH19 13 M6 3
Kingscott Cl BEXW TN39 160 A6
Kingsdale Cl BAT TN33 137 M3
SLVH TN37 139 J8
King's Dr EAST BN21 196 C6
HPPT/KEY BN6 122 F2
King's Esp HOVE BN3 186 A1
King's Gdns HOVE BN3 186 B1
Kingsgate La TENT TN30 67 J1
King's Hill Rd BUR/ETCH TN19 83 H2
Kingsland Cl SHOR BN43 166 C7
Kingsley Cl SLVH TN37 162 C1
Kingsley Rd BRI BN1 168 D5
LEW BN7 2 C3
Kingsmarsh La LYDD TN29 95 J2
Kingsmead SEAF BN25 202 D1 3
Kingsmead Cl SEAF BN25 202 E2 2
King's Mead La SEAF BN25 202 D2
Kingsmead Wk SEAF BN25 202 E2
Kingsmead Wy SEAF BN25 202 E2
Kingsmere Wy LGNY BN23 197 L6
Kings Ms HOVE BN3 168 B8 1
Kings Ride BURH RH15 97 K5
POLE BN26 193 M4
SEAF BN25 202 D2
King's Rd BRI BN1 6 A7
HWH RH16 71 M4
SLVH TN37 4 B8
STHW BN42 166 D5
Kingsthorpe Rd HOVE BN3 167 L6
Kingston Av SEAF BN25 203 H3
Kingston Bay Rd SHOR BN43 166 C8
Kingston Broadway
SHOR BN43 166 C5
Kingston Cl BRI BN1 146 E8
HOVE BN3 167 L4
SEAF BN25 203 H3
SHOR BN43 166 C6
Kingston Gn SEAF BN25 203 H3
Kingston La SHOR BN43 166 D7
Kingston Rdg LEW BN7 148 D8
Kingston Rd LEW BN7 149 H7
LW/ROSE BN22 196 F4
Kingston Wy SEAF BN25 203 H4
SHOR BN43 166 C5
King St BRI BN1 6 E6 1
Kings Wy BURH RH15 97 J5
Kingsway HOVE BN3 167 M8
SEAF BN25 202 D2
Kingswood Av BEXW TN39 159 M8
Kingswood Rd RTWE/PEM TN2 20 C3
Kingswood St ROTT BN2 6 F7
King Wood Hl RYE TN31 114 B3
Kinver La BEX TN40 161 G8
Kipling Av ROTT BN2 170 E6
Kipling Wy EGRIN RH19 13 J5
Kirby Dr PEAHV BN10 190 A5
Kirkford Cl BURH RH15 97 J5 3
Kirkdale Rd RTW TN1 20 B2
Kirkstall Cl LW/ROSE BN22 196 E3
Kirk Wy EDN/EASTW BN20 206 B1
Kitchenour La RYE TN31 89 L1
Kite Cl STLEO TN38 161 L6
Kitewell La LYDD TN29 95 K6
Knebworth Rd BEXW TN39 182 F1
Knelle Rd RBTBR TN32 84 F2
Knepp Cl ROTT BN2 169 M4
Knightsbridge Cl
SBGH/RUST TN4 19 M1
Knights Gdn HAIL BN27 155 H8
Knights Meadow UCK TN22 76 E6 2
Knock Hl TENT TN30 69 G4
Knole Gv EGRIN RH19 13 J3
Knole Rd BEX TN40 183 K3
ROTT BN2 189 G5
Knoll Cl HOVE BN3 167 K5
Knoll Ri STLEO TN38 161 M4
Knoll Rd LW/ROSE BN22 197 G4
Knowle Av RHAS TN35 164 E1 1
Knowle Cl CROW TN6 40 C6
RRTW TN3 18 E3
Knowle Hl MAYF TN20 57 G5
Knowle Pk CROW TN6 39 K4
Knowle Park Rd MAYF TN20 57 G4
Knowle Rd RHAS TN35 164 E1
Knoyle Rd BRI BN1 168 E4
Kymer Gdns HPPT/KEY BN6 123 G3

L

Laburnum Av HOVE BN3 167 L5
Laburnum Gdns BEX TN40 160 F8
Laburnum Wy HWH RH16 72 B2
Lacys Hl RING/NEW BN8 150 E6
Ladies Mile RRTW TN3 27 K2
Ladies Mile Cl BRI BN1 145 M8
Ladies' Mile Rd BRI BN1 145 L8
Ladycross Cl SEAF BN25 203 J3 3
Ladymead BURH RH15 97 J1 1
Ladysmith Rd ROTT BN2 169 K6
Lagwood Cl HPPT/KEY BN6 122 E3
Laine Cl BRI BN1 168 E3
Lake Dr PEAHV BN10 190 B6
Lake House Cl BEXW TN39 182 D2
Lakehurst La BAT TN33 108 F6
Lakelands Cl LW/ROSE BN22 197 G4
Lakelands Dr BEXW TN39 182 D2
Lake Rd SBGH/RUST TN4 19 L2
Lake St CROW TN6 42 A5
MAYF TN20 42 C6
Lake View Rd CRAWE RH10 12 B3
EGRIN RH19 13 M1
Laleham Cl EAST BN21 10 A4
SLVH TN37 162 C1 3
Lambert Pl LEW BN7 3 G1
Lambert Rd LGNY BN23 197 L3 3
Lambourn Cl EGRIN RH19 13 L3 3
Lambourne Cl BRI BN1 169 J4
Lambourne Rd BRI BN1 169 J4
Lambourn Wy RTWE/PEM TN2 20 D5
Lampington Rw RRTW TN3 18 E3 2
Lancaster Dr EGRIN RH19 14 A3
Lancaster Rd BRI BN1 6 C2
STLEO TN38 161 M1
Lancaster St LEW BN7 3 G5 1
Lancing Cl HAS TN34 162 D3
Lancing Wy POLE BN26 195 M2
Landgate RYE TN31 91 J8
Landport Rd LEW BN7 2 E4
Landsdowne Wy BEX TN40 183 L1
Landsdown Rd SEAF BN25 203 H1 2
Landseer Rd HOVE BN3 168 A6
The Lane RRTW TN3 18 C1
Langdale Cl LGNY BN23 197 J2
Langdale Gdns HOVE BN3 167 M8
Langdale Rd HOVE BN3 167 M8
Langham Cl HAS TN34 162 F2
RING/NEW BN8 150 D1 3
Langham Rd HAS TN34 162 F2
RBTBR TN32 84 F2
Langholm Rd RRTW TN3 18 F3
Langley Cl BEXW TN39 160 B6
Langley Crs ROTT BN2 170 D5
Langney Gn LGNY BN23 197 L6
Langney Ri LGNY BN23 197 K4
Langney Rd EAST BN21 11 G6
Langridge Dr EGRIN RH19 13 L6 4
PTSD BN41 167 H4
Langridge La HWH RH16 72 A1 1
Langridge Wy BURH RH15 96 E1
Langton Cl BAT TN33 137 L2
Langton Rd RRTW TN3 18 F3
Langtye La RING/NEW BN8 152 E8
Lansdowne Crs HAIL BN27 155 G4
Lansdowne Dr HAIL BN27 155 G4
Lansdowne Gdns HAIL BN27 155 H4 2
Lansdowne Ms HOVE BN3 168 D8 2
Lansdowne Pl HOVE BN3 168 D8
HOVE BN3 186 D1
Lansdowne Rd HAIL BN27 155 G4
HOVE BN3 168 D8
RTW TN1 20 C2 4
Lansdowne Sq HOVE BN3 186 D1 1
RTW TN1 20 B2 3
Lansdowne St HOVE BN3 168 D8
Lansdowne Wy HAIL BN27 155 G3
Lansdown Pl LEW BN7 3 G7
Lapierre Rd NEWHV BN9 8 D3
Lapwing Cl LGNY BN23 197 J4
Larch Cl HTHF TN21 106 B1
ROTT BN2 170 F7
STLEO TN38 162 A5
Larches Wy CRAWE RH10 12 C6
Larch Gdns LW/ROSE BN22 196 D3
Larch Wy HWH RH16 72 B2
Larke Cl SHOR BN43 166 C7
Larkfield Cl STLEO TN38 162 A3 2
Larkfield Wy BRI BN1 169 G2
Larkhill BEX TN40 183 J2
Lark Hl HOVE BN3 167 L3
Larkspur Dr LGNY BN23 197 H3
Larnach Cl UCK TN22 76 D6
Lascelles Ter EAST BN21 10 F9
Lashbrooks Rd UCK TN22 76 B7
Latimer Rd LW/ROSE BN22 11 K2
Laton Rd HAS TN34 5 G2
Laughton Cl LW/ROSE BN22 197 G2 3
Laughton Rd RING/NEW BN8 128 D8
RING/NEW BN8 129 J7
ROTT BN2 170 F6
Laundry La RHWH RH17 36 D6
Laurel Cl BURH RH15 97 K1 2
Laurel Dene EGRIN RH19 13 M5
Laurel La WSEA TN36 141 M1
The Laurels UCK TN22 76 E6 3
Lauriston Rd BRI BN1 168 E4
Lavant Cl BEXW TN39 159 J8
Lavender Cl LGNY BN23 197 H3 1
Lavender Gdns WADH TN5 45 L5 1
Lavender Hl SHOR BN43 166 B5
Lavender St ROTT BN2 7 H8
Lawes Av NEWHV BN9 8 E3
Lawns Av EAST BN21 206 D2
The Lawn STLEO TN38 4 A8
Lawrence Cl LGNY BN23 197 K5 3
Lawrence Rd HOVE BN3 167 M7
Lawrie La HWH RH16 72 B1
Laylands Rd PTSD BN41 167 G7
Lea Av RYE TN31 91 G8
Leaf Hall Rd LW/ROSE BN22 11 H5
Leaf Rd EAST BN21 10 F5
Leahurst Court Rd BRI BN1 168 E3
Lealands Cl RRTW TN3 18 C7
Lealands Dr UCK TN22 76 C6
Lea Rd PEAHV BN10 190 B6
Leasam La RYE TN31 91 H6
Leasingham Gdns
BEXW TN39 183 G1 1
The Leas PEAHV BN10 200 F1
WADH TN5 32 A8
Le Brun Rd EAST BN21 10 B2
Ledsham Av SLVH TN37 162 B1
Ledsham Cl SLVH TN37 162 B1 1
Ledsham Pk SLVH TN37 162 B1
Ledsham Wy SLVH TN37 162 B1
Leeds Av LGNY BN23 197 K6
Leeds Cl RHAS TN35 163 K3
Leeds La MAYF TN20 56 C8
Lee Rd LEW BN7 2 D3
Leeves Cl HTHF TN21 80 A8
Leeves Wy HTHF TN21 79 M8
Leeward Quay LGNY BN23 197 M6 3
Lee Wy NEWHV BN9 8 E2
Leggs' La RRTW TN3 18 E1
Legsheath La EGRIN RH19 23 M7
Leicester Dr RTWE/PEM TN2 19 M6 3
Leicester Rd LEW BN7 2 C6
Leicester St ROTT BN2 7 H7
Leicester Vls HOVE BN3 167 K7
Leighton Rd HOVE BN3 168 A6
RHWH RH17 50 C1
Leneda Dr RTWE/PEM TN2 19 L6
Lenham Av ROTT BN2 189 H5
Lenham Rd East ROTT BN2 189 H5
Lenham Rd West ROTT BN2 189 G5
Lennox Cl EDN/EASTW BN20 206 B1 1
Lennox Rd HOVE BN3 167 M6
SHOR BN43 166 B6
Lennox St ROTT BN2 7 H6
Leopold Rd BEXW TN39 183 H2
BRI BN1 6 C5
Lepeland HAIL BN27 155 G5 2
Lesley Cl BEX TN40 160 F7
Leslie St LW/ROSE BN22 11 H3
Leveller Rd RING/NEW BN8 74 D7
Levett Av POLE BN26 178 C7
Levett Cl POLE BN26 178 C8 2
Levett Rd POLE BN26 178 C8
Levetts La RBTBR TN32 63 K5
Levett Wy POLE BN26 178 C8 3
Lewes Cl BEXW TN39 160 A8
ROTT BN2 189 L5
Lewes Crs ROTT BN2 187 L2
Lewes Rd BRI BN1 147 G8
EAST BN21 10 D3
EGRIN RH19 13 M6
FROW RH18 24 E3
HPPT/KEY BN6 123 L4
HWH RH16 49 H7
HWH RH16 72 B3
NEWHV BN9 8 F3
POLE BN26 177 H8
RHWH RH17 36 D5
RHWH RH17 50 C2
RHWH RH17 51 G3
RING/NEW BN8 150 D1
ROTT BN2 7 H2
ROTT BN2 169 J5
UCK TN22 101 L8
Lewes St ROTT BN2 7 G4
Lewis Cl NEWHV BN9 191 M4
Lewis Rd STLEO TN38 162 A3
Lewry Cl NEWHV BN9 8 C4
Lexden Ct SEAF BN25 203 G2 1
Lexden Dr SEAF BN25 202 F1
Lexden Rd SEAF BN25 192 F8
SEAF BN25 202 F1
Leybourne Cl ROTT BN2 170 A5 1
Leybourne Gdns SLVH TN37 162 C2
Leybourne Rd ROTT BN2 170 A4
Leyland Rd PEV BN24 198 D2
Leylands Pk BURH RH15 97 H1
Leylands Rd BURH RH15 97 G2
Library Wy UCK TN22 76 C7
Lilac Cl LW/ROSE BN22 196 D4
Lillywhite Cl BURH RH15 96 F1
Limden Cl WADH TN5 44 F8
Lime Cl RRTW TN3 30 B3
STLEO TN38 162 A5
UCK TN22 76 D6
Lime Hill Rd RTW TN1 20 A2 2
Limekiln Ct CROW TN6 40 B3
Limes Gv HAWK TN18 47 M1
Limes La UCK TN22 77 K3
The Limes EGRIN RH19 13 G1
Limetree Av LW/ROSE BN22 196 D3 2
Lime Tree Av UCK TN22 76 D7
Lime Wy HTHF TN21 106 B1
Limney Rd ROTT BN2 169 L7
Linchmere Av ROTT BN2 189 J5
Lincoln Av PEAHV BN10 190 A7
Lincoln Av South
PEAHV BN10 190 A7 1
Lincoln Cl EDN/EASTW BN20 206 C6
STLEO TN38 161 M2
Lincoln Cottages ROTT BN2 7 H4 1
Lincoln Rd PTSD BN41 167 H7
Lincoln St ROTT BN2 7 H4
Lincoln Wy CROW TN6 40 A6
Lincoln Wd RHWH RH17 71 J1
Linden Av EGRIN RH19 13 J4
Linden Cha UCK TN22 76 C7
Linden Cl LW/ROSE BN22 196 E3
RTWE/PEM TN2 19 M4 1
Linden Ct UCK TN22 76 C7 2
Linden Gdns RTWE/PEM TN2 19 M5
Linden Gv HAIL BN27 155 J3
HWH RH16 49 G8
Linden Park Rd RTWE/PEM TN2 19 M5
Linden Rd BEX TN40 183 J3
Lindfield Av SEAF BN25 203 J4
Lindfield Cl ROTT BN2 189 H4
Lindfield Dr HAIL BN27 155 H7
Lindfield Rd LW/ROSE BN22 196 D5
RHWH RH17 34 C8
Lindon Cl EDN/EASTW BN20 205 H5 2
Lindsay Cl EDN/EASTW BN20 206 C4
Lingfield Rd EGRIN RH19 13 K3 1
Link Rd EDN/EASTW BN20 206 D5
Links Av NEWHV BN9 8 A4
Links Cl CROW TN6 39 K5
PTSD BN41 167 J6
SEAF BN25 203 G3
Links Dr BEX TN40 183 L2
Links Rd PTSD BN41 167 J6
SEAF BN25 203 G4
The Links STLEO TN38 161 M6
Links Wy RYE TN31 118 E4
The Link EDN/EASTW BN20 205 J4
RYE TN31 117 G1
Linkway EDN/EASTW BN20 196 A7

The Linkway *BRI* BN1 .... 169 H5
Linley Cl *BEX* TN40 .... 183 K2
Linley Dr *HAS* TN34 .... 163 G3
Linnet Cl *LGNY* BN23 .... 197 J4
Linnet Gn *UCK* TN22 .... 102 D1 🔲
Linthouse Pl *PEAHV* BN10 .... 190 D4 🔲
Linton Crs *HAS* TN34 .... 4 E6
HOVE BN3 .... 167 M6
Linton Rd *HAS* TN34 .... 4 E4
HOVE BN3 .... 167 M6
Lionel Rd *BEX* TN40 .... 183 L3
Lion Hl *PEV* BN24 .... 197 H1
Lion La *CRAWE* RH10 .... 22 A2
LW/ROSE BN22 .... 11 H6
Lions Pl *SEAF* BN25 .... 202 F4
Lion St *RYE* TN31 .... 117 J1
Liphook Cl *BRI* BN1 .... 169 J5 🔲
Lismore Rd *EAST* BN21 .... 10 F7
Lister Av *EGRIN* RH19 .... 13 L8
Little Bentswood *HWH* RH16 .... 71 M1 🔲
Little Black Hl *HWH* RH16 .... 49 H7
Little Common Rd *BEXW* TN39 .. 182 D2
Little Copse Rd *HPPT/KEY* BN6 .. 122 E1
Little Crs *ROTT* BN2 .... 189 H5
Little East St *LEW* BN7 .... 3 G5
Little Footway *RRTW* TN3 .... 18 F3
Little King St *EGRIN* RH19 .... 13 L5 🔲
Little London Rd *HTHF* TN21 .... 105 L6
Little Mallett *RRTW* TN3 .... 18 F3 🔲
Little Md *RING/NEW* BN8 .... 126 A7
Little Mount Sion *RTW* TN1 .... 20 A4 🔲
Little Paddock *CROW* TN6 .... 39 L5
RING/NEW BN8 .... 127 L8
Little Pk *WADH* TN5 .... 43 L1
Little Preston St *BRI* BN1 .... 6 B7
Little Ridge Av *BEXW* TN39 .... 139 H8
Little Sunnyside *CROW* TN6 .... 39 M5 🔲
Little Trogers La *MAYF* TN20 .... 57 H2
Little Twitten *BEXW* TN39 .... 182 C3
Littlewood La *UCK* TN22 .... 77 J2
Littleworth Cl *ROTT* BN2 .... 170 F7
Livingstone Rd *BURH* RH15 .... 96 F3
HOVE BN3 .... 168 B7
Livingstone St *ROTT* BN2 .... 7 L6 🔲
Lloyd Cl *HOVE* BN3 .... 168 C6
Lloyd Rd *HOVE* BN3 .... 168 C6
Lloyds Gn *TENT* TN30 .... 67 K2
Lockitt Wy *LEW* BN7 .... 171 L1
Locks Crs *PTSD* BN41 .... 167 H5
Locks Hl *PTSD* BN41 .... 167 H5
Lockwood Cl *ROTT* BN2 .... 170 E7
Lockwood Crs *ROTT* BN2 .... 170 E7
Loder Pl *BRI* BN1 .... 168 F4
Loder Rd *BRI* BN1 .... 168 F4
Lodge Av *LW/ROSE* BN22 .... 196 C4
Lodge Cl *EGRIN* RH19 .... 13 J5
LEW BN7 .... 2 B7
PTSD BN41 .... 166 F4 🔲
Lodge Hill La *HPPT/KEY* BN6 .. 123 J2
Lodgelands *RHWH* RH17 .... 34 B8
Lodge La *HPPT/KEY* BN6 .... 123 G3
Lodge Rd *RHAS* TN35 .... 163 J5 🔲
Lodsworth Cl *ROTT* BN2 .... 169 M7
Lomas La *HAWK* TN18 .... 64 F1
Lomond Av *BRI* BN1 .... 146 A7
London Rd *BAT* TN33 .... 111 J4
BEXW TN39 .... 183 H1
BRI BN1 .... 6 F2
BRI BN1 .... 145 K6
BRI BN1 .... 168 E3
BUR/ETCH TN19 .... 62 A1
BURH RH15 .... 96 F3 🔲
CROW TN6 .... 39 L2
EGRIN RH19 .... 13 L5
FROW RH18 .... 24 E2
HAIL BN27 .... 155 H6
HPPT/KEY BN6 .... 122 E1
RBTBR TN32 .... 62 B8
RBTBR TN32 .... 111 K1
RHWH RH17 .... 51 G2
RING/NEW BN8 .... 129 M1
SBGH/RUST TN4 .... 20 A3
STLEO TN38 .... 4 A4
STLEO TN38 .... 162 B4
UCK TN22 .... 76 B2
WADH TN5 .... 46 D3
London Ter *BRI* BN1 .... 6 F2
Long Acre *CRAWE* RH10 .... 12 A6
Long Acre Cl *EAST* BN21 .... 206 D1
Longacre Cl *SLVH* TN37 .... 139 J8
Long Av *BEX* TN40 .... 161 G8
Longbury *UCK* TN22 .... 102 C1
Longhill Cl *ROTT* BN2 .... 188 E2
Longhill Rd *ROTT* BN2 .... 188 D2
Longhurst *BURH* RH15 .... 97 K4
Longland Rd
EDN/EASTW BN20 .... 206 C2
Long La *BAT* TN33 .... 112 C5
Long Meads *RRTW* TN3 .... 19 H3
Long Park Cnr *HPPT/KEY* BN6 .. 123 K4
Longridge Av *SLVH* TN37 .... 139 J8
Long Slip *RRTW* TN3 .... 19 G3
Longstone Rd *EAST* BN21 .... 10 F6
Longview *HTHF* TN21 .... 106 A1
Lonsdale Gdns *RTW* TN1 .... 20 A3 🔲
The Lookout *PEAHV* BN10 .... 190 C3
Lordine Cl *RBTBR* TN32 .... 87 H2
Lordslaine Cl
EDN/EASTW BN20 .... 206 C6
Lords La *RHAS* TN35 .... 163 K3
The Lords *SEAF* BN25 .... 192 E8
Lordswell La *CROW* TN6 .... 39 L6
Lorna Rd *HOVE* BN3 .... 168 D7
Lorne Rd *BRI* BN1 .... 6 F1
Lorraine Rd *NEWHV* BN9 .... 9 G2
Lossenham La *HAWK* TN18 .... 65 K2
Lottbridge Dro *LW/ROSE* BN22 .. 196 F5
LW/ROSE BN22 .... 197 H6
Love La *MAYF* TN20 .... 56 F4
RYE TN31 .... 91 H8
Lover's Wk *BRI* BN1 .... 146 F8
Lowdells Cl *EGRIN* RH19 .... 13 J2
Lowdells Dr *EGRIN* RH19 .... 13 K2
Lowdells La *EGRIN* RH19 .... 13 J3
Lower Bevendean Av
ROTT BN2 .... 169 L5
Lower Chalvington Pl
ROTT BN2 .... 187 L1 🔲
Lower Church Rd *BURH* RH15 .. 96 F3

Lower Dene *EGRIN* RH19 .... 14 A5
Lower Dr *SEAF* BN25 .... 202 F1
STHW BN42 .... 166 E5
Lower Glen Rd *SLVH* TN37 .... 162 B2
Lower Green Rd *RRTW* TN3 .... 19 J1
SBGH/RUST TN4 .... 19 J2
Lower Hazelhurst *WADH* TN5 .. 45 H3
Lower High St *WADH* TN5 .... 44 M1
Lower Market St *HOVE* BN3 .. 186 D1 🔲
Lower Mere *EGRIN* RH19 .... 13 M6
Lower Park Rd *HAS* TN34 .... 4 E3
Lower Pl *NEWHV* BN9 .... 8 F3
Lower Platts *WADH* TN5 .... 45 L5
Lower Rd *EAST* BN21 .... 206 D2
HAIL BN27 .... 156 D3
Lower Rock Gdns *ROTT* BN2 .... 7 H8
Lower Saxonbury *CROW* TN6 .. 39 M4 🔲
Lower South Rd *STLEO* TN38 .. 4 A4
Lower Station Rd
RING/NEW BN8 .... 74 A8
Lower Stoneham
RING/NEW BN8 .... 149 L2
Lower St *BAT* TN33 .... 159 H2
EDN/EASTW BN20 .... 205 H6
Lower Waites La *RHAS* TN35 .. 164 F2
Lowfield Rd *HWH* RH16 .... 71 M3
Lowlands Rd *BURH* RH15 .... 97 H1
The Lowlands *HAIL* BN27 .... 155 H6
Lowther Cl *LGNY* BN23 .... 197 K3
Lowther Rd *BRI* BN1 .... 169 G4
Loxfield Cl *MAYF* TN20 .... 57 G4
Loxwood Cl *BEXW* TN39 .... 182 C1
LW/ROSE BN22 .... 196 C5
Lucas *RHWH* RH17 .... 50 D1
Lucas Cl *EGRIN* RH19 .... 13 M5 🔲
Lucas Gra *RHWH* RH17 .... 71 K1
Lucas Shadwell Wy *RYE* TN31 .. 117 M4
Lucastes Av *HWH* RH16 .... 48 C8
Lucastes La *RHWH* RH17 .... 48 C8
RHWH RH17 .... 71 J1
Lucastes Rd *HWH* RH16 .... 71 J1
Lucas Wy *HWH* RH16 .... 71 J1
Lucerne Cl *PTSD* BN41 .... 167 H5
Lucerne Rd *BRI* BN1 .... 168 F5
Lucinda Wy *SEAF* BN25 .... 202 F1
Lucraft Rd *ROTT* BN2 .... 169 M1
Ludley Hl *RYE* TN31 .... 89 G8
Ludlow Ri *ROTT* BN2 .... 170 A3
Ludpit La *BUR/ETCH* TN19 .... 61 J8
Lulham Cl *PEAHV* BN10 .... 190 B5 🔲
Lullington Av *HOVE* BN3 .... 167 M6
Lullington Cl *BEX* TN40 .... 161 G8
EAST BN21 .... 196 C7
SEAF BN25 .... 203 H4
Lullington Gdns *SLVH* TN37 .. 162 C1 🔲
Lunce's Hl *RHWH* RH17 .... 71 M6
Lundy Wk *HAIL* BN27 .... 154 F4 🔲
Lurgashall *BURH* RH15 .... 97 J5 🔲
Lushington La *EAST* BN21 .... 10 E7
Lushington Rd *EAST* BN21 .... 10 E7
Lustrells Cl *ROTT* BN2 .... 189 H4
Lustrells Crs *ROTT* BN2 .... 189 H4
Lustrells V *ROTT* BN2 .... 189 H4
Luther St *ROTT* BN2 .... 7 J3
Luton Cl *EAST* BN21 .... 196 C8
Luxford Dr *CROW* TN6 .... 40 A5
Luxford La *CROW* TN6 .... 40 A5
Luxford Rd *CROW* TN6 .... 40 A7
HWH RH16 .... 49 H7
Luxford's La *EGRIN* RH19 .... 14 B8
EGRIN RH19 .... 24 B1
Lychgates Cl *BEX* TN40 .... 183 K1
Lydd Cl *LGNY* BN23 .... 197 K4 🔲
Lydd Rd *RYE* TN31 .... 118 E4
Lydd Town Crossing *LYDD* TN29 .. 95 K6
Lymden La *WADH* TN5 .... 45 G7
Lyminster Av *BRI* BN1 .... 169 C1
Lynchet Cl *BRI* BN1 .... 169 J4
Lynchet Down *BRI* BN1 .... 169 J4
Lynchets Crs *HOVE* BN3 .... 167 K3
The Lynchets *LEW* BN7 .... 3 J2
Lynchet Wk *BRI* BN1 .... 169 J4
Lyndhurst Av *HAS* TN34 .... 163 G2
Lyndhurst Farm Cl *EGRIN* RH19 .. 12 D1
Lyndhurst Rd *HOVE* BN3 .... 168 D7
Lynholm Rd *POLE* BN26 .... 178 B8
Lynton Cl *HPPT/KEY* BN6 .... 122 B1
Lynton Park Av *EGRIN* RH19 .. 14 A4
Lynton St *ROTT* BN2 .... 7 K3
Lynwood *RRTW* TN3 .... 18 C8
Lynwood Cl *HAS* TN34 .... 162 D1
Lynwood Rd *ROTT* BN2 .... 189 J6
Lyon Cl *HOVE* BN3 .... 168 D7
Lyoth La *HWH* RH16 .... 72 B1
Lytham Cl *STLEO* TN38 .... 161 M6

M

Maberley Rd *BEX* TN40 .... 160 C8 🔲
Mackerel Hl *RYE* TN31 .... 89 M1
Mackerel's Rocks
RING/NEW BN8 .... 100 F3
Mackie Av *BRI* BN1 .... 145 M8
HPPT/KEY BN6 .... 123 G1
Macmichaels Wy
BUR/ETCH TN19 .... 62 A3 🔲
Macmillan Dr *EAST* BN21 .... 206 C1
Madehurst Cl *ROTT* BN2 .... 7 H7
Madeira Dr *ROTT* BN2 .... 7 G8
Madeira Pk *RTW* TN1 .... 20 B4 🔲
Madeira Rd *ROTT* BN2 .... 7 G8
Maderia Dr *SLVH* TN37 .... 162 C3
Mafeking Rd *ROTT* BN2 .... 7 M6
Magdalen Cl *LGNY* BN23 .... 197 J3 🔲
Magdalen Rd *BEX* TN40 .... 183 K2
SLVH TN37 .... 4 C7
Magellan Wy *LGNY* BN23 .... 198 A8
Magnolia Cl *HTHF* TN21 .... 106 B1
Magnolia Dr *LW/ROSE* BN22 .. 196 D4
Magpie Cl *BEXW* TN39 .... 159 J8
STLEO TN38 .... 161 L6
Magpie Rd *LGNY* BN23 .... 197 J3
Magreed La *HTHF* TN21 .... 80 E4
Main Rd *RHAS* TN35 .... 139 L2
RHAS TN35 .... 141 H2

Mainstone Rd *HOVE* BN3 .... 167 M7 🔲
Main St *RYE* TN31 .... 65 H8
RYE TN31 .... 90 B4
RYE TN31 .... 91 H3
Maitland Cl *HAS* TN34 .... 139 L8
Major Cl *BRI* BN1 .... 169 H5
Major York's Rd
SBGH/RUST TN4 .... 19 M3
Malcolm Gdns *POLE* BN26 .... 178 A7
Maldon Rd *BRI* BN1 .... 168 D4
Malines Av *PEAHV* BN10 .... 190 B7
Malines Av South *PEAHV* BN10 .. 190 A7
Mallard Cl *LW/ROSE* BN22 .... 196 F5
Mallard Dr *UCK* TN22 .... 102 D1
Mallard Pl *EGRIN* RH19 .... 13 M6
Mallard Rd *SEAF* BN25 .... 202 E4 🔲
Malling Cl *LEW* BN7 .... 3 G2
Malling Down *LEW* BN7 .... 3 J2
Malling Hl *LEW* BN7 .... 3 J2
Malling St *LEW* BN7 .... 3 J5
Mallory Rd *HOVE* BN3 .... 168 C4
Malthouse Cl *HPPT/KEY* BN6 .. 96 C3
ROTT BN2 .... 7 G4 🔲
RYE TN31 .... 90 B4
Malthouse Wy *RING/NEW* BN8 .. 126 A7
The Maltings *BURH* RH15 .... 96 D2
Malvern St *HOVE* BN3 .... 168 B7 🔲
Malvern Wy *HAS* TN34 .... 163 H3
Manaton Cl *HWH* RH16 .... 71 M2
Manchester Rd *BAT* TN33 .... 136 A8
Manchester St *ROTT* BN2 .... 6 F8
Manifold Rd *LW/ROSE* BN22 .. 11 G4
Manning Cl *EGRIN* RH19 .... 13 K4
Mann St *HAS* TN34 .... 5 G6
Manor Av *HPPT/KEY* BN6 .... 123 C1
Manor Cl *BURH* RH15 .... 97 K2
EDN/EASTW BN20 .... 196 A4
HTHF TN21 .... 105 M6
RING/NEW BN8 .... 127 M7 🔲
ROTT BN2 .... 187 L1
SBGH/RUST TN4 .... 19 L2
SEAF BN25 .... 203 H3
STHW BN42 .... 167 G6
UCK TN22 .... 76 C6
WSEA TN36 .... 141 M1
Manor Dr *PEAHV* BN10 .... 190 B5
Manor End *UCK* TN22 .... 76 C6
Manor Gdns *ROTT* BN2 .... 187 L1
Manor Hall Rd *STHW* BN42 .... 166 E6
Manor Hl *ROTT* BN2 .... 169 L8
Manor Paddock *ROTT* BN2 .... 187 L2
Manor Pk *SBGH/RUST* TN4 .... 19 L3
Manor Park Rd *HAIL* BN27 .... 155 G3
Manor Pl *ROTT* BN2 .... 187 L2
Manor Rd *BEX* TN40 .... 183 K2
BURH RH15 .... 97 J2
BURH RH15 .... 97 K3
EGRIN RH19 .... 13 J4
HAS TN34 .... 5 J3
HTHF TN21 .... 105 M6
LW/ROSE BN22 .... 197 G4
LYDD TN29 .... 121 J1
PTSD BN41 .... 167 H5
ROTT BN2 .... 187 L2
SBGH/RUST TN4 .... 19 J2
SEAF BN25 .... 203 H3
Manor Rd North *SEAF* BN25 .. 203 H3
Manor Wy *CROW* TN6 .... 39 L6
EDN/EASTW BN20 .... 196 B6
POLE BN26 .... 178 A8
ROTT BN2 .... 187 L1
UCK TN22 .... 76 C6
The Martlet *HOVE* BN3 .... 168 D6
Mansell Cl *BEXW* TN39 .... 182 C2
Mansfield Rd *SHOR* BN43 .... 166 B6
Mansers La *HAIL* BN27 .... 154 C3
Mansfield Rd *HOVE* BN3 .... 167 L7
Mansion Cl *BURH* RH15 .... 97 K3
Manston Wy *HAS* TN34 .... 4 E2
Mantell Cl *LEW* BN7 .... 149 J2
Manton Rd *ROTT* BN2 .... 7 K7
Manvers Rd *EDN/EASTW* BN20 .. 206 B3
Maple Av *BEXW* TN39 .... 182 C3
Maple Cl *BEXW* TN39 .... 182 C3
BURH RH15 .... 97 H1
HWH RH16 .... 72 B3
ROTT BN2 .... 170 E7
UCK TN22 .... 76 A2 🔲
Maple Gdns *HOVE* BN3 .... 167 L5
Maple Hts *SLVH* TN37 .... 139 H7
Maplehurst Cl *SLVH* TN37 .... 139 H7
Maplehurst Dr *SLVH* TN37 .... 139 J6
Maplehurst Ri *SLVH* TN37 .... 139 H7 🔲
Maplehurst Rd *LW/ROSE* BN22 .. 196 D4
PTSD BN41 .... 167 G5
Maple Leaf Cl *NEWHV* BN9 .... 8 C3
Mapleleaf Gdns *POLE* BN26 .. 178 A6 🔲
Maple Wk *BEXW* TN39 .... 182 C3
Marbles Rd *RING/NEW* BN8 .. 74 D7
Marchants *HPPT/KEY* BN6 .... 96 A8
Marchants Dr *RYE* TN31 .... 118 E4
Marchants Rd *HPPT/KEY* BN6 .. 96 A8
Marchants Wy *BURH* RH15 .... 96 F1
Marcia Cl *EDN/EASTW* BN20 .. 196 A6
Marcus Gdns *STLEO* TN38 .... 162 A1
Marden's Hl *CROW* TN6 .... 27 H8
Mare Bay Cl *STLEO* TN38 .... 138 E7
Maresfield Dr *PEV* BN24 .... 180 E8
Maresfield Rd *ROTT* BN2 .... 187 L1
Margaret St *ROTT* BN2 .... 7 G8
Margery Rd *HOVE* BN3 .... 167 K6
Marina *BEX* TN40 .... 183 J3
STLEO TN38 .... 162 A8
Marina Court Av *BEX* TN40 .... 183 J3
Marina Wy *ROTT* BN2 .... 187 L3
Marine Av *HOVE* BN3 .... 167 K8
Marine Cl *PEV* BN24 .... 180 C1
Marine Crs *SEAF* BN25 .... 202 E4
Marine Dr *ROTT* BN2 .... 187 M3
SEAF BN25 .... 192 A8
Marine Gdns *ROTT* BN2 .... 7 H8
Marine Pde *HAS* TN34 .... 5 J7

LW/ROSE BN22 .... 11 H7
ROTT BN2 .... 7 G8
SEAF BN25 .... 202 B2
Marine Parade Rd
LW/ROSE BN22 .... 11 H6
Marine Rd *LW/ROSE* BN22 .... 11 H6
PEV BN24 .... 198 D1
Marine Sq *ROTT* BN2 .... 7 K9
Marine Terrace Ms *ROTT* BN2 .. 7 G8
Marine Vw *ROTT* BN2 .... 7 H6
Marjoram Pl *SHOR* BN43 .... 166 B5 🔲
Mark Cl *SEAF* BN25 .... 203 J4 🔲
Market La *LEW* BN7 .... 3 G5
Market Pl *HAIL* BN27 .... 155 J7
HWH RH16 .... 71 K1
Market Rd *BAT* TN33 .... 137 J1
RYE TN31 .... 117 J1 🔲
Market St *BRI* BN1 .... 6 E7
LEW BN7 .... 3 G6
RTWE/PEM TN2 .... 20 A4 🔲
RYE TN31 .... 117 J1 🔲
STLEO TN38 .... 4 A9
Markland Wy *UCK* TN22 .... 76 A7
Mark La *EAST* BN21 .... 10 E7
Marklye La *HTHF* TN21 .... 80 B5
HTHF TN21 .... 107 J3
Markstakes Cnr *RING/NEW* BN8 .. 99 L5
Markstakes La *RING/NEW* BN8 .. 99 L5
Markwick Ter *STLEO* TN38 .... 162 B6
Marlborough Cl *LGNY* BN23 .. 197 K3 🔲
SBGH/RUST TN4 .... 19 L2
STLEO TN38 .... 162 A5
Marlborough Dr *BURH* RH15 .. 97 J3
Marlborough Ms *BRI* BN1 .... 6 C6 🔲
Marlborough Pl *BRI* BN1 .... 6 F6 🔲
Marlborough St *BRI* BN1 .... 6 F6 🔲
Marle Av *BURH* RH15 .... 97 G2 🔲
Marley Cl *BAT* TN33 .... 137 M2
Marley Gdns *BAT* TN33 .... 137 M2
Marley La *BAT* TN33 .... 137 M2
Marley Ri *BAT* TN33 .... 137 M2
Marley Rd *RYE* TN31 .... 91 G8
Marline Av *STLEO* TN38 .... 162 A3
Marline Rd *STLEO* TN38 .... 162 A3
Marlow Av *LW/ROSE* BN22 .... 197 K8
SLVH TN37 .... 162 B1
Marlow Dr *HWH* RH16 .... 72 B2
Marlow Rd *ROTT* BN2 .... 187 M2
Marlpit Cl *EGRIN* RH19 .... 13 L3
Marlpit Rd *EGRIN* RH19 .... 23 G8
Marlpits La *BAT* TN33 .... 136 A7
The Marlpit *WADH* TN5 .... 43 L1
Marmion Rd *HOVE* BN3 .... 167 M7
Marsden Rd *LGNY* BN23 .... 197 L5
Marshall La *NEWHV* BN9 .... 8 F3
Marshalls Rw *BRI* BN1 .... 6 F3
Marshall Wy *HOVE* BN3 .... 167 M5
Marshfoot La *HAIL* BN27 .... 155 J6
Marshlands La *HTHF* TN21 .... 80 A6
Marsh Quarter La *HAWK* TN18 .. 64 C2
Martello Rd *LW/ROSE* BN22 .... 197 K8
SEAF BN25 .... 202 E4
Martha Gunn Rd *ROTT* BN2 .. 169 K5
Martineau La *RHAS* TN35 .... 163 M1
Martingale Cl *SLVH* TN37 .... 162 C1 🔲
Martin Rd *HOVE* BN3 .... 167 K5
The Martins *CRAWE* RH10 .... 12 C6
PEAHV BN10 .... 190 B5 🔲
Martlets *BEX* TN40 .... 183 L1 🔲
The Martlets *CROW* TN6 .... 39 M5
LEW BN7 .... 3 H2 🔲
RYE TN31 .... 114 C2
The Martlet *HOVE* BN3 .... 168 D6
The Martletts
RING/NEW BN8 .... 127 L8 🔲
Martyn's Cl *ROTT* BN2 .... 188 E2
Martyns Pl *EGRIN* RH19 .... 14 A6
Martyns Wy *BEX* TN40 .... 184 A1
Maryan Ct *HAIL* BN27 .... 155 H6
Maryland Rd *RTWE/PEM* TN2 .. 20 D5
Marylands *HWH* RH16 .... 71 M1 🔲
Mary Stamford Gn
RYE TN31 .... 118 A3 🔲
Maskelyne Rd *HAIL* BN27 .... 157 G6
Mason Cl *EDN/EASTW* BN20 .. 13 L4
Mason Rd *RYE* TN31 .... 117 G5
SEAF BN25 .... 202 F2
Matlock Rd *BRI* BN1 .... 168 D5
Maurice Rd *SEAF* BN25 .... 202 F5
Maxfield Cl
EDN/EASTW BN20 .... 206 B1 🔲
Maxfield La *RHAS* TN35 .... 140 D4
May Av *SEAF* BN25 .... 203 H3
Mayfair Cl *POLE* BN26 .... 195 M2
Mayfield Av *PEAHV* BN10 .... 190 D8
Mayfield Cl *BRI* BN1 .... 168 F1
Mayfield Flat *HTHF* TN21 .... 79 G6
Mayfield La *STLEO* TN38 .... 161 K4
WADH TN5 .... 43 K2
Mayfield Pk *WADH* TN5 .... 43 K1
Mayfield Pl *LW/ROSE* BN22 .. 10 E3
Mayfield Rd *CROW* TN6 .... 42 A4
SBGH/RUST TN4 .... 19 M2
Mayfield Wy *BEX* TN40 .... 183 L1
Mayflower Ct *HWH* RH16 .... 71 M2 🔲
Mayflower Rd *HWH* RH16 .... 71 M2
Mayhew Wy *LEW* BN7 .... 3 G3
Mayhouse Rd *BURH* RH15 .... 96 F5 🔲
Mayne Waye *HAS* TN34 .... 163 G2
Mayo Cl *BEXW* TN39 .... 160 A6
Mayo Ri *BEXW* TN39 .... 160 A6
Mayo Rd *ROTT* BN2 .... 169 H6
Maypole Cottages *UCK* TN22 .. 54 B6
Maypole Rd *EGRIN* RH19 .... 13 K4
EGRIN RH19 .... 14 E8
May Rd *ROTT* BN2 .... 187 L3
May Tree Gdns *BEX* TN40 .... 160 F8
Maytree Wk *HOVE* BN3 .... 167 L5
Maywood Av *LW/ROSE* BN22 .. 196 D4
Mcindoe Rd *EGRIN* RH19 .... 13 K3
Mciver Cl *EGRIN* RH19 .... 12 F1
Mcwilliam Rd *ROTT* BN2 .... 170 C5
Meadow Cl *HAIL* BN27 .... 155 H5
HOVE BN3 .... 168 B3
PTSD BN41 .... 167 H4 🔲

ROTT BN2 .... 188 E3
STHW BN42 .... 167 G6
STLEO TN38 .... 162 A2 🔲
Meadow Crs *BEXW* TN39 .... 160 C7
Meadowcroft Cl *EGRIN* RH19 .. 13 J4
Meadow Dr *HWH* RH16 .... 49 H8
Meadow Hill Rd *RTW* TN1 .... 20 B3 🔲
Meadowlands Av
LW/ROSE BN22 .... 196 D4
Meadow La *BAT* TN33 .... 112 D5
BURH RH15 .... 96 F5
HWH RH16 .... 49 H8
Meadow Pde *ROTT* BN2 .... 188 E3
Meadow Rd *HAIL* BN27 .... 155 G8
RRTW TN3 .... 18 B7
SBGH/RUST TN4 .... 19 J2
Meadows *HPPT/KEY* BN6 .... 122 E1
Meadows Rd *LW/ROSE* BN22 .. 196 B4
The Meadows *HOVE* BN3 .... 167 J3
LEW BN7 .... 3 J1
SLVH TN37 .... 139 J8
Meadow Vw *CROW* TN6 .... 41 G7
Meadowview *ROTT* BN2 .... 169 L5
Meadow Wy *HTHF* TN21 .... 106 A1
RHAS TN35 .... 164 E2
SEAF BN25 .... 203 G3
Meads Av *BEXW* TN39 .... 182 C2
HOVE BN3 .... 167 J3
Meads Brow
EDN/EASTW BN20 .... 206 D6 🔲
Meads Cl *HOVE* BN3 .... 167 J3 🔲
Meads Rd *BEXW* TN39 .... 182 C2
EDN/EASTW BN20 .... 206 E6
SEAF BN25 .... 202 F5
Meads St *EDN/EASTW* BN20 .. 206 E6
The Meads *BRI* BN1 .... 169 K1
EGRIN RH19 .... 13 L7
RTWE/PEM TN2 .... 20 C4
The Mead *BEXW* TN39 .... 182 D2
Meadway Ct *STHW* BN42 .... 166 D6
Meadway Crs *HOVE* BN3 .... 167 M4
The Meadway *ROTT* BN2 .... 187 M1
Mealla Cl *LEW* BN7 .... 2 F1
Medina Dr *PEV* BN24 .... 197 H1
Medina Pl *HOVE* BN3 .... 186 B1
Medina Ter *HOVE* BN3 .... 186 B1 🔲
Medina Vls *HOVE* BN3 .... 186 B1
Medmerry Hl *ROTT* BN2 .... 169 L4
Medway *CRAWE* RH10 .... 22 A1
CROW TN6 .... 40 C5
HAIL BN27 .... 155 G4
Medway Dr *EGRIN* RH19 .... 13 K8
FROW RH18 .... 25 G4
Medway La *PEV* BN24 .... 197 G1
Medway Rd *RTW* TN1 .... 20 B3
Meeching Ri *NEWHV* BN9 .... 8 F4
Meeching Rd *NEWHV* BN9 .... 9 G4 🔲
Meeds Rd *BURH* RH15 .... 97 G4
Meeting House La *BRI* BN1 .... 6 E7 🔲
Melbourne Rd *LW/ROSE* BN22 .. 11 G5
Melbourne St *ROTT* BN2 .... 7 J1
Melfort Rd *CROW* TN6 .... 39 K5
Melrose Av *PTSD* BN41 .... 167 G5
Melrose Cl *BRI* BN1 .... 169 J4
HAIL BN27 .... 155 G6
Melville Rd *HOVE* BN3 .... 6 B3
Melvill La *EDN/EASTW* BN20 .. 196 B6
Mendip Av *LGNY* BN23 .... 197 J3
Mendip Gdns *HAS* TN34 .... 163 H3
Menzies Rd *SLVH* TN37 .... 162 B3 🔲
Meon Cl *PEV* BN24 .... 197 G1
Mercatoria *STLEO* TN38 .... 4 A9
Mercers *RRTW* TN3 .... 19 G3
Mercer St *RTW* TN1 .... 20 B1 🔲
Mercread Rd *SEAF* BN25 .... 202 F3
Meres La *MAYF* TN20 .... 56 D6
MAYF TN20 .... 79 H3
Merevale *BRI* BN1 .... 169 H4
Meridian Rd *LEW* BN7 .... 2 C3
Meridian Wy *EGRIN* RH19 .... 13 M3
Merlin Cl *HOVE* BN3 .... 168 C6
Merlin Wy *EGRIN* RH19 .... 14 A3
Mermaid St *RYE* TN31 .... 117 H1
Merrimede Cl *STLEO* TN38 .... 162 A7
Merriments La *BUR/ETCH* TN19 .. 62 A2
Merston Cl *ROTT* BN2 .... 170 E8
Metcalfe Av *NEWHV* BN9 .... 8 C3
Mews Ct *EGRIN* RH19 .... 13 M8
The Mews *RING/NEW* BN8 .... 130 A1
Meyners Cl *HOVE* BN3 .... 167 J4
Michael Flds *FROW* RH18 .... 24 E4
Michelbourne Cl *BURH* RH15 .. 96 E5 🔲
Michel Cl *EDN/EASTW* BN20 .. 205 H5
Michel Dene Cl
EDN/EASTW BN20 .... 205 J5 🔲
Michel Dene Rd
EDN/EASTW BN20 .... 205 H5
Michele Cl *STLEO* TN38 .... 162 B5 🔲
Michel Gv *EAST* BN21 .... 10 A4
Micheham La *LGNY* BN23 .... 197 G2 🔲
Micheham Rd *UCK* TN22 .... 76 E5
Michelson Cl *STLEO* TN38 .... 161 M2
Middle Dr *UCK* TN22 .... 53 G8
Middle Furlong Cl *RING/NEW* BN8 .. 150 C2
Middleham Cl *RING/NEW* BN8 .. 150 C2
Middleham Cl *RING/NEW* BN8 .. 197 J2 🔲
Middle Rd *BRI* BN1 .... 168 E5
RHAS TN35 .... 163 K3
RRTW TN3 .... 31 G1
SHOR BN43 .... 166 B7
Middlesex Rd *BEX* TN40 .... 183 K3
Middle St *BRI* BN1 .... 6 D8
BRI BN1 .... 147 J4
HAS TN34 .... 5 G6
PTSD BN41 .... 167 H8
Middleton Av *NEWHV* BN9 .... 8 D3
Middleton Dr *LGNY* BN23 .... 197 L7 🔲
Middleton Ri *BRI* BN1 .... 169 L1
Middle Wy *BURH* RH15 .... 97 H3
LEW BN7 .... 2 A5
Midfields Cl *BURH* RH15 .... 97 H2 🔲
Midfields Dr *BURH* RH15 .... 97 H2
Midfields Wk *BURH* RH15 .... 97 H2 🔲
Midhurst Ri *BRI* BN1 .... 146 B8
Midhurst Rd *LW/ROSE* BN22 .. 196 F4
Midhurst Wk *HOVE* BN3 .... 167 M3 🔲
Midway Rd *ROTT* BN2 .... 170 C6

The Midway SBGH/RUST TN4 ...... 19 K4
Mighell St ROTT BN2 ...... 7 G6
Milcote Av HOVE BN3 ...... 167 M6
Mildenhall Dr SLVH TN37 ...... 162 B2
Mildmay Rd HOVE BN8 BN41 ...... 127 K8
Mildmay Rd LEW BN7 ...... 2 B5
Mile Oak Crs STHW BN42 ...... 166 F5
Mile Oak Gdns PTSD BN41 ...... 167 G5
Mile Oak Rd PTSD BN41 ...... 166 F5
Milfoil Dr LGNY BN23 ...... 197 J5 ▣
Military Rd RYE TN31 ...... 91 K5
Milland Cl BEX TN40 ...... 160 E8
Milland Rd HAIL BN27 ...... 155 H5
Millbank BURH RH15 ...... 97 H2
Millberg Rd SEAF BN25 ...... 203 H2
Millbrook Cl HTHF TN21 ...... 106 A7
Millbrook Gdns
  EDN/EASTW BN20 ...... 196 B8
Millbrook Rd CROW TN6 ...... 40 E4
Mill Brooks RING/NEW BN8 ...... 99 K7
Mill Cl EDN/EASTW BN20 ...... 205 G5
  EGRIN RH19 ...... 13 L7
  HTHF TN21 ...... 79 M7
  POLE BN26 ...... 195 M2
  POY/PYE BN45 ...... 144 C1
  PTSD BN41 ...... 167 J5
  RBTBR TN32 ...... 86 E4
  RHAS TN35 ...... 139 L1
  RHAS TN35 ...... 163 L2
Mill Crs CROW TN6 ...... 39 M3 ▣
Millcroft BRI BN1 ...... 168 C1
Millcroft Av STHW BN42 ...... 166 E5
Millcroft Gdns STHW BN42 ...... 166 E5
Millcross Rd PTSD BN41 ...... 167 H5
Mildown Rd SEAF BN25 ...... 202 F2
Mill Dr CROW TN6 ...... 39 M4
  HOVE BN3 ...... 168 A3
  SEAF BN25 ...... 203 G3
Mill Dro UCK TN22 ...... 76 C8
Miller Rd BRI BN1 ...... 168 E5
Miller's Hill Cottage La
  RHAS TN35 ...... 113 K7
Millers Rd HAIL BN27 ...... 155 C8
Miller's Rd BRI BN1 ...... 168 E5 ▣
Millers Wy BURH RH15 ...... 97 G2
Millfield BAT TN33 ...... 136 A8
Millfield Cl RING/NEW BN8 ...... 74 C7
  SEAF BN25 ...... 203 G2
Millfield Cottages ROTT BN2 ...... 7 L9
Millfield Ri BEX TN40 ...... 183 J2
Mill Gap Rd EAST BN21 ...... 10 C4
Mill Gdns HTHF TN21 ...... 106 A1
  RING/NEW BN8 ...... 150 D1
Mill Green Rd HWH RH16 ...... 48 E8
Milham Cl BEXW TN39 ...... 182 F1
Mill Hill Cl HWH RH16 ...... 48 E7
Mill La BAT TN33 ...... 158 F4
  CROW TN6 ...... 39 L4
  EGRIN RH19 ...... 12 D1
  HAIL BN27 ...... 155 G1
  HPPT/KEY BN6 ...... 96 A3
  HPPT/KEY BN6 ...... 122 C7
  LEW BN7 ...... 172 C7
  LYDD TN29 ...... 95 J7
  POY/PYE BN45 ...... 144 C1
  PTSD BN41 ...... 167 J4
  RHAS TN35 ...... 139 L1
  RHAS TN35 ...... 163 L1
  RING/NEW BN8 ...... 99 K7
  RING/NEW BN8 ...... 126 D4
  RING/NEW BN8 ...... 130 A1
  RYE TN31 ...... 89 M3
  UCK TN22 ...... 76 C8
Mill Md RING/NEW BN8 ...... 150 D1
Mill Race HPPT/KEY BN6 ...... 96 E6
The Millrace POLE BN26 ...... 195 M2
Mill Ri BRI BN1 ...... 168 C1
  RBTBR TN32 ...... 85 G3
Mill Rd BRI BN1 ...... 145 J8
  BURH RH15 ...... 97 H2
  EAST BN21 ...... 206 D1
  HAIL BN27 ...... 155 J7
  HTHF TN21 ...... 79 M7
  LEW BN7 ...... 3 J2
  LYDD TN29 ...... 95 K8
  PTSD BN41 ...... 167 H7
  RING/NEW BN8 ...... 150 D1
  RYE TN31 ...... 91 J7
  WSEA TN36 ...... 116 A6
Millstream Cl RRTW TN3 ...... 17 K4 ▣
Millstream Gdns POLE BN26 ...... 195 M2
Mill Stream Meadow
  HWH RH16 ...... 48 D7 ▣
Mill St BRI BN1 ...... 147 J7
Mill Vw RING/NEW BN8 ...... 150 C2
Mill Vw Cl PEV BN24 ...... 179 K8
Mill View Rd BEXW TN39 ...... 160 B7
Millward Rd PEV BN24 ...... 198 C3
Mill Wy EGRIN RH19 ...... 13 L7
  POLE BN26 ...... 195 L5
Mill Wd BURH RH15 ...... 97 H3
Millwood EGRIN RH19 ...... 22 E1
Millwood Cl UCK TN22 ...... 76 D2
Millwood La UCK TN22 ...... 76 D2
Millwood Rd BEXW TN39 ...... 160 A6
Millyard Crs ROTT BN2 ...... 170 D7
Milner Rd ROTT BN2 ...... 169 J5
Milnthorpe Rd
  EDN/EASTW BN20 ...... 206 E6
  HOVE BN3 ...... 167 L6
Milton Crs EAST BN21 ...... 206 C2
  EGRIN RH19 ...... 13 J5
Milton Dr STHW BN42 ...... 166 F6
Milton Rd EAST BN21 ...... 206 C2
  HWH RH16 ...... 71 K1
  ROTT BN2 ...... 7 H3
Milton St PEV BN24 ...... 179 M8
Milward Rd HAS TN34 ...... 5 J5
Milward Rd HAS TN34 ...... 5 J6
Mimosa Cl POLE BN26 ...... 178 A7 ▣
Mimram Rd PEV BN24 ...... 197 G1
Mindleheim Av EGRIN RH19 ...... 14 B4
The Minnels HPPT/KEY BN6 ...... 122 F3
Minsted Sq BEXW TN39 ...... 182 C4
Minster Cl POLE BN26 ...... 178 A7 ▣
The Mint RYE TN31 ...... 117 H1 ▣
Mistley Cl BEX TN40 ...... 161 G8
Mitchelldean PEAHV BN10 ...... 190 B5

Mitten Rd BEX TN40 ...... 183 J2
Moat Croft Rd EAST BN21 ...... 10 A5
Moat Farm RTWE/PEM TN2 ...... 20 A7
Moat La BAT TN33 ...... 139 H4
  RHAS TN35 ...... 104 D5
Moat Rd EGRIN RH19 ...... 13 L5 ▣
Mocatta Wy BURH RH15 ...... 96 D1
Modena St HOVE BN3 ...... 167 M7
Molesworth St HOVE BN3 ...... 167 M6
Molyneux Park Rd
  SBGH/RUST TN4 ...... 19 M2
Monarch Gdns LGNY BN23 ...... 197 L5
  SEAF BN25 ...... 203 G1 ▣
Monarchs Wy HOVE BN3 ...... 168 C7
  PTSD BN41 ...... 144 D8
  STHW BN42 ...... 166 E3
Mona Rd LW/ROSE BN22 ...... 11 H2
Monceux Rd
  EDN/EASTW BN20 ...... 206 C2
  HAIL BN27 ...... 133 L8
Monckton Wy LEW BN7 ...... 171 L1
Monger's Md RING/NEW BN8 ...... 126 E2
Monk Cl LEW BN7 ...... 146 E8
Monks La WADH TN5 ...... 32 B7
Monks Wy LEW BN7 ...... 2 E1
  RYE TN31 ...... 65 H6
Monmouth St HOVE BN3 ...... 168 B7 ▣
Monson Rd RTW TN1 ...... 20 B2 ▣
Monson Wy RTW TN1 ...... 20 B2 ▣
Montacute Gdns
  RTWE/PEM TN2 ...... 19 M4 ▣
Montacute Rd LEW BN7 ...... 2 A8
  RTWE/PEM TN2 ...... 20 A5
Montacute Wy UCK TN22 ...... 76 D5 ▣
Montague Cl SHOR BN43 ...... 166 D7 ▣
Montague Pl ROTT BN2 ...... 7 J8
Montague St ROTT BN2 ...... 7 J8
Montague Wy PEV BN24 ...... 197 M1
Montefiore Rd HOVE BN3 ...... 6 A3
Monteith Cl RRTW TN3 ...... 19 G3
Monterey Gdns BEXW TN39 ...... 182 D3
Montes HI HWH RH16 ...... 49 M6
Monteswood La RHWH RH17 ...... 50 B6
Montford Cl SHOR BN43 ...... 166 D6
Montfort Pl PEV BN24 ...... 179 M8
Montfort Rd PEV BN24 ...... 179 M8
Montgomery Rd RHAS TN35 ...... 163 K1
Montgomery St HOVE BN3 ...... 167 M7
Montpelier Crs BRI BN1 ...... 6 B4
Montpelier Pl BRI BN1 ...... 6 A5
Montpelier Rd BRI BN1 ...... 6 A6
Montpelier St BRI BN1 ...... 6 B5
Montpelier Ter BRI BN1 ...... 6 B5
Montpelier Vls BRI BN1 ...... 6 B5
Montreal Rd ROTT BN2 ...... 7 H5
Monument Vw ROTT BN2 ...... 7 M5
Moons HI BAT TN33 ...... 136 B8
Moore's La RYE TN31 ...... 88 E7
Moor Hall Dr BAT TN33 ...... 135 M8
Moor HI HAWK TN18 ...... 47 M6
The Moorings EGRIN RH19 ...... 13 G3
  SHOR BN43 ...... 166 C3
Moor La RHAS TN35 ...... 139 L3
  RING/NEW BN8 ...... 151 G3
Moor Pl EGRIN RH19 ...... 13 K4
Moor Rd RHAS TN35 ...... 139 L3
The Moor HAWK TN18 ...... 47 M6
Morecambe Rd BRI BN1 ...... 146 A8
Morestead PEAHV BN10 ...... 190 D5
Morgan Cl BEXW TN39 ...... 160 B6 ▣
Morgay Wood La RHAS TN35 ...... 140 E4
Morlais Pl WSEA TN36 ...... 117 H8
Morlais Rdg WSEA TN36 ...... 117 H8
Morland Cl BAT TN33 ...... 159 H1 ▣
Morley Cl LEW BN7 ...... 2 D9
Morley St ROTT BN2 ...... 6 F5
Morningside Cl SEAF BN25 ...... 202 F2
Mornington Crs HOVE BN3 ...... 167 K7 ▣
Morris Rd LEW BN7 ...... 3 J6
Mortain Rd PEV BN24 ...... 179 M8
Mortimer Gdns POLE BN26 ...... 195 M2
Mortimer Rd HOVE BN3 ...... 167 M6
  LW/ROSE BN22 ...... 197 G8
Morton Rd EGRIN RH19 ...... 13 L7
Moscow Rd RHAS TN35 ...... 163 J3
Motcombe La EAST BN21 ...... 206 D2
Motcombe Rd EAST BN21 ...... 206 D2
Motte Fld HRTF TN7 ...... 26 E2
Mottins HI CROW TN6 ...... 40 D6
Moulsecoomb Wy ROTT BN2 ...... 169 L1
Mountain Ash Cl HAIL BN27 ...... 155 G6
Mountbatten Cl RHAS TN35 ...... 163 K1
Mountbatten Dr LGNY BN23 ...... 197 L7
Mount Caburn Crs
  PEAHV BN10 ...... 190 C4 ▣
Mount Cl NEWHV BN9 ...... 9 L1
Mount Dr ROTT BN2 ...... 189 K4
Mount Edgcumbe Rd
  SBGH/RUST TN4 ...... 20 A3
Mount Ephraim RTW TN1 ...... 20 A2
Mount Ephraim Rd RTW TN1 ...... 20 A2 ▣
Mountfield Gdns
  RTWE/PEM TN2 ...... 20 B3
Mountfield La RBTBR TN32 ...... 84 B7
Mountfield Rd LEW BN7 ...... 3 G8
  RTWE/PEM TN2 ...... 20 B3
Mountfields BRI BN1 ...... 169 J4
Mount Idol Vw BEXW TN39 ...... 159 M6
Mount Joy BAT TN33 ...... 137 K1
Mount La CRAWE RH10 ...... 22 A2
Mountney Dr PEV BN24 ...... 180 F8
Mountney Rd EAST BN21 ...... 206 C2
Mount Noddy RHWH RH17 ...... 70 C2
Mount Pl LEW BN7 ...... 2 F6
Mount Pleasant CROW TN6 ...... 40 C7
  ROTT BN2 ...... 7 H7
  UCK TN22 ...... 78 A8
  WADH TN5 ...... 43 L1 ▣
Mount Pleasant Av
  RTWE/PEM TN2 ...... 20 B3 ▣
Mount Pleasant Rd HAS TN34 ...... 5 J2
  RTW TN1 ...... 20 A3
Mountreed MAYF TN20 ...... 56 B7
Mount Rd EDN/EASTW BN20 ...... 206 F6
  NEWHV BN9 ...... 9 L1

RHAS TN35 ...... 163 J4
Mount Sion RTW TN1 ...... 20 A4
Mount St BAT TN33 ...... 137 K1
  LEW BN7 ...... 2 F6
The Mount HAIL BN27 ...... 155 M8
  UCK TN22 ...... 76 C6
Mount View Ter HAIL BN27 ...... 155 J8 ▣
Mount Zion Pl BRI BN1 ...... 6 D5 ▣
Moy Av LW/ROSE BN22 ...... 11 G2
Moyne Cl HOVE BN3 ...... 167 L5
Muirfield Ri STLEO TN38 ...... 161 M7
Mulberry Cl BEXW TN39 ...... 168 F3 ▣
  BRI BN1 ...... 168 F3 ▣
  LW/ROSE BN22 ...... 196 E3
  SHOR BN43 ...... 166 D5
Mulberry La HPPT/KEY BN6 ...... 123 K5
Mulberry Wk SLVH TN37 ...... 162 D1
Mulberry Wy HTHF TN21 ...... 106 B1
Munnion Rd RHWH RH17 ...... 34 E7
Munns Dr BURH RH15 ...... 97 H2
Munster Gn RING/NEW BN8 ...... 126 E2 ▣
Murray Av NEWHV BN9 ...... 8 E3
Musgrave Av EGRIN RH19 ...... 13 L7
Mushroom Fld LEW BN7 ...... 171 L1
Muster Gn North HWH RH16 ...... 71 K2
Muster Gn South HWH RH16 ...... 71 K2
Mutton Hall HI HTHF TN21 ...... 80 A6
Mutton Hall La HTHF TN21 ...... 80 A6
Myrtle Rd CROW TN6 ...... 39 M5
  LW/ROSE BN22 ...... 197 K8

N

Namrik Ms HOVE BN3 ...... 168 A8
Nanson Rd BRI BN1 ...... 146 D8
Nan Tucks La UCK TN22 ...... 77 J3
Napier Rd RTWE/PEM TN2 ...... 20 A7
  STLEO TN38 ...... 161 L1
Nash La RHWH RH17 ...... 73 H2
Natal Rd ROTT BN2 ...... 169 K5
Neale Cl EGRIN RH19 ...... 13 H3
Neath Rd LYDD TN29 ...... 119 M5
Neaves La RING/NEW BN8 ...... 151 G3
Neill's Cl NEWHV BN9 ...... 8 F4
Neills Rd RRTW TN3 ...... 32 D4
Nellington Rd RRTW TN3 ...... 19 G3
Nelson Dr LGNY BN23 ...... 197 L8 ▣
Nelson Rd HAS TN34 ...... 5 J4
  RTWE/PEM TN2 ...... 20 D4
Nelson Rw ROTT BN2 ...... 7 G6
Nesbitt Rd ROTT BN2 ...... 169 K5
Ness Rd LYDD TN29 ...... 95 J8
Netherfield Av LGNY BN23 ...... 197 M4
Netherfield Gn ROTT BN2 ...... 170 F6
Netherfield HI BAT TN33 ...... 111 H7
Netherfield Rd BAT TN33 ...... 110 C4
Netherfield Wy BAT TN33 ...... 110 E4
Nether La UCK TN22 ...... 52 C3
Netherwood Cl HAS TN34 ...... 162 L1
Nevill Av HOVE BN3 ...... 167 M5
  LW/ROSE BN22 ...... 196 E5
Nevill Cl HOVE BN3 ...... 168 A4
Nevill Crs LEW BN7 ...... 2 A2
Neville Rd LW/ROSE BN22 ...... 11 G3
  PEAHV BN10 ...... 190 D8
Nevill Gdns HOVE BN3 ...... 168 A4
Nevill Ga HPPT/KEY BN6 ...... 123 G3
Nevill Pk SBGH/RUST TN4 ...... 19 L3
Nevill Pl HOVE BN3 ...... 168 A4
Nevill Rdg SBGH/RUST TN4 ...... 19 K3
Nevill Rd CROW TN6 ...... 39 M3
  HOVE BN3 ...... 168 A4
  LEW BN7 ...... 2 C6
  ROTT BN2 ...... 188 F5
  UCK TN22 ...... 76 D5
Nevill St RTWE/PEM TN2 ...... 20 A4
Nevill Ter RTWE/PEM TN2 ...... 19 M4 ▣
Nevill Wy HOVE BN3 ...... 168 A4
Newark Pl ROTT BN2 ...... 7 G4
New Barn Cl HAIL BN27 ...... 155 J8
  PTSD BN41 ...... 167 H4
  SHOR BN43 ...... 166 B5 ▣
New Barn La UCK TN22 ...... 102 C1
New Barn Rd ROTT BN2 ...... 188 E3
  SHOR BN43 ...... 166 B5
Newbury La RHWH RH17 ...... 70 E1
  WADH TN5 ...... 32 C6
New Church Rd HOVE BN3 ...... 167 K7
Newcomen Rd SBGH/RUST TN4 ...... 20 A1
New Cut RBTBR TN32 ...... 111 J1
  RHAS TN35 ...... 139 L2
New Dorset St BRI BN1 ...... 6 D5
Newells Cl ROTT BN2 ...... 170 E5
New England La BAT TN33 ...... 138 E1
New England Ri PTSD BN41 ...... 167 G2
New England Rd BRI BN1 ...... 6 D2
  HWH RH16 ...... 71 L2
New England St BRI BN1 ...... 6 E2
Newfield La NEWHV BN9 ...... 8 E3
Newfield Rd NEWHV BN9 ...... 8 E3
Newgate Rd SLVH TN37 ...... 4 A4
Newhaven Rd SEAF BN25 ...... 202 A1
Newhaven St ROTT BN2 ...... 7 G4
Newick Cl SEAF BN25 ...... 203 J4 ▣
Newick Dr RING/NEW BN8 ...... 74 C7
Newick HI RING/NEW BN8 ...... 74 C6
Newick La MAYF TN20 ...... 57 G6
Newick Rd BRI BN1 ...... 169 L2
  EDN/EASTW BN20 ...... 196 C8 ▣
Newlands RRTW TN3 ...... 19 G2
Newlands Av BEXW TN39 ...... 183 G1
Newlands Cl HAS TN34 ...... 162 E1
  HPPT/KEY BN6 ...... 123 G3
Newlands Crs EGRIN RH19 ...... 13 K4
Newlands Rd ROTT BN2 ...... 189 G5
New La UCK TN22 ...... 76 B7
New Lydd Rd RYE TN31 ...... 118 D3 ▣
Newmans Wy RHAS TN35 ...... 163 K2
Newmarket Rd ROTT BN2 ...... 169 J6 ▣
New Moorsite RHAS TN35 ...... 139 M3
Newnham Rd HTHF TN21 ...... 80 A6
Newnham Wy HTHF TN21 ...... 80 A7
New Pde EAST BN21 ...... 206 D3 ▣
New Pl EAST BN21 ...... 206 D3 ▣
  UCK TN22 ...... 102 C1
New Pond HI HTHF TN21 ...... 79 K8

Newport Rd BURH RH15 ...... 96 F3
Newport St ROTT BN2 ...... 7 H2
New Rd BRI BN1 ...... 6 E6
  CROW TN6 ...... 39 M3
  CROW TN6 ...... 41 H6
  HAIL BN27 ...... 155 J2
  HPPT/KEY BN6 ...... 122 F5
  LEW BN7 ...... 2 F6
  LW/ROSE BN22 ...... 11 G4
  NEWHV BN9 ...... 191 K5
  POLE BN26 ...... 178 B8
  RHAS TN35 ...... 163 K4
  RHAS TN35 ...... 164 D3
  RING/NEW BN8 ...... 150 D3
  RYE TN31 ...... 88 A3
  RYE TN31 ...... 91 K8
  UCK TN22 ...... 102 D3
New Steine ROTT BN2 ...... 7 G8
New Steine Ms ROTT BN2 ...... 7 G8
New St LYDD TN29 ...... 95 J8
Newtimber Dr PTSD BN41 ...... 167 G5
Newton Av EGRIN RH19 ...... 13 M8
Newton Cl HWH RH16 ...... 49 H7
Newton Rd HWH RH16 ...... 49 H7
  LEW BN7 ...... 2 D4
  PEAHV BN10 ...... 190 C7 ▣
  RTW TN1 ...... 20 B2 ▣
Newton Willows RRTW TN3 ...... 18 C7
Newtown Rd ROTT BN2 ...... 168 B6
New Upperton Rd EAST BN21 ...... 10 A4
New Way La HPPT/KEY BN6 ...... 122 B4
New Winchelsea Rd RYE TN31 ...... 117 H4
Nightingale Cl EGRIN RH19 ...... 13 K7 ▣
  LGNY BN23 ...... 197 J3
Nightingale La BURH RH15 ...... 96 F4
Nightingale Ri UCK TN22 ...... 102 D2 ▣
Nile St BRI BN1 ...... 6 E7
Ninfield Pl ROTT BN2 ...... 169 L7
Ninfield Rd BEXW TN39 ...... 159 L5
Nizells Av HOVE BN3 ...... 168 C5
Noahs Ark La HWH RH16 ...... 49 J7
Nodes La HAIL BN27 ...... 155 M2
Noel Gn BURH RH15 ...... 97 H2
Noel Ri BURH RH15 ...... 97 H2
Nolan Rd ROTT BN2 ...... 170 E7
Nook Cl RHAS TN35 ...... 163 K3 ▣
The Nook UCK TN22 ...... 102 D2 ▣
Norbury Cl CROW TN6 ...... 39 L2
Nore Rd NEWHV BN9 ...... 8 E5
Norfolk Buildings BRI BN1 ...... 6 A6 ▣
Norfolk Cl BEXW TN39 ...... 160 B7
Norfolk Dr STLEO TN38 ...... 161 M2
Norfolk Ms BRI BN1 ...... 6 A6 ▣
  RTW TN1 ...... 20 B4 ▣
Norfolk Sq BRI BN1 ...... 6 A6 ▣
Norfolk St BRI BN1 ...... 6 A7
Norfolk Ter BRI BN1 ...... 6 A5
Norlington Ct RING/NEW BN8 ...... 127 K8
Norlington Flds
  RING/NEW BN8 ...... 127 J7
Norlington La RING/NEW BN8 ...... 127 K6
Norman Cl BAT TN33 ...... 137 M2
  SEAF BN25 ...... 192 B8 ▣
Normandale BEXW TN39 ...... 160 B7
Normandy Cl EGRIN RH19 ...... 13 M6 ▣
Normandy Rd SLVH TN37 ...... 162 C3
Norman Rd BURH RH15 ...... 96 F3
  HOVE BN3 ...... 167 L8
  NEWHV BN9 ...... 8 F4
  PEV BN24 ...... 198 D2
  RTW TN1 ...... 20 B1 ▣
  SLVH TN37 ...... 4 B3
  STLEO TN38 ...... 4 A9
Northampton Wy
  STLEO TN38 ...... 162 A2 ▣
North Av EDN/EASTW BN20 ...... 206 B1
North Barn HPPT/KEY BN6 ...... 122 C7
North Barnes La LEW BN7 ...... 124 F1
North Beeches Rd CROW TN6 ...... 40 A4
Northbourne Rd
  LW/ROSE BN22 ...... 197 H7
Northbridge St RBTBR TN32 ...... 85 H1
North Camp La SEAF BN25 ...... 202 F7
Northcliffe Cl SEAF BN25 ...... 202 F2 ▣
North Cl POLE BN26 ...... 178 B7
  PTSD BN41 ...... 167 G4
North Common Rd RHWH RH17 ...... 98 D1
Northcote La PEAHV BN10 ...... 190 A5 ▣
North Ct HPPT/KEY BN6 ...... 122 E2
  LEW BN7 ...... 3 J5
Northdown Cl NEWHV BN9 ...... 8 E5
Northdown Rd NEWHV BN9 ...... 8 E5
North Dr ROTT BN2 ...... 7 J5
Northease Cl HOVE BN3 ...... 167 K4
Northease Dr HOVE BN3 ...... 167 K4
Northease Gdns HOVE BN3 ...... 167 L5 ▣
North End HPPT/KEY BN6 ...... 123 K2
Northern Av POLE BN26 ...... 178 B7
Northfield Cl SEAF BN25 ...... 202 F1
Northfield Ri HOVE BN3 ...... 167 K2
  ROTT BN2 ...... 189 G4
Northfield Wy BRI BN1 ...... 169 G2
North Gdns BRI BN1 ...... 6 D5
Northgate Cl ROTT BN2 ...... 170 F6
Northgrove Rd HAWK TN18 ...... 47 M4 ▣
North Heath Cl HAIL BN27 ...... 155 J4 ▣
North Hill Rd HAWK TN18 ...... 47 J5
Northiam St ROTT BN2 ...... 7 G8
Northiam Rd
  EDN/EASTW BN20 ...... 206 C2
  RYE TN31 ...... 88 D2
Northlands Av HWH RH16 ...... 72 A3
North La EGRIN RH19 ...... 34 E1
  PTSD BN41 ...... 167 G4
  RHAS TN35 ...... 140 C1
North Pl BRI BN1 ...... 6 E5
North Quay Rd NEWHV BN9 ...... 191 M5
Northridge Rd ROTT BN2 ...... 188 C4
North Rd BEXW TN39 ...... 160 C7
  BRI BN1 ...... 6 D5
  BRI BN1 ...... 168 D5
  HAIL BN27 ...... 134 C4

HWH RH16 ...... 72 A2
PEV BN24 ...... 198 D2
POLE BN26 ...... 193 L3
PTSD BN41 ...... 167 G4
RING/NEW BN8 ...... 127 K8
STLEO TN38 ...... 4 A4
North Rw UCK TN22 ...... 76 C6
North Salts RYE TN31 ...... 91 H3
North St BRI BN1 ...... 6 D5
  CRAWE RH10 ...... 22 A2
  CROW TN6 ...... 41 H6
  EAST BN21 ...... 10 F6
  HAIL BN27 ...... 131 M8
  HAIL BN27 ...... 154 F2
  HAIL BN27 ...... 155 H6
  HTHF TN21 ...... 104 F1
  HTHF TN21 ...... 107 K1
  LEW BN7 ...... 3 G5 ▣
  MAYF TN20 ...... 57 H3
  POLE BN26 ...... 194 A3
  PTSD BN41 ...... 167 H7
  RTWE/PEM TN2 ...... 20 C3
  STLEO TN38 ...... 4 A4
  WSEA TN36 ...... 116 A6
North Ter HAS TN34 ...... 5 M2
North Trade Rd BAT TN33 ...... 136 F2
Northway BURH RH15 ...... 97 J2
North Wy LEW BN7 ...... 2 A4
  NEWHV BN9 ...... 9 G3
  SEAF BN25 ...... 192 F8
  SEAF BN25 ...... 202 F1
Northwood Av ROTT BN2 ...... 189 L5
Norton Cl HOVE BN3 ...... 168 B3 ▣
Norton Dr ROTT BN2 ...... 170 D5
Norton Rd HOVE BN3 ...... 168 B8
  NEWHV BN9 ...... 9 J4
Norton Ter NEWHV BN9 ...... 9 J4
Norway Rd LW/ROSE BN22 ...... 197 K8
Norway St PTSD BN41 ...... 167 J7
Norwich Cl ROTT BN2 ...... 170 A4
Norwich Dr ROTT BN2 ...... 170 A4
Nottidge Rd SBGH/RUST TN4 ...... 19 K5 ▣
Novington La LEW BN7 ...... 125 C5
Nunnery Stable LEW BN7 ...... 2 D6 ▣
Nursery Cl HAIL BN27 ...... 155 J6 ▣
  HWH RH16 ...... 71 K1
  POLE BN26 ...... 178 B8
  PTSD BN41 ...... 166 E2 ▣
  SHOR BN43 ...... 166 B6
  WADH TN5 ...... 46 B3
Nursery Fld UCK TN22 ...... 77 H2
Nursery La HAIL BN27 ...... 157 H1
  UCK TN22 ...... 52 C2
  UCK TN22 ...... 76 B1
  UCK TN22 ...... 78 E5
  UCK TN22 ...... 102 D2
The Nursery BURH RH15 ...... 97 J2
Nursery Wy HTHF TN21 ...... 79 L7
Nuthatch Rd LGNY BN23 ...... 197 J3
Nuthurst Cl ROTT BN2 ...... 169 M8
Nuthurst Pl ROTT BN2 ...... 187 M1
Nutley Av ROTT BN2 ...... 189 K6
Nutley Cl HOVE BN3 ...... 167 M3 ▣
  RYE TN31 ...... 91 G8
Nutley Mill Rd PEV BN24 ...... 197 H1
Nye Cl CROW TN6 ...... 39 M5
Nye La HPPT/KEY BN6 ...... 123 K6
Nye Rd BURH RH15 ...... 97 H3
Nyetimber HI ROTT BN2 ...... 169 L4

O

Oakapple Rd STHW BN42 ...... 166 D4
Oak Bank HWH RH16 ...... 48 F7
Oak Cl BRI BN1 ...... 168 C3
Oak Cft EGRIN RH19 ...... 14 A6
Oakdale Rd HWH RH16 ...... 71 M3 ▣
  SBGH/RUST TN4 ...... 19 M2
Oakdene Av PTSD BN41 ...... 166 E3
Oakdene Cl PTSD BN41 ...... 166 E3
Oakdene Crs PTSD BN41 ...... 166 E3
Oakdene Gdns PTSD BN41 ...... 166 E3
Oakdene Ri PTSD BN41 ...... 166 E3
Oakdene Wy PTSD BN41 ...... 166 E2
Oakenfield BURH RH15 ...... 96 F1
Oakfield HAWK TN18 ...... 47 M4
Oakfield Cl HWH RH16 ...... 49 G7
Oakfield Court Rd
  RTWE/PEM TN2 ...... 20 C3 ▣
Oakfield Rd RHAS TN35 ...... 163 J3
The Oak Fld RYE TN31 ...... 141 M5
The Oakfield RYE TN31 ...... 91 H6
Oakfield Wy BEXW TN39 ...... 159 J8
  EGRIN RH19 ...... 13 M3
Oak Hall Pk BURH RH15 ...... 97 H5
Oakhill Dr RYE TN31 ...... 114 H3
Oakhurst Cl HAS TN34 ...... 162 E1
Oakhurst Dr CROW TN6 ...... 40 A4
Oakhurst Gdns EGRIN RH19 ...... 13 J4
Oakhurst La HWH RH16 ...... 48 D7
Oakhurst Rd BAT TN33 ...... 111 K8
Oakland Dr RBTBR TN32 ...... 84 D2
Oaklands PEV BN24 ...... 179 K8
  RRTW TN3 ...... 34 B6
Oaklands Av ROTT BN2 ...... 189 J5
Oaklands Cl POLE BN26 ...... 178 B8 ▣
Oaklands Rd HAWK TN18 ...... 47 M5
  HWH RH16 ...... 71 K1
  RRTW TN3 ...... 18 B3
Oaklea Wy HAIL BN27 ...... 155 G8 ▣
Oak La LYDD TN29 ...... 95 H8 ▣
Oaklea Cl SLVH TN37 ...... 162 C2
Oakleaf Cl POLE BN26 ...... 178 A7
Oaklea Wy UCK TN22 ...... 76 B7
Oakleigh Dr HTHF TN21 ...... 80 B8 ▣
Oakleigh Rd BEXW TN39 ...... 182 C2
Oakley Cl EGRIN RH19 ...... 14 D7
Oakmead Rd BURH RH15 ...... 96 F5
Oakmede Wy RING/NEW BN8 ...... 150 C1
Oakroyd Cl BURH RH15 ...... 97 J1
Oaks Cl BUR/ETCH TN19 ...... 61 H5
Oaks Forstal HAWK TN18 ...... 64 C1
The Oaks BURH RH15 ...... 96 C2
  EGRIN RH19 ...... 14 A6
  HTHF TN21 ...... 80 B8
  HWH RH16 ...... 71 K1

HWH RH16............72 A2 🛈
SLVH TN37............162 D1
Oaktree *RING/NEW* BN8....126 E2 🛈
Oak Tree Cl *RTW* TN1........20 A5
Oak Tree Ct *UCK* TN22........76 D6
Oak Tree La *LGNY* BN23....197 J2
Oak Tree Wy *HAIL* BN27....155 J4
Oakwood Av *BEXW* TN39....160 B7 🛈
Oakwood Cl *BURH* RH15....97 H4
HAS TN34............162 F3
Oakwood Dr *UCK* TN22........76 E6
Oakwood Pk *UCK* TN22........52 C1
Oakwood Rd *BURH* RH15....97 H4
HWH RH16............71 K2
Oasthouse Cl *HAS* TN34....162 D1 🛈
Oast House Dr *RYE* TN31....116 F2
Oast House Fld *WSEA* TN36...115 M8
Oast House Rd *WSEA* TN36...141 M1 🛈
Oathall Av *HWH* RH16........48 F8
Oathall Rd *HWH* RH16........71 L1
Oban Rd *SLVH* TN37........162 B3
Observatory Vw *HAIL* BN27...155 K8
Ochiltree Cl *HAS* TN34....163 G2
Ochiltree Rd *HAS* TN34....163 G2
Ockenden Wy *HPPT/KEY* BN6...122 E3
Ockley Hi *HPPT/KEY* BN6....123 G2
Ockley La *BURH* RH15........97 H7
HPPT/KEY BN6........123 G2
Ockley Wy *HPPT/KEY* BN6...123 G2
Ocklynge Cl *BEXW* TN39....182 D1
Ocklynge Rd *EAST* BN21....206 D2
Ockman La *RYE* TN31........117 J1 🛈
Offa Rd *RHAS* TN35........163 K3
Offham Cl *LW/ROSE* BN22....196 F3
SEAF BN25............202 F1 🛈
Offham Rd *LEW* BN7..........2 C3
Okehurst Rd *EAST* BN21....206 C3
Oldaker Rd *RING/NEW* BN8...74 D7
Old Barn Cl *EDN/EASTW* BN20...196 B5
Old Barn Wy *STHW* BN42....167 G2
Old Boat Wk *BRI* BN1........146 B7
Old Camp Rd
EDN/EASTW BN20........206 C4
Old Church Rd *STLEO* TN38....162 A2
Old Court Cl *BRI* BN1........168 C7
Old Dr *POLE* BN26..........177 M8
Old Dro *LGNY* BN23........197 J3
Olde Place Ms *ROTT* BN2....188 F5
Old Farm Rd *BEXW* TN39....160 B8
BRI BN1............168 F1
Oldfield Av *EDN/EASTW* BN20...196 A3
Oldfield Crs *HAIL* BN27....155 H5
STHW BN42..........166 D7
Oldfield Rd *EDN/EASTW* BN20...196 A4
Old Forest La *CROW* TN6....40 E6
Old Forewood La *BAT* TN33...137 M7
Old Forge La *UCK* TN22........52 F6
Old Fort Rd *SHOR* BN43....166 A8
Old Gardens Rd *RTWE/PEM* TN2...20 B6
Old Ghyll Rd *HTHF* TN21....106 A1
Old Harrow Rd *SLVH* TN37....162 B2
Old Heath Cl *RING/NEW* BN8...103 J8
The Old Hop Gdn *RYE* TN31...90 C4
Old House Gdns *HAS* TN34...162 F2
Old House La *RRTW* TN3........18 D1
Oldlands Av *HPPT/KEY* BN6...123 G2
Oldlands Hi *UCK* TN22........53 J4
Old La *CROW* TN6..........39 K3
CROW TN6............40 B5
MAYF TN20............56 F4
Old London Rd *BRI* BN1....168 E1
HAS TN34............5 M3
RHAS TN35............163 K2 🛈
Old Lydd Rd *RYE* TN31....118 E4
Old Malling Wy *LEW* BN7......2 E6
Old Manor Cl *BEX* TN40....183 K2
Old Mansion Cl
EDN/EASTW BN20........196 A6
HAIL BN27............155 G3 🛈
Old Mill Cl *BRI* BN1..........168 E1
Old Mill La *POLE* BN26....195 L3
Old Mill Pk *BEXW* TN39....160 A8
Old Motcombe Ms
EAST BN21............206 D2 🛈
Old Orch *HAWK* TN18........64 B1
Old Orchard Pl *HAIL* BN27...155 H7
Old Orchard Rd *EAST* BN21...10 C7
Old Parish La *ROTT* BN2....170 D6
Old Park Cl *RHWH* RH17....48 A8 🛈
Old Patcham Ms *BRI* BN1....145 L8
Old Rectory Gdns *STHW* BN42...166 D7
Old River Wy *WSEA* TN36...117 M1
Old Rd *EGRIN* RH19........13 M6
HAIL BN27............155 M2
Old Roar Rd *SLVH* TN37....162 C2
Old School Cl *RING/NEW* BN8...127 L8 🛈
Old School La *POLE* BN26....178 A7 🛈
Old School Pl *BURH* RH15....96 F4
Old Shoreham Rd *HOVE* BN3...168 C6
STHW BN42............166 F6
Old Station Cl *CRAWE* RH10...12 B7
Old Station Rd *WADH* TN5....31 L8
Old Steine *BRI* BN1............6 F7
ROTT BN2............7 K6
Old Swan La *HAIL* BN27....178 D1
Old Timbers La *UCK* TN22....76 C8
Old Top Rd *RHAS* TN35....163 K6
Old Wardsdown *WADH* TN5....46 B3
Old Wickham La *HWH* RH16....48 D7
Old Willingdon Rd
EDN/EASTW BN20........205 C5
Old Wish Rd *EAST* BN21....10 D9
Oliver Cl *CROW* TN6........40 A5
ROTT BN2............7 K6
Olive Rd *HOVE* BN3........167 L6
Olives Meadow *UCK* TN22....76 D7
Onslow Rd *HOVE* BN3........168 C5
Orchard Cl *HOVE* BN3........168 A5
Orchard Cl *HAS* TN34........162 F3
HWH RH16............48 D6
RHWH RH17............72 F3 🛈
STHW BN42............166 F6
Orchard Cnr *HWH* RH16........72 B1
Orchard Gdns *HOVE* BN3....168 B5
Orchard Ms *NEWHV* BN9....191 M4 🛈
Orchard Ri *RRTW* TN3........18 B7

Orchard Rd *BEX* TN40........160 C8
BURH RH15............96 E3
HOVE BN3............168 A5
LEW BN7............3 J3
The Orchard *BUR/ETCH* TN19...61 J5
RYE TN31............114 B2
UCK TN22............102 D6
Orchard Wy *BURH* RH15....96 F3 🛈
EGRIN RH19............13 L5
HWH RH16............48 D6
RYE TN31............90 C5
Orchid Cl *LGNY* BN23........197 H3 🛈
Orchid Pk *HWH* RH16........72 C2
Orchid Vw *BRI* BN1........146 C8
Oriental Pl *BRI* BN1..........6 A7
Orion Cl *HAIL* BN27........155 K6
Ormerod Av *STLEO* TN38....162 A2
Orpen Rd *HOVE* BN3........168 D5
Osbern Cl *BEXW* TN39....159 M6
Osborne Cl *HAS* TN34........4 F1
Osborne Hi *CROW* TN6........40 C6
Osborne Rd *BRI* BN1........168 A5
CROW TN6............40 C5 🛈
EDN/EASTW BN20........206 B2
Osborne Vls *HOVE* BN3....186 B1
Osmers Hi *WADH* TN5........31 M1
Osmond Rd *HOVE* BN3........6 A3
Osprey Dr *UCK* TN22........102 E1
Otham Court La *POLE* BN26...178 A6
Otham Rd *LW/ROSE* BN22....197 G4
Otteham Cl *POLE* BN26....178 B8
Oulton Cl *LGNY* BN23........197 H3
Ousedale Cl *LEW* BN7........2 D6 🛈
Outlook Av *PEAHV* BN10....190 C5
The Outlook *EDN/EASTW* BN20...205 G5
Oval Cl *PEAHV* BN10........190 C4
Overdown Ri *PTSD* BN41....166 F2
Overhill *STHW* BN42........166 E5
Overhill Dr *BRI* BN1........168 E1
Overhill Gdns *BRI* BN1....168 E1
Overhill Wy *BRI* BN1........145 L8
Over St *BRI* BN1............6 E5
Overton Shaw *EGRIN* RH19....13 L3
Ovingdean Cl *BRI* BN2....188 D1
Ovingdean Rd *ROTT* BN2....188 D2
Owen Cl *BURH* RH15........96 F5
Oxbottom Cl *RING/NEW* BN8...74 D8
Oxenbridge La *BUR/ETCH* TN19...61 H6
Oxendean Gdns
LW/ROSE BN22........196 B2
Oxford Cl *BRI* BN1..........6 F3 🛈
Oxford Ms *HOVE* BN3........168 C7
Oxford Pl *BRI* BN1..........6 F3
Oxford Rd *LW/ROSE* BN22....11 H4
STLEO TN38............162 A3
Oxford St *BRI* BN1..........6 F3 🛈
Ox Lea *RRTW* TN3............19 G3
Oyster Creek *RYE* TN31....117 M3

P

Packham Wy *BURH* RH15....96 F2 🛈
Paddock Cl *LYDD* TN29....95 H8
RRTW TN3............18 B1
Paddock Gdns *EGRIN* RH19...13 L7
POLE BN26............195 M2
Paddockhall Rd *HWH* RH16...71 K1
Paddock La *LEW* BN7..........2 E6
Paddock Rd *LEW* BN7..........2 E6
The Paddocks *HAIL* BN27....155 G4
LEW BN7............98 E8 🛈
LEW BN7............172 D6
The Paddock *HOVE* BN3....168 C5
LW/ROSE BN22........196 F4
RYE TN31............65 H7
UCK TN22............76 A2
Padgham La *HTHF* TN21....108 D6
Pages Av *BEXW* TN39........182 F3
Pages Cl *HTHF* TN21..........79 L7
Pages Hi *HTHF* TN21..........79 L7
Pages La *BEXW* TN39........182 E3
The Pagets *RING/NEW* BN8...74 D7
Pagham La *PEV* BN24........197 H2
Paine Av *LYDD* TN29........95 J4
Pain's Flat *RHWH* RH17........70 D6
Palace Pl *BRI* BN1............6 F7
Palesgate La *CROW* TN6....40 E6
Palliser Cl *LGNY* BN23....197 L8 🛈
Palma Cl *POLE* BN26........178 A7
Palmeira Av *HOVE* BN3....168 C8
Palmeira Sq *HOVE* BN3....186 C1
Palmerston Rd *NEWHV* BN9...191 M5
Pangdean La *HPPT/KEY* BN6...96 C2
Pangdene Cl *BURH* RH15....96 E5
Pankhurst Av *ROTT* BN2........7 K4
Pankhurst Ri *BEXW* TN39....160 A6 🛈
Pannel La *RHAS* TN35........141 M4
Pannell Cl *EGRIN* RH19........13 K5
Pannett *BURH* RH15........96 E2 🛈
The Pantiles *RTWE/PEM* TN2...20 A4 🛈
The Parade *PEV* BN24........198 E1
Paradise Cl *EDN/EASTW* BN20...206 D4
Paradise Dr *EDN/EASTW* BN20...206 D5
The Paragon
EDN/EASTW BN20........195 M3
Parham Cl *ROTT* BN2..........7 L6
Park Av *BEXW* TN39........183 H3
EAST BN21............196 C7
HAS TN34............162 D3
HOVE BN3............167 L7
HPPT/KEY BN6........122 C1
PEAHV BN10........190 A6
SHOR BN43............166 A6
Park Cl *BRI* BN1............169 L1
BURH RH15............96 F3
EDN/EASTW BN20........206 D3 🛈
HAIL BN27............155 H8
HAS TN34............163 G2
HOVE BN3............167 L3
PTSD BN41............167 G3
SBGH/RUST TN4........19 L4
Park Crs *CROW* TN6........39 M3 🛈
FROW RH18............25 G4
HAS TN34............4 D1
PTSD BN41............167 G6

ROTT BN2............188 F5
Park Crescent Pl *ROTT* BN2....7 H2 🛈
Park Crescent Rd *ROTT* BN2....7 G2
Park Crescent Ter *ROTT* BN2....7 G2
Park Dr *HAS* TN34..........4 D1
Park Drive Cl *NEWHV* BN9...191 M4
Parker Rd *HAS* TN34........5 J1
Park Farm Cl *BUR/ETCH* TN19...61 H6
Parkfield Av *LW/ROSE* BN22...196 D5
Park Ga *HAIL* BN27........155 K3
Park Hi *ROTT* BN2..........7 H6
Parkhurst Rd *BEXW* TN39....183 J5
Parklands *SHOR* BN43........166 C6
UCK TN22............76 A1
Parklands Rd *HPPT/KEY* BN6...122 F3
Park La *BAT* TN33..........137 K2
BEXW TN39............160 A8
EAST BN21............196 C6
HWH RH16............49 K4
RBTBR TN32............112 A1
RING/NEW BN8........129 L8
STHW BN42............166 D7
Parkmore Ter *ROTT* BN2........6 D1
Park Ri *HOVE* BN3........167 L3
Park Rd *BEXW* TN39........183 H3
BRI BN1............169 L1
BURH RH15............96 F3
CROW TN6............39 M3
EGRIN RH19............13 K5
FROW RH18............25 G4
HAIL BN27............155 H3
HTHF TN21............80 B7
HWH RH16............71 K2
LEW BN7............2 E5
PEAHV BN10........200 F1
ROTT BN2............188 F5
SBGH/RUST TN4........20 B1
SHOR BN43............166 A6
Park Road Ter *ROTT* BN2........7 H6
Park Shaw *BAT* TN33........112 E5
Parkside *EGRIN* RH19........13 J5
HPPT/KEY BN6........123 G3
HTHF TN21............80 B8
SHOR BN43............166 A5
Parkside Rd *SEAF* BN25....202 F2
The Parks *PTSD* BN41........167 H3 🛈
Parkstone Rd *HAS* TN34....162 D2
Park St *BRI* BN1............147 J8
LYDD TN29............95 H8
ROTT BN2............189 G5
RTWE/PEM TN2........20 C3 🛈
The Park *CROW* TN6........39 M4
ROTT BN2............189 G5
Park Vw *HAS* TN34........162 D3
HWH RH16............48 E8
RYE TN31............65 G4
RYE TN31............90 B4
UCK TN22............77 J2
Park View Cl *PEAHV* BN10....190 A5
Park View Ri *PEAHV* BN10....190 A6 🛈
Park View Rd *HOVE* BN3....168 B5
Parkview *UCK* TN22........76 D5
Parkway *EDN/EASTW* BN20....196 B6
Park Wy *HAS* TN34........162 D3
STHW BN42............166 F6
Park Way *STHW* BN42........166 F6
Parkwood *RYE* TN31........91 H2
Park Wood Rd *HAS* TN34....139 M8
Parrock La *HRTF* TN7........25 K4
Parry Cl *LGNY* BN23........197 L3
Parsonage Cl *SBGH/RUST* TN4...19 H1 🛈
Parsonage La *RHAS* TN35....139 J2
WSEA TN36............115 M4
Parsonage Rd *EAST* BN21....206 D2
SBGH/RUST TN4........19 H1
Parsons Cl *STLEO* TN38....161 M2
Partridges La *WADH* TN5....42 A1
Pashley Rd *EDN/EASTW* BN20...206 B4
Paston Pl *ROTT* BN2........7 L9
Pasture Hill Rd *HWH* RH16...48 D8
Patcham By-pass *BRI* BN1...145 J8
BRI BN1............168 E1
Patcham Gra *BRI* BN1........168 E1
Patcham Mill Rd *PEV* BN24...197 H1
Patchdean *BRI* BN1........168 E1
Paton Rd *BEXW* TN39........159 M6
Paul Cl *HAIL* BN27........155 G3
Pavilion Buildings *BRI* BN1....6 E7
Pavilion Cl *HPPT/KEY* BN6...122 C1
Pavilion Pde *ROTT* BN2........6 F6
Pavilion St *ROTT* BN2........6 F7 🛈
Pavilion Wy *EGRIN* RH19....13 L6
Paxhill Cl *STLEO* TN38....161 L2
Paygate Rd *BAT* TN33....112 E7
Payne Av *HOVE* BN3........167 M6
Paynsbridge Wy *HTHF* TN21...105 M7
Paynters Wy *RING/NEW* BN8...74 C7
Paynton Rd *SLVH* TN37....162 B3
Paythorne Cl *STHW* BN42...166 D5 🛈
Payton Dr *BURH* RH15........96 F4
Peace Cl *BRI* BN1............169 J5
Peacock La *BRI* BN1........168 E2
Peakdean Cl
EDN/EASTW BN20........205 H4
Peakdean La
EDN/EASTW BN20........205 H4
Pearse Pl *RRTW* TN3........33 G1
Peartree Cl *BURH* RH15........96 E3
Peartree Fld *WSEA* TN36....115 M8 🛈
Peartree Hi *WADH* TN5........59 K3
Peartree La *BEXW* TN39....182 D1
Pebble Rd *PEV* BN24........198 E1
Pebsham Dr *BEX* TN40........161 G8
Pebsham La *BEX* TN40........160 F8
Peckham Cl *LEW* BN7........2 F2 🛈
Peelings La *PEV* BN24........179 H8
Peel Rd *ROTT* BN2..........187 M2
Pegasus Wy *EGRIN* RH19....14 A3
Pegler Av *NEWHV* BN9........8 C6
Pegwell Cl *HAS* TN34........4 D1
Pelham Cl *PEAHV* BN10....190 D5 🛈
PEV BN24............197 M1
Pelham Crs *HAIL* BN27....155 J8
HAS TN34............5 H1
Pelham Pl *HAS* TN34........5 J7
Pelham Rd *PEAHV* BN10....190 C5

Pelham Rd *HWH* RH16........49 G8
SEAF BN25............202 E4
Pelham Sq *BRI* BN1..........6 F4 🛈
Pelham St *BRI* BN1..........6 F4
HAS TN34............5 H7
Pelham Ter *LEW* BN7..........2 F5
Pelham Yd *SEAF* BN25....202 E4 🛈
Pellbrook Rd *LEW* BN7........2 B2
Pell Cl *WADH* TN5............32 A8
Pellings Farm Cl *CROW* TN6...40 B4
Pellings Ri *CROW* TN6........40 B3
Pelwood Rd *RYE* TN31........119 G4
Pembroke Av *HOVE* BN3....168 A8
Pembroke Cl *HAIL* BN27....155 J3 🛈
Pembroke Crs *HOVE* BN3....168 A7
Pembroke Gdns *HOVE* BN3...168 A8
Pembury Cl *HWH* RH16........72 B3
Pembury Gv *BEXW* TN39....160 A7
Pembury Rd *LGNY* BN23....197 K5
RTWE/PEM TN2........20 C3
Pendean *BURH* RH15........97 J5 🛈
Penhale Rd *LW/ROSE* BN22...11 L2
Penhurst Dr *BEX* TN40........160 F8
Penhurst La *BAT* TN33....135 L1
Penhurst Pl *ROTT* BN2....169 M8
Penland Cl *HWH* RH16........48 D7
Penland Rd *BEX* TN40........183 L1
HWH RH16............48 D8
Penn Crs *HWH* RH16........72 A1
RING/NEW BN8........150 D1
Pennine Ri *HAS* TN34........163 H2
Pennine Wy *LGNY* BN23....197 K2
Pennybridge La *MAYF* TN20...57 K1
Penny La *BEX* TN40........184 A1
Penrith Wy *LGNY* BN23....197 J2
Pensford Dr *LGNY* BN23....197 K4
Pentland Cl *LGNY* BN23....197 K3 🛈
SLVH TN37............162 C1 🛈
Peppercombe Rd
EDN/EASTW BN20........206 B2
Pepper Dr *BURH* RH15....96 F5 🛈
Percival Crs *LW/ROSE* BN22...196 F3
Percival Rd *LW/ROSE* BN22...196 F3
Percival Ter *ROTT* BN2........7 M9
Percy Rd *RHAS* TN35........163 J3
Perry Av *EGRIN* RH19........13 L3
Perryfields *BURH* RH15....96 E2
Perry Hi *ROTT* BN2........189 J4
Perryman's La *RHWH* RH17...51 K1
Perrymount Rd *HWH* RH16...71 L1
Perth Cl *SEAF* BN25........203 J3
Perth Rd *SLVH* TN37........162 B3
Peter James Cl *RYE* TN31...118 E4 🛈
Peter James La *RYE* TN31...118 D4
Petlands Gdns *HWH* RH16...71 M3
Petlands Rd *HWH* RH16....71 L3
Pett Cl *ROTT* BN2........169 M8 🛈
Pett La *WSEA* TN36........142 B2
Pett Level Rd *RHAS* TN35...141 M8
WSEA TN36............143 G3
Pett Rd *RHAS* TN35........141 G7
Petworth Dr *BURH* RH15....97 G2
Petworth Pl *LW/ROSE* BN22...196 E4 🛈
Petworth Rd *BRI* BN1....146 B8
Pevensey Bay Rd *LGNY* BN23...197 L6
Pevensey Cl *SEAF* BN25....203 H2
Pevensey Park Rd *PEV* BN24...179 M8
Pevensey Rd *EAST* BN21....11 G6
NEWHV BN9............8 B7
POLE BN26............178 B8
ROTT BN2............7 J1
STLEO TN38............162 B1
The Peverells *SEAF* BN25...203 G1 🛈
Peyton Cl *LGNY* BN23....197 M7
Phoenix Cswy *LEW* BN7........3 H5
Phoenix Crs *STHW* BN42....166 D6
Phoenix La *EGRIN* RH19....14 E8
Phoenix Pl *LEW* BN7..........3 G5
ROTT BN2............7 G4 🛈
Phoenix Ri *ROTT* BN2........7 G4
Phoenix Wy *STHW* BN42....166 D6
Phyllis Av *PEAHV* BN10....190 B7
Picardy Cl *BAT* TN33........137 L2
Piccadilly La *MAYF* TN20....57 K5
Pickers Gn *HWH* RH16........49 G6
Picketts La *UCK* TN22........52 D7
Pickforde La *WADH* TN5....45 L5
Picton St *ROTT* BN2..........7 J2
Piddinghoe Av *PEAHV* BN10...190 D8
Piddinghoe Cl *PEAHV* BN10...190 D7
Pilmer Rd *CROW* TN6........39 M3
Pilot Rd *HAS* TN34........163 G2
Piltdown Cl *BEXW* TN39....183 H2
HAS TN34............4 F3
Piltdown Ri *UCK* TN22........76 D6
Piltdown Rd *ROTT* BN2....169 M8
Piltdown Wy *LW/ROSE* BN22...197 G2
Pinders Rd *RHAS* TN35....163 K4
Pine Av *HAS* TN34........163 H3
Pine Gv *CROW* TN6........39 L4
EGRIN RH19............13 H5
Pineham Copse *HWH* RH16...71 M2
Pinehurst *BURH* RH15........97 G5
The Pines *HWH* RH16........72 B2
Pine Tree Cl *HPPT/KEY* BN6...122 B1
Pine Tree Rd *HTHF* TN21....106 A1
Pine Wk *UCK* TN22........76 D6
Pine Way *HAIL* BN27........155 G3
Pine Wy *EGRIN* RH19........13 L7
Pinewood Cha *CROW* TN6....39 K3
Pinewood Cl *LW/ROSE* BN22...196 D4
SEAF BN25............202 F2 🛈
Pinewood Rd
RTWE/PEM TN2........20 D1 🛈
Pinewoods *BEXW* TN39....182 E2
Pinewood Wy *HWH* RH16....71 K4 🛈
STLEO TN38............161 L3
Pinfold Cl *ROTT* BN2........170 E8
Pinton Hi *WADH* TN5........45 H3
Pinwell Rd *LEW* BN7..........3 H5
Pipers Cl *BEX* TN40........183 J1 🛈
HOVE BN3............167 J3
WADH TN5............44 A2
Pipers Fld *UCK* TN22........102 D2
Piper's Ga *UCK* TN22........102 D2
Pipit Meadow *UCK* TN22....102 D1
Pitreavie Dr *HAIL* BN27....155 G6

Pit Rd *HPPT/KEY* BN6........122 A1
Pitt Dr *SEAF* BN25........203 G1
Pitt Gdns *ROTT* BN2........170 D6
Place La *SEAF* BN25........202 E3
Plainfields Av *BRI* BN1....146 A7
Plaistow Cl *ROTT* BN2....169 M8
The Plat *RYE* TN31..........65 H8
Plaw Hatch La *EGRIN* RH19...35 L1
Playden Cl *ROTT* BN2....187 L2
Playden Gdns *HAS* TN34....163 H2
Playden La *RYE* TN31........91 H3
Pleasant View Rd *CROW* TN6...39 L2
Plemont Gdns *BEXW* TN39...160 A8
Pleyden Ri *BEXW* TN39....181 M2
Plough La *SLVH* TN37........162 B1
Plover Cl *LGNY* BN23........197 J4
Plover Ct *STLEO* TN38....161 L3
Plummerden La *HWH* RH16...49 L4
Plumpton Bostall *LEW* BN7...124 D8
Plumpton Cl *BEX* TN40....160 C8
LW/ROSE BN22........197 G2
Plumpton La *LEW* BN7....124 C6
Plumpton Rd *ROTT* BN2........7 L4
Plymouth Av *ROTT* BN2....169 M5
Plymouth Cl *LGNY* BN23....197 M6 🛈
Plynlimmon Rd *HAS* TN34....5 J5
Pocock's Rd *EAST* BN21....206 D1
Polegate By-pass *POLE* BN26...177 M7
Polesden Rd *RTWE/PEM* TN2...20 C3
Pollington Pl *CROW* TN6....39 M4 🛈
Pomper La *HPPT/KEY* BN6....96 A4
Pond Cl *RYE* TN31..........114 B1
Pondcroft Rd *HWH* RH16....49 H7
Pond Wy *EGRIN* RH19........14 B5
Ponswood Rd *STLEO* TN38...162 B4 🛈
Pont Cl *HTHF* TN21..........81 J8
Pook Reed La *HTHF* TN21....79 L8
Pool Va *BRI* BN1............6 E8
Poona Rd *RTWE/PEM* TN2....20 B4
Poplar Av *HOVE* BN3........167 L5
Poplar Cl *BRI* BN1..........168 F4
HOVE BN3............167 L5
Poplar La *LYDD* TN29........95 K7
Poplar Rd *TENT* TN30........67 K2
The Poplars *HPPT/KEY* BN6...123 G3 🛈
Poppinghole La *RBTBR* TN32...85 K5
Popps La *BEXW* TN39........182 C3
Porters Wy *POLE* BN26....178 A7
Portfield Av *BRI* BN1........146 A8
Portfield Cl *BEX* TN40........183 K1
Port Hall Av *BRI* BN1....168 E6 🛈
Port Hall Ms *BRI* BN1..........6 A1
Port Hall Pl *BRI* BN1........168 E6
Port Hall Rd *BRI* BN1........6 B1
Port Hall St *BRI* BN1........168 E6
Portland Av *HOVE* BN3....167 L7
Portland Gdns *HAIL* BN27...155 G5
Portland Pl *HAS* TN34........5 H6
ROTT BN2............7 K9
Portland Rd *BURH* RH15....96 F3
EGRIN RH19............13 L6
HOVE BN3............167 K7
The Portlands *LGNY* BN23...197 M7
Portland St *BRI* BN1..........6 D6
Portland Vls *HOVE* BN3....167 K7
Port Rd *LW/ROSE* BN22....197 G5
Portsdown Wy
EDN/EASTW BN20........196 B4
Portsmouth La *HWH* RH16...48 F7
Portsmouth Wd *HWH* RH16...48 F6 🛈
Portsmouth Wood Cl
HWH RH16............48 F6
Port Vw *NEWHV* BN9........191 L4
Possingworth Cl *HTHF* TN21...78 F6
Post Horn La *FROW* RH18....25 G5
Post Office La *HAWK* TN18...47 M4 🛈
Potato La *RING/NEW* BN8....150 L1
Potman's Mill La *MAYF* TN20...80 F2
Pottens Mill La *MAYF* TN20...80 F2
The Potteries *UCK* TN22....102 C2
Potters Fld *RING/NEW* BN8...127 K8
Potters La *BURH* RH15........96 F5
LEW BN7............2 E8
Pottery Cl *RYE* TN31........113 M4
Pottery La *RYE* TN31........113 M4
Pottingfield Rd *RYE* TN31....91 G8
Pound Cl *LGNY* BN23....197 M8 🛈
Poundfield Rd *CROW* TN6....40 A4
HAWK TN18............64 B1
Pound La *RING/NEW* BN8....129 J7
UCK TN22............77 K8
The Pound *BURH* RH15........96 F2
Poveys Cl *BURH* RH15........96 D2
Powdermill La *BAT* TN33....136 E6
RYE TN31............113 K3
Powell Gdns *NEWHV* BN9....191 L5 🛈
Powell Rd *RING/NEW* BN8....74 D7
Powis Gv *BRI* BN1............6 C5
Powis Rd *BRI* BN1............6 B4
Powis Sq *BRI* BN1............6 B4
Powis Vls *BRI* BN1........6 C5 🛈
Poynings Cl *SEAF* BN25....203 J4 🛈
Poynings Dr *HOVE* BN3....167 M3
Poynter Rd *HOVE* BN3....168 A6
Pratt's Folly La *CROW* TN6...39 L5 🛈
Precincts Castle *LEW* BN7....2 F6
Preemans La *UCK* TN22........53 L4
Preston Dro *BRI* BN1........168 F4
Preston Gv *UCK* TN22........77 H8
Preston Park Av *BRI* BN1...168 E5
Preston Rd *BEXW* TN39....160 B7
BRI BN1............168 E5
Preston St *BRI* BN1..........6 C7
Prestonville Rd *BRI* BN1....6 C3
Price Wy *RHWH* RH17........34 B7
Prideaux Rd *EAST* BN21....10 A2
Primrose Cl *BURH* RH15....96 D2
LGNY BN23............197 H3
Primrose Hi *BEXW* TN39....159 M8
RHAS TN35............164 F1
Primrose La *FROW* RH18....25 G5
Prince Albert St *BRI* BN1....6 E7 🛈
Prince Charles Cl *STHW* BN42...166 F4
Prince Charles Rd *LEW* BN7...3 J2
Prince Edward's Rd *LEW* BN7...2 C5
Prince Regent's Cl *ROTT* BN2...187 L2
Princes Av *HOVE* BN3....168 A8

Princes Cl *SEAF* BN25 .... 202 E2
   UCK TN22 .... 76 A7
Princes Crs *HOVE* BN3 .... 168 A8
   ROTT BN2 .... 7 G1
Prince's Pl *BRI* BN1 .... 6 E7
Princes Rd *LGNY* BN23 .... 197 L7
   ROTT BN2 .... 169 H6
   SLVH TN37 .... 4 C8
Princess Dr *SEAF* BN25 .... 202 D1 🡒
Princess Sq *HOVE* BN3 .... 168 A8
Prince's St *ROTT* BN2 .... 6 F7
   RTWE/PEM TN2 .... 20 C3 🡒
Prince's Ter *ROTT* BN2 .... 187 L2
Prince William Pde *LGNY* BN23.. 197 L8
Prinkle La *HAIL* BN27 .... 134 C5
Prinsep Rd *HOVE* BN3 .... 168 A6
Priory Av *HAS* TN34 .... 4 F4
Priory Cl *HAS* TN34 .... 4 F4
   PEV BN24 .... 198 D1
Priory Crs *LEW* BN7 .... 2 F8
Priory Hts *EDN/EASTW* BN20 .. 206 A1 🡒
Priory La *LGNY* BN23 .... 197 L3
Priory Orch *LGNY* BN23 ...... 197 L3
Priory Rd *BURH* RH15 .... 97 G5
   FROW RH18 .... 24 A8
   HAS TN34 .... 5 J6
   HPPT/KEY BN6 .... 122 F1
   LGNY BN23 .... 197 L3
Priory St *HAS* TN34 .... 4 F6
   LEW BN7 .... 2 F8
Priory Wy *HWH* RH16 .... 71 M2
Promenade *PEAHV* BN10 ..... 190 A8
The Promenade *PEV* BN24 .. 198 D3
Prospect Gdns *EAST* BN21 ... 206 D2 🡒
Prospect Pl *HAS* TN34 .... 4 F7
Prospect Rd *HTHF* TN21 .... 80 B8 🡒
   RTWE/PEM TN2 .... 20 B3
Providence Pl *BRI* BN1 .... 6 F4
Prowting Md *BEXW* TN39 ... 182 C2
Pudding Cake La *UCK* TN22 . 76 C7 🡒
Pulborough Av *LW/ROSE* BN22.. 196 E6
Pulborough Cl *ROTT* BN2 .... 169 M7 🡒
Pump La *UCK* TN22 .... 103 K4
Purbeck Cl *LGNY* BN23 .... 197 J3
Pyecombe St *POY/PYE* BN45 .. 122 A8

Q

The Quadrant *EAST* BN21 ...... 10 A3
   HPPT/KEY BN6 .... 123 G2
Quakers La *HWH* RH16 .... 72 A1
Quantock Cl *LGNY* BN23 ..... 197 K3
   RTWE/PEM TN2 .... 20 D1
Quantock Gdns *HAS* TN34 ... 163 H3
Quarry Bank Rd *BRI* BN1 ... 169 H4 🡒
Quarry Cl *BURH* RH15 .... 97 K3
Quarry Crs *HAS* TN34 .... 5 J3
Quarry Hl *RHWH* RH17 .... 48 C8
   STLEO TN38 .... 162 B7
Quarry La *SEAF* BN25 .... 203 C1
Quarry Ri *EGRIN* RH19 .... 14 A3
Quarry Rd *HAS* TN34 .... 5 J3
   NEWHV BN9 .... 8 F7
   RTW TN1 .... 20 B1
Quebec Cl *BEXW* TN39 .... 183 C1
   LGNY BN23 .... 197 M7
Quebec Rd *STLEO* TN38 .... 162 A2
Quebec St *ROTT* BN2 .... 7 H5
Queen Alexandra Av
   HOVE BN3 .... 168 A3
Queen Anne's Cl *LEW* BN7 ... 2 E5 🡒
Queen Caroline Cl *HOVE* BN3 .. 168 A3 🡒
Queen Elizabeth Av *BURH* RH15.. 96 F4
Queen Mary Av *HOVE* BN3 .. 168 A3
Queens Av *UCK* TN22 .... 76 D5 🡒
Queensbury Ms *BRI* BN1 .... 6 B7 🡒
Queen's Colonnade Gdns
   LW/ROSE BN22 .... 11 H6
Queens Cottages *WADH* TN5.. 43 L1
Queens Crs *BURH* RH15 .... 97 G4
   LGNY BN23 .... 197 K7
Queensdown School Rd
   BRI BN1 .... 169 J3
Queens Dr *HPPT/KEY* BN6 .. 122 F2
   UCK TN22 .... 75 M7
Queen's Gdns *BRI* BN1 .... 6 E5
   HOVE BN3 .... 186 C1
Queensmount *MAYF* TN20 ..... 56 B7
Queens Park Gdns *SEAF* BN25 .. 202 C2
Queen's Park Ri *ROTT* BN2 ..... 7 K5
Queen's Park Rd *ROTT* BN2 ..... 7 H6
Queen's Park Ter *ROTT* BN2 ..... 7 J4
Queen's Pl *BRI* BN1 .... 6 F3 🡒
   HOVE BN3 .... 168 C8
Queen Sq *BRI* BN1 .... 6 D6
Queen's Rd *BRI* BN1 .... 6 E4 🡒
   CROW TN6 .... 39 M6
   EGRIN RH19 .... 13 L6
   HAIL BN27 .... 156 C1
   HAS TN34 .... 5 G7
   HWH RH16 .... 48 E8
   LEW BN7 .... 3 H2
   LGNY BN23 .... 197 K7
   LYDD TN29 .... 95 J8
   STHW BN42 .... 166 E5
Queen St *HAWK* TN18 .... 64 C1
Queensway *EGRIN* RH19 .... 13 L6 🡒
   LYDD TN29 .... 95 J8
   ROTT BN2 .... 7 L5
   SEAF BN25 .... 203 C1
   STLEO TN38 .... 161 L1
Queen Victoria Av *HOVE* BN3.. 168 A3
Querneby Cl *SHOR* BN43 ...... 166 D7 🡒
Quickbourne La *RYE* TN31 ..... 65 J7
Quinnell Dr *HAIL* BN27 .... 155 H4
Quintin Cl *HAIL* BN27 .... 178 A1 🡒

R

Radcliffe Cl *SLVH* TN37 .... 162 C3
Radinden Dr *HOVE* BN3 .... 168 D5
Radinden Manor Rd
   HOVE BN3 .... 168 C6
Radnor Ms *STLEO* TN38 .... 161 L4 🡒

Ragged Dog La *HTHF* TN21 .. 105 H3
Railway Ap *EGRIN* RH19 .... 13 K5
   NEWHV BN9 .... 9 H3
Railway La *LEW* BN7 .... 3 H6
Railway Rd *NEWHV* BN9 .... 9 H3
Railway St *BRI* BN1 .... 6 D4
Raleigh Cl *LGNY* BN23 .... 197 L7
Ramsay Wy *LGNY* BN23 ...... 197 L7
Ramslye Rd *SBGH/RUST* TN4 .. 19 K5
Randolph La *RYE* TN31 .... 91 G3
Ranelagh Vls *HOVE* BN3 .... 168 B6
Rangemore Dr *EAST* BN21 ... 196 D7
Rannoch Rd *CROW* TN6 .... 39 K4
Rannoch Rd West *CROW* TN6 .. 39 K4 🡒
Ranscombe Hl *RING/NEW* BN8.. 150 A8
Ranscombe La *RING/NEW* BN8.. 150 B8
Ranworth Cl *LGNY* BN23 ..... 197 H2 🡒
Rapson's Rd
   EDN/EASTW BN20 .... 195 M3
Rastrick Cl *BURH* RH15 .... 96 F5
Rattle La *PEV* BN24 .... 197 K1
Ratton Dr *EDN/EASTW* BN20 .. 196 B7
Ratton Rd *EAST* BN21 .... 10 A3
Raven Ct *BAT* TN33 .... 137 M2 🡒
   STLEO TN38 .... 161 L3
Ravens Cl *BEXW* TN39 .... 182 C3
Ravens Cft
   EDN/EASTW BN20 .... 206 F6 🡒
Ravenswood Dr *ROTT* BN2 ... 170 F8
Ravenswood Rd *BURH* RH15 .. 97 H3
Ravine Cl *HAS* TN34 .... 163 G3
Rayford Cl *PEAHV* BN10 ...... 190 C7 🡒
Raymond Cl *SEAF* BN25 .... 203 C1
Readers La *RYE* TN31 .... 90 F1
Reading Rd *ROTT* BN2 .... 187 M2
Rectory Cl *BUR/ETCH* TN19 ... 60 B8
   EDN/EASTW BN20 .... 206 D3
   NEWHV BN9 .... 8 E5
   RING/NEW BN8 .... 130 A1
   SHOR BN43 .... 166 D7
   STLEO TN38 .... 162 B5 🡒
Rectory Fld *HRTF* TN7 .... 26 E2
Rectory La *RYE* TN31 .... 88 F1
   RYE TN31 .... 91 H6
   WSEA TN36 .... 116 E8
Rectory Rd *NEWHV* BN9 ...... 191 L4
   SHOR BN43 .... 166 C7
Rectory Wy *BEX* TN40 .... 183 K1
Redbridge La *CROW* TN6 .... 54 D1
Redbrook La *UCK* TN22 .... 77 K2
Redcross St *BRI* BN1 .... 6 F4
Redford Cl *EDN/EASTW* BN20.. 197 L5 🡒
Redgarth Ct *EGRIN* RH19 ...... 13 H3
Redgeland Ri *STLEO* TN38 ... 161 M4 🡒
Redgill La *RING/NEW* BN8 ..... 74 B5
Redhill Cl *BRI* BN1 .... 168 C2
Redhill Dr *BRI* BN1 .... 168 C1
Red Lake Ter *RHAS* TN35 ..... 163 K2 🡒
Red Oak *HAWK* TN18 .... 47 L6
Redoubt Rd *LW/ROSE* BN22 ... 11 J3
Redvers Rd *ROTT* BN2 .... 169 K5
Redwell Av *BEXW* TN39 .... 160 B6 🡒
Redwood Dr *HWH* RH16 .... 71 K4
Reedham Rd *LGNY* BN23 ..... 197 H2 🡒
Reed Pond Wk *HWH* RH16 .... 72 A2
Reedswood Rd *RYE* TN31 ..... 114 B2
   STLEO TN38 .... 161 L6
Reeves Hl *BRI* BN1 .... 169 K1
Reeves Ter *WADH* TN5 .... 45 L5 🡒
Regal Dr *EGRIN* RH19 .... 13 M6
Regency Cl *UCK* TN22 .... 76 C7
Regency Gdns *STLEO* TN38 .. 162 A6
Regency Ms *BRI* BN1 .... 6 B6
   EDN/EASTW BN20 .... 207 G5 🡒
Regency Rd *BRI* BN1 .... 6 C7
Regency Sq *BRI* BN1 .... 6 B7
Regent Pl *STLEO* TN38 .... 138 F7
Regent Rw *BRI* BN1 .... 6 C6 🡒
Regents Cl *SEAF* BN25 .... 202 E1
Regent St *BRI* BN1 .... 6 E6
Reginald Rd *BEXW* TN39 ...... 183 H2
Regnum Cl *LW/ROSE* BN22 .. 196 E2
Reigate Rd *BRI* BN1 .... 168 D5
Resting Oak Hl *RING/NEW* BN8.. 125 M2 🡒
Reynolds Dr *BEXW* TN40 ...... 183 L1
Reynolds Rd *HOVE* BN3 .... 167 M7
   LGNY BN23 .... 197 K5
Reynoldstown La
   POLE BN26 .... 177 M8 🡒
Riccards La *BAT* TN33 .... 112 A4
Rices Hl *EGRIN* RH19 .... 13 L5
Richardson Rd *HOVE* BN3 .... 167 M7
Richborough Cl *HAS* TN34 ... 162 D2 🡒
Richington Wy *SEAF* BN25 ... 203 H1
Richland Cl *RHAS* TN35 .... 163 K2
Richmead Gdns *MAYF* TN20 .. 57 H4
Richmond Av *BEXW* TN39 ... 182 F3
Richmond Cl *BEXW* TN39 ... 183 G3
Richmond Gv *BEXW* TN39 ... 183 G4
Richmond Pde *ROTT* BN2 .... 6 F5
Richmond Pl *ROTT* BN2 .... 6 F5
Richmond Rd *BEXW* TN39 ... 182 F3
   SEAF BN25 .... 202 D3
Richmond St *HAS* TN34 .... 163 J4 🡒
   ROTT BN2 .... 7 H5
Richmond Ter *SEAF* BN25 ... 202 E3 🡒
Richmond Wy *EGRIN* RH19 .. 13 M6
Riddens Cl *LEW* BN7 .... 124 E1
Riddens La *LEW* BN7 .... 98 E8
   LEW BN7 .... 124 E1
Riders Bolt *BEXW* TN39 .... 182 E1
The Ride *BRI* BN1 .... 168 F5
Ridge Cl *PTSD* BN41 .... 167 G2 🡒
   UCK TN22 .... 52 C1
Ridge Lands Cl
   EDN/EASTW BN20 .... 206 C3 🡒
Ridge Rd *BRI* BN1 .... 147 J6
Ridgeside Av *BRI* BN1 .... 168 E1
The Ridge *HAS* TN34 .... 163 H2
   SLVH TN37 .... 139 J8
   WSEA TN36 .... 143 H1
Ridge Vw *BRI* BN1 .... 169 L1
Ridgeway *BUR/ETCH* TN19 .... 61 M3
   EGRIN RH19 .... 13 L7
Ridge Wy *HWH* RH16 .... 72 B4

Ridgeway *PTSD* BN41 .... 166 F5 🡒
Ridgeway Cl *HTHF* TN21 .... 80 A6
   STHW BN42 .... 166 F5
Ridgeway Gdns *ROTT* BN2 ... 170 E7 🡒
The Ridgeway *BURH* RH15 .... 97 H2 🡒
   EDN/EASTW BN20 .... 205 G5
   HAIL BN27 .... 133 L8
   SEAF BN25 .... 202 F7
The Ridge West *SLVH* TN37 .. 139 G7
Ridgewood Av *ROTT* BN2 .... 189 J3
Ridgewood Cl *UCK* TN22 ...... 52 C1
Ridgewood Gdns *BEX* TN40 .. 183 M2
   HAS TN34 .... 162 E1
Ridgway Cl *ROTT* BN2 .... 170 D6
Ridgway Paddock *LEW* BN7 .. 148 D8
The Ridgway *ROTT* BN2 .... 170 D6
The Ridings *BEXW* TN39 ...... 159 M7
   BURH RH15 .... 97 J5
   PEAHV BN10 .... 190 B5
   RING/NEW BN8 .... 74 C7
   SEAF BN25 .... 202 F1
   SLVH TN37 .... 162 C1 🡒
Ridleys *EGRIN* RH19 .... 22 E3
Rigden Rd *HOVE* BN3 .... 168 C6
Riley Rd *ROTT* BN2 .... 169 J5
Rill Wk *EGRIN* RH19 .... 14 B5
Ringmer Cl *BRI* BN1 .... 169 L2
Ringmer Rd *BRI* BN1 .... 169 M2
   NEWHV BN9 .... 8 C6
   SEAF BN25 .... 202 E4
Ringmer Wy *LGNY* BN23 ..... 197 G2 🡒
Ringwood Cl *LW/ROSE* BN22.. 11 G1
Ringwood Rd *BEXW* TN39 ... 160 C7
   LW/ROSE BN22 .... 10 E1
Ripe La *RING/NEW* BN8 .... 152 F3
Riseden Rd *WADH* TN5 .... 43 H3
Rise Park Gdns *LGNY* BN23 .. 197 K4
The Rise *EGRIN* RH19 .... 13 M6
   HWH RH16 .... 72 B1
   PTSD BN41 .... 166 F4
The Rising *LGNY* BN23 .... 197 L4
Riverdale *LEW* BN7 .... 2 F7
River La *POLE* BN26 .... 194 A3
Riverside *FROW* RH18 .... 24 E3
   NEWHV BN9 .... 9 H6
   PTSD BN41 .... 166 E8
   UCK TN22 .... 78 D5
Riverside Gdns *CROW* TN6 ... 40 C6
River's Rd *HWH* RH16 .... 48 D3
River Wy *UCK* TN22 .... 76 C7
Rixons Cl *SEAF* BN25 .... 203 G2 🡒
Rixons Orch *RHWH* RH17 ..... 50 C1
Roadean Cl *SEAF* BN25 .... 203 G2 🡒
Robert's Hl *WSEA* TN36 .... 116 E7
Robertson Pas *HAS* TN34 .... 4 F7
Robertson Rd *BRI* BN1 .... 168 D4
Robertson St *HAS* TN34 .... 4 F7
Robertsons Hl *HAS* TN34 .... 5 M2
Robert St *BRI* BN1 .... 6 E5
Robert Tressell Cl *HAS* TN34 ... 4 E4
Robian Cl *UCK* TN22 .... 76 A2
   LGNY BN23 .... 197 J4 🡒
Robin Cl *EGRIN* RH19 .... 13 L4
   LGNY BN23 .... 197 J4 🡒
Robin Davis Cl *ROTT* BN2 .... 169 L6
Robin Dene *ROTT* BN2 .... 187 L2
Robin Hl West *ROTT* BN2 ..... 189 J3
Robin Hood La *LYDD* TN29 .. 121 J1
Robin La *LYDD* TN29 .... 95 J3
Robin Post La *POLE* BN26 .... 177 H5
Robin Rd *HPPT/KEY* BN6 ...... 96 D4
Robinson Rd *NEWHV* BN9 ...... 8 E5
Roborough Cl *LW/ROSE* BN22.. 10 F4
Robsack Av *STLEO* TN38 ...... 161 L4
Rochester Cl
   EDN/EASTW BN20 .... 206 C4
Rochester Gdns *HOVE* BN3 .. 168 D8
Rochester Rd *SLVH* TN37 ..... 162 B4 🡒
Rochester St *ROTT* BN2 .... 7 L6
Rochester Wy *CROW* TN6 ...... 40 C5 🡒
Rochford Wy *SEAF* BN25 ..... 192 B8
Rochmans Wy *CROW* TN6 ..... 40 A6
Rockall Av *LGNY* BN23 .... 197 M6 🡒
Rockall Dr *HAIL* BN27 .... 155 G4
Rock-a-nore Pde *HAS* TN34 .... 5 M6
   RHAS TN35 .... 163 J6
Rock-a-nore Rd *HAS* TN34 ...... 5 L7
Rock Channel *RYE* TN31 ...... 117 J1
Rock Cl *RHAS* TN35 .... 163 J6
Rock Gv *ROTT* BN2 .... 7 M9
Rockhurst Dr
   EDN/EASTW BN20 .... 196 B8
Rockington Wy *CROW* TN6 .... 40 B6
Rocklands La *RHAS* TN35 .... 163 J5
Rockla La *RHAS* TN35 .... 140 D6
Rockmead Rd *RHAS* TN35 .... 164 F2 🡒
Rock Pl *ROTT* BN2 .... 7 H8
Rocks Hl *RBTER* TN32 .... 62 E8
Rocks La *UCK* TN22 .... 53 M7
Rocks Park Rd *UCK* TN22 ...... 76 B7
The Rocks *EDN/EASTW* BN20.. 14 C8
Rock St *ROTT* BN2 .... 187 L2
Rock Villa Rd *RTW* TN1 .... 20 A2 🡒
Rocky La *HWH* RH16 .... 71 J7
Roderick Av *PEAHV* BN10 .... 190 C5
Roderick Av North
   PEAHV BN10 .... 190 C4
Rodmell Av *ROTT* BN2 .... 189 K5
Rodmell Rd *RTWE/PEM* TN2 .. 20 A5
   SEAF BN25 .... 203 H4
Rodmill Dr *EAST* BN21 .... 206 D1
Rodmill Rd *EAST* BN21 .... 206 D1
Rodney Cl *LGNY* BN23 .... 197 M7 🡒
Rodwell Cl *CROW* TN6 .... 40 C5 🡒
Roebuck St *HAS* TN34 .... 5 L6
Roedale Rd *BRI* BN1 .... 169 H5
Roedean Cl *BEXW* TN39 ...... 183 G4
Roedean Crs *ROTT* BN2 .... 188 A2
Roedean Hts *ROTT* BN2 .... 188 A2
Roedean Pth *ROTT* BN2 .... 188 B3
Roedean Rd *ROTT* BN2 .... 187 M2
   RTWE/PEM TN2 .... 20 A5
Roedean V *ROTT* BN2 .... 188 B3
Roffrey Av *LW/ROSE* BN22 ... 196 D5
Rolfe Dr *BURH* RH15 .... 97 K3
Romaine Cl *BURH* RH15 .... 97 K1
Roman Cl *SEAF* BN25 .... 192 B8 🡒
Roman Crs *STHW* BN42 .... 166 E6

Roman Rd *HOVE* BN3 .... 167 K8
   STHW BN42 .... 166 E6
Romans Wy *PEV* BN24 .... 179 L8
Roman Wy *STHW* BN42 .... 166 E6
   UCK TN22 .... 76 E7
Romany Cl *PTSD* BN41 .... 167 H6
Romney Cl *SEAF* BN25 .... 203 J3 🡒
   POLE BN26 .... 178 B8
   ROTT BN2 .... 189 G5
Romney Rd *LYDD* TN29 .... 95 L1
Romney St *LW/ROSE* BN22 .... 11 K1
Romsey Cl *BRI* BN1 .... 169 H4
Rookery Cl *BRI* BN1 .... 168 E5
   NEWHV BN9 .... 191 L4 🡒
Rookery La *WSEA* TN36 .... 116 F7
Rookery Wy *HWH* RH16 .... 71 L5
   NEWHV BN9 .... 191 M4
   SEAF BN25 .... 202 B1
Rookhurst Rd *BEX* TN40 .... 183 M1
Rookley Cl *RTWE/PEM* TN2 .. 20 D6 🡒
Rookwood Cl *UCK* TN22 .... 76 E6 🡒
Rope Wk *HAIL* BN27 .... 155 H6
   RYE TN31 .... 91 J3
The Rope Wk *HAWK* TN18 ..... 64 B1
Rosebarn Cl *BURH* RH15 .... 97 J5
Rosebery Av *LW/ROSE* BN22.. 196 E5
   ROTT BN2 .... 170 C3
Rosedale Pl *LW/ROSE* BN22 .. 196 D3 🡒
Rosedene Cl *ROTT* BN2 .... 170 D8
Rose Hl *ROTT* BN2 .... 7 G2
   TENT TN30 .... 68 B1
Rose Hill Cl *BRI* BN1 .... 6 F2
Rose Hill Ter *BRI* BN1 .... 6 F2
Rosehill Wk *RTW* TN1 .... 20 A3 🡒
Roselands *BEXW* TN39 .... 159 M8 🡒
Roselands Av *LW/ROSE* BN22.. 197 H8
   MAYF TN20 .... 56 F5
Roselands Rd *LW/ROSE* BN22.. 11 J1
Roseleigh Gdns *RHWH* RH17.. 72 F3
   RHWH RH17 .... 48 B8
Rosemary Cl *PEAHV* BN10 ... 190 C6
   RHWH RH17 .... 48 B8
Rosemary Dr *SHOR* BN43 .... 166 B5
Rosemary La *RHAS* TN35 ..... 141 L8
   WADH TN5 .... 46 A1
Rosemount Cl *SEAF* BN25 ... 192 A8
Rosetti Rd *PEV* BN24 .... 198 C2
Roseveare Rd
   LW/ROSE BN22 .... 197 J8 🡒
Rose Wk *SEAF* BN25 .... 202 F3
Rose Walk Cl *NEWHV* BN9 ..... 8 D4
The Rose Wk *NEWHV* BN9 ...... 8 D4
Rossdale *RTWE/PEM* TN2 ..... 20 C1
Rosslyn Av *SHOR* BN43 .... 166 B4
Rothbury Rd *HOVE* BN3 .... 167 K7
Rother Av *POLE* BN26 .... 196 F4 🡒
Rother Cl *BUR/ETCH* TN19 .... 60 B8
   CROW TN6 .... 40 A7
Rotherfield Av *BEX* TN40 ..... 183 K2
   LW/ROSE BN22 .... 197 G2
Rotherfield Cl *BRI* BN1 .... 146 B8
Rotherfield Crs *BRI* BN1 .... 169 H1
Rotherfield La *MAYF* TN20 .... 56 F2
Rotherfield Rd *CROW* TN6 .... 40 E6
Rotherhill Rd *CROW* TN6 .... 41 G8
Rotherhurst La *CROW* TN6 .... 41 G8
Rothermead *MAYF* TN20 .... 56 F5
Rother Rd *SEAF* BN25 .... 203 G4
Rother Vw *BUR/ETCH* TN19 .. 60 B7
Rotherview *RBTER* TN32 .... 85 J1
Rothley Cha *HWH* RH16 .... 71 M2
Rothwell Ct *NEWHV* BN9 .... 8 B4
Rotten Rw *LEW* BN7 .... 2 F7
Rotunda Rd *LGNY* BN23 ...... 197 K6
The Rotyngs *ROTT* BN2 .... 188 F4
Rough Brow *SEAF* BN25 .... 203 J5 🡒
Rough Fld *EGRIN* RH19 .... 13 K2 🡒
The Rough *RING/NEW* BN8 ..... 74 C7
Roundacres Wy *BEX* TN40 .... 160 E8
The Roundel *SLVH* TN37 ...... 162 D1
Roundhay Av *PEAHV* BN10 .. 190 E8 🡒
Round Hill Rd *BRI* BN1 .... 7 G1
Roundhill Crs *ROTT* BN2 .... 7 H1
Roundway *BRI* BN1 .... 169 L1
Roundwood La *HWH* RH16 .... 48 F6
Roundwood Rd *SLVH* TN37 .. 162 B1
Rowan Av *HOVE* BN3 .... 167 L5
   LW/ROSE BN22 .... 196 D3
Rowan Cl *HAS* TN34 .... 139 K8
   HTHF TN21 .... 106 A1
   HWH RH16 .... 72 B2
   PTSD BN41 .... 166 F5
   SEAF BN25 .... 203 J5 🡒
Rowan Gdns *BEX* TN40 .... 160 F8
Rowan Tree Rd
   RTWE/PEM TN2 .... 19 L5 🡒
Rowan Wy *ROTT* BN2 .... 188 E3
Rowbarns *BAT* TN33 .... 111 J8
Rowe Av *PEAHV* BN10 .... 190 B6
Rowplatt La *EGRIN* RH19 ...... 12 E3
Rowsley Rd *EDN/EASTW* BN20.. 206 D7
Royal Cha *SBGH/RUST* TN4 ... 19 M2
Royal Crs *ROTT* BN2 .... 7 J8
Royal Crescent Ms *ROTT* BN2.. 7 J8
Royal Dr *SEAF* BN25 .... 192 E8
Royal George Pde *SHOR* BN43.. 166 B5
Royal George Rd *BURH* RH15.. 96 E3
Royal Military Canal Pth
   TENT TN30 .... 69 G6
Royal Military Rd *WSEA* TN36.. 117 G6
Royal Oak La *UCK* TN22 .... 54 B5
Royal Pde *LW/ROSE* BN22 ..... 11 K3
Royal Sovereign Vw
   LGNY BN23 .... 197 M8 🡒
Royal Sussex Crs
   EDN/EASTW BN20 .... 206 B1 🡒
Royles Cl *ROTT* BN2 .... 189 G4
Royston Cl *EDN/EASTW* BN20.. 205 G5
Royston Gdns *BEX* TN40 ...... 183 J3 🡒
Rudyard Cl *ROTT* BN2 .... 170 E6
Rudyard Rd *ROTT* BN2 .... 170 E6
Rue De Bayeux *BAT* TN33 .... 137 K1 🡒
Rufus Cl *LEW* BN7 .... 2 F6
Rugby Cl *SEAF* BN25 .... 203 H2
Rugby Pl *ROTT* BN2 .... 187 L2
Rugby Rd *BRI* BN1 .... 169 G5
Rumbolds La *HWH* RH16 .... 71 K4
Rusbridge La *LEW* BN7 .... 3 J6

The Rushes *HWH* RH16 .... 72 C2 🡒
Rushetts *RRTW* TN3 .... 18 F2
Rushey Cl *RING/NEW* BN8 ... 150 E1
Rushlake Cl *BRI* BN1 .... 169 L1
Rushlake Crs *EAST* BN21 ...... 196 D8
Rushlake Rd *BRI* BN1 .... 146 B8
Rushlye Cl *FROW* RH18 .... 30 F1
Rushmere Ri *STLEO* TN38 .... 161 L5 🡒
Rushwood Cl *HWH* RH16 .... 72 B2 🡒
Ruskin Rd *EDN/EASTW* BN20.. 196 B5
   HOVE BN3 .... 167 M6
Rusper Rd *BRI* BN1 .... 146 B8
   EDN/EASTW BN20 .... 196 B8
Ruspers *BURH* RH15 .... 97 K4
Russell Crs *BRI* BN1 .... 6 B2
Russell Pl *BRI* BN1 .... 6 C7
Russell Rd *BRI* BN1 .... 6 C7
Russell Sq *BRI* BN1 .... 6 C7
Russet Cl *HAS* TN34 .... 5 H7
Russet Cl *POLE* BN26 .... 178 C8
Rusthall Gra *SBGH/RUST* TN4.. 19 K2 🡒
Rusthall High St
   SBGH/RUST TN4 .... 19 H2
Rusthall Pk *SBGH/RUST* TN4.. 19 K3
Rusthall Rd *SBGH/RUST* TN4.. 19 K3
Rustic Cl *PEAHV* BN10 .... 190 B5
Rustic Rd *PEAHV* BN10 .... 190 B4
Rustington Rd *BRI* BN1 .... 169 L1 🡒
Rustlings Cl *HWH* RH16 .... 72 B1 🡒
Rustwick *SBGH/RUST* TN4 ..... 19 K2 🡒
Rutland Cl *EAST* BN21 .... 196 D8
Rutland Gdns *HOVE* BN3 ..... 167 M7
Rutland Rd *HOVE* BN3 .... 168 A7
Rydal Cl *SBGH/RUST* TN4 ...... 19 L1
Rydal Dr *SBGH/RUST* TN4 ..... 19 L1
Rydal Wy *LGNY* BN23 .... 197 H2
Ryde Rd *ROTT* BN2 .... 7 L2
Ryders *RRTW* TN3 .... 19 G3
Rye Cl *POLE* BN26 .... 178 C7
   ROTT BN2 .... 189 L4
   SEAF BN25 .... 203 J2
Ryecroft *HWH* RH16 .... 71 K3
Ryefield Cl *EAST* BN21 .... 196 C7
Ryelands Dr *ROTT* BN2 .... 169 K3
Rye Rd *RHAS* TN35 .... 163 K2
   RYE TN31 .... 90 F4
   TENT TN30 .... 68 A4
Rye St *LW/ROSE* BN22 .... 197 J8 🡒
Rylstone Rd *LW/ROSE* BN22 .. 11 J4
Rymill Rd *STLEO* TN38 .... 162 A3
Rype Cl *LYDD* TN29 .... 121 J1
Ryst Wood Rd *FROW* RH18 .... 25 H4

S

Sackville Cl *EGRIN* RH19 .... 13 J3
   LEW BN7 .... 2 E5 🡒
Sackville Gdns *HOVE* BN3 .... 167 M8
Sackville La *EGRIN* RH19 .... 13 H3
Sackville Rd *BEXW* TN39 ..... 183 H3
   HAIL BN27 .... 155 J8
   HOVE BN3 .... 168 A8
   LW/ROSE BN22 .... 196 F4
Saddlers Cl *BURH* RH15 .... 97 K5
Sadlers Wy *RING/NEW* BN8 .. 150 D2
Sadler Wy *ROTT* BN2 .... 169 M8
Saffron Cl *SHOR* BN43 .... 166 C5
Saffron Gdns *POLE* BN26 ..... 193 M3
Saffrons Pk *EDN/EASTW* BN20.. 10 C9
Saffrons Rd *EAST* BN21 .... 10 C6
The Saffrons *EAST* BN21 .... 10 C6
St Agnes Rd *EGRIN* RH19 ...... 13 L4
St Andrews Cl *HAIL* BN27 ..... 155 G5
St Andrew's Dr *SEAF* BN25 .. 192 A8
St Andrew's La *LEW* BN7 .... 2 F6
St Andrew's Rd *BEX* TN40 ... 183 J1
   BRI BN1 .... 169 G5 🡒
   BURH RH15 .... 97 K3 🡒
   PTSD BN41 .... 167 H7
St Andrew's Sq *HAS* TN34 ...... 5 H5
St Anne's Crs *LEW* BN7 .... 2 C7
St Anne's Rd *EAST* BN21 .... 10 D5
   LW/ROSE BN22 .... 196 B3
St Anthony's Av *LGNY* BN23.. 197 K7
St Aubyns *HOVE* BN3 .... 168 A8
St Aubyn's Crs *PTSD* BN41 .. 167 H7 🡒
St Aubyn's Md *ROTT* BN2 .... 189 G5
St Aubyn's Rd *LW/ROSE* BN22.. 11 K5
   PTSD BN41 .... 167 G7
St Aubyns South *HOVE* BN3.. 186 A1 🡒
St Augustine Cl *RHWH* RH17.. 72 F3 🡒
St Augustine's Cl
   BEXW TN39 .... 182 F3 🡒
St Barnabas' Cl *RTW* TN1 ..... 20 B1 🡒
St Boswells Cl *HAIL* BN27 ... 154 F6
St Catherine's La *SLVH* TN37.. 4 C6
St Crispians *SEAF* BN25 .... 202 D3
St Cuthmans Cl *ROTT* BN2 .. 169 L8
St David's Av *BEX* TN40 .... 183 J1
St Davids Cl *LW/ROSE* BN22.. 196 D3
St Edmund's Rd *HWH* RH16 .. 71 M3
St Edward's Cl *EGRIN* RH19 .. 13 J5
St Francis Cha *BEXW* TN39 .. 183 G1
St Francis Cl *HWH* RH16 .... 71 L4
St George's La *HPPT/KEY* BN6.. 122 B1 🡒
St George's Ms *BRI* BN1 .... 6 F5
St George's Pk *RTWE/PEM* TN2.. 19 M6
St George's Rd *BRI* BN1 .... 6 F5 🡒
   HPPT/KEY BN6 .... 122 B1
   HAS TN34 .... 5 K3
   LW/ROSE BN22 .... 11 H4
   ROTT BN2 .... 7 M9 🡒
St George's Ter *ROTT* BN2 ..... 7 J8
St Giles Cl *SHOR* BN43 .... 166 B6
   WSEA TN36 .... 116 F7
St Gregory Cl
   EDN/EASTW BN20 .... 206 E6
St Helen's Av *HAS* TN34 .... 162 F1
St Helen's Crs *HAS* TN34 .... 4 F1
   HOVE BN3 .... 167 K3 🡒
St Helen's Down *HAS* TN34 .. 163 G3
St Helen's Dr *HOVE* BN3 ...... 167 K3
St Helen's Park Rd *HAS* TN34.. 5 H2
St Helen's Rd *ROTT* BN2 .... 7 L2

SLVH TN37 .... 162 D3
St Helens's Wood Rd
HAS TN34 .... 162 E1
St Heliers Av HOVE BN3 .... 167 L7
Saint Hill Rd EGRIN RH19 .... 13 H8
St James' Av BEX TN40 .... 160 D8
St James' Crs BEX TN40 .... 160 D7
St James' Pk RTW TN1 .... 20 C1
RTWE/PEM TN2 .... 20 C1
St James' Rd BEX TN40 .... 160 C8
LW/ROSE BN22 .... 11 J4
RTW TN1 .... 20 C1
Stjames' Rd RTW TN1 .... 20 C2
St James's Av ROTT BN2 .... 7 H8
St James's Rd EGRIN RH19 .... 13 K5
HAS TN34 .... 5 H4
St James's St ROTT BN2 .... 6 F7 2
St James's Street Ms ROTT BN2 .. 7 G7
St James St LEW BN7 .... 2 F7
St John Bank RING/NEW BN8 .... 99 K6
St John's Av BURH RH15 .... 96 F3
St John's Cl CROW TN6 .... 39 L3
EGRIN RH19 .... 13 L4
St John's Dr PEV BN24 .... 179 L8
St John's Hl LEW BN7 .... 2 F5
St John's Pl HOVE BN3 .... 168 C8 1
ROTT BN2 .... 7 G6
St John's Rd BEX TN40 .... 160 C8
BURH RH15 .... 97 G3
CROW TN6 .... 39 J1
EDN/EASTW BN20 .... 206 E6
EGRIN RH19 .... 13 L4
HOVE BN3 .... 186 C1
HWH RH16 .... 71 L3
POLE BN26 .... 178 A8
SEAF BN25 .... 202 E4
SLVH TN37 .... 4 B7
St John's Ter LEW BN7 .... 2 F5
St John St LEW BN7 .... 3 G5
St Joseph's Cl HOVE BN3 .... 168 A6
St Josephs Wy HWH RH16 .... 71 L2
St Julians Cl SHOR BN43 .... 166 C7
St Julian's La SHOR BN43 .... 166 C7
St Keyna Av HOVE BN3 .... 167 K8
St Laurence Cl PEAHV BN10 .... 190 A5 5
St Lawrence Rd BEXW TN39 .... 160 B7
St Lawrence Wy
HPPT/KEY BN6 .... 96 A7
St Leonard's Av HOVE BN3 .... 167 J8
St Leonards Cl NEWHV BN9 .... 191 M4
St Leonard's Gdns HOVE BN3 .... 167 K8
St Leonard's Pl
EDN/EASTW BN20 .... 206 C3
St Leonard's Rd EAST BN21 .... 10 D5
HOVE BN3 .... 167 J8
NEWHV BN9 .... 191 M4
ROTT BN2 .... 7 J1 3
St Leonards Ter POLE BN26 .... 177 M7
St Louie Cl STHW BN42 .... 167 G6 1
St Luke's Rd ROTT BN2 .... 7 K4
St Luke's Ter ROTT BN2 .... 7 J4
St Margaret's Pl BRI BN1 .... 6 B7
St Margaret's Ri SEAF BN25 .... 192 A8
St Margaret's Rd EGRIN RH19 .. 13 M3 2
SLVH TN37 .... 4 C8
St Margaret's Ter SLVH TN37 .... 4 C8
St Marks Cl BEXW TN39 .... 182 D2
St Marks Fld UCK TN22 .... 78 B1
St Mark's Rd RTWE/PEM TN2 .... 19 M7
St Mark's St ROTT BN2 .... 187 L2
St Martins Crs NEWHV BN9 .... 191 K5 2
St Martin's La LEW BN7 .... 2 F7
St Martin's Pl ROTT BN2 .... 7 H2
St Martins Rd
LW/ROSE BN22 .... 196 D3 4
St Martin's St ROTT BN2 .... 7 H1
St Mary-in-the-fields
MAYF TN20 .... 57 H4
St Mary Magdalene St
ROTT BN2 .... 7 H1
St Marys Av HAIL BN27 .... 155 J7
St Mary's Cl LW/ROSE BN22 .... 196 B4
RYE TN31 .... 114 A4
WADH TN5 .... 45 K5
St Mary's Cottages
EDN/EASTW BN20 .... 206 D3 5
Saint Marys Garth UCK TN22 .... 77 J2
St Mary's La BEXW TN39 .... 159 M5
WADH TN5 .... 45 K5
St Mary's Pl ROTT BN2 .... 7 H8
St Mary's Rd EAST BN21 .... 206 D2
HAS TN34 .... 5 J3
St Mary's Rd West BURH RH15 .... 96 E2
St Mary's Sq ROTT BN2 .... 7 M9
St Mary's Ter HAS TN34 .... 5 J4
St Matthew's Gdns
STLEO TN38 .... 162 B5
St Matthew's Rd STLEO TN38 .... 162 B5
St Mellion Cl HAIL BN27 .... 154 F6 1
St Michaels Cl CROW TN6 .... 40 B6
PEV BN24 .... 179 G8
St Michael's Pl BRI BN1 .... 6 B5
HAS TN34 .... 4 F7
St Michaels Rd EGRIN RH19 .... 13 L4
PTSD BN41 .... 167 H7
St Michael's Ter LEW BN7 .... 3 G2
St Nicholas La LEW BN7 .... 3 G6
St Nicholas Rd BRI BN1 .... 6 D5
PTSD BN41 .... 167 H7
St Nicolas Cl PEV BN24 .... 180 B8
St Olive's Cl HTHF TN21 .... 79 J7
St Pancras Gdns LEW BN7 .... 2 D8
St Pancras Gn LEW BN7 .... 171 K1
St Pancras Rd LEW BN7 .... 2 D7
St Patrick's Crs BEX TN40 .... 183 J1
St Patrick's Rd HOVE BN3 .... 168 A7
St Paul's Cl HWH RH16 .... 71 M1
LW/ROSE BN22 .... 196 D3 5
St Paul's Pl SLVH TN37 .... 4 C6
St Paul's Rd SLVH TN37 .... 4 B4
St Paul's St ROTT BN2 .... 7 H1
SBGH/RUST TN4 .... 19 J2
St Peter's Av PEAHV BN10 .... 190 A6
St Peter's Cl HOVE BN3 .... 167 M4
SEAF BN25 .... 202 E1
St Peter's Crs BEX TN40 .... 183 K1
St Peter's Pl BRI BN1 .... 6 F4
LEW BN7 .... 2 E6
St Peters Rd BURH RH15 .... 97 G2
PTSD BN41 .... 167 H7
SEAF BN25 .... 202 E1
SLVH TN37 .... 4 A4
St Peters Rw RRTW TN3 .... 18 B1
St Peter's St BRI BN1 .... 6 F3
RTWE/PEM TN2 .... 20 C3 7
St Philip's Av LW/ROSE BN22 .... 11 G2
St Philips Ms HOVE BN3 .... 167 M7
St Richards Rd CROW TN6 .... 40 A7
PTSD BN41 .... 167 H7
St Saviour's Rd STLEO TN38 .... 161 L8
St Stephons Ct RTW TN1 .... 20 B1 5
St Swithun's Cl EGRIN RH19 .... 13 M5 5
St Swithun's La LEW BN7 .... 2 F7 2
St Swithun's Ter LEW BN7 .... 2 F7 3
St Thomas's Rd HAS TN34 .... 5 K3
St Thomas's St WSEA TN36 .... 116 F7
St Vincents Pl
EDN/EASTW BN20 .... 206 E5 6
St Vincents Rd STLEO TN38 .... 161 M7
St Wilfred's Pl SEAF BN25 .... 203 H4
St Wilfreds Rd BURH RH15 .... 97 H2
St Wilfrid's Gn HAIL BN27 .... 155 H6
St Wilfrid's Wy HWH RH16 .... 71 L2
Salcey Cl STLEO TN38 .... 161 L4
Salehurst Gdns STLEO TN38 .... 161 K4 2
Salehurst Rd EAST BN21 .... 206 C3
Salisbury Cl LW/ROSE BN22 .... 196 C4
Salisbury Rd BEXW TN39 .... 183 H1
EDN/EASTW BN20 .... 206 C6
HOVE BN3 .... 168 C8
RRTW TN3 .... 18 F3
SEAF BN25 .... 202 E3
SLVH TN37 .... 4 B4
Saltcote St RYE TN31 .... 91 J6
Saltdean Cl BEXW TN39 .... 182 E3
Saltdean Dr ROTT BN2 .... 189 H5
Saltdean Park Rd ROTT BN2 .... 189 J5
Saltdean V ROTT BN2 .... 189 K3
Saltdean Wy BEXW TN39 .... 182 D3
Saltwood Rd SEAF BN25 .... 203 J2
Salvador Cl LGNY BN23 .... 197 M7
Salvington Crs BEXW TN39 .... 182 F2
Sancroft Rd EDN/EASTW BN20 .. 206 B3
The Sanctuary
EDN/EASTW BN20 .... 206 B2 1
Sandbanks Cl HAIL BN27 .... 178 A1
Sandbanks Gdns HAIL BN27 .... 178 B1 1
Sandbanks Gv HAIL BN27 .... 155 H8 5
Sandbanks Rd HAIL BN27 .... 155 G8
Sandbanks Wy HAIL BN27 .... 155 H8
Sandgate Cl SEAF BN25 .... 203 J1
Sandgate Rd BRI BN1 .... 169 G4
Sandhawes Hl EGRIN RH19 .... 14 A2 1
Sandhill La CRAWE RH10 .... 12 B7
CROW TN6 .... 28 E7
HAIL BN27 .... 134 A1
Sand Hill La RING/NEW BN8 .... 103 G8
UCK TN22 .... 103 J5
Sandhurst Av ROTT BN2 .... 170 D5
Sandhurst Gdns HAS TN34 .... 139 M8
Sandhurst La BEXW TN39 .... 182 A2
Sandore Cl SEAF BN25 .... 203 G2 5
Sandore Rd SEAF BN25 .... 203 G2
Sandown Cl LGNY BN23 .... 197 H2
Sandown Pk RTWE/PEM TN2 .... 20 F1
Sandown Rd RHAS TN35 .... 163 J3 1
ROTT BN2 .... 7 L2
STHW BN42 .... 166 D6
Sandown Wy BEX TN40 .... 160 E8
Sandridge CROW TN6 .... 39 M5 2
Sandridge La HWH RH16 .... 48 F5
Sandringham Cl HOVE BN3 .... 168 A3 3
SEAF BN25 .... 193 G8 2
Sandringham Dr HOVE BN3 .... 168 A3
Sandringham Hts
STLEO TN38 .... 161 K3 2
Sand Rd RRTW TN3 .... 33 G2
Sandrock Hl BAT TN33 .... 161 G2
Sandrock Pk HAS TN34 .... 162 F1
Sandrock Rd RTWE/PEM TN2 .... 20 C2
Sandrocks Wy HWH RH16 .... 71 L4
Sandwich Dr STLEO TN38 .... 161 M7
Sandwich St LW/ROSE BN22 .... 197 J8
Sandy Cl SLVH TN37 .... 162 B1
Sandy Cross La HTHF TN21 .... 106 B1
Sandy La CRAWE RH10 .... 12 A6
EGRIN RH19 .... 13 L5
EGRIN RH19 .... 22 E8
HRTF TN7 .... 25 K8
HTHF TN21 .... 105 L5
RHWH RH17 .... 36 C6
UCK TN22 .... 76 F7
Sandy V HWH RH16 .... 71 K4
San Feliu Ct EGRIN RH19 .... 14 B4
Santa Cruz Dr LGNY BN23 .... 197 M7
Sanyhils Av BRI BN1 .... 145 M7
Saunders Cl HAS TN34 .... 5 J3
UCK TN22 .... 76 A6
Saunders Hl BRI BN1 .... 146 D7
Saunders Park Vw ROTT BN2 .... 169 J5
Saunders Rd SBGH/RUST TN4 .... 19 L5
Saunders Wy RYE TN31 .... 119 G4 1
Savill Rd HWH RH16 .... 49 G6
Sawyers Cl BURH RH15 .... 97 K5
Saxby Cl LGNY BN23 .... 197 L5
Saxby Rd BEXW TN39 .... 183 G2
BURH RH15 .... 96 D2
Saxonbury Cl CROW TN6 .... 39 M4
Saxon Cl EAST BN21 .... 196 C8
ROTT BN2 .... 189 J4
Saxon La SEAF BN25 .... 202 E4
Saxon Ri BEX TN40 .... 183 L2
Saxon Rd HOVE BN3 .... 167 K8
NEWHV BN9 .... 8 F4
RHAS TN35 .... 163 K3
Saxon Shore Wy HAS TN34 .... 5 M6
RHAS TN35 .... 142 C6
RHAS TN35 .... 163 K5
RYE TN31 .... 91 L6
WSEA TN36 .... 116 F8
Saxon St SLVH TN37 .... 4 B9
Saxonwood Rd BAT TN33 .... 137 J1
Sayerland La POLE BN26 .... 178 A6
Sayerland Rd POLE BN26 .... 177 M7
The Sayers EGRIN RH19 .... 13 J5
Scamps Hl HWH RH16 .... 49 J8
Scanlon Cl EDN/EASTW BN20 .. 196 A3 3
Scarborough Rd BRI BN1 .... 168 D5 1
Scarletts Cl UCK TN22 .... 76 B7
Schofield Wy LGNY BN23 .... 197 M7
School Cl BURH RH15 .... 96 F4
STHW BN42 .... 166 E7 3
School Fld RING/NEW BN8 .... 126 E2
School Gdns RING/NEW BN8 .... 126 D2
School Hl RING/NEW BN8 .... 126 E2
WSEA TN36 .... 116 E6
School La CROW TN6 .... 39 J2
EGRIN RH19 .... 14 D8
FROW RH18 .... 24 F4
POLE BN26 .... 178 A7
POY/PYE BN45 .... 122 C8
RHWH RH17 .... 51 G2
RYE TN31 .... 90 A5
RYE TN31 .... 91 J5
UCK TN22 .... 52 C1
UCK TN22 .... 55 H8
UCK TN22 .... 78 A8
School Pl BEX TN40 .... 184 A1
School Ri ROTT BN2 .... 169 L8 2
RTWE/PEM TN2 .... 19 M5 3
School Rd HOVE BN3 .... 167 M7
RHAS TN35 .... 163 J3
School Ter HAWK TN18 .... 47 M4
Schwerte Wy SLVH TN37 .... 4 E8
Scotland St ROTT BN2 .... 7 H5
Scotsford Hl MAYF TN20 .... 57 L4
Scotsford Rd HTHF TN21 .... 80 F5
Scott Rd HOVE BN3 .... 167 M7 2
Scotts Acre RYE TN31 .... 118 E3
Scotts Wy RTWE/PEM TN2 .... 19 L6
Scraper's Hl RING/NEW BN8 .... 130 F6
Scutes Cl HAS TN34 .... 162 F3
Seabeach La LW/ROSE BN22 .... 11 K2
Seabourne Rd BEXW TN40 .... 160 F8
Seafield Cl SEAF BN25 .... 203 H1 3
Seafield Rd HOVE BN3 .... 186 B1
Seaford Rd HOVE BN3 .... 167 J8
LW/ROSE BN22 .... 11 K1
NEWHV BN9 .... 9 L2
Seagrave Cl SEAF BN25 .... 192 A8 2
Seagrove Wy SEAF BN25 .... 192 F8
Searle Av PEAHV BN10 .... 190 E8
Sea Rd BEX TN40 .... 183 K3
PEV BN24 .... 198 D1
RHAS TN35 .... 165 G1
RYE TN31 .... 118 F4
STLEO TN38 .... 161 M8
WSEA TN36 .... 116 F6
Seasaw Wy ROTT BN2 .... 169 M7
Seaside LW/ROSE BN22 .... 11 H5
Seaside Rd EAST BN21 .... 11 G7
STLEO TN38 .... 161 M8
Seaside Wy STLEO TN38 .... 161 M8
Seaview Av PEAHV BN10 .... 190 E8
PEAHV BN10 .... 200 E1
Seaview Rd NEWHV BN9 .... 191 M5
PEAHV BN10 .... 200 E1
ROTT BN2 .... 170 B6
Seaville Dr LGNY BN23 .... 197 K6
PEV BN24 .... 198 D1
Second Av BEX TN40 .... 183 M1
HOVE BN3 .... 186 C1
NEWHV BN9 .... 8 E4
RYE TN31 .... 118 F4
Second Rd PEAHV BN10 .... 190 A7 2
Sedgebrook Gdns HAS TN34 .... 4 E2
Sedgewick Rd BEXW TN39 .... 160 C8
BRI BN1 .... 146 C8
Sedlescombe Gdns
STLEO TN38 .... 162 B4
Sedlescombe Rd North
BAT TN33 .... 112 B4
SLVH TN37 .... 4 A1
SLVH TN37 .... 162 B1
Sedlescombe Rd South
STLEO TN38 .... 162 B5
Sefton Cha CROW TN6 .... 40 A3
Sefton Rd PTSD BN41 .... 166 F5
Sefton Wy CROW TN6 .... 40 A3 2
Segrave Cl LEW BN7 .... 2 C4
Selba Dr ROTT BN2 .... 169 L4
Selborne Pl HOVE BN3 .... 168 C7 2
Selborne Rd HOVE BN3 .... 168 C8
Selby Ct HWH RH16 .... 71 L3
Selby Gdns UCK TN22 .... 102 D1
Selby Ri UCK TN22 .... 102 D1
Selby Rd EAST BN21 .... 206 D1
UCK TN22 .... 76 D8
Selham Cl BRI BN1 .... 146 E8 1
Selham Dr BRI BN1 .... 146 D8
Selhurst Rd ROTT BN2 .... 170 E8
Sellbourne Pk RRTW TN3 .... 30 C2
Selmeston Cl HAS TN34 .... 4 D4
Selmestone Rd ROTT BN2 .... 187 M1 1
Selmeston Pl ROTT BN2 .... 169 M8 3
Selmeston Rd EAST BN21 .... 196 C7
Selsey Cl BRI BN1 .... 146 E8
Selsfield Cl EAST BN21 .... 196 D8
Selsfield Dr ROTT BN2 .... 169 K3
Selsfield Rd CRAWE RH10 .... 22 A3
EGRIN RH19 .... 22 C7
RHWH RH17 .... 34 B5
Selwyn Dr EAST BN21 .... 10 A3
Selwyn Rd EAST BN21 .... 10 A2
Semley Rd BRI BN1 .... 169 G5
HPPT/KEY BN6 .... 122 E2
Sempstead La RBTBR TN32 .... 87 J3
Senlac Rd NEWHV BN9 .... 9 G3
Senlac Wy SLVH TN37 .... 162 C1
Sergison Cl HWH RH16 .... 71 J1
Sergison Rd HWH RH16 .... 71 K1
Setfords Fld RING/NEW BN8 .... 99 L5
Sevelands Cl ROTT BN2 .... 169 M7 2
Seven Acre Cl SLVH TN37 .... 162 A1
Sevenoaks Rd LGNY BN23 .... 197 K5
Seven Sisters Rd
LW/ROSE BN22 .... 196 B3
Seville St ROTT BN2 .... 7 J2
Sewell Av BEX TN40 .... 183 J1
Seymour St ROTT BN2 .... 7 L9
Shaftesbury Pl BRI BN1 .... 6 F1 1
Shaftesbury Rd BRI BN1 .... 6 F1
Shakespeare St HOVE BN3 .... 168 A6
Shalesbrook La FROW RH18 .... 24 F5
Shalfleet Cl LGNY BN23 .... 197 H3
Shandon Cl RTWE/PEM TN2 .... 20 C2
Shanklin Cl LGNY BN23 .... 197 H2
Shanklin Rd ROTT BN2 .... 7 K1
Shannon Cl PEAHV BN10 .... 190 A5
Shannon Wy LGNY BN23 .... 197 M6
Sharpthorne Crs PTSD BN41 .... 167 J4
Shawfield CROW TN6 .... 40 B5 2
The Shaw RTWE/PEM TN2 .... 20 C4
Sheddingdean Cl BURH RH15 ... 97 G2 2
Sheen Rd LW/ROSE BN22 .... 11 H4
Sheepbell Cl PTSD BN41 .... 167 H3
Sheepfair LEW BN7 .... 2 A3
Sheep Pen La SEAF BN25 .... 203 G3
Sheep Pln CROW TN6 .... 39 K7
Sheepsetting La HTHF TN21 .... 79 L7
Sheepstreet La BUR/ETCH TN19 .. 60 E2
Sheep Wk ROTT BN2 .... 188 F5
Sheepwash La UCK TN22 .... 78 C6
Sheerwater Crs HAS TN34 .... 162 D2
Sheffield Br UCK TN22 .... 74 B2
Sheffield Mill La UCK TN22 .... 51 J6
Sheffield Park Wy
LW/ROSE BN22 .... 197 G2
Shelling Rd CROW TN6 .... 39 L3
Shelldale Av PTSD BN41 .... 167 H7
Shelldale Crs PTSD BN41 .... 167 H7
Shelldale Rd PTSD BN41 .... 167 G6
Shelley Cl LEW BN7 .... 2 C6
Shelley Rd EGRIN RH19 .... 13 K5 1
HOVE BN3 .... 167 M7
RING/NEW BN8 .... 150 D1
Shenfield Wy BRI BN1 .... 169 H4
Shenstone HWH RH16 .... 49 H6
Shepham Av ROTT BN2 .... 189 J5
Shepham La POLE BN26 .... 178 C7
Shepherd's Cl BEXW TN39 .... 182 C2
NEWHV BN9 .... 191 H4 2
POLE BN26 .... 196 F3 1
RING/NEW BN8 .... 150 E1 2
Shepherds Cot PEAHV BN10 .... 190 D4 4
Shepherds Cft BRI BN1 .... 168 C3
Shepherdsgrove La
EGRIN RH19 .... 14 F1
Shepherd's Hl HRTF TN7 .... 25 K5
Shepherds Md BURH RH15 .... 96 F2 2
Shepherd St STLEO TN38 .... 4 A9
Shepherds Wk CROW TN6 .... 40 C5 5
HPPT/KEY BN6 .... 122 E1
RTWE/PEM TN2 .... 20 D2 1
Shepherds Wy RHAS TN35 .... 164 E2
RING/NEW BN8 .... 99 J7
RING/NEW BN8 .... 150 E1
UCK TN22 .... 102 C1
Sheppard Wy PTSD BN41 .... 167 G3
Sheppeys HWH RH16 .... 71 K4
Sheppey Wk HAIL BN27 .... 155 G3
The Shepway SEAF BN25 .... 203 H2
Sheraton Cl EAST BN21 .... 10 D8
Sherbourne Cl HOVE BN3 .... 167 K3
Sherbourne Rd HOVE BN3 .... 167 K3
Sherbourne Wy HOVE BN3 .... 167 K3
Sheridan Cl EGRIN RH19 .... 13 J5
Sheridan Ter HOVE BN3 .... 168 A6
Sheriff's La CROW TN6 .... 41 J8
Sheringham Cl RBTBR TN32 .... 86 E4
Sherman Br POLE BN26 .... 176 C7
Sherrington Rd ROTT BN2 .... 170 F6
Sherwood Cl HAS TN34 .... 5 H3
Sherwood Dr HWH RH16 .... 71 J1
Sherwood Gn HAIL BN27 .... 155 H8 4
Sherwood Pl RRTW TN3 .... 18 E3 3
Sherwood Ri SEAF BN25 .... 202 F2
Sherwood Rd
RTWE/PEM TN2 .... 20 D2 2
SEAF BN25 .... 202 F2
Shinewater La LGNY BN23 .... 197 H3
Shingle Ct STLEO TN38 .... 138 E7
Shingle Rd SHOR BN43 .... 166 A8
Shipley La BEXW TN39 .... 182 D4
Shipley Mill Cl PEV BN24 .... 197 H1
Shipley Rd ROTT BN2 .... 170 E7
Ship St BRI BN1 .... 6 D7
EGRIN RH19 .... 13 L6
NEWHV BN9 .... 8 F2
Shirlea Vw BAT TN33 .... 137 L2
Shirley Av HOVE BN3 .... 168 B4
Shirley Cl SHOR BN43 .... 166 C6
Shirley Dr HOVE BN3 .... 168 C5
SLVH TN37 .... 162 B2
Shirley Gdns SBGH/RUST TN4 .... 19 J2 1
Shirley Gv SBGH/RUST TN4 .... 19 K1
Shirley Rd HOVE BN3 .... 168 C6
Shirleys HPPT/KEY BN6 .... 123 L4
Shirley St HOVE BN3 .... 168 B7
Short Brow SEAF BN25 .... 203 G2
Short Brow Cl
LW/ROSE BN22 .... 196 B3 1
Shortdean Pl EAST BN21 .... 206 D2 5
Shortgate La RING/NEW BN8 .... 129 G4
Shortgate Rd ROTT BN2 .... 169 M2
Shortlands Cl
LW/ROSE BN22 .... 196 C5 1
Shovelstrode La EGRIN RH19 .... 14 E4
Showfields Rd RTWE/PEM TN2 .. 19 M5
The Shrublands BEXW TN39 .... 182 E3
Shrub La WADH TN5 .... 60 B1
Sicklehatch La HTHF TN21 .... 106 A4
Sidcup Cl LGNY BN23 .... 197 K4 2
Sidehill Dr PTSD BN41 .... 166 F4
Sidley Gn BEXW TN39 .... 160 C7
Sidley Rd LW/ROSE BN22 .... 11 K2
Sidley St BEXW TN39 .... 160 B7
Sidney Cl RTWE/PEM TN2 .... 19 L6
Silchester Rd STLEO TN38 .... 4 A8
Sillwood Pl BRI BN1 .... 6 A6
Sillwood Rd BRI BN1 .... 6 B6
Sillwood St BRI BN1 .... 6 A6
Silva Cl BEX TN40 .... 161 G8
Silvan Rd STLEO TN38 .... 161 L3 2
Silver Birches HWH RH16 .... 72 A2
Silverdale HPPT/KEY BN6 .... 123 H3
Silverdale Av HOVE BN3 .... 168 D7
Silverdale La HAWK TN18 .... 63 M2
Silverdale Rd BURH RH15 .... 97 H4
EDN/EASTW BN20 .... 206 F5
HOVE BN3 .... 168 D7
Silverhill Av SLVH TN37 .... 162 C2
Silverlands Rd SLVH TN37 .... 162 B4
Silvester Rd BEX TN40 .... 183 J1
Simons Cl CROW TN6 .... 40 A5 2
Singleton Mill Rd PEV BN24 .... 197 J1
Singleton Rd BRI BN1 .... 146 A8
Singleton Wy BURH RH15 .... 97 J5
Six Bells Ms RYE TN31 .... 88 C1
Skinner Rd LYDD TN29 .... 121 J1 1
Skinner's La BAT TN33 .... 136 C7
Skyline Vw PEAHV BN10 .... 190 D5
The Slade RRTW TN3 .... 33 G3
Sleepers Stile Rd WADH TN5 .... 32 D5
Slider's La UCK TN22 .... 50 F8
The Slides STLEO TN38 .... 161 M3
Slimbridge Rd BURH RH15 .... 96 F3
Slindon Av PEAHV BN10 .... 190 D8
Slindon Crs LGNY BN23 .... 197 L5 3
Slinford Cl ROTT BN2 .... 7 M7
Slip Mill Rd HAWK TN18 .... 47 L4
Sliverick's La HTHF TN21 .... 108 F7
Sloe La POLE BN26 .... 194 A3
Slonk Hill Rd SHOR BN43 .... 166 A4
Slugwash La RHWH RH17 .... 98 B1
Smeatons La WSEA TN36 .... 143 H1
Smith Cl BAT TN33 .... 159 H1
Smithy's Cl SLVH TN37 .... 162 C1 11
The Smithy UCK TN22 .... 76 B8
Smolletts EGRIN RH19 .... 13 J6 1
Smugglers Cl POLE BN26 .... 193 M3
Smugglers La CROW TN6 .... 39 K1
Smugglers Wy RHAS TN35 .... 164 F2
Snape La WADH TN5 .... 43 L5
Snape Vw WADH TN5 .... 43 M2
Snatt's Rd UCK TN22 .... 76 C5
Snednore LEW BN7 .... 171 M1
Snowdon Cl LGNY BN23 .... 197 K3
Snowdrop La HWH RH16 .... 72 C2
Snowflakes La HWH RH16 .... 49 K8
Solomon's La RBTBR TN32 .... 111 J2
Solway HAIL BN27 .... 155 G4
Solway Av BRI BN1 .... 145 M7
Somerhill Av HOVE BN3 .... 168 D7
Somerhill Rd HOVE BN3 .... 168 D8
Somerset St ROTT BN2 .... 7 J7 1
Somerville Cl LGNY BN23 .... 197 L7 5
Somerville Gdns
SBGH/RUST TN4 .... 19 M2
Sompting Cl ROTT BN2 .... 169 M7 5
Soper's La HAWK TN18 .... 47 K2
Sorrel Cl LGNY BN23 .... 197 J3 5
Sorrel Dr LGNY BN23 .... 197 J3
Southall Av ROTT BN2 .... 169 K4
Southampton Cl LGNY BN23 .. 197 M6 5
Southampton St ROTT BN2 .... 7 H4
South Av EDN/EASTW BN20 .... 206 B1
HPPT/KEY BN6 .... 122 A1
ROTT BN2 .... 7 J6
South Bank HPPT/KEY BN6 .... 122 E3
Southbourne Rd
LW/ROSE BN22 .... 197 J8
South Brooks Rd LYDD TN29 .... 120 E6
South Cliff BEXW TN39 .... 182 E4
EDN/EASTW BN20 .... 206 F6
South Cliff Av BEXW TN39 .... 182 E4
EDN/EASTW BN20 .... 206 F5 5
South Cliffe LEW BN7 .... 3 J6
South Cl BURH RH15 .... 96 E3
HAIL BN27 .... 155 H8
PEV BN24 .... 180 F8
South Coast Rd PEAHV BN10 .... 189 L6
ROTT BN2 .... 189 K6
Southcourt Av BEXW TN39 .... 182 F3
Southdown Av BRI BN1 .... 169 G5
EDN/EASTW BN20 .... 196 A3
HAS TN34 .... 163 H3
LEW BN7 .... 2 A7
PEAHV BN10 .... 190 E8
PTSD BN41 .... 167 J6 1
Southdown Cl HWH RH16 .... 71 K4
NEWHV BN9 .... 8 C5
Southdown Pl BRI BN1 .... 169 G5 2
Southdown Rd BRI BN1 .... 169 G5
EDN/EASTW BN20 .... 196 B7
NEWHV BN9 .... 8 D6
PTSD BN41 .... 167 G4
SEAF BN25 .... 202 F3
STHW BN42 .... 166 E7
South Downs LEW BN7 .... 124 F1 1
South Downs Rd LEW BN7 .... 3 H3
South Downs Wy
EDN/EASTW BN20 .... 206 B5
HPPT/KEY BN6 .... 123 J7
LEW BN7 .... 148 A6
LEW BN7 .... 170 F2
POLE BN26 .... 194 E3
POY/PYE BN45 .... 122 E8
RING/NEW BN8 .... 173 K6
RING/NEW BN8 .... 193 J1
SEAF BN25 .... 204 A3
South Dr BURH RH15 .... 96 E3
Southerden Cl HAIL BN27 .... 155 J7
Southern Av POLE BN26 .... 178 B8
Southern Rd LW/ROSE BN22 .... 196 F4
Southfield POLE BN26 .... 195 M1
Southfields WADH TN5 .... 31 M8
Southfields Rd EAST BN21 .... 10 C6
South Gv RTW TN1 .... 20 A4 5
Southlands EGRIN RH19 .... 13 L7
Southlands Av BEXW TN39 .... 160 A7
Southlands Rd BEXW TN39 .... 160 A7
South La HTHF TN21 .... 108 E4
NEWHV BN9 .... 9 G3
South Lodge Cl BURH RH15 .... 96 F2 3
South Lynn Dr EAST BN21 .... 10 C3
Southmead Cl MAYF TN20 .... 57 K3
Southmount ROTT BN2 .... 169 H5
Southon Cl PTSD BN41 .... 166 F3
Southover High St LEW BN7 .... 2 C9
Southover Pl ROTT BN2 .... 7 G3
Southover Rd LEW BN7 .... 2 F7
Southover St ROTT BN2 .... 7 G3
Southridge Ri CROW TN6 .... 39 L6
Southridge Rd CROW TN6 .... 39 L6
South Rd BRI BN1 .... 168 E5
HAIL BN27 .... 155 G8
HWH RH16 .... 71 L2
NEWHV BN9 .... 9 G3
RHWH RH17 .... 98 C2

South Rough RING/NEW BN8 ...... 74 C8
South St BRI BN1 ...... 6 D7
 BRI BN1 ...... 147 J8
 CROW TN6 ...... 39 M5
 CROW TN6 ...... 41 H7
 EAST BN21 ...... 10 D7
 HPPT/KEY BN6 ...... 123 K3
 LEW BN7 ...... 3 J6
 LYDD TN29 ...... 95 J8
 MAYF TN20 ...... 57 H4
 PTSD BN41 ...... 167 G5
 RHWH RH17 ...... 70 E1
 RING/NEW BN8 ...... 129 M2
 SEAF BN25 ...... 202 E4
 SLVH TN37 ...... 4 B8
South Ter HAS TN34 ...... 5 C5
South Undercliff RYE TN31 ...... 117 J1
South Vw HPPT/KEY BN6 ...... 123 K1
South View Cl BUR/ETCH TN19 ...... 61 M3
Southview Cl CROW TN6 ...... 39 L5 [2]
 SHOR BN43 ...... 166 C7
 STHW BN42 ...... 166 E5 [1]
Southview Dr UCK TN22 ...... 76 C3
South View Rd CROW TN6 ...... 39 L5
Southview Rd PEAHV BN10 ...... 190 C6
 STHW BN42 ...... 166 E6
South View Rd WADH TN5 ...... 31 M8
Southwater Cl ROTT BN2 ...... 7 L5
Southwater Rd SLVH TN37 ...... 4 A6
Southway BURH RH15 ...... 96 D3
South Wy LEW BN7 ...... 2 A5
 NEWHV BN9 ...... 9 G3
 SEAF BN25 ...... 203 J5
Southwick Cl EGRIN RH19 ...... 13 K4
Southwick Sq STHW BN42 ...... 166 C7
Southwick St STHW BN42 ...... 166 C7
Southwood Cl STLEO TN38 ...... 162 B5 [3]
South Woodlands BRI BN1 ...... 168 C3
Southwood Rd
 SBGH/RUST TN4 ...... 19 H1
Sovereign Cl HAS TN34 ...... 163 G2
 SEAF BN25 ...... 203 G1 [4]
The Spaldings STLEO TN38 ...... 161 L3
The Sparrows PEAHV BN10 ...... 190 D5 [5]
Sparrow Wy HPPT/KEY BN6 ...... 96 D3
Spatham La HPPT/KEY BN6 ...... 123 H8
Speldhurst Rd RRTW TN3 ...... 18 F1
Spencer Av HOVE BN3 ...... 167 K3
Spencer Rd EAST BN21 ...... 10 E4
Spences Fld LEW BN7 ...... 3 J5
Spences La LEW BN7 ...... 3 H5
Spicers Cl BURH RH15 ...... 96 F1 [6]
Spindlewood Dr BEXW TN39 ...... 182 C2
Spinnals Gv STHW BN42 ...... 166 D7
Spinney Cl CRAWE RH10 ...... 12 C6
 HPPT/KEY BN6 ...... 122 C1
The Spinneys HTHF TN21 ...... 80 B8 [7]
 LEW BN7 ...... 3 J4
The Spinney BAT TN33 ...... 137 M3
 BEXW TN39 ...... 182 D3
 HAS TN34 ...... 4 B6
 HOVE BN3 ...... 168 C5
 HPPT/KEY BN6 ...... 122 F1
 RBTBR TN32 ...... 84 F3
 RHWH RH17 ...... 48 D7
Spital Rd LEW BN7 ...... 2 C6
Spithurst Rd RING/NEW BN8 ...... 100 E7
Spotted Cow La UCK TN22 ...... 77 L1
Spout Hl CROW TN6 ...... 41 K5
Spray Hl RRTW TN3 ...... 33 H2
Spray's La RRTW TN3 ...... 139 H2
Springate Rd STHW BN42 ...... 166 F6
Spring Cl EDN/EASTW BN20 ...... 196 B5
Springett Av RING/NEW BN8 ...... 150 D1
Springfield EGRIN RH19 ...... 13 K2
Springfield Av PEAHV BN10 ...... 189 M6
Springfield Cl CROW TN6 ...... 40 B4 [8]
 PEV BN24 ...... 179 M8
Springfield Rd BEX TN40 ...... 160 C8
 BRI BN1 ...... 169 C6
 LW/ROSE BN22 ...... 11 K3
 RRTW TN3 ...... 18 C7
 STLEO TN38 ...... 162 B5
Springfields WADH TN5 ...... 45 L5
Springfields Valley Rd
 STLEO TN38 ...... 162 B5
Spring Gdns BRI BN1 ...... 6 D4
 LEW BN7 ...... 3 G5
Springhead RTWE/PEM TN2 ...... 20 D1
Springhead Wy CROW TN6 ...... 39 L6
Spring Hl RYE TN31 ...... 65 H7
Spring La BEXW TN39 ...... 182 C1
 BUR/ETCH TN19 ...... 59 J6
 HPPT/KEY BN6 ...... 122 C1
 HWH RH16 ...... 49 H5
 UCK TN22 ...... 78 F1
Spring Lodge Cl LGNY BN23 ...... 197 L4 [9]
Spring Meadow FROW RH18 ...... 24 F5
Springside Wk STLEO TN38 ...... 161 M5
Spring St BRI BN1 ...... 6 B5
 SLVH TN37 ...... 4 A4
Spring Wy EGRIN RH19 ...... 14 A2
Springwood Rd HTHF TN21 ...... 79 M6
Spruce Cl LW/ROSE BN22 ...... 196 D4
Spur Rd POLE BN26 ...... 196 B1
Spurway Pk POLE BN26 ...... 196 B1
Squab La HAIL BN27 ...... 156 A2
The Square PEV BN24 ...... 180 F8
Squires Cl CRAWE RH10 ...... 12 A6
Squirrel Cl BEXW TN39 ...... 182 L1
Squirrel Wy RTWE/PEM TN2 ...... 20 E1
Stablefield RHAS TN35 ...... 139 L2 [10]
Stables La EAST BN21 ...... 10 E6
Stafford Rd BRI BN1 ...... 6 B1
 RTWE/PEM TN2 ...... 20 B2
 SEAF BN25 ...... 202 F3
Stafford Wy HPPT/KEY BN6 ...... 123 G1
Stainsby St SLVH TN37 ...... 4 B7
Stalkers La RING/NEW BN8 ...... 104 D8
Stanam Rd RTWE/PEM TN2 ...... 21 L1
Stanbridge Rd RHWH RH17 ...... 34 A7
Standard Hill Cl BAT TN33 ...... 135 M8
Standean Cl BRI BN1 ...... 146 D8
Standen St EGRIN RH19 ...... 13 G3
Standen St SBGH/RUST TN4 ...... 20 A1
Standgrove Pl RHWH RH17 ...... 34 A1
Stanford Av BRI BN1 ...... 169 C6
 HPPT/KEY BN6 ...... 122 E2

Stanford Cl HOVE BN3 ...... 168 C5
 HPPT/KEY BN6 ...... 122 E2 [2]
Stanford Rd BRI BN1 ...... 168 E6
Stanhope Rd RTW TN1 ...... 20 C1 [1]
Stanley Av PTSD BN41 ...... 166 F2
Stanley Rd BRI BN1 ...... 6 E2
 HAS TN34 ...... 4 F5
 LW/ROSE BN22 ...... 11 H3
 RHWH RH10 ...... 190 B5
 PTSD BN41 ...... 167 G6
 RTW TN1 ...... 20 B1
Stanley St ROTT BN2 ...... 7 H6
Stanmer Av ROTT BN2 ...... 189 K3
Stanmer Dr LW/ROSE BN22 ...... 196 D5
Stanmer Park Rd BRI BN1 ...... 169 G4
Stanmer St BRI BN1 ...... 169 H4 [3]
Stanmer Vls BRI BN1 ...... 169 H3
Stansfield Rd LEW BN7 ...... 2 D4
Stanstead Crs ROTT BN2 ...... 170 F8
Stanstead La LW/ROSE BN22 ...... 10 F3
Staplefield Dr ROTT BN2 ...... 169 M3
Stapley Rd HOVE BN3 ...... 167 K6
Starfield CROW TN6 ...... 39 L5
Star La MAYF TN20 ...... 57 H4 [2]
 POLE BN26 ...... 193 M3
Star Rd EAST BN21 ...... 10 E2
Starling Cl HPPT/KEY BN6 ...... 96 C3
Starr Rd EAST BN21 ...... 10 A4
Starr's Green La BAT TN33 ...... 137 H3
Starrs Md BAT TN33 ...... 137 M3
Starvecrow La RYE TN31 ...... 89 H8
Starwell Cl HAS TN34 ...... 162 D3
Station Ap BAT TN33 ...... 137 L3
 BRI BN1 ...... 147 H8
 BUR/ETCH TN19 ...... 61 J3 [7]
 HAS TN34 ...... 4 F6
 HPPT/KEY BN6 ...... 122 E2 [3]
 HTHF TN21 ...... 80 A7
 LW/ROSE BN22 ...... 196 F5
 MAYF TN20 ...... 56 F4
 RHWH RH17 ...... 48 E5
 RYE TN31 ...... 91 H8 [8]
 SEAF BN25 ...... 202 E5
 SLVH TN37 ...... 4 B7
Station Rd BAT TN33 ...... 138 A8
 BAT TN33 ...... 160 F1
 BEX TN40 ...... 183 J2
 BRI BN1 ...... 168 D3
 BUR/ETCH TN19 ...... 61 M3
 BURH RH15 ...... 96 F4
 CRAWE RH10 ...... 12 B6
 CROW TN6 ...... 41 J5
 EGRIN RH19 ...... 13 K5
 EGRIN RH19 ...... 23 G8
 FROW RH18 ...... 24 F3
 HAIL BN27 ...... 155 H1
 HAIL BN27 ...... 155 G1
 HAS TN34 ...... 5 G6
 HRTF TN7 ...... 27 H1
 HTHF TN21 ...... 80 A7
 LEW BN7 ...... 3 G8
 LEW BN7 ...... 98 E8
 LYDD TN29 ...... 95 K7
 MAYF TN20 ...... 56 F4
 NEWHV BN9 ...... 191 M5
 POLE BN26 ...... 178 A8
 RBTBR TN32 ...... 85 G3
 RHWH RH17 ...... 50 C1
 RING/NEW BN8 ...... 73 L7
 RRTW TN3 ...... 18 C7
 RYE TN31 ...... 65 H6
 SEAF BN25 ...... 202 B2
 STHW BN42 ...... 166 E7
 UCK TN22 ...... 101 K6
 WADH TN5 ...... 31 J8
 WADH TN5 ...... 59 L1
 WSEA TN36 ...... 116 E5
Station St BRI BN1 ...... 6 E4
 EAST BN21 ...... 10 D6
Station Ter SLVH TN37 ...... 162 B3 [9]

Stonecross Rd ROTT BN2 ...... 169 M2
Stone Cross Rd WADH TN5 ...... 44 A3
Stonedene Cl FROW RH18 ...... 25 H4
Stonefield Pl HAS TN34 ...... 5 H5
Stonefield Rd HAS TN34 ...... 5 H5
Stonefield Wy BURH RH15 ...... 96 F1
Stonegate Cl LW/ROSE BN22 ...... 197 G2
Stonegate Rd WADH TN5 ...... 44 C5
Stoneham Cl LEW BN7 ...... 2 F1
Stoneham Rd HOVE BN3 ...... 167 M7
Stonehouse Dr BAT TN33 ...... 138 F5
 STLEO TN38 ...... 162 A4
Stonehurst Ct ROTT BN2 ...... 7 K4
Stonehurst La MAYF TN20 ...... 56 A6
 UCK TN22 ...... 55 J8
Stoneleigh Av BRI BN1 ...... 145 M8
Stoneleigh Cl BRI BN1 ...... 145 M8
 EGRIN RH19 ...... 13 M4 [1]
Stonelink Cl STLEO TN38 ...... 138 F7
Stonepark Dr FROW RH18 ...... 25 G4
Stone Pit La HAWK TN18 ...... 64 E1
Stonepound Rd
 HPPT/KEY BN6 ...... 122 E2
Stone Quarry Rd RHWH RH17 ...... 36 D7
Stonery Cl PTSD BN41 ...... 167 G4
Stonery Rd PTSD BN41 ...... 167 G4
Stonestile La RHAS TN35 ...... 139 L3
Stone St BRI BN1 ...... 6 B6
 HAS TN34 ...... 5 H6
 RTW TN1 ...... 20 B2
Stonewall Park Rd RRTW TN3 ...... 18 F3
Stonewood Cl SEAF BN25 ...... 203 J2 [6]
Stoney La SHOR BN43 ...... 166 C6
Stonhouse Dr STLEO TN38 ...... 162 B3
Storrington Cl HOVE BN3 ...... 167 L4 [2]
Straight Half Mile UCK TN22 ...... 76 B7
Strand RYE TN31 ...... 117 H1
Strand Hl WSEA TN36 ...... 116 F7
Strand Meadow
 BUR/ETCH TN19 ...... 60 B7
The Strand ROTT BN2 ...... 188 A3
Stratford St RTW TN1 ...... 20 C1
Strathfield Cl HWH RH16 ...... 71 M2 [1]
Strawberry Cl RRTW TN3 ...... 19 L6
Strawberry Flds RYE TN31 ...... 65 G7
Stream La BAT TN33 ...... 112 B4
 HAWK TN18 ...... 47 M7
 RHAS TN35 ...... 142 A4
Stream Pk PEAHV BN10 ...... 13 G3
Stream Pit La HAWK TN18 ...... 64 B1
Streamside Cl HAS TN34 ...... 138 F3
Streat Bostall HPPT/KEY BN6 ...... 124 C7
Streatfield Gdns HTHF TN21 ...... 79 M6
Streatfield Rd HTHF TN21 ...... 79 M6
 UCK TN22 ...... 76 B7
Streat La HPPT/KEY BN6 ...... 98 C6
Streele La UCK TN22 ...... 77 K5
Streele Vw UCK TN22 ...... 76 D6
Street End La HTHF TN21 ...... 80 D6
 MAYF TN20 ...... 80 F2
Streetlands BAT TN33 ...... 112 F5
Street La RHWH RH17 ...... 34 A6
The Street BAT TN33 ...... 112 F6
 HPPT/KEY BN6 ...... 123 M6
 LEW BN7 ...... 171 L1
 RING/NEW BN8 ...... 174 B2
 TENT TN30 ...... 67 K4
 TENT TN30 ...... 69 G1
 UCK TN22 ...... 103 H1
Stringer Wy BRI BN1 ...... 168 F3
The Stringwalk HAIL BN27 ...... 155 J7
Stroma Gdns HAIL BN27 ...... 154 F4
Strood Ga RHWH RH17 ...... 98 C1
Strood Rd SLVH TN37 ...... 4 A2
Stuart Av BAT TN33 ...... 196 C8
Stuart Cl RTWE/PEM TN2 ...... 19 M6
Stuart Wy EGRIN RH19 ...... 13 M6
Stubb La RYE TN31 ...... 114 B5
Studdens La HAIL BN27 ...... 133 K5
Sturdee Cl LGNY BN23 ...... 197 M7
Sudeley Pl ROTT BN2 ...... 7 M9
Sudeley St ROTT BN2 ...... 7 L8
Sudeley Ter ROTT BN2 ...... 7 L8
Suffolk Rd BEXW TN39 ...... 182 F1
Suffolk St HOVE BN3 ...... 167 M6
Sugar La RHWH RH17 ...... 50 B1
Sugworth Cl HWH RH16 ...... 48 D7 [8]
Sullington Cl ROTT BN2 ...... 169 M2
Sullington Wy SHOR BN43 ...... 166 A6
Sumach Cl RING/NEW BN22 ...... 196 E4
Summer Cl PTSD BN41 ...... 167 G7
Summercourt HAIL BN27 ...... 155 H6 [2]
Summerdale Rd HOVE BN3 ...... 167 K4
Summerdown Cl
 EDN/EASTW BN20 ...... 206 D3
Summerdown La
 EDN/EASTW BN20 ...... 205 J5
Summerdown Rd
 EDN/EASTW BN20 ...... 206 C3
Summerfields SLVH TN37 ...... 4 C6
Summerfields Av HAIL BN27 ...... 155 G6
Summerheath Rd HAIL BN27 ...... 155 G6
Summer Hl STLEO TN38 ...... 162 A6
Summerhill Cl HWH RH16 ...... 48 F7
Summerhill Dr HWH RH16 ...... 48 F7
Summerhill Gra HWH RH16 ...... 48 F7
Summerhill La HWH RH16 ...... 48 F7
Summerlands Rd
 LW/ROSE BN22 ...... 196 B4
Summersdeane STHW BN42 ...... 166 F5
Summervale Rd
 SBGH/RUST TN4 ...... 19 K5
Sumners RHWH RH17 ...... 34 A7
Sunningdale Cl BEX TN40 ...... 183 L1
 HAIL BN27 ...... 155 G5
 SEAF BN25 ...... 203 G4 [1]
Sunningdale Dr STLEO TN38 ...... 161 M5
Sunninghill Av HOVE BN3 ...... 167 L4
Sunninghill Cl HOVE BN3 ...... 167 L4 [8]
Sunny Av CRAWE RH10 ...... 12 A6
Sunnybrooke Cl UCK TN22 ...... 76 D7 [3]
Sunnycroft Cl RHWH RH17 ...... 72 E4
Sunnydale Av BRI BN1 ...... 146 A8
Sunnydale Cl BRI BN1 ...... 146 A8
Sunnyhill Cl CRAWE RH10 ...... 12 A6 [1]
Sunnyside Rd SBGH/RUST TN4 ...... 19 J2

Sunnywood Dr HWH RH16 ...... 71 K3
Sunset Cl PEAHV BN10 ...... 190 B5 [7]
 PEV BN24 ...... 180 E8
Sunstar La POLE BN26 ...... 177 L8
Sun St LEW BN7 ...... 3 G7
Sunte Av HWH RH16 ...... 48 F7
Sunte Cl HWH RH16 ...... 48 E7
Sunview Av PEAHV BN10 ...... 190 D8
Surrenden Cl BRI BN1 ...... 168 F2
Surrenden Crs BRI BN1 ...... 168 F3
Surrenden Holt BRI BN1 ...... 168 F3
Surrenden Pk BRI BN1 ...... 169 G2
Surrenden Rd BRI BN1 ...... 168 F3
Surrey Cl RTWE/PEM TN2 ...... 19 M6
Surrey Rd SEAF BN25 ...... 202 C2
Surrey St BRI BN1 ...... 6 D4
Susans Cl RING/NEW BN8 ...... 130 A1
Susan's Rd EAST BN21 ...... 10 F5
Sussex Av HWH RH16 ...... 48 F7
Sussex Border Pth BRI BN1 ...... 144 F1
 EGRIN RH19 ...... 12 D7
 EGRIN RH19 ...... 14 A5
 EGRIN RH19 ...... 24 A1
 PTSD BN41 ...... 144 A5
 RHWH RH17 ...... 35 K6
 RRTW TN3 ...... 17 K2
 TENT TN30 ...... 67 K7
 WADH TN5 ...... 31 K6
 WADH TN5 ...... 42 F1
 WADH TN5 ...... 46 A2
Sussex Cl BEXW TN39 ...... 182 F1
 HAIL BN27 ...... 155 H6
 RTWE/PEM TN2 ...... 20 C5
Sussex Gdns
 EDN/EASTW BN20 ...... 205 J5
 HWH RH16 ...... 72 B3
Sussex Ms RTWE/PEM TN2 ...... 20 A4 [8]
Sussex Pl ROTT BN2 ...... 7 G5
Sussex Rd HOVE BN3 ...... 186 B1 [8]
 HWH RH16 ...... 71 J3
 STLEO TN38 ...... 162 A8
Sussex Sq ROTT BN2 ...... 187 L2
Sussex St ROTT BN2 ...... 7 G6
Sussex Wy BURH RH15 ...... 96 E1
 PEAHV BN10 ...... 189 M7
Sutherland Av BEXW TN39 ...... 183 C5
Sutherland Cl BEXW TN39 ...... 182 F2
Sutherland Rd ROTT BN2 ...... 7 K7
 RTW TN1 ...... 20 B4
Sutton Av PEAHV BN10 ...... 190 B7
 SEAF BN25 ...... 203 C4
Sutton Av North PEAHV BN10 ...... 190 B6
Sutton Cl ROTT BN2 ...... 170 E5
Sutton Croft La SEAF BN25 ...... 202 E3 [8]
Sutton Dro SEAF BN25 ...... 202 E3
Sutton Park Rd SEAF BN25 ...... 202 E3
Sutton Pl BEX TN40 ...... 183 L2
Sutton Rd EAST BN21 ...... 10 E6
 SEAF BN25 ...... 202 F3
The Suttons RYE TN31 ...... 118 F5
 STLEO TN38 ...... 161 M4
Swaines Wy HTHF TN21 ...... 80 A8
Swainham La BAT TN33 ...... 161 G3
Swainsthorpe Cl HWH RH16 ...... 71 M3 [3]
Swallow Bank STLEO TN38 ...... 161 M4
Swallow Cl LGNY BN23 ...... 197 H4
Swallow Ct UCK TN22 ...... 102 D1 [8]
Swallow Dr BAT TN33 ...... 137 M2 [8]
The Swallows PEAHV BN10 ...... 190 B5 [8]
Swamp Rd LYDD TN29 ...... 95 G2
Swanborough Dr ROTT BN2 ...... 169 M7
Swanborough Dro LEW BN7 ...... 171 M3
Swanborough Hollow
 LEW BN7 ...... 172 A2
Swanborough Pl ROTT BN2 ...... 169 M7 [9]
Swan Cl RING/NEW BN8 ...... 99 L7
Swan Cottages TENT TN30 ...... 67 K3
Swanley Cl LGNY BN23 ...... 197 J4
Swann Cl BURH RH15 ...... 97 K3
Swannee Cl PEAHV BN10 ...... 190 D5 [2]
Swan Rd HAIL BN27 ...... 155 J8
Swansbrook La HTHF TN21 ...... 131 K5
Swans Ghyll FROW RH18 ...... 24 E3
Swan St TENT TN30 ...... 67 H3
Swan Ter HAS TN34 ...... 5 K6
Swaylands Av BEXW TN39 ...... 39 M7
Sweethaws La CROW TN6 ...... 39 G6
Sweetings La RRTW TN3 ...... 32 D5
Sweetlands HPPT/KEY BN6 ...... 123 H1 [8]
Swife La HTHF TN21 ...... 81 J3
Swift Cl CROW TN6 ...... 39 K5
 HPPT/KEY BN6 ...... 96 D3
 UCK TN22 ...... 102 D1 [8]
Swinburne Av LW/ROSE BN22 ...... 196 B3
Swynford Dr STLEO TN38 ...... 161 M1
Sybron Wy CROW TN6 ...... 40 D6
Sycamore Cl BEXW TN39 ...... 182 C1
 HTHF TN21 ...... 80 B8
 LW/ROSE BN22 ...... 196 D3 [3]
 LYDD TN29 ...... 95 K7
 PTSD BN41 ...... 167 J3 [3]
 ROTT BN2 ...... 170 C6
 STLEO TN38 ...... 162 A5 [1]
Sycamore Ct UCK TN22 ...... 76 D6
Sycamore Dr EGRIN RH19 ...... 14 A5
 HAIL BN27 ...... 155 J7
The Sycamores PEAHV BN10 ...... 190 D5 [2]
Sydney Cl STLEO TN38 ...... 162 B3
Sydney Little Rd STLEO TN38 ...... 161 K2
Sydney Rd HWH RH16 ...... 48 E8
 LW/ROSE BN22 ...... 11 G5
Sydney St BRI BN1 ...... 6 E5
Sylvan Cl HWH RH16 ...... 72 B2
Sylvester Wy HOVE BN3 ...... 167 J3
Symbister Rd PTSD BN41 ...... 167 J7 [3]
Syresham Gdns HWH RH16 ...... 71 J2

T

Tackleway HAS TN34 ...... 5 L6
Taddington Rd BRI BN2 ...... 11 J3
Tainter's Brook UCK TN22 ...... 76 E6
Talbot Cl BRI BN1 ...... 146 D8
Talbot Pk RTWE/PEM TN2 ...... 20 C1
Talbot Rd HAWK TN18 ...... 47 M6

Talbot Ter LEW BN7 ...... 2 F5
Tall Ash Dr SLVH TN37 ...... 162 C2
Tamarack Cl LW/ROSE BN22 ...... 196 D4
Tamar Cl PEV BN24 ...... 197 G1
Tamplin Ter ROTT BN2 ...... 7 G4
Tamworth Rd HOVE BN3 ...... 167 M7
Tanbridge Rd LGNY BN23 ...... 197 M5
Tandridge Rd HOVE BN3 ...... 167 L8
Tangier La RRTW TN3 ...... 20 B8
Tangle Oak EGRIN RH19 ...... 12 E2
Tanglewood Coppice
 BEXW TN39 ...... 182 E3 [8]
Tangmere Cl BEXW TN39 ...... 182 E3 [8]
Tangmere Rd BRI BN1 ...... 146 A8
Tanhouse La RYE TN31 ...... 89 M4
Tanners Brook LEW BN7 ...... 3 G7
Tanners Fld RHWH RH17 ...... 35 K4
Tanners Wy CROW TN6 ...... 40 A5 [8]
Tanyard HAWK TN18 ...... 64 B1
Tanyard Av EGRIN RH19 ...... 14 A6
Tanyard La RHWH RH17 ...... 51 J2
 WSEA TN36 ...... 116 E6
Tapsell's La WADH TN5 ...... 43 J1
Tarner Rd ROTT BN2 ...... 7 H6
Tarragon Wy SHOR BN43 ...... 166 C5
Tarring Cl NEWHV BN9 ...... 191 K4 [8]
Tas Combe Wy
 EDN/EASTW BN20 ...... 196 B4
Tate Crs BURH RH15 ...... 96 F1 [8]
Taunton Rd ROTT BN2 ...... 169 M5
Taunton Wy ROTT BN2 ...... 170 A5 [8]
Tavistock Down BRI BN1 ...... 169 J4
Taylor Cl STLEO TN38 ...... 161 M2
Tea Garden La RRTW TN3 ...... 19 H5
Teal Ct STLEO TN38 ...... 161 L3
Teg Cl PTSD BN41 ...... 167 J4
Telegraph St ROTT BN2 ...... 7 K8 [8]
Telford Rd STLEO TN38 ...... 162 A1
Telham Cl HAS TN34 ...... 163 G1
Telham La BAT TN33 ...... 137 L5
Telscombe Cliffs Wy
 PEAHV BN10 ...... 189 M7
Telscombe Pk PEAHV BN10 ...... 190 C4 [8]
Telscombe Rd LGNY BN23 ...... 197 M4
 PEAHV BN10 ...... 190 C4
Temple Gdns HOVE BN3 ...... 6 A4
Temple Gv BURH RH15 ...... 96 D2
Temple St BRI BN1 ...... 6 A6
Tenantry Down Rd ROTT BN2 ...... 169 L7
Tenantry Rd ROTT BN2 ...... 169 K6
Tennis Cl HAIL BN27 ...... 155 H7
Tennis Rd HOVE BN3 ...... 167 L8
Tennyson Ri EGRIN RH19 ...... 13 J5
Tenterden Cl LGNY BN23 ...... 197 M5
Tenterden Ri HAS TN34 ...... 4 D1
Terminus Av BEXW TN39 ...... 182 F3
Terminus Pl BRI BN1 ...... 6 D3 [8]
Terminus Rd BEXW TN39 ...... 183 G3
 BRI BN1 ...... 6 D3
 EAST BN21 ...... 10 F6
Terminus St BRI BN1 ...... 6 D4
Terrace Rd SLVH TN37 ...... 4 B8
Thackeray Cl LGNY BN23 ...... 197 L3
Thakeham Cl BEX TN40 ...... 161 G8
Thames Cl ROTT BN2 ...... 7 J8
Thanet Wy HAS TN34 ...... 4 E2
Thatchers Cl BURH RH15 ...... 97 K5
The Thatchings POLE BN26 ...... 196 A1
Theobalds HAWK TN18 ...... 47 M4
Theobalds Gn HTHF TN21 ...... 106 A1
Theobalds Rd BURH RH15 ...... 71 J8
Third Av HOVE BN3 ...... 186 B1
 NEWHV BN9 ...... 8 E5
Third Rd PEAHV BN10 ...... 190 A7 [8]
Third St RRTW TN3 ...... 18 F3
Thirlmere Rd SBGH/RUST TN4 ...... 19 K1
Thomas Brassey Cl
 SLVH TN37 ...... 162 B1 [8]
Thomas St LEW BN7 ...... 3 J4
 SBGH/RUST TN4 ...... 20 A1
Thomas Turner Dr
 RING/NEW BN8 ...... 130 A1
Thompson Rd BRI BN1 ...... 169 J5
 NEWHV BN9 ...... 191 M4
Thornbank Crs BEXW TN39 ...... 182 F3
Thornbush Crs PTSD BN41 ...... 167 H3
Thorndean Rd ROTT BN2 ...... 169 J5
Thorne Crs BEXW TN39 ...... 159 L5
Thornfield Gdns
 RTWE/PEM TN2 ...... 20 F1
Thornhill Av BRI BN1 ...... 146 A7
Thornhill Cl HOVE BN3 ...... 167 L4 [8]
Thornhill Ri PTSD BN41 ...... 167 G3
Thornhill Wy PTSD BN41 ...... 167 G3
The Thorns RHAS TN35 ...... 141 G6
Thornwell Rd POLE BN26 ...... 176 F7
Thornwood Cl
 LW/ROSE BN22 ...... 196 B4
Thorny Cl HTHF TN21 ...... 80 A7
Three Leg Cross Rd WADH TN5 ...... 45 K3
Three Oaks La WADH TN5 ...... 31 J7
Thurrock Cl
 EDN/EASTW BN20 ...... 196 B2 [8]
Thyme Cl SHOR BN43 ...... 166 C5 [8]
Thyssel La RYE TN31 ...... 65 H8
Tibbs Mill La UCK TN22 ...... 54 C5
Ticehurst Av BEXW TN39 ...... 181 M1
Ticehurst Rd ROTT BN2 ...... 187 M1
Tichborne St BRI BN1 ...... 6 C4
Tickerage La UCK TN22 ...... 77 M8
Tidebrook Gdns LGNY BN23 ...... 197 M4
Tidewell Rd EAST BN21 ...... 10 F4
Tidy St BRI BN1 ...... 6 E3
Tilbury Pl ROTT BN2 ...... 7 G6
Tilbury Wy ROTT BN2 ...... 7 H5
Tile Barn Cl UCK TN22 ...... 101 K6
Tile Barn Rd STLEO TN38 ...... 161 M2
Tilehurst Dr HAIL BN27 ...... 155 C6
Tilekiln La RHAS TN35 ...... 163 L2
Tilers Cl BURH RH15 ...... 97 K3 [8]
Tilgate Cl EAST BN21 ...... 196 D7
 ROTT BN2 ...... 7 L5
Tilgate Dr BEXW TN39 ...... 182 D3
Tilley La HAIL BN27 ...... 157 K1
Tillingham Av RYE TN31 ...... 117 H1
Tillingham La RYE TN31 ...... 89 M8
 RYE TN31 ...... 116 D1
Tillingham Vw RYE TN31 ...... 114 A2

Tillingham Wy PEV BN24 .... 197 G1
Tillstone Cl ROTT BN2 .... 169 K4
Tillstone St ROTT BN2 .... 7 H7
Tilsmore Cnr HTHF TN21 .... 79 M7
Tilsmore Rd HTHF TN21 .... 79 M7
Tiltwood Dr CRAWE RH10 .... 12 C5
Timberlaine Rd PEV BN24 .... 198 C2
Timberley Rd LW/ROSE BN22 .... 196 D5
Timbers Cl HAIL BN27 .... 155 J7
Timber Yard Cottages LEW BN7 .... 3 J6
Tindal Cl BURH BN1 .... 97 K3
Tinker's La UCK TN22 .... 78 E2
  WADH TN5 .... 45 K3
Tintern Cl BRI BN1 .... 169 H5
  LW/ROSE BN22 .... 196 D3
Tisbury Rd HOVE BN3 .... 168 C8
Titchfield Cl ROTT BN2 .... 7 H7
Tithe Barn Fld WSEA TN36 .... 141 M1
Tithe Orch EGRIN RH19 .... 12 C2
Titian Rd HOVE BN3 .... 167 M7
Tiverton Dr BEX TN40 .... 183 L1
Tivoli Crs BRI BN1 .... 168 D5
Tivoli Crs North BRI BN1 .... 168 D4
Tivoli Pl BRI BN1 .... 168 D4
Tivoli Rd BRI BN1 .... 168 D4
Tolhurst La WADH TN5 .... 45 C5
Tolkien Rd LGNY BN23 .... 197 L4
Tollgate PEAHV BN10 .... 190 B5
Tollgates BAT TN33 .... 137 H2
Toll La UCK TN22 .... 52 F5
Tollwood Pk CROW TN6 .... 40 B6
Tollwood Rd CROW TN6 .... 40 B6
Toll Wood Rd HTHF TN21 .... 105 M7
Tompset's Bank FROW RH18 .... 24 F6
Tomtits La FROW RH18 .... 24 E5
Tonbridge Wy RYE TN31 .... 118 E4
Tongdean Av HOVE BN3 .... 168 C3
Tongdean La BRI BN1 .... 168 D2
Tongdean Ri BRI BN1 .... 168 C2
Tongdean Rd HOVE BN3 .... 168 B3
Top Cross Rd BEX TN40 .... 161 G7
Top Dr UCK TN22 .... 53 G8
Top Rd EGRIN RH19 .... 34 F1
  TENT TN30 .... 68 E3
Torcross Cl ROTT BN2 .... 169 L5
Torfield Rd EAST BN21 .... 10 B4
Toronto Ter LEW BN7 .... 2 F5
  ROTT BN2 .... 7 H5
Torrance Cl HOVE BN3 .... 167 M5
Tor Rd PEAHV BN10 .... 190 C4
Tor Rd West PEAHV BN10 .... 190 B4
Totland Rd ROTT BN2 .... 7 L2
Tottington Wy SHOR BN43 .... 166 B5
Tott Yew Rd EDN/EASTW BN20 .... 194 A6
Tourney Rd LYDD TN29 .... 121 H1
Tovey Cl ROTT BN2 .... 196 D8
Tower Cl EGRIN RH19 .... 13 L4
  PEV BN24 .... 180 F8
Towergate BRI BN1 .... 168 E4
Tower Ride UCK TN22 .... 76 D5
Tower Rd ROTT BN2 .... 7 J4
  STLEO TN38 .... 4 A4
Tower Rd West STLEO TN38 .... 162 B6
Towerscroft Av SLVH TN37 .... 162 B1
Tower St HTHF TN21 .... 80 B6
  RYE TN31 .... 91 J8
Tower Vw UCK TN22 .... 76 D6
Town HI RRTW TN3 .... 33 G2
Trafalgar Cl PEAHV BN10 .... 190 C5
  STLEO TN38 .... 138 F7
Trafalgar Ct BRI BN1 .... 6 F4
Trafalgar Ga ROTT BN2 .... 187 M3
Trafalgar La BRI BN1 .... 6 E4
Trafalgar Pl BRI BN1 .... 6 E4
Trafalgar St BRI BN1 .... 6 E4
Tram Rd RYE TN31 .... 118 A4
Transit Rd NEWHV BN9 .... 9 H4
Travellers La RHAS TN35 .... 163 J2
Treblers Rd CROW TN6 .... 40 D7
Tredcroft Rd HOVE BN3 .... 168 B4
Treemans Rd RHWH RH17 .... 50 B4
Tree Tops Cl ROTT BN2 .... 170 E6
Tremola Av ROTT BN2 .... 189 H4
Trenches Rd CROW TN6 .... 39 M5
Treyford Cl ROTT BN2 .... 170 E5
Triangle Rd HWH RH16 .... 71 L3
The Triangle
  EDN/EASTW BN20 .... 196 A3
Trinity Cl RTWE/PEM TN2 .... 20 D2
Trinity Fld RING/NEW BN8 .... 127 L8
Trinity Pl EAST BN21 .... 10 F7
Trinity Rd HPPT/KEY BN6 .... 96 A8
Trinity St HAS TN34 .... 4 F7
  ROTT BN2 .... 7 H2
Trinity Trees EAST BN21 .... 10 F7
Tristan Gdns SBGH/RUST TN4 .... 19 K2
Troon Cl SEAF BN25 .... 192 A8
Trossachs Cl LGNY BN23 .... 197 K3
Troy Cl CROW TN6 .... 40 A5
Truleigh Cl ROTT BN2 .... 170 F4
Truleigh Dr PTSD BN41 .... 167 G2
Truleigh Wy SHOR BN43 .... 166 A5
Truman Dr STLEO TN38 .... 138 F8
Trumpet La HAIL BN27 .... 134 B4
Tubwell La CROW TN6 .... 40 D7
  HTHF TN21 .... 105 M4
Tudor Av STLEO TN38 .... 162 A7
Tudor Cl EGRIN RH19 .... 13 M7
  HOVE BN3 .... 167 M4
  SEAF BN25 .... 202 F2
Tudor Ct RTWE/PEM TN2 .... 19 L5
Tudor Gdns BURH RH15 .... 96 F2
Tudor Wk UCK TN22 .... 103 H1
Tugwell Rd LW/ROSE BN22 .... 196 F4
Tumulus Rd ROTT BN2 .... 189 J4
Tunbridge Wells Rd CROW TN6 .... 41 L8
  MAYF TN20 .... 56 F1
Tunnel Rd RTW TN1 .... 20 B1
Turkey La BURH RH15 .... 97 H3
Turkey Rd BEXW TN39 .... 159 K7
Turk's Br HTHF TN21 .... 58 E6
Turnberry Cl STLEO TN38 .... 161 M7
Turnberry Dr HAIL BN27 .... 155 C6
Turner Cl BEX TN40 .... 183 K1
  LGNY BN23 .... 197 K5
Turner Ct EGRIN RH19 .... 14 A3
Turners Green La WADH TN5 .... 31 M8
Turners Green Rd WADH TN5 .... 31 M7

Turner's Hill Rd EGRIN RH19 .... 23 G1
Turners Mill Cl HWH RH16 .... 48 D7
Turners Mill Rd HWH RH16 .... 48 D8
Turners Wy BURH RH15 .... 96 F2
Turnpike Cl PEAHV BN10 .... 190 C6
  RING/NEW BN8 .... 128 C2
Turton Cl ROTT BN2 .... 7 L7
Tutts Barn La LW/ROSE BN22 .... 10 D2
Tuxford Rd SBGH/RUST TN4 .... 19 H1
Twineham Cl ROTT BN2 .... 169 M7
Twineham Rd EAST BN21 .... 196 D8
Twitten Cl STHW BN42 .... 166 E7
Twitten La EGRIN RH19 .... 12 E2
  CROW TN6 .... 39 L5
  STHW BN42 .... 166 E7
Twyford Crs SLVH TN37 .... 162 C2
Twyford Rd BRI BN1 .... 146 D8
Twyfords CROW TN6 .... 39 L5
Twyhurst Ct EGRIN RH19 .... 13 K3
Tye Cl ROTT BN2 .... 189 K6
Tyedean Rd PEAHV BN10 .... 189 M6
Tye Hill Rd POLE BN26 .... 176 F2
Tye Vw PEAHV BN10 .... 190 A5
Tyler's Gn RHWH RH17 .... 71 H2
Tylers La UCK TN22 .... 52 E5
Tyndale Av BEXW TN39 .... 182 C3

U

Uckfield Cl ROTT BN2 .... 169 M8
Uckfield Rd CROW TN6 .... 39 H8
  RING/NEW BN8 .... 127 H7
Uckham La BAT TN33 .... 111 L8
Udimore Rd RYE TN31 .... 116 B2
  RYE TN31 .... 116 E2
Undercliff STLEO TN38 .... 4 A9
Underdown Rd STHW BN42 .... 166 E6
Underhill UCK TN22 .... 76 B1
Underhill La HPPT/KEY BN6 .... 122 E6
Under Rd HAIL BN27 .... 156 B3
Underwood Cl CRAWE RH10 .... 12 B6
Union Cl HAIL BN27 .... 155 H4
Union Rd ROTT BN2 .... 7 G3
Union St BRI BN1 .... 6 D7
  STLEO TN38 .... 4 A8
Upland Rd EDN/EASTW BN20 .... 206 C3
Uplands Cl BEXW TN39 .... 159 M8
  UCK TN22 .... 76 C5
Uplands Pk HTHF TN21 .... 80 E5
Uplands Rd BRI BN1 .... 169 J4
Upper Abbey Rd ROTT BN2 .... 7 L8
Upper Av EAST BN21 .... 10 E3
  LW/ROSE BN22 .... 10 E3
Upper Bannings Rd ROTT BN2 .... 189 L3
Upper Bedford St ROTT BN2 .... 7 J8
Upper Belgrave Rd SEAF BN25 .... 202 F1
Upper Bevendean Av
  ROTT BN2 .... 169 L5
Upper Broomgrove Rd
  HAS TN34 .... 163 H3
Upper Carlisle Rd
  EDN/EASTW BN20 .... 206 C6
Upper Chalvington Pl
  ROTT BN2 .... 187 L1
Upper Church Rd SLVH TN37 .... 162 B4
Upper Chyngton Gdns
  SEAF BN25 .... 203 H1
Upper Cl FROW RH18 .... 24 F4
Upper Cumberland Wk
  RTW TN1 .... 20 B5
The Upper Dr HOVE BN3 .... 168 C6
Upper Duke's Dr
  EDN/EASTW BN20 .... 206 D7
Upper Gardner St BRI BN1 .... 6 E3
Upper Glen Rd SLVH TN37 .... 162 A1
Upper Gloucester Rd BRI BN1 .... 6 D5
Upper Greenwoods La
  HTHF TN21 .... 81 H8
Upper Grosvenor Rd
  SBGH/RUST TN4 .... 20 B1
Upper Hamilton Rd BRI BN1 .... 6 B1
Upper Hollingdean Rd
  BRI BN1 .... 169 H5
Upper Horsebridge Rd
  HAIL BN27 .... 155 G3
Upper King's Dr
  EDN/EASTW BN20 .... 196 B5
Upper Kingston La
  STHW BN42 .... 166 D5
Upper Lake BAT TN33 .... 137 K2
Upper Lewes Rd ROTT BN2 .... 7 G2
Upper Market St HOVE BN3 .... 186 D1
Upper Maze HI STLEO TN38 .... 162 B6
Upper Nellington RRTW TN3 .... 19 H2
Upper North St BRI BN1 .... 6 B5
Upper Park Pl ROTT BN2 .... 7 J8
Upper Park Rd SLVH TN37 .... 4 B3
Upper Profit RRTW TN3 .... 19 G3
Upper Ratton Dr
  EDN/EASTW BN20 .... 196 B6
Upper Rock Gdns ROTT BN2 .... 7 H8
Upper St James's St ROTT BN2 .... 7 H8
Upper St Johns Rd BURH RH15 .... 97 G3
Upper Sea Rd BEX TN40 .... 183 K2
Upper Sherwood Rd
  SEAF BN25 .... 202 F2
Upper Shoreham Rd
  STHW BN42 .... 166 D5
Upper Sth Rd SLVH TN37 .... 4 A4
Upper Station Rd HTHF TN21 .... 80 A7
Upper Stephens RRTW TN3 .... 19 G3
Upper Stoneham
  RING/NEW BN8 .... 149 M2
Upper St EDN/EASTW BN20 .... 205 H6
Upper Sudeley St ROTT BN2 .... 7 L8
Upperton Gdns EAST BN21 .... 10 D5
Upperton La EAST BN21 .... 10 A4
Upperton Rd EAST BN21 .... 10 A4
Upper Valley Rd NEWHV BN9 .... 8 C5
Upper Wellington Rd ROTT BN2 .... 7 J2
Upper Winfield Av BRI BN1 .... 145 M8
Upper Wish HI
  EDN/EASTW BN20 .... 196 B6
Upton Av STHW BN42 .... 166 E5
Upton Quarry RRTW TN3 .... 18 F3

Upwick Rd EDN/EASTW BN20 .... 206 C3

V

Vale Av BRI BN1 .... 145 L7
  RTW TN1 .... 20 A3
Valebridge Cl BURH RH15 .... 71 J8
Valebridge Dr BURH RH15 .... 97 J1
Valebridge Rd BURH RH15 .... 97 J1
Vale Cl SEAF BN25 .... 203 J1
Vale Gdns PTSD BN41 .... 167 H7
Valence Rd LEW BN7 .... 2 C5
Valentine Dr BURH RH15 .... 96 E2
Valerie Cl PTSD BN41 .... 167 H4
Vale Rd BAT TN33 .... 137 H1
  HAWK TN18 .... 47 M3
  HWH RH16 .... 71 K4
  MAYF TN20 .... 57 H4
  PTSD BN41 .... 167 J7
  ROTT BN2 .... 189 K3
  RTW TN1 .... 20 A3
  SEAF BN25 .... 202 F2
  SLVH TN37 .... 4 A1
The Vale ROTT BN2 .... 188 E1
Vale View Rd HTHF TN21 .... 80 B8
Vallance Cl BURH RH15 .... 96 E2
Vallance Gdns HOVE BN3 .... 168 A8
Vallance Rd HOVE BN3 .... 168 A8
Valley Cl BRI BN1 .... 168 C2
  NEWHV BN9 .... 8 D2
Valley Dene NEWHV BN9 .... 8 D4
Valley Dr BRI BN1 .... 168 C2
  SEAF BN25 .... 203 G1
Valley Ri SEAF BN25 .... 202 F6
Valley Rd CROW TN6 .... 39 M5
  LEW BN7 .... 2 B8
  NEWHV BN9 .... 8 B4
  PEAHV BN10 .... 190 C4
  PTSD BN41 .... 167 G4
  SBGH/RUST TN4 .... 19 K3
Valley Side Rd HAS TN34 .... 163 J3
Valley View Cl CROW TN6 .... 39 M5
Val Prinseps Rd PEV BN24 .... 198 C2
Vanguard Wy CROW TN6 .... 38 F7
  EGRIN RH19 .... 14 F1
  POLE BN26 .... 175 M4
  RING/NEW BN8 .... 130 F4
  SEAF BN25 .... 203 C5
  UCK TN22 .... 54 C6
  UCK TN22 .... 104 A3
Varndean Cl BRI BN1 .... 168 E3
Varndean Dr BRI BN1 .... 168 E3
Varndean Gdns BRI BN1 .... 168 E3
Varndean Holt BRI BN1 .... 168 F3
Varndean Rd BRI BN1 .... 168 E3
Vega Cl HAIL BN27 .... 155 K7
Ventnor Cl LGNY BN23 .... 197 H2
Ventnor Vls HOVE BN3 .... 168 B8
Venture Cl BEX TN40 .... 183 M2
Verbania Wy EGRIN RH19 .... 14 B5
Verdant Cl HAS TN34 .... 5 D5
Vere Rd BRI BN1 .... 6 F1
Vermont Rd SBGH/RUST TN4 .... 19 J2
Vernon Av PEAHV BN10 .... 190 D8
  ROTT BN2 .... 170 C5
Vernon Cl LGNY BN23 .... 197 L7
Vernon Rd UCK TN22 .... 76 D8
Vernons Rd RING/NEW BN8 .... 74 C7
Vernon Ter BRI BN1 .... 6 B4
Veronica Wy ROTT BN2 .... 7 K1
Verulam Pl SLVH TN37 .... 4 E8
Viaduct Rd BRI BN1 .... 6 E2
Vian Av LGNY BN23 .... 197 M8
Vicarage Cl NEWHV BN9 .... 191 L4
  RING/NEW BN8 .... 150 C1
  SEAF BN25 .... 202 F3
Vicarage Dr EDN/EASTW BN20 .... 206 D3
Vicarage La BUR/ETCH TN19 .... 82 A3
  EDN/EASTW BN20 .... 206 D3
  HAIL BN27 .... 132 A8
  HAIL BN27 .... 155 J6
  RHAS TN35 .... 139 K3
  RHWH RH17 .... 72 F3
  ROTT BN2 .... 188 F5
Vicarage Rd BUR/ETCH TN19 .... 82 A3
  CRAWE RH10 .... 12 A7
  EDN/EASTW BN20 .... 206 D3
  HAIL BN27 .... 155 J7
  HAS TN34 .... 5 J4
Vicarage Ter ROTT BN2 .... 188 F5
Vicarage Wy BUR/ETCH TN19 .... 62 A3
  RING/NEW BN8 .... 150 D1
Victor Cl SEAF BN25 .... 202 D1
Victoria Av BURH RH15 .... 96 E3
  PEAHV BN10 .... 190 C8
  RHAS TN35 .... 163 J2
Victoria Cl BURH RH15 .... 96 E3
  POLE BN26 .... 177 M7
Victoria Dr EAST BN21 .... 206 C1
  EDN/EASTW BN20 .... 196 B8
  EDN/EASTW BN20 .... 206 C2
Victoria Gdns BURH RH15 .... 96 E4
  EDN/EASTW BN20 .... 206 C2
Victoria Pl BRI BN1 .... 6 B5
Victoria Gv HOVE BN3 .... 168 C8
Victoria Rd BEXW TN39 .... 183 H2
  BRI BN1 .... 6 B5
  BURH RH15 .... 96 E4
  CROW TN6 .... 40 C6
  EDN/EASTW BN20 .... 206 B1
  HAIL BN27 .... 155 J7
  HAIL BN27 .... 157 H1
  HWH RH16 .... 71 M5
  MAYF TN20 .... 57 G3
  POLE BN26 .... 177 M7
  PTSD BN41 .... 167 H6
  RTW TN1 .... 20 B2
  SLVH TN37 .... 4 C8
  STHW BN42 .... 166 D7
Victoria St BRI BN1 .... 6 B5
Victoria Wy BURH RH15 .... 96 E4
  EGRIN RH19 .... 13 M7
  WSEA TN36 .... 143 G1
Victory Ms ROTT BN2 .... 188 A3
View Bank RHAS TN35 .... 163 K4
View Rd PEAHV BN10 .... 190 C6

Viking Cl SEAF BN25 .... 192 A8
The Village Barn BRI BN1 .... 145 L7
Village Ms BEXW TN39 .... 160 C8
The Village EDN/EASTW BN20 .... 206 D6
Village Wy BRI BN1 .... 147 J8
Villa Rd SLVH TN37 .... 4 C8
Villiers Cl ROTT BN2 .... 170 E6
Vincent Cl LGNY BN23 .... 197 M7
Vinehall Cl HAS TN34 .... 163 G1
Vinehall Rd RBTBR TN32 .... 85 L8
Vine Lands LYDD TN29 .... 95 H8
The Vineries BURH RH15 .... 97 K3
  LGNY BN23 .... 197 K4
Vines Cross Rd HTHF TN21 .... 106 A6
  ROTT BN2 .... 169 M7
Vine Sq LW/ROSE BN22 .... 197 K8
Vine St BRI BN1 .... 6 F5
Vineyard La WADH TN5 .... 45 H4
Virgin's Cft BAT TN33 .... 111 K8
Virgin's La BAT TN33 .... 111 K8
Vowels La EGRIN RH19 .... 22 D4

W

Wade Cl LGNY BN23 .... 197 M7
Wadhurst Cl LW/ROSE BN22 .... 196 F4
  SLVH TN37 .... 162 B1
Wadhurst Ri BRI BN1 .... 187 M1
Wadhurst La BAT TN33 .... 136 E1
Wadhurst Rd CROW TN6 .... 42 F3
  RRTW TN3 .... 30 C5
  WADH TN5 .... 30 F6
Wadlands Brook Rd
  EGRIN RH19 .... 13 K1
Wagg Cl EGRIN RH19 .... 14 A5
Waghorns La UCK TN22 .... 78 C1
Wainwright Cl STLEO TN38 .... 161 K3
Wainwright Rd BEXW TN39 .... 183 H2
Waite Cl LEW BN7 .... 3 H3
Waites La RHAS TN35 .... 164 E1
Wakefield Rd ROTT BN2 .... 7 G1
Wakehurst La RHWH RH17 .... 34 A6
Waldegrave Rd BRI BN1 .... 168 F4
Waldegrave St HAS TN34 .... 5 H5
Waldene Cl HAS TN34 .... 5 H1
Waldron Av BRI BN1 .... 146 D8
Waldron Cl LW/ROSE BN22 .... 196 D6
Waldron Rd RING/NEW BN8 .... 130 A1
Waldron Thorns HTHF TN21 .... 80 A8
Waldshut Rd LEW BN7 .... 2 B2
Walesbeech Rd ROTT BN2 .... 189 K6
Walker Cl LGNY BN23 .... 197 M7
Wallace Cl RTWE/PEM TN2 .... 20 A6
Wallands Crs LEW BN7 .... 2 E4
The Walled Gdn UCK TN22 .... 76 D2
Wall Hill Rd FROW RH18 .... 24 D1
Wallis Av LGNY BN23 .... 197 L7
Wallis Cl CROW TN6 .... 40 A5
Wallis Wy BURH RH15 .... 96 E2
Wallsend Rd PEV BN24 .... 180 B8
Walmer Crs ROTT BN2 .... 170 A5
Walmer Rd SEAF BN25 .... 203 J2
Walnut Cl BRI BN1 .... 168 E3
  HTHF TN21 .... 80 B8
Walnut Pk HWH RH16 .... 72 B2
Walnut Tree Wk
  EDN/EASTW BN20 .... 196 B6
Walnut Wk POLE BN26 .... 178 A8
Walpole Rd ROTT BN2 .... 7 K8
Walpole Ter ROTT BN2 .... 7 L7
Walshes Rd CROW TN6 .... 40 A7
Walsingham Cl
  LW/ROSE BN22 .... 196 D3
Walsingham Rd HOVE BN3 .... 167 M8
Walton Bank BRI BN1 .... 145 M4
Walton Cl SLVH TN37 .... 162 C1
Walton Rd BEXW TN39 .... 182 F2
Wanderdown Cl ROTT BN2 .... 188 E2
Wanderdown Dr ROTT BN2 .... 188 E2
Wanderdown Rd ROTT BN2 .... 188 D2
Wanderdown Wy ROTT BN2 .... 188 E2
Wannock Av
  EDN/EASTW BN20 .... 195 M3
Wannock Cl BEX TN40 .... 161 G8
Wannock Dr POLE BN26 .... 195 M1
Wannock Gdns
  EDN/EASTW BN20 .... 195 M3
Wannock La EDN/EASTW BN20 .... 195 M3
Warbleton Cl ROTT BN2 .... 187 L1
Warburton Cl EAST BN21 .... 196 C6
  EGRIN RH19 .... 14 A5
Ward Cl WADH TN5 .... 43 L1
Wardsbrook Rd WADH TN5 .... 45 K7
Ward's La WADH TN5 .... 44 E3
Ward Wy BEXW TN39 .... 160 A8
Warelands BURH RH15 .... 96 F5
Warenne Rd HOVE BN3 .... 167 J3
Wares Fld UCK TN22 .... 102 D3
Wares Rd UCK TN22 .... 102 D2
Warleigh Rd BRI BN1 .... 6 F1
Warmdene Av BRI BN1 .... 145 M8
Warmdene Cl BRI BN1 .... 168 F1
Warmdene Rd BRI BN1 .... 145 M8
Warmdene Wy BRI BN1 .... 145 M8
Warminster Rd PEV BN24 .... 198 D1
Warnham Gdns BEXW TN39 .... 182 D4
Warnham Ri BRI BN1 .... 169 G1
Warren Av ROTT BN2 .... 170 C5
Warren Cl CROW TN6 .... 39 K4
  EDN/EASTW BN20 .... 205 H5
  EGRIN RH19 .... 13 L8
  HTHF TN21 .... 78 F8
  LEW BN7 .... 2 C2
  ROTT BN2 .... 170 B6
  STLEO TN38 .... 161 L6
Warren Dr LEW BN7 .... 2 B7
Warren Farm La RRTW TN3 .... 17 G8
Warren Gdn CROW TN6 .... 39 L4
Warren HI EDN/EASTW BN20 .... 206 A5
Warren La EDN/EASTW BN20 .... 205 H5
  HTHF TN21 .... 79 G6
  RING/NEW BN8 .... 73 L6
Warren Rdg CROW TN6 .... 39 K4
  RRTW TN3 .... 30 C3
Warren Ri ROTT BN2 .... 170 B6
Warren Rd CROW TN6 .... 39 J5
  RHAS TN35 .... 164 C2
  ROTT BN2 .... 169 L7
  ROTT BN2 .... 170 C6
The Warren BURH RH15 .... 97 J5
  MAYF TN20 .... 57 J4
  WADH TN5 .... 45 L5
Warren Wy PEAHV BN10 .... 190 A5
  RING/NEW BN8 .... 73 M6
  ROTT BN2 .... 170 D6
Warrenwood RING/NEW BN8 .... 74 A6
Warr Gn LEW BN7 .... 2 C2
Warrior Cl PTSD BN41 .... 167 H4
Warrior Gdns SLVH TN37 .... 4 B7
Warrior Sq SLVH TN37 .... 4 B8
Warrs Hill La RING/NEW BN8 .... 73 L5
Wartling Cl STLEO TN38 .... 161 M3
Wartling Dr BEXW TN39 .... 181 M1
Wartling Rd HAIL BN27 .... 157 K6
  LW/ROSE BN22 .... 11 K1
Warwick Cl HAIL BN27 .... 155 J3
Warwick Pk RTWE/PEM TN2 .... 20 B5
Warwick Rd BEXW TN39 .... 182 F1
  RTW TN1 .... 20 A4
  SEAF BN25 .... 202 E3
Washington Av STLEO TN38 .... 138 F8
Washington Rd HWH RH16 .... 71 M1
Washington St ROTT BN2 .... 7 H4
Washwell La WADH TN5 .... 43 M3
Watchbell La RYE TN31 .... 117 J1
Watchbell St RYE TN31 .... 117 H1
Waterbury Rd RHWH RH17 .... 35 H8
Waterdown Rd SBGH/RUST TN4 .... 19 K5
Waterdyke Av STHW BN42 .... 166 E7
Waterfield RTWE/PEM TN2 .... 20 A7
Waterford Cl PEAHV BN10 .... 190 C4
Watergate BEXW TN39 .... 160 B6
Watergate La LEW BN7 .... 2 F6
Waterhall Rd BRI BN1 .... 145 J8
Waterloo Dr STLEO TN38 .... 138 F7
Waterloo Pl LEW BN7 .... 3 G5
Waterloo Sq POLE BN26 .... 194 C4
Waterloo St HOVE BN3 .... 186 D1
Watermen's Cl HAS TN34 .... 162 E3
Watermill Cl BEXW TN39 .... 160 B6
  POLE BN26 .... 196 A1
Watermill Dr STLEO TN38 .... 161 K3
Watermill La BEXW TN39 .... 160 B6
  RHAS TN35 .... 141 J5
  RYE TN31 .... 88 D3
Waters Cottages WADH TN5 .... 44 A2
Waterside EGRIN RH19 .... 14 B5
Waterside Cl HAS TN34 .... 163 H3
Waterworks Rd HAS TN34 .... 5 H5
  LW/ROSE BN22 .... 10 F3
Watling Cl STHW BN42 .... 166 E7
Wattle's Wish BAT TN33 .... 111 J8
Watts Cl WADH TN5 .... 45 M2
Watts La EAST BN21 .... 10 A4
Watts' Palace La RYE TN31 .... 87 K6
Waverley Crs BRI BN1 .... 169 H5
Waverley Gdns PEV BN24 .... 198 D1
Wayfaring Down POLE BN26 .... 195 K3
Wayfield Av HOVE BN3 .... 167 L5
Wayfield Cl HOVE BN3 .... 167 M5
Wayford Cl LGNY BN23 .... 197 K4
Wayland Av BRI BN1 .... 168 C2
Wayland Hts BRI BN1 .... 168 C2
Wayside BRI BN1 .... 145 K8
  EDN/EASTW BN20 .... 205 H6
Wayside Wk HTHF TN21 .... 79 M8
Weald Av HOVE BN3 .... 167 M5
Weald Cl LEW BN7 .... 2 E4
  RING/NEW BN8 .... 126 E2
Wealden BUR/ETCH RH19 .... 60 B7
Wealden Cl CROW TN6 .... 39 M3
Wealden Pk LW/ROSE BN22 .... 196 C4
Wealden Wy BEXW TN39 .... 159 J8
  HWH RH16 .... 71 K2
Weald Ri HWH RH16 .... 71 L5
Weald Rd BURH RH15 .... 96 E3
The Weald EGRIN RH19 .... 13 M3
Weald Vw RBTBR TN32 .... 86 E5
  RING/NEW BN8 .... 126 D2
  WADH TN5 .... 31 M8
Wealdview Rd HTHF TN21 .... 79 L7
Wealdway CROW TN6 .... 38 C4
  EDN/EASTW BN20 .... 195 L5
  EDN/EASTW BN20 .... 206 A3
  HAIL BN27 .... 131 J5
  HAIL BN27 .... 153 M7
  HRTF TN7 .... 17 G8
  HRTF TN7 .... 26 F6
  HTHF TN21 .... 131 L6
  POLE BN26 .... 176 E1
  POLE BN26 .... 176 F2
  RING/NEW BN8 .... 103 M7
  RING/NEW BN8 .... 129 M1
  UCK TN22 .... 38 C6
  UCK TN22 .... 53 J2
  UCK TN22 .... 103 L2
Weatherby Cl EAST BN21 .... 196 C6
Weavers Cl BURH RH15 .... 97 K5
Weavers La POLE BN26 .... 193 M3
Weavers Rock La HTHF TN21 .... 106 C1
Wedderburn Rd
  EDN/EASTW BN20 .... 196 B6
Week La RING/NEW BN8 .... 150 D4
Welbeck Av HOVE BN3 .... 167 L8
  STLEO TN38 .... 162 A7
Welbeck Cl BURH RH15 .... 97 K2
  LW/ROSE BN22 .... 196 D3
Welbeck Dr BURH RH15 .... 97 J1
The Welkin HWH RH16 .... 49 G6
Welland Cl CROW TN6 .... 40 A7
Wellcombe Crs
  EDN/EASTW BN20 .... 206 D7
Weller Rd SBGH/RUST TN4 .... 19 J2
Wellesley Cl BEXW TN39 .... 182 D3
  CROW TN6 .... 39 K5
Wellesley Rd EAST BN21 .... 10 F5

Wellfield EGRIN RH19 ..... 14 C7
Wellgreen La LEW BN7 ..... 171 M1
Wellhouse La BURH RH15 ..... 97 H7
Well House Pl LEW BN7 ..... 2 E6
Wellingham La
 RING/NEW BN8 ..... 127 G7
Wellington Cottages HAWK TN18 47 J3
Wellington Ms HAS TN34 ..... 5 H6
Wellington Pk SEAF BN25 ..... 203 G3
Wellington Pl HAS TN34 ..... 5 G7
Wellington Rd HAS TN34 ..... 5 J6
 NEWHV BN9 ..... 191 L4
 PEAHV BN10 ..... 190 E8
 PTSD BN41 ..... 167 H8
 ROTT BN2 ..... 7 H2
Wellington Sq HAS TN34 ..... 5 H7
Wellington St LEW BN7 ..... 3 G5
 ROTT BN2 ..... 7 J3
Wellington Town Rd
 EGRIN RH19 ..... 13 K3
Wellis Gdns STLEO TN38 ..... 162 A6
Wellsbourne Rd PEV BN24 ..... 197 C1
Wells Cl EDN/EASTW BN20 ..... 206 C6
 LEW BN7 ..... 98 E8
 RTW TN1 ..... 20 A3
Wells Lea EGRIN RH19 ..... 13 K3
Wells Meadow EGRIN RH19 ..... 13 K3
Wendale Dr PEAHV BN10 ..... 190 D4
Wenthill Cl EDN/EASTW BN20 ..... 205 H5
Went Hill Pk SEAF BN25 ..... 203 G3
Went La EDN/EASTW BN20 ..... 205 H5
Went Wy EDN/EASTW BN20 ..... 205 H6
Wentworth Cl BEX TN40 ..... 183 M1
 HAIL BN27 ..... 154 F5
Wentworth St ROTT BN2 ..... 7 G8
Wentworth Wy STLEO TN38 ..... 161 M6
Westaway Dr BEXW TN39 ..... 183 G2
West Beeches Rd CROW TN6 ..... 40 A4
Westbourne Gdns HOVE BN3 ..... 168 A8
Westbourne Pl HOVE BN3 ..... 168 A8
Westbourne St HOVE BN3 ..... 168 A7
Westbourne Vls HOVE BN3 ..... 167 M8
Westbrook La RHAS TN35 ..... 139 L1
Westbrook Wy STHW BN42 ..... 166 F7
West Cl POLE BN26 ..... 178 B7
 POLE BN26 ..... 193 M3
West Common HWH RH16 ..... 48 F7
West Common Dr HWH RH16 ..... 49 C7
Westcourt Dr BEXW TN39 ..... 182 F3
Westdean Av NEWHV BN9 ..... 8 B7
West Dean Ri SEAF BN25 ..... 203 G2
Westdene Cl SLVH TN37 ..... 139 J8
Westdene Dr BRI BN1 ..... 168 C1
Westdown La BUR/ETCH TN19 ..... 82 A3
West Down Rd BEXW TN39 ..... 183 L1
Westdown Rd SEAF BN25 ..... 202 D2
West Dr ROTT BN2 ..... 7 H6
West End HAIL BN27 ..... 133 L8
Westergate Rd ROTT BN2 ..... 169 L2
Westerham Rd LGNY BN23 ..... 197 K5
Westerleigh Cl STLEO TN38 ..... 162 A6
Western Av HAWK TN18 ..... 47 M4
 POLE BN26 ..... 178 B8
Western Gdns CROW TN6 ..... 40 D7
Western Rd BEX TN40 ..... 183 J3
 BURH RH15 ..... 96 E3
 CROW TN6 ..... 40 C7
 HAIL BN27 ..... 155 C6
 HAWK TN18 ..... 47 M4
 HWH RH16 ..... 71 M3
 LEW BN7 ..... 2 C6
 LW/ROSE BN22 ..... 11 G3
 NEWHV BN9 ..... 8 E5
 RING/NEW BN8 ..... 74 C7
 RTW TN1 ..... 20 C1
 SLVH TN37 ..... 4 A3
 WADH TN5 ..... 31 M8
Western St BRI BN1 ..... 186 D1
Western Ter HAS TN34 ..... 6 A6
Westfield Av ROTT BN2 ..... 189 K3
Westfield Av North ROTT BN2 ..... 189 K3
Westfield Av South ROTT BN2 ..... 189 K3
Westfield Cl BRI BN1 ..... 169 G2
 MAYF TN20 ..... 56 B8
 POLE BN26 ..... 178 A7
Westfield Cl POLE BN26 ..... 178 A7
Westfield Crs BRI BN1 ..... 169 C1
Westfield La SLVH TN37 ..... 139 L7
Westfield Ri ROTT BN2 ..... 189 K3
Westfield Rd EAST BN21 ..... 196 D8
West Furlong La
 HPPT/KEY BN6 ..... 122 A1
West Ga LEW BN7 ..... 98 E8
Westgate St LEW BN7 ..... 3 G5
Westham Cl BEXW TN39 ..... 182 E3
Westham Dr PEV BN24 ..... 180 F8
West Hl EGRIN RH19 ..... 13 K6
Westhill Dr BURH RH15 ..... 96 E3
West Hill Pl BRI BN1 ..... 6 C4
West Hill Rd BRI BN1 ..... 6 C4
 STLEO TN38 ..... 162 A6
West Hill St BRI BN1 ..... 6 C4
West Hoathly Rd EGRIN RH19 ..... 23 J3
Westlands Rd HWH RH16 ..... 72 B1
West La EGRIN RH19 ..... 13 K6
West Leigh EGRIN RH19 ..... 13 M7
Westmeston Av ROTT BN2 ..... 189 H4
Westminster Cl
 LW/ROSE BN22 ..... 196 D3
Westminster Crs HAS TN34 ..... 163 G2
Westmoreland Cl STLEO TN38.. 161 M3
Westmount Cl STHW BN42 ..... 166 D6
West Pde BEXW TN39 ..... 183 C4
West Park Crs BURH RH15 ..... 96 D2
Westpoint RING/NEW BN8...... 74 C7
West Rd CRBK TN17 ..... 33 M3
 PTSD BN41 ..... 167 J7
West St BRI BN1 ..... 6 D7
 BURH RH15 ..... 96 E1
 EAST BN21 ..... 10 D7
 EGRIN RH19 ..... 13 L6
 HAS TN34 ..... 5 K7
 HPPT/KEY BN6 ..... 123 J3
 LEW BN7 ..... 3 G5
 MAYF TN20 ..... 57 G5
 POLE BN26 ..... 193 M2
 PTSD BN41 ..... 167 J7

ROTT BN2 ..... 188 F5
RYE TN31 ..... 117 J1
SEAF BN25 ..... 202 E4
West Street La HTHF TN21 ..... 105 M4
West Ter EAST BN21 ..... 10 D7
 HAIL BN27 ..... 133 L8
West Undercliff RYE TN31 ..... 117 G1
West Vw HAS TN34 ..... 5 M2
 HWH RH16 ..... 49 H8
West View Gdns EGRIN RH19 ..... 13 L6
Westville Rd BEXW TN39 ..... 183 G2
West Wy HOVE BN3 ..... 167 K4
Westway Cl PTSD BN41 ..... 166 E2
Westway Gdns PTSD BN41 ..... 166 E2
Westwood Rd SBGH/RUST TN4.. 19 H1
Wharf Rd EAST BN21 ..... 10 D6
Whatlington Rd BAT TN33 ..... 111 L8
Whatlington Wy STLEO TN38 ..... 161 K4
Wheatfield Ct SLVH TN37 ..... 162 C1
Wheatfield Wy ROTT BN2 ..... 169 M3
Wheatland Cl PEAHV BN10 ..... 190 B4
Wheatsheaf Cl BURH RH15 ..... 96 E1
Wheatsheaf Gdns LEW BN7 ..... 3 K4
Wheatsheaf La RHWH RH17 ..... 48 A8
Wheelers La UCK TN22 ..... 55 K8
Wheelers Wy EGRIN RH19 ..... 12 E3
Wheel La RHAS TN35 ..... 139 K3
Wheelwright Cl
 LW/ROSE BN22 ..... 196 D2
Wheelwright La BURH RH15 ..... 97 K5
Whichelo Pl ROTT BN2 ..... 7 J4
Whin Croft Pk CROW TN6 ..... 39 M4
Whippingham Rd ROTT BN2 ..... 7 K1
Whippingham St ROTT BN2 ..... 7 K1
Whipping Post La ROTT BN2 ..... 188 F5
White Bear Pas
 SBGH/RUST TN4 ..... 20 A4
White Bread La RYE TN31 ..... 65 K6
Whitecross St BRI BN1 ..... 6 E4
Whitefriars Rd HAIL BN27 ..... 155 K3
Whitegates Cl RING/NEW BN8 ..... 99 K7
Whitegates La WADH TN5 ..... 31 J6
Whitehawk Cl ROTT BN2 ..... 169 L8
Whitehawk Crs ROTT BN2 ..... 187 L1
Whitehawk Hill Rd ROTT BN2 ..... 7 L1
Whitehawk Rd ROTT BN2 ..... 169 L8
Whitehawk Wy ROTT BN2 ..... 169 M8
White Hl LEW BN7 ..... 2 F5
White Hill Av BEXW TN39 ..... 182 E6
Whitehill Cl CROW TN6 ..... 39 M5
White Hill Dr BEXW TN39 ..... 182 E6
Whitehill Rd CROW TN6 ..... 39 M6
Whitehouse Av BEXW TN39 ..... 160 B7
Whitehouse La HTHF TN21 ..... 105 G3
Whitelot Cl STHW BN42 ..... 166 E5
Whitelot Wy STHW BN42 ..... 166 E4
White Rock Gdns HAS TN34 ..... 4 F7
Whiterock Pl STHW BN42 ..... 166 E4
White Rock Rd SLVH TN37 ..... 4 E8
White's Cl HPPT/KEY BN6 ..... 96 A7
White St ROTT BN2 ..... 7 G7
Whitethorn Dr BRI BN1 ..... 168 B2
White Wy LEW BN7 ..... 172 B5
 POLE BN26 ..... 193 M5
Whiteway Cl SEAF BN25 ..... 192 E8
Whiteway La ROTT BN2 ..... 189 G4
Whitfeld La RING/NEW BN8 ..... 126 C8
Whitley Rd LW/ROSE BN22 ..... 11 H3
Whittingehame Gdns BRI BN1 ..... 168 F3
Whittington's Wy HAS TN34 ..... 163 H2
Whittlewood Cl STLEO TN38 ..... 161 L4
Whybourne Crest
 RTWE/PEM TN2 ..... 20 D5
Whydown Hl BAT TN33 ..... 112 E8
Whydown Rd BEXW TN39 ..... 159 H6
The Wickets BURH RH15 ..... 96 F1
Wickham Av BEXW TN39 ..... 183 H3
Wickham Cl HWH RH16 ..... 48 E7
Wickham Dr HPPT/KEY BN6 ..... 122 B1
Wickham Gdns SBGH/RUST TN4 .. 19 K1
Wickham Hl HPPT/KEY BN6... 122 C2
Wickham La RING/NEW BN8 ..... 125 L4
Wickham Rock La WSEA TN36 ..... 142 D1
Wickham Wy HWH RH16 ..... 48 E7
Wickhurst Cl PTSD BN41 ..... 166 F3
Wickhurst Ri PTSD BN41 ..... 166 F3
Wickhurst Rd PTSD BN41...... 166 F4
Wicklands Av ROTT BN2 ..... 189 K5
Wick St RING/NEW BN8 ..... 174 C1
Widbury Cl RRTW TN3 ..... 18 F3
Widdicombe Wy ROTT BN2 ..... 169 L3
Wigmore Cl BRI BN1 ..... 169 H5
Wilbury Av HOVE BN3 ..... 168 C6
Wilbury Crs HOVE BN3 ..... 168 D7
Wilbury Gdns HOVE BN3 ..... 168 C6
Wilbury Gv HOVE BN3 ..... 168 C8
Wilbury Rd HOVE BN3 ..... 168 C7
Wilbury Vls HOVE BN3 ..... 168 C7
Wilby Av STHW BN42 ..... 166 E5
Wilderness Gdns RYE TN31 ..... 65 C7
Wilderness La UCK TN22 ..... 78 C2
Wilderness Pk CROW TN6 ..... 39 L4
Wilderness Ri EGRIN RH19 ..... 14 A1
Wilderness Rd HPPT/KEY BN6 ..... 96 A6
The Wilderness HWH RH16 ..... 49 H6
Wilderwick Rd EGRIN RH19 ..... 14 A1
Wild Park Cl ROTT BN2 ..... 169 L3
Wildwood Cl LGNY BN23 ..... 197 J2
Wilfrid Rd HOVE BN3 ..... 167 K6
Wilkinson Cl ROTT BN2 ..... 188 F3
Wilkinson Wy SEAF BN25 ..... 202 E2
Wilkins Wy BEX TN40 ..... 160 F8
Willard Cl LW/ROSE BN22 ..... 197 G3
Willetts Fld RING/NEW BN8 ..... 100 D5
Willetts La RRTW TN3 ..... 17 J2
William Allen La HWH RH16 ..... 49 H8
 HWH RH16 ..... 72 B1
William Rd STLEO TN38....... 161 L7
William Sandys Rd SHOR BN43 ..... 166 B6
William St PTSD BN41 ..... 167 H7
 ROTT BN2 ..... 7 F6
 SBGH/RUST TN4 ..... 20 A4
Willingdon Av BEXW TN39 ..... 159 H8
 STLEO TN38 ..... 162 A1
Willingdon Cl
 EDN/EASTW BN20 ..... 196 B5

STLEO TN38 ..... 162 A1
Willingdon Ct
 EDN/EASTW BN20 ..... 196 A3
Willingdon Dro LGNY BN23 ..... 197 H5
 LW/ROSE BN22 ..... 197 G5
Willingdon La POLE BN26 ..... 195 J7
Willingdon Park Dr
 LW/ROSE BN22 ..... 196 D4
Willingdon Rd EAST BN21 ..... 196 C5
 EAST BN21 ..... 206 D2
 LW/ROSE BN22 ..... 196 C5
 ROTT BN2 ..... 169 L5
Willingdon Wy
 LW/ROSE BN22 ..... 196 B4
 STLEO TN38 ..... 162 A1
Willingford La
 BUR/ETCH TN19 ..... 82 C4
Willoughby Crs
 EAST BN21 ..... 197 J8
Willow Av HAIL BN27 ..... 155 H5
Willow Bank RBTBR TN32 ..... 85 H3
Willowbed Wk HAS TN34 ..... 162 E1
Willowbrook Wy
 HPPT/KEY BN6 ..... 123 G3
Willow Cl BUR/ETCH TN19 ..... 61 H6
 EGRIN RH19 ..... 13 K3
 HTHF TN21 ..... 80 B6
 ROTT BN2 ..... 170 E6
Willow Dr BEXW TN39 ..... 182 C1
 POLE BN26 ..... 196 A1
 SEAF BN25 ..... 203 J3
Willow End HAS TN34 ..... 162 F2
Willowfield Rd LW/ROSE BN22 ..... 11 H5
Willowfield Sq LW/ROSE BN22 ..... 11 H5
Willow La WSEA TN36 ..... 117 H8
Willowmead CROW TN6 ..... 39 L6
Willow Md EGRIN RH19 ..... 13 M6
Willow Ms RBTBR TN32 ..... 85 H3
Willow Pk HWH RH16 ..... 72 B2
Willow Rdg CRAWE RH10 ..... 22 A3
Willows Ri UCK TN22 ..... 103 H1
The Willows BURH RH15 ..... 97 H1
 RING/NEW BN8 ..... 126 E1
Willow Stream Cl RHAS TN35 ..... 140 E3
Willow Tree Rd RTWE/PEM TN2 ..... 19 L5
Willow Wk NEWHV BN9 ..... 8 E2
Willow Wy HPPT/KEY BN6 ..... 96 A6
Wilmington Cl BRI BN1 ..... 169 G1
 HPPT/KEY BN6 ..... 122 F2
Wilmington Pde BRI BN1 ..... 168 F1
Wilmington Rd HAS TN34 ..... 163 G3
 NEWHV BN9 ..... 8 C6
 SEAF BN25 ..... 202 D2
Wilmington Sq EAST BN21 ..... 10 E9
Wilmington St POLE BN26 ..... 194 F1
Wilmington Wy BRI BN1 ..... 168 F1
 HWH RH16 ..... 72 A1
Wilmot Rd SHOR BN43 ..... 166 C6
Wilson Av ROTT BN2 ..... 187 M2
Wilson Gv UCK TN22 ..... 76 A7
Wilton Av LW/ROSE BN22 ..... 196 F3
Wilton Rd BEX TN40 ..... 183 J3
Winceby Cl BEXW TN39 ..... 182 E4
Winchcombe Rd
 LW/ROSE BN22 ..... 10 F4
Winchelsea Cl SEAF BN25 ..... 203 J1
Winchelsea La RHAS TN35 ..... 163 L1
 RYE TN31 ..... 115 M4
Winchelsea Rd LW/ROSE BN22 ..... 197 K8
 RHAS TN35 ..... 140 F8
 RYE TN31 ..... 91 H1
 RYE TN31 ..... 117 H1
Winchester St BRI BN1 ..... 6 E1
Winchester Wy
 LW/ROSE BN22 ..... 196 B4
Wincombe Rd BRI BN1 ..... 168 D5
Windermere Crs
 LW/ROSE BN22 ..... 11 J1
Windermere Rd HWH RH16 ..... 71 M1
Winding St HAS TN34 ..... 5 K6
Windlesham Av HOVE BN3 ..... 6 A4
Windlesham Cl PTSD BN41 ..... 167 G5
Windlesham Gdns BRI BN1 ..... 6 A4
Windlesham Rd BRI BN1 ..... 6 A4
Windmill Av HPPT/KEY BN6... 122 F3
Windmill Cl EAST BN21 ..... 196 C8
 HOVE BN3 ..... 167 M4
 HTHF TN21 ..... 80 B6
Windmill Dr BRI BN1 ..... 145 J8
 BURH RH15 ..... 97 G2
Windmill Gn PEV BN24 ..... 197 H1
Windmill La EDN/EASTW BN20 ..... 205 C5
 EGRIN RH19 ..... 13 K3
 EGRIN RH19 ..... 14 C7
 WADH TN5 ..... 32 C3
 WADH TN5 ..... 43 K2
Windmill Pl POLE BN26....... 196 A1
Windmill Rd POLE BN26 ..... 196 A1
 STHW BN42 ..... 166 E5
 STLEO TN38 ..... 162 B4
Windmill St ROTT BN2 ..... 7 H6
 RTWE/PEM TN2 ..... 20 C3
Windmill Ter ROTT BN2 ..... 7 H5
Windmill Vw BRI BN1 ..... 146 A8
Windmill Wy WSEA TN36 ..... 117 H7
Windover Crs LEW BN7 ..... 2 A4
Windover Wy LW/ROSE BN22 ..... 196 B3
Windsor Cl HOVE BN3........ 168 A3
 HWH RH16 ..... 71 M1
 SEAF BN25 ..... 192 B8
Windsor Dr CROW TN6 ..... 40 C5
Windsor Pl CROW TN6 ..... 40 C6
 EGRIN RH19 ..... 14 A6
Windsor Rd BEXW TN39 ..... 183 H2
 CROW TN6 ..... 40 C6
 HAIL BN27 ..... 155 H8
 SLVH TN37 ..... 162 B3
Windsor St BRI BN1 ..... 6 D6
Windsor Wy POLE BN26 ..... 178 A4
 WSEA TN36 ..... 143 G2
Windward Quay LGNY BN23 ..... 197 M6
Wineham Wy BEX TN40 ..... 183 M2
Winfield Av BRI BN1 ..... 145 M8
Winfield Cl BRI BN1 ..... 167 F1
 PTSD BN41 ..... 167 G2
Wingate Cl STLEO TN38 ..... 162 A5
Wingle Tye Rd BURH RH15... 97 G6
Winkhurst Wy BURH RH15 ..... 97 K5
Winkney Rd LW/ROSE BN22 ..... 196 F3

Winscote Cl CROW TN6 ..... 39 K5
Winston Crs LGNY BN23 ..... 197 K7
Winston Dr BEXW TN39 ..... 182 E2
Winstone Scott Av RRTW TN3 ..... 18 E2
Winterbourne Cl HAS TN34 ..... 4 D5
 LEW BN7 ..... 2 B8
Winterbourne Hollow LEW BN7 ..... 2 B8
 LEW BN7 ..... 2 B8
 LEW BN7 ..... 2 C8
Winterton Wy SHOR BN43 ..... 166 B8
Winton Av ROTT BN2 ..... 189 J4
Winton St POLE BN26 ..... 193 M2
Wisden Av BURH RH15 ..... 96 E1
Wiseacre RRTW TN3 ..... 33 G3
Wish Hl EDN/EASTW BN20 ..... 196 B5
Wishing Tree Cl STLEO TN38 ..... 161 M4
Wishing Tree La STLEO TN38 ..... 161 M4
Wishing Tree Rd STLEO TN38 ..... 161 M4
Wishing Tree Rd North
 STLEO TN38 ..... 162 A2
Wish Rd EAST BN21 ..... 10 E7
 HOVE BN3 ..... 167 H8
Wish Ward RYE TN31 ..... 117 H1
Withdean Av BRI BN1 ..... 168 D4
Withdean Cl BRI BN1 ..... 168 D3
Withdean Court Av BRI BN1 ..... 168 D3
Withdean Crs BRI BN1 ..... 168 D3
Withdean Ri BRI BN1 ..... 168 D3
Withdean Rd BRI BN1 ..... 168 D4
Witherenden Rd MAYF TN20 ..... 57 L5
Withy Bush BURH RH15 ..... 96 E2
 BURH RH15 ..... 96 E1
Withyham Av ROTT BN2 ..... 189 J6
Withyham Cl LW/ROSE BN22 ..... 196 F5
Withyham Rd BEXW TN39 ..... 182 C4
 RRTW TN3 ..... 18 A2
Withypitts CRAWE RH10 ..... 22 A3
Withypitts East CRAWE RH10 ..... 22 A3
Wittersham La RYE TN31 ..... 91 H1
Wittersham Rd CRBK TN17 ..... 66 D2
 RYE TN31 ..... 68 A6
 RYE TN31 ..... 91 H1
 TENT TN30 ..... 67 H1
Wivelsfield Rd HWH RH16 ..... 71 L4
 ROTT BN2 ..... 189 J3
Woburn Cl HAIL BN27 ..... 155 C5
Woburn Pl BRI BN1 ..... 169 M1
 LW/ROSE BN22 ..... 196 D3
Wode Rd BAT TN33 ..... 159 C3
Wolfe Cl CROW TN6 ..... 40 A6
Wolseley Rd BRI BN1 ..... 146 D8
 PTSD BN41 ..... 167 G6
Wolstonbury Rd HOVE BN3... 6 A2
Wolstonbury Wy BURH RH15 ..... 97 G4
Wolverstone Dr BRI BN1 ..... 169 J4
Woodbourne Av BRI BN1 ..... 169 F2
Woodbrook Rd HAS TN34 ..... 162 F3
Woodbury Av EGRIN RH19 ..... 14 B6
Woodbury Cl EGRIN RH19 ..... 14 B6
Woodbury Park Gdns
 SBGH/RUST TN4 ..... 20 B1
Woodbury Park Rd
 SBGH/RUST TN4 ..... 20 A1
Woodcombe HAS TN34 ..... 162 F2
Woodcote Rd FROW RH18 ..... 24 E4
Woodcrest Rd BURH RH15 ..... 96 F5
Woodcroft BURH RH15 ..... 96 F1
Woodcroft Dr EAST BN21 ..... 196 C7
Woodgate Meadow LEW BN7 ..... 98 E7
Woodgate Rd LW/ROSE BN22 ..... 11 H1
Woodhams Cl BAT TN33 ..... 137 K2
Woodhouse Rd HOVE BN3.... 167 L7
Woodland Av BURH RH15 ..... 97 J2
 HOVE BN3 ..... 168 B2
 LW/ROSE BN22 ..... 196 C6
Woodland Cl BURH RH15 ..... 97 J2
 HOVE BN3 ..... 168 B4
Woodland Dr CRAWE RH10 ..... 12 B6
 HOVE BN3 ..... 168 B3
Woodland Ms HTHF TN21 ..... 80 B8
Woodland Ri BEX TN40 ..... 183 L2
 HOVE BN3 ..... 168 C4
Woodlands CRAWE RH10 ..... 12 B7
 HAIL BN27 ..... 155 J4
 HPPT/KEY BN6 ..... 122 F2
 HTHF TN21 ..... 106 B1
 PEAHV BN10 ..... 190 B5
 UCK TN22 ..... 76 D6
Woodlands Rd EGRIN RH19 ..... 14 A2
 HPPT/KEY BN6 ..... 122 F2
 HWH RH16 ..... 71 M2
The Woodlands BRI BN1 ..... 168 E1
 HAS TN34 ..... 162 E1
Woodlands Vale Rd STLEO TN38 ..... 4 A5
Woodland Vw TENT TN30 ..... 67 L2
Woodland Wk BURH RH15 ..... 188 D2
Woodland Wy BAT TN33 ..... 160 F2
 BRI BN1 ..... 168 F2
 CROW TN6 ..... 39 M6
 HTHF TN21 ..... 80 B8
 RHAS TN35 ..... 164 E1
Woodpecker Crs
 HPPT/KEY BN6 ..... 96 D3
Woodpecker Dr HAIL BN27 ..... 155 G6
Woodpecker Rd LGNY BN23 ..... 197 H4
Woodpecker Wy UCK TN22 ..... 102 D1
Wood Ride HWH RH16 ..... 71 K3
Woodridge Cl HWH RH16 ..... 72 A3
Woodruff Av HOVE BN3 ..... 168 C4
Woodsgate Av BEX TN40 ..... 160 C8
Woodsgate Pk BEXW TN39 ..... 160 A8
Woods Hill Cl EGRIN RH19 ..... 14 D8
Woods Hill La EGRIN RH19 ..... 14 D8
Woodside CROW TN6 ..... 39 L4
Woodside Av BRI BN1 ..... 168 D4
Woodside Rd SBGH/RUST TN4 ..... 19 K2
Woodside Wy HAIL BN27 ..... 178 A2
Woodspring Cl SLVH TN37 ..... 162 B1
Woodstock EGRIN RH19 ..... 13 J4
Woodstock Rd BEXW TN39 ..... 159 J8
Wood St EGRIN RH19 ..... 13 K5
 RTW TN1 ..... 20 B2

Woodview Cl BRI BN1 ..... 146 D8
Woodville Rd BEXW TN39 ..... 183 H3
Woodward Cl LGNY BN23 ..... 197 L7
Woodwards Cl BURH RH15 ..... 97 H5
Woolven Cl BURH RH15 ..... 96 E5
Worcester Vls HOVE BN3 ..... 167 J7
Wordsworth Dr LGNY BN23 ..... 197 L4
Wordsworth St HOVE BN3 ..... 168 A7
Workhouse La WSEA TN36 ..... 141 M1
Worsham La BEX TN40 ..... 160 F7
Worsted La EGRIN RH19 ..... 14 B7
Wray Cl EGRIN RH19 ..... 14 D8
Wren Cl HTHF TN21 ..... 80 A7
Wren Ct BAT TN33 ..... 137 M2
 STLEO TN38 ..... 161 L3
Wrestwood Av LW/ROSE BN22 ..... 196 C5
Wrestwood Rd BEX TN40 ..... 160 D8
Wrotham Cl HAS TN34 ..... 162 E1
 LGNY BN23 ..... 197 K5
Wroxham Rd LGNY BN23 ..... 197 H2
Wyatts La RHWH RH17 ..... 50 D1
Wyberlye Rd BURH RH15 ..... 97 G2
Wychperry Rd HWH RH16 ..... 71 K1
Wychurst Gdns BEX TN40 ..... 160 D8
Wykeham Rd HAS TN34 ..... 4 E4
Wykeham Wy BURH RH15 ..... 97 J4
Wyndham St ROTT BN2 ..... 7 H8
Wynlea Cl CRAWE RH10 ..... 12 A6
Wynnes Ms HOVE BN3 ..... 168 A7
The Wyshe POY/PYE BN45 ..... 122 C8
Wythwood HWH RH16 ..... 71 L5

Y

Yardley St BRI BN1 ..... 6 E1
Yates Cl RYE TN31 ..... 119 G4
Yeomans RING/NEW BN8 ..... 128 A7
Yew La EGRIN RH19 ..... 13 H3
Yew Tree Cl HAS TN34 ..... 139 L8
 HTHF TN21 ..... 80 A8
 RING/NEW BN8 ..... 127 M7
Yewtree La CROW TN6 ..... 39 M6
Yielding's Cl EAST BN21 ..... 206 D1
York Av EGRIN RH19 ..... 14 A6
 HOVE BN3 ..... 6 A4
York Gdns HAS TN34 ..... 5 C7
York Gv BRI BN1 ..... 6 F4
York Hl BRI BN1 ..... 6 F4
York Pl BRI BN1 ..... 6 F4
York Rd BEX TN40 ..... 184 A1
 EAST BN21 ..... 10 D7
 HOVE BN3 ..... 6 A4
 PEAHV BN10 ..... 190 E8
 RTW TN1 ..... 20 A2
 SLVH TN37 ..... 4 A2
York Vls BRI BN1 ..... 6 C2
Youngsmere Cl BRI BN1 ..... 146 B8

Abbotsford School
BURH RH15...........................70 F8

A B C Cinema
HAS TN34.............................5 G7

A B C Cinema
RTW TN1.............................20 A3

Adur District Council
STHW BN42.......................166 E7

Aids Positive
Underground Theatre
ROTT BN2.............................7 J7

Albion Doctors Surgery
ROTT BN2.............................7 G4

Aldrington House Hospital
HOVE BN3........................167 M8

Alfriston County
Primary School
POLE BN26.......................193 M3

The Alfriston Gallery
POLE BN26.......................194 A3

All Saints Hospital
EDN/EASTW BN20............206 E7

All Saints Infant School
BEXW TN39.......................160 B7

All Saints Junior School
RHAS TN35.......................163 J4

Alwin Gallery
SBGH/RUST TN4................20 A4

Amberstone Hospital
HAIL BN27........................132 D8

Amberstone Hospital
HAIL BN27........................155 L2

Ambulance Station
LW/ROSE BN22...................10 F4

The Arden Foot & Health Clinic
ROTT BN2.............................6 F7

Arndale Shopping Centre
EAST BN21.........................10 E6

Art Gallery
BRI BN1...............................6 E5

Arthur Blackman Clinic
SLVH TN37.......................162 B2

Ashdown Forest Health Centre
FROW RH18.......................24 E3

The Ashdown Hospital
HWH RH16.........................48 D8

Ashwyn Business Centre
BURH RH15.......................97 G1

Assembly Hall Theatre
RTWE/PEM TN2..................20 B3

The Audrey Wickens
School of Music
EAST BN21.........................10 A5

The Avenue Surgery
BURH RH15.......................96 F4

Bad Apple Theatre Co
RTW TN1.............................20 C2

Baldwins Hill CP School
EGRIN RH19.......................13 J3

Balfour Junior School
BRI BN1...........................169 G3

Bandstand
EAST BN21.........................11 G8

Barclays Business Centre
HTHF TN21.........................80 A6

Barcombe Primary School
RING/NEW BN8.................126 D1

Bartholomews Tutorial College
BRI BN1...............................6 E7

Barton School
STLEO TN38.....................162 B5

Battle Abbey
Preparatory School
BEX TN40........................183 L1

Battle Abbey School
BAT TN33........................137 K2

Battle Hospital
BAT TN33........................137 G2

Battle & Langton School
BAT TN33........................137 J2

Battle Museum
BAT TN33........................137 K2

Beacon Community College
CROW TN6.........................40 A4

Beacon Community College
CROW TN6.........................40 B3

Beckley Gallery
RYE TN31...........................89 J2

Beckley School
RYE TN31...........................89 G2

Beeching Park Industrial Estate
BEXW TN39.....................183 H2

Bellerbys College
HOVE BN3........................168 C7

Bellerbys College Mayfield
WADH TN5.........................43 J2

Bell Tower Industrial Estate
ROTT BN2........................187 M2

Belmont Surgery
WADH TN5.........................44 A2

Benfield County Junior School
PTSD BN41.......................167 J6

Benfield Valley Golf Course
PTSD BN41.......................167 J3

Bentley Wildfowl &
Motor Museum
RING/NEW BN8.................128 F2

Bethany House Surgery
HAIL BN27........................155 J5

Bevendean County
Primary School
ROTT BN2........................169 M5

Bexhill Amateur Athletic Club
BEXW TN39.....................183 H1

Bexhill C of E Primary
Junior School
BEX TN40........................183 J2

Bexhill College
BEXW TN39.....................160 A7

Bexhill Costume Museum
BEX TN40........................183 K2

Bexhill High School
BEXW TN39.....................183 H1

Bexhill Hospital
BEX TN40........................160 C8

Bexhill Leisure Centre
BEXW TN39.....................183 H1

Bexhill Sailing Club
BEX TN40........................183 K3

Bexhill Squash Rackets Club
BEX TN40........................183 L2

The Birman Gallery
HWH RH16.........................49 H6

The Bishop Bell C of E School
LGNY BN23......................197 L5

Bishops Down CP School
SBGH/RUST TN4................19 L1

Blackboys C of E School
UCK TN22..........................78 A8

Blackwell CP School
EGRIN RH19.......................13 L3

Blatchington Mill School
HOVE BN3........................168 A5

Bodiam Castle (Nt)
RBTBR TN32......................63 M6

Bodiam Manor School
RBTBR TN32......................63 L6

Bodiam Primary School
RBTBR TN32......................63 L6

Boltons Clinic
MAYF TN20.......................56 B8

Boltons Clinic
STLEO TN38....................162 B5

Booth Museum of
Natural History
BRI BN1.........................168 E6

Bourne County Primary School
LW/ROSE BN22.................11 G4

Bowden House School
SEAF BN25......................202 E2

Brambletye School
EGRIN RH19.......................24 C1

Braybon Business Park
BURH RH15........................96 E4

Brede County Primary School
RYE TN31........................114 B2

Bridge Road Business Park
HWH RH16.........................48 E7

Brighton Business Centre
BRI BN1...............................6 F2

Brighton Business Centre
BRI BN1...........................168 F6

The Brighton Centre
BRI BN1...............................6 C7

Brighton College
ROTT BN2...........................7 K7

Brighton College of Technology
BRI BN1...............................6 F4

Brighton College of Technology
HOVE BN3........................167 L6

Brighton College of Technology
HOVE BN3........................168 B8

Brighton College of Technology
ROTT BN2...........................7 G3

Brighton County Court
ROTT BN2...........................6 F6

Brighton Fishing Museum
BRI BN1...............................6 D8

Brighton Framing Gallery
ROTT BN2...........................7 K8

Brighton General Hospital
ROTT BN2...........................7 M3

Brighton & Hove Council
BRI BN1...............................6 F3

Brighton & Hove Council
BRI BN1...........................146 B8

Brighton & Hove Council
HOVE BN3........................167 M5

Brighton & Hove Council
HOVE BN3........................168 B7

Brighton & Hove Council
HOVE BN3........................168 C8

Brighton & Hove Council
PTSD BN41.......................167 J6

Brighton & Hove Council
PTSD BN41.......................167 G5

Brighton & Hove Council
ROTT BN2...........................7 K2

Brighton & Hove Council
ROTT BN2........................169 L3

Brighton & Hove Girls
Day School
BRI BN1...............................6 A5

Brighton & Hove Golf Course
HOVE BN3........................144 E8

Brighton & Hove High Schools
BRI BN1...............................6 A4

Brighton & Hove Islamic
Centre & Mosque
HOVE BN3...........................6 B2

Brighton & Hove Progressive
Synagogue
HOVE BN3........................168 D8

Brighton Hove &
Sussex Sixth Form College
HOVE BN3...........................6 B1

Brighton Library & Museum
BRI BN1...............................6 E6

Brighton Media Centre
BRI BN1...............................6 D7

Brighton Municipal Market
ROTT BN2...........................6 F5

Brighton Racecourse
ROTT BN2........................170 A6

Brighton Rugby Club
BRI BN1...........................145 H8

Brighton Technical College
BRI BN1...............................6 D1

Brighton Youth Centre
ROTT BN2...........................7 H7

Broad Oak Primary School
HTHF TN21.........................80 F4

Broadwater CP School
RTWE/PEM TN2..................19 M6

Broadway Surgery
ROTT BN2........................187 M2

The Brook Health Centre
CROW TN6.........................40 C5

Broomham School
RHAS TN35......................141 G3

Bross Estate
HWH RH16...........................9 H1

Buchanan Hospital
STLEO TN38....................162 B5

Buckingham Middle School
SHOR BN43......................166 A6

Burfield Park Industrial Estate
HAIL BN27........................155 G6

Burgess Hill Clinic
BURH RH15........................96 F3

Burgess Hill School
BURH RH15........................97 H4

Burgess Hill Town Football Club
BURH RH15........................97 H1

Burrswood Medical Centre
RRTW TN3.........................18 A6

Burwash School
BUR/ETCH TN19................60 B8

Buxted C of E Primary School
UCK TN22..........................76 F3

Camber Castle
RYE TN31.........................117 J4

Cambridge Gardens College
HAS TN34............................4 F7

The Cameron Practice
EAST BN21.........................10 F8

Campion Gallery
RYE TN31.........................117 H1

Cardinal Newman School
HOVE BN3........................168 D6

Carlton Hill CP School
ROTT BN2...........................7 G6

Castledean School
BRI BN1...........................169 H4

Castletown County
Primary School
HAS TN34............................5 K3

Catsfield C of E Primary School
BAT TN33........................136 E6

Causeway Secondary School
LW/ROSE BN22................197 G3

The Cavendish School
EAST BN21......................206 D1

Centenary Industrial Estate
BRI BN1...........................169 H5

The Central Hove Surgery
HOVE BN3........................168 B8

Central Library
EAST BN21.........................10 C6

Chailey Comprehensive School
RING/NEW BN8...................99 K7

Chailey Heritage
Clinical Services
RING/NEW BN8...................73 J7

Chailey Heritage School
RING/NEW BN8...................73 J7

Chantry CP School
BEX TN40........................183 J1

Charlwoods Industrial Estate
EGRIN RH19.......................13 L3

Charter Medical Centre
HOVE BN3........................168 D7

Charters Ancaster School
BEX TN40........................183 L1

Chaucer Industrial Estate
POLE BN26.......................178 D8

Chiddingly CP School
RING/NEW BN8.................130 E6

Chiddingly Cricket Club
RING/NEW BN8.................130 E5

Child Clinic
ROTT BN2...........................6 F6

Churchfields Industrial Estate
STLEO TN38....................161 K2

Churchill Square
Shopping Centre
BRI BN1...............................6 C7

Church of England School
RHWH RH17.......................51 H2

Church Surgery
ROTT BN2........................169 J5

Churchwood Primary School
STLEO TN38....................161 M3

Churchwood Surgery
STLEO TN38....................161 M2

Cinema
EAST BN21.........................10 F6

Cinque Ports Surgery
RYE TN31...........................91 H8

Circe Health & Beauty Clinic
UCK TN22..........................76 C7

Civic Centre
SHOR BN43......................166 A7

Clairmonte Galleries
BRI BN1...............................6 E6

Clanricarde Medical Centre
RTW TN1...........................20 A3

Claremont CP School
RTWE/PEM TN2..................20 B4

Claverham Community College
BAT TN33........................137 G2

Clermont C P U School
BRI BN1...........................168 E4

Cliffe Business Centre
LEW BN7.............................3 J6

Cliffe Industrial Estate
LEW BN7.............................3 L8

Club House
EDN/EASTW BN20............206 A4

Cofe Primary School
MAYF TN20.......................57 H3

Coghurst Hall County Primary
RHAS TN35......................140 C6

Coldean Junior & Infant School
BRI BN1...........................146 D8

Community Mental
Health Centre
BURH RH15........................97 G2

The Congress Theatre
EAST BN21.........................10 E9

Conquest Hospital
HAS TN34........................139 K8

Conway Court Clinic
HOVE BN3........................168 B6

Cooden Beech Golf Club
BEXW TN39.....................182 B4

Coombe Road County
Primary School
ROTT BN2........................169 K5

The Corner Gallery
HWH RH16.........................49 H6

Cornerstones Independent School
HOVE BN3........................168 D8

Corn Exchange Theatre
BRI BN1...............................6 E6

The Cottage Clinic
BEX TN40........................183 J3

Cottage Surgery
PEAHV BN10....................190 C8

Cottesmore St Marys RC Primary
School
HOVE BN3........................168 D6

Count Primary School
BURH RH15........................97 J5

County Hall
LEW BN7.............................3 H5

County Middle School
STHW BN42......................166 F6

County Primary School
BRI BN1...........................169 H4

County Primary School
RING/NEW BN8.................129 J8

Court Meadow School
RHWH RH17.......................48 A6

Cradle Hill CP School
SEAF BN25......................203 G1

The Craftsman Gallery
HPPT/KEY BN6.................123 K3

Crawley Down C of E
Infant School
CRAWE RH10....................12 B6

Crawley Down C of E School
CRAWE RH10....................12 B6

Crawley Down Health Centre
CRAWE RH10....................12 A6

Cross In Hand C of E
Primary School
HTHF TN21.........................79 M7

Crowborough Beacon Golf Club
CROW TN6.........................39 K6

Crowborough War
Memorial Hospital
CROW TN6.........................39 L5

Crowhurst School
BAT TN33........................160 F1

Crown Court
HOVE BN3........................168 D8

Crown Prosecution Service
EAST BN21.........................10 E4

Cumnor House School
RHWH RH17.......................51 H1

The Cyril Richings Business
Centre
SHOR BN43......................166 A7

Dale Hill Hotel & Golf Club
WADH TN5.........................45 M5

Dallington School
HTHF TN21.......................108 D3

Davigdor County Infants School
HOVE BN3........................168 D7

Denton County Primary School
NEWHV BN9.....................191 L1

Devonshire Park Cricket Ground
EAST BN21.........................10 E9

Devonshire Park Theatre
EAST BN21.........................10 E9

Ditchling Gallery
HPPT/KEY BN6.................123 J3

Ditchling Health Centre
HPPT/KEY BN6.................123 K3

Ditchling Museum
HPPT/KEY BN6.................123 J3

Ditchling Primary School
HPPT/KEY BN6.................123 K3

Dolphin House Clinic for Adults
BRI BN1...............................6 E6

Dolphin Leisure Centre
HWH RH16.........................48 D8

Douglas Moat Practice
SBGH/RUST TN4................20 A4

Downland Medical Centre
POLE BN26.......................178 A8

Downlands School
HPPT/KEY BN6.................122 F3

Downs County First School
BRI BN1...........................169 G6

Downs Junior School
BRI BN1...........................169 G5

Downs Leisure Centre
SEAF BN25......................203 G2

Downs Park School
PTSD BN41.......................167 H4

Downs Special School
EDN/EASTW BN20............206 B2

Downs View School
ROTT BN2........................170 C6

The Dr Jan De Winter Clinic for
Cancer Prevention Advice
BRI BN1...............................6 E6

Drusillas Zoo Park
POLE BN26.......................176 B8

DSS
EAST BN21.........................10 D5

DSS
ROTT BN2...........................7 G2

Dudley Infants School
RHAS TN35..........................5 M3

Dunnings Squash Club
EGRIN RH19.......................13 L8

Durgates Industrial Estate
WADH TN5.........................43 L1

The Eastbourne Clinic
EDN/EASTW BN20............10 C8

Eastbourne College
EAST BN21.........................10 D8

Eastbourne College
EDN/EASTW BN20............10 C8

Eastbourne College of Arts &
Technology
EAST BN21......................196 E2

Eastbourne County Court
EAST BN21.........................10 C5

Eastbourne District
General Hospital
EAST BN21......................196 E2

Eastbourne Downs Golf Club
EDN/EASTW BN20............206 A4

Eastbourne & Hailsham
Magistrates Court
EAST BN21.........................10 C7

Eastbourne Health Authority
EAST BN21.........................10 E3

Eastbourne Hospitals N H S Trust
EAST BN21.........................10 E4

Eastbourne Pier
LW/ROSE BN22.................11 H7

Eastbourne Rugby Football Club
LW/ROSE BN22...............196 D6

Eastbourne Saffrons Sports Club
EAST BN21.........................10 B8

Eastbourne Sovereign
Sailing Club Ltd
LW/ROSE BN22.................11 L3

Eastbourne United Football Club
LW/ROSE BN22.................11 L1

East Court
EGRIN RH19.......................13 M4

East Grinstead Health Clinic
EGRIN RH19.......................13 L4

East Grinstead Sports Club
EGRIN RH19.......................23 J1

East Hoathly C of E School
RING/NEW BN8.................129 M1

East Hoathly Surgery
RING/NEW BN8.................130 A1

East Sussex Brighton &
Hove Health Auth
LEW BN7.............................3 H4

East Sussex County Council
BRI BN1...............................6 E6

East Sussex County Council
HOVE BN3........................167 L3

East Sussex County Council
HTHF TN21.........................80 C6

East Sussex County Council
LEW BN7.............................2 D6

East Sussex County Council
LEW BN7.............................3 H4

East Sussex County Council
LEW BN7.............................3 J9

East Sussex County Council
NEWHV BN9........................8 E4

East Sussex County Council
NEWHV BN9........................8 F3

East Sussex County Council
PEAHV BN10....................190 E8

East Sussex County Council
PEAHV BN10....................190 C7

East Sussex County Council
POLE BN26.......................178 A8

East Sussex County Council
ROTT BN2........................169 L8

East Sussex County Council
SEAF BN25......................202 E3

East Sussex County
Music School
LEW BN7.............................2 F7

East Sussex Health Authority
NEWHV BN9........................9 G2

East Sussex National Golf Club
UCK TN22........................102 D6

Eaton Place Surgery
ROTT BN2...........................7 M9

E F International School of
English
SLVH TN37..........................4 B7

Elm Grove CP School
ROTT BN2...........................7 K2

Elphinstone Junior School
HAS TN34............................5 J1

Emerson College
FROW RH18.......................25 H3

Enterprise Shopping Centre
EAST BN21.........................10 D6

Escotts County Primary School
EGRIN RH19.......................14 A5

Esperance Private Hospital
EAST BN21.........................10 F8

Etchingham C of E
Primary School
BUR/ETCH TN19................61 K4

Eversfield Hospital
STLEO TN38....................162 A8

Evolution Health Centre
BRI BN1...............................6 B5

Fairfax Gallery
RTW TN1...........................20 A4

Fairfield Surgery
BUR/ETCH TN19................60 A8

Fairlight County Primary School
ROTT BN2...........................7 J1

Faques Gallery
ROTT BN2...........................7 J8

Felbridge CP School
EGRIN RH19.......................12 F2

Felix Gallery
LEW BN7.............................3 G5

Fermor School
CROW TN6.........................40 A4

Ferryfield Industrial Estate
NEWHV BN9........................9 J4

Filching Manor
POLE BN26.......................195 K4

Filsham Valley
Secondary School
STLEO TN38....................161 M7

Firle C of E School
RING/NEW BN8.................174 A2

Firle Place
RING/NEW BN8.................174 C3

The Firs Surgery
HTHF TN21.........................79 L6

The Fishermans Museum
HAS TN34............................5 M7

Fishersgate First School
PTSD BN41.......................167 G8

Five Ashes Primary School
MAYF TN20.......................56 B8

Fletching C of E School
UCK TN22..........................74 F3

The Fold School
HOVE BN3........................167 K7

Fonthill Lodge School
EGRIN RH19.......................13 J8

Fordcombe C of E
　Primary School
　　RRTW TN3 .... 18 B1
Forest Row Business Park
　FROW RH18 .... 24 F3
Forest Row C of E Infant
　School
　FROW RH18 .... 24 F4
Fort
　NEWHV BN9 .... 9 H8
Foxhill Surgery
　PEAHV BN10 .... 190 B5
Framfield C of E School
　UCK TN22 .... 77 H8
Frant C of E School
　RRTW TN3 .... 30 B2
Freda Gardham Cp School
　RYE TN31 .... 91 K8
The Gallery
　BEXW TN39 .... 183 H3
The Gallery
　BRI BN1 .... 6 C6
The Gallery
　HOVE BN3 .... 168 A7
Gattons Cp School
　BURH RH15 .... 96 E3
Gemini Business Centre
　HOVE BN3 .... 168 A6
George Street Gallery
　ROTT BN2 .... 6 F7
Georgian House
　Business Centre
　ROTT BN2 .... 6 F7
Gerald Dale Motor
　Sports Centre
　STLEO TN38 .... 161 M1
Glebe CP School
　STHW BN42 .... 166 D7
Glennys Estate
　LW/ROSE BN22 .... 11 J2
Glynde Palace
　RING/NEW BN8 .... 150 F7
Goldsmith Leisure Centre
　CROW TN6 .... 39 M2
Goldstone Junior School
　HOVE BN3 .... 167 L5
The Good Start School
　POY/PYE BN45 .... 144 C1
Graham Gallery
　SBGH/RUST TN4 .... 20 A3
Graham Whitehouse Practice
　BURH RH15 .... 96 E2
Granary Business Centre
　HAIL BN27 .... 131 M8
Grays County Infants School
　NEWHV BN9 .... 9 C5
Great Walstead School
　HWH RH16 .... 49 M8
Greenfield School
　FROW RH18 .... 24 C5
Green Street Clinic
　EAST BN21 .... 206 C2
Grosvenor Medical Centre
　RTW TN1 .... 20 A2
Grovelands County
　Primary School
　HAIL BN27 .... 155 G5
Grove Park School
　CROW TN6 .... 39 L1
The Grove School
　STLEO TN38 .... 161 M5
Guestling School
　RHAS TN35 .... 141 G6
Guestling Surgery
　RHAS TN35 .... 141 G6
Hailsham School
　HAIL BN27 .... 155 H6
Hailsham Town Council
　HAIL BN27 .... 155 J2
Hailsham Whitehouse Cp School
　HAIL BN27 .... 155 H6
Halsford Park Primary School
　EGRIN RH19 .... 13 H4
Ham Business Centre
　SHOR BN43 .... 166 A7
Hamilton Lodge School
　ROTT BN2 .... 7 J2
Hammerwood Park
　EGRIN RH19 .... 15 J4
Hampden Park Infants School
　LW/ROSE BN22 .... 196 E4
Hampden Park Secondary
　School
　LW/ROSE BN22 .... 196 E4
Hampden Park Sports Centre
　LW/ROSE BN22 .... 196 D5
Hamsey CP School
　RING/NEW BN8 .... 126 A3
Hangleton County
　Junior & Infant School
　HOVE BN3 .... 167 L4
Hankham CP School
　PEV BN24 .... 179 H6
Hapstead Business Centre
　RHWH RH17 .... 34 B6
Harden Road Industrial Estate
　LYDD TN29 .... 95 K7
Harlands CP School
　RHWH RH17 .... 48 D7
Harlands Farm County
　Primary School
　UCK TN22 .... 102 D1
Harvington Business Park
　LW/ROSE BN22 .... 196 F6
Hassocks County Infant School
　HPPT/KEY BN6 .... 122 F2
Hassocks Golf Club
　HPPT/KEY BN6 .... 122 E1
Hasting Medical Centre
　HAS TN34 .... 5 G6
Hastings Castle
　HAS TN34 .... 5 J6
Hastings College of Arts &
　Technology
　HAS TN34 .... 5 K3
Hastings College of Arts &
　Technology
　STLEO TN38 .... 162 B8

Hastings Education College
　STLEO TN38 .... 161 M7
Hastings Golf Club
　BAT TN33 .... 138 F6
Hastings Indoor Market
　HAS TN34 .... 5 H7
Hastings Museum & Art Gallery
　HAS TN34 .... 4 E7
Hastings & St Leonards
　Sailing Club
　STLEO TN38 .... 4 A9
Hastings & St Leonards
　Sailing Club
　STLEO TN38 .... 162 B8
Hastings Town Football Club
　HAS TN34 .... 163 G2
Hawkes Farm CP School
　HAIL BN27 .... 155 H4
Hawkhurst C of E
　Primary School
　HAWK TN18 .... 47 M6
Hawkhurst Squash Club
　HAWK TN18 .... 47 L4
Haywards Heath College
　HWH RH16 .... 48 D8
Haywards Heath Football Club
　HWH RH16 .... 72 A1
Haywards Heath Golf Club
　HWH RH16 .... 48 F5
Haywards Heath Hospital
　HWH RH16 .... 71 J1
Hazel Cottage Clinic
　ROTT BN2 .... 170 C6
Hazel Court School
　LGNY BN23 .... 197 H3
Heathfield C of E Primary School
　HTHF TN21 .... 80 D8
Heathfield School
　HTHF TN21 .... 80 E7
Helenswood Lower School
　SLVH TN37 .... 139 K7
Helenswood Upper School
　HAS TN34 .... 163 G2
Hellingly CP School
　HAIL BN27 .... 154 F1
Hellingly Hospital
　HAIL BN27 .... 155 K1
Herbert Hone Clinic
　ROTT BN2 .... 7 G2
Herne School
　CROW TN6 .... 39 M6
Herons Dale School
　SHOR BN43 .... 166 C5
Herstmonceux Castle
　HAIL BN27 .... 157 H5
Herstmonceux C of E School
　HAIL BN27 .... 156 E1
Hesketh Gallery &
　Potters Supplies
　LEW BN7 .... 3 G6
Heyworth County Primary
　School
　HWH RH16 .... 71 L1
High Beech Hotel &
　Country Club
　STLEO TN38 .... 138 F8
Highfield Business Park
　STLEO TN38 .... 161 K2
Highfield County Junior School
　LW/ROSE BN22 .... 196 F5
High Hurstwood C of E School
　UCK TN22 .... 54 A5
Highwoods Golf Club Ltd
　BEXW TN39 .... 159 M7
Hillcrest School
　RHAS TN35 .... 163 L1
Hillside School
　PTSD BN41 .... 167 H4
Hippodrome Bingo
　BRI BN1 .... 6 D7
Hoddern County Junior School
　PEAHV BN10 .... 190 B6
Hollington Junior School
　STLEO TN38 .... 162 A2
Hollington Lodge Country Club
　SLVH TN37 .... 139 G7
Holmbush County
　Infants School
　SHOR BN43 .... 166 C5
Holmewood House School
　RRTW TN3 .... 19 G4
Homecare Business Centre
　LEW BN7 .... 3 J6
Home Farm Business Centre
　BRI BN1 .... 169 K3
Homeopathic Hospital
　RTW TN1 .... 20 A3
Horsted Keynes C of E School
　RHWH RH17 .... 35 J8
Hospital
　HAWK TN18 .... 47 K4
Hove Business Centre
　HOVE BN3 .... 168 B6
Hove General Hospital
　HOVE BN3 .... 168 A7
Hove Medical Centre
　HOVE BN3 .... 167 K4
Hove Metal Galleries
　BRI BN1 .... 6 C3
Hove Park Upper School
　HOVE BN3 .... 168 A5
Hove Polyclinic
　HOVE BN3 .... 167 M5
Hove Rugby Football Club
　HOVE BN3 .... 168 B5
How We Lived Then
　Museum of Shops
　EAST BN21 .... 10 E7
Hubbard School
　EGRIN RH19 .... 13 L5
Hurstpierpoint College
　HPPT/KEY BN6 .... 96 B6
Hurstwood Park Hospital
　HWH RH16 .... 72 A4
The Hutchinson Gallery
　HWH RH16 .... 71 L1
Ice Rink
　BRI BN1 .... 6 D6

Icklesham Primary School
　WSEA TN36 .... 115 L8
Iford & Kingston C of E School
　LEW BN7 .... 171 M1
Imberhorne School
　EGRIN RH19 .... 13 H4
The Imber Sports Centre
　EGRIN RH19 .... 13 K3
Independent Business Park
　EGRIN RH19 .... 13 G3
The Indooer Market
　HAS TN34 .... 5 G7
Indoor Market
　SLVH TN37 .... 4 B8
Inglesea School
　STLEO TN38 .... 161 M2
Inside Out Theatre Co Ltd
　SLVH TN37 .... 4 A5
International Lawn
　Tennis Centre
　EAST BN21 .... 10 E8
Jarvis Brook Cp School
　CROW TN6 .... 40 C7
Jempsons Trading Estate
　RYE TN31 .... 117 H1
Kent & Sussex Hospital
　SBGH/RUST TN4 .... 20 A2
King Offa Cp School
　BEXW TN39 .... 183 H1
Kings Manor School
　SHOR BN43 .... 166 D6
Kingston Buci School
　SHOR BN43 .... 166 A6
Kingswood Surgery
　RTWE/PEM TN2 .... 20 C3
Knoll Business Centre
　HOVE BN3 .... 167 K6
Lamberhurst Surgery
　RRTW TN3 .... 33 G1
Langney CP School
　LGNY BN23 .... 197 L5
Langney Shopping Centre
　LGNY BN23 .... 197 J3
Langney Sports Club
　LGNY BN23 .... 197 M3
Langton Green Cp School
　RRTW TN3 .... 18 E2
Lansdowne Road Clinic
　RTW TN1 .... 20 B2
Law Courts
　ROTT BN2 .... 7 G6
Lawn Tennis Club
　EAST BN21 .... 10 E8
Leap Cross Small
　Business Centre
　HAIL BN27 .... 155 G4
Lewes Business Centre
　LEW BN7 .... 2 F4
Lewes Castle & Museums
　LEW BN7 .... 2 F6
Lewes District Council
　LEW BN7 .... 3 G7
Lewes District Council
　NEWHV BN9 .... 8 F2
Lewes District Council
　SEAF BN25 .... 202 E3
Lewes Gallery
　LEW BN7 .... 2 F7
Lewes Grammar School
　LEW BN7 .... 2 E6
Lewes Leisure Centre
　LEW BN7 .... 3 J3
Lewes Little Theatre
　LEW BN7 .... 3 G5
Lewes Magistrates Court
　LEW BN7 .... 3 H6
Lewes Natural Health Centre
　LEW BN7 .... 3 J5
Lewes Sports Club
　LEW BN7 .... 149 H7
Lewes Tertiary College
　LEW BN7 .... 3 H7
Lewes Victoria Hospital
　LEW BN7 .... 2 B5
Lewes Wallands Cp School
　LEW BN7 .... 2 B3
Lexden Lodge Industrial Estate
　CROW TN6 .... 40 D6
Life Boat Museum
　EAST BN21 .... 10 F9
Lindfield Infant School
　HWH RH16 .... 49 G7
Lindfield Junior School
　HWH RH16 .... 49 H7
Lindfield Medical Centre
　HWH RH16 .... 49 H6
Lingfield School
　LW/ROSE BN22 .... 196 D4
Liongate Clinic
　SBGH/RUST TN4 .... 20 A1
Little Common Primary School
　BEXW TN39 .... 182 D2
Little Horsted School
　UCK TN22 .... 102 C5
Little Ridge School
　SLVH TN37 .... 162 C1
Little Ridge Surgery
　SLVH TN37 .... 162 C1
Little Theatre
　SEAF BN25 .... 202 E4
London Meed CP School
　BURH RH15 .... 97 G5
Longhill School
　ROTT BN2 .... 188 E2
Longley Industrial Estate
　BRI BN1 .... 6 E2
Lower Glen Surgery
　SLVH TN37 .... 162 B2
L T C International College
　EAST BN21 .... 10 B8
Lydd County Primary School
　LYDD TN29 .... 95 J8
Lydd Town Council
　LYDD TN29 .... 95 J8
Malthouse Business Park
　RYE TN31 .... 90 C4
Manor CP School
　UCK TN22 .... 76 D6

Manor Farm Business Centre
　POY/PYE BN45 .... 144 D1
Manor Field Cp School
　BURH RH15 .... 97 J2
Manor House Hospital
　HOVE BN3 .... 168 A7
Manor Oak Surgery
　HTHF TN21 .... 105 M7
Manor Park Medical Centre
　POLE BN26 .... 177 M8
Marefield Leisure Centre
　UCK TN22 .... 76 A2
Maresfield Bonners School
　UCK TN22 .... 76 B2
Marine Clinic
　ROTT BN2 .... 189 G5
Mark Cross C of E School
　CROW TN6 .... 42 A3
Market Place
　BURH RH15 .... 97 G4
Marlborough House School
　HAWK TN18 .... 47 L4
Marshlands CP School
　HAIL BN27 .... 155 K6
Martins Oak Surgery
　BAT TN33 .... 137 K2
Mayfield Gallery
　MAYF TN20 .... 57 H3
Maynards Green Cp School
　HTHF TN21 .... 106 A4
The Meadows Surgery
　BURH RH15 .... 96 D2
The Mead School
　RTWE/PEM TN2 .... 20 A5
Meads School
　EGRIN RH19 .... 13 L7
The Meads Surgery
　UCK TN22 .... 76 C2
The Medical Centre
　PEV BN24 .... 198 D1
Meeching Valley Cp School
　NEWHV BN9 .... 8 C3
Megabowl
　BEX TN40 .... 184 A2
Memorial Art Gallery
　HAS TN34 .... 5 G7
Mercantia Business Centre
　STLEO TN38 .... 4 A9
Meridian CP School
　PEAHV BN10 .... 190 C5
Meridian Leisure Centre
　PEAHV BN10 .... 190 C7
Meridian Surgery
　PEAHV BN10 .... 190 B6
The Mews Clinic
　EAST BN21 .... 10 A4
Michael Hall School
　FROW RH18 .... 24 D5
Michelham Priory
　HAIL BN27 .... 154 B7
Middle Street Primary School
　BRI BN1 .... 6 D7
Mid Sussex Golf Club
　HPPT/KEY BN6 .... 124 A1
Mile Oak Clinic
　PTSD BN41 .... 166 F3
Mile Oak Junior School
　PTSD BN41 .... 166 F3
Millbrook Business Park
　CROW TN6 .... 40 D6
Mill Green Industrial Estate
　HWH RH16 .... 48 E8
Mill View Hospital
　HOVE BN3 .... 167 L5
Moatfield Surgery
　EGRIN RH19 .... 13 L4
Moira House School
　EDN/EASTW BN20 .... 206 D5
Morley Street Health Centre
　ROTT BN2 .... 7 G5
The Mosque
　STLEO TN38 .... 4 A8
Motcombe County
　Infant School
　EAST BN21 .... 206 C1
Moulsecoomb Clinic
　ROTT BN2 .... 169 L3
Moulsecoomb County
　Junior School
　ROTT BN2 .... 169 L3
Mountfield & Whatlington
　C of E Primary Sch
　RBTBR TN32 .... 85 K7
Mount Pleasant Hospital
　SLVH TN37 .... 162 A2
Mount School
　WADH TN5 .... 31 H8
Mowden School
　HOVE BN3 .... 168 D5
Museum of Local History
　HAS TN34 .... 5 K6
Netherfield C of E
　Primary School
　BAT TN33 .... 110 C4
Nevill Golf Club
　RTWE/PEM TN2 .... 20 D7
Newhaven Flea Market
　NEWHV BN9 .... 8 F4
Newhaven Health Centre
　NEWHV BN9 .... 9 G3
Newhaven Town Council
　NEWHV BN9 .... 9 G4
Newick Health Centre
　RING/NEW BN8 .... 74 D7
Newick House Special School
　BURH RH15 .... 97 J5
Newick School
　RING/NEW BN8 .... 74 C8
Newlands Health Clinic
　HWH RH16 .... 71 L2
Newlands Preparatory School
　SEAF BN25 .... 203 H2
Newlands Senior School
　SEAF BN25 .... 203 G2
New Life School
　EGRIN RH19 .... 13 K4
Newmans Loner School
　HOVE BN3 .... 168 D6

Ninfield C of E School
　BAT TN33 .... 159 H1
Northbourne Medical Centre
　SHOR BN43 .... 166 A6
Northease Manor School
　LEW BN7 .... 172 C5
Northfield Business Park
　HAIL BN27 .... 154 A5
Northiam Primary School
　RYE TN31 .... 88 B1
Northlands Wood Cp School
　HWH RH16 .... 72 B2
Northlands Wood Surgery
　HWH RH16 .... 72 B2
Nutley Primary School
　UCK TN22 .... 52 C2
Oakmeads Community School
　BURH RH15 .... 97 G4
Oathall Community College
　HWH RH16 .... 48 F8
Ocklynge County Junior School
　EAST BN21 .... 196 C8
Odeon Cinema
　BRI BN1 .... 6 C7
Old Grammar School
　LEW BN7 .... 2 D5
Old Grammar School
　LEW BN7 .... 2 E6
The Old Museum
　RYE TN31 .... 88 F4
Old Salehurst School
　RBTBR TN32 .... 85 H1
Old School Surgery
　SEAF BN25 .... 202 E1
Old Town Art Gallery
　HAS TN34 .... 5 K6
The Open University
　EGRIN RH19 .... 13 L5
Ore Business Park
　HAS TN34 .... 5 M1
Our Lady of Lourdes School
　ROTT BN2 .... 188 F4
Ovingdean Hall School
　ROTT BN2 .... 188 D2
Palace Pier
　ROTT BN2 .... 6 F9
Park College Eastbourne
　EAST BN21 .... 196 D7
Parklands Junior & Infant
　School
　LW/ROSE BN22 .... 196 D5
Park Mead School
　HAIL BN27 .... 154 C4
Parkside County Primary
　School
　HTHF TN21 .... 106 C1
Park View Leisure Centre
　HOVE BN3 .... 167 L7
Pashley Down County
　Infant School
　EDN/EASTW BN20 .... 206 B2
Patcham Cp School
　BRI BN1 .... 145 M8
Patcham First School
　BRI BN1 .... 145 L8
Patcham High School
　BRI BN1 .... 145 M8
Patcham House School
　BRI BN1 .... 145 L8
The Pavilion Clinic
　BRI BN1 .... 6 B6
Pavilion Theatre
　BRI BN1 .... 6 E6
Paxton Business Centre
　HOVE BN3 .... 167 K6
Peacehaven Infant School
　PEAHV BN10 .... 190 B7
Peacehaven Sports Centre
　PEAHV BN10 .... 190 B7
Peacehaven Town Council
　PEAHV BN10 .... 190 B7
Peacock Industrial Estate
　HOVE BN3 .... 168 C7
Peasmarsh C of E
　Primary School
　RYE TN31 .... 90 B5
Pebsham Primary School
　BEX TN40 .... 184 A1
Pells C of E Infant School
　LEW BN7 .... 2 D4
Pells Primary School
　LEW BN7 .... 2 F5
Penns Gallery
　EAST BN21 .... 10 D7
Peter Gladwin School
　PTSD BN41 .... 167 G4
Pevensey Bay Sailing Club
　PEV BN24 .... 198 C4
Pevensey Castle
　PEV BN24 .... 180 B8
Pevensey & Westham
　C of E Primary School
　PEV BN24 .... 180 A8
Philpots Manor School
　EGRIN RH19 .... 34 C1
Phoenix Industrial Estate
　LEW BN7 .... 3 G4
Phoenix Industrial Estate
　LEW BN7 .... 3 H5
The Picture House
　UCK TN22 .... 76 C2
The Piltdown Golf Club
　UCK TN22 .... 75 L4
Playden School
　RYE TN31 .... 91 J4
Plumpton New Primary School
　LEW BN7 .... 124 F1
Polegate CP School
　POLE BN26 .... 178 A7
Polegate Town Council Office
　POLE BN26 .... 195 M1
Police Station and
　Magistrates Court
　RTW TN1 .... 20 A2
Portfolio Studio Gallery
　BRI BN1 .... 6 E7
Portland Business Park
　HOVE BN3 .... 167 K7

Portland Industrial Estate *HOVE* BN3 ...... 167 L6
Portland Road Industrial Estate *HOVE* BN3 ...... 167 K6
Portland Surgery *HOVE* BN3 ...... 167 M7
Portslade Community College *PTSD* BN41 ...... 167 G3
Portslade Community College *PTSD* BN41 ...... 167 G5
Portslade Community College *STHW* BN42 ...... 166 F4
Portslade Health Centre *PTSD* BN41 ...... 167 H7
Practice *SBGH/RUST* TN4 ...... 20 A4
Premier Gallery *EAST* BN21 ...... 10 D7
Preston Furniture Gallery *BRI* BN1 ...... 168 F4
Preston Park Clinic *BRI* BN1 ...... 169 G5
Preston Park Surgery *BRI* BN1 ...... 169 G6
Priest House *EGRIN* RH19 ...... 22 E8
Prince Regent Swimming Complex *BRI* BN1 ...... 6 F6
The Princes Royal Hospital *HWH* RH16 ...... 71 M4
Prinnys Antique Gallery *BRI* BN1 ...... 6 D7
Priory Hill Shopping Centre *HAS* TN34 ...... 5 G6
Priory School *LEW* BN7 ...... 3 H8
Punnetts Town School *HTHF* TN21 ...... 81 H8
Queensdown School *BRI* BN1 ...... 169 J3
Queens Park County Primary School *ROTT* BN2 ...... 7 J7
Queen Victoria Hospital N H S Trust *EGRIN* RH19 ...... 13 M3
Quintin Medical Centre *HAIL* BN27 ...... 155 J3
Ranalah Estate *NEWHV* BN9 ...... 9 H1
Ratton County Secondary School *EAST* BN21 ...... 196 C7
Red Lake CP School *RHAS* TN35 ...... 163 K2
Regent Business Centre *BURH* RH15 ...... 96 E4
Rich Industrial Estate *NEWHV* BN9 ...... 191 L5
Ringmer Business Centre *RING/NEW* BN8 ...... 127 M8
Ringmer CP School *RING/NEW* BN8 ...... 150 E1
Ringmer Football Club *RING/NEW* BN8 ...... 150 D1
Ringmer Parish Council *RING/NEW* BN8 ...... 150 D1
River Lodge Surgery *LEW* BN7 ...... 3 H5
Riverside Industrial Estate *LEW* BN7 ...... 3 G4
Robertsbridge Community College *RBTBR* TN32 ...... 84 F2
Roborough Day Hospital *EAST* BN21 ...... 10 E4
Robsack Infant School *STLEO* TN38 ...... 161 L4
Rock & Bowl Bowling Alley *EGRIN* RH19 ...... 13 L5
Rocks Park CP School *UCK* TN22 ...... 76 B6
Rockys Leisure Centre *HAS* TN34 ...... 4 F8
Rodmell Primary School *LEW* BN7 ...... 172 E5
Roebuck House Surgery *HAS* TN34 ...... 5 L5
Roedean School *ROTT* BN2 ...... 188 C3
Rose Hill School *SBGH/RUST* TN4 ...... 19 L1
Roselands County Infants School *LW/ROSE* BN22 ...... 11 H1
Rother District Council *BAT* TN33 ...... 137 J1
Rotherfield CP School *CROW* TN6 ...... 41 H6
Rotherfield Surgery *CROW* TN6 ...... 41 H6
Rottingdean Football Club *ROTT* BN2 ...... 188 F3
Rottingdean Primary School *ROTT* BN2 ...... 189 G4
Rottingdean Surgery *ROTT* BN2 ...... 188 E3
Royal Alexandra Hospital *BRI* BN1 ...... 6 C4
Royal Ashdown Forest Golf Club *FROW* RH18 ...... 25 G5
Royal Eastbourne Golf Club *EAST* BN21 ...... 10 A7
Royal Eastbourne Golf Club *EDN/EASTW* BN20 ...... 206 D4
Royal George Clinic *BURH* RH15 ...... 96 E3
Royal Hippodrome Theatre *EAST* BN21 ...... 11 G6
Royal Pavilion *BRI* BN1 ...... 6 F6
Royal Sussex County Hospital N H S Trust *ROTT* BN2 ...... 7 L8
Royal Victoria Place Shopping Centre *RTW* TN1 ...... 20 B2

Rudyard Kipling Primary School *ROTT* BN2 ...... 170 E7
Rugby Club *EGRIN* RH19 ...... 23 J1
Rusthall School *SBGH/RUST* TN4 ...... 19 H2
Rutherfords Business Park *BAT* TN33 ...... 112 B7
Rye Art Gallery *RYE* TN31 ...... 117 J1
Rye Bay Club House *WSEA* TN36 ...... 143 G1
Rye Castle Museum *RYE* TN31 ...... 117 J1
Rye Community Clinic *RYE* TN31 ...... 117 H1
Rye Football & Cricket Club *RYE* TN31 ...... 91 J8
Rye Golf Club *RYE* TN31 ...... 118 B3
Rye Harbour Sailing Club *RYE* TN31 ...... 118 A3
Rye Industrial Estate *RYE* TN31 ...... 117 K2
Sackville School *EGRIN* RH19 ...... 14 A5
Sacred Heart School *RTWE/PEM* TN2 ...... 20 E2
Sacred Heart School *WADH* TN5 ...... 43 K1
St Andrews C of E Infant School *LW/ROSE* BN22 ...... 197 J8
St Andrews C of E School *HOVE* BN3 ...... 168 B8
St Andrews Market *HAS* TN34 ...... 5 H6
St Andrews School *EDN/EASTW* BN20 ...... 206 D7
St Andrews Surgery *LEW* BN7 ...... 3 G7
St Annes Special School *LEW* BN7 ...... 2 D7
St Aubyns School *ROTT* BN2 ...... 189 G5
St Barnabas C of E Primary School *RTW* TN1 ...... 20 B1
St Bartholomews C of E Primary School *BRI* BN1 ...... 6 E3
St Bedes School *EDN/EASTW* BN20 ...... 206 E7
St Bedes School *HAIL* BN27 ...... 153 M6
St Bernadettes First Middle Va School *BRI* BN1 ...... 168 E4
St Christophers School *HOVE* BN3 ...... 168 A7
St Dominics Gallery *HPPT/KEY* BN6 ...... 123 J3
St Faith Clinic *ROTT* BN2 ...... 187 L2
St Georges School *RTWE/PEM* TN2 ...... 21 G1
St Giles College *EDN/EASTW* BN20 ...... 206 F5
St James's Junior & Infant School *RTWE/PEM* TN2 ...... 20 C2
St Johns Church School *CROW* TN6 ...... 39 J2
St Johns Infant School *SBGH/RUST* TN4 ...... 20 A1
St Johns Residential School *ROTT* BN2 ...... 7 L7
St John the Baptist RC Primary School *ROTT* BN2 ...... 7 M6
St Josephs R C Primary School *HWH* RH16 ...... 71 L2
St Josephs RC School *LW/ROSE* BN22 ...... 11 J2
St Leonards C of E Primary School *STLEO* TN38 ...... 162 A7
St Leonards Football Club *HAS* TN34 ...... 163 G3
St Lukes Junior & Infant School *ROTT* BN2 ...... 7 K5
St Lukes Swimming Pool *ROTT* BN2 ...... 7 K4
St Marks C of E Primary School *ROTT* BN2 ...... 187 L1
St Marks C of E Primary School *SBGH/RUST* TN4 ...... 19 K5
St Marks C of E Primary School *UCK* TN22 ...... 78 C1
St Martins C of E Primary School *ROTT* BN2 ...... 7 J1
St Martins C of E Primary School *ROTT* BN2 ...... 169 J6
St Mary Magdalene School *BEX* TN40 ...... 160 E8
St Mary Magdalene School *BRI* BN1 ...... 6 B6
St Marys C of E School *EGRIN* RH19 ...... 13 K4
St Marys Primary Catholic School *CROW* TN6 ...... 39 M4
St Marys RC School *PTSD* BN41 ...... 167 H7
St Marys School *BEX* TN40 ...... 160 E8
St Marys School *HTHF* TN21 ...... 106 A5
St Mary the Virgin School *HRTF* TN7 ...... 26 D2
St Michaels Cp School *HRTF* TN7 ...... 27 H1
St Nicholas & St. Mary School *SHOR* BN43 ...... 166 A6
St Pancras RC Primary School *LEW* BN7 ...... 2 C6
St Pauls C of E Infant School *RRTW* RH17 ...... 19 H2
St Pauls C of E Junior School *SBGH/RUST* TN4 ...... 19 H2
St Pauls C of E School *BRI* BN1 ...... 6 D5

St Pauls RC Comprehensive School *HWH* RH16 ...... 71 M1
St Pauls School *SLVH* TN37 ...... 4 C4
St Peters C of E School *RHWH* RH17 ...... 34 A6
St Peters County Infant School *PTSD* BN41 ...... 167 H8
St Peters Medical Centre *BRI* BN1 ...... 6 F3
St Peters Primary School *RING/NEW* BN8 ...... 99 L2
St Peters Primary School *RTWE/PEM* TN2 ...... 20 C3
St Peters RC School *EGRIN* RH19 ...... 13 J5
St Peters R C School *SHOR* BN43 ...... 166 A6
St Phillips R C Primary School *UCK* TN22 ...... 102 C1
St Richards School *BEX* TN40 ...... 183 L2
St Thomas A Becket RC Infants School *EAST* BN21 ...... 10 D2
St Thomas A Becket RC Junior School *EAST* BN21 ...... 10 D1
St Thomas C of E Primary School *RRTW* TN3 ...... 18 C8
St Thomas C of E Primary School *WSEA* TN36 ...... 116 F7
St Vincent School *STLEO* TN38 ...... 161 M8
St Wilfrids C of E School *HWH* RH16 ...... 72 H3
St Wilfrids RC School *BURH* RH15 ...... 97 G4
Salehurst C of E Primary School *RBTBR* TN32 ...... 85 H2
Saltdean County Primary School *ROTT* BN2 ...... 189 J4
Salvation Army *LW/ROSE* BN22 ...... 11 G5
Sandhurst CP School *HAWK* TN18 ...... 64 C1
Sandown School *RHAS* TN35 ...... 163 J2
Saxonborough Surgery *CROW* TN6 ...... 39 M4
Saxon Mount School *STLEO* TN38 ...... 161 M7
The Seaford Business Centre *SEAF* BN25 ...... 202 E3
Seaford CP School *SEAF* BN25 ...... 202 E2
Seaford Day Hospital *SEAF* BN25 ...... 202 F3
Seaford Golf Club *SEAF* BN25 ...... 192 F8
Seaford Head Community College *SEAF* BN25 ...... 202 F4
Seaford Head Community College *SEAF* BN25 ...... 203 G4
Seaford Head Lower School *SEAF* BN25 ...... 202 F4
Seaford Health Centre *SEAF* BN25 ...... 202 E3
Seaford Sports & Leisure Centre *SEAF* BN25 ...... 202 E3
Sea Life Centre *ROTT* BN2 ...... 6 F8
Sea Road Surgery *BEX* TN40 ...... 183 K3
Seaside Medical Centre *LW/ROSE* BN22 ...... 11 H4
Secondary School *ROTT* BN2 ...... 169 L8
Sedlescombe C of E School *BAT* TN33 ...... 112 E5
Sedlescombe Golf Club *BAT* TN33 ...... 138 E1
The Seven Dials Medical Centre *BRI* BN1 ...... 6 C4
Shankill Surgery *RHAS* TN35 ...... 163 K2
Sheddindean Business Centre *BURH* RH15 ...... 96 F1
Sheddingdean First School *BURH* RH15 ...... 97 G1
Sheila Cashin Gallery *BRI* BN1 ...... 6 C5
Sheriffs Gallery *HAIL* BN27 ...... 155 J7
The Ship Street Surgery *EGRIN* RH19 ...... 13 L6
Shoe Gallery *LEW* BN7 ...... 3 G6
Shoreham Beach County First School *SHOR* BN43 ...... 166 A8
Shoreham College *SHOR* BN43 ...... 166 D7
Shoreham Football Club *PTSD* BN41 ...... 167 H7
Sidley Primary School *BEXW* TN39 ...... 160 C8
Sidley Sports Club *BEXW* TN39 ...... 160 C7
Sidley Surgery *BEXW* TN39 ...... 160 B7
Silverhill Natural Health Centre *STLEO* TN38 ...... 162 B4
Silver Springs Medical Practice *SLVH* TN37 ...... 4 B5
Simpsons Industrial Estate *RYE* TN31 ...... 117 J3
Skippers Hill Manor Preparatory School *MAYF* TN20 ...... 56 B6
Snowhill Business Centre *CRAWE* RH10 ...... 12 A2
Somerhill County Junior School *HOVE* BN3 ...... 168 D8
Southdown Business Park *LEW* BN7 ...... 3 J3

South Downs Health Clinic *BRI* BN1 ...... 6 D4
South Malling Primary School *LEW* BN7 ...... 3 H2
Southover C of E Primary School *LEW* BN7 ...... 2 E7
Southover C of E Primary School *LEW* BN7 ...... 2 F8
South Saxon Howe Surgery *STLEO* TN38 ...... 161 L7
Southway County Junior School *HPPT/KEY* BN6 ...... 96 D3
Southwick Business Centre *PTSD* BN41 ...... 166 E8
Southwick Manor Hall County First School *STHW* BN42 ...... 166 F7
Spinney School *HTHF* TN21 ...... 105 K3
Springfield Industrial Estate *HAWK* TN18 ...... 47 M3
Springfield Industrial Estate *RHWH* RH17 ...... 97 M1
Squash Club *EAST* BN21 ...... 10 C8
Squires Farm Industrial Estate *UCK* TN22 ...... 103 L5
Stafford County Junior School *LW/ROSE* BN22 ...... 197 G8
Stanford Junior School *BRI* BN1 ...... 6 C1
Stanley Deason Leisure Centre *ROTT* BN2 ...... 187 M1
Staplecross School *RBTBR* TN32 ...... 86 E4
Stevenson Gallery *RYE* TN31 ...... 117 H1
Stewart Gallery *BEX* TN40 ...... 183 J3
Stone Cross CP School *PEV* BN24 ...... 197 G1
Stonegate C of E Primary School *WADH* TN5 ...... 59 M1
Stonelands School of Ballet & Theatre *HOVE* BN3 ...... 168 B8
Summerfields Business Centre *SLVH* TN37 ...... 4 C5
Summerfield Sports Centre *HAS* TN34 ...... 4 D6
Sussex County Cricket Club *HOVE* BN3 ...... 168 C7
Sussex Eye Hospital *ROTT* BN2 ...... 7 L8
Sussex House Industrial Estate *HOVE* BN3 ...... 167 M6
Sussex Nuffield Hospital *HOVE* BN3 ...... 167 M8
Sussex Nuffield Hospital *ROTT* BN2 ...... 170 C6
Sussex Private Clinic *STLEO* TN38 ...... 162 B6
The Sussex Toy & Model Museum *BRI* BN1 ...... 6 D4
Sussex University *LEW* BN7 ...... 3 J4
Sutton Industrial Park *WSEA* TN36 ...... 117 G7
Swan Barn Business Centre *HAIL* BN27 ...... 155 K8
Sydney West Sports Centre *BURH* RH15 ...... 97 G2
Synagogue *BRI* BN1 ...... 6 D7
Synagogue *EAST* BN21 ...... 10 F6
TA Centre *LW/ROSE* BN22 ...... 11 H4
Tavistock & Summerhill School *HWH* RH16 ...... 48 F7
Teacher Training School *HAS* TN34 ...... 5 K4
Telscombe Cliffs Primary School *PEAHV* BN10 ...... 190 A6
Temple Grove with St Nicholas School *UCK* TN22 ...... 53 L3
Tennis Club *CROW* TN6 ...... 39 L4
Theatre Royal *BRI* BN1 ...... 6 E6
Thomas Peacocke Community College *RYE* TN31 ...... 91 H8
Ticehurst Clinic *HOVE* BN3 ...... 168 A8
Ticehurst C of E Primary School *WADH* TN5 ...... 45 H6
Tideway School *NEWHV* BN9 ...... 8 D6
Tilling Green School *RYE* TN31 ...... 117 G1
Tobias School of Art *EGRIN* RH19 ...... 13 L8
Tollgate Junior School *LGNY* BN23 ...... 197 K7
Torfield School *HAS* TN34 ...... 5 L4
Towner Art Gallery & Local History Museum *EDN/EASTW* BN20 ...... 206 D3
Town Hall *BRI* BN1 ...... 6 E8
Town Hall *EAST* BN21 ...... 10 C7
Town Hall *HOVE* BN3 ...... 168 B8
Town Hall *RTW* TN1 ...... 20 A2
Tree Tops Tree Surgery *STLEO* TN38 ...... 161 M8
Trinity Theatre & Arts Association *RTW* TN1 ...... 20 A3
Tunbridge Wells Borderers Sports Club *RTWE/PEM* TN2 ...... 20 A6
Tunbridge Wells Centre *RTW* TN1 ...... 20 A2

Tunbridge Wells Golf Club *SBGH/RUST* TN4 ...... 19 L3
Tunbridge Wells Hockey Club *RTW* TN1 ...... 20 B5
Tunbridge Wells Independent Hospital *RRTW* TN3 ...... 18 B3
Tunbridge Wells Museum & Art Gallery *SBGH/RUST* TN4 ...... 20 A2
Tunbridge Wells Nuffield Hospital *RTWE/PEM* TN2 ...... 20 D3
Turners Hill C of E School *CRAWE* RH10 ...... 22 A3
Uckfield Civic Centre *UCK* TN22 ...... 76 C7
Uckfield Community Hospital *UCK* TN22 ...... 76 D8
Uckfield Community School *UCK* TN22 ...... 76 D6
Uckfield Holy Cross School *UCK* TN22 ...... 76 C7
Uckfield Rugby Football Club *UCK* TN22 ...... 76 E6
Uckfield Sports Centre *UCK* TN22 ...... 76 C7
University of Brighton *BRI* BN1 ...... 146 E8
University of Brighton *BRI* BN1 ...... 170 A1
University of Brighton *EAST* BN21 ...... 10 C4
University of Brighton *EDN/EASTW* BN20 ...... 10 A9
University of Brighton *EDN/EASTW* BN20 ...... 206 D7
University of Brighton *EDN/EASTW* BN20 ...... 206 D5
University of Brighton *ROTT* BN2 ...... 6 F6
University of Brighton *ROTT* BN2 ...... 169 J4
University of Sussex *BRI* BN1 ...... 147 H7
Uplands Community College *WADH* TN5 ...... 43 M2
Uplands School *BRI* BN1 ...... 169 J4
Utopia Leisure Centre *UCK* TN22 ...... 76 D6
Vals Swim School *BEXW* TN39 ...... 160 B6
Varndean College *BRI* BN1 ...... 168 F3
Varndean High School *BRI* BN1 ...... 169 G3
Venture Industrial Park *STLEO* TN38 ...... 162 A4
Vicarage Field Surgery *HAIL* BN27 ...... 155 J6
Virgin Cinemas *LGNY* BN23 ...... 197 M5
Virgin Cinemas *ROTT* BN2 ...... 187 L3
Wadhurst Business Park *WADH* TN5 ...... 31 H7
Wadhurst C of E Primary School *WADH* TN5 ...... 43 M1
Warden Park School *RHWH* RH17 ...... 71 G1
Warrior Square Surgery *SLVH* TN37 ...... 4 B9
Waterhall Golf Course *BRI* BN1 ...... 145 H7
Wayfield Clinic *BRI* BN1 ...... 168 E4
Wealden College *CROW* TN6 ...... 39 M6
Wealden District Council *HAIL* BN27 ...... 155 J6
Wealden Industrial Estate *CROW* TN6 ...... 40 C6
Websters Gallery *EAST* BN21 ...... 11 G6
Welfare Clinic *HOVE* BN3 ...... 167 L4
Wellington Square Medical Centre *HAS* TN34 ...... 5 H7
Wellshurst Golf & Country Club *HAIL* BN27 ...... 132 A4
Westdene Primary School *BRI* BN1 ...... 168 C1
Westerleigh School *STLEO* TN38 ...... 162 A6
Western Road Primary School *LEW* BN7 ...... 2 C6
Westham Medical Centre *PEV* BN24 ...... 198 A1
West Hoathly School *EGRIN* RH19 ...... 22 E8
West Hove Middle School *HOVE* BN3 ...... 167 L7
West Pier (Under Repair) *BRI* BN1 ...... 6 B8
West Rise Junior & Infant School *LGNY* BN23 ...... 197 J4
West St Leonards County Primary School *STLEO* TN38 ...... 161 M6
West Sussex County Council *SHOR* BN43 ...... 166 B7
West Terrace Clinic *EAST* BN21 ...... 10 D7
Wheel Park Farm Industrial Estate *RHAS* TN35 ...... 139 K2
The White Gallery *HOVE* BN3 ...... 168 C8
Whitehawk Clinic *ROTT* BN2 ...... 187 M1
The Whitehawk College *EAST* BN21 ...... 10 E6
Whitehawk Infant School *ROTT* BN2 ...... 169 L8
Whitehawk Junior School *ROTT* BN2 ...... 169 L8

Notes